THE OXFORD HANDBOOK OF

CRITICAL IMPROVISATION STUDIES

VOLUME 1

THE OXFORD HANDBOOK OF

CRITICAL IMPROVISATION STUDIES

VOLUME 1

Edited by

GEORGE E. LEWIS

and

BENJAMIN PIEKUT

OXFORD

UNIVERSITY PRESS

OXFORD
UNIVERSITY PRESS

Oxford University Press is a department of the University of Oxford. It furthers
the University's objective of excellence in research, scholarship, and education
by publishing worldwide. Oxford is a registered trade mark of Oxford University
Press in the UK and certain other countries.

Published in the United States of America by Oxford University Press
198 Madison Avenue, New York, NY 10016, United States of America.

Library of Congress Cataloging-in-Publication Data
Names: Lewis, George E., 1952– editor. | Piekut, Benjamin, 1975– editor.
Title: The Oxford handbook of critical improvisation studies / edited by George E. Lewis and Benjamin Piekut
Description: New York : Oxford University Press, 2016. | Series: Oxford handbooks |
Includes bibliographical references and index.
Identifiers: LCCN 2015041014 | ISBN 978–0–19–537093–5 (hardcover, vol. 1 : alk. paper) |
ISBN 978–0–19–989292–1 (hardcover, vol. 2 : alk. paper)
Subjects: LCSH: Improvisation (Music) | Creation (Literary, artistic, etc.)
Classification: LCC MT68 .O97 2016 | DDC 001—dc23 LC record available at http://lccn.loc.gov/2015041014

1 3 5 7 9 8 6 4 2
Printed by Sheridan Books, Inc., United States of America

This *Handbook* is dedicated to the memory of Derek Bailey (1930–2005), Jeff Pressing (1946–2002), and Marvin Minsky (1927–2016).

CONTENTS

PART III CULTURAL HISTORIES

PART IV MOBILITIES

PREFACE

It is far too early to create a history or prehistory of what many are now calling "critical improvisation studies," but we can point to some significant early irruptions. Properly speaking, the project that resulted in this two-volume *Handbook* began around the turn of the twenty-first century with an important early conference, "Improvising Across Borders: An Inter-Disciplinary Symposium on Improvised Music Traditions." The conference, which took place in April 1999, was conceived by Dana Reason, then an innovation-minded graduate student in the Department of Music at the University of California, San Diego (UCSD), and produced in collaboration with her fellow graduate students Michael Dessen and Jason Robinson. The conference featured performances as well as paper presentations from both scholars and practitioners, and the call for papers welcomed proposals from

> musicologists, ethnomusicologists, and musicians, and also from scholars in other disciplines such as cultural studies, sociology, women's studies, and literature. We are interested not only in performative notions of improvisation but also the cultural contexts that influence and shape improvised traditions. Possible topics include: cultural location with regard to cross-cultural trends in current music-making, the politics of reception, theorizing the social and political implications of improvised traditions, the role of gender and body, and the relationship of improvisation to current changes in music—or other—pedagogies.[1]

In 2002, a trio of scholar-artists, also based in the University of California system, Adriene Jenik and George Lewis from UCSD and Susan Leigh Foster from UCLA, built on this earlier effort by co-convening a Residential Research Group at the University of California Humanities Research Institute with the title "Global Intentions: Improvisation in the Contemporary Performing Arts." The co-conveners developed an introductory guiding narrative for the research project that declared an intent to focus on

> (1) how improvisation mediates cross-cultural, transnational and cyberspatial (inter) artistic exchanges that produce new conceptions of identity, history, and the body; (2) how improvisation functions as a key element in emerging postcolonial forms of aesthetics and cultural production; and (3) how improvisative production of meaning and knowledge provides models for new forms of social mobilization that foreground agency, personality, and difference. The group will ask questions concerning

how improvisation expresses notions of ethnicity, race, nation, class, and gender, as well as how improvisative works are seen as symbolizing history, memory, agency, difference, personal narrative, and self-determination.[2]

The conveners observed that any practice for which such expansive claims could even be entertained, much less sustained, obviously deserved serious study. Their narrative also identified issues of power, authority, resistance, dominance and subalterity, the role of the individual in relation to the social, and models for social responsibility and action, as salient to the study of improvisation. Improvisation in the arts was seen to subvert hierarchies; challenge totalizing narratives; empower audiences; exemplify new (and quite often utopian) models of social, economic, and political relations; and in one memorable phrase, "overthrow the patriarchal organization of the art world, preparing fertile ground for a contestatory politics."[3]

The research group discussions at UCHRI, which took place weekly over a three-month period, often manifested a distinct unease with then-dominant portrayals of improvisation, as well as with some of the scholarship that proceeded from those understandings. In pursuing a critical review of the already substantial literature on the topic, the group gradually realized that the purview of a new kind of improvisation studies needed to range well beyond the arts. That discovery crucially informed the current project.

In the first of this two-volume set, we hear from scholars examining topics in cognition, philosophy, anthropology, cultural history, critical theory, economics, classics, organization science, and mobility on stages of various kinds. We expect readers to jump across sections and volumes, so for both volumes, we have created a nonlinear order of chapters to foster surprise. We encourage readers to extend their engagement into Volume 2, which includes investigations into city planning, music, creativity, media, literature, computing technologies, and theology.

George E. Lewis and Benjamin Piekut

Notes

1. Dana Reason and Michael Dessen, "Call for Papers: Improvising Across Borders: An inter-disciplinary symposium on improvised music traditions," (1999), http://goldenpages.jpehs.co.uk/static/conferencearchive/99-4-iab.html. Accessed December 23, 2014. Presenters included Douglas Ewart, Ed Sarath, Ingrid Monson, Ajay Heble, David Borgo, Sarita Gregory, Bennetta Jules-Rosette, Catherine Sullivan, Eleanor Antin, Eddie Prévost, Alvin Curran, Tom Nunn, Jonathan Glasier, and Jason Stanyek. A visionary keynote address was delivered by Pauline Oliveros, later published as "Quantum Improvisation: The Cybernetic Presence," in *Sound Unbound: Sampling Digital Music and Culture*, ed. Paul D. Miller aka DJ Spooky That Subliminal Kid (Cambridge: MIT Press, 2008). For an account of the conference, see La Donna Smith, "Improvising Across Borders, the Symposium on Improvisation: A Review and Personal Account," (1999), http://www.the-improvisor.com/improvising_across_borders.htm. Accessed December 23, 2014.

2. Susan Leigh Foster, Adriene Jenik, and George E. Lewis, "Proposal for a 2002–2003 Resident Research Group: Global Intentions: Improvisation in the Contemporary Performing Arts," (2002). The UCHRI research group included Georgina Born, Renee Coulombe, Anthea Kraut, Antoinette LaFarge, Simon Penny, Eric Porter, and Jason Stanyek.
3. Foster, Jenik, and Lewis, "Proposal for a 2002–2003 Resident Research Group."

Acknowledgments

These volumes were over a half-decade in the making, during which time we accrued countless debts. In many ways, this journey began at the University of California Humanities Research Institute, and we'd like to thank UCHRI director David Theo Goldberg, who in 2002 sponsored a scholarly Residential Research Group whose members became the core of this *Handbook*. At Oxford University Press, we would like to recognize the expansive vision of our editor, Suzanne Ryan, who originally suggested the handbook format as the most effective way to bring together a wide range of perspectives that can sometimes elude more modest edited volume formats. Oxford also provided the finest cat-wrangling support we could ask for from Molly Davis, Lisbeth Redfield, Amy Chang, and Andrew Maillet. We want to offer a special thank you to Swaathi Venugopal, Preethi Sundar, and Kathrin Immanuel at Newgen KnowledgeWorks for keeping us on track. Several PhD students at Cornell University provided crucial proofreading and copyediting services; our gratitude goes to Samuel Dwinell, Dietmar Friesenegger, Ji Young Kim, Mat Langlois, Erica Levenson, Becky Lu, and Mackenzie Pierce. We received invaluable support from the Edwin H. Case Chair in American Music at Columbia University.

Our greatest thanks go to our authors, who matched their excitement for this project with commensurate patience and good humor. We also wish to thank the many colleagues and friends who shared their thoughts and opinions on critical improvisation studies over the years, and who, like the contributors, humored us by maintaining straight faces when we repeatedly issued assurances of imminent publication.

CONTRIBUTORS TO VOLUME 1

Philip Alperson is professor emeritus of philosophy at Temple University, where he is also a senior scholar at the Center for Vietnamese Philosophy, Culture, and Society. He was the editor of *The Journal of Aesthetics and Art Criticism* for ten years. His main interests are in aesthetics, the philosophy of the arts, the theory of culture, value theory, and theories of interpretation and criticism. A long-time jazz musician, he has special interests in the philosophy of music and philosophical questions concerning creativity, performance, improvisation, personal and musical authenticity, music education, and the cultural placement of music. Professor Alperson was the Styrian Endowed Professor at the Institute of Music Aesthetics at the Universität für Musik und darstellende Kunst in Graz, Austria, and Fulbright Scholar at the Sibelius Academy of the University of the Arts in Helsinki, Finland.

Freya Bailes is a lecturer in music at the University of Hull. Prior to her current appointment, she was a senior research fellow at the MARCS Institute at the University of Western Sydney, collaborating with Roger Dean on research into the perception and emotional expression of contemporary music and the role of leadership in musical improvisation. This research draws on Bailes's previous postdoctoral experience at the Laboratoire d'Etude de l'Apprentissage et du Développement (Université de Bourgogne), the Cognitive and Systematic Musicology Laboratory (Ohio State University), and the Sonic Communications Research Group (University of Canberra). Her doctoral thesis, "Musical Imagery: Hearing and Imagining Music" (University of Sheffield), explored the nature and prevalence of musical imagery.

Daniel Belgrad is an associate professor in the Department of Humanities and Cultural Studies at the University of South Florida. His research focuses on post–World War II American culture. He is the author of *The Culture of Spontaneity: Improvisation and the Arts in Postwar America* (Chicago, 1998), which describes the intellectual and social currents informing the trend toward spontaneous improvisation in American art, music, and literature in the 1940s, 1950s, and 1960s that resulted in such movements as Abstract Expressionism, bebop jazz, and Beat poetry. In 2002 he won the Oscar O. Winther Award from the Western Historical Association. His current research interests include dance studies, biofeedback, and affect theory.

Aaron L. Berkowitz completed his PhD in music at Harvard University, his MD at Johns Hopkins University, and his postgraduate training in neurology in the Harvard Partners Neurology Residency. He is the author of *The Improvising Mind: Cognition and*

Creativity in the Musical Moment (Oxford, 2010). As a pianist and fortepianist, he has performed throughout Europe and the United States, and as a composer his compositions have been performed in Europe and the United States, including Carnegie Hall. He is currently an associate neurologist and director of the Global Neurology Program at Brigham and Women's Hospital, an instructor in neurology at Harvard Medical School, and a health and policy advisor in neurology to nongovernmental organization Partners in Health.

David Borgo is a saxophonist, ethnomusicologist, and professor of music at the University of California, San Diego, where he teaches in the Music Department's programs in Integrative Studies, Jazz, and Music of the African Diaspora. His primary areas of interest include improvisation, creativity research, technocultural studies, chaos and complexity theories, and non-Cartesian cognitive science. His book, *Sync or Swarm: Improvising Music in a Complex Age* (Continuum, 2005) won the Alan P. Merriam Prize in 2006 from the Society for Ethnomusicology as the most distinguished English-language book published during the previous year. As a saxophonist, Borgo has toured internationally and released eight CDs and one DVD.

Jared Burrows is a performer, composer, author, community organizer, and musical instigator in Vancouver, BC. He leads the Jared Burrows Quartet and Sextet and the Vancouver Improvisers Orchestra, and works in many other ensembles in jazz, new music, and world music. Jared is the head of the Jazz Studies Department at Capilano University, where he teaches improvisation and directs the new music ensemble Narwhal. Since 2008 he has co-curated Vancouver's weekly Jazz at Presentation House concert series, and from 2003 to 2013 was co-director of the South Delta Jazz Festival. He holds a PhD in arts education from Simon Fraser University. www.jaredburrows.com.

Yves Citton is professor of French literature at the Université de Grenoble, a member of the UMR LIRE (CNRS 5611, Littérature, idéologies, représentations, XVIIIe-XIXe siècles), and co-director of the journal *Multitudes*. He taught for twelve years in the Department of French and Italian of the University of Pittsburgh, and has been an invited professor at New York University, Harvard, and Sciences-Po Paris. He recently published *Pour une écologie de l'attention* (Seuil, 2014), *Gestes d'humanités: Anthropologie sauvage de nos expériences esthétiques* (Armand Colin, 2012), *Renverser l'insoutenable* (Seuil, 2012), *Zazirocratie* (Éditions Amsterdam, 2011), and *Mythocratie: Storytelling et imaginaire de gauche* (Éditions Amsterdam, 2010), along with a dozen articles on jazz and collective improvisation.

Arnold I. Davidson is Robert O. Anderson Distinguished Service Professor at the University of Chicago and professor of the philosophy of cultures at the Università Ca'Foscari Venezia. He is also the jazz critic for *Il Sole 24 Ore Domenica*. He is the series editor of the English language edition of Michel Foucault's courses at the Collège de France and has contributed to critical editions of several of Foucault's works in French. He has also edited works of Pierre Hadot in English, French, and Italian, as well as coauthored a book of conversations with Hadot, *La philosophie comme manière de vivre*

(Albin Michel, 2004). Among his other works are *The Emergence of Sexuality* (Harvard, 2004) and *Religión, razón y espiritualidad* (Alpha Decay, 2014). His major writings are in Italian, French, and Spanish, as well as in English.

Roger T. Dean is a composer/improviser and researcher in music cognition and computation. His performances on the bass, piano, and laptop range from the Academy of Ancient Music to the London Sinfonietta; his improvising collaborations, from Ted Curson to Evan Parker. Dean's work is available on 50 commercial recordings and many multimedia and installation pieces (with Keith Armstrong, Will Luers, Hazel Smith, and others). His creative work centers on keyboard/ensemble improvisation and computer music composition. These merge in his solo MultiPiano Event (live grand piano, real-time audio processing, generative piano, and electroacoustic sound). He founded the ensemble austraLYSIS, which has performed in 30 countries, and has previously been a research biochemist, foundation director of the Heart Research Institute, and vice-chancellor and president of the University of Canberra.

Thomas F. DeFrantz is chair of African and African American Studies at Duke University, and director of SLIPPAGE: Performance, Culture, Technology, a research group that explores emerging technology in live performance applications. His books include the edited volume *Dancing Many Drums: Excavations in African American Dance* (Wisconsin, 2002), *Dancing Revelations: Alvin Ailey's Embodiment of African American Culture* (Oxford, 2004), and *Black Performance Theory*, co-edited with Anita Gonzalez (Duke, 2014). A director and writer, he is the former president of the Society of Dance History Scholars.

William Duggan is on the faculty of Columbia Business School, where he teaches strategic intuition in MBA and Executive MBA courses and Executive Education sessions. In 2007 the journal *Strategy+Business* named his book, *Strategic Intuition*, "Best Strategy Book of the Year." Professor Duggan has also given talks and workshops on strategic intuition to thousands of executives from companies in countries around the world. He has BA, MA and PhD degrees from Columbia University.

Angela Esterhammer is principal of Victoria College and professor of English and comparative literature at the University of Toronto. Her publications include *Creating States: Studies in the Performative Language of John Milton and William Blake* (Toronto, 1994), *The Romantic Performative: Language and Action in British and German Romanticism* (Stanford, 2000), *Romanticism and Improvisation, 1750–1850* (Cambridge, 2008), and the edited volumes *Romantic Poetry* (John Benjamins, 2002) and *Spheres of Action: Speech and Performance in Romantic Culture* (Toronto, 2009). Her current research examines interrelations among improvisational performance, print culture, periodicals, and fiction in the early nineteenth century.

Susan Leigh Foster, choreographer and scholar, is distinguished professor in the Department of World Arts and Cultures/Dance at UCLA. She is the author of *Reading Dancing: Bodies and Subjects in Contemporary American Dance* (California, 1986), *Choreography and Narrative: Ballet's Staging of Story and Desire* (Indiana, 1996), *Dances* *that Describe Themselves: The Improvised Choreography of Richard Bull* (Wesleyan, 2002), and *Choreographing Empathy: Kinesthesia in Performance* (Routledge, 2010). She is also the editor of three anthologies: *Choreographing History* (Indiana, 1995), *Corporealities* (Routledge, 1996), and *Worlding Dance* (Palgrave Macmillan, 2009). Three of her danced lectures can be found at the Pew Center for Arts and Heritage website, http://danceworkbook.pcah.us/susan-foster/index.html.

Michael Gallope is an assistant professor in the Department of Cultural Studies and Comparative Literature at the University of Minnesota. His research examines music and sound from a problem-based perspective that brings together the disciplines of philosophy, critical theory, aesthetics, and cultural history. He taught previously at the University of Chicago, where he was a member of the Society of Fellows, and at New York University, where he completed his PhD in historical musicology. As a practicing musician, he has worked in a variety of genres from avant-garde composition, experimental music, and free improvisation to rock and electronic dance music.

Lydia Goehr is professor of philosophy at Columbia University. She is the author of *The Imaginary Museum of Musical Works: An Essay in the Philosophy of Music* (Oxford, 1992/ 2007); *The Quest for Voice: Music, Politics, and the Limits of Philosophy* (Oxford, 1998); and *Elective Affinities: Musical Essays on the History of Aesthetic Theory* (Columbia, 2008); and co-editor with Daniel Herwitz of *The Don Giovanni Moment: Essays on the Legacy of an Opera* (Columbia, 2006).

Danielle Goldman is an assistant professor of critical dance studies and dance program coordinator at Eugene Lang College, The New School. She is the author of *I Want to Be Ready: Improvised Dance as a Practice of Freedom* (Michigan, 2010), and she has published articles in *Dance Research Journal, Dance Research, Etcetera, Movement Research Performance Journal, The Drama Review*, and *Women & Performance*. She has danced with DD Dorvillier and Beth Gill.

Garry L. Hagberg is the James H. Ottaway Professor of Philosophy and Aesthetics at Bard College. His books include *Meaning and Interpretation: Wittgenstein, Henry James, and Literary Knowledge* (Cornell, 1994) and *Art as Language: Wittgenstein, Meaning, and Aesthetic Theory* (Cornell, 1995); his most recent book is *Describing Ourselves: Wittgenstein and Autobiographical Consciousness* (Oxford, 2011). He has edited *Art and Ethical Criticism* (Blackwell, 2008), co-edited *A Companion to the Philosophy of Literature* (Blackwell, 2010), and is editor of the journal *Philosophy and Literature*. He is also co-author of *The Guitar Compendium: Technique, Improvisation, Musicianship, Theory* (three vols., Advance, 1989), is presently working on a book on aesthetic issues in jazz improvisation, and continues to record as a jazz guitarist.

Timothy Hampton teaches comparative literature and French at the University of California at Berkeley. He has written widely on literature and politics, focusing primarily on early modern Europe. Among his publications are *Fictions of Embassy: Literature and Diplomacy in Early Modern Europe* (Cornell, 2009), "La foi des traités" (*Yale French*

Studies, 2013), and "Tangled Generation: Dylan, Petrarch, Kerouac, and the Poetics of Escape" (*Critical Inquiry*, 2013). His current projects touch on the history of the emotions and on popular music.

Paul Ingram is the Kravis Professor of Business at the Columbia Business School and faculty director of the Columbia Advanced Management Program. The courses he teaches on leadership and strategy benefit from his research on organizations in the United States, Canada, Israel, Britain, China, and Australia. His research has been published in more than fifty articles, book chapters, and books. Ingram's current research projects examine the structure and impact of executives' professional values, the impact of income inequality on life satisfaction, and the question of how social structure and culture influenced participation in the Liverpool slave trade.

Vijay Iyer is a pianist, composer, improviser, bandleader, and electronic musician, and the Franklin D. and Florence Rosenblatt Professor of the Arts in the Department of Music at Harvard University. He holds an interdisciplinary PhD in Technology and the Arts from the University of California, Berkeley. His recent honors include a MacArthur Fellowship, a Doris Duke Performing Artists Award, a Grammy nomination, and the Pianist of the Year award in the *DownBeat* International Critics Poll. He has published in *Music Perception, Journal of Consciousness Studies, Critical Studies in Improvisation*, and various anthologies, and has released nineteen recordings as a leader.

Anthea Kraut is an associate professor in the Department of Dance at the University of California, Riverside, where she teaches courses in critical dance studies. Her first book, *Choreographing the Folk: The Dance Stagings of Zora Neale Hurston* (Minnesota, 2008), received a Special Citation from the Society of Dance History Scholars' de la Torre Bueno Prize® for a distinguished book of dance scholarship. Her next book, *Choreographing Copyright: Race, Gender, and Intellectual Property Rights in American Dance,* is forthcoming from Oxford University Press.

George E. Lewis is the Edwin H. Case Professor of American Music at Columbia University. A fellow of the American Academy of Arts and Sciences, his honors include a MacArthur Fellowship (2002) and a Guggenheim Fellowship (2015). A member of the Association for the Advancement of Creative Musicians (AACM) since 1971, Lewis's creative work has been presented by the BBC Scottish Symphony Orchestra, London Philharmonia Orchestra, Radio-Sinfonieorchester Stuttgart, International Contemporary Ensemble, and others. His widely acclaimed book, *A Power Stronger Than Itself: The AACM and American Experimental Music* (Chicago, 2008) received the American Book Award and the American Musicological Society's first Music in American Culture Award. In 2015, Lewis received the degree of Doctor of Music (DMus, *honoris causa)* from the University of Edinburgh.

Tracy McMullen is an assistant professor of music at Bowdoin College and an improvising musician (saxophone). Her teaching and research engage a variety of issues in popular music, jazz, and American culture. Her articles have appeared or are forthcoming in journals including *Current Musicology*, *The Journal of Popular Music Studies*, and *Critical Studies in Improvisation/Études Critiques en Improvisation*; the edited volumes *Big Ears: Listening for Gender in Jazz Studies* (Duke, 2008); and *People Get Ready: The Future of Jazz Is Now* (Duke, 2013); and the reference works *The Encyclopedia of African American Music*, *The Encyclopedia of African American Culture*, *The Oxford Handbooks Online in Music*; and the *Grove Dictionary of American Music*.

Fred Moten lives in Los Angeles and teaches at the University of California, Riverside. His books include *In the Break: The Aesthetics of the Black Radical Tradition* (Minnesota, 2003), *Hughson's Tavern* (Leon, 2008), *B. Jenkins* (Duke, 2010), *The Undercommons* (with Stefano Harney; Autonomedia, 2013), *The Feel Trio* (Letter Machine, 2014), and *The Little Edges* (Wesleyan, 2014).

Glyn P. Norton is Willcox B. and Harriet M. Adsit Professor of International Studies, Emeritus, at Williams College. He is the editor of Volume 3 (The Renaissance) of *The Cambridge History of Literary Criticism* (2008), and author of *Montaigne and the Introspective Mind* (Mouton, 1975), *The Ideology and Language of Translation in Renaissance France and Their Humanist Antecedents* (Droz, 1984), and numerous essays on French Renaissance and neo-Latin rhetoric, literature and criticism, and Quintilian. He has received fellowships and awards from the Guggenheim Foundation, The National Endowment for the Humanities, and the École Normale Supérieure. He is currently completing a book, *Eloquence Beside Itself: The Theory and Art of Improvisation in the French Renaissance and Neoclassical Texts*.

Gary Peters is professor of critical and cultural theory at York St. John University, England. His books include *Irony and Singularity: Aesthetic Education from Kant to Levinas* (Ashgate, 2005) and *The Philosophy of Improvisation* (Chicago, 2009). He is currently working on a book entitled *Improvisations on Improvisation* (also Chicago). With his wife Fiona Peters, he co-edited *Thoughts of Love* (Cambridge Scholars, 2013). He plays the pedal steel guitar and has performed with improvisers such as Lol Coxhill, Steve Beresford, Veryan Weston, and John Stevens.

Benjamin Piekut is a historian of experimental music, jazz, and rock after 1960, and an associate professor of musicology at Cornell University. He is the author of *Experimentalism Otherwise: The New York Avant-Garde and Its Limits* (California, 2011) and the editor of *Tomorrow Is the Question: New Directions in Experimental Music Studies* (Michigan, 2014). With David Nicholls, he co-edited a special issue of *Contemporary Music Review* for John Cage's 100th birthday. He has published articles in *Jazz Perspectives*, *The Drama Review*, *American Quarterly*, *Twentieth-Century Music*, *Cultural Critique*, and the *Journal of the American Musicological Society*.

Alexandre Pierrepont, an anthropologist whose work focuses on the concept of *diversalité* and the phenomena of internal otherness in Western societies—more specifically on African American music as an alternative social institution—divides his time between North America and France, between different "jazz worlds" and the academy. He is an associate researcher for the laboratories CANTHEL (Centre d'anthropologie culturelle) at the Human and Social Sciences Faculty at the University Paris 5—Sorbonne, and CERILAC, Centre d'étude et de recherche interdisciplinaire de l'UFR (lettres, arts et cinema) at the Department of Literature, Arts, and Cinema at the University Paris 7—Denis Diderot, and served as postdoctoral fellow at the Improvisation, Community, and Social Practice group at McGill University.

Clyde G. Reed is professor emeritus in the Department of Economics at Simon Fraser University. He received his PhD in economics from the University of Washington. His recent work on inequality was published in the *Journal of Political Economy* and the *European Review of Economic History* in 2013. As a double bass player, Reed has performed at major jazz festivals in North America and Europe. Recent recordings with the Rich Halley 4, *Back From Beyond* (2012) and *Crossing the Passes* (2013), received prestigious 4-star reviews in *DownBeat*.

Paul Richards was professor of anthropology at University College London and professor of technology and agrarian development at Wageningen University, The Netherlands. He retired in 2010 and is now director of junior faculty research programs at Njala University, Sierra Leone, where he runs several research projects on post-conflict social and institutional change. His books include *Coping with Hunger* (Unwin Hyman, 1986) and *Fighting for the Rain Forest* (Heinemann, 1996). His recent articles include items on war as performance, the distribution of witchcraft cases in post-war settlements around the Gola forest, and social pathways for Ebola Virus Disease in Sierra Leone.

Philosopher and musician **David Rothenberg** is the author of *Why Birds Sing* (Basic, 2005), now published in eight languages and turned into a feature-length BBC TV documentary. Rothenberg has also written *Thousand Mile Song* (Basic, 2008), about making music live with whales, *Survival of the Beautiful* (Bloomsbury, 2011), on evolution and beauty, and *Bug Music* (St. Martin's, 2013), on insects and their million-years old music. His music, recorded on ECM, Gruenrekorder, and the Terra Nova labels, usually involves an integration with his clarinet improvisations with live and recorded natural sounds. Rothenberg has issued nine CDs under his own name. He is professor of philosophy and music at the New Jersey Institute of Technology. www.davidrothenberg.net

Amy Seham is the author of *Whose Improv Is It, Anyway? Beyond Second City* (Mississippi, 2001), a book analyzing the workings of gender, race, and power in six important improv troupes in Chicago. She has given workshops on "Resisting Stereotypes in Improv" at Second City-Toronto, Fringe Benefits, The Funny Woman Festival, and numerous universities across the United States. Director, playwright, and coach, Seham is a professor of theater and dance at Gustavus Adolphus College, in a program that focuses on performance for social justice. She lives in St. Peter, Minnesota, with her daughter, Miranda.

Erik Simpson is professor of English at Grinnell College. He is the author of *Literary Minstrelsy, 1770–1830: Minstrels and Improvisers in British, Irish, and American Literature* (Palgrave Macmillan, 2008) and *Mercenaries in British and American Literature, 1790–1830: Writing, Fighting, and Marrying for Money* (Edinburgh, 2010), in addition to articles on British literature, transatlantic literature, and the use of digital technologies in undergraduate teaching.

Davide Sparti has written 11 books and over 90 articles in journals such as the *Deutsche Zeitschrift für Philosophie, European Journal of Social Theory, European Journal of Philosophy, Philosophy and Literature,* and *Philosophy and Social Criticism*. Co-founder of the journal *Studi culturali*, Sparti's work deals with the epistemology of the social sciences and the relation between identity and recognition, as well as improvised action, Wittgenstein, Cavell, and Foucault. After having taught at the Universities of Milano and Bologna, he is currently professor at the University of Siena. Sparti is a fellow of the Humboldt Stiftung and the Collegium Budapest and holds a PhD from the European University Institute.

Samuel Wells is vicar of St. Martin-in-the-Fields, Trafalgar Square, and visiting professor of Christian ethics at King's College, London. He was previously dean of the chapel and research professor of Christian ethics at Duke University. He is the author of 22 books in ethical, devotional, and exegetical fields, including *Improvisation: The Drama of Christian Ethics* (Brazos, 2004), *God's Companions: Reimagining Christian Ethics* (Blackwell, 2006), *Learning to Dream Again* (Eerdmans, 2013) and *A Nazareth Manifesto: Being with God* (Wiley-Blackwell, 2015).

THE OXFORD HANDBOOK OF

CRITICAL IMPROVISATION STUDIES

VOLUME 1

INTRODUCTION

On Critical Improvisation Studies

GEORGE E. LEWIS AND BENJAMIN PIEKUT

CULTURAL historian Andreas Huyssen has perceptively observed that Fluxus, an art movement that featured improvisation as a key element, was "an avant-garde born out of the spirit of music. . . . [F]or the first time in the twentieth century, music played the leading part in an avant-garde movement that encompassed a variety of artistic media and strategies."[1] We would like to venture that critical improvisation studies was born out of a similar spirit: music scholars and practitioner-scholars have taken important leadership roles in the field. Reflecting the pre-eminent position of music in discussions of improvisation in performance, critical improvisation studies draws substantially from musical experience. In his essay for this *Handbook*, ethnomusicologist Bruno Nettl, one of the pioneers of twentieth-century scholarship on improvisation, found it "surprising that the word 'improvisation' (or any of its synonyms) appears rarely, if ever, in the early literature of ethnomusicology, and the concept is virtually untouched by the early scholars in this field." While acknowledging that music historians had been interested in improvisation since at least the late nineteenth century, Nettl cites the work of Hungarian scholar Ernest Ferand as "the first attempt to synthesize the various kinds of improvisation in Western art music as a single concept."[2]

Around the 1960s, ethnomusicologists began producing detailed case studies of musical improvisation, concentrating on jazz, Hindustani and Carnatic classical music, and Iranian (Persian) music—a particular focus of Nettl's that formed the basis for his important article, "Thoughts on Improvisation: A Comparative Approach."[3] Since the mid-1970s and moving into the 1980s, historical musicology's increasing interest in improvisation has gone hand in hand with the field's turn to cultural history, popular music studies, and the investigation of experimental music scenes, as expressed by the term "new musicology." William Kinderman's work on Beethoven; Annette Richards and Kenneth Hamilton's work on European Romanticism (a topic Dana Gooley extends in this *Handbook*); John Rink's work in music theory on Heinrich Schenker; the work of Anna Maria Busse Berger, Julie Cumming, Peter Schubert, and *Handbook* contributor

Leo Treitler on medieval music; and the editors' engagement with experimental music, sound art, and interactive technology constitute only a small part of musicology's current engagement with improvisation studies.[4]

Proceeding from the example of Fluxus, however, critical improvisation studies is creating an agenda in which the arts become part of a larger network tracing the entire human condition of improvisation. Critical improvisation studies has "exploded" in recent years, with a surge in interdisciplinary inquiry across many artistic and nominally nonartistic fields; for this *Handbook*, we commissioned new articles from a sizable group of distinguished senior and emerging scholars representing a wide variety of disciplines in the humanities, sciences, and the arts.

One might look to musicology and ethnomusicology as among the earliest areas in which the study of improvisation might have gained traction, but we have evidence from *Handbook* essays by literary scholars Glyn Norton, Timothy Hampton, Angela Esterhammer, and Erik Simpson, as well as a recent edited volume by Timothy McGee, that serious scholarly and informed lay attention to improvisation's effects and histories, both within and outside of the arts, have been an integral part of world intellectual history since early in the Common Era.[5] For example, spontaneous oral composition has a very long history, appearing in the political arena well before the advent of the eighteenth-century Italian *improvvisatori*. One of the earliest focused critical works on improvisation, the first-century *Institutio Oratoria* of Quintilian, was forgotten for over a millennium until the sixteenth-century recrudescence of the theory and practice of extemporaneous rhetoric in Europe. A 1947 book by a Catholic nun, Sister Miriam Joseph's *Shakespeare's Use of the Arts of Language*, neatly analyzes and classifies the vast number of rhetorical devices that Elizabethan schoolchildren of Shakespeare's time were expected to learn to deploy in extemporaneous debate.[6]

Thus, while recognizing the important historical role played by music in the practice of improvisation, it is entirely in keeping with this larger history of improvisation as an aspect of the broader human condition that our *Handbook* is intended to explore both artistic and non-artistic ways in which improvisation functions in culture. We therefore asked authors to take particular care to contextualize their work in dialogue with larger debates and histories in their own and other fields.

We also decided to concentrate on theoretical, metatheoretical, critical, and historical engagements with improvisation. We fully recognize that this focus tended to leave out other encounters with the topic, some of which have been influential and even predominant, particularly in treatments of artistic practice. For instance, we decided not to feature (auto)ethnographies, analytical case studies, or treatments of particular traditions, methods, practices, genres, or works. Also essentially absent here are some regularly recurring features of edited volumes on traditional artistic media (in particular, the performing arts), such as (auto)biographies, interviews, first-person narratives, and how-to discussions of practice. Finally, although some of our contributors discuss music pedagogy, we decided to forgo discussions of skill development, and/or working with children on musical improvisation.[7] Although these kinds of writing on improvisation have produced important texts for the field, we took the view that critical and theoretical approaches would best enable cross-disciplinary conversation.

DEFINITIONS AND ISSUES

Once upon a time (at least in musical scholarship), constructing a definition of improvisation seemed a relatively straightforward matter. The *Oxford Dictionary of Music*'s pithy definition was typical, framing improvisation as a performance conducted "according to the inventive whim of the moment, i.e. without a written or printed score, and not from memory."[8] These perspectives appeared to draw implicitly upon an ideologically driven dialectic between improvisation and composition, reflecting widespread contention regarding not just the nature of improvisation, but its propriety as well. This debate dovetailed with improvisation's fraught status in Western classical music history and culture, in which improvisation, particularly since the eighteenth century, was compared with the practice of composition, with clear prejudices in favor of the latter's presumed advantages of unity and coherence in musical utterance.

The British experimental guitarist Derek Bailey's *Improvisation: Its Nature and Practice in Music*, one of the most widely cited books on the subject, simply avoids creating a definition at all, preferring to describe cases in which improvisation—as Bailey understands it—works, in order to fulfill the remit of the book to divine its nature and practice. Similarly, this *Handbook* makes no explicit attempt to negotiate a single overarching definition of improvisation. Rather, as we see it, the critical study of improvisation seeks to examine improvisation's effects, interrogate its discourses, interpret narratives and histories related to it, discover implications of those narratives and histories, and uncover its ideologies.

Particularly before 1995, scholarly commentary on improvisation in the West was found largely in discussions of traditional artistic expressive media—most centrally, music, dance, theater, and their tributaries. Reflecting its status as the West's preeminent improvised music, jazz received a large share of scholarly attention early on, both appreciative and disapprobative, from social scientists and philosophers in particular, including Alan Merriam, Howard S. Becker, and Theodor Adorno.[9]

In dance, as Cynthia Novack, Melinda Tufnell, and Ann Cooper Albright have extensively documented, the emergence of contact improvisation in the 1970s was crucial to an emerging experimentalism. In theater, the first-person accounts and methodological interventions of Keith Johnstone were highly influential, while the work of Chicago's Second City scene looked back to the work of Konstantin Stanislavski and the sixteenth-century commedia dell'arte. The work of *Handbook* contributors Susan Leigh Foster, Amy Seham, Thomas DeFrantz, Danielle Goldman, and Anthea Kraut has opened up this area of scholarship with additional perspectives on issues of race, class, gender, and sexuality.[10]

All three media attracted the attention of specialists in wellbeing and pedagogy—such as Émile Jaques-Dalcroze, Fritz Hegi, Tony Wigram, and Patricia Shehan Campbell—who developed therapies based in improvisation.[11] The issues in this literature are well summarized and extended in the *Handbook* article by Raymond MacDonald and Graeme Wilson. Psychological, psychiatric, and psychoanalytic strategies employed improvisation as well, as in work by John Byng-Hall on family counseling.[12]

A large number of key themes resonate throughout much earlier commentary. However, most of them can be taxonomized under a number of master tropes, the first of which concerns a certain reluctance actually to use the term *improvisation* in discussions of the practice. As a 2002 research proposal by Susan Foster, Adriene Jenik, and George E. Lewis noted, in art and music histories and criticism, "improvisative practices were often erased, masked, or otherwise discussed without reference to the term. Substitutions such as 'happening,' 'action,' and 'intuition' often masked the presence of improvisation."[13] Even one of the most frequently cited texts among later generations in improvisation studies, sociologist Erving Goffman's 1959 *The Presentation of Self in Everyday Life*, never invokes the term.[14]

Related to the trope of masking is the trope of neglect, a point made by Nettl in the title of the introduction to his 1998 co-edited volume, *In The Course of Performance*: "An Art Neglected in Scholarship." This trope tends to animate first-generation new improvisation studies; thus, in compensation for the massive Western cultural investment in neglect, dismissal, parody, and general opposition to improvisation amid which their work was appearing, later scholars often (over)valorized the practice. For instance, as David Gere noted in a 2003 collection of essays on dance improvisation, "To improvise, it is held, is to engage in aimless, even talentless, noodling."[15] Gere provides his own riposte, averring that "improvisation is by its very nature among the most rigorous of human endeavors."[16]

Indeed, writers have emphasized that exhibitions of mastery and virtuosity compose part of the pleasure of improvisation. Domenico Pietropaolo identifies this as a preoccupation of long standing, to be found not only in musical genres, but also in the tradition of medieval rhetoric and its forebears in Greek and Roman oratory: "[A] great legacy of the second sophistic with its celebrated emphasis on virtuosity, improvisation was for medieval rhetoric a skill to be mastered after long hours of practice."[17]

Another trope that appears frequently concerns a binary opposition between process and product. An influential 1989 article by sociologist Alan Durant, "Improvisation in the Political Economy of Music," maintains that the experimental improvised music that emerged in the United States and especially in Europe in the mid-1960s "foregrounds—in its practice as well as in its name—the relationship between the *product* of performance (the musical 'text') and the *process* through which that product comes into being."[18] Particularly in music, it is frequently asserted that improvisers are more interested in the process of creation than in its products. In the influential formulation of Ted Gioia, this renders artistic improvisation (and jazz improvisation in particular) an "imperfect" art, governed by an "aesthetic of imperfection."[19]

For Andy Hamilton, writing in 2000, "Gioia's point about the 'haphazard art' was that improvisation fails *more often* than art music; not that it always fails." Hamilton's formulation reminds us that the process-product opposition inevitably becomes mapped onto the improvisation-composition binary in Western music scholarship, as well as the great divide between low and high culture that is now so regularly bridged. His essay is one of many that invoke the process-product discussion as a way of opening the door to discussions of whether improvised music meets the criteria of the work concept in Western music.

Anticipating the 1990s work of ethnomusicologist Paul Berliner on jazz, Berliner, architectural designer Charles Jencks's 1972 book *Adhocism: The Case for Improvisation* used the term *improvisation* as a trope for a process of "using an available system or dealing with an existing situation in a new way to solve a problem."[20] Jencks declared that the principle/practice of adhocism was observable in and applicable to "many human endeavours," an observation also made by philosopher Gilbert Ryle, writing in 1976. In one of his last essays, titled simply "Improvisation," Ryle intimates that "I shall soon be reminding you of some of the familiar and unaugust sorts of improvisations which, just *qua* thinking beings, we all essay every day of the week, indeed in every hour of the waking day."[21] Even if we may admit that, on some level, not all of our activities are improvised, the line between improvised and nonimprovised activities may not be as bright as we suppose, and it may well be that it is the non-improvised event that stands out as an anomalous event in the flow of everyday life. For example, in his influential book, *The Improvisation of Musical Dialogue*, philosopher-theologian and *Handbook* contributor Bruce Ellis Benson identifies several improvisative moments within the nominally non-improvised activity of music composition.[22]

Ryle's essay invokes the quotidian and transposes the language of adhocism to a near-universal register that sounds a lot like "using an available system or dealing with an existing situation in a new way":

> I want now to go further and to show that . . . to be thinking what he is here and now up against, he must both be trying to adjust himself to just this present once-only situation *and* in doing this to be applying lessons already learned. There must be in his response a union of some Ad Hockery with some know-how. If the normal human is not at once *improvising* and improvising *warily,* he is not engaging his somewhat trained wits in some momentarily live issue, but perhaps acting from sheer unthinking habit. So thinking, I now declare quite generally, is, at the least, the engaging of partly trained wits in a partly fresh situation. It is the pitting of an acquired competence or skill against an unprogrammed opportunity, obstacle or hazard. It is a bit like putting some *new* wine into *old* bottles.[23]

Remarkably, Ryle's essay does not mention music at all, an omission that could well be strategic rather than unmindful. After all, had philosophers of music of his day wanted to think about improvisation, numerous examples were on offer, but other than the work of Vladimir Jankélévitch and Philip Alperson, the philosophy of music offered little where improvisation was concerned.[24] In this *Handbook*, Alperson directly confronts this near-erasure, while Gary Peters, whose 2009 book, *The Philosophy of Improvisation*, constitutes a new departure in the field, explores the relation between improvisation and Edmund Husserl's ideas on time-consciousness.[25]

One area that could be taken up by scholars working on the aesthetics of improvisation is the relation between an aesthetics of perfection/imperfection and issues of moral perfectionism taken up by philosophers working largely outside of music but with significant musical interests, such as Stanley Cavell. Arnold I. Davidson's *Handbook* essay addresses moral perfectionism and improvisation, relating it to Pierre Hadot's ideas on the spiritual exercises conceived by philosophers of antiquity as a means toward transformation of the self, and taking as his example the music of Sonny Rollins. For Hadot,

> Attention (*prosoche*) is the fundamental Stoic spiritual attitude. It is a continuous vigilance and presence of mind, self-consciousness which never sleeps, and a constant tension of the spirit. Thanks to this attitude, the philosopher is fully aware of what he does at each instant, and he *wills* his actions fully. . . . We could also define this attitude as "concentration on the present moment." . . . Attention (*prosoche*) allows us to respond immediately to events, as if they were questions asked of us all of a sudden.[26]

Samuel Wells's essay for the *Handbook* approaches ethics from an ecclesiastical perspective that invokes improvisational theater. Other philosophers engage improvisation without often invoking aesthetics or artistic examples, such as Martha Nussbaum and Barbara Herman's writing on moral improvisation and situational ethics, as well as J. David Velleman's work on collective intentions,[27] an issue that Garry Hagberg's article in this *Handbook* takes up in detail.[28]

Issues of identity have been strongly connected with discussions of musical improvisation through such putatively African American cultural tropes as signifying, storytelling and narrative, personal voice, and individuality within an aggregate.[29] The emergence of jazz studies as an important academic discipline has attracted both senior and emerging scholars in film, literature, history, social science, and cultural studies, as well as music, generating a set of new questions around jazz that are explored in edited volumes by Daniel Fischlin and Ajay Heble, Robert G. O'Meally, Brent Hayes Edwards, Farah Jasmine Griffin, Sherrie Tucker, and many others.[30] As a field, literary studies has made significant contributions to jazz and improvisation studies, and this is reflected in *Handbook* articles by Walton Muyumba, Patricia Ryan, Hazel Smith, Sara Villa, and Rob Wallace.

Particularly in earlier jazz studies literature, the identity of the artist was often deemed homologous with the musical results, a relationship that Gioia has forcefully asserted:

> Indeed, only a particular type of temperament would be attracted to an art form which values spur-of-the-moment decisions over carefully considered choices, which prefers the haphazard to the premeditated, which views unpredictability as a virtue and sees cool-headed calculation as a vice. If Mingus, Monk, Young, and Parker had been predictable and dependable individuals, it seems unlikely that their music could have remained unpredictable and innovative.[31]

It is but a short step from an assumption of this nature to the invocation of notions of genius and self-expression, as Edgar Landgraf, one of the most wide-ranging among recent improvisation theorists, points out:

Instead of challenging the aesthetic tradition whose concepts fail to account for the specificities of this improvisational art form, Gioia propagates an understanding of jazz in terms of nineteenth-century aesthetics of genius that asks us to ignore this art form's "imperfections" and appreciate improvisation as "the purest expression possible of the artist's emotions and feelings."[32]

Homologies between musical improvisative practice and sociopolitical expression were given powerful voice in LeRoi Jones's 1963 book, *Blues People*.[33] Around the same time, the phenomenological sociology of Alfred Schutz, in his well-known 1964 essay, "Making Music Together," asserted that "a study of the social relationships connected with the musical process may lead to some insights valid for many other forms of social intercourse."[34] Anthropologist John Szwed noted that

> The esthetics of jazz demand that a musician play with complete originality, with an assertion of his own musical individuality. . . . At the same time jazz requires that musicians be able to merge their unique voices in the totalizing, collective improvisations of polyphony and heterophony. The implications of this esthetic are profound and more than vaguely threatening, for no political system has yet been devised with social principles which reward maximal individualism within the frame work of spontaneous egalitarian interaction.[35]

In this way, improvisation is also frequently symbolically endowed with the potential for the overthrow of hierarchical practices. A contrary turn in this discussion is provided by political theorist Yves Citton's invocation of improvisation's "diagonality in relation to the traditional parameters of vertical domination and horizontal equality: its (fundamentally political) challenge is to devise collective forms of agency which articulate the outstanding power of the participating singularities with the principle of equal respect necessary to find non-oppressive strength in numbers."[36] In his *Handbook* article, Citton notices that Bruno Latour's declaration, "Il n'a pas de monde commun; il faut le composer" can easily be redirected toward a view of an improvised common world in which, following fellow contributor Daniel Belgrad, a "culture of spontaneity" exercises strong sociopolitical effects.[37]

In any case, as pointed out by both Stephen Greenblatt and Tzvetan Todorov, improvisation can easily support imperial ideologies.[38] Greenblatt and Todorov see in improvisation a practice vital to the European conquest of the New World, in particular via what the former calls "the ability to both capitalize on the unforeseen and transform given materials into one's own scenario." Greenblatt calls this ability "opportunistic," a term that speaks to the oft-invoked foregrounding of attention and awareness in discussions of improvisation but without ceding to the practice any kind of moral high ground.

The mobile, improvisatory sensibility that Greenblatt identifies in imperial conquest (and the machinations of Iago) also marks epochal change: the sensibility, according to Greenblatt, emerges with the early modern period. We can identify a similar periodizing turn in Michel Foucault's late fascination with Kant's essay on *Aufklärung* and the specific qualities of modernity, which Foucault understood to be a kind of improvisational attitude or ethos toward the self, its contemporary moment, and its historical contingency—in short, a "mode of reflective relation to the present."[39] Although he does not use the term *improvisation*, Foucault adopts many of its key characteristics in his description of the modern ethos, which is one of continual performance and testing of the self as an "object of a complex and difficult elaboration."[40]

The point of this experimental historico-critical attitude, for Foucault, is "both to grasp the points where change is possible and desirable, and to determine the precise form this change should take."[41] The critic therefore attempts to convert states of domination, in which power relations are frozen or blocked, into mobile sites for the conscious practice of freedom.[42] The philosopher's employment of improvisational language (experimentation, adaptation, reflection on the present, mobility) in relation to considerations of freedom in his final years was not a coincidence—as many authors have noted, including Ali Jihad Racy in this *Handbook*, improvisation is frequently represented as symbolic of freedom and liberation. At the same time, however, moderating this image of improvisation as an engine for change is the binary opposition of freedom/structure (or freedom/constraint), routinely invoked in response to portrayals of musical "free improvisation."

In these invocations, improvisation must always be entirely unfettered, leading the analyst to develop fettered alternatives in the form of "regulated," "constrained," or "structured" improvisation. For example, in her 2004 book *Undoing Gender*, Judith Butler presents a model of how constraint is encountered in social interaction:

> If gender is a kind of a doing, an incessant activity performed, in part, without one's knowing and without one's willing, it is not for that reason automatic or mechanical. On the contrary, it is a practice of improvisation within a scene of constraint. Moreover, one does not "do" one's gender alone. One is always "doing" with or for another, even if the other is only imaginary. What I call my "own" gender appears perhaps at times as something that I author or, indeed, own. But the terms that make up one's own gender are, from the start, outside oneself, beyond oneself in a sociality that has no single author (and that radically contests the notion of authorship itself).[43]

On this view, the primary constraints on human freedom lie in the social encounter with multiple agents, mediated as they may be through convention, language, tradition, or idiom.

Often enough, discussions of constraint turn from the simple presumption of their presence in any situation to a further assertion of a fundamental need for constraint as a precondition for a "successful" improvisation, an assertion that can appear surprisingly bereft of corroboration. For example, in his 1964 book on the anthropology of music, Alan Merriam admitted, "While it is clear that there must always be limits imposed upon improvisation, we do not know what these limits are."[44] Perceptions of conceptual rigidity in the frequent mapping of the freedom/structure binary onto low/high culture oppositions, as well as the improvisation-composition binary (which Merriam adopted in his book), have prompted more nuanced approaches based in theories of mediation, such as in the recent work of Georgina Born.[45]

In any event, attempts to elucidate the nature of constraint have suffered from a discourse that frames constraints as somehow outside of the system of improvisative production itself. Sociologist of science Andrew Pickering saw this discourse as "the language of the prison: constraints are always there, just like the walls of the prison, even though we only bump into them occasionally (and can learn not to bump into them at all)."[46] Against this static, essentialist model, Pickering substitutes a related but more flexible notion of resistance:

> In the real-time analysis of practice, one has to see resistance as genuinely emergent in time, as a block arising in practice to this or that passage of goal-oriented practice. Thus, though resistance and constraint have an evident conceptual affinity, they are, as it were, perpendicular to one another in time: constraint is synchronic, antedating practice and enduring through it, while resistance is diachronic, constitutively indexed by time. Furthermore, while constraint resides in a distinctively human realm, resistance, as I have stressed, exists only in the crosscutting of the realms of human and material agency.[47]

Another frequently encountered trope of the constraints on improvisation involves the notion of a knowledge base from which improvisers are said to draw. In music this can involve larger questions of an idiom, genre, or cultural milieu that grounds musical expression—in Derrida's formulation, "the logic that ties repetition to alterity."[48] In his 1978 book Derek Bailey advanced the now-influential yet still theoretically rocky opposition between idiomatic and non-idiomatic music,[49] and analogously, sociologist Pierre Bourdieu's 1977 book *Outline of a Theory of Practice* asserted that improvisation in social life draws from a *habitus* that forecloses the possibility of "unpredictable novelty." Bourdieu's notion of the *habitus*, worked out with and against his ethnography of rural Berber kinship practices, critiques the romantic notion of unmediated spontaneity. He discovers a "durably installed generative principle of regulated improvisations."[50] For Bourdieu, the *habitus* exists (again) within a recursive logic, both producing and being produced through praxis. Each individual agent, acting without objectively structured correlation with others, "wittingly or unwittingly, willy nilly, is a producer and reproducer of objective meaning."[51] Those who produce these actions manifest a kind of "intentionless invention."[52]

More routinely offered than this early irruption of the notion of emergence is the idea of improvisation as a process of concatenation and recombination. Ethnomusicologist Paul Berliner's 1994 book on improvisation in jazz described the practice as "reworking precomposed material and designs in relation to unanticipated ideas conceived, shaped, and transformed under the special conditions of performance."[53] Often these materials were portrayed in jazz parlance as "licks"—stock, memorized phrases (or as the saxophonist Eddie Harris called them in his book-length compilation, "cliché capers")—that the players concatenate to produce the music.[54] Cognitive psychologist Philip Johnson-Laird terms this (somewhat dismissively) the "motif theory,"[55] and points out the theory's inability to account for change and novelty. Organizational scientists Kathleen McGinn and Angela Keros, on the other hand, had no trouble asserting in a 2002 paper

that, "improvisations are inherently both active and interactive and contain both familiar moves and unique approaches."[56]

Though distinct, motif theory is commonly linked to the notion of the referent or
model to which improvising musicians take recourse[57] and to the most widely referenced of all early knowledge-base theories, Albert Lord's 1960 book, *The Singer of
Tales*. Milman Parry's pioneering discovery of recurring formulas in Homeric verse,
combined with the fieldwork on Serbo-Croatian oral improvising poets conducted by
Parry and his student Lord in the 1930s, uncovered major structural analogues between
that poetry and Homeric verse, leading to the development of the now influential oral-
formulaic theory.[58] However, Parry was ambivalent about calling Homer himself an oral
poet, and possibly reprising the trope of masking, Lord was wary of conflating oral composition with improvisation.[59] Both of these cautions, as Angela Esterhammer shows in
this volume and other writings, had been thrown to the winds by nineteenth-century
commentators.[60] Theodor Adorno's anti-jazz polemics again raised the topic of formulas in the middle of the twentieth century, but in the context of his critique of a capitalist
"culture industry" that only offered pseudo-individualized performances, standardization, and feigned authenticity.[61]

Psychologist R. Keith Sawyer's wide-ranging and influential work on improvisation,
pedagogy, music, and theater is crucially informed by his work as a jazz pianist. Sawyer
rethinks the notion of the "knowledge base," this time in terms of higher-level cultural
references rather than individual formulas:

> It's difficult for casual audiences to believe that improvisers do not draw on material
> that has been at least partially worked up in rehearsal, but I've performed with many
> improv groups repeatedly—and attended rehearsals—and I have never seen even a
> single line used twice. However, all groups draw on culturally shared emblems and
> stereotypes, which in some sense are "preexisting structures."

As might be expected, the nature of improvisative temporality became a major point of
commentary. An influential formulation in art music distinguishes between aleatoric or
indeterminate modes of expression and the improvisative. One well-expressed theoretical binary opposition is found in a 1971 essay by French musicologist Célestin Deliège,
but in the United States the issue is best known through the writings of composer John
Cage.[62]

Reflecting reaction to the composition-improvisation binary, musical improvisation is frequently characterized as "real-time composition," "instant composition," and
the like. Most frequently, however, artistic improvisation is portrayed as an immediate
(and even unmediated), spontaneous, intuitive creation in real time that bears significant analogues to everyday experience. As dance theorist Cynthia Novack portrayed the
expectations generated by contact improvisation,

> The experience of the movement style and improvisational process itself were thought
> to teach people how to live (to trust, to be spontaneous and "free," to "center" oneself,

and to "go with the flow"), just as the mobile, communal living situations of the young, middle-class participants provided the setting and values which nourished this form. Dancers and audiences saw contact improvisation as, to use Clifford Geertz's phrase, a "model of" and a "model for" an egalitarian, spontaneous way of life.[63]

Here, the role played by memory and history becomes a particularly thorny issue. In a complex contradiction, improvisation is viewed as iterative and repetition-oriented, habit-based, and essentially unrepeatable—all at once. The presumed ephemerality of improvisative products became provisionally forestalled via sound recording technologies, and yet the emergence of these technologies also led to novel formulations of the iterability/alterity binary in comparisons between the ontology of a real-time improvisation and its recorded version.

Another dimension of musical improvisation, this time of an aesthetic nature, is the expectation that a good improvisation be, as Bailey wrote, "a celebration of the moment."[64] The best improvisation will be unique, avoid stagnation and the commonplace, and constantly display or embody innovation, originality (albeit via recombination of existing elements), novelty, freshness, and surprise. The improvisation must also take risks, which come in at least two flavors. Dance theorist Curtis L. Carter maintained that "improvisation as a form of performance runs the risk of falling into habitual repetitive patterns that may become stale for both performers and viewers."[65] The other kind of risk, as expressed by philosopher David Davies, draws upon the composition-improvisation opposition, in that an improviser is "creating a musical structure without the resources for revision available to the composer."[66]

In his discussion of key issues and ideologies surrounding ethnomusicological interpretations of musical improvisation, Stephen Blum writes, "We are not likely to speak of improvisation unless we believe that participants in an event, however they are motivated, share a sense that something unique is happening in their presence at the moment of performance."[67] However, improvisation can take place on much larger time scales than "the moment," and with much larger forces, such as the long-term coping strategies that anthropologist Paul Richards discussed in his *Handbook* essay on farming communities in Sierra Leone, where shifting rice cultivation requires dynamic analysis and response in real—if extended—time to changing natural and social conditions. A number of improvisative methods are deployed that must also change dynamically, and an extensive knowledge base is one result.

Before concluding an overview of this nature, one would need to consider the frequently invoked metaphorical relation between music and spoken language. Johnson-Laird's description presents the fundamental idea:

If you are not an improvising musician, then the best analogy to improvisation is your spontaneous speech. If you ask yourself how you are able to speak a sequence of English sentences that make sense, then you will find that you are consciously aware of only the tip of the process. That is why the discipline of psycholinguistics exists: psychologists need to answer this question too.[68]

Linguist François Grosjean also maintains that spontaneous language production shares important features with music improvisation, including recourse to knowledge bases. Most directly, Grosjean asserts that "spontaneous language production is a form of improvisation."[69] Extending this insight, Sawyer finds that everyday conversation is "both improvised and collaborative."[70]

> [M]ost everyday conversation is *improvisational*—no one joins a conversation with a written script, and participants generally cannot predict where the conversation will go. Everyday conversation is also collaborative, because no single person controls or directs a conversation; instead, the direction of its flow is collectively determined, by all of the participants' contributions. This view of conversation as both improvised and collaborative will be my starting point, leading me into a discussion of several key characteristics of group improvisation, characteristics that I will argue apply equally to both verbal and musical improvisation.[71]

For Sawyer, the key characteristics of improvisation include

- Unpredictable outcome, rather than a scripted, known endpoint;
- Moment-to-moment contingency: the next dialogue turn depends on the one just before;
- Open to collaboration;
- An oral performance, not a written product;
- Embedded in the social context of the performance.[72]

In Sawyer's work, these features come together to describe a phenomenon of "collaborative emergence." In a 2003 book on the topic, he presents an ethnographic study of improvisational theater in early 1990s Chicago that explores how conversations work, using analytic techniques developed for the study of everyday conversation. The result, in Sawyer's terms, presents a challenge to traditional "individualist" psychological methods.[73]

Ingrid Monson's 1996 book, *Saying Something: Jazz Improvisation and Interaction*, provides an important perspective on the ongoing metaphor of music-as-language by situating jazz improvisation as a kind of conversation taking place in the context of African American cultural styles.[74] The work draws upon the linguistics of Michael Silverstein, for whom an everyday conversation amounts to an "improvisational performance of culture" in which "an interactional text . . . is a structure-in-realtime of organized, segmentable, and recognizable event-units of the order of social organizational regularity. . . . [S]ocial action in event-realtime has the capacity to be causally effective in the universe of identities as a basis for relationships and further social action."[75]

What emerges from this extended, yet necessarily incomplete, discussion of issues is the futility of drawing boundaries around the critical study of improvisation. Rather, in this project, we defer definitions in order to allow the scholarly conversation to wander into unforeseen areas. Our intent is to place scholars in virtual dialogue, where the totality of the compendium itself formulates an articulated, emergent, yet unbounded set of issues, drawn from multiple fields and thereby moving beyond the preoccupations of any one.

IMPROVISATION AS A WAY OF LIFE

The view of artistic improvisation as symbolizing social and political formations was dear to many authors in an earlier moment of improvisation studies. Newer critical engagements with the practice tended to turn this view on its head, finding that social and political formations themselves improvise and that improvisation not only enacts such formations directly but also is fundamentally constitutive of them. This turn allows the new critical improvisation studies to free itself from musical and artistic models while encouraging novel theoretical models of musical improvisation that can invoke the social in a higher register.

The kinds of theorizations found in abundance in this *Handbook* tend to feel comfortable invoking the term *improvisation* without either special pleadings or the earlier problematizations and maskings. This is in part because important new discussions of improvisation are taking place across a large range of fields: anthropology and sociology; organizational, political, cognitive, and computer science; economics, theology, neuroscience, and psychology; philosophy, cultural studies, and literary theory; gender and sexuality studies; architecture and urban planning; education; and many others. In working with the contributors for this *Handbook*, we realized early on that scholars working in these areas did not necessarily situate their work in dialogue with the tropes identified in the previous section of this Introduction, and often had little or no investment in musical histories and ideologies, such as the cherished opposition between improvisation and composition. For instance, McGinn and Keros sought to "define an improvisation in the context of a negotiation as a coherent sequence of relational, informational, and procedural actions and responses created, chosen, and carried out by the parties during the social interaction."[76] The prosaic and provisional nature of this definition, in expanding the frame of reference beyond the artistic, places considerable pressure on ideologies that impose upon the concept of improvisation the special sense of creative autonomy and uniqueness that so many commentators on music portrayed as fundamental.

Nonetheless, musical improvisation continues to play an important role as a model for how various fields of scholarship pursue the identification and theorization of improvisative structure and function in human endeavor more generally. For instance, in 1998 the influential journal *Organization Science* devoted an entire issue to the possibilities of conceptually migrating concepts from improvisation toward theories and practices of business management. The issue, which was later published in book form, was one outcome of a 1995 symposium held in Vancouver, Canada, "Jazz as a Metaphor for Organizing in the 21st Century." The conference included performances by noted Canadian jazz musicians as well as organization scholars such as Frank Barrett, an accomplished pianist.

The title of the issue's introduction, "The Organization Science Jazz Festival: Improvisation as a Metaphor for Organizing," playfully cast individual articles as performances on a festival. Influenced by Berliner's *Thinking in Jazz*, contributions by Barrett, Karl Weick, and Mary Jo Hatch spurred the field's now influential "jazz metaphor" for reconceiving interaction and creativity in business and management interactions. This metaphor provides one route toward thinking of improvisation in ways that could be applied to both artistic and nonartistic exchanges.[77]

Around this same time, Claudio Ciborra, whose work combined organizational theory and information systems theory, published another influential book, *The Labyrinths of Information: Challenging the Wisdom of Systems*, in which he introduced notions of bricolage and what he called "drift" in his work on improvisation in management systems and their associated technologies, including his early studies of the Internet. In Ciborra's words,

> Drifting describes a slight, or sometimes significant, shift of the role and function in concrete situations of usage, compared to the planned, pre-defined, and assigned objectives and requirements that the technology is called upon to perform (irrespective of who plans or defines them, whether they are users, sponsors, specialists, vendors, or consultants).[78]

For Ciborra, drifting in the life of technological systems takes place in two related arenas:

> the openness of the technology, its plasticity in response to the re-inventions carried out by users and specialists, who gradually learn to discover and exploit features, affordances, and potentialities of systems. On the other hand, there is the sheer unfolding of the actors' being-in-the-workflow and the continuous stream of interventions, tinkering, and improvisations that colour perceptions of the entire system life cycle.[79]

The encounter between freedom and structure ostensibly played out in musical improvisation also becomes connected with notions of planning. What is frequently heard is that the best improvisations are unscripted and unplanned, appearing with little or no preconceptions or premeditation, and/or drawing upon intuition and the unconscious mind. Hamilton quotes trumpeter-composer Wadada Leo Smith to the effect that "at its highest level, improvisation [is] created entirely within the improviser at the moment of improvisation without any prior structuring."[80]

As it happens, both Ciborra's work and the improvisative approach to organization and management theory more generally do call into question the efficacy of traditional models and practices of planning. A 1999 Ciborra article contrasts planning-oriented views of organization, such as the work of Allan Newell, Herbert Simon, and the artificial intelligence research of Terry Winograd, with research that he sees as more compatible with real-time choice and memory processes, such as the social theory of Anthony Giddens, the sociology of Alfred Schutz, and the philosophy of Edmund Husserl. While the discourse of rules and constraints is never far from a discussion of improvisation, Ciborra's conclusion is that "ordinary decisions on markets and in hierarchies are de facto improvised, no matter how rules and norms are supposed to guide and constrain behavior."[81]

Research in ethnomethodology has exercised significant impact on improvisation studies. Tamotsu Shibutani's 1966 book *Improvised News* anticipated actor-network theory in its investigation of the circulation of rumor, an outgrowth of his experience in a Japanese American detention camp during World War II. "If enough news is not available to meet the problematic situation," Shibutani wrote, "a definition must be improvised. Rumor is the collective transaction in which such improvisation occurs."[82]

Like Ciborra, later generations of computer science theorists working on interactive systems design, such as Paul Dourish and Philip Agre, also draw upon ethnomethodology. Dourish's interpretation of the ideas of Harold Garfinkel maintains that "work is not so much 'performed' as *achieved* through improvisation and local decision-making."[83]

> The ethnomethodological view emphasises the way in which social action is not achieved through the execution of pre-conceived plans or models of behaviour, but instead is *improvised* moment-to-moment, according to the particulars of the situation. The sequential structure of behaviour is *locally organised*, and is *situated* in the context of particular settings and times.[84]

Agre's late-1990s work is critical of the notion of planning as intrinsic to the operation of a real-time, real-world, situated computational system. For Agre, a central question concerns how

> human activity can take account of the boundless variety of large and small contingencies that affect our everyday undertakings while still exhibiting an overall orderliness and coherence and remaining generally routine? In other words, how can flexible adaptation to specific situations be reconciled with the routine organization of activity?[85]

Agre maintains that

> Schemes that rely on the construction of plans for execution will operate poorly in a complicated or unpredictable world such as the world of everyday life. In such a world it will not be feasible to construct plans very far in advance; moreover, it will routinely be necessary to abort the execution of plans that begin to go awry. If contingency really is a central feature of the world of everyday life, computational ideas about action will need to be rethought.[86]

Asserting that "when future states of the world are genuinely uncertain, detailed plan construction is probably a waste of time,"[87] Agre concludes that

> activity in worlds of realistic complexity is inherently a matter of improvisation. By "inherently" I mean that this is a necessary result, a property of the universe and not

simply of a particular species of organism or a particular type of device. In particular, it is a computational result, one inherent in the physical realization of complex things.[88]

Agre's use of improvisation as a computational metaphor brings him to a definition of improvisation that focuses less on materials, as with Berliner's notion of recombination, than on an interactionist dynamics of decision making. Agre proposes a view of improvisation as "a running argument in which an agent decides what to do by conducting a continually updated argument among various alternatives," where "individuals continually choose among options presented by the world around them. Action is not realized fantasy but engagement with reality. In particular, thought and action are not alternated in great dollops as on the planning view but are bound into a single, continuous phenomenon."[89]

The relationship of improvisation to planning has been explored at the level of management of software projects, particularly the emerging "agile project management" (APM) model. Stephen Leybourne sees agile models moving away from "plan-then execute" paradigms toward a multistage model: "envision, speculate, explore, adapt, and close."[90] "If the known attributes of APM are mapped onto these accepted and empirically derived constructs of improvisational working," Leybourne maintains, "the overlaps and common areas can then emerge. These constructs are creativity, innovation, bricolage, adaption, compression, and learning."[91]

Of course, not everyone views bricolage as an unalloyed good. Togolese economist Kako Nubukpo's scathing critique of African economic planning deploys the term pejoratively:

> Few African economists have a clear theoretical positioning. We are primarily in the register of bricolage, of opportunism, or if you want to be kinder, of pragmatism! There are two kinds of bricolage. Some are not bothered by the inconsistencies, provided their power positions are assured. . . . The others have no clear theoretical positioning: we are in situations characterized by the absence of discussion of macroeconomic paradigms, with improvisation in the face of societal challenges.[92]

The result of this lack of expertise, as Nubukpo sees it, results in improvisation: "Economic improvisation is the contextually rational response of African governments to events perceived as random. The lack of control of the instruments of economic sovereignty (currency, budget) translates in practice to an obligation to react instead of acting."[93] On the surface, Nubukpo's lament is reminiscent of Richards's account, in this *Handbook*, of shifting cultivation in Sierra Leone. However, what emerges from the economist's account seems more in tune with a remark by *Handbook* contributors Ton Matton and Christopher Dell, who in their book on improvisation and urban studies, point out that "improvisation is often experienced as something rather forced than as emancipatory. . . . Well, we had to improvise, is what people say, in the hope that soon a situation will be established where order rules again."[94]

Rethinking traditional approaches to planning has become a focus of the field of emergency management, as with recent work by Tricia Wachtendorf, James Kendra, and David Mendonca. Noting that "improvisation has had something of a checkered history in the emergency management field since its appearance in a disaster response seems to suggest a failure to plan for a particular contingency,"[95] Wachtendorf and Kendra nonetheless assert that "while planning encompasses the normative 'what ought to be done,' improvisation encompasses the emergent and actual 'what needs to be done.'"[96] Indeed, the authors assert, following sociologist Kathleen Tierney, that "improvisation is a significant feature of every disaster. . . . [I]f an event does not require improvisation, it is probably not a disaster."[97]

One notes in this work on computation and emergency management a very different viewpoint on the relation between the indeterminate and the improvisative. Rather than posing a distinction between the two based on directed acts of aesthetic choice, these non-artistic theorists assert an understanding of indeterminacy as an aspect of everyday life that is addressed improvisatively. Also absent in this expanded context are ideological debates common in musical research concerning whether or not improvisations must inevitably rely upon preset, memorized formulae, rules, and cultural models. Finally, as we see in a number of this *Handbook*'s articles, freedom and structure are not taken as oppositional.[98] Rather, structure and freedom—as well as power, agency and constraint—become emergent in improvisative interaction. Indeed, in concert with those *fin de siècle* claims that improvisation is uniformly subversive, resistant, or utopian, we might also wish to see more research into the many *other* kinds of communities and institutions that have been "empowered" by their mastery of improvisational practices, such as the global financial industries, or the nation-state, which has proven remarkably resilient in spite of the rumors of its passing.

Computer scientists have also deployed mathematical analogues to improvisation, notably in process control algorithms, and in experimental models of Internet search engines. The evolutionary "harmony search" algorithm, in wide use in civil engineering and industrial applications, is a metaheuristic path optimization algorithm that adopts the metaphor of a jazz trio searching for the ideal harmony.

> Musical performances seek a best state (fantastic harmony) determined by aesthetic estimation, as the optimization algorithms seek a best state (global optimum—minimum cost or maximum benefit or efficiency) determined by objective function evaluation. Aesthetic estimation is determined by the set of the sounds played by joined instruments, just as objective function evaluation is determined by the set of the values produced by component variables; the sounds for better aesthetic estimation can be improved through practice after practice, just as the values for better objective function evaluation can be improved iteration by iteration.[99]

Beyond such specific applications in search algorithms, the general relation between technology and improvisation is explored by a number of contributors in this *Handbook*. Tim Blackwell and Michael Young explore both the mathematics and the

social aesthetics of "live algorithms." Computer programs that can be said to improvise, as well as interacting in meaningful ways with improvising musicians, go back to
the 1970s advent of relatively small, portable minicomputers and microcomputers that
made live, interactive computer music a practical possibility. During the 1970s and
1980s, composer-performers such as Joel Chadabe, Salvatore Martirano, Frankie Mann,
David Behrman, George Lewis, David Rosenboom, and the California Bay Area scene
surrounding the League of Automatic Music Composers (Jim Horton, John Bischoff,
Rich Gold, Tim Perkis, Mark Trayle, and others) began creating computer programs
that interacted with each other and human musicians to create music collectively,
blurring the boundaries between improvisation (in the traditional sense of purposive
human activity) and machine interactivity. Much of this work was influenced by discourses in artificial intelligence, and MIT's Marvin Minsky, one of the founders of the
field and a virtuoso improvising pianist, was one of the first to propose musical improvisation as a gateway to understanding larger issues of knowledge representation.[100] Later,
as computing technology underwent its second wave of miniaturization, new possibilities opened up for collaborative, networked improvisation; Ge Wang surveys some of
these new possibilities for mobile music making in his contribution to these volumes.
Another widely influential figure in this area was the groundbreaking psychologist-per-
cussionist-computer scientist David Wessel, who passed away suddenly while preparing
his article for this *Handbook*.

Technologists often adopt improvisational theater as an area of focus. Research on
computers as intelligent agents in virtual theater is the subject of *Handbook* articles by
Celia Pearce and Brian Magerko, while installation and gaming contexts are explored by
Simon Penny and D. Fox Harrell. Psychologist Clément Canonne, working on Collective
Free Improvisation (CFI), references earlier work by Michael Pelz-Sherman, who calls
free improvisation "heteroriginal" music, in which artistic decisions are made in performance relationships between multiple agents who seek to construct a shared representation of the improvisation.[101] Other models of real-time performances, both over
the Internet and in live broadcasts, are recounted in *Handbook* articles by Sher Doruff,
Antoinette LaFarge, and Adriene Jenik (in the human-to-human domain) and by David
Rothenberg, who discusses his sound improvisation with a very tractable humpback
whale. These articles also consider ways in which improvisation fosters new imaginings
of the aesthetic, social, cultural, and political dimensions of human-computer and interspecies interactivity.

Research at the nexus of improvisation, neuroscience, music, and cognitive science
has also provided new discoveries about the brain, as Aaron Berkowitz, David Borgo,
Ellie Hisama, Roger Dean and Freya Bailes, and Vijay Iyer discuss here. This research is
presaged by the 1980s and 1990s work of Jeff Pressing, a crucially important early figure
in improvisation studies. His models of how people improvise encompass physiology
and neuropsychology, motor control, skill, and timing; music theory and oral folklore;
artificial intelligence; and much more.[102]

CONCLUSION

Since we began this project, a number of influential volumes have emerged that engage improvisation in unusual and exciting ways that challenge prior orthodoxies within fields, revise histories that preserve traditional lacunae in the areas of gender and race, and construct new historiographies. Spearheaded by University of Guelph scholars Ajay Heble (literary theory) and Daniel Fischlin (theater studies), the Improvisation, Community, and Social Practice (ICASP) international research initiative has consistently provided leadership in the field. Founded with a grant from Canada's Social Sciences and Humanities Research Council (SSHRC), ICASP's remit begins with the assertion that "musical improvisation is a crucial model for political, cultural, and ethical dialogue and action."[103]

ICASP features seven interrelated research areas: gender and the body, law and justice, pedagogy, social aesthetics, social policy, text and media, and transcultural understanding, all of which come together to produce an ongoing series of colloquia, summer institutes, publications, postdoctoral fellowships, and its open-source peer-reviewed web journal, *Critical Studies in Improvisation/Études critiques en improvisation*.[104] One important focus of ICASP's social policy team is on ethics, democracy, and human rights, as represented in recent books by Tracey Nicholls, as well as Heble, Fischlin, George Lipsitz, and Jesse Stewart. Other ICASP-affiliated authors have contributed to legal studies, with recent books and articles by Sara Ramshaw, Tina Piper, and Desmond Manderson.[105] For example, Ramshaw's analysis of Jacques Derrida's remarks on improvisation cites the "openly responsive dimension of improvisation, which, although never complete or absolute, glances toward the singular other and keeps alive the possibility of democracy, ethics, resistance and justice in society."[106] In fact, both scholars and journalists routinely offer the notion of musical improvisation as symbolic of democracy itself.

Like ICASP, this *Handbook* is designed to serve as a marker for what the interdisciplinary study of improvisation has already achieved in terms of an exemplary literature. Particularly influential on this project has been the work of many scholars we have not already cited in this Introduction. The five edited volumes on improvisation in Walter Fähndrich's *Improvisation* series (1992–2003) have included work on improvisative dimensions in semiotics, psychology, anthropology, music therapy, aesthetics, film, dance, and linguistics, among other fields.

As this *Handbook* goes to press, we'd like to make mention of some recently published books that bode well for the diverse future of the field: *Improvising Medicine*, Julie Livingstone's ethnographic study of an African oncology ward; Peter Goodwin Heltzel's ringing Pentecostal call to justice, *Resurrection City: A Theology of Improvisation*; Edgar Landgraf's *Improvisation as Art*; and the important volume edited by Hans-Friedrich Bromann, Gabriele Brandstetter, and Annemarie Matzke, *Improvisieren: Paradoxien des Unvorhersehbaren*.[107]

With scholarship of this quality emerging, we can be sure that this *Handbook* will become a spur to further exploration. So much work has been going on in so many fields that as researchers and readers become more familiar with the diversity of new approaches to improvisation—perhaps more than ever before—they will be surprised to find analogies and similarities between findings in disciplines seemingly far distant from their own. In the coming years, we hope to see new work that engages with topic areas in the posthumanities: new materialism, vitalism, and assemblage theory, among others. Spanning a wide range of disciplines in the humanistic, natural, and social sciences, this research examines concepts—like adaptation, self-organization, uncertainty, translation, and emergence—that could be profitably viewed through an improvisational squint. If, as Rosi Braidotti has recently observed, new work on the posthuman has already begun (and will continue) to bridge the two cultures of science and the humanities, then critical improvisation studies is well poised to make significant contributions to these unfolding conversations.[108] Indeed, one important outcome of the volume is to demonstrate that at levels of theory and practice, improvisation provides a site for the most fruitful kind of interdisciplinarity. One can also expect that a volume of this magnitude and scope will generate some controversies as to the propriety and usefulness of studying improvisation. In our view, sparking this kind of debate is a prime objective.

We feel that the study of improvisation presents a new animating paradigm for scholarly inquiry. Borrowing a conceit of David Harvey's, we can consider a fundamental "condition" of improvisation, and the essays we have commissioned for this *Handbook* demonstrate the ways in which the study of improvisation is now informing a vast array of fields of inquiry. Our hope is for these volumes to serve as both reference and starting point for a new, exciting, and radically interdisciplinary field.

NOTES

1. Andreas Huyssen, "Back to the Future: Fluxus in Context," in *Twilight Memories: Marking Time in a Culture of Amnesia* (New York: Routledge, 1994), 198.
2. Bruno Nettl, Volume 2. See Ernest T. Ferand, *Die Improvisation in der Musik: Eine entwicklungsgeschichtliche und psychologische Untersuchung* (Zurich: Rhein-Verlag, 1938).
3. Bruno Nettl, "Thoughts on Improvisation: A Comparative Approach," *The Musical Quarterly* 60, no. 1 (1974): 1–19.
4. See William Kinderman, "Improvisation in Beethoven's Creative Process," in *Musical Improvisation: Art, Education, and Society*, ed. Gabriel Solis and Bruno Nettl, 296–312 (Urbana and Chicago: University of Illinois Press, 2009); Annette Richards, *The Free Fantasia and the Musical Picturesque* (Cambridge: Cambridge University Press, 2001); Anna Maria Busse Berger, *Medieval Music and the Art of Memory* (Berkeley: University of California Press, 2005); Leo Treitler, *With Voice and Pen: Coming to Know Medieval Song and How It Was Made* (New York: Oxford University Press, 2007); Leo Treitler, "Medieval Improvisation," *World of Music* 33, no. 3 (1991): 66–91; Kenneth Hamilton, *After the Golden Age: Romantic Pianism and Modern Performance* (Oxford: Oxford University Press, 2008);

John Rink, "Schenker and Improvisation," *Journal of Music Theory* 37, no. 1 (Spring 1993); George E. Lewis, "Improvised Music after 1950: Afrological and Eurological Perspectives," *Black Music Research Journal* 16, no. 1 (1996): 91–123; Benjamin Piekut, *Experimentalism Otherwise: The New York Avant-Garde and Its Limits* (Berkeley: University of California Press, 2011); Melina Esse, "Encountering the *Improvvisatrice* in Italian Opera," *Journal of the American Musicological Society* 66, no. 3 (Fall 2013): 709–770; Benjamin Piekut, "Indeterminacy, Free Improvisation, and the Mixed Avant-Garde: Experimental Music in London, 1965–75," *Journal of the American Musicological Society* 67, no. 3 (Fall 2014): 769–824.

5. See Timothy J. McGee, *Improvisation in the Arts of the Middle Ages and Renaissance* (Kalamzoo: Medieval Institute Publications, 2003).

6. Sister Miriam Joseph, C.S.C., *Shakespeare's Use of the Arts of Language* (New York: Columbia University Press, 1947).

7. For excellent examples of these kinds of writings on improvisation, see Patricia Shehan Campbell and Lee Higgins, *Free to Be Musical: Group Improvisation in Music* (Lanham MD: Rowman and Littlefield, 2010); Cornelius Cardew, "Towards an Ethic of Improvisation," in *Treatise Handbook* (London: Edition Peters, 1971); Cornelius Cardew, *Scratch Music* (London: Latimer New Dimensions, 1972); William Forsythe, *Improvisation Technologies: A Tool for the Analytical Dance Eye (with CD-ROM)* (Ostfildern: Hatje Cantz, [1999] 2012); Malcolm Goldstein, *Sounding The Full Circle: Concerning Music Improvisation and Other Related Matters* (Sheffield, Vt: Self-published, 1988), http://www.frogpeak.org/unbound/goldstein/goldstein_fullcircle.pdf?lbisphpreq=1; Keith Johnstone, *Impro: Improvisation and the Theatre* (London: Methuen, 1981); Stephen Nachmanovitch, *Free Play: Improvisation in Life and Art* (New York: Jeremy P. Tarcher/Putnam, 1990); Pauline Oliveros, *Software for People* (Baltimore: Smith Publications, 1984); Leo Smith, *Notes (8 Pieces) Source, A New World Music: Creative Music* (New Haven, CT: Kiom Press, 1973); Viola Spolin, *Improvisation for the Theatre* (Evanston: Northwestern University Press, [1963] 1983); Miranda Tufnell and Chris Crickmay, *Body Space Image: Notes Toward Improvisation and Performance* (London: Virago Press, 1993); Frances-Marie Uitti, "Impossible Music" [special issue on improvisation], *Contemporary Music Review* 25, no. 5/6 (2006); Ruth Zaporah, *Improvisation on the Edge: Notes from On and Off Stage* (Berkeley, CA: North Atlantic Books, 2014); John Zorn, ed. *Arcana: Musicians on Music*, Vols 1–7 (New York: Hips Road/Tzadik, 2000–2014). Also see the classic autoethnographic account of the acquisition of improvisational skill, David Sudnow, *Ways of the Hand: The Organization of Improvised Conduct* (Cambridge: Harvard University Press, 1978).

8. "Improvisation," in *The Oxford Dictionary of Music*, 2nd revised edition (New York: Oxford University Press, 2006). Available at http://www.oxfordmusiconline.com:80/subscriber/article/t237/e5140. Accessed December 5, 2011.

9. See Theodor Adorno, "Perennial Fashion—Jazz," in *Prisms*, trans. Samuel Weber and Shierry Weber (Cambridge: MIT Press, 1981); Alan P. Merriam, *The Anthropology of Music* (Evanston: Northwestern University Press, 1964), 119–132; Howard S. Becker, *Outsiders: Studies in the Sociology of Deviance* (New York: Free Press, 1963).

10. Essays by these *Handbook* contributors are in Volume 1. Also see Amy Seham, *Whose Improv Is It Anyway? Beyond Second City* (Jackson: University Press of Mississippi, 2001); Susan Leigh Foster, *Dances That Describe Themselves: The Improvised Choreography of Richard Bull* (Middletown: Wesleyan University Press, 2002); Danielle Goldman, *I Want to Be Ready: Improvised Dance as a Practice of Freedom* (Ann Arbor: University of

Michigan Press, 2010); Thomas F. DeFrantz and Anita Gonzalez, eds., *Black Performance Theory* (Durham: Duke University Press, 2014).

11. See Campbell, *Free to Be Musical: Group Improvisation in Music*; John Byng-Hall, *Rewriting Family Scripts: Improvisation and Systems Change* (New York: Guilford Press, 1995); Émile Jaques-Dalcroze, *Rhythm, Music, and Education*, trans. Harold F. Rubinstein (New York: G. P. Putnam's Sons, 1921); Fritz Hegi, *Improvisation und Musiktherapie: Möglichkeiten und Wirkungen von freier Musik* (Wiesbaden: Dr. Ludwig Reichert Verlag, [1986] 2010); Tony Wigram, *Improvisation: Methods and Techniques for Music Therapy—Clinicians, Educators, and Students* (London: Jessica Kingsley, 2004).

12. Byng-Hall, *Rewriting Family Scripts*.

13. Susan Foster, Adriene Jenik, and George E. Lewis, "Proposal for a 2002–2003 Resident Research Group: Global Intentions: Improvisation in the Contemporary Performing Arts."

14. See Erving Goffman, *The Presentation of Self in Everyday Life* (New York: Anchor Books, 1959).

15. David Gere and Ann Cooper Albright, eds., *Taken by Surprise: A Dance Improvisation Reader* (Middletown, CT: Wesleyan University Press), xv.

16. Gere and Albright, *Taken by Surprise*, xlv.

17. Domenico Pietropaolo, "Improvisation in the Arts," in Timothy J. McGee, ed., *Improvisation in the Arts of the Middle Ages and Renaissance* (Kalamzoo: Medieval Institute Publications, 2003), 9.

18. Alan Durant, "Improvisation in the Political Economy of Music," in *Music and the Politics of Culture*, ed. Christopher Norris (New York: St. Martin's Press, 1989), 253.

19. See Ted Gioia, "Jazz: The Aesthetics of Imperfection," *The Hudson Review* 39, no. 4 (1987): 585–600. Also see Andy Hamilton, "The Art of Improvisation and the Aesthetics of Imperfection," *British Journal of Aesthetics* 40, no. 1 (2000): 168–185.

20. Charles Jencks, *Adhocism: The Case for Improvisation* (Cambridge: MIT Press, 2013 [1972]), vii.

21. Gilbert Ryle, "Improvisation," *Mind* 85, no. 337 (1976): 69.

22. Bruce Ellis Benson, *The Improvisation of Musical Dialogue: A Phenomenology of Music* (Cambridge: Cambridge University Press, 2003).

23. Ryle, "Improvisation," 77.

24. Philip Alperson, "On Musical Improvisation," *The Journal of Aesthetics and Art Criticism* 43, no. 1, Autumn (1984): 17–29; Vladimir Jankélévitch, *Liszt: Rhapsodie et Improvisation* (Paris: Flammarion, [1955] 1998).

25. Gary Peters, *The Philosophy of Improvisation* (Chicago: University of Chicago Press, 2009). Coincidentally, a recent PhD dissertation uses evidence from the personal archives of Derek Bailey to advance the possibility that the guitarist was also influenced by Husserl, via his engagement with an unpublished treatment of Husserlian time-consciousness, written as an undergraduate senior thesis by one of us (Lewis) in 1974 and borrowed by the guitarist sometime in the 1980s. See Dominic Lash, "Metonymy as a Creative Structural Principle in the Work of J. H. Prynne, Derek Bailey and Helmut Lachenmann, with a Creative Component" (PhD dissertation, Brunel University, 2010).

26. Pierre Hadot, *Philosophy as a Way of Life: Spiritual Exercises from Socrates to Foucault*, ed. Arnold I. Davidson (Malden: Wiley-Blackwell, 1995), 84–85. A contrasting approach to consciousness is presented by Edward Sarath's *Handbook* essay.

27. See William Day, "Knowing as Instancing: Jazz Improvisation and Moral Perfectionism," *The Journal of Aesthetics and Art Criticism* 58, no. 2 (Spring 2000): 99–111; J. David Velleman, "How to Share an Intention," *Philosophy and Phenomenological Research* 57, no. 1 (March 1997): 29–50; Barbara Herman, *Moral Literacy* (Cambridge: Harvard University Press, 2007); Martha C. Nussbaum, *Love's Knowledge: Essays on Philosophy and Literature* (New York: Oxford University Press, 1990).

28. Hagberg's many contributions to the philosophy of improvisation include his guest editorship of the special issue of the *Journal of Aesthetics and Art Criticism* (58, no. 2, Spring 2000) on improvisation in the arts, as well as contributing, along with William Day, Philip Alperson, and others, to that journal's 2010 "Symposium on Improvisation" (68, no. 3, Summer 2010).

29. Henry Louis Gates's notion of signifying, developed in the context of literary theory, has become highly influential in jazz studies. See Henry Louis Gates, Jr., *The Signifying Monkey: A Theory of African-American Literary Criticism* (New York: Oxford University Press, 1988). Among the many articles invoking notions of storytelling and personal voice, see Lewis, "Improvised Music after 1950: Afrological and Eurological Perspectives." For Samuel Floyd's notion of "individuality within the aggregate," see Samuel A. Floyd, Jr., *The Power of Black Music: Interpreting Its History from Africa to the United States* (New York: Oxford University Press, 1995).

30. Among the many new and exciting volumes that have appeared under the aegis of jazz studies in recent years are Paul Berliner, *Thinking in Jazz: The Infinite Art of Improvisation* (Chicago: University of Chicago Press); Daniel Fischlin, Ajay Heble, and George Lipsitz, eds., *The Fierce Urgency of Now: Improvisation, Rights, and the Ethics of Co-Creation* (Durham and London: Duke University Press, 2013); Ingrid Monson, *Saying Something: Jazz Improvisation and Interaction* (Chicago: University of Chicago Press, 1996); Robert G. O'Meally, ed., *The Jazz Cadence of American Culture* (New York: Columbia University Press, 1998); Robin D. G. Kelley, "Dig They Freedom: Meditations on History and the Black Avant-Garde," *Lenox Avenue* 3 (1997): 13–27; Brent Hayes Edwards and John F. Szwed, "A Bibliography of Jazz Poetry Criticism," *Callaloo* 25, no. 1 (2002): 338–346; Krin Gabbard, ed., *Representing Jazz, Jazz Among the Discourses* (two books) (Durham, NC: Duke University Press, 1995); Aldon Lynn Nielsen, *Black Chant: Languages of African-American Postmodernism* (Cambridge: Cambridge University Press, 1997); Charles O. Hartman, *Jazz Text: Voice and Improvisation in Poetry, Jazz, Song* (Princeton, NJ: Princeton University Press, 1991); Robert G. O'Meally, Brent Hayes Edwards, and Farah Jasmine Griffin, eds., *Uptown Conversation: The New Jazz Studies* (New York: Columbia University Press, 2004); Nichole T. Rustin and Sherrie Tucker, eds., *Big Ears: Listening for Gender in Jazz Studies* (Durham, NC: Duke University Press, 2008).

31. Gioia, "Jazz: The Aesthetics of Imperfection," 590.

32. Edgar Landgraf, "Improvisation: Form and Event, A Spencer-Brownian Calculation," in *Emergence and Embodiment: New Essays on Second-Order Systems Theory*, ed. Bruce Clarke and Mark B. N. Hansen (Durham and London: Duke University Press, 2009), 202n26.

33. LeRoi Jones, *Blues People: Negro Music in White America* (New York: William Morrow, 1963).

34. Alfred Schutz, "Making Music Together: A Study in Social Relationship," in *Alfred Schutz, Collected Papers 2: Studies in Social Theory*, ed. Arvid Broderson (The Hague: Martinus Nijhoff, 1964), 159.

35. John Szwed, "Josef Skvorecky and the Tradition of Jazz Literature," *World Literature Today* 54, no. 4 (1980): 588.

36. Citton, this *Handbook*, vol. 1.

37. Daniel Belgrad, *The Culture of Spontaneity: Improvisation and the Arts in Postwar America* (Chicago: University of Chicago Press, 1998).

38. Stephen J. Greenblatt, "Improvisation and Power," in *Literature and Society*, ed. Edward Said (Baltimore: Johns Hopkins University Press, 1980); Tzvetan Todorov, *The Conquest of America: The Question of the Other* (New York: Harper & Row, 1984).

39. Michel Foucault, "What Is Enlightenment?," in *Ethics: Subjectivity and Truth*, trans. Robert Hurley and others, ed. Paul Rabinow (New York: New Press, 1997), 313.

40. Foucault, "What Is Enlightenment?," 311.

41. Foucault, "What Is Enlightenment?," 316.

42. Michel Foucault, "The Ethics of the Concern of the Self as a Practice of Freedom," in *Ethics: Subjectivity and Truth*, trans. Robert Hurley and others, ed. Paul Rabinow, 281–301 (New York: New Press, 1997).

43. Judith Butler, *Undoing Gender* (New York: Routledge, 2004), 1.

44. Merriam, *The Anthropology of Music*, 179.

45. See Georgina Born, "Digital Music, Relational Ontologies and Social Forms," in *Bodily Expression in Electronic Music: Perspectives on Reclaiming Performativity*, ed. Deniz Peters, Gerhard Eckel, and Andreas Dorschel (New York: Routledge, 2012), 163–180.

46. Andrew Pickering, "The Mangle of Practice: Agency and Emergence in the Sociology of Science," *American Journal of Sociology* 99, no. 3 (November, 1993): 583. One detects a certain anxious Puritanism in the insistence on the inherent presence and power of constraints in improvisation. It is as though there is a deeply rooted fear that an improvisation, like noise, slaves, or subjects of authoritarian regimes, could simply get out of hand and run buck wild, de-authorizing the authorities, overturning well-formed arrangements, and putting out its tongue at the judgments of theorists.

47. Pickering, "The Mangle of Practice," 584–585.

48. Jacques Derrida, "Signature Event Context," in *Limited Inc* (Evanston: Northwestern University Press, 1988 [1977]), 7. Quoted in Edgar Landgraf, *Improvisation as Art: Conceptual Challenges, Historical Perspectives* (New York: Continuum, 2011), 22.

49. See Derek Bailey, *Improvisation: Its Nature and Practice in Music* (New York: Da Capo Press, 1992).

50. Pierre Bourdieu, *Outline of a Theory of Practice*, trans. Richard Nice (Cambridge and New York: Cambridge University Press, 1977), 78.

51. Bourdieu, *Outline of a Theory of Practice*, 79.

52. Bourdieu, *Outline of a Theory of Practice*, 79.

53. Berliner, *Thinking in Jazz*, 241.

54. Philosopher Jerrold Levinson has spoken of how his "concatenationist" notion of the apprehension of musical form might coexist with the experience of improvisation. See Clément Canonne and Pierre Saint-Germier, "De la philosophie de l'action à l'écoute musicale: Entretien avec Jerrold Levinson," *Traces* 18, no. 1 (2010): 211–221. For a detailed explication of Levinson's theory, see Jerrold Levinson, *Music in the Moment* (Ithaca: Cornell University Press, 1997).

55. See Philip N. Johnson-Laird, "Jazz Improvisation: A Theory at the Computational Level," in *Representing Musical Structure*, ed. Peter Howell, Robert West, and Ian Cross (London:

Academic Press, 1991): 291–326. The long-out-of-print Harris book is Eddie Harris, *Jazz Cliché Capers* (Chicago: Wardo Enterprises, 1973).

56. Kathleen L. McGinn and Angela T. Keros, "Improvisation and the Logic of Exchange in Socially Embedded Transactions," *Administrative Science Quarterly* 47 (2002): 445.

57. See Nettl's article in this *Handbook*.

58. See Nettl's article in this *Handbook*. Also see Milman Parry, *The Making of Homeric Verse: The Collected Papers of Milman Parry*, ed. Adam Parry (Oxford: Clarendon Press, 1971).

59. According to Adam Parry, Milman Parry "almost never discussed Homer, that is, the author or authors of the *Iliad* and the *Odyssey*, as opposed to the tradition in which Homer worked; nor did he ever demonstrate, although at times he seems to assume it, that Homer was himself an oral poet." *The Making of Homeric Verse: The Collected Papers of Milman Parry*, lx–lxi." As Lord put it, "If we equate [oral composition] with improvisation in a broad sense, we are again in error. Improvisation is not a bad term for the process, but it too must be modified by the restrictions of the particular style. The exact way in which oral composition differs from free improvisation will, I hope, emerge from the following chapter." Lord, *The Singer of Tales*, 5.

60. See Angela Esterhammer, *Romanticism and Improvisation, 1750–1850* (Cambridge: Cambridge University Press, 2008). The range of scholarship in this area is far too great to summarize in this short Introduction, but the work of Gregory Nagy and D. Gary Miller provide two contrasting viewpoints.

61. See Adorno, "Perennial Fashion—Jazz." Among Adorno's critics, sociologist Heinz Steinert stands out because of his impatience with the tendency to explain away Adorno's standpoints on jazz. See Heinz Steinert, *Die Entdeckung der Kulturindustrie, oder: Warum Professor Adorno Jazz-Musik nicht ausstehen konnte* (Vienna: Verlag für Gesellschaftskritik, 1992).

62. See Célestin Deliège, "Indetermination et Improvisation," *International Review of the Aesthetics and Sociology of Music* 2, no. 2 (December, 1971): 155–191. John Cage's fraught relationship with improvisation is explored by Sabine Feisst, a contributor to the present *Handbook*, in Sabine Feisst, "John Cage and Improvisation: An Unresolved Relationship," in *Musical Improvisation: Art, Education, and Society*, ed. Gabriel Solis and Bruno Nettl, 38–51 (Urbana, IL: University of Illinois Press, 2009).

63. Cynthia J. Novack, "Looking at Movement as Culture: Contact Improvisation to Disco," *TDR* 32, no. 4 (Winter, 1988): 105.

64. Bailey, *Improvisation*, 142.

65. Curtis L. Carter, "Improvisation in Dance," *The Journal of Aesthetics and Art Criticism* 58, no. 2 (Spring 2000): 182.

66. David Davies, *Philosophy of the Performing Arts* (Malden, MA: Wiley-Blackwell, 2011), 140.

67. Stephen Blum, "Recognizing Improvisation," in *In the Course of Performance: Studies in the World of Musical Improvisation*, ed. Bruno Nettl with Melinda Russell (Chicago: University of Chicago Press, 1998), 27.

68. Philip N. Johnson-Laird, "How Jazz Musicians Improvise," *Music Perception* 19, no. 3 (Spring 2002): 417.

69. Francois Grosjean, "Language: From Set Patterns to Free Patterning," in *Improvisation III*, ed. Walter Fähndrich (Winterthur: Amadeus, 2005), 71.

70. R. Keith Sawyer, "Improvised Conversations: Music, Collaboration, and Development," *Psychology of Music* 27, no. 2 (October 1999): 192.

71. Sawyer, "Improvised Conversations," 192.

72. "Improvisation and Narrative," *Narrative Inquiry* 12, no. 2 (2002): 321.

73. See *Improvised Dialogues: Emergence and Creativity in Conversation* (Westport, CT: Greenwood Publishing Group, 2003).

74. Monson, *Saying Something*.

75. Silverstein, "The Improvisational Performance of Culture in Realtime Discursive Practice," 268.

76. McGinn, "Improvisation and the Logic of Exchange in Socially Embedded Transactions," 445.

77. One of the most frequently cited articles is Karl E. Weick, "Improvisation as a Mindset for Organizational Analysis," *Organization Science* 9, no. 5 (September–October 1998): 543–555. Weick's work, as well as a recent book by Frank Barrett, draws on the notion of the aesthetics of imperfection. See Frank J. Barrett, *Yes to the Mess: Surprising Leadership Lessons from Jazz* (Boston: Harvard Business Review Press, 2012). For a compilation of key articles on the topic, see the chapter in this volume by management theorists Paul Ingram and Bill Duggan, which serves as an overview of the scholarship in this area, with particular attention to issues of individual and group decision making, strategy, trust, intuition, and divergent thinking.

78. Claudio Ciborra, *The Labyrinths of Information: Challenging the Wisdom of Systems* (Oxford: Oxford University Press, 2002), 85.

79. Ciborra, *The Labyrinths of Information*, 87. Ciborra's ideas on improvisation were integral to his work on systems. A list of his publications can be found at http://is2.lse.ac.uk/Staff/Ciborra/publications.htm.

80. Hamilton, "The Aesthetics of Imperfection," 337.

81. Claudio U. Ciborra, "Notes on Improvisation and Time in Organizations," *Accounting, Management and Information Technologies* 9, no. 2 (1999): 85.

82. Tamotsu Shibutani, *Improvised News: A Sociological Study of Rumor* (Indianapolis: Bobbs-Merrill, 1966), 57.

83. Paul Dourish, Annette Adler, and Brian Cantwell Smith, "Organising User Interfaces Around Reflective Accounts" (paper presented at the Reflections '96 Conference, San Francisco, CA) http://www.dourish.com/publications/1996/refl96-electronic.pdf.

84. Dourish, Adler, and Smith, "Organising User Interfaces Around Reflective Accounts."

85. Philip E. Agre, *Computation and Human Experience* (Cambridge: Cambridge University Press, 1997), 149.

86. Agre, *Computation and Human Experience*, 155.

87. Agre, *Computation and Human Experience*, 147.

88. Agre, *Computation and Human Experience*, 156.

89. Agre, *Computation and Human Experience*, 161.

90. Stephen A. Leybourne, "Improvisation and Agile Project Management: A Comparative Consideration," *International Journal of Managing Projects in Business* 2, no. 4 (2009): 524.

91. Leybourne, "Improvisation and Agile Project Management," 524.

92. Béatrice Hibou and Boris Samuel, with Kako Nubukpo, "Les macroéconomistes africains: Entre opportunisme théorique et improvisation empirique—Entretien de Béatrice Hibou et Boris Samuel avec Kako Nubukpo," *Politique Africaine*, no. 124 (Décembre 2011): 89. In the original French: "Peu d'économistes africains ont un positionnement théorique bien défini. Nous sommes avant tout dans le registre du bricolage, de l'opportunisme ou, si l'on veut être plus gentil, du pragmatisme! Il y a deux sortes de bricolage. Les uns ne sont pas gênés par

les incohérences, pourvu que leurs positions de pouvoir soient assurées.... Les autres n'ont pas de positionnement théorique clair: on est dans des situations caractérisées par l'absence de discussion des paradigmes macroéconomiques et par l'improvisation face aux défis sociaux."

93. Kako Nubukpo, *L'improvisation économique en Afrique de l'Ouest: Du coton au franc CFA* (Paris: Karthala, 2011). "L'improvisation économique est la réponse contextuellement rationnelle des pouvoirs publics africains à des événements perçus comme aléatoires. L'absence de maîtrise des instruments de souveraineté économique (la monnaie, le budget) se traduit concrètement par une obligation de réagir au lieu d'agir."

94. Ton Matton and Christopher Dell, *Improvisations on Urbanity: Trendy Pragmatism in a Climate of Change* (Rotterdam: Post Editions, 2010), n.p.

95. James M. Kendra and Tricia Wachtendorf, "Improvisation, Creativity, and the Art of Emergency Management," in *Understanding and Responding to Terrorism*, ed. Huseyin Durmaz, Bilal Sevinc, Ahmet Sait Yayla and Siddik Ekici (Amsterdam: IOS Press, 2007), 324.

96. Kendra and Wachtendorf, "Improvisation, Creativity, and the Art of Emergency Management," 324–325.

97. Kendra and Wachtendorf, "Improvisation, Creativity, and the Art of Emergency Management," 324. Also see David Mendonça, Gary Webb, Carter Butts, and James Brooks, "Cognitive Correlates of Improvised Behaviour in Disaster Response: the Cases of the Murrah Building and the World Trade Center," *Journal of Contingencies and Crisis Management* 22, no. 4 (December 2014). The impromptu/extempore dynamic in improvisation pursued by Lydia Goehr in this *Handbook* provides a certain corroboration from a philosophical perspective.

98. For instance, see *Handbook* contributions by Christopher Dell and Ton Matton, Eric Porter, and David P. Brown.

99. Zong Woo Geem, Joong Hoon Kim, and G. V. Loganathan, "A New Heuristic Optimization Algorithm: Harmony Search," *Simulation* 76, no. 2 (February 2001): 62. The *Handbook* essay by Clyde Reed and Jared Burrows deploys an economics theory based on path dependence to investigate the dynamics of musical choice.

100. See Marvin Minsky, "Music, Mind, and Meaning," in *Machine Models of Music*, edited by Stephen Schwanauer and David Levitt, 327–354 (Cambridge: MIT Press, 1981). Recent accounts of work with musical computers that explore its improvisative character include John Bischoff, Rich Gold, and Jim Horton, "Music for an Interactive Network of Microcomputers," *Computer Music Journal* 2, no. 3 (1978): 24–29; Jim Horton, "Unforeseen Music: The Autobiographical Notes of Jim Horton," *Leonardo Music Journal Online* 9 (1999); George E. Lewis, "The Secret Love between Interactivity and Improvisation, or Missing in Interaction: A Prehistory of Computer Interactivity," in *Improvisation V: 14 Beiträge*, ed. Walter Fähndrich, 193–203 (Winterthur: Amadeus, 2003); "Living with Creative Machines: An Improvisor Reflects," in *AfroGEEKS: Beyond the Digital Divide*, ed. Anna Everett and Amber J. Walllace, 83–99 (Santa Barbara: Center for Black Studies Research, 2007); Chris Salter, with foreword by Peter Sellars, *Entangled: Technology and the Transformation of Performance* (Cambridge: MIT Press, 2010); Scot Gresham-Lancaster, "The Aesthetics and History of the Hub: The Effects of Changing Technology on Network Computer Music," *Leonardo Music Journal* 8 (1998): 38–44.

101. Michael Pelz-Sherman, "A Framework for the Analysis of Performer Interactions in Western Improvised Music" (PhD dissertation, University of California, San Diego,

1998); Clément Canonne, "Focal Points in Collective Free Improvisation," *Perspectives of New Music* 51, no. 1 (Winter 2013): 40–55.

102. See Jeff Pressing, "Improvisation: Methods and Models," in *Generative Processes in Music: The Psychology of Performance, Improvisation, and Composition*, ed. John A. Sloboda, 129–178 (Oxford: Clarendon Press, 1988). Psychologists John Sloboda and Eric Clarke are particularly significant in this area as well. Important early work includes John A. Sloboda, "Improvisation," in *The Musical Mind: The Cognitive Psychology of Music* (Oxford: Clarendon Press, 1985), 138–150. Also see Eric F. Clarke, "Creativity in Performance," *Musicae Scientiae* 19, no. 1 (Spring 2005): 157–182; David Dolan, John Sloboda, Henrik Jeldtoft Jensen, Björn Crüts, and Eugene Feygelson, "The Improvisatory Approach to Classical Music Performance: An Empirical Investigation into its Characteristics and Impact," *Music Performance Research* 6 (2013): 1–38.

103. Improvisation, Community and Social Practice website, http://www.improvcommunity.ca/about.

104. The ICASP website is http://www.improvcommunity.ca. The journal is at http://www.criticalimprov.com. For some of the work produced under ICASP's auspices, see Tracey Nicholls, *An Ethics of Improvisation: Aesthetic Possibilities for a Political Future* (Lanham, MD: Lexington Books, 2012); Fischlin, Heble, and Lipsitz, *The Fierce Urgency of Now: Improvisation, Rights, and the Ethics of Co-Creation*; Rebecca Caines and Ajay Heble, eds. *The Improvisation Studies Reader: Spontaneous Acts* (New York: Routledge, 2014); Ajay Heble and Daniel Fischlin, eds., *Rebel Musics: Human Rights, Resistant Sounds, and the Politics of Music Making* (Montréal and New York: Black Rose Books, 2003). Also see Sara Ramshaw, *Justice as Improvisation: The Law of the Extempore* (New York: Routledge, 2013).

105. Ramshaw, *Justice as Improvisation*; Tina S. Piper, "The Improvisational Flavour of Law, the Legal Taste of Improvisation," *Critical Studies in Improvisation/Études Critiques en Improvisation* 6, no. 1 (2010), http://www.criticalimprov.com/article/view/1191/1725; Desmond Manderson, "Fission and Fusion: From Improvisation to Formalism in Law and Music," *Critical Studies in Improvisation/Études Critiques en Improvisation* 6, no. 1 (2010), http://www.criticalimprov.com/article/view/1167/1726.

106. Ramshaw, *Justice as Improvisation*, 14. Also see Sara Ramshaw, "Deconstructin(g) Jazz Improvisation: Derrida and the Law of the Singular Event," *Critical Studies in Improvisation/Études critiques en improvisation* 2, no. 1 (2006): http://www.criticalimprov.com/article/viewArticle/81/179. Derrida's remarks on improvisation appear in a published transcript of a 1982 documentary: Kirby Dick, Amy Ziering Kofman, and Jacques Derrida, *Derrida: Screenplay and Essays on the Film*. (Manchester, UK: Manchester University Press, 2005). In addition, a fascinating colloquy between the philosopher and Ornette Coleman appears in Timothy S. Murphy, "The Other's Language: Jacques Derrida Interviews Ornette Coleman, 23 June 1997," *Genre* 37, No. 2 (2004): 319–329. Michael Gallope's *Handbook* article examines this encounter in considerable detail. The interface between critical theory and improvisation is also explored here in essays by Alexandre Pierrepont, Davide Sparti, Tracy McMullen, and Fred Moten.

107. Peter Goodwin Heltzel, *Resurrection City: A Theology of Improvisation* (Grand Rapids, MI and Cambridge, England: William B. Eerdmans, 2012); Landgraf, *Improvisation as Art*; Julie Livingston, *Improvising Medicine: An African Oncology Ward in an Emerging Cancer Epidemic* (Durham, NC: Duke University Press, 2012); Hans-Friedrich Bromann, Gabriele Brandstetter, and Annemarie Matzke, eds., *Improvisieren: Paradoxien des Unvorhersehbaren, Kunst-Medien-Praxis* (Bielefeld: Transcript, 2010).

108. Rosi Braidotti, *The Posthuman* (Cambridge: Polity Press, 2013).

Bibliography

Adorno, Theodor. "Perennial Fashion—Jazz," In *Prisms*, translated by Samuel Weber and Shierry Weber, 119–132. Cambridge, MA: MIT Press, 1981.

Agre, Philip E. *Computation and Human Experience*. Cambridge: Cambridge University Press, 1997.

Alperson, Philip. "On Musical Improvisation." *The Journal of Aesthetics and Art Criticism* 43, no. 1 (Autumn, 1984): 17–29.

Bailey, Derek. *Improvisation: Its Nature and Practice in Music*. New York: Da Capo Press, 1992.

Barrett, Frank J. *Yes to the Mess: Surprising Leadership Lessons from Jazz*. Boston: Harvard Business Review Press, 2012.

Becker, Howard S. *Outsiders: Studies in the Sociology of Deviance*. New York: Free Press, 1963.

Belgrad, Daniel. *The Culture of Spontaneity: Improvisation and the Arts in Postwar America*. Chicago: University of Chicago Press, 1998.

Benson, Bruce Ellis. *The Improvisation of Musical Dialogue: A Phenomenology of Music*. Cambridge: Cambridge University Press, 2003.

Berliner, Paul. *Thinking in Jazz: The Infinite Art of Improvisation*. Chicago: University of Chicago Press, 1994.

Bischoff, John, Rich Gold, and Jim Horton. "Music for an Interactive Network of Microcomputers." *Computer Music Journal* 2, no. 3 (1978): 24–29.

Blum, Stephen. "Recognizing Improvisation." In *In The Course of Performance: Studies in the World of Musical Improvisation*, edited by Bruno Nettl with Melinda Russell, 27–45. Chicago: University of Chicago Press, 1998.

Born, Georgina. "Digital Music, Relational Ontologies and Social Forms." In *Bodily Expression in Electronic Music: Perspectives on Reclaiming Performativity*, edited by Deniz Peters, Gerhard Eckel, and Andreas Dorschel, 163–180. New York: Routledge, 2012.

Bourdieu, Pierre. *Outline of a Theory of Practice*, translated by Richard Nice. Cambridge and New York: Cambridge University Press, 1977.

Braidotti, Rosi. *The Posthuman*. Cambridge: Polity Press, 2013.

Bromann, Hans-Friedrich, Gabriele Brandstetter, and Annemarie Matzke, eds. *Improvisieren: Paradoxien des Unvorhersehbaren, Kunst-Medien-Praxis*. Bielefeld: Transcript, 2010.

Busse Berger, Anna Maria. *Medieval Music and the Art of Memory*. Berkeley: University of California Press, 2005.

Butler, Judith. *Undoing Gender*. New York: Routledge, 2004.

Byng-Hall, John. *Rewriting Family Scripts: Improvisation and Systems Change*. New York: Guilford Press, 1995.

Caines, Rebecca, and Ajay Heble, eds. *The Improvisation Studies Reader: Spontaneous Acts*. New York: Routledge, 2014.

Campbell, Patricia Shehan, and Lee Higgins. *Free to Be Musical: Group Improvisation in Music*. Lanham MD: Rowman and Littlefield, 2010.

Canonne, Clément, and Pierre Saint-Germier. "De la philosophie de l'action à l'écoute musicale: Entretien avec Jerrold Levinson." *Traces* 18, no. 1 (2010): 211–221.

Canonne, Clément. "Focal Points in Collective Free Improvisation." *Perspectives of New Music* 51, no. 1 (Winter, 2013): 40–55.

Cardew, Cornelius, ed. *Scratch Music*. London: Latimer New Dimensions, 1972.

Cardew, Cornelius. "Towards an Ethic of Improvisation." In *Treatise Handbook*. London: Edition Peters, 1971.

Carter, Curtis L. "Improvisation in Dance." *The Journal of Aesthetics and Art Criticism* 58, no. 2 (Spring, 2000): 181–190.

Ciborra, Claudio. *The Labyrinths of Information: Challenging the Wisdom of Systems.* Oxford: Oxford University Press, 2002.

Ciborra, Claudio U. "Notes on Improvisation and Time in Organizations." *Accounting, Management and Information Technologies* 9, no. 2 (1999): 77–94.

Clarke, Eric F. "Creativity in Performance." *Musicae Scientiae* 19, no. 1 (Spring 2005): 157–182.

Davies, David. *Philosophy of the Performing Arts.* Malden, MA: Wiley-Blackwell, 2011.

Day, William. "Knowing as Instancing: Jazz Improvisation and Moral Perfectionism." *The Journal of Aesthetics and Art Criticism* 58, no. 2 (Spring, 2000): 99–111.

DeFrantz, Thomas F., and Anita Gonzalez, eds. *Black Performance Theory.* Durham: Duke University Press, 2014.

Dèliege, Célestin. "Indetermination et Improvisation." *International Review of the Aesthetics and Sociology of Music* 2, no. 2 (December, 1971): 155–191.

Derrida, Jacques. "Signature Event Context." In *Limited Inc,* 1–24. Evanston: Northwestern University Press, 1988 [1977].

Dick, Kirby, Amy Ziering Kofman, and Jacques Derrida. *Derrida: Screenplay and Essays on the Film.* Manchester, UK: Manchester University Press, 2005.

Dolan, David, John Sloboda, Henrik Jeldtoft Jensen, Björn Crüts, and Eugene Feygelson. "The Improvisatory Approach to Classical Music Performance: An Empirical Investigation into its Characteristics and Impact." *Music Performance Research* 6 (2013): 1–38.

Dourish, Paul, Annette Adler, and Brian Cantwell Smith. "Organising User Interfaces Around Reflective Accounts." Paper presented at the Reflections '96 Conference (San Francisco, CA) http://www.dourish.com/publications/1996/refl96-electronic.pdf.

Durant, Alan. "Improvisation in the Political Economy of Music." In *Music and the Politics of Culture,* edited by Christopher Norris, 252–282. New York: St. Martin's Press, 1989.

Edwards, Brent Hayes, and John F. Szwed. "A Bibliography of Jazz Poetry Criticism." *Callaloo* 25, no. 1 (2002): 338–346.

Esse, Melina. "Encountering the *Improvvisatrice* in Italian Opera." *Journal of the American Musicological Society* 66, no. 3 (Fall, 2013).

Esterhammer, Angela. *Romanticism and Improvisation, 1750–1850.* Cambridge: Cambridge University Press, 2008.

Feisst, Sabine. "John Cage and Improvisation: An Unresolved Relationship." In *Musical Improvisation: Art, Education, and Society,* edited by Gabriel Solis and Bruno Nettl, 38–51. Urbana: University of Illinois Press, 2009.

Ferand, Ernest T. *Die Improvisation in der Musik: Eine entwicklungsgeschichtliche und psychologische Untersuchung.* Zurich: Rhein-Verlag, 1938.

Fischlin, Daniel, Ajay Heble, and George Lipsitz, eds. *The Fierce Urgency of Now: Improvisation, Rights, and the Ethics of Co-Creation.* Durham and London: Duke University Press, 2013.

Floyd, Samuel A. Jr. *The Power of Black Music: Interpreting its History from Africa to the United States.* New York: Oxford University Press, 1995.

Forsythe, William. *Improvisation Technologies: A Tool for the Analytical Dance Eye (with CD-ROM).* Ostfildern: Hatje Cantz, [1999] 2012.

Foster, Susan, Adriene Jenik, and George E. Lewis. "Proposal for a 2002–2003 Resident Research Group: Global Intentions: Improvisation in the Contemporary Performing Arts." Unpublished narrative, University of California Humanities Research Institute, 2002.

Foster, Susan Leigh. *Dances That Describe Themselves: The Improvised Choreography of Richard Bull*. Middletown: Wesleyan University Press, 2002.

Foucault, Michel. "The Ethics of the Concern of the Self as a Practice of Freedom." In *Ethics: Subjectivity and Truth*. Translated by Robert Hurley and others. Edited by Paul Rabinow, 281–301. New York: New Press, 1997.

Foucault, Michel. "What Is Enlightenment?" In *Ethics: Subjectivity and Truth*. Translated by Robert Hurley and others. Edited by Paul Rabinow, 303–320. New York: New Press, 1997.

Gabbard, Krin, ed. *Representing Jazz, Jazz Among the Discourses* (two books). Durham, NC: Duke University Press, 1995.

Gates, Henry Louis, Jr. *The Signifying Monkey: A Theory of African-American Literary Criticism*. New York: Oxford University Press, 1988.

Geem, Zong Woo, Joong Hoon Kim, and G. V. Loganathan. "A New Heuristic Optimization Algorithm: Harmony Search." *Simulation* 76, no. 2 (February 2001): 60–68.

Gere, David, and Ann Cooper Albright, eds. *Taken by Surprise: A Dance Improvisation Reader*. Middletown, CT: Wesleyan University Press.

Gioia, Ted. "Jazz: The Aesthetics of Imperfection." *The Hudson Review* 39, no. 4 (1987): 585–600.

Goffman, Erving. *The Presentation of Self in Everyday Life*. New York: Anchor Books, 1959.

Goldman, Danielle. *I Want to Be Ready: Improvised Dance as a Practice of Freedom*. Ann Arbor: University of Michigan Press, 2010.

Goldstein, Malcolm. *Sounding the Full Circle: Concerning Music Improvisation and Other Related Matters*. Sheffield, VT: Self-published, 1988. http://www.frogpeak.org/unbound/goldstein/goldstein_fullcircle.pdf?lbisphpreq=1.

Greenblatt, Stephen J. "Improvisation and Power." In *Literature and Society*, edited by Edward Said, 57–99. Baltimore: Johns Hopkins University Press, 1980.

Gresham-Lancaster, Scot. "The Aesthetics and History of the Hub: The Effects of Changing Technology on Network Computer Music." *Leonardo Music Journal* 8 (1998): 39–44.

Grosjean, Francois. "Language: From Set Patterns to Free Patterning." In *Improvisation III*, edited by Walter Fähndrich, 71–84. Winterthur: Amadeus, 2005.

Hadot, Pierre, edited by Arnold I. Davidson. *Philosophy as a Way of Life: Spiritual Exercises from Socrates to Foucault*. Malden: Wiley-Blackwell, 1995.

Hamilton, Andy. "The Aesthetics of Imperfection." *Philosophy* 65, no. 253 (July, 1990): 323–340.

Hamilton, Andy. "The Art of Improvisation and the Aesthetics of Imperfection." *British Journal of Aesthetics* 40, no. 1 (2000): 168–185.

Hamilton, Kenneth. *After the Golden Age: Romantic Pianism and Modern Performance*. Oxford: Oxford University Press, 2008.

Harris, Eddie. *Jazz Cliché Capers*. Chicago: Wardo Enterprises, 1973.

Hartman, Charles O. *Jazz Text: Voice and Improvisation in Poetry, Jazz, Song*. Princeton, NJ: Princeton University Press, 1991.

Heble, Ajay, and Daniel Fischlin, eds. *Rebel Musics: Human Rights, Resistant Sounds, and the Politics of Music Making*. Montréal and New York: Black Rose Books, 2003.

Hegi, Fritz. *Improvisation und Musiktherapie: Möglichkeiten und Wirkungen von freier Musik*. Wiesbaden: Dr. Ludwig Reichert Verlag, [1986] 2010.

Heltzel, Peter Goodwin. *Resurrection City: A Theology of Improvisation*. Grand Rapids, MI and Cambridge, England: William B. Eerdmans, 2012.

Herman, Barbara. *Moral Literacy*. Cambridge: Harvard University Press, 2007.

Hibou, Béatrice, and Boris Samuel, avec Kako Nubukpo. "Les macroéconomistes africains: Entre opportunisme théorique et improvisation empirique—Entretien de Béatrice

Hibou et Boris Samuel avec Kako Nubukpo." *Politique Africaine*, no. 124 (Décembre 2011): 87–106.

Horton, Jim. "Unforeseen Music: The Autobiographical Notes of Jim Horton." *Leonardo Music Journal Online* 9 (1999): http://leonardo.info/lmj/horton.html.

Huyssen, Andreas. "Back to the Future: Fluxus in Context." In *Twilight Memories: Marking Time in a Culture of Amnesia*, 191–208. New York: Routledge, 1994.

"Improvisation." In *The Oxford Dictionary of Music*. 2nd revised edition. New York: Oxford University Press, 2006. Available at oxfordmusiconline.com.

Jankélévitch, Vladimir. *Liszt: Rhapsodie et Improvisation*. Paris: Flammarion, [1955] 1998.

Jaques-Dalcroze, Émile. *Rhythm, Music, and Education*, translated by Harold F. Rubinstein. New York: G. P. Putnam's Sons, 1921.

Jencks, Charles. *Adhocism: The Case for Improvisation*. Cambridge: MIT Press, 2013 [1972].

Johnson-Laird, Philip N. "How Jazz Musicians Improvise." *Music Perception* 19, no. 3 (Spring 2002): 415–442.

Johnson-Laird, Philip N. "Jazz Improvisation: A Theory at the Computational Level." In *Representing Musical Structure*, edited by Peter Howell, Robert West, and Ian Cross, 291–325. London: Academic Press, 1991.

Johnstone, Keith. *Impro: Improvisation and the Theatre*. London: Methuen, 1981.

Jones, LeRoi. *Blues People: Negro Music in White America*. New York: William Morrow, 1963.

Joseph, Sister Miriam, C. S. C. *Shakespeare's Use of the Arts of Language*. New York: Columbia University Press, 1947.

Kelley, Robin D. G. "Dig They Freedom: Meditations on History and the Black Avant-Garde." *Lenox Avenue* 3 (1997): 13–27.

Kendra, James M., and Tricia Wachtendorf. "Improvisation, Creativity, and the Art of Emergency Management." In *Understanding and Responding to Terrorism*, edited by Huseyin Durmaz, Bilal Sevinc, Ahmet Sait Yayla, and Siddik Ekici, 325–335. Amsterdam: IOS Press, 2007.

Kinderman, William. "Improvisation in Beethoven's Creative Process." In *Musical Improvisation: Art, Education, and Society*, edited by Gabriel Solis and Bruno Nettl, 296–312. Urbana: University of Illinois Press, 2009.

Landgraf, Edgar. *Improvisation as Art: Conceptual Challenges, Historical Perspectives*. New York: Continuum, 2011.

Landgraf, Edgar. "Improvisation: Form and Event: A Spencer-Brownian Calculation." In *Emergence and Embodiment: New Essays on Second-Order Systems Theory*, edited by Bruce Clarke and Mark B. N. Hansen, 179–204. Durham and London: Duke University Press, 2009.

Lash, Dominic. "Metonymy as a Creative Structural Principle in the Work of J. H. Prynne, Derek Bailey, and Helmut Lachenmann, with a Creative Component." PhD dissertation, Brunel University, 2010.

Levinson, Jerrold. *Music in the Moment*. Ithaca: Cornell University Press, 1997.

Lewis, George E. "Improvised Music after 1950: Afrological and Eurological Perspectives." *Black Music Research Journal* 16, no. 1 (1996): 91–122.

Lewis, George E. "Living with Creative Machines: An Improvisor Reflects." In *AfroGEEKS: Beyond the Digital Divide*, edited by Anna Everett and Amber J. Walllace, 83–99. Santa Barbara: Center for Black Studies Research, 2007.

Lewis, George E. "The Secret Love between Interactivity and Improvisation, or Missing in Interaction: A Prehistory of Computer Interactivity." In *Improvisation V: 14 Beiträge*, edited by Walter Fähndrich, 193–203. Winterthur: Amadeus, 2003.

Leybourne, Stephen A. "Improvisation and Agile Project Management: A Comparative Consideration." *International Journal of Managing Projects in Business* 2, no. 4 (2009): 519–535.

Livingston, Julie. *Improvising Medicine: An African Oncology Ward in an Emerging Cancer Epidemic*. Durham, NC: Duke University Press, 2012.

Lord, Albert B. *The Singer of Tales*. New York: Athenaeum, 1960.

Manderson, Desmond. "Fission and Fusion: From Improvisation to Formalism in Law and Music." *Critical Studies in Improvisation/Études Critiques en Improvisation* 6, no. 1 (2010). http://www.criticalimprov.com/article/view/1167/1726.

Matton, Ton, and Christopher Dell. *Improvisations on Urbanity: Trendy Pragmatism in a Climate of Change*. Rotterdam: Post Editions, 2010.

McGee, Timothy J. *Improvisation in the Arts of the Middle Ages and Renaissance*. Kalamazoo: Medieval Institute Publications, 2003.

McGinn, Kathleen L., and Angela T. Keros. "Improvisation and the Logic of Exchange in Socially Embedded Transactions." *Administrative Science Quarterly* 47 (2002): 442–473.

Mendonça, David, Gary Webb, Carter Butts, and James Brooks. "Cognitive Correlates of Improvised Behaviour in Disaster Response: The Cases of the Murrah Building and the World Trade Center." *Journal of Contingencies and Crisis Management* 22, no. 4 (December 2014): 185–195.

Merriam, Alan P. *The Anthropology of Music*. Evanston: Northwestern University Press, 1964.

Minsky, Marvin. "Music, Mind, and Meaning." In *Machine Models of Music*, edited by Stephen Schwanauer and David Levitt, 327–354. Cambridge: MIT Press, 1981.

Monson, Ingrid. *Saying Something: Jazz Improvisation and Interaction*. Chicago: University of Chicago Press, 1996.

Murphy, Timothy S., trans. "The Other's Language: Jacques Derrida Interviews Ornette Coleman, 23 June 1997." *Genre* 36 (2004): 319–328.

Nachmanovitch, Stephen. *Free Play: Improvisation in Life and Art*. New York: Jeremy P. Tarcher/Putnam, 1990.

Nettl, Bruno. "Thoughts on Improvisation: A Comparative Approach." *The Musical Quarterly* 60, no. 1 (1974): 1–19.

Nicholls, Tracey. *An Ethics of Improvisation: Aesthetic Possibilities for a Political Future*. Lanham, MD: Lexington Books, 2012.

Nielsen, Aldon Lynn. *Black Chant: Languages of African-American Postmodernism*. Cambridge: Cambridge University Press, 1997.

Novack, Cynthia J. "Looking at Movement as Culture: Contact Improvisation to Disco." *TDR* 32, no. 4 (Winter, 1988): 102–119.

Nubukpo, Kako. *L'improvisation économique en Afrique de l'Ouest: Du coton au franc CFA*. Paris: Karthala, 2011.

Nussbaum, Martha C. *Love's Knowledge: Essays on Philosophy and Literature*. New York: Oxford University Press, 1990.

O'Meally, Robert G., ed. *The Jazz Cadence of American Culture*. New York: Columbia University Press, 1998.

O'Meally, Robert G., Brent Hayes Edwards, and Farah Jasmine Griffin, eds. *Uptown Conversation: The New Jazz Studies*. New York: Columbia University Press, 2004.

Oliveros, Pauline. "Quantum Improvisation: The Cybernetic Presence." In *Sound Unbound: Sampling Digital Music and Culture*, edited by Paul D. Miller aka DJ Spooky That Subliminal Kid, 119–130. Cambridge: MIT Press, 2008.

Oliveros, Pauline. *Software for People*. Baltimore: Smith Publications, 1984.

Parry, Milman, edited by Adam Parry. *The Making of Homeric Verse: The Collected Papers of Milman Parry*. Oxford: Clarendon Press, 1971.

Pelz-Sherman, Michael. "A Framework for the Analysis of Performer Interactions in Western Improvised Music." PhD dissertation, University of California, San Diego, 1998.

Peters, Gary. *The Philosophy of Improvisation*. Chicago: University of Chicago Press, 2009.

Pickering, Andrew. "The Mangle of Practice: Agency and Emergence in the Sociology of Science." *American Journal of Sociology* 99, no. 3 (November 1993): 559–589.

Piekut, Benjamin. *Experimentalism Otherwise: The New York Avant-Garde and Its Limits*. Berkeley: University of California Press, 2011.

Piekut, Benjamin. "Indeterminacy, Free Improvisation, and the Mixed Avant-Garde: Experimental Music in London, 1965–75." *Journal of the American Musicological Society* 67, no. 3 (Fall 2014): 769–824.

Pietropaolo, Domenico. "Improvisation in the Arts." In *Improvisation in the Arts of the Middle Ages and Renaissance*, edited by Timothy J. McGee, 1–28. Kalamzoo: Medieval Institute Publications, 2003.

Piper, Tina S. "The Improvisational Flavour of Law, the Legal Taste of Improvisation." *Critical Studies in Improvisation/Études Critiques en Improvisation* 6, no. 1 (2010). http://www.criticalimprov.com/article/view/1191/1725.

Pressing, Jeff. "Improvisation: Methods and Models." In *Generative Processes in Music: The Psychology of Performance, Improvisation, and Composition*, edited by John A. Sloboda, 129–178. Oxford: Clarendon Press, 1988.

Ramshaw, Sara. "Deconstructin(g) Jazz Improvisation: Derrida and the Law of the Singular Event." *Critical Studies in Improvisation/Études critiques en improvisation* 2, no. 1 (2006): http://www.criticalimprov.com/article/viewArticle/81/179.

Ramshaw, Sara. *Justice as Improvisation: The Law of the Extempore*. New York: Routledge, 2013.

Reason, Dana, and Michael Dessen. "Call for Papers: Improvising Across Borders: An Inter-Disciplinary Symposium on Improvised Music Traditions." (1999). http://goldenpages.jpehs.co.uk/static/conferencearchive/99-4-iab.html. Accessed December 23, 2014.

Richards, Annette. *The Free Fantasia and the Musical Picturesque*. Cambridge: Cambridge University Press, 2001.

Rink, John. "Schenker and Improvisation." *Journal of Music Theory* 37, no. 1 (Spring, 1993): 1–54.

Rustin, Nichole T., and Sherrie Tucker, eds. *Big Ears: Listening for Gender in Jazz Studies*. Durham, NC: Duke University Press, 2008.

Ryle, Gilbert. "Improvisation." *Mind* 85, no. 337 (1976): 69–83.

Salter, Chris, with foreword by Peter Sellars. *Entangled: Technology and the Transformation of Performance*. Cambridge: MIT Press, 2010.

Sawyer, R. Keith. "Improvisation and Narrative." *Narrative Inquiry* 12, no. 2 (2002): 319–349.

Sawyer, R. Keith. "Improvised Conversations: Music, Collaboration, and Development." *Psychology of Music* 27, no. 2 (October 1999): 192–205.

Sawyer, R. Keith. *Improvised Dialogues: Emergence and Creativity in Conversation*. Westport, CT: Greenwood Publishing Group, 2003.

Schutz, Alfred. "Making Music Together: A Study in Social Relationship." In *Alfred Schutz, Collected Papers 2: Studies in Social Theory*, edited by Arvid Broderson, 159–178. The Hague: Martinus Nijhoff, 1964.

Seham, Amy. *Whose Improv Is It Anyway? Beyond Second City*. Jackson: University Press of Mississippi, 2001.

Shibutani, Tamotsu. *Improvised News: A Sociological Study of Rumor*. Indianapolis: Bobbs-Merrill, 1966.

Silverstein, Michael. "The Improvisational Performance of Culture in Realtime Discursive Practice." In *Creativity in Performance*, edited by R. Keith Sawyer, 265–312. London: Ablex Publishing Group, 1997.

Sloboda, John A. "Improvisation." In *The Musical Mind: The Cognitive Psychology of Music*, 138–150. Oxford: Clarendon Press, 1985.

Smith, La Donna. "Improvising Across Borders, the Symposium on Improvisation: A Review and Personal Account." (1999). http://www.the-improvisor.com/improvising_across_borders.htm. Accessed December 23, 2014.

Smith, Leo. *Notes (8 Pieces) Source, a New World Music: Creative Music*. New Haven, CT: Kiom Press, 1973.

Spolin, Viola. *Improvisation for the Theatre*. Evanston: Northwestern University Press, [1963] 1983.

Steinert, Heinz. *Die Entdeckung der Kulturindustrie, oder: Warum Professor Adorno Jazz-Musik nicht ausstehen konnte*. Vienna: Verlag für Gesellschaftskritik, 1992.

Sudnow, David. *Ways of the Hand: The Organization of Improvised Conduct*. Cambridge: Harvard University Press, 1978.

Szwed, John. "Josef Skvorecky and the Tradition of Jazz Literature." *World Literature Today* 54, no. 4 (1980): 586–590.

Todorov, Tzvetan. *The Conquest of America: The Question of the Other*. New York: Harper & Row, 1984.

Treitler, Leo. "Medieval Improvisation." *World of Music* 33, no. 3 (1991): 66–91.

Treitler, Leo. *With Voice and Pen: Coming to Know Medieval Song and How It Was Made*. New York: Oxford University Press, 2007.

Tufnell, Miranda, and Chris Crickmay. *Body Space Image: Notes Toward Improvisation and Performance*. London: Virago Press, 1993.

Uitti, Frances-Marie. "Impossible Music [special issue on improvisation]." *Contemporary Music Review* 25, no. 5/6 (2006).

Velleman, J. David. "How to Share an Intention." *Philosophy and Phenomenological Research* 57, no. 1 (March, 1997): 29–50.

Weick, Karl E. "Improvisation as a Mindset for Organizational Analysis." *Organization Science* 9, no. 5 (September–October 1998): 543–555.

Wigram, Tony. *Improvisation: Methods and Techniques for Music Therapy—Clinicians, Educators, and Students*. London: Jessica Kingsley, 2004.

Zaporah, Ruth. *Improvisation on the Edge: Notes from On and Off Stage*. Berkeley CA: North Atlantic Books, 2014.

Zorn, John, ed. *Arcana: Musicians on Music*, Vols. 1–7. New York: Hips Road/Tzadik, 2000–2014.

PART I

COGNITIONS

CHAPTER 1

....

COGNITIVE PROCESSES IN MUSICAL IMPROVISATION

....

ROGER T. DEAN AND FREYA BAILES

INTRODUCTION

....

IN this article we discuss the conceptual frameworks in which current empirical studies of cognition in musical improvisation are being undertaken. We take as our starting point the significant theoretical and empirical contributions of the late Jeff Pressing, musician and researcher, several of which were directed toward opening up this area of investigation. It is on the theoretical bases of such a model that one can most readily construct experimentally accessible hypotheses about improvisation. We make some cross-cultural and cross-medium comparisons, though briefly; we do not address closely the sociological, philosophical, or educational bases and uses of improvisation, though we have contributed to these areas in previous work (Dean 1989, 1992; Smith and Dean 1997; Dean 2003).

MODELS OF IMPROVISATION BASED ON JEFF PRESSING'S IDEAS

....

Pressing laid the groundwork for a cognitive understanding of musical improvisation. In spite of his focus on cognition, his work is characterized by recognition of the integral and often dominant role of motor function in the performative act of improvisation. This perspective is a natural consequence of his considering the chain of neural processing involved in perceiving and producing sound (e.g., Pressing 1988). These two elements, of perceiving and producing sound, share a special relationship during any musical performance, since the musicians receive feedback from their performance, allowing them to detect errors and correct them by comparison with the intended output. In improvisation, the concept of error is somewhat different from that in the realization of compositions, because any event can potentially be incorporated into an improvisation, and while a sonic event cannot be withdrawn, it can be subject to retrospective "erasure," reinterpretation, or repositioning (Smith and Dean 1997). While motoric function is normally central to musical improvisation, even in this idiom it may be somewhat evaded, as in the case of the computer-interactive improviser. More generally, improvisation in some spheres, such as dance, involves an intensive reliance on motor function, whereas in others, such as text generation and performance, this reliance can be more distant.

In musical improvisation, perceptual feedback also shapes the improviser's decisions as to the course that the music will take. Influenced by "closed-loop" theories of motor learning, Pressing describes the establishment of "perceptual traces," which are representations of intended movements established by practice. These perceptual traces come to form the basis of comparison between intended and realized performance (Pressing 1988). With increasing experience, Pressing argues, improvising musicians refine their perceptual abilities as well as their perceptual traces and error correction, such that performance is nuanced, flexible, and largely automatized. For Pressing, improvisational control is heterarchical more than hierarchical, characterized by redundancy and consequent flexibility, and by a feeling of "going with flow" more than a "top-down" conscious monitoring of decisions. The concept of "flow" has been elaborated by Csíkszentmihályi (1996) and championed in relation to free jazz by Mazzola (Mazzola and Cherlin 2009). Thus the flow of microstructural events can generate macrostructure in the resultant musical stream. That is not to say that there is no role for conscious attention in improvisation. "Tonal imagery" may also play a part, acting as the perception of internal images of either reproduced (recalled) or produced (created) material, at the same time as perception of the actual sensory environment (Pressing 1988). Pressing clearly did not intend the term "tonal" to refer to degrees of tonality, but rather used the term to refer to the structure of tone material.

Improvisation is of special interest for cognitive science since real-time processes place great demands on available resources. In relation to this argument, Pressing (1988) writes that "the need of the improviser is for a good solution, not the best," since the search for an optimum would be too time-consuming and resource-intensive. Reviewing physiological and neurological literature, Pressing concludes that improvisers have the biological capacity to react to unexpected changes, and hence to one another's new ideas, about twice a second. This feature of improvisation is of course one of the aspects that contributes to its potential for unique outputs and unique interactions between musicians.

Pressing outlined a model of improvisation with aims to explain how people improvise, how they learn to improvise, and to explain the genesis of novel behavior (Pressing 1988). The model is simple in its starting point as a sequence of non-overlapping sections. Each section comprises musical events and is called an event cluster. Each new event cluster is generated on the basis of previous events, long-term memory, current goals, and, where applicable, a referent. The model allows for variations in cognitive strength associated with different "objects" (cognitive units or entities such as a chord or gesture), reflecting attentional loading, which is tantamount to the object's importance within the improviser's internal representation. In producing a new event cluster, Pressing proposes two types of continuation, namely "associative" and "interrupt" generation. In associative generation, continuity is sought between event clusters with objects high in cognitive strength assuming a continued importance, while interrupt generation represents a break with previous events.

Objects, which can in some ways be conceptualized as musical content, are not the most crucial elements of Pressing's model. Rather, what he terms "features" and "processes" allow for control of the improvisation. Features are the common parameters of multiple objects. Processes describe changes in objects or features over time. Features and processes together form dynamic patterns, and these are at the core of improvisational cognition. In the modest development of this theoretical stance to which the first author contributed (Dean 1989, 1992; Smith and Dean 1997; Dean 2003), the role of ongoing process is emphasized and generalized to the other arts beside music. The process may be such as to generate the objects rather than simply acting on them. In addition, the distinction between process and object readily permits the conception that event-clusters might be non-overlapping in some situations but overlapping in others, particularly by means of continuity of a single process, while the features differ between segments, or by continuity of an object set while the process differs.

The concept of process readily accommodates the situation in which improvisers play together: they may each bring different processes to bear on shared objects, or vice versa, hence generating a diversity of features. A related issue put forward in our earlier work (Dean 1989, 1992; Smith and Dean 1997; Dean 2003) is the possibility that within certain limits improvisers may choose whether or not to adopt what we then described as a "sensory" stance, that is, one in which they respond to ongoing streams besides their own. Somewhat as John Cage encouraged us to perceive environmental sounds outside the control of a performer as part of the musical process, improviser A may construe the musical stream of co-improviser B either as mutable, susceptible to influence from A, or vice versa. And similarly, A may consciously or unconsciously adopt an exogenous (which is a more appropriate term in the context of cognitive studies than our previous "sensory") or endogenous (previously "non-sensory") orientation in relation to whether to respond to B's stream. Extreme cases of such endogenously oriented interactions occur during improvisations in which the participants do not hear each other (for example, sometimes in trans-internet improvisation), or in which one participant is a computer agent that does not "hear" the input of its partner(s). The work of the Hub, our co-editor George Lewis, and many others, including the first author, have exploited such possibilities of computer-interactive improvisation, and mostly emphasized the capacity of computer-agents not only to generate autonomously, but also to process and exploit incoming musical streams from their partners. Large-scale evolutionary processes in musical generation may also occur with such computer-agents (c.f. McCormack et al. 2009).

Overall, Pressing's model, together with an enhanced emphasis on process as a separable element, and on interaction as an additional dimension, may be thought of as an Interactive Object/Feature/Process (IOFP) model. This appropriately brings to mind many of the core concepts of the cognitive processes in creativity in general, such as those in Finke's GENEPLORE model. Here, repeated cycles of generation (of *objects* in our terminology), followed by exploration (giving rise to detectable features as a result of ongoing process), and then by a refinement or selection step, take place. We have proposed a similar model for the long-term processes of research-led practice in the creative arts (Smith and Dean 2009). But even in a short-term improvisation, the aspect of refinement and selectivity can occur, both when a solo improviser chooses which objects, features, or processes to continue and which to discontinue, and when a group improviser selects, among all the available objects, features and processes present or preceding in the performance. It is the selection step that is central to biological or social evolution in the large time frame, and to the iterative cycle of research-led practice we have identified. And while selectivity in evolutionary biology operates largely on the basis of fitness (for survival and reproduction), it may operate on any basis in a creative or socio-cultural system. In the case of socio-cultural systems this brings attendant ethical risks, since many of the selective bases might not produce outcomes that are beneficial for all or a majority of people. This is not to say that creative work is ethically free of risk, but rather that the appropriate and potentially valuable range of selective approaches is exceedingly broad, since they are not bound by purely functional considerations.

SOME IMPLICATIONS OF THE IOFP MODEL FOR COGNITIVE RESEARCH

In this brief section we illustrate the kinds of experimental questions that can be raised on the basis of the simple model just described. These illustrations are meant to be suggestive rather than exhaustive. Commonly, the ideas one can develop prove difficult to investigate directly, because of the complexity of human cognition and the moderate development of the research field, as well as the complexity implied by an interactive model. So it is necessary first to investigate what often seem like the most simplistic questions. To those outside experimental science these reductive experiments and their conclusions may seem obvious, predictable, and even intrinsic, but they nevertheless form a necessary step in the long-term project to understand the cognition of improvisation. In what follows we mix examples of the inaccessible and complex with the reductively simple, again, for our suggestive purposes.

The possible primacy of the motoric considerations emphasized by Pressing leads to the suggestion that improvisation is largely unconscious, since it necessitates the learning of basic structures and movements. Can one readily distinguish a conscious from an unconscious process experimentally? Sometimes in cognitive science such a question is reinterpreted as one that asks: is attention required for the task at hand, or not? As Pressing argued, it may be necessary to learn to minimize the attention required for many motor actions (musical or during walking, etc.) such that the organism has enough attention available for other impinging perceptual streams. A reciprocal possibility when improvising on an instrument is that it is the motoric demands that drive the production of the musical objects, features or processes. The experience of David Sudnow in learning slowly to improvise at the piano (Sudnow 1978) could be seen partly in this light, and most improvisers would also recognize the influence of the physical structure of their instrument, and the process of playing it, on the range of musical outputs they generate. To take an extreme example, playing chordally is much more obvious for a pianist than a trombonist, yet both can ultimately achieve this if they wish, the trombonist through the use of a variety of techniques for multiphonic generation of sounds.

Returning to attention, a common empirical approach to the question of how much attention is applied to some particular activity is to enquire whether the precision and speed with which another task is undertaken is reduced when it is done at the same time as the specified activity (say, improvising a flurry of notes). It is probably obvious that this is not an easy experiment to achieve. For example, if attentional resources are in abundance in relation to demand, there will be no interaction. And if attentional resources are modality-specific (for example, hearing calls upon distinct resources from vision), then again there can be no interference between cross-modal tasks. Even when it can be demonstrated that performance on one task is decreased by the simultaneous demands of another, this is clearly a quite indirect assessment of attentional demands and even less directly related to the issue of conscious versus unconscious behaviors. The field of attention is huge and developing (Pashler 1998; Pashler and Johnston 1998; Knudsen 2007), but there are indications that musical activity can focus it. For example, Jones and colleagues have demonstrated that if participants are familiarized with a metrical rhythmic pattern, they develop an expectation of the sonic event that occurs on the emphasized beat of the pattern, and at that point in time they also show greater acuity in detecting certain sonic features of the sound than when the sound is heard at an unexpected (non-metrical) time (Jones and McAuley 2005; Jones 1992). On the other hand, there is evidence for pre-attentive processing of auditory timing and intensity changes (e.g., Repp 2005; Tervaniemi et al. 2006).

Returning to the IOFP model, one might readily envisage that increased attention would occur at moments of associative or interrupt generation (i.e., at section boundaries). In our own studies, we have reinterpreted this idea as suggesting that there should be changed skin conductance at such points, since skin conductance is a physiological response reflective of psychological arousal (which is commonly related to increased attention), and it is a response that is seemingly not open to our conscious control. The response is part of what is therefore termed the autonomic nervous system, because of its resistance to conscious control. Unlike many neuroimaging techniques, such as magnetoencephalography (MEG) and functional magnetic resonance imaging (fMRI), skin conductance can be measured under fairly normal keyboard performing conditions.

This line of discussion suggests that ultimately such studies of the roles of attention in improvisation will be meaningful, but there is a very long way to go as yet to translate the observations of neurophysiology and neuroimaging into clear-cut interpretations specific to this framework.

When we consider the psychology of interactions between co-improvisers, clearly the difficulties just discussed are magnified hugely, but there are also new questions. For example, are there leadership functions expressed across the "interruptions" when musicians are improvising in an exogenously oriented manner? Some experimental hypotheses can be made as the first step toward addressing such a complex issue. For example, if changes in skin conductance (or some other neurophysiological response) distinguish interruptions from the surrounding periods in the work of a solo improviser, then one would expect a distinction in the nature or degree of these changes between different co-improvisers. Similarly, someone leading an interruption should show a characteristic skin conductance change signature in advance of a co-improviser. The co-improviser would show different responses thereafter according to whether or not he chooses to cooperate and cohere with the form of the interruption (e.g., takes up a newly introduced process). Such hypotheses become accessible providing one has the musicological tools and hypotheses to distinguish the postulated leaderly interruption from a follower's behavior and to distinguish cooperation from a decision to ignore the instigated idea. Such distinctions can be made by computational analysis of musical and acoustic features, providing one can distinguish among the musical contributions of different participants. We mention later some simple experiments in which such musicological analyses are facilitated in some cases by providing clear-cut referents for improvisers to use, requiring particular types of interruption: for example, requiring transition from soft to loud or from sparse to dense playing. We complement these referents with free improvisations to allow totally realistic conditions also.

A Brief Survey of Empirical Studies on Cognition in Musical Improvisation

There have been numerous empirical studies of the performance of music, but there is a relative paucity of such work on improvised music. Moreover, music psychology is often interested in improvisation primarily as a simple departure from score-based music rather than as a sophisticated object in itself. One example can be found in the work of Bengtsson, Csíkszentmihályi, and Ullén (2007). They hoped to uncover the cortical regions associated with simple improvisations by pianists. In one condition, pianists were asked to improvise around a visually displayed melody, while in a subsequent condition they were asked to reproduce their improvisation. A third condition encouraged improvisation without the need to memorize. Improvisation complexity was measured so that it could be aligned with the isolated brain regions active during the condition.

Brain activity was measured using fMRI, which images blood flow. One finding was an increase in activity in the dorsolateral prefrontal cortex during improvisation compared to during recall. This brain region is associated with a number of cognitive functions, including "top-down" attending to activity, monitoring working memory (namely the short-term memory necessary for us to relate current perceptions to immediately preceding events), response selection, and the suppression of stereotypical response (Bengtsson, Csíkszentmihályi, and Ullén 2007). All such functions are potentially important in improvisation, and it is perhaps remarkable that such a result was found in the context of such a simple improvisation context. On the other hand, changes in blood flow bear variable relationships to changes in neural activity (Logothetis 2008) and are in any case representative of massive regions of the brain, comprising millions of neurons, commonly coordinated with millions in other regions. Thus the interpretation of such changes is complex, but their occurrence is encouraging.

It stands to reason that Pressing's event clusters and their associative or interruptive generation can be traced by a musicological-statistical analysis of improvised music along the lines mentioned above. Pressing himself was one of the first to attempt a detailed and systematic analysis of the micro-structure of "free" improvisations (Pressing 1987), contrasting with the broader, more macro-structural studies of Jost (1974), Dean (1992), and others. Recording himself performing two short synthesizer improvisations and simultaneously recording the MIDI output, Pressing conducted various computational analyses of both traditional musical features (pitch, rhythm, phrase structure, articulation, dynamics, texture) and what he termed microstructure (essentially expressive properties of music such as rubato, chordal spread, legato-ness). One of his findings was that even his free improvisations seem to comprise organized interval and pitch class structures. A second finding of interest to music cognition was the apparent categorical production of performance dynamics, similar to the phenomenon of categorical perception. In other words, dynamics did not seem to vary continuously; rather, they clustered around certain key velocity means, reminiscent of the perceptual bias to perceive dimensions of sound as discrete categories. It should be noted, though, that when playing with most synthesizers of the time, the relationship between key velocity and apparent loudness was not as satisfactory or nuanced as with an acoustic instrument, which might have accentuated the tendency to clustering that Pressing observed. One of Pressing's two improvisations was suitable as a test of his model of improvisation, and he conducted a partitioning of the music into event clusters and higher-level event cluster classes. The segmenting into event clusters was determined on a musical, motoric, and "cognitive" (i.e., based on recorded comments) basis.

In addition to studying free improvisations by retrospectively identifying the objects, features, and processes, one can simplify the situation experimentally by providing referent bases for improvisation. In such improvisations, the musicians improvise around a particular structural or thematic idea, and these ideas may be arbitrarily simple (for empirical studies) or complex. For example, we are studying a series of three section referent-improvisations by professional improvising pianists, in which the referents are simple musical "features." We request an ABA improvisation, over a few minutes, where

A might be soft and B loud, but the performance is otherwise unconstrained. An alternative might be sparse-dense-sparse. In an experiment we have a series of improvisation referents, preceded and concluded by a free improvisation (no referent whatsoever). We record MIDI data from a Yamaha Disklavier, an acoustic grand piano with MIDI detection. We record all aspects of the keyboard and pedal performance, together with acoustic and video data, and skin conductance of the performer. After the participants have recorded their improvisations, we ask them to listen back to some of the recordings, and to give a continuous response via a computer interface about their perception of musical "change" (which we leave them to define, and take as an index of their perception of musical structure) and their perception of the expressed arousal and valence (positivity to negativity) of the music. We have conducted extensive studies of such continuous response measures of change and affect during listening tasks undertaken by both non-musicians and musicians (Bailes and Dean 2009, in press; Dean, Bailes, and Schubert 2011).

With this approach, we can use computational analyses informed by the referent instruction to detect whether segmentation (into ABA) is achieved as judged by the musical note stream. Having determined segmentation points, we can also assess whether skin conductance changes were related to this segmentation, thus testing a core implication of the IOFP model. We have developed a range of computational analyses to do with key velocity (relating to loudness produced), pitch and pitch range, tonality versus atonality, rhythmic pulse, and event density. Many of these are based on algorithms developed in the literature previously for use with the performance of composed tonal music. In dealing with the free improvisations we recorded, we apply a multiplicity of these computational analyses, and we are developing a range of approaches that take into account the multivariate nature of our data streams: that is, the performance may use several simultaneous processes acting on several objects to generate the features of any particular part of the improvisation. A combination of quite simple analytical algorithms is surprisingly successful in segmenting even the free improvisations we recorded.

Each of the component processes, objects, and features is potentially a continuously variable stream throughout the performance, from an analytical-computational point of view. We use detailed techniques of Time Series Analysis, a statistical approach that takes account of the "autocorrelation" between successive events in these streams: that is, the fact that if one note is sounded in a high register, the next is more likely to be adjacent than distant; or if a note is sounded loudly, the next is also likely to be loud rather than soft. This feature of autocorrelation is very strong in all the music and perceptual responses we have studied, and if it is not considered, statistical analyses and conclusions can be insecure (Dyson and Quinlan 2010). This quite elaborate data gathering approach has generated a few simple conclusions, generally in support of the hypotheses we generated from the IOFP model. For example, improvisers are entirely capable of generating the "interruptions" requested by our referents, and this is readily revealed by our computational analyses of their outputs. More interesting, it does seem that at points of interruption, there generally are changes in skin conductance, and that

segments defined by the interruption points are commonly distinct in their skin conductance characteristics.

In the retrospective perception studies, we find that the improvisers identify change
in such a way that it coheres with both the referent and the computational analysis. We
have yet to complete studies on the perception of affect. We hypothesize that acoustic
intensity profiles will be strong predictors of perceived arousal, as we have shown in
some depth with composed and improvised electroacoustic and composed piano music
previously. Our FEELA hypothesis (see Dean and Bailes 2010), which suggests a Force-
Effort-Energy-Loudness-Affect chain, may thus link an improviser with listeners and
with other improvisers. This role for energy and loudness, corresponding to the physical
property of acoustic intensity and its perceptual counterpart loudness, would be consistent with the suggestions of categorical velocity generation made by Pressing. The role
would also cohere with our other observations that statistical patterns of intensity in
electroacoustic music (both composed and improvised, see Dean and Bailes 2010) and
in a wide range of improvised music (Dean and Bailes 2010) share recurrent patterns of
intensity in which crescendi are shorter and show faster dynamic change than dimin-
uendi. This can readily be interpreted as a device, perhaps originating from statistical
learning of environmental sounds, by which musicians are able to modulate attention
on the part of the listener and sometimes of their fellow performers. In agreement with
these suggestions that intensity and timing/rhythm are of particular importance in the
perception of improvisation, Keller, Weber, and Engel (2011) indeed report that a majority of participants in a study in which the task was to listen to performances and try to
distinguish which were improvised and which were imitated indicated that they used
information about timing/rhythm (16/22 listeners) and intensity (12/22). These parameters also correlated with activity in the left amygdala, an area of the brain with which
many functions, including fear and aversion, have been associated. It is difficult to interpret this functionally, but the existence of anatomic specificity in the response supports
the idea that it is distinctive.

In ongoing work we will also be assessing the capacity of the various object, feature,
and process streams, discussed earlier, to predict the affect that listeners of the music
perceive, based on our computational analysis of the performances. In other work
(Gingras et al., unpublished), we have indeed found that expressive performance features (in a baroque harpsichord fantasia by Louis Couperin), such as event timing,
can be predicted by the information and entropy flow of the composition, using the
Information Dynamics of Music (IDyoM) model of Pearce and Wiggins in collaboration with them. In the near future our improvisation studies will assess whether there
are separable contributions of the object/feature/process streams that relate to pitch,
timbre, rhythm, and the acoustic intensity profile. From a computational perspective,
a feature, as characterized by Pressing, would be an amalgam of several objects that first
occur together apposed in time.

These studies of solo improvisers are currently being extended to apply to pairs of
keyboard improvisers playing together. Again we record the same complex set of data
for each performer as described above, except that they play digital instruments. In this

development, we also ask the musicians to alternate in adopting the role of leader in some of the improvised pieces, preceding and succeeding them by improvisations in which the concept of leadership is not mentioned (and not forewarning them that the issue will be raised, since this produces psychological "demand" that may alter their performance).

During the retrospective listening task, after the improvisers have performed, we request some perceptual responses about the music (as above), but also, separately, we ask for an identification of "musical leadership" on a continuous scale and continuously across the pieces. Thus, each player hears the performance back with one player in each headphone ear, is not reminded who is who, and judges which "side" of the audio is musically leading. Again, we do not provide guidance as to what constitutes leadership, leaving that for our musicians to consider in their own terms. Our analyses of this data are in the early stages, but it does seem that interruption is achieved well, and leadership is recognized, both in perceptual retrospection and in skin conductance. There are complex statistical interactions between the various data strands, such that some features of one improviser may be quite predictive of those of another, supporting the idea of there being interactions such as would be expected from a leader-follower relationship, or for that matter, from competitive interactions. We hope to gain much more understanding of these data during the completion of our analyses.

COMPARATIVE AND CROSS-CULTURAL ISSUES IN STUDIES OF COGNITION OF IMPROVISATION

Of interest is to ask whether the IOFP model is useful in describing the structure of compositions that have not been improvised. Lehmann and Kopiez (2010) asked whether musical experts could discern when a piece had been improvised rather than composed in a listening experiment. The task was found to be hard, and the authors surmised that the cues listeners used to identify an improvisation had little to do with structure and more to do with its performative character. Studies by Engel and Keller mentioned earlier were consistent with this view, revealing the importance of "instability" in timing and intensity patterns and the possible role of the amygdala. This could have important implications for our understanding of the cognitive processes involved in improvisation. Indeed, Engel and Keller showed that musically experienced listeners had greater facility in making the distinction between improvised and imitated performances, and suggested that this ability "depends upon whether an individual's action-related experience and perspective taking skills enable faithful internal simulation of the given behaviour." Keller, Weber, and Engel (2011) pursued their study of instability in improvised music by comparing the entropy of keystroke variables in improvisations with imitations of those improvisations. They interpret their finding of greater entropy in keystroke intensity in improvisations as indicative of irregularities in motor control associated with greater uncertainty than occur during the certainty of an imitated performance. While these differences might say more about the impact of rehearsal on performance manner-isms than the relative spontaneity associated with improvisation versus imitation, the approach holds promise for its potential application to compare the entropy associated with different styles of improvisation. For example, it seems likely that the entropy of performance variables would be greater in a free improvisation than in a referent-based improvisation. Keller et al. (2011) measure the entropy of the distribution of keystrokes across an entire piece. A potentially fruitful alternative would be to measure the short-term information content of an unfolding improvisation to explore the time course of uncertainty in both solo and ensemble improvisations, as we have already been doing with the Couperin Fantasia, which is closely related to a long-standing tradition of pre-classical improvisation.

Improvisation can occur in highly defined musical conventions, such as in the per-formance of baroque music and in the cadenzas of classical concertos, where the song structure is often fixed and recurrent, although it occurs most dominantly in idioms such as jazz and rock. Berkowitz (2010), focusing on classical music, defines improvi-sation as "spontaneous creativity within constraints" and provides neuroimaging data related to models of improvisation in the classical music context. One can quibble with the somewhat romantic word *spontaneous* given the many hours of training and prac-tice required to achieve proficiency in the required function in classical music as in jazz (Sudnow 1978) or free improvisation. But for the purpose of contrast, composi-tion could be construed in the same terms but as lacking in spontaneity. The cogni-tive demands placed on improvisers and composers are likely to differ substantially. Recognizing that improvisers both create and perform, Eisenberg and Thompson (2011) examined the effects of competition on their creative production. They found that improvisations were judged to be more creative when improvisers had been told that musical experts would be looking for the "best improvisers." The link is intrigu-ing, and invites future research into the contextual factors that shape spontaneous creativity.

Jazz has been the focus of empirical study in other work designed to examine the neu-ral activity associated with musical improvisation (Limb and Braun 2008). An fMRI approach was again taken in which professional jazz pianists were required to play on specially adapted keyboards while lying with their head in the MRI scanner. Comparing regions of the brain that were activated during improvisation with those activated dur-ing the performance of overlearned material revealed that the improvisations activated brain regions associated with internally generated, stimulus-independent processes, with concomitant deactivation of regions associated with conscious self-regulation. Limb and Braun suggest that "rather than operating in accordance with conscious strat-egies and expectations, musical improvisation may be associated with behaviors that conform to rules implemented . . . outside of conscious awareness" (2008, 4). We have already noted the complexity and difficulty of such a claim; yet it is stimulating and wor-thy of intensive follow-up.

Others have studied jazz as an essentially social process. For example, Bastien and Hostager (1988) analyzed the performance of a jazz ensemble that had not previously improvised together through the observation of video footage. Focusing on inter-musician communication, they describe the observed importance of shared information and attention. For them, ensemble improvisation is inherently turbulent, and this "produces uncertainty for performers insofar as each musician cannot fully predict the behavior of the other musicians or, for that matter, the behavior of the collectivity" (Bastien and Hostager 1988, 586). Uncertainty requires a focused attention, and this is particularly high at moments of structural change. The authors found that the attention of the musicians was high around moments of potential change in the solo, with dips in between. This attentional focus is consistent with the overarching IOFP model of improvisation outlined above, whereby the structure comprises event clusters that transition by means of either associative or interrupt generation. A further cognitive level is that of the establishment of a shared history of improvisation between the players, during the course of the performance (or more broadly, an improvisation session or stream of sessions). This serves to reduce uncertainty with respect to the behavior of the other musicians and, perhaps, to focus attention efficiently. Bastien and Hostager (1988) argue that the greater the "center of shared information" between musicians, the greater the affordance for increased musical complexity. But many improvisers thrive on the opportunity to play with new musicians, and quite possibly exploit such situations equally toward the generation of complexity and of IOFP components that for them are novel and hardly experienced previously. R. Keith Sawyer has provided frameworks of social psychology for consideration of group interactions, notably in improvisation in both theater and music (Sawyer 2003).

Correspondingly, improvisation is the foundation of many approaches to music therapy (e.g., Nordhoff Robbins), and this may be construed in light of its capacity to encourage both coherent interaction and personalized novelty of expression. The communication and regulation of emotions are important goals, and it is perhaps these goals that prompted Luck et al. (2008) to investigate listener perceptions of the emotion expressed in music therapy improvisations, relating these to their musical content. This musical content tends to be stylistically "free," which is typically less easily described in traditional analytic terms. Luck et al. (2008) summarize the problem as follows: "there is a need to be able to capture the most essential musical features—whatever they are—and connect them to the psychological meanings, especially those relating to emotional content, that they represent. In other words, there is a need to be able to define and extract the clinically relevant combinations of musical features that are 'hiding' within the improvisation" (Luck et al. 2008, 27). The authors were interested in studying the perception of music for which listeners have minimal associations, arguing that this is the case for free improvisation (see our comparable motivation for exploring perceptions of unfamiliar electroacoustic music in Bailes and Dean [2009]), though acknowledging that stylistic associations could always exist for any given listener. A therapist and client jointly improvised at keyboards, with separate MIDI tracks being recorded for each. As in our work, listeners (but in this case not the improvisers themselves) rated continuously their perceptions of the emotion they felt was being expressed by the improvisations. A relationship was found between the mean velocity of the key strikes of the music and listener ratings of the activity (arousal) of the music. This is consistent with other reports of a robust relationship between sound intensity and perceptions of loudness with heightened perceptions of arousal (Dean, Bailes, and Schubert 2011), including in improvisation (Dean and Bailes 2010).

We have suggested that in the social context of improvisation, acoustic intensity may be a cross-culturally shared expressive resource (Dean and Bailes 2010), which is consistent with the work of Balkwill and Thompson (1999). In particular, intensity is a powerful predictor of judgments of affect even in cross-cultural studies of Hindustani and Japanese listeners, who come from very different musical cultures. Thus, an improviser might be involved in a real-time collaboration with someone from another culture (say an African-American from the jazz tradition with an Indian classical musician) and yet be able to interact successfully in improvisation. Control of dynamic intensity as a means of projecting an affective profile could be very important here.

Rhythmic structures differ considerably between, say, Western classical music and jazz (mostly symmetric meters), Indian music (quite commonly involving asymmetric meters), and Balkan dance music, with its characteristic aksak ("limping") asymmetric rhythms (such as 3+3+2+3). Yet as can be extrapolated from the discussions by fellow improvising pianists Vijay Iyer on microrhythms (Iyer 2002) and Pressing on "Black Atlantic" rhythm (Pressing 2002), what is shared by improvisers from these different musical and cultural environments is an ability to adapt instantly (or in about half a second) to a rhythmic event and a perception of the relative accentuation of particular events. Accentuation is a combination of acoustic intensity with many features of articulation and timbre (as discussed by Pressing). Thus again, intensity is among the features that may assist musical cross-cultural improvisation, and also perhaps verbal cross-cultural or conflicted discussion through prosody. This may have practical applications in post-dialogic community discussions contributing to social policy development. We have developed this argument in more depth elsewhere (Dean and Bailes 2010).

A cross-cultural study of improvisation was reported by Matare (2009), who was interested in the practice as a manifestation of creativity or musical intelligence among twelve European and twelve African musicians. Musicians from each background were recorded improvising and asked to listen back and provide a commentary on problems, decisions, points of interest, and directions taken. On the whole, the commentaries of the European musicians were focused on aspects of the music itself, such as characteristics of the structure or details of the sound produced, while the African musicians made no explicit mention of music.

There are higher-level issues that relate to cross-cultural cognition in improvisation, such as those adumbrated by George E. Lewis in his contrast between Afro-logic and Euro-logic in improvisation (Lewis 1996). One aspect of his interesting dissection is the idea of "telling a story" as central to Afro-logic improvisation, in contrast to more of a structural/process approach in Euro-logic. This is not to do justice to these ideas (see also discussion in Smith and Dean 1997 and Dean and Bailes 2010), but rather to indicate that both narrative and structural approaches can be readily envisaged as outcomes an IOFP model: both are formed at the interaction of feature and process, and where microstructure meets macrostructure.

OUTLOOK

Cognitive studies of musical improvisation are still at a very early stage of development, but they show great potential. Besides giving insight into improvisational processes, might such studies eventually contribute to them? We would argue they have strong potential to do so. As discussed by Wiggins and colleagues with reference to classical music, a computational approach to the generation of music can use models of cognition as part of the generative mechanism. This may occur by using a statistical corpus of information, as in information content approaches to the prediction of segmentation timing and emphasis in composition and performance (Wiggins, Pearce, and Müllensiefen 2009). More interesting, another computational approach could be to use an ongoing computer analysis of an incoming musical stream in conjunction with a cognitive model of whatever degree of elaboration is available. As mentioned, real-time analysis of input is intrinsic to many computer-interactive improvisation systems that have been developed since the early efforts of the Hub, George Lewis (*Voyager*; Lewis 2000), and Richard Teitelbaum, and large-scale cognitive architecture models (such as ACT-R; Anderson et al. 2004) are also under long-term development. A combination of such real-time analysis, particular generative models, and a cognitive architecture model may suffice to help take computer interactive sound improvisation to another level (see also discussion in Dean 2003; Dean and Bailes 2010). For example, computational "conceptual blending" is an idea of current importance in improvisation with text (see chapters in this handbook by Smith, and by Harrell), and it involves exploiting "domains" of knowledge or of arbitrary codification so as to perform crossovers between them with a flexibility and variability of outcome that is shared by genetic crossovers in organismal evolution. This approach can be applied much more freely with the relatively non-referential components of music than with highly referential words and verbal concepts. Not surprisingly, it has a long tradition of related antecedents in the improvisation systems just mentioned and in commercial software such as the classic program M from the first days of desktop computers in the 1980s. The potential of such approaches (discussed in Dean 2009) has probably only been glimpsed.

BIBLIOGRAPHY

Anderson, J. R., D. Bothell, M. D. Byrne, S. Douglass, C. Lebiere, and Y. Qin. "An Integrated Theory of the Mind." *Psychological Review* 111, no. 4 (2004): 1036–1060.

Bailes, F., and R. T. Dean. "Listeners Discern Affective Variation in Computer-Generated Musical Sounds." *Perception* 38, no. 9 (2009): 1386–1404.

Bailes, F., and R. T. Dean. "Comparative Time Series Analysis of Perceptual Responses to Electroacoustic Music." *Music Perception* 29, no. 4 (April 2012): 359–375.

Balkwill, L.-L., and W. F. Thompson. "A Cross-cultural Investigation of the Perception of Emotion in Music: Psychophysical and Cultural Cues." *Music Perception* 17, no. 1 (1999): 43–64.

Bastien, D. T., and T. J. Hostager. "Jazz as a Process of Organizational Innovation." *Communication Research* 15, no. 5 (1988): 582–602.

Bengtsson, S. L., M. Csíkszentmihályi, and F. Ullén. "Cortical Regions Involved in the Generation of Musical Structures during Improvisation in Pianists." *Journal of Cognitive Neuroscience* 19, no. 5 (2007): 830–842.

Berkowitz, A. L. *The Improvising Mind: Cognition and Creativity in the Musical Moment.* New York: Oxford University Press, 2010.

Csíkszentmihályi, M. *Creativity: Flow and the Psychology of Discovery and Invention.* New York: HarperCollins, 1996.

Dean, R. T. *Creative Improvisation: Jazz, Contemporary Music and Beyond.* Milton Keynes: Open University Press, 1989.

Dean, R. T. *New Structures in Jazz and Improvised Music since 1960.* Milton Keynes: Open University Press, 1992.

Dean, R. T. *Hyperimprovisation: Computer Interactive Sound Improvisation; with CD(R) of Sound Works, Intermedia, and Performance Software Patches.* Middleton, WI: A-R Editions, 2003.

Dean, R. T., and F. Bailes. "The Control of Acoustic Intensity during Jazz and Free Improvisation Performance: Possible Transcultural Implications for Social Discourse and Community." *Critical Studies in Improvisation/Études Critiques en Improvisation* 6, no. 2, December 2010. Available at http://www.criticalimprov.com/article/view/1193/1889, accessed December 21, 2013.

Dean, R. T., and F. Bailes. "A Rise-Fall Temporal Asymmetry of Intensity in Composed and Improvised Electroacoustic Music." *Organised Sound* 15, no. 2 (2010): 147–158.

Dean, R. T., F. Bailes, and E. Schubert. "Acoustic Intensity Causes Perceived Changes in Arousal Levels in Music." *PLoS One* 6, no. 4 (April 20, 2011), e18591. Available at http://www.ncbi.nlm.nih.gov/pmc/articles/PMC3080387/, accessed December 21, 2013.

Dean, R. T., ed. *The Oxford Handbook of Computer Music.* New York: Oxford University Press, 2009.

Dyson, B. J., and P. T. Quinlan. "Decomposing the Garner Interference Paradigm: Evidence for Dissociations between Macrolevel and Microlevel Performance." *Attention, Perception, & Psychophysics* 72, no. 6 (2010): 1676–1691.

Eisenberg, J., and W. F. Thompson. "The Effects of Competition on Improvisers' Motivation, Stress, and Creative Performance." *Creativity Research Journal* 23, no. 2 (2011): 129–136.

Iyer, V. "Embodied Mind, Situated Cognition, and Expressive Microtiming in African-American Music." *Music Perception* 19, no. 2 (2002): 387–414.

Jones, M. R., and J. D. McAuley. "Time Judgments in Global Temporal Contexts." *Perception & Psychophysics* 67, no. 3 (2005): 398–417.

Jones, M. R. "Attending to Musical Events." In *Cognitive Bases of Musical Communication*, edited by M. R. Jones and S. Holleran, 91-110. Washington, DC: American Psychological Association, 1992.

Jost, E. *Free Jazz* (English ed.). Graz: Universal Edition, 1974.

Keller, P. E., A. Weber, and A. Engel. "Practice Makes Too Perfect: Fluctuations in Loudness Indicate Spontaneity in Musical Improvisation." *Music Perception* 29, no. 1 (2011): 107–112.

Knudsen, E. I. "Fundamental Components of Attention." *Annual Review of Neuroscience* 30 (2007): 57–78.

Lehmann, A. C., and R. Kopiez. "Can Expert Listeners Hear if a Piece Is Improvised or Composed?" *Proceedings of the 11th International Conference on Music Perception and Cognition*, edited by S. M. Demorest, S. J. Morrison, and P. S. Campbell, 577–580. Seattle, Washington: ICMPC (2010).

Lewis, G. E. "Improvised Music after 1950: Afrological and Eurological Perspectives." *Black Music Research Journal* 16, no. 1 (1996): 91–122.

Lewis, G. E. "Too Many Notes: Computers, Complexity and Culture in Voyager." *Leonardo Music Journal* 10 (December 2000): 33–39.

Limb, C. J., and A. R. Braun. "Neural Substrates of Spontaneous Musical Performance: An fMRI Study of Jazz Improvisation." *PLoS ONE* 3, no. 2 (2008). Available at http://www.plosone.org/article/info%3Adoi%2F10.1371%2Fjournal.pone.0001679, accessed December 28, 2013.

Logothetis, N. K. 2008. "What We Can Do and What We Cannot Do with fMRI." *Nature* 453, no. 7197 (2008): 869–878.

Luck, G., P. Toiviainen, E. Jaako, O. Lartillot, K. Riillilä, A. Mäkelä, K. Pyhäluoto, et. al. "Modelling the Relationships between Emotional Responses to, and Musical Content of, Music Therapy Improvisations." *Psychology of Music* 36, no. 1 (2008): 24–45.

Matare, J. "Creativity or Musical Intelligence? A Comparative Study of Improvisation/Improvisation Performance by European and African Musicians." *Thinking Skills and Creativity* 4, no. 3 (2009): 194–203.

Mazzola, G. B., and P. B. Cherlin. *Flow, Gesture, and Spaces in Free Jazz: Towards a Spirit of Collaboration*. Berlin: Springer, 2009.

McCormack, J., A. Eldridge, A. Dorin, and P. McIlwain. "Generative Algorithms for Making Music: Emergence, Evolution, and Ecosystems." In *The Oxford Handbook of Computer Music*, edited by R. T. Dean, 354–382. New York: Oxford University Press, 2009.

Pashler, H. E. *The Psychology of Attention*. Cambridge, Mass.: MIT Press, 1998.

Pashler, H., and J. C. Johnston. "Attentional Limitations in Dual-Task Performance." In *Attention*, edited by H. Pashler, 155–189. Hove, England: Taylor & Francis, 1998.

Pressing, J. "The Micro- and Macrostructural Design of Improvised Music." *Music Perception* 5, no. 2 (1987): 133–172.

Pressing, J. "Improvisation: Methods and Models." In *Generative Processes in Music: The Psychology of Performance, Improvisation, and Composition*, edited by J. Sloboda, 129–178. Oxford: Clarendon Press, 1988.

Pressing, J. "Black Atlantic Rhythm: Its Computational and Transcultural Foundations." *Music Perception* 19, no. 3 (2002): 285–310.

Repp, B. H. "Sensorimotor Synchronization: A Review of the Tapping Literature." *Psychonomic Bulletin & Review* 12, no. 6 (2005): 969–992.

Sawyer, R. K. *Group Creativity: Music, Theater, Collaboration*. Mahwah, NJ: Lawrence Erlbaum Associates, 2003.

Smith, H., and R. T. Dean. *Improvisation, Hypermedia and the Arts Since 1945*. London: Harwood Academic, 1997.

Smith, H., and R. T. Dean, eds. Practice-led Research, Research-led Practice in the Creative Arts. Edinburgh: Edinburgh University Press, 2009.

Sudnow, D. *Ways of the Hand: The Organization of Improvised Conduct*. Cambridge, MA: Harvard University Press, 1978.

Tervaniemi, M., A. Castaneda, M. Knoll, and M. Uther. "Sound Processing in Amateur Musicians and Nonmusicians: Event-related Potential and Behavioural Indices." *NeuroReport* 17, no. 11 (2006): 1225–1228.

Wiggins, G. A., M. T. Pearce, and D. Müllensiefen. "Computational Modeling of Music Cognition and Musical Creativity." In *The Oxford Handbook of Computer Music*, edited by R. T. Dean, 383–420. New York: Oxford University Press, 2009.

CHAPTER 2

THE COGNITIVE NEUROSCIENCE OF IMPROVISATION

AARON L. BERKOWITZ

THE relationship between music and the mind has fascinated some of Western history's greatest thinkers, including Pythagoras, Galileo, and Descartes.[1] Broadly defined, the field referred to as "music cognition" or "the psychology of music" seeks to answer two complementary questions:

1. How does the brain carry out musical processes?
2. What can the study of music tell us about how the brain works?

The first question examines which cognitive processes—and their neural substrates—allow for the perception, understanding, and production of music. For example, research addressing this first question has sought to understand how we recognize, remember, read, understand, compose, perform, and have an emotional response to music, and what regions of the brain may be responsible for these features of music cognition.[2]

The second question treats music as a specialized substrate through which to study more general cognitive processes. For example, studying the ability to know how a piece of music sounds by looking at the score allows for the exploration of mental imagery, as well as transformations between one sensory modality and another.[3] High-level musical performance is a case study in expertise.[4] Investigating musical learning and memory can provide insights into these higher-order cognitive processes and their neural substrates outside the verbal or visual domains.[5] If areas of the brain are discovered to be involved in musical processes in addition to previously ascribed roles, such findings can provide insights into the more general functionality of these brain regions.

Most early research in music cognition explored music perception, but more recent work has also begun to explore the psychology and neurobiology of musical performance.[6] From a cognitive perspective, musical performance requires extraordinary motor dexterity, control, and coordination; the ability to link the motor system with the auditory system; and, in the case of performance traditions that use written scores, the transformation of visual input into motor output. Improvised performance additionally requires the capacity to generate spontaneously novel musical structures in real time. This chapter explores the two complementary questions presented at the beginning of the chapter with respect to improvisation: What can studying the brain tell us about improvisation? What can studying improvisation tell us about the brain?

Exploring the neural basis of musical improvisation can aid in understanding the more general cognitive processes called upon in this specialized instance of auditory-motor expertise and creativity. This inquiry has the potential to provide insights into both practice and pedagogy. In turn, discovering which areas of the brain are involved in musical improvisation may influence how the function(s) of these regions are understood.

Improvisation can be defined most generally as "the creation of a musical work, or the final form of a musical work, as it is being performed."[7] Spontaneous creation in the moment is of course not unique to music. Improvisation occurs in theater, dance, and to some degree in any artistic expression that evolves in real time. Improvisation is also part of our everyday speech and movement. Just as infinite possibilities exist in how the blues or a Beethoven cadenza can be improvised while still maintaining its stylistic and formal identity, so too can we create infinite possible sentences, all the while using a finite vocabulary and obeying the finite grammatical rules that together allow for the comprehensibility of a novel utterance. Our everyday actions also incorporate some degree of improvisation, as we dexterously enact spontaneously created motor solutions to challenges as mundane as balancing grocery bags while we unlock the front door and as important as life-saving, split-second maneuvers to avoid accidents while driving.[8] Therefore, while musical improvisation is a fascinating feat of human cognition worthy of study in its own right, it also provides a specific instance of a much more general phenomenon in human behavior: spontaneous rule-based combinations of elements to create novel sequences that are appropriate for a given moment in a given context. This chapter presents data from recent brain imaging studies that explore the neural basis of improvisation. It then discusses findings of these studies from the perspective of the questions: What can studying the brain tell us about improvisation? What can studying improvisation tell us about the brain?

The Neural Basis of Improvisation

To date there have been five published studies of the neuroscience of improvisation.[9] This review focuses on the studies of Berkowitz and Ansari (2008 and 2010) and Limb and Braun (2008), since their work is complementary both at the methodological level and with respect to results, and because both studies use functional magnetic resonance imaging (fMRI) to assess brain activity during improvisation.

fMRI uses a magnetic field to detect changes in blood oxygenation in the brain as an index of the relative activity of different brain regions when the brain is engaged in a cognitive process. Because many areas of the brain are highly active even at rest, fMRI studies often employ a subtraction technique in an attempt to precisely localize activation during a cognitive task of interest by comparing this with a control condition. When using a subtraction technique, brain activity during a control task is "subtracted" from brain activity during the cognitive task of interest. For example, if neural activity were to be examined while someone listens to music, many areas involved in more general cognitive processes would be involved (e.g., basic auditory perception, attention). While these regions are surely involved in music perception, their role would not necessarily be specific to music perception. Comparing brain activity while listening to music with that during a control task, such as listening to a less complex auditory stimulus (e.g., pure tones or white noise), allows for the subtraction of the activity stimulated by these more basic processes. This subtraction would thus demonstrate the areas involved in music perception above and beyond basic cognitive functions such as auditory perception and general attention to an external stimulus.[10]

Berkowitz and Ansari (2008)

To study improvisation with fMRI, we designed a simple experimental set-up that consisted of four tasks allowing for varying degrees of improvisatory freedom.[11] These tasks were performed on a five-key piano-like keyboard. In the most constrained task, subjects played simple patterns that were taught to them before the experiment, and they performed these patterns in the order of their choosing, with one note per beat with a metronome click. This experimental condition will be referred to here as Patterns/Metronome. The only freedom of choice provided during this condition was that of which pattern to play at any given time; the internal melodic and rhythmic structure of each pattern was fixed. Two conditions provided freedom in one musical parameter only (melody or rhythm): in Melodic Improvisation/Metronome, subjects invented five-note melodies, but these melodies were rhythmically constrained by the metronome (one note per beat); in Patterns/Rhythmic Improvisation, subjects were free to improvise the rhythms of the pre-learned five-note patterns. In the final condition, Melodic Improvisation/Rhythmic Improvisation, subjects improvised five-note melodies and their rhythms. Comparing brain activity in Melodic Improvisation tasks with that during Patterns tasks allowed for the isolation of the neural correlates of melodic improvisation, whereas comparison of Rhythmic Improvisation tasks with the Metronome tasks demonstrated the regions of brain involved in rhythmic improvisation.

Melodic improvisation requires creativity in the pitch domain (or, from a motor perspective, in the spatial domain), whereas rhythmic improvisation can be thought of as the generation of novel musical structures in the temporal realm. Melodic and rhythmic generativity would be expected to have distinct but overlapping neural networks underlying them.[12] Areas of nonoverlap between melodic and rhythmic improvisation would presumably be taking part in processes unique to spatial/melodic and temporal/rhythmic generativity, respectively. We were particularly interested in the areas subserving both melodic improvisation and rhythmic improvisation. The areas of overlap between these two types of improvisation would ostensibly be the brain regions giving rise to musical generativity at the most fundamental (or, alternatively, the "supra-domain") level, irrespective of whether the improvisation involves pitch/space or rhythm/time. We thus performed a conjunction analysis of melodic improvisation (brain activity in Melodic Improvisation tasks minus brain activity in Patterns tasks) and rhythmic improvisation (brain activity in Rhythmic Improvisation tasks minus brain activity in Metronome tasks) in order to identify the network of brain regions involved in improvisation, whether that improvisation is in the melodic or rhythmic domain.

This conjunction analysis revealed three areas of the brain that participated in both melodic and rhythmic improvisation: the dorsal premotor cortex (dPMC), the anterior cingulate cortex (ACC), and the inferior frontal gyrus/ventral premotor cortex (IFG/vPMC).

The dPMC is involved in the selection and execution of movement sequences.[13] It would thus be expected to be involved in any task involving motor activity. Our results show that this area is more active in improvisation as opposed to playing patterns and/or playing with a metronome, consistent with a possible increased demand on this brain region as movement complexity increases.

The ACC is known to play a role in a wide variety of cognitive tasks, including monitoring conflict between stimuli or responses, unrehearsed movements, decision making, voluntary selection, and willed action.[14] These cognitive functions are of course intertwined. Making a decision involves voluntary, willed choice between potentially conflicting responses to a stimulus. Improvisation involves near-constant decision making among a multitude of musical possibilities available to the improviser at any given moment. A brain-imaging study of performance of a memorized composition by Bach compared to playing scales did not show differential activation of this region,[15] thus suggesting that the ACC plays a role in our experiment in improvisation specifically (i.e., beyond a role in mere musical or motor complexity, since in that role it would likely have been active in the Bach versus scales comparison of the cited study).

The IFG/vPMC has been found to play a role in language perception and production as well as music perception.[16] The aforementioned study of piano performance of a memorized composition did not show activation of this area in that context, suggesting that its role in our experiment is unique to the improvisatory/generative nature of our experimental tasks. Given that this region is involved in both perception and production of language and music, it can be postulated that, on the most general level, it subserves "analysis, recognition, and prediction of sequential auditory information"[17] as well as the production of such sequential auditory-motor information.

Limb and Braun (2008)

Our experiment sought to isolate and study one particular aspect of improvisation: spontaneous generation of novel sequences. Charles Limb and Allen Braun designed more ecologically valid tasks in their 2008 study to explore a broader array of neural activity in improvisation. In the main experimental condition, jazz musicians improvised over the chord structure of a jazz composition. Brain activity during this task was compared to that in a control condition in which subjects played a fixed composition from memory.

Since their tasks were far more complex than those of Berkowitz and Ansari and allowed their subjects to improvise based on an actual compositional structure that evolved in time, Limb and Braun elicited changes in brain activity in over forty regions when comparing their improvisation tasks to control tasks, including the network of IFG/vPMC, ACC, and dPMC described in Berkowitz and Ansari (2008). Additional areas included the superior temporal lobe (likely to be involved in processing and memory for musical materials), limbic regions (probably involved in emotion and memory), the medial prefrontal cortex (MPFC) (activation is associated with self-expression and higher-level goals and intentions), and the lateral orbital prefrontal cortex (LOFC) and dorsolateral prefrontal cortex (DLPFC) (deactivation is suggestive of inhibition of regions involved in monitoring and correction). With regard to these latter findings in the prefrontal cortex, the authors suggest that

> Musical creativity vis-à-vis improvisation may be a result of the combination of intentional, internally generated self-expression (MPFC-mediated) with the suspension of self-monitoring and related processes (LOFC—and DLPFC-mediated) that typically regulate conscious control of goal-directed, predictable, or planned actions.[18]

In conjunction, the studies of Berkowitz and Ansari and Limb and Braun complement one another. The precise focus of Berkowitz and Ansari on a limited type of improvisation with a very small set of possibilities allowed for relatively specific attribution of functional roles to the brain areas that were active but probably did not activate the full range of regions of the brain involved in real-world improvisation. By studying improvisation in as close to its real-world form as possible in the laboratory, Limb and Braun offer a more panoramic view of the full panoply of neural activity involved in improvising.

Berkowitz and Ansari (2010)

In a follow-up study to Berkowitz and Ansari (2008), the brain activity in musicians and nonmusicians was compared during the performance of the four improvisation tasks described earlier.[19] The behavioral results were essentially equivalent between the two groups in that the degree of novelty of the improvised melodies did not differ between them. Comparison of the three areas described earlier (IFG/vPMC, ACC, and dPMC) showed no difference in activation between the two groups. The neural substrates of the generation, selection, and execution of musical sequences therefore appear to be fundamental to the process of spontaneous motor performance, whether the intention behind it is that of a trained musician or not. The pattern of neural activation did, however, reveal one difference outside of this network. The single difference in brain activity between the two groups was in an area known as the right temporoparietal junction (rTPJ), which plays a role in attention. While nonmusicians did not show any significant change in the activity in this area when melodic improvisation was compared to pattern performance, musicians showed deactivation of this region. The difference between a musical mind approaching improvisation and an untrained mind performing the same task therefore appears to be not one of generativity, selection, or execution, but rather one of attention.

Activation of the rTPJ region is associated with stimulus-driven or bottom-up attention (i.e., the type of attention stimulated by salient characteristics of the stimulus itself).[20] Deactivation of the rTPJ occurs in contexts of goal-driven, or top-down attention (i.e., the type of attention driven by intention based on one's pre-existing knowledge, experience, and memory about a particular stimulus). Specifically, the rTPJ is involved in the reorienting of attention to task-relevant but unexpected stimuli. Imagine the example of an archer aiming an arrow at a target. The target, the tension in the bow, and the wind are all relevant to whether the archer will succeed in hitting the target. However, the archer would ideally want to "tune out" any task-irrelevant stimuli that could be distracting—for example, a bird chirping or the shifting shadows of a tree branch blowing in the wind in the archer's peripheral vision. This "tuning out" of stimuli that could cause an inappropriate reorientation of attention away from one's intended focus is thought to be accomplished in part by deactivating the rTPJ. That is, during sustained attention, the rTPJ is deactivated to allow for focus on one task while filtering out potentially disruptive stimuli to which reorientation would prove disruptive to the goal behavior.

Musicians' deactivation of the rTPJ when improvising as compared to nonmusicians performing the same tasks suggests that musical training may allow for an increase in goal-directed attention and the filtering out of task-irrelevant stimuli in this context. Such an effect can also be interpreted as an increase in top-down processing of improvisational output as musicians may have chunked their phrases as musical units rather than strings of individual notes in sequence; the latter may have been the cognitive strategy utilized by nonmusicians.[21]

WHAT CAN STUDYING THE BRAIN TELL US ABOUT IMPROVISATION?

Underlying Processes: Loci for Practice and Pedagogy

The fundamental cognitive processes supporting improvisation appear to be the generation and recombination of musical sequences (IFG/vPMC), the selection among such sequences (ACC), and the execution of the chosen sequence (dPMC). In addition, when trained musicians improvise, they appear to enter a top-down state of goal-directed attentional control (deactivation of rTPJ) when compared to nonmusicians performing the same tasks. Broken down into its cognitive components, this portrait of the improvising brain provides insights into loci for improvisational practice and pedagogy.[22]

In order to generate musical sequences appropriate for a given musical context, the improviser must be well versed in a stylistic idiom. For jazz musicians, this entails the knowledge of chords, scales/modes, forms, and a large vocabulary of "riffs," some self-composed, others absorbed through transcription and imitation of solos by the great masters.[23] For Indian musicians, a long germination period in which fixed compositions and melodic and rhythmic patterns are learned in various *ragas* (modes) and *talas* (rhythmic cycles) precedes the stage at which the musician can improvise.[24] Robert Levin, a classical pianist who has learned to improvise in the styles of many classical composers, first internalized the composed repertoire of those composers.[25] It is this learned material that provides the primordial musical soup from which materials are recombined and selected in the moment of improvised performance.

With this knowledge base in place, the improviser must learn how to navigate it to draw on stylistically idiomatic and artistically coherent sequences of musical materials in the moment of musical improvisation.[26] Such selection is governed by "history" on a number of levels: the history of the style in which the performer is improvising, the history of all of the improvisational choices by the performer up to that performance, and the more local history of the musical choices up to that moment in the performance. The education of an improviser therefore involves not only the internalization of fundamental musical elements and forms, but also the acquisition of the ability to appropriately select from them in real time in a stylistically idiomatic way. To learn to improvise therefore involves rehearsal of the act of improvisation itself. In this rehearsal process, the improviser-in-training acquires experiential knowledge about how to navigate through the knowledge base and develops a personal style for doing so.

These aspects of learning to improvise ostensibly train the network of IFG/vPMC-ACC-dPMC in the actions of sequence generation, recombination, selection, and execution. In a review of the pedagogy of improvisation in a wide variety of musical traditions across different cultures, I have described how these principles are incorporated seemingly universally in improvisational pedagogy and learning.[27] Beyond these principles, improvisers across cultures describe a particular state of mind when improvising in which creation and a partially detached observation of what is being created are carefully balanced, referred to as being both "creator and witness" by Levin and "inventor and recipient" by Paul Berliner in his study of jazz musicians.[28] These ideas seem to resonate with Limb and Braun's interpretation of their findings in the prefrontal cortex as representing a balance between self-expression and self-monitoring. Thus, the neuroscience of improvisation reflects a near-universal intuitive understanding by improvising musicians of the component processes necessary for improvisation and how to cultivate them in practice and pedagogy, and also appears to correlate with improvisers' subjective experience of improvisation.[29]

Music and Language Comparisons

One widely explored area in music cognition research has been the comparison of music and language cognition.[30] Broadly speaking, these two systems of human sound communication can be compared at three loci: production (i.e., the speaker or musical performer), the sound systems themselves (i.e., the underlying sound structures and the rules that govern them), and perception/comprehension (i.e., how the listener understands the utterance of the speaker or musical performer). The majority of research and theoretical speculation comparing music and language cognition has focused on the latter two. Improvisation is ideally suited to the study of production because it can be considered analogous to spontaneous speech; in both improvisation and spontaneous linguistic production, one needs both a knowledge base (e.g., vocabulary, grammatical rules, pronunciation in language; melodic figures, rhythms, timbres, harmonies, musical structures, and stylistic parameters in music) and the skill set to generate recombinations of the elements of this knowledge base in real time in a way that follows linguistic or stylistic norms so that utterances are comprehensible to the listener.

In Berkowitz and Ansari (2008), we demonstrated that the IFG/vPMC, an area known to be important in language, is also involved in musical improvisation. In fact, the triad of regions elicited in this study (i.e., dPMC, ACC, and IFG/vPMC) is also at the core of a network that brain imaging studies have shown to be involved in spontaneous speech.[31] Musical improvisation and spontaneous speech therefore appear to be analogous at both theoretical and neurobiological levels. Many parallels can also be drawn between how musicians learn to improvise and how languages are learned.[32] This begs the tantalizing question of whether training in musical improvisation can facilitate language learning and/or whether the data and experience derived from the extensive research in the pedagogy and learning of language can be applied to training methods for musical improvisation. Given the effects of musical training on the brain (discussed later in the chapter), this seems to be an area ripe for research that could have implications for both language pedagogy and music pedagogy.

Is music a language? Or, as David Lidov once titled a collection of essays, "Is language a music?"[33] Music and language clearly share much in terms of cognitive processes, the neural substrates that appear to underlie them in both perception and performance, and the learning processes involved in acquiring these two systems of sound communication. The exploration of such connections between music and language provides one example of the types of insights that the study of music cognition may provide about brain function more generally.

WHAT CAN STUDYING IMPROVISATION TELL US ABOUT THE BRAIN?

The research described demonstrates that musical improvisation, albeit a highly specialized capacity, occurs through the coordinated activity of brain regions that are involved in numerous other domain-general cognitive processes such as motor sequencing, decision making, and attention, to name a few. This underscores the fact that such networks of brain areas are highly flexible in the functions in which they can participate. Just as studying the neural basis of improvisation can yield insights into the nature of its component cognitive operations, so too can the study of improvisation provide insights into the functions of the brain regions upon which improvisation relies.

Mirror Systems

Our finding that the IFG/vPMC is involved in musical generativity complements data showing that this area is involved in music perception.[34] A dual role in production and perception in this region has also been described for language. Such perception-action coupling in the brain is referred to as a "mirror system."[35] A mirror system is one involved in both the performance of actions and the understanding of such actions as performed by others. Such systems may encode an overarching (or underlying) concept of an action that can be utilized both in the performance of that action and in the understanding of the intention behind the action when observing it performed by someone else. Roles for such systems in higher-level cognitive functions such as language and empathy have been postulated.[36] What purpose might such a mirror system serve in music? Itvan Molnar-Szakacs and Katie Overy propose that a mirror system for music "allows for co-representation of the musical experience, emerging out of the shared and temporally synchronous recruitment of similar neural mechanisms in the sender and the perceiver of the musical message.[37]

As described previously, non-generative musical performance (e.g., playing from a score) does not appear to stimulate activity in the IFG/vPMC. It was therefore through the study of the neurobiological basis of improvisation that it was discovered that this area plays a role in music production. This finding, in conjunction with previous work identifying that this region participates in music perception, provides possible evidence for a mirror system for music in this region, and it expands our conception of the range of such a system's possible functionality beyond the realms of intentional action and linguistic communication. As Molnar-Szakacs and Overy summarize, "a mirror neuron system may provide a domain-general neural mechanism for processing combinatorial rules common to language, action, and music, which in turn can communicate meaning and human affect."[38]

Music, Language, and Neural Plasticity

As discussed earlier, improvisation provides an ideal musical substrate for comparison with linguistic processes. In a now (in)famous and oft-quoted statement, psychologist of language Steven Pinker referred to music as "auditory cheesecake, an exquisite confection crafted to tickle the sensitive spots of . . . our mental faculties."[39] Pinker argues that the brain did not evolve for music, per se, but rather that music "tickles" brain regions evolved for other purposes (e.g., language). He has even gone so far as to suggest that music is "useless" from an evolutionary perspective, and that it could "vanish from our species and the rest of our lifestyle would be virtually unchanged."[40] Pinker's suggestions have, understandably, been controversial,[41] and indeed others have proposed the alternative possibility that language may have evolved from music.[42] We will probably never know whether music or language "came first," evolutionarily speaking, although intriguing theories exist for how music and language may have co-evolved from a common progenitor.[43] Perhaps what is most striking about the accumulating evidence that music and language share neural resources and cognitive processes in both perception and production is what this signifies with respect to the extraordinary flexibility of the brain. An area such as the IFG/vPMC may have evolved, generally speaking, for the production and perception of sequences, with the capacity to produce and perceive music and language, as well as a wide variety of combinations of elements of actions. Music is probably not "auditory cheesecake," tickling innate linguistic areas, nor is language the "auditory bread and butter" of a musically predisposed neural architecture. Rather, highly flexible neural circuits can process a veritable buffet of inputs and outputs. Just as improvising musicians can produce infinite musical possibilities out of a finite set of musical elements and rules for combining them, so too can the improvising mind support an infinite variety of processes out of a finite number of neurons and their interconnections.

This versatility begs the question of whether musical training can actually foster such flexibility beyond merely drawing on it. A growing literature suggests that music does indeed change the brain. These changes are both structural and functional. In terms of structure, musicians have been shown to have 10 percent more fibers in the corpus callosum, the fiber tract that connects the left and right hemispheres of the brain.[44] This data on increased size of fiber tracts has been complemented by more recent data using newer imaging techniques that reveal increases in fiber tract organization in trained musicians.[45] In addition to such changes in white matter tracts that connect brain regions, increases in the volume of gray matter in such regions throughout the brain (not merely in auditory and motor areas) have been demonstrated in musicians.[46]

Functionally, it has been shown that musical training expands auditory and sensory representations in the brain.[47] Also, in certain contexts, musicians demonstrate different patterns of brain activity when perceiving and processing auditory input,[48] as well as in performance of motor tasks,[49] when compared to nonmusicians. Research by Nadine Gaab and Gottfried Schlaug has shown that musicians are more successful—and utilize a different set of neural substrates and cognitive operations—in the performance of a pitch memory task when compared to nonmusicians.[50] In a follow-up study, Gaab and colleagues showed that when training nonmusicians on a pitch memory task yielded improved performance in certain subjects, there was a concomitant shift from using the network of brain regions that they were using previously (with poorer performance) to recruiting the group of areas used by trained musicians.[51] These studies reflect that musical training can lead to shifts in how the brain processes auditory input and motor output, demonstrating the neural correlates of musical expertise.

Such findings raise the age-old nature-nurture question: Are certain individuals born with brains predisposed to music, and do these individuals therefore excel at it and seek musical training—or does musical training itself lead to such changes? Through studies comparing brain and cognitive development of children receiving musical training with that of those who do not, evidence is emerging that musical training changes the brain.[52]

What insights can the study of the neurobiology of improvisation provide about neural plasticity? As described above, activation in areas involved in auditory processing and motor production appears to be identical between the two groups. The unique difference was that the musicians deactivated the rTPJ, an area involved in bottom-up stimulus-driven attention that is deactivated in top-down, goal-directed attention. The finding of rTPJ deactivation in improvising musicians as compared to nonmusicians suggests that musical training appears to yield cognitive benefits that are not merely music-related. If improvisation training leads to a shift in the ability to activate goal-directed, top-down attention, further research could explore whether training in improvisation actually enhances the ability to modulate attention in this way, and whether this remains limited to improvisatory tasks or is available across domains.

Conclusion

Improvisation is one of many musical processes that have inspired recent investigation with the experimental techniques of cognitive neuroscience. These studies allow for a deeper understanding of the cognitive processes—and the neural correlates of such processes—that support such highly specialized feats of human behavior. Discovering the networks of brain regions that are involved in music contributes to our understanding of the more generalized function of such networks and underscores their remarkable plasticity. Musical training draws on such plasticity in the development of auditory-motor expertise, but it also appears to cultivate changes in brain structure and function that extend beyond musical perception and performance.[53] The brain itself can therefore be considered an improviser in its own right, and the study of improvisation and other musical processes has and will continue to play a role in shaping our understanding of this improvising mind.

Notes

1. Diana Deutsch, et al., "Psychology of Music," in *Grove Music Online. Oxford Music Online*, http://www.oxfordmusiconline.com/subscriber/article/grove/music/42574 (accessed May 17, 2011); Robert Gjerdingen, "The Psychology of Music," in *The Cambridge History of Western Music Theory*, ed. Thomas Christensen (Cambridge: Cambridge University Press, 2002), 956–981.

2. Isabelle Peretz and Robert J. Zatorre, *The Cognitive Neuroscience of Music* (New York: Oxford University Press, 2010); Diana Deutsch, ed., *The Psychology of Music*, 2nd ed. (San Diego, CA: Academic Press, 1999).

3. D. A. Hodges, W. D. Hairston, and J. H. Burdette, "Aspects of Multisensory Perception: The Integration of Visual and Auditory Information in Musical Experiences," *Annals of the New York Academy of Sciences* 1060 (2005): 175–185.

4. Jeff Pressing, "Psychological Constraints on Improvisational Expertise and Communication," in *In the Course of Performance: Studies in the World of Musical Improvisation*, ed. Bruno Nettl and Melinda Russell (Chicago, IL: University of Chicago Press, 1998), 47–68.

5. N. Gaab and G. Schlaug, "The Effect of Musicianship on Pitch Memory in Performance Matched Groups," *Neuroreport* 14 (2003): 2291–2295; N. Gaab, C. Gaser, and G. Schlaug, "Improvement-related Functional Plasticity Following Pitch Memory Training," *NeuroImage* 31 (2006): 255–263.

6. For discussion, see Diana Deutsch, et al. "Psychology of Music," in *Grove Music Online. Oxford Music Online*, http://www.oxfordmusiconline.com/subscriber/article/grove/music/42574pg4 (accessed May 27, 2011).

7. Bruno Nettl et al., "Improvisation," in *Grove Music Online. Oxford Music Online*, http://www.oxfordmusiconline.com/subscriber/article/grove/music/13738 (accessed May 17, 2011). For a review of a wide range of published definitions of improvisation, see Bruno Nettl, "Introduction: An Art Neglected in Scholarship," in *In the Course of Performance: Studies in the World of Musical Improvisation*, ed. Bruno Nettl and Melinda Russell (Chicago, IL: University of Chicago Press, 1998), 10–12.

8. The improvisatory nature of human behavior is eloquently described in Gilbert Ryle, "Improvisation," *Mind* 85, no. 337 (1976): 69–83; R. Keith Sawyer, "The Improvisational Performance of Everyday Life," *Journal of Mundane Behavior* 2 (2001): 149–162; and R. Keith Sawyer, *Creating Conversations: Improvisation in Everyday Discourse* (Cresskill: Hampton, 2001). For further discussion, see Aaron L. Berkowitz, *The Improvising Mind: Cognition and Creativity in the Musical Moment* (Oxford: Oxford University Press, 2010), 1–14, 177–184.

9. S. Brown, et al., "Music and Language Side by Side in the Brain: A PET Study of the Generation of Melodies and Sentences," *European Journal of Neuroscience* 23 (2006): 2791–2803; S. L. Bengtsson, M. Csíkszentmihályi, and F. Ullén, "Cortical Regions Involved in the Generation of Musical Structures During Improvisation in Pianists," *Journal of Cognitive Neuroscience* 19 (2007), 830–842; Aaron L. Berkowitz and Daniel Ansari, "Generation of Novel Motor Sequences: The Neural Correlates of Musical Improvisation," *NeuroImage* 41 (2008): 535–543; Charles J. Limb and Allen R. Braun, "Neural Substrates of Spontaneous Musical Performance: An fMRI Study of Jazz Improvisation," *PLoS ONE* 3 (2008): e1679. doi:10.1371/journal.pone.0001679; Aaron L. Berkowitz and Daniel Ansari, "Expertise-related Deactivation of the Right Temporoparietal Junction During Musical Improvisation," *NeuroImage* 49 (2010): 712–719. By neuroscience studies, I refer to studies actually examining brain activity during improvisation with brain imaging techniques. For theoretical work on the cognitive psychology of improvisation, see the following brilliant discussions by Jeff Pressing: "Cognitive Processes in Improvisation," in *Cognitive Processes in the Perception of Art*, ed. W. Ray Crozier and Anthony J. Chapman (Amsterdam: Elsevier, 1984), 345–366; "Improvisation: Methods and Models," in *Generative Processes in Music: The Psychology of Performance, Improvisation, and Composition*, ed. John Sloboda (Oxford

and New York: Oxford University Press, 1988), 129–178; "Psychological Constraints on Improvisational Expertise and Communication," in *In the Course of Performance: Studies in the World of Musical Improvisation*, ed. Bruno Nettl and Melinda Russell (Chicago, IL: University of Chicago Press, 1998), 47–68.

10. For an example of a very elegant solution to creating a control task to be compared in order to elicit the areas involved in hearing musical structure, see D. J. Levitin and V. Menon, "Musical Structure Is Processed in 'Language' Areas of the Brain: A Possible Role for Brodmann Area 47 in Temporal Coherence," *NeuroImage* 20 (2003): 2142–2152.

11. Berkowitz and Ansari, "Generation of Novel Motor Sequences." For discussion, see also Berkowitz, *The Improvising Mind*, 131–144.

12. For discussion of the neural correlates of melodic and rhythmic performance, see S. L. Bengtsson et al., "Dissociating Brain Regions Controlling the Temporal and Ordinal Structure of Learned Movement Sequences," *European Journal of Neuroscience* 19 (2004): 2591–2602; S. L. Bengtsson and F. Ullén, "Dissociation between Melodic and Rhythmic Processing During Piano Performance from Musical Scores," *NeuroImage* 30 (2006): 272–284.

13. For review, see P. A. Chouinard and T. Paus, "The Primary Motor and Premotor Areas of the Human Cerebral Cortex," *Neuroscientist* 12 (2006): 143–152.

14. For review and discussion, see Berkowitz and Ansari, "Generation of Novel Motor Sequence," 541; Berkowitz, *The Improvising Mind*, 139–140.

15. L. M. Parsons et al., "The Brain Basis of Piano Performance," *Neuropsychologia* 43 (2005): 199–215.

16. S. Koelsch, "Significance of Broca's Area and Ventral Premotor Cortex for Music-Syntactic Processing," *Cortex* 42 (2006): 518–520.

17. Ibid., 219.

18. Limb and Braun, "Neural Substrates of Spontaneous Musical Performance," 4–5.

19. Berkowitz and Ansari, "Expertise-related Deactivation of the Temporoparietal Junction."

20. For review and discussion see M. Corbetta and G. L. Shulman, "Control of Goal-directed and Stimulus-driven Attention in the Brain," *Nature Reviews Neuroscience* 3 (2002): 201–215; M. Corbetta, G. Patel, and G. L. Shulman, "The Reorienting System of the Human Brain: From Environment to Theory of Mind," *Neuron* 58 (2008): 306–324.

21. For further discussion, see Berkowitz and Ansari "Expertise-related Deactivation of the Temporoparietal Junction," 7–8.

22. For a review and discussion of improvisation pedagogy and learning across musical cultures, see Berkowitz, *The Improvising Mind*, 39–96.

23. For review and discussion, see Paul Berliner, *Thinking in Jazz* (Chicago: University of Chicago Press, 1994).

24. For review and discussion, see Stephen Slawek, "Keeping It Going: Terms, Practices, and Processes of Improvisation in Hindustani Music," in *In the Course of Performance: Studies in the World of Musical Improvisation*, ed. Bruno Nettl and Melinda Russell, (Chicago: University of Chicago Press, 1998), 335–368; George Ruckert and Richard Widdess, "Hindustani Raga," in *The Garland Encyclopedia of World Music*, Vol. 5, *South Asia: The Indian Subcontinent*, ed. Alison Arnold (New York: Routledge, 1999), 64–88.

25. For review and discussion, see Berkowitz, *The Improvising Mind*, 81–96.

26. See Berkowitz, *The Improvising Mind*, 39–96 and 121–130; Pressing, "Improvisation: Methods and Models." In *Generative Processes in Music: The Psychology of Performance, Improvisation, and Composition*, ed. John Sloboda (Oxford: Oxford University

Press, 1988), 129–178; Pressing, "Cognitive Processes in Improvisation"; Pressing, "Psychological Constraints on Improvisational Expertise and Communication."

27. Berkowitz, *The Improvising Mind*, 15–96.

28. Berliner, *Thinking in Jazz*, 208. For discussion of this creator-witness phenomenon see Berkowitz, *The Improvising Mind*, 121–130.

29. For further discussion, see Berkowitz, *The Improvising Mind*, 143–144.

30. For comprehensive review and discussion, see Aniruddh Patel, *Music, Language and the Brain* (Oxford: Oxford University Press, 2007). See also Berkowitz, *The Improvising Mind*, 97–120 and 145–152; Erin McMullen and Jenny Saffran, "Music and Language: A Developmental Comparison," *Music Perception* 21 (2004): 289–311.

31. For review and discussion, see Berkowitz, *The Improvising Mind*, 145–52.

32. For review and discussion, see Berkowitz, *The Improvising Mind*, 97–120; McMullen and Saffran, "Music and Language."

33. David Lidov, *Is Language a Music?: Writings on Musical Form and Signification* (Bloomington: Indiana University Press, 2004).

34. For review and discussion, see Koelsch, "Significance of Broca's Area and Ventral Premotor Cortex for Music-Syntactic Processing."

35. G. Rizzolatti et al., "The Mirror-Neuron System," *Annual Review Neuroscience* 27 (2004): 169–192; F. Binkofski, "The Role of Ventral Premotor Cortex in Action Execution and Action Understanding," *Journal of Physiology Paris* 99 (2006): 396–405.

36. For recent review, see M. Iacoboni, "Imitation, Empathy, and Mirror Neurons," *Annual Review of Psychology* 60 (2009): 653–670.

37. I. Molnar-Szakacs and K. Overy, "Music and Mirror Neurons: From Motion to 'E'motion," *Social Cognitive and Affective Neuroscience* 1 (2006): 235–236.

38. Ibid., 239.

39. Stephen Pinker, *How the Mind Works* (New York: W.W. Norton and Company, 1997), 534.

40. Ibid., 528–529.

41. See for example, Ian Cross, "Music and Biocultural Evolution," in *The Cultural Study of Music*, ed. Martin Clayton, Trevor Herbert, and Richard Middleton (New York: Routledge, 2003), 19–30; Elizabeth Tolbert, "Theorizing the Musically Abject," in *Bad Music: The Music We Love to Hate*, ed. Christopher Washburne and Maiken Derno (New York: Routledge, 2004), 104–119; Philip Ball, *The Music Instinct: How Music Works and Why We Can't Do Without It* (New York: Oxford University Press, 2010), 1–31; Daniel Levitin, *This Is Your Brain on Music* (London: Penguin Group, 2006), 241–262.

42. For review and discussion, see W. Tecumseh Fitch, "The Biology and Evolution of Music: A Comparative Perspective," *Cognition* 100 (2006): 173–215.

43. Stephen Brown, "The 'Musilanguage' Model of Music Evolution," in *The Origins of Music*, ed. Nils L Wallin, Bjorn Merker, and Steven Brown (Cambridge: MIT Press, 2000), 271–300.

44. G. Schlaug et al., "Increased Corpus Callosum Size in Musicians," *Neuropsychologia* 33 (1995): 1047–1055.

45. S. L. Bengtsson et al., "Extensive Piano Practicing Has Regionally Specific Effects on White Matter Development," *Nature Neuroscience* 8 (2005): 1148–1150.

46. M. Bangert and G. Schlaug, "Specialization of the Specialized in Features of External Human Brain Morphology," *European Journal of Neuroscience* 24 (2006): 1832–1834; C. Gaser and G. Schlaug, "Brain Structures Differ Between Musicians and Nonmusicians," *Journal of Neuroscience* 23 (2003): 9240–9245.

47. T. Elbert et al., "Increased Cortical Representation of the Fingers of the Left Hand in String Players," *Science* 270 (1995): 305–307; C. Pantev et al., "Increased Auditory Cortical Representation in Musicians," *Nature* 392 (1998): 811–814.
48. N. Gaab, C. Gaser, and G. Schlaug, "Improvement-related Functional Plasticity Following Pitch Memory Training," *NeuroImage* 31 (2006): 255–263.
49. M. Hund-Georgiadis and D. Y. von Cramon, "Motor-Learning-Related Changes in Piano Players and Non-Musicians Revealed by Functional Magnetic-Resonance Signals," *Experimental Brain Research* 125 (1999): 417–425; T. Krings et al., "Cortical Activation Patterns During Complex Motor Tasks in Piano Players and Control Subjects. A Functional Magnetic Resonance Imaging Study," *Neuroscience Letters* 278 (2000): 189–193; M. Lotze et al., "The Musician's Brain: Functional Imaging of Amateurs and Professionals During Performance and Imagery," *NeuroImage* 20 (2003): 1817–1829.
50. N. Gaab and G. Schlaug, "The Effect of Musicianship on Pitch Memory in Performance Matched Groups."
51. Gaab, Gaser, and Schlaug, "Improvement-related Functional Plasticity Following Pitch Memory Training."
52. K. L. Hyde et al., "Musical Training Shapes Structural Brain Development," *Journal of Neuroscience* 29 (2009): 3019–3025. G. Schlaug et al., "Training-induced Neuroplasticity in Young Children," *Annals of the New York Academy of Science* 1169 (2009): 205–208.
53. For discussion, see C. Y. Wan and G. Schlaug, "Music Making as a Tool for Promoting Brain Plasticity Across the Life Span," *Neuroscientist* 16 (2010): 566–577.

BIBLIOGRAPHY

Ball, Philip. *The Music Instinct: How Music Works and Why We Can't Do Without It.* New York: Oxford University Press, 2010.
Bangert, M., and G. Schlaug. "Specialization of the Specialized in Features of External Human Brain Morphology." *European Journal of Neuroscience* 24 (2006): 1832–1834.
Bengtsson, S. L., et al. "Dissociating Brain Regions Controlling the Temporal and Ordinal Structure of Learned Movement Sequences." *European Journal of Neuroscience* 19 (2004): 2591–2602.
Bengtsson, S. L., et al. "Extensive Piano Practicing Has Regionally Specific Effects on White Matter Development." *Nature Neuroscience* 8 (2005): 1148–1150.
Bengtsson, S. L., and F. Ullén. "Dissociation Between Melodic and Rhythmic Processing During Piano Performance from Musical Scores." *NeuroImage* 30 (2006): 272–284.
Bengtsson, S. L., M. Csíkszentmihályi, and F. Ullén. "Cortical Regions Involved in the Generation of Musical Structures During Improvisation in Pianists." *Journal of Cognitive Neuroscience* 19 (2007): 830–842.
Berkowitz, Aaron L. *The Improvising Mind: Cognition and Creativity in the Musical Moment.* Oxford: Oxford University Press, 2010.
Berkowitz, Aaron L., and Daniel Ansari. "Generation of Novel Motor Sequences: The Neural Correlates of Musical Improvisation." *NeuroImage* 41 (2008): 535–543.
Berkowitz, Aaron L., and Daniel Ansari. "Expertise-related Deactivation of the Right Temporoparietal Junction During Musical Improvisation." *NeuroImage* 49 (2010): 712–719.
Berliner, Paul. *Thinking in Jazz: The Infinite Art of Improvisation.* Chicago: University of Chicago Press, 1994.

Binkofski, F. "The Role of Ventral Premotor Cortex in Action Execution and Action Understanding." *Journal of Physiology Paris* (2006): 396–405.

Brown, Stephen. "The "Musilanguage" Model of Music Evolution." In *The Origins of Music*, edited by Nils L. Wallin, Bjorn Merker, and Steven Brown, 271–300. Cambridge, MA: MIT Press, 2000.

Brown, S., et al. "Music and Language Side by Side in the Brain: A PET Study of the Generation of Melodies and Sentences." *European Journal of Neuroscience* 23 (2006): 2791–2803.

Chouinard, P. A., and T. Paus. "The Primary Motor and Premotor Areas of the Human Cerebral Cortex." *Neuroscientist* 12 (2006): 143–152.

Corbetta, M., and G. L. Shulman. "Control of Goal-directed and Stimulus-driven Attention in the Brain." *Nature Reviews Neuroscience* 3 (2002): 201–215.

Corbetta, M., G. Patel, and G. L. Shulman, "The Reorienting System of the Human Brain: From Environment to Theory of Mind." *Neuron* 58 (2008): 306–324.

Cross, I. "Music and Biocultural Evolution". In *The Cultural Study of Music*, edited by Martin Clayton, Trevor Herbert, and Richard Middleton, 19–30. New York: Routledge, 2003.

Deutsch, Diana, ed. *The Psychology of Music*, 2nd ed. San Diego, CA: Academic Press, 1999.

Deutsch, D., et al., "Psychology of Music." In *Grove Music Online. Oxford Music Online*, http://www.oxfordmusiconline.com/subscriber/article/grove/music/42574 (accessed May 17, 2011).

Elbert T., et al. "Increased Cortical Representation of the Fingers of the Left Hand in String Players." *Science* 270 (1995): 305–307.

Fitch, W. T. "The Biology and Evolution of Music: A Comparative Perspective." *Cognition* 100 (2006): 173–215.

Gaab N., and G. Schlaug. "The Effect of Musicianship on Pitch Memory in Performance Matched Groups." *Neuroreport* 14 (2003): 2291–2295.

Gaab, N., C. Gaser, and G. Schlaug. "Improvement-related Functional Plasticity Following Pitch Memory Training." *NeuroImage* 31 (2006): 255–263.

Gjerdingen, Robert. "The Psychology of Music." In *The Cambridge History of Western Music Theory*, edited by Thomas Christensen, 956–981. Cambridge, UK: Cambridge University Press, 2002.

Hodges, D. A., W. D. Hairston, and J. H. Burdette. "Aspects of Multisensory Perception: The Integration of Visual and Auditory Information in Musical Experiences." *Annals of the New York Academy of Sciences* 1060 (2005): 175–185.

Hund-Georgiadis, M., and D. Y. von Cramon. "Motor-Learning-Related Changes in Piano Players and Non-musicians Revealed by Functional Magnetic-Resonance Signals." *Experimental Brain Research* 125 (1999): 417–425.

Hyde, K. L., et al. "Musical Training Shapes Structural Brain Development." *Journal of Neuroscience* 29 (2009): 3019–3025.

Gaser, C., and G. Schlaug, "Brain Structures Differ Between Musicians and Nonmusicians." *Journal of Neuroscience* 23 (2003): 9240–9245.

Iacoboni, M., et al. "Grasping the Intentions of Others with One's Own Mirror Neuron System." *PLoS Biology* 3 (2005): e79.

Iacoboni, M. "Imitation, Empathy, and Mirror Neurons." *Annual Review of Psychology* 60 (2009): 653–670.

Koelsch, S. "Significance of Broca's Area and Ventral Premotor Cortex for Music-Syntactic Processing." *Cortex* 42 (2006): 518–520.

Krings, T. et al. "Cortical Activation Patterns During Complex Motor Tasks in Piano Players and Control Subjects. A Functional Magnetic Resonance Imaging Study." *Neuroscience Letters* 278 (2000): 189–193.

Levitin, D. J., and V. Menon. "Musical Structure is Processed in 'Language' Areas of the Brain: A Possible Role for Brodmann Area 47 in Temporal Coherence." *NeuroImage* 20 (2003): 2142–2152.

Levitin, Daniel. *This Is Your Brain on Music: The Science of a Human Obsession*. London: Penguin Group, 2006.

Lidov, David. *Is Language a Music?: Writings on Musical Form and Signification*. Bloomington: Indiana University Press, 2004.

Limb, Charles J., and Allen R. Braun. "Neural Substrates of Spontaneous Musical Performance: An fMRI Study of Jazz Improvisation." *PLoS ONE* 3 (2008): e1679. doi:10.1371/journal. pone.0001679

Lotze, M., et al. "The Musician's Brain: Functional Imaging of Amateurs and Professionals During Performance and Imagery." *NeuroImage* 20 (2003): 1817–1829.

McMullen, Erin, and Jenny Saffran. "Music and Language: A Developmental Comparison." *Music Perception* 21 (2004): 289–311.

Molnar-Szakacs, I., and K. Overy. "Music and Mirror Neurons: From Motion to 'E'motion." *Social Cognitive and Affective Neuroscience* 1 (2006): 235–241.

Nettl, B. "Introduction: An Art Neglected in Scholarship." In *In the Course of Performance: Studies in the World of Musical Improvisation*, edited by Bruno Nettl and Melinda Russell, 1– 26. Chicago: University of Chicago Press, 1998.

Nettl, B. et al. "Improvisation." In *Grove Music Online. Oxford Music Online*. http://www. oxfordmusiconline.com/subscriber/article/grove/music/13738 (accessed May 17, 2011).

Pantev, C. et al. "Increased Auditory Cortical Representation in Musicians." *Nature* 392 (1998): 811–814.

Patel, Aniruddh. *Music, Language, and the Brain*. New York: Oxford University Press, 2007.

Peretz, Isabelle, and Robert J. Zatorre. *The Cognitive Neuroscience of Music*. New York: Oxford University Press, 2010.

Pinker, Stephen. *How the Mind Works*. New York: W.W. Norton and Company, 1997.

Pressing, Jeff. "Cognitive Processes in Improvisation." In *Cognitive Processes in the Perception of Art*, edited by W. Ray Crozier and Anthony J. Chapman, 345–366. Amsterdam: Elsevier, 1984.

Pressing, Jeff. "Improvisation: Methods and Models." In *Generative Processes in Music: The Psychology of Performance, Improvisation, and Composition*, edited by John Sloboda, 129–178. Oxford: Oxford University Press, 1988.

Pressing, Jeff. "Psychological Constraints on Improvisational Expertise and Communication." In *In the Course of Performance: Studies in the World of Musical Improvisation*, edited by Bruno Nettl and Melinda Russell, 47–68. Chicago: University of Chicago Press, 1998.

Rizzolatti, G., et al. "The Mirror-Neuron System." *Annual Review of Neuroscience* 27 (2004): 169–192.

Ruckert, George, and Richard Widdess. "Hindustani Raga." In *The Garland Encyclopedia of World Music*. Vol. 5, *South Asia: The Indian Subcontinent*, edited by Alison Arnold, 64–88. New York: Routledge, 1999.

Ryle, Gilbert. "Improvisation." *Mind* 85, no. 337 (1976): 69–83.

Sawyer, R. Keith. "The Improvisational Performance of Everyday Life." *Journal of Mundane Behavior* 2 (2001): 149–162.

Sawyer, R. Keith. *Creating Conversations: Improvisation in Everyday Discourse*. Cresskill: Hampton, 2001.

Schlaug, G. et al. "Increased Corpus Callosum Size in Musicians." *Neuropsychologia* 33 (1995): 1047–1055.

Schlaug, G., et al. "Training-induced Neuroplasticity in Young Children." *Annals of the New York Academy of Science* 1169 (2009): 205–208.

Slawek, Stephen. "Keeping It Going: Terms, Practices, and Processes of Improvisation in Hindustani Music." In *In the Course of Performance: Studies in the World of Musical Improvisation*, edited by Bruno Nettl and Melinda Russell, 335–368. Chicago: University of Chicago Press, 1998.

Sloboda, John. "Musical Expertise." In *Toward a General Theory of Expertise*, edited by K. A. Ericsson and J. Smith, 153–171. Cambridge: Cambridge University Press, 1991.

Tolbert, Elizabeth. "Theorizing the Musically Abject." In *Bad Music: The Music We Love to Hate*, edited by Christopher Washburne and Maiken Derno, 104–119. New York: Routledge, 2004.

Wan, C. Y., and G. Schlaug. "Music Making as a Tool for Promoting Brain Plasticity Across the Life Span." *Neuroscientist* 16 (2010): 566–577.

CHAPTER 3

IMPROVISATION, ACTION UNDERSTANDING, AND MUSIC COGNITION WITH AND WITHOUT BODIES

VIJAY IYER

WHAT are we referring to when we use the word "improvisation"? The term is used in innumerable ways, but always with the implicit assumption that there are acts that are improvised and acts that are not, and that those two kinds of acts are distinguishable. Two main aspects of that class of acts we call "improvised" seem to be (1) a real-time process of making choices and acting on them, and (2) the sense of temporal embeddedness: the fact that these actions take time, and that the time taken matters. With this understanding, we might take improvisation to denote that semi-transparent, multi-stage process through which we sense, perceive, think, decide, and act in real time.

But when construed this broadly, improvisation seems to encompass most of our behavior, including acts as disparate as walking through a forest or an airport, hunting and gathering, conversational speech, sport, climbing, driving, courtship, parenting, social dancing, and surfing the web. The class of improvisational behaviors is so vast that it may be easier to list behaviors that are *not* improvised—the carrying out of routines, plans, checklists, pre-routed or pre-ordained actions, well-rehearsed songs and dances, rituals, recitations, pageants, ceremonies, scripted performances of fully composed works—these last few exemplifying what Edward Said called "extreme occasions" (Said 1991). It seems that this class of non-improvised behaviors are the overall exception, a relatively small (but important) subset of human behavior as a whole.

Improvisation would also seem to encompass the noisy processes by which we acquire most skills. Babies learn to talk by babbling; they learn to walk by staggering, finding their balance, stumbling, finding something to hold onto; they learn to eat efficiently by first making a lot of messes. Improvisation is also the means by which we solve problems, by resorting to a repertoire of skills and adapting them to the situation at hand: putting out a fire, fixing a leak, doubling back to catch a missed turn, or building a shelter.

As we expand and refine these lists, we realize that most behaviors include improvised and non-improvised components. For improvisation also seems to govern the ways in which we do things; even if we go to a store to buy the items on a grocery list, we might find ourselves making moment-to-moment decisions in how we navigate the store, how we choose specific tomatoes, how and with what (and indeed whether) we decide to pay. We make choices based on what's at hand, what's allowed, and what's desired, and also based on what we are taught, trained, forced, or empowered to do, or on what we are experienced in doing.

And similarly, acts of improvisation can readily incorporate patterns of behavior. Seemingly spontaneous speech acts can easily lapse into routine exchanges, or the re-narrating of previously told stories and jokes; a politician may answer a question from a reporter with a previously crafted statement; an improvising musician may develop a "personal sound" that might include hallmark melodic ideas, specific techniques, a habitual way of producing a certain sound. These facts do not deny their improvised or real-time quality; rather, they reveal how decades of choosing can lead to patterned responses to similar conditions.

In light of these observations, it becomes more and more problematic to identify moments of "pure" improvisation, or to disambiguate them from the execution of pre-ordained programs. We might think that we can recognize improvised acts in extreme moments—uncontrolled facial expressions, slips of the tongue, non-grammatical for-mulations, or graceful witticisms on an unscripted television show, for example—but it is still difficult to prove their unscriptedness; we merely trust or believe that they are so.

What we seem to be doing, instead of literally *identifying* improvisation according to some intrinsic attribute, is allowing cultural and contextual factors to *regulate* the presence or absence of improvisation. To attend a play or a narrative film or a symphony, for example, is to witness what one knows to be a series of carefully scripted and sculpted human actions, while to watch emcees in a street corner "cipher," to hear a performance of Hindustani classical music, or to attend an "improv comedy" event or a jazz club is to knowingly witness individual and collective acts of improvisation, and to parse them in those terms. We may also use visual and auditory cues to signal an event's compos-edness, its un-improvised character: a moment of ensemble synchrony in music or dance, for example, might seem statistically unlikely to be improvised, so we take it to be somehow planned. But in this realm, we can also be tricked: the improvisational dance technique known as "flocking" can create the illusion of choreographed group movement; similarly, systems of cues are frequently embedded in improvised musical settings, whereby moments of synchrony can emerge from apparent disorder. We there-fore arrive at a crucial question for music cognition: when construed this broadly, does improvisation "sound like" anything? We will return to this question.

EMBODIED MUSIC COGNITION

A central theme in my work is the trace of the body in music. My dissertation and sub-sequent publications (Iyer 1998, 2002, 2004a, 2004b, 2009) explore the role of physical embodiment and sociocultural situatedness in music cognition. Drawing from recent advances in cognitive science, I claimed that music cognition should be understood as intimately tied in with the body and its physical and sociocultural environment—a per-spective that was previously neglected in the music cognition literature.

The paradigm of embodied cognition emerged in the late 1980s as a corrective response to the Cartesian "dualist" theories of mind that had prevailed in cognitive science since the field's inception in the mid-twentieth century. Dualism held that the mind exists in a realm separate from the brain—that is, that the mind could be understood as "the software" and the brain and body as "the hardware." The dualist paradigm known as "cognitivism" thereby presupposed that cognition was a kind of rule-based computation that could happen in any machine using the same rules, and that there was therefore nothing special about the bodies that housed our brains. The cognition-as-computation view then influenced the field of music cognition, where music was treated primarily as a disembodied flow of forms in an abstract space. Early research in the field focused on perception of timbre, harmony, and pitch, largely neglecting subjects such as rhythm, performance, or the physical act of making music, not to mention the cultural forces that might lead one to prioritize harmony at all.

Theories of embodiment hold that the body, the brain, and the mind must be under-stood as one system, and that the brain is an organ optimized for producing motor (i.e., bodily) output in response to sensory stimuli. This "sensory-motor loop" becomes the basis for what we call cognition. Rather than seeing thought as a process separate from sensation or action, we understand the faculties of perception, thought, and action as codependent, having developed together both ontologically (from birth through child-hood and into adulthood) and phylogenetically (in the evolution of the species).

It should be noted that adopting this framework does not inherently refute the idea of abstraction or "concepts." Intermediate theories such as the "grounding by interaction" framework (Mahon and Camerazza 2008) allow for abstract or symbolic concepts to be instantiated in the context of specific sensory and motor information. Such a framework offers a view of cognition that is neither fully embodied nor fully disembodied, but con-tains aspects of both.

From the embodiment paradigm, or some intermediate form of it, we can develop a body-based view of musical cognition. This view is borne out, for example, by brain imaging studies that have highlighted a fundamental identification between rhythm and human movement. It is understood that to perceive rhythm is to "imagine move-ment"; musical rhythm provokes the brain to prepare the body to move, facilitating or activating a physical response (Todd 1999, Todd et al. 1999). In consideration of some recent claims about mirror neurons (Kohler et al. 2002), this might be considered as a kind of "aural mirroring." In this view (discussed critically below), we tend to respond *in kind* to what we think we hear another body doing, imagining or actually generating an action that is suggested by the rhythmic character of the sounds we hear.

Music is then understood as the sound of human bodies in motion; to listen to music is to perceive the actions of those bodies, and a kind of sympathetic, synchronous bodily action (i.e., dance) is one primary response. Of course, this is mediated by culture. Certain cultural settings may foreground bodily responses to music, while others conceal or suppress them; these variations express "situated cognition" (Robbins and Aydede 2008, Clancey 1997)—the interrelationship of mind and world, the interdependence between knowledge and its context.

The notion of music cognition as an embodied, situated phenomenon ties in well with contemporary ethnomusicological accounts of African diasporic musics, in which embodiment, performativity, and cultural context play a crucial role in the production of meaning. The idea of embodiment can also bring the field of music perception and cognition into a healthier dialogue with the music humanities, which has in recent decades seen robust critical engagement with "the body" in terms of race, gender, and sexuality. When we hear bodies but do not see them, we instead fantasize about them; listening to music (especially in the disembodied way that it circulates today) is deeply informed by that same process of racialized, sexualized fantasy-formation about the virtual bodies that made those sounds. While interdisciplinarity can, at its worst, provoke an unproductive confrontation of epistemological incongruities between paradigms, bodies can still offer a strong focus for dialogue, critique, and new productions of knowledge across many fields of inquiry. Although bodies are described from many different standpoints, somehow we can all agree on their sheer, stubborn presence (or absence, as the case may be).

EMBODIED RHYTHM PERCEPTION

The central idea that music is an embodied, situated activity means that music depends crucially on the structure of our bodies, and also on the environment and culture in which our musical awareness emerges. Rhythm, especially, is a complex, whole-body experience, and its role in music makes use of the embodied, situated status of the participant. Such claims have a variety of implications; they lead us to appreciate traces of the embodiment in instrumental and vocal music, to notice how musical cultures and individuals variously deal with the role of physicality in music-making, and to understand music perception as an active, culturally contingent process.

The claim that music perception and cognition are embodied activities also means that they are actively constructed by the listener, rather than passively transferred from performer to listener. This active nature of music perception highlights the role of culture and context. For example, the discernment of qualities such as pulse and meter from a piece of music is not perceptually inevitable; rather, the music may offer perceptual ambiguities whose resolution depends on an observer's culturally contingent listening strategies (Iyer 1998: 83–104). In addition, I have argued that rhythmic expression is often directly related to the role of the body in making music, and to certain cultural aesthetics that privilege this role. In particular, certain subtle microrhythmic variations in rhythmic performance display striking systematic structure, carrying an encoded trace of the culturally situated music-making body (for a detailed explanation, see Iyer 2002).

The salience of fine-grained musical rhythm at this level of detail is borne out by more recent neuroscientific studies of timing perception (see Patel 2008, 96–154; Levitin 2009). In particular, microrhythmic perception appears to take advantage of our ability to differentiate between phonemes (Patel 2008), and, crucially, our ability to aurally locate and track human movement around us (Changizi 2011). The assertion of the existence in the microrhythmic realm of meaningful musical structure, activating our faculties for perception of human movement and speech, runs counter to more common descriptions of microrhythmic variation as "discrepancies" (Keil 1987), "imperfections" or "being slightly off" (Hennig et al. 2012), or, for *The New York Times*, "essentially mistakes" and "error[s]" (Belluck 2011).

Rhythm—in music, speech, bodily acts, or some interleaved combination thereof—offers one productive line of inquiry for theories of embodied cognition. Another such category is improvisation. Rhythm and improvisation are not mutually exclusive categories in this regard, but two overlapping fields of behavior, both treating *time* as a central parameter.

TIME AND TEMPORAL SITUATEDNESS

A fundamental consequence of physical embodiment and environmental situatedness is the fact that *things take time*. Temporality must ground our conception of physically embodied cognition. Smithers (1996) draws a useful distinction between processes that occur "in-time" and those that exist "over-time." The distinction is similar to that between process-oriented activity, such as speech or walking, and product-oriented activity, such as writing a novel or composing a symphony.

In-time processes are *embedded* in time; not only does the time taken matter, but, in fact, it contributes to the overall structure. The speed of a typical walking gait relates to physical attributes like leg mass and size and shoulder-hip torsional moment; this is why we cannot walk one-tenth or ten times as fast as we do. Similarly, the rate at which we speak exploits the natural timescales of lingual and mandibular motion as well as respiration. Changizi (2011) further argues that human speech is made of vocalized imitations of real-world solid-object events—"hits, slides, and rings"—with speech's rhythmic profiles derived from this physical "grammar." Accordingly, we learn to process speech at precisely such a rate. Recorded speech played at slower or faster speeds rapidly becomes unintelligible, even if the pitch is held constant. The perceived flow of conversation, while quite flexible, is sensitive to the slowdown caused by an extra few seconds taken to think of a word or recall a name.

Over-time processes, by contrast, are merely *contained* in time; the fact that they take time is of no fundamental consequence to the result. Most of what we call computation occurs over time. The fact that all computing machines were originally considered computationally equivalent regardless of speed suggests that time was not a concern in the original theory of computation, and that the temporality of a computational process was theoretically immaterial. Though computational theory is more nuanced today, "real-time" computer applications make use of the speed of modern microprocessors, performing computations so fast that the user doesn't notice how much time is taken. However, this is not what the mind does when immersed in a dynamic, real-time environment; rather, it exploits both the constraints and the allowances of the natural time-scales of the body and the brain as a total physical system. In other words, Smithers (1996) claims, *cognition chiefly involves in-time processes.* Furthermore, this claim is not limited simply to cognitive processes that require interpersonal interaction; it pertains to all thought, perception, and action.

The Temporality of Performance

In intersubjective activities, such as speech or music making, one remains aware of a sense of mutual embodiment. This sense brings about the presupposition of "shared time" between the listener and the performer. This sense is a crucial aspect of the temporality of performance. The experience of listening to music is qualitatively different from that of reading a book. The experience of music requires the listener's "co-performance" within a shared temporal domain (Schutz 1964). While the essentially solitary act of reading a book also takes time, the specific amount of time is of little consequence. (Literary notions of co-performance, such as Roland Barthes' idea of "writerly texts" [1975], do not fundamentally incorporate the temporality of experience.) The notion of musical co-performance is made literal in musical contexts primarily meant for dance; the participatory act of marking time with rhythmic bodily activity physicalizes the sense of shared time and could be viewed as embodied listening.

The performance situation itself might be understood as a context-framing device. In his study of the music of a certain community in South Africa, ethnomusicologist John Blacking wrote, "Venda music is distinguished from nonmusic by the creation of a special world of time. The chief function of music is to involve people in shared experiences within the framework of their cultural experience" (Blacking 1973: 48). There is no doubt that this is true to some degree in all musical performance, and we can take this concept further in the case of improvised music.

WHAT DOES IMPROVISATION SOUND LIKE?

Can one *hear* the fact that a sound was just decided in its moment of creation? Does music have any characteristic that announces itself as such? My sense, from my own performing, teaching, and listening experiences, is that most listeners can't tell the difference in isolation; the perception of the relative presence or absence of improvisation is largely imagined and profoundly contextual, based on cultural factors and assumptions. And analytically, it is difficult to find any such traits on the musical surface; the tendency in the West is to focus on so-called "mistakes" as an indicator of improvisation, as if they somehow verify the fragile and risky process.

Limb and Braun (2008), in their fMRI brain imaging studies of skilled musicians in the act of improvising, found that in a focused state of improvisation, a soloist has lowered self-correcting inhibitions and enhanced activation of a self-narrative function. "Just relax and be yourself," might be another way to put it; it's the kind of advice given before a date or a job interview, both of which are also instances of heightened, carefully framed improvisation. But Limb (private communication, 2012) further suggests that there is something else happening in moments of highly skilled musical improvisation, something like what Csikszentmihalyi (1990) calls a "flow state," a mental and physical state of utmost relaxation, focus, and concentration, known to be conducive to creative thinking. Such a criterion (if it is indeed a criterion, and not merely a correlated phenomenon or perhaps an outcome of the "overlearning" involved in improvisational skill) may enable us to qualitatively set apart sustained creative musical improvisation, for example, from our more everyday spontaneous acts.

However, that doesn't tell us anything about what improvisation "sounds like" to an observer. So another question is, does the distinction matter? Why are we, in music, so bound up with the issue? The reason is that the experience of listening to music that is understood to be improvised differs significantly from listening knowingly to composed music. The main source of drama in improvised music is the sheer fact of the shared sense of time: the sense that the improviser is working, creating, generating musical material in the same time in which we are co-performing as listeners (Iyer 1998, 80). As listeners to any music, we experience a kind of *empathy* for the performer, an awareness of physicality and an understanding of the effort required to create music. This empathy is one facet of our listening strategies in any context. In improvisational music, this embodied empathy extends to an awareness of the performers' coincident physical and mental exertion, of their "in-the-moment" processes of creative activity and interactivity, the risks taken in the face of unbounded possibilities, the inherent constraints of the mind deciding and the body acting in time. Perhaps it can be said that improvisational music magnifies the role of embodiment in musical performance. The perception of improvisation seems to involve the perception of another body or bodies engaged in embodied, situated, real-time experience. If so, then a sense of mutual embodiment, of the shared space, time, and bodily presence of performers and observers, would seem to open the door to specific kinds of *empathy*.

A Science of Empathy

A flurry of recent, intensely debated findings in neuroscience have suggested a neural basis for empathy that seems to reinforce this view. The body of research on so-called "mirror neurons" (Gallese et al. 1996; Kohler et al. 2002; Rizzolatti and Sinigaglia 2010; Gallese et al. 2011) promotes the idea of *action understanding*, a kind of empathy at the neural level, and claims the existence of a "mirroring mechanism" for action understanding, in which the perception of certain familiar actions in another body can trigger the activation of similar motor programs in the observer's brain: "[E]ach time an individual observes another individual performing an action, a set of neurons that encode that action is activated in the observer's cortical motorsystem" (Rizzolatti and Sinigaglia 2010: 264). These activations may manifest as analogous bodily motion, action or stance to that of the observed body, or they may just remain at the level of an "imagined movement." There is evidence in primates for the existence of such a neural system—as famously depicted in photographs of a baby macaque sticking its tongue out in response to a scientist doing the same (Gross 2006)—suggesting something quite fundamental about this process, even applying across species in primates (Buccino et al. 2004).

Unfortunately, we cannot allow these findings to paint too rosy a picture of universal "understanding." Recent studies on mirror neurons and racial identification (Gutsell and Inzlicht 2010) actually suggest that the perception of racialized difference may inhibit or constrain empathy. It was observed that test subjects (all whites from North America) displayed a greater mirror neuron-type response to images of other whites than they did to non-whites. In some cases, whites displayed practically zero empathy-like mental simulation of actions of non-whites. This finding has been extended to more fluid "in-group/out-group" affiliations, suggesting a profound neuroplasticity in this "mirroring" mechanism associated with empathy. For reviews of such findings, see Eres and Molenberghs (2013) and Matusall (2013).

That science might find empathy to be instinctively possible across real species boundaries, and yet also suppressed across imagined racial boundaries, suggests that there could be both innate and learned aspects to action understanding, and that it can be informed by both structural and superficial qualities visually perceived in the other. It would appear that there is no such thing as "clean" mirroring; there is perhaps always some distortion of the metaphorical mirror, since the problematic visual "perception" of racial difference can seemingly interfere with action understanding.

However, crucially for music cognition, some recent research suggests that mirror neurons might be involved in both visual *and* auditory processing. Whereas early research in this mirror neuron system focused on action understanding activated through visual stimuli (Rizzolatti et al. 1996), subsequent work has revealed a similar mechanism at work through auditory channels (Kohler et al. 2002). It is claimed that "these audiovisual mirror neurons code actions independently of whether these actions are performed, heard, or seen" (Kohler et al. 2002). The notion that this process could occur through sound—that we may undergo a kind of empathetic action understanding when we merely *hear* someone do something without *seeing* that person do it—offers quite radical implications for how we listen to music (and especially what happens when we hear music without seeing).

This offers a tantalizing reading of the history of recorded music, as bound up as it is with race and twentieth-century American history. Is it possible that music-heard-and-not-seen (which, of course, was a rarity before the advent of recorded music, Pythagoras's "acousmatic" scenario notwithstanding) might have overridden the visual, racialized, culturally imposed constraints on empathy? Could the essential humanity of African Americans have been newly revealed for white American listeners in the twentieth century through the disembodied circulation of "race records," by activating in these listeners a neural "understanding" of the actions of African American performers? These were, after all, among the first recordings to circulate on a mass scale in the United States. Could a new kind of cross-racial empathy, or at least a new quasi-utopic racial imaginary, have been inaugurated through the introduction and sudden ubiquity of recorded sound? As the above line of inquiry suggests, this very idea—that disembodied human sound can elicit in the listener a mirroring or empathic understanding of the imagined movements of an imagined other—carries the disruptive potential to restructure our knowledge of what music is, why it exists, and how it works.

Mirror neurons and their identification with action understanding have received intense scientific scrutiny and critique, especially in the last few years (Hickok 2009, Hickok and Hauser 2010, Hutto 2013). Contributing to the issue has been the fact that "the concept of 'action understanding' has been evolving" (Hickok 2009) due to the persistent, irresolvable question of what it means to "understand" the action of another. To confirm "understanding," must one reproduce the other's action identically, or does it suffice simply to "know how" to do the action, or perhaps to understand its intended goal? Can there be generative mis-"understandings" of the actions of others, and how are they distinguished from "true" action understanding?

Still, underlying most instances of the phrase "action understanding" is the idea that, in certain cases, "self-generated actions have an inherent semantics and that observing the same action in others affords access to this action semantics" (Hickok 2009). A recent review by Rizzolatti and Sinigaglia (2010) concedes that there may be types of action understanding attributable to non-mirror mechanisms in the brain, and then turns its focus to a specific type of mirror mechanism "that allows an individual to understand the action of others 'from the inside'" (264), which seems to specifically mean the knowledge of *how* to perform an action that one is observing.

A tidy resolution of the rapidly evolving mirror-neuron debate is beyond the scope of this article (or indeed of any article, as of this writing). What is of direct relevance to our discussion here is *the concept of action understanding*—not its exact neural mechanism, but its very existence, and its explanatory power as an intersubjective framework for music cognition. The last century's global cultural transformation—from humankind's longstanding identification of music with embodied action to the sudden propagation of recorded music and its concomitant abundance of music without bodies—offers us a productive conceptual space to consider the role of action understanding (or its com-modified 20th century replacement—which can only be called *fantasy*) in the act of lis-tening to music.

EXPECTATIONS

If improvisation and rhythm are central to embodied musical cognition, are these claims borne out in the current literature in music cognition? Curiously, recent "big-picture" treatises in music cognition have avoided discussions of improvisation, despite its seem-ing primacy in musical and cognitive experience. David Huron's work on expectation (2008) considers the evolutionary advantages of humankind's ability to predict events based on cues: "Those who can predict the future are better prepared to take advantage of opportunities and sidestep dangers. . . . Accurate expectations are adaptive mental functions that allow organisms to prepare for appropriate action and perception" (3). These functions, he continues, are entangled with emotional response: " [T]he emotions accompanying expectations are intended to reinforce accurate prediction, promote appropriate event-readiness, and increase the likelihood of future positive outcomes. . . . [M]usic-making taps into these primordial functions to produce a wealth of com-pelling emotional experiences . . . including surprise, awe, 'chills,' comfort, and even laughter" (4). Building on Meyer's (1956) proposed correspondence between expecta-tion, emotion, and meaning in the perception of musical form, Huron develops a per-spective on music perception grounded in the science of expectation.

It becomes apparent that Huron's theory of expectation, while building on Meyer's composer-centered theory, is fundamentally similar to embodied and situated cogni-tion. Expectation is a capacity that guides our understanding of real-world, real-time events in a way that helps us make efficacious, life-sustaining actions, to "predict the future" and "take advantage of opportunities." This view would seem completely com-patible with, and indeed nearly identical with, our working understanding of improvisa-tion. It is therefore ironic and unfortunate that Huron's sole discussions of improvisation focus on how improvisers cover for "wrong" notes (234–235, 291). Indeed, the improvi-sational orientation of Huron's entire theory—grounded in an understanding of percep-tion as optimized for interacting in real time with an information-rich environment—is somehow repressed in his discussions of music. The reason seems to be that improvisa-tion is not compatible with his working model of music, which is characterized by a divi-sion between music and its listeners; his and Meyer's basic thrust is that music makers (which for Huron and Meyer essentially means *composers*) make choices to manipulate the expectations of a passive audience of listeners. Music, in his view and in the views of many other researchers in the field, is something that *happens to* listeners, or something that they perceive without very much direct engagement; music is rarely framed as an *activity* that listeners *coexist with* as well as *participate in* throughout their entire lives, and are always already acculturated to.

The presupposition of a division between music and listener, between performer and audience, stems from a fundamentally non-participatory understanding of music, which runs counter to most anthropological evidence about how music tends to function in culture. That kind of separation is of course a widespread paradigm in the West and in the court musics of many non-western cultures, but that does not make it meaningful in evolutionary terms. We stand to learn more about music's origins by attention to humankind's vernacular and folk musics, which are participatory almost by definition. Just as we humans have not evolved very much in the millennia since writing was introduced, we certainly haven't evolved significantly in the century since recordings became popular, or even in the last few centuries since composers started writing for orchestras.

The point here is that the embodied improvising agent, situated in a real-world physical and cultural environment, is most often the listener *and* the doer in the equation. Expectation is perhaps best understood as a capacity of the improviser—that is, all of us—to take in information, make predictions, and carry out informed, situated actions based on those predictions, with real-world consequences. Just as the theory of musical expectation is a consequence of a more general theory of expectation, this view of expectation as an improvisational skill has both "real-world" and musical implications. For example, it has been observed in simulations (Friston, Mattout, and Kilner 2011) that "mirror neurons will emerge naturally in any agent that acts on its environment to avoid surprising events"—a startling conclusion that brings together notions of situated cognition and improvisation (the agent acting on its environment), expectation (learning to reduce predictive error, i.e., avoiding surprises), and action understanding—with repercussions for cognition in intersubjective situations, musical or otherwise.

MUSIC AND SPEECH

A recent treatise by Patel (2008) considers fundamental connections between music and language from a neuroscience perspective. Drawing from a huge range of research in music and speech perception, Patel presents a thorough view of the state of our current understanding of the connections between these two systems.

Given the exhaustive nature of this work, the absence of any substantial consideration of improvisation is again striking. But certain conceptual biases about what music *is* soon reveal themselves, which help explain this strange gap. In a discussion of linguistic meaning in relation to musical meaning, Patel imagines composers trying to write short pieces that "mean" common nouns or verbs ("school," "eye," "know"). Would listeners be able to "hear" their meanings? Most probably they would not, he answers. However, "lacking specificity of semantic reference is not the same as being utterly devoid of referential power. . . . Instrumental music lacks specific semantic *content*, but it can at times suggest semantic *concepts*. Furthermore, it can do this with some consistency in terms of the concepts activated in the minds of listeners within a culture" (Patel 2008: 328).

This uncovers a certain assumption about music and speech—that it is all received, never generated; that composers make music, and others learn to hear it. The assumption is that language is both simply created by others for us to learn to use, that it has inherent meanings that we can "hear," and so forth—as if language were not itself a vast, improvisational, arbitrary, and continually evolving system of signs. The inherent bias is that music is not something that we do, but instead something that we merely accept from those who have the authority to do it for us. This removes music from the realm of action into the passive realm of "reception."

Meanwhile, is the meaning of a speech act simply a question of processing—of decoding sounds and hearing their meaning? There is also something very important going on in real time, in the realm of expectation. A speech act comes into being in the void, in a sense; it not only conveys a meaning, but it also fills up an experiential space where there might just as easily not have been such an act. And once it is done, it cannot be undone. So the very fact of it having been *decided* in those moments under those constraints— decided often not even as a complete thought but *word by word*—marks it undeniably as improvisation. In other words, to speak is necessarily to improvise. At some level, to listen to speech is always to bear this fact in mind; the improvisational nature of speech is essentially axiomatic, seemingly a precondition for our ever communicating at all. "Speech acts" are performative in the sense that they represent a filling-in of shared time with an improvisation that aims to construct meaning. Certainly in retrospect, speech acts also "are" their semantic meanings, but before they acquire meaning, they are, first and foremost, *acts*.

Perhaps one reason that listeners cling to "mistakes" in music as evidence of improvisation is that "gaffes" do exactly the same thing for speech. Such "mistakes" (and of course it is difficult to name anything as such) underscore the fragility of the improvisational act. So we must bear in mind also the similarity between acts of musical improvisation and speech acts on this level: they always move *forward in time*, and they always are in some way a replacement for their own absence. Their existence is always the result of a set of choices: that of whether to say anything at all, of what to say, and of when to say it. The gravity of an improvisational act is the very fact that it happened at all, as opposed to anything else that could have happened, including nothing.

Those choices exist within a dynamic web of interacting constraints—particularly the more social considerations of what is appropriate, what is expected, what is individually desired, and what is "right." One of Charles Limb's (2008) discoveries is that when we improvise, questions of what is "right" diminish in importance. In this way a set of constraints is relaxed, perhaps making it easier to choose, or allowing more choice.

Harnessing

The latest body of research to support the embodied and situated view of music is summarized in Changizi (2011). Here it is argued that music takes advantage of the existing skills we have of recognizing and decoding audible traces of human action. Instead of emphasizing pitch, harmony, and the other hallmarks of music perception research, the author focuses on our perceptual attunement to the specific sounds of human motion.

Since much of the time in everyday life we hear our fellow human beings in our peripheries without seeing them, Changizi suggests that we have evolved to decode and respond to these stimuli—to hear everyday human moving-around noises not as abstract sounds but as markers of bodies in motion. From an evolutionary perspective, we are optimized to communicate with and "read" our fellow humans. Building on this idea, the author argues that the details of music take advantage of our aural grounding in the perception of specifically *human* motion: the sound and rhythmic profile of footsteps as a marker of locomotive behavior; small Doppler shifts as an indicator of direction of motion (Oechslin et al. 2008); the correspondence between loudness and distance; and other such sonic hallmarks. Rather than suggest that humans evolved to hear music, he argues that humans "harnessed" an existing perceptual apparatus, which had evolved for the perception of human motion, to develop music, which, he suggests, mimics human action.

Changizi argues that music takes advantage of our aural ability to notice human action in the same way that written language takes advantage of our visual ability to notice contours, edges, and joints, the building blocks of human vision. Furthermore, human movement is emotionally evocative; we can recognize the emotion from someone's gait. Music "can often sound like *contagious* expressive human behavior and movement, and trigger a similar expressive movement in us" (Changizi 2011: 116). But we can take this argument a step further, since from the perspective of embodiment, music is more than a mere sonic imitation of human action; indeed, it was never anything *but* human action. Until the last century, music was only ever made by *bodily* engagement with available sound-producing technology; whether it was mediated by objects adapted from the natural world (gourds and logs, animal skins and bones) or pure bodily acts (stomping, clapping, and singing), the sound of music *always was* the sound of people in motion—perhaps a stylized, synchronized, or sustained kind of motion, but never disconnected from bodily presence or action, nor ever outside of the realm of plausible human actions. This means that we don't perceive rhythms in implausible frequency ranges of 1000 Hz or .001 Hz, because they do not correspond to any human action. We don't readily integrate a stream of stimuli from physically separated sources as if it were a single source, but, rather, we notice harmonic tones because we are sharply attuned to the harmonicity of human voices.

In this perspective, crucially, music is inherently social; it taps into parts of our brains that connect us to other people. We can hear and immediately understand what people are doing in our midst; their gaits indicate their behaviors and emotions; the direction of their motion is indicated by changes in volume and pitch. Working with these very perceptual ingredients, music recreates for us the sensation and emotional thrill of people in our midst. Such reasoning falls in line with what J. J. Gibson called the "ecological mode of perception," in which our perceptual systems are tuned to apprehend real-world *sound sources* in an environment, rather than only to pure sound itself (Gibson

1979; Shove and Repp 1995). It also aligns squarely with the views on embodied music cognition—the idea of bodies listening to bodies—as well as with the neural foundations of empathy and the notion of auditory action understanding.

CONCLUSION

To summarize the extravagant claims in this rather speculative article: improvisation "matters" in music because a knowing listener experiences some kind of empathy for the embodiment of the performer, or some kind of understanding of the effortfulness of real-time performance. There is evidence that this phenomenon possibly has a neural basis, which is grounded in our ability to perceive, recognize, and decode the sights *and* sounds of bodies in motion. And this phenomenon is also linked to the foundations of rhythm perception, since the sound of a humanly generated rhythm (i.e., the sound of a body in motion) can activate an analogous body motion in a listener.

Our skill at perceiving, "understanding," and/or imitating the sonorous actions of another enables us to synchronize our actions, to operate in rhythmic unison or in sustained antiphony, to move, sing, dance, or work together. Improvisation and rhythm, two foundational elements of music and creativity, both have at their core some kind of embodied perception and cognition of the other, and therefore they seem to be what enable us, as human beings, to do anything together in the same time and space.

Music is born of our actions—its ingredients are the sound of bodies in motion—and therefore *music cognition begins as action understanding*. This does not mean that we cannot process musical information without bodies, but it does mean that our sensations and actions provide the context for abstraction, symbolic music cognition, and the fantasies brought about by music-without-bodies.

CODA

What do we mean when we use the word "experience"? It refers to both (1) the stream of sensation and perception and (2) the accumulation of cognition through sustained immersion in this stream. (Let us set aside any notion of "consciousness.") Our very language suggests an assumed relationship between the first and second meanings: an "experienced" person is someone who has "experienced" enough to gain knowledge from these experiences. So the second sense of "experience" would seem to encompass the first; to be "experienced," to have field knowledge, to know how to handle things in a given situation, is to have undergone prior "experiences" of a similar sort. In the embodiment perspective, we understand the first sense of "experience"—sensation and perception—as connected to and dependent upon embodied action; cognition becomes an umbrella term for all of these processes, as well as the mental structures that connect these different stages of the "sensorimotor loop"—sensation, perception, thought, action.

We might reconsider whether we have cast too wide a net with the expansive conception of improvisation posed in this chapter. But if we were to refuse to dignify an infant's babbling with so exalted a term as improvisation—if we were to insist instead, for example, that a true act of improvisation first requires a coherent self, or some threshold level of "creativity," or some move away from what is "habitual," or that it must display some sort of "resistance" or "non-normativity" or "soul"—then we might limit the more radical implications of this overall perspective. For I am suggesting instead that improvisation, in this broad sense, might be considered as the means by which we *acquire selfhood*. It is not only a means of self-transformation, as Arnold Davidson (2005) has eloquently described it, but of self-generation. In other words, I am positing a relationship—or more to the point, an *identity*, a *sameness*—between what we call "improvisation" and what we call "experience." A corollary is that an observer's perception of improvisation is contingent upon an "understanding" of its status as experience—which, again, underscores the essential intersubjectivity of music cognition.

This broad view does not reject the possibility of political action or engagement. Indeed, political struggles for selfhood have been advanced by concurrent transformative improvisations in culture, whether it was the possible problematization of race brought on by the circulation of music-without-bodies, or the improvised musical expressions of an African American subculture defiantly asserting its collective humanity. It is in our interest to consider these perspectives on the origins of music, so that we may better understand how fundamental it is to the origins and elaborations of the self.

> Improvisation is a human response to necessity.
>
> Muhal Richard Abrams (2007)

> It seems to me what music *is* is *everything that you do*.
>
> Cecil Taylor (Mann 1981)

BIBLIOGRAPHY

Abrams, M. R., M. Jefferson, Y. Komunyakaa, G. Lewis, and P. Williams. "Improvisation in Everyday Life: A Conversation." Public lecture, Columbia University, New York, September 25, 2007. Available at http://www.worldleaders.columbia.edu/events/conversations-series-improvisation-everyday-life. Accessed December 31, 2013.

Barthes, R. *S/Z*, translated by Richard Miller. London: Cape Publishers, 1975.

Belluck, P. "To Tug at the Heart, Music First Must Tickle the Neurons." *New York Times*, April 19, 2011, D1.

Blacking, J. *How Musical Is Man?* Seattle: University of Washington Press, 1973.

Buccino, G., F. Lui, N. Canessa, I. Patteri, G. Lagravinese, et al. "Neural Circuits Involved in the Recognition of Actions Performed by Nonconspecifics: An fMRI Study." *Journal of Cognitive Neuroscience* 16, no. 1 (Jan.–Feb. 2004): 114–126.

Changizi, M. A.. *Harnessed: How Language and Music Mimicked Nature and Transformed Ape to Man*. Dallas, TX: BenBella Books, 2011. Kindle edition.

Clancey, W. *Situated Cognition: On Human Knowledge and Computer Representation*. New York: Cambridge University Press, 1997.

Csikszentmihalyi, M. *Flow: The Psychology of Optimal Experience*. New York: Harper and Row, 1990.

Davidson, A. I. "Introduction." In *Michel Foucault: The Hermeneutics of the Subject, Lectures at the College de France, 1981–1982*, translated by Graham Burchell, and edited by Arnold I. Davidson, xix–xxx. New York: Palgrave Macmillan, 2005.

Eres, R., and P. Molenberghs. "The Influence of Group Membership on the Neural Correlates Involved in Empathy." *Frontiers in Human Neuroscience* 7 (May 2013): 176.

Friston, K., J. Mattout, and J. Kilner. "Action Understanding and Active Inference." *Biological Cybernetics* 104, nos. 1–2 (February 2011): 137–160.

Gallese, V., L. Fadiga, L. Fogassi, and G. Rizzolatti. "Action Recognition in the Premotor Cortex." *Brain* 119, nos. 2 (1996): 593–609.

Gallese, V., M. A. Gernsbacher, C. Heyes, G. Hickok, and M. Iacoboni. "Mirror Neuron Forum." *Perspectives on Psychological Science* 6, vol. 4 (2011): 369–407.

Gibson, J. J. *The Ecological Approach to Visual Perception*. Boston: Houghton Mifflin, 1979.

Gross, L. "Evolution of Neonatal Imitation." *PLoS Biology* 4, no. 9 (2006): e311.

Gutsell, J. N., and M. Inzlicht. "Empathy Constrained: Prejudice Predicts Reduced Mental Simulation of Actions during Observation of Outgroups." *Journal of Experimental Social Psychology* 46, nos. 5 (2010): 841–845.

Hennig, H., R. Fleischmann, and T. Geisel. "Musical Rhythms: The Science of Being Slightly Off." *Physics Today* 65, no. 7 (2012), Quick Study.

Hickok, G. "Eight Problems for the Mirror Neuron Theory of Action Understanding in Monkeys and Humans." *Journal of Cognitive Neuroscience* 21, no. 7 (2009): 1229–1243.

Hickok, G., and M. Hauser. "(Mis)understanding Mirror Neurons." *Current Biology* 20, no. 14 (2010): R593–R594.

Huron, D. *Sweet Anticipation*. Cambridge, MA: MIT Press, 2008.

Hutto, D. D. "Action Understanding: How Low Can You Go?" *Consciousness and Cognition* 22, no. 3 (September 2013): 1142–1151.

Iyer, V. "Microstructures of Feel, Macrostructures of Sound: Embodied Cognition in West African and African-American Musics." Ph.D. dissertation, University of California, Berkeley, 1998.

Iyer, V. "Embodied Mind, Situated Cognition, and Expressive Microtiming in African-American Music." *Music Perception* 19, no. 3 (2002): 387–414.

Iyer, V. "Exploding the Narrative in Jazz Improvisation." In *Uptown Conversation: The New Jazz Studies*, edited by R. O'Meally, B. Edwards, and F. Griffin, 393–403. New York: Columbia University Press, 2004.

Iyer, V. "Improvisation, Temporality, and Embodied Experience." *Journal of Consciousness Studies* 11, nos. 3–4 (2004): 159–173.

Iyer, V. "Improvisation: Terms and Conditions." In *Arcana IV: Musicians on Music*, edited by John Zorn, 171–175. New York: Hips Road/Tzadik, 2009.

Keil, C. "Participatory Discrepancies and the Power of Music." *Cultural Anthropology* 2, no. 3 (1987): 275–283.

Kohler, E., C. Keysers, M. A. Umiltà, L. Fogassi, V. Gallese, and G. Rizzolatti. "Hearing Sounds, Understanding Actions: Action Representation in Mirror Neurons." *Science* 297 (2 August 2002): 846–848.

Levitin, D. J. "The Neural Correlates of Temporal Structure in Music." *Music and Medicine* 1, no. 1 (2009): 9–13.

Levitin, D. J., and A. K. Tirovolas. "Current Advances in the Cognitive Neuroscience of Music." *The Year in Cognitive Neuroscience 2009: Annals of the New York Academy of Sciences* 1156, no. 1 (2009): 211–231.

Limb, C. J., and A. R. Braun. "Neural Substrates of Spontaneous Musical Performance: An fMRI Study of Jazz Improvisation." *PLoS ONE* 3, no. 2 (2008): e1679. doi:10.1371/journal.pone.0001679.

Mahon, B. Z., and Caramazza, A. "A Critical Look at the Embodiment Hypothesis and a New Proposal for Grounding Conceptual Content." *Journal of Physiology—Paris* 102, nos. 1–3 (January-May 2008): 59–70.

Mann, R. *Imagine the Sound* (documentary feature film). New York: Janus Films, 1981.

Matusall, S. "Social Behavior in the "Age of Empathy"? A Social Scientist's Perspective on Current Trends in the Behavioral Sciences." *Frontiers in Human Neuroscience* 7 (May 31, 2013): 236.

Meyer, Leonard. *Emotion and Meaning in Music.* Chicago: University of Chicago Press, 1956.

Oechslin, M., M. Neukom, and G. Bennett. "The Doppler Effect—An Evolutionary Critical Cue for the Perception of the Direction of Moving Sound Sources." In *Proceedings of International Conference on Audio, Language and Image Processing, Shanghai, China, July 2008.* ICALIP 2008.

Patel, A. *Music, Language, and the Brain.* Oxford: Oxford University Press, 2008.

Rizzolatti, G., L. Fadiga, V. Gallese, and L. Fogassi. "Premotor cortex and the recognition of motor actions." *Cognitive Brain Research* 3, no. 2 (March 1996): 131–141.

Rizzolatti, G., and C. Sinigaglia. "The Functional Role of the Parieto-frontal Mirror Circuit: Interpretations and Misinterpretations." *Nature Reviews Neuroscience* 11, no. 4 (2010): 264–274.

Robbins, P., and M. Aydede, ed. *The Cambridge Handbook of Situated Cognition.* Cambridge: Cambridge University Press, 2008.

Said, E. W. *Musical Elaborations.* New York: Columbia University Press, 1991.

Schutz, A. "Making Music Together." In *Collected Papers II: Studies in Social Theory*, edited by Arvid Brodersen, 159–178. The Hague: Martinus Nijhoff, 1964.

Shove, P., and B. Repp. "Musical Motion and Performance: Theoretical and Empirical Perspectives." In *The Practice of Performance*, edited by J. Rink, 55–83. Cambridge: Cambridge University Press, 1995.

Smithers, T. "On What Embodiment Might Have to Do with Cognition (Technical Report FS-96–02)." In *Embodied Cognition and Action: Papers from the 1996 AAAI Fall Symposium*, edited by M. Mataric, 113–116. Menlo Park, CA: AAAI Press, 1996.

Todd, N. P. M. "Motion in Music: A Neurobiological Perspective." *Music Perception* 17, no. 1 (1999): 115–126.

Todd, N. P. M., D. J. O'Boyle, and C. S. Lee. "A Sensory-Motor Theory of Rhythm, Time Perception, and Beat Induction." *Journal of New Music Research* 28, no. 1 (1999): 5–28.

CHAPTER 4

....

THE GHOST IN THE MUSIC, OR THE PERSPECTIVE OF AN IMPROVISING ANT

....

DAVID BORGO

ANTS are remarkable creatures. They inhabit almost every landmass on Earth, survive in most every climate, and make up nearly one quarter of the total biomass on the planet. They are industrious and exhibit impressive physical abilities. They are masters of exploiting the cracks, crevices, gaps, and hollows that other creatures often avoid or ignore.[1]

Ants work together. They are fearless, even militaristic and conniving at times, but also generous to the point of self-sacrifice. Most often they appear to follow their own agenda, yet they secretly communicate with each other, solving complex problems together and organizing the group without supervision. The largest ant colonies are frequently described as superorganisms or vivisystems, since the individuals operate as a unified entity to maintain the colony. Yet from the perspective of humans, ants are barely noticeable. And when they are noticed, they are most often perceived as a nuisance.

Although I briefly discussed actor-network theory in my book *Sync or Swarm: Improvising Music in a Complex Age*, Bruno Latour's recent overview of the field, *Reassembling the Social*, has reinvigorated my belief that ANT offers an important "material-semiotic approach" that could be invaluable to the study of improvisation.[2] Briefly, ANT begins with the realization that any given interaction overflows with elements from some other time, some other place, and generated by some other agency. But rather than becoming paralyzed by the "actor/system quandary" (essentially the question of whether the actor is "in" a system, or the system is made up of actors), or even attempting to articulate a "happy medium" that considers at once the actor and the network in which it is embedded, ANT redraws the map of the social such that "action is always dislocated, articulated, delegated, translated."[3]

In other words, ANT resists the temptation to invoke social "context" or social "forces," or to invoke the "social" or "society" at all as a type of material with specific properties, since to do so is to accept a collection of assemblages as being fully formed and no longer open to investigation and scrutiny. Latour frequently stresses that society, like nature, is "a premature assemblage" that should be put ahead of us and not behind. His credo for ANT is to "follow the actors themselves!"[4]

Critically, Latour argues for an understanding of actor as *any thing* that modifies a state of affairs by making a difference: any *participant* in the course of action waiting to be given a figuration. The questions to ask, according to Latour, are, "Does it make a difference in the course of some other agent's action or not? Is there some trial that allows someone to detect this difference?"[5] To turn to the contemporary musical domain, it seems clear that things like hardware and software interfaces and their design, the underlying code and coding itself, and even the Internet and its propensity for sharing, collaboration, and institutional gerrymandering, all make a difference.

In ANT, material objects do not "determine" the action. Hardware and software clearly do not determine musical style alone any more than instrument choice does, but neither do they constitute an inert or inconsequential backdrop to the human actor. Latour argues that objects can "authorize, allow, afford, encourage, permit, suggest, influence, block, render possible, forbid, and so on."[6] ANT analysts should be prepared to investigate who and what participates in the action in order to account for the durability and extension of any interaction. We cannot content ourselves, for instance, with the ways in which interactivity is often discussed in computer music circles or in the music industry itself as if it were a quality that is designed into a system a priori. John Bowers's important work on "Ethnographically Informed Design for Improvised Electro-Acoustic Music" goes a considerable distance in this regard.[7]

In my own work in the electro-acoustic environment with trumpeter/computer musician Jeff Kaiser as the duo KaiBorg, our reigning aesthetic has been to devise hybrid instruments that both extend and complicate our sense of agency and control. We wish to avoid the more conventional divisions of performative labor in electro-acoustic music between artists and technologists and between acoustic and electronic performers, as well as any hard and fast distinctions between the so-called "technical" and "non-technical" aspects of our work. To paraphrase Donna Haraway's discourse on the cyborg, we seek pleasure in the confusion of boundaries and accept the responsibility for their construction.[8] One of the challenges we perceive in the current computer-mediated environment for musical improvisation is to avoid a situation in which, to again reference Haraway, our machines are disturbingly lively, and we become frighteningly inert. Instead, we seek a relationship between the cybernetic and organic in which the organism becomes one part of elaborate feedback mechanisms and the cybernetic, in turn, incorporates the sophistication of the organic into its systems. In an earlier essay, I suggested the term "configuring," as it has been used in ANT—and even gave it a Gatesian twist as *configurin'*—as a means of understanding the mutually constitutive processes through which users, technologies, and environments configure one another.[9]

My title for the present article references Gilbert Ryle's well-known critique of the Cartesian duality of mind and body, "the ghost in the machine." In his 1949 book *The Concept of Mind*, in which the phrase first appeared, Ryle challenged the "official doctrine" that mind is "self-luminous," knowing all that it does, including its causation of action.[10] For Ryle, the "dogma" or the "myth" of the "ghost in the machine" is that the "will" is a faculty within the mind, and that mental acts determine physical acts. While Ryle was primarily challenging the views of René Descartes, he was equally critical of B. F. Skinner's behaviorism for its insistence that the actions of conscious individuals were governed exclusively by stimulus-response mechanisms.

In 1967, Arthur Koestler used Ryle's turn of phrase as the title of a book in which he argued that the primitive brain structures upon which the frontal cortex has developed are the true "ghost in the machine," in that they can overpower reason and the higher faculties with destructive impulses.[11] Although unconnected to Ryle's "ghost," we might also add to this list Avery Gordon's provocative book titled *Ghostly Matters*, in which she explores the consequences of the historically situated divide between the social and the individual, the abstract and the concrete, the analytical and the imaginary, and ultimately argues that we desperately need greater knowledge of "the things behind the things."[12]

In this chapter, I wish to extend the thrust, if not always the character, of these perspectives into the realm of musical improvisation, arguing that one of the particular joys of improvising music together is not knowing precisely the relationship either between one's own actions and thoughts or between one's actions and the actions of others (broadly defined). Ultimately, I would like to move the site of inquiry beyond the corporeal and the "social," as it is normally conceived, in order to investigate more fully (following Latour) "the trail of associations between heterogeneous elements." In addition to actor-network theory, I will draw on insight concerning "distributed agency" or "interagency" between humans and technology and on the "extended mind" theory in cognitive science.

CHALLENGING THE OFFICIAL DOCTRINE

The conventional understanding of improvisation, at least in psychological circles, goes something like this: information, in the form of sound waves, impinges on the sensorium (perception); we compute an internal representation of what we are hearing and how we wish to engage/respond (cognition); and we use this to control action (motor). Work by Philip Johnson-Laird and Jeff Pressing, for instance, offers a formalized, computational account of improvisation by maintaining a rather rigid distinction between perceptual and motor considerations and cognitive factors.[13] Philosopher Susan Hurley amusingly characterizes this general orientation: "The mind is a kind of sandwich, and cognition is the filling."[14]

Researchers with interests in phenomenology or embodied cognition tend instead to focus on the physicality of performance, on the instrument itself as a kind of structured environment, and on the intelligence of the body.[15] Others have looked beyond the individual and her instrument to take greater account of evolving group dynamics and shared understandings.[16] Herbert Simon, a Nobel Prize winning psychologist, famously compared the human mind to a pair of scissors: one blade was the brain, while the other blade was the specific environment in which the brain was operating. If you want to understand the function of cognition, Simon reasoned by analogy, you have to look at both blades simultaneously.[17]

It is perhaps uncontentious in the modern era to argue that cognition is both embodied and embedded, in that cognitive processes rely heavily on features of human bodily experience and depend on the use of external resources. The extended mind thesis, however, goes further in arguing that human cognition literally includes elements that lie beyond the boundary of the human organism.[18] Researchers with this orientation argue that we may be better served, in certain instances, by viewing biological, material, and semiotic resources as functionally integrated into an "extended" cognitive system.[19] Ultimately, the extended mind thesis is not simply about the epistemology of mind—how we "talk about" or view cognition—but about the ontology of mind: what literally counts as cognitive.

This is a challenging proposition for many reasons, not the least of which is the simple fact that the terms we use—including "mind," "cognition," and "consciousness," among others—tend to convey the sense of an entity or activity that goes on entirely inside an organism, and most often entirely inside the head. To be clear, the agenda here is not to argue that external artifacts are in and of themselves cognitive, or even that they get to be part of cognition just because they are causally coupled to a preexisting cognitive agent. For example, when we pick up a pencil and paper to write something down, the pencil does not become "cognitive" in its own right. Rather, the goal is to explain, as Richard Menary writes, "why X and Y are so coordinated that they together function as Z, which causes further behavior."[20] Extended mind researchers share a focus on studying the active exercise of cognitive capacities in the real world and a belief that by examining just what is involved in the exercise of some particular cognitive capacity, one finds that it actually does or could well involve causal loops that extend beyond the body of the individual agent.[21]

Coupling through language is the paradigmatic example for many extended mind researchers, since it offers "cognitive scaffolding" to the individual in a way that depends on its social practice. Hilary Putnam's influential work on the social division of linguistic labor demonstrates that there is no requirement that each individual carry the burden of securing meaningful reference for words.[22] For instance, I might use the word "sousaphone" or "crumhorn" and have no idea what the instrument looks like or how it functions. Cognitive neuroscientist and philosopher Alva Noë, in his recent book titled *Out of Our Heads: Why You Are Not Your Brain, and Other Lessons from the Biology of Consciousness*, writes: "Insofar as language is itself socially manufactured and shared by linguistic communities, then to that extent our cognitive powers require for their very exercise the existence of a sociolinguistic environment."[23] Although music does not factor into Noë's argument for a body- and world-involving conception of ourselves, he concludes the book with an explicit analogy: "It is now clear, as it has not been before, that consciousness, *like a work of improvisational music*, is achieved in action, by us, thanks to our situation in and access to a world we know around us. We are in the world and of it."[24]

The perspective of improvising musicians frequently offers compelling motivation for moving beyond a "head-bound" interpretation of cognition. In the 2009 film by Phil Hopkins titled *Amplified Gesture*, saxophonist Evan Parker explains:

> You couple yourself to that instrument and it teaches you as much as you tell it what to do. So you're sensitive to . . . how it's responding to your efforts to control it. By hearing it, the way it's feeding back to you, you learn to control it better. So it's a very dynamic and very sensitive process. And the instrument at the same time seems to be giving you additional information. So [there are] things that you have under your control, but every so often something will go wrong. You'll lose control. In that moment you are given an opportunity to learn something else that the instrument can do. Then gradually the nature of the instrument and its will—it sounds a bit mystical—in relation to its destiny—it sounds Steinerian! [laughs] But let's say the saxophone has a destiny, has a will, and it has a set of intentions in its relationship with you, and you start to find it difficult to distinguish yourself and your intentions from the instrument's intentions, or let's say I've found it difficult to do that.[25]

Parker's comment attests to the idea that our cognitive system can be extended beyond mind-body to mind-body-coupled-with-instrument. Elsewhere Parker reflected on the social dynamics of improvisation:

> However much you try, in a group situation what comes out is group music and some of what comes out was not your idea, but your response to somebody else's idea. . . . The mechanism of what is provocation and what is response—the music is based on such fast interplay, such fast reactions that it is arbitrary to say, "Did you do that because I did that? Or did I do that because you did that?" And anyway the whole thing seems to be operating at a level that involves . . . certainly intuition, and maybe faculties of a more paranormal nature.[26]

If the instrument itself and the social dynamics of performance can affect one's sense of agency, what role might newer musical technologies play? Increasingly the electro-acoustic improvised music landscape involves technologies that can share generation, memory, and judgment capabilities during performance. In Parker's view, "It would sort of be crazy not to work with what's available. . . . The creative and the technological always have a constant kind of interaction, or a feedback relationship with one another. Your notion of what is achievable affects your intentions."[27]

The complex relationship between technological affordances and creative intentions can be even more tangled in the context of a group performance. Reflecting on the practice of his Electro-Acoustic Ensemble, Parker notes: "If you work like this . . . there's a kind of uncertainty about whether that was the first time that sound happened, or 'Did I miss it the first time and that's a replay of a sample of the first time?'"[28]

Among some contemporary improvisers there also appears to be a concerted effort to either reduce, deflect, or decenter human agency and intentionality, whether or not advanced technologies are involved. For instance, the term "lowercase music" describes a fairly recent subgenre of free improvisation that, as the name suggests, tends to avoid overt displays of individual "uppercase" virtuosity. And a recent article by David Toop titled "The Feeling of Rooms" explores the notion of "atmosphere" in improvised music (a concept Toop borrows from guitarist Keith Rowe).[29] Or for one more example, a recent DVD released on the EcoSono label showcasing emergent technological systems and human group improvisation (in many cases recorded together outdoors) is titled *Agents Against Agency*.[30]

I would like to suggest that the agency wielded by the environment is becoming increasingly important, and that artists often articulate this interrelationship in compelling ways. In particular, I argue that free improvisation, especially but not only in the context of its interface with advanced audio and computer technology, affords simultaneously an inroad to participating in complexity and the possibility of creating some provisional closure, some fleeting reduction of complexity, in a world increasingly characterized by relentless machinic heterogenesis.[31] In other words, if machines are to serve as mediators of human co-evolution with the environment, then improvising music under the conditions of hybrid constellations of human and technological actions can offer a situated practice for exploring interagency and the extended mind—in essence providing an avenue for exorcising the ghost in the music.

DISTRIBUTED AGENCY AND THE PUZZLE OF COACTION

In an article exploring distributed agency between humans, machines, and programs, Werner Rammert argues that the meaning of "agent" in the social sciences associated with human intentionality is being transferred to software; we "interact" with machines, and personal software "agents" do much of the communicating, searching, and aggregating for us.[32] In an era of Google algorithms and biotechnology, it often seems as if we are the ones being "objectified"—turned into "standing reserve," to reference Heidegger—as profiling programs multiply and evolved machines and manufactured organisms coexist in the same frame of reference. Lev Manovich, whose theoretical work has been influential in new media studies and what he now terms "software studies," highlights that "transcoding" between the computer layer and the cultural layer—essentially a process of mutual influence—is an intrinsic and unavoidable dimension of our interactions with digital and networked media.[33]

Taking a historical perspective, Rammert identifies a gradual drift over the past several centuries from crafted tools to mechanical machines to automatic systems, and, in terms of their agency, a drift through "passive," "semi-active," "re-active," "pro-active" and, most recently, "co-operative" systems. Rammert argues that a mechanistic vocabulary suffices for describing passive, semi-active, and re-active behaviors, but that we must adopt a notion of interagency with regard to humans and machines when discussing systems capable of actively searching for new information, either to select behavior or to change a pre-given frame of action.

Adopting for the moment Rammert's engineering terminology, most conventional musical instruments are "passive," in that they are completely moved from outside (from a phenomenological perspective, however, the relationship created as a musician *plays* an instrument is often anything but passive!). "Semi-active" instruments are those that have one aspect of self-acting, including things like mechanical organs and vibraphones. More recent electric and electronic instruments often exploit the "re-active" aspects of feedback loops and delay, among other things, while "pro-active" instruments are increasingly those that operate in the digital realm. Here we might think of sequencers, score-following programs, and other intelligent accompaniment systems that utilize self-activating programs and subroutines.

The final category of "co-operative" agency could describe both the distributed and self-coordinating systems and networks that compose the "workflow" of countless contemporary musicians and, more specifically, the technical design for many interactive environments for improvisation. Describing the earliest generation of these "interactive composing instruments," as he terms them, Joel Chadabe writes that they "made musical decisions as they responded to a performer, introducing the concept of shared symbiotic control of a musical process."[34]

If technical objects can exhibit multiple and often overlapping levels of agency, then what of human beings? I am tempted to employ a similar five-part taxonomy to describe levels of human agency, moving from "repressed," "rote," and "routine" behaviors (for which mechanistic vocabulary may often suffice) to "reflexive" and "reflective" agency. Contrary to the "free-from-habit-and-influence" discourse that all too often circulates around free improvisation, much of the effort involved in cultivating expertise—whether musical or not—involves building up fluency and automaticity so that one may be more "reflexive" and "reflective" in performance. "As I write my mind is not preoccupied with how my fingers form the letters," wrote Sir Charles Sherrington in 1906, "my attention is fixed simply on the thoughts the words express. But there was a time when the formation of the letters, as each one was written, would have occupied my whole attention."[35] Envisioning the five "Rs" of human agency positioned in a spiral configuration rather than in a linear or even circular arrangement might help conceptualize the way in which many improvisers do use reflective agency to confront their own repressed, rote, and routine activities, or just as often to challenge those of the musicians with whom they improvise.[36]

Yet I fear that this perspective subscribes all too easily to Ryle's ghost in the machine, presenting agency—or at least that agency that matters most—in the form of an independent, internal, and fully controllable "will" that reflects and in turn authors one's thoughts and actions. Experimental evidence demonstrates that our actions are often either initiated from below the level of our "conscious" awareness or inflected by social dynamics of which we are seldom aware.[37] For example, when a professional baseball player "decides" to tip his bat just up or just down as the pitch crosses the plate, he is performing a feat that, due to processing speed considerations alone, cannot possibly be conscious or involve the frontal cortex. A similar process may be involved in the rapid-fire aspects of Parker's solo saxophone playing. For a more commonplace example, consider that when raising one's arm the brain can actually prepare the action before its "conscious" operator is aware that it is doing so. And perhaps even more surprising, one's experience of "authorship" can be enhanced or undermined relatively easily by externally directed attention or by manipulation of environmental and social conditions.

Harvard social psychologist Daniel M. Wegner uses some deceptively simple alphabet pointing experiments (involving paired participants working simultaneously and in leading and following arrangements) to demonstrate how one's experience of "authorship" can be extremely sensitive to external social pressures.[38] Wegner argues that people come to understand their actions as their own by using proprioception (the mind's ability to learn from the body itself), establishing how the mind may have contributed to action (via intention, planning, and premeditation), and incorporating external information about the social circumstance of the action (the presence and potential contribution of other agents).

For Wegner, these three indicators of authorship may add or subtract from each other such that the experience of conscious will is the final common pathway that produces the sense of "I did it," "I didn't do it," or any gradations in between. In place of a "ghostly" faculty within the mind that controls action, Wegner envisions a conscious will that *emerges from* the mind's efforts to understand its own authorship. He uses this insight, and our propensity for social accounting (to constantly keep track of who does what), to conclude that "authorship judgments have evolved to account for own agency in a social world where agency in coaction is the measure of all things."[39]

Following Wegner's insight, I would like to argue that a similar balancing act is at play in improvised music, as individual musicians combine informational pathways from proprioception, intention/planning/premeditation (inspiration?), and the social circumstance of performance gleaned from the shared acoustic, visual, and material space and the presence and potential contribution of other agents writ large. It may be that improvised music also offers a shared experience by which we can, at least temporarily, lessen our grip on social accounting and celebrate—rather than merely puzzle over—coaction.[40]

WHO IS REALLY MAKING THE MUSIC?

The notion of "own agency" in improvisation is an important subject about which there is little agreement. It may seem incontrovertible that improvisation is about human agency and intentionality. To improvise requires the capacity to act, and for it to mean anything at all it must surely be "about" something, a common definition of intentionality. Duke Ellington famously remarked: "Improvisation? Anyone who plays anything worth hearing knows what he's going to play, no matter whether he prepares a day ahead or a beat ahead. It has to be with intent."[41] And yet, while improvising it can remain unclear at times from where and whence intention and agency actually arise. "The best bits of my solo playing," Evan Parker reflects, "I can't explain to myself."[42]

Scholarship on musical improvisation tends to be either concerned with the ways in which creative expression is structured and confined by certain rules and traditions, usually conceived of as a model or referent stored in long-term memory, or the ways in which individual artists variously confront their influences (in culturally informed ways ranging from anxiety-ridden to ecstatic).[43] While I find these discussions illuminating, and it is often useful to explore free improvisation as a fascinating boundary case for these various contentions, I wish here to return to the question of distributed agency between humans, machines, and programs and, in particular, to extend the inquiry further into the realm of electro-acoustic music.

One reason for pursuing this is that electronics, on a purely technical level, can easily produce dissociating factors in musical production and reception. The history and impact of sound recording technology, for instance, has been a favorite topic of scholars pursuing this argument,[44] but additional shifts over the last century or so in sound reinforcement (microphones, amplifiers, loud speakers), sound production (synthesis, sampling), sound transformation (signal processing), and sound control (gesture mapping, for example) offer equally pronounced dissociative potential.

Since the late 1960s, amplification and electronics have played an important role in free improvisation, and arguably much electro-acoustic improvisation begins from the realization that the "one-gesture-to-one-acoustic-event" paradigm has been broken.[45] Pioneering groups such as Musica Elettronica Viva, AMM, and Music Improvisation Company used "homemade" electronics to amplify "small" sounds, frequently introducing unexpected sonic elements that seemed unconnected to human agency. Writing about his time with Musica Elettronica Viva, Alvin Curran recounts:

> We found ourselves busily soldering cables, contact mikes, and talking about "circuitry" as if it were a new religion. By amplifying the sounds of glass, wood, metal, water, air, and fire, we were convinced we had tapped into the sources of the natural musics of "everything." We were in fact making a spontaneous music which could be said to be coming from "nowhere" and made out of "nothing"—all somewhat a wonder and a collective epiphany.[46]

In the wake of noise, techno, house, and hip-hop, and the ceaseless development of sampling, sequencing, synthesizing, and signal processing technologies, among other things, the scene today seems decidedly different. Following Rammert, we might wish to argue that a qualitative shift in the level of technical agency—or, better stated, human-machine *interagency*—is now achieved when advanced computer programs participate in or take over planning and control activities and their intelligent coordination.

To illustrate this point, Rammert asks the compelling question: "Who is really flying the Airbus?" While we may commonly assign agency to the pilot, in reality the plane transports a load of passengers safely from point A to point B only if the entire system of people (e.g., pilot, co-pilot, radio operator, flight controller, tourist office, airline company, and aviation industry), machines (e.g., engines, rudders, radio equipment, radar, booking machine, aviation technology, and air traffic system), and programs (auto-pilot software, navigation systems, radio signals, radar screening, reservation software, and R&D, and infrastructure plans) are operating successfully and together.

We might ask a similar question about electro-acoustic improvised music performance: "Who is really making the music?" Although we may wish to attribute agency only to the human performers (and undoubtedly this is still a primary draw for audiences, especially in the context of "live" performance), similar systemic relationships between people, machines, and programs are deeply implicated and coordinated. Rough analogies to the human and technical infrastructure involved in flying an Airbus can be located in the musical realm as performers, audiences, sound reinforcement technicians, instrument designers, interface programmers, promoters, and many others exhibit interagency with an enormous variety of musical, audio, and computer hardware, software, and media, the performance space(s), and institutional programs and plans, among other things.

Another possible approach to answering the question of "Who is really making the music?" is to focus instead on the "perceptual agency" of the listener, or the idea that what we hear in a particular performance depends, in part, on where we focus our attention.[47] Reflecting on his work with the Electro-Acoustic Ensemble, Parker comments: "There's so much going on, so I think the ideal mix is beyond anybody's imagination because no one knows what is the total complement of sonic activity—you only know what you hear."[48] But returning us to the individual cognitive agent as the locus of activity does not necessarily reduce or remove the complexity from the situation, and it runs the risk of keeping us embroiled in the methodological individualism and representationalist paradigm that has historically dominated studies of music cognition and psychology.

Even our most mundane tasks now occur across the backdrop of complex computational infrastructures, what geographer Nigel Thrift has dubbed the "technological unconscious."[49] Drawing on Thrift's work, philosopher Mark B. N. Hansen argues that a pressing question for contemporary cultural theorists is: "How can one recognize the certain consistency, perhaps even the autonomy, of the (individual or collective) human mindbody and at the same time account for the certain non-autonomy that accrues from its unavoidable reliance on the agency of informationally complex environments to achieve its cognitive tasks?"[50]

Hansen's question has a particular relevance to the realm of technologically mediated improvised music performance. Can (or should?) we continue to speak of the autonomy of the improviser even as her performance practice is ever more embedded in a network of agents and informationally complex environments? Not only has the "one gesture to one acoustic event paradigm" been broken, but physical, cognitive, spatial, and even geographic constraints no longer adhere in quite the same way.[51] The mandate in improvisation to compose music together "in the course of performance" does provide an important aspect of "operational closure," as does the flexibility of our autopoietic nature, our "organismic closure," but increasingly we are being asked to, in Hansen's words, "combine multiple and heterogeneous closures in order to act in the world."[52]

Katherine Hayles's frequently cited book, *How We Became Posthuman*, details the complex and conflicted history of this emerging orientation while also cautioning us against capitulating too easily to dominant strains of thought in cybernetics and information theory.[53] Andy Clark's equally influential work argues that the overriding question is not how we became posthuman, but rather how we have always been posthuman, or as he prefers, "natural-born cyborgs" or "open-ended opportunistic controllers."[54] Alexander Weheliye, conversely, focuses on the racial and cultural dimensions of posthuman discourse and argues that people in the African diaspora, in particular, were never human to begin with, and therefore the desired "escape" from the liberal humanist subject so often found in writing about the posthuman actually begins from rather tenuous footing.[55] Similarly, George E. Lewis, drawing on the important work of Lucy Suchman on interactivity, argues that dominant discourses and research directions in artificial intelligence continue to assume Euro-American models of human agency and subjectivity.[56] Improvising in a technologically saturated realm may offer an avenue through which we can explore the active role that the environment plays in driving cognitive processes, but the choices we make, and the relationships we forge, remain critical in this endeavor.

WHERE DO WE GO FROM HERE?

Even if we take the dissociative dimensions of musical technology as a given—a position, I should add, that may subscribe too easily to technological determinism and run counter to much of the extended mind argument—where do we go from here? Some may simply view the current situation as another opportunity for humans to shape the environment according to their creative whims. For instance, Simon Emmerson seems to subscribe to this view when he writes: "We no longer assert our human presence only by hitting, scraping, and blowing the objects around us, but through reasserting our power over the new medium—using it as source."[57]

Lewis, however, has repeatedly stressed in both his musical and scholarly work that "the improvised musical encounter may be seen as a negotiation between musicians, some of whom are people, others not." Lewis is willing not only to extend agency to machines but also a certain empathy to his non-human partners. "Decisions taken by the computer have consequences for the music that must be taken into account by the human improvisors, an aesthetic of variation and difference," Lewis reminds us, "that is clearly at variance with the information retrieval and control paradigm that late capitalism has found useful in the encounter with interactive multimedia and hypertext discourses."[58]

Despite Lewis's insightful critique, I worry that we are in danger of replacing the false dichotomy between mind and body—the ghost in the machine—with a trichotomy of mind/body/machine that continues to avoid complex issues foregrounded by human/ non-human entanglements. Simply admitting machines into the realm of agency, as Rammert and Lewis are willing to do, may not be enough. This alone cannot adequately confront the still dominant tendency to make a stark division between humans and their technological environment: in other words, to separate arbitrarily "what we make" from "who we (think we) are." Further, in separating machines and programs, as Rammert suggests, are we simply recreating the mind/body split in the technical realm?[59]

In some ways, ANT extends the "material-semiotic" understanding of the extended mind thesis outward beyond individual cognition to gain a better understanding of how assemblages and collectives are formed. Latour asks that we "restudy what we are made of and extend the repertoire of ties and the number of associations way beyond the repertoire proposed by social explanations." He equally insists that we make ourselves "sensitive again to the sheer difficulty of assembling collectives made of so many new members once nature and society have been simultaneously put aside." I find this orientation to be, in interesting ways, analogous to the challenges posed and faced by contemporary musicians. The musician-to-musician interactions that we experience through improvised music are undoubtedly the terminus point of a great number of agencies swimming toward them. And in the wake of the significant rupturing and rethinking of music and musical style that took place in the last century, contemporary musicians are now often faced with the daunting challenge of "assembling collectives," both for their own personal musical use (as in "technical" assemblages of instruments, devices, and interfaces, or as in a personal "vocabulary" of techniques, among other things) and for the purpose of creating a communal sensibility and shared commitment (as evidenced by the many artist-run and community-oriented collectives that nurture the music).

Although Latour considered many times renaming the field that he helped to initiate—due in no small part to the many misrepresentations it has spawned in the intervening decades—in *Reassembling the Social* he fully embraces the name as well as its acronym, since ants, after all, are "myopic, workaholic, trail-sniffing and collective traveller(s)."

As an improviser, I proudly wear the moniker of ant as well. Improvisers, like their ANT counterparts, can be equally single-minded and dedicated, while also supportive and community-minded. Free improvisation, filled as it sometimes is with quick reactions and dense soundscapes, has even inspired literal analogies to insect behavior. Toop writes: "Perhaps it was no coincidence that in the wake of drummer John Stevens and the Spontaneous Music Ensemble, certain strands of English improvised music were known, half-disparagingly as insect music."[60] And John Corbett once compared the improvisation community to "ants stripping a carcass," working "from the inside and outside of codes."[61]

Latour argues that "it is only the freshness of the results of social science that can guarantee its relevance." He stresses that ANT researchers must work to counteract the premature transformation of what he calls "matters of concern" into "matters of fact," a position that seems equally applicable to musical improvisers, who must work to counteract premature closures on interactional strategies and sonic techniques/resources, among other things.

Ultimately, how we conceive of and value ant-like behavior also tells us as much about ourselves as it does about ants. The discourse that has surrounded improvisation, and the presumed binary between it and composition, reveals much about the ways in which cultural understandings are often reflected, reshaped, or remain concealed as we continue assembling collectives together. Lewis notes, "In Euro-American art-music culture this binary [between improvisation and composition] is routinely and simplistically framed as involving the 'effortless spontaneity' of improvisation, versus the careful deliberation of composition—the composer as ant, the improviser as grasshopper."[62]

In addition to their impressive individual and collective behaviors, ants also co-evolve with other species to form complex interrelationships ranging from mimetic (involving mimicry) and parasitic (where one organism benefits and the other is harmed), to commensal (where one organism benefits and the other is unharmed) and mutualistic (where both organisms benefit). It may be that these relationships also capture an essence of the ways in which improvisation plays a role in all musical traditions, and, writ large, dynamically informs our shared existence.

A PROVISIONAL CLOSURE

In this chapter I have focused on electro-acoustic improvisation as a useful site of inquiry, since in this domain musicians are entering into increasingly immersive relations with their instruments and forming increasingly complex machine-body assemblages. All music, however, relies on an interconnected series of material mediations involving sound sources and spaces, for instance, as well as other mediations that may be more tradition-dependent, such as scores and staging in Western European art music. Ultimately, I have argued that we are better served by notions of interagency and interactive contingency between heterogeneous sources of activities than with the dual concept of human action as intentional and creative and material and machine activity as inert, repetitive, or rule-following.

This realization, however, does not preclude the need to interrogate the ways in which notions of the "technical" and the "non-technical" are used—when, by whom, and to what effect—as well as to what extent this distinction itself performs different communities. In an article discussing glitch music and ANT (as well as Bourdieu), Nick Prior argues that we need to give increased attention to "how machines produce as well as get produced, enable as well as constrain, act as well as react," but that in addition to opening the "black box of technology," we must do the same for the "well-regulated ballet of the field."[63]

Although the current essay makes only limited inroads in that regard, my contention is that the provisional closure provided by electro-acoustic improvised music performance—it begins, it ends, it starts anew—can celebrate our fundamental and shared humanity even as it tracks the alterations imposed on it by our ever accelerating environmental complexity. Undoubtedly, one of the ongoing challenges that artists face while working in the rapidly evolving musical technoscape is the extent to which one chooses to spend one's time either negotiating new "interface" environments or developing knowledge, connection, and intuition within more familiar ones. The trend in recent years toward "ubiquitous," "social," "tangible," and "wearable" computing, as well as advances in audio and gesture recognition technology, among other things, has the potential to make our interfaces more intuitive, but also portends to make the computer even more entangled in our daily and artistic lives.

Hansen argues that we face an ethical imperative "to avoid the twin temptations posed by contemporary environmental complexity": either "to dissolve boundaries altogether" and therefore flatten our notions of agency across human and technical configurations, or "to harden boundaries into a handful of durable autopoietic system types," which may only redraft previous distinctions between the human and the technical. In the end, Hansen believes that we must maintain a commitment to "the irreducibility of the human perspective" and to "the human as a form of living, in the face of its ever more complexly configured technical distribution."[64]

While I agree with Hansen's well-honed argument and heartfelt position, our cognitive and creative abilities are not, nor have they ever been, achievements we reach in isolation. Creativity is an interactive process and a consequence of the material-semiotic scaffolding of culture. One goal of Gary Peters's recent book *The Philosophy of Improvisation* is to liberate improvisation studies from "the foibles and idiosyncrasies of individual practitioners and their self-legitimizing discourses" and to strip it of "the humanistic and expressionistic cultural garb that clings to it."[65] Admittedly, this is still a daunting and potentially dangerous challenge.

An approach inspired by ANT and the "extended mind" theories of cognition might, however, give us some theoretical and empirical teeth to speak more precisely about the evolving "group mind" or "group flow"—ideas that many improvisers already feel comfortable discussing—by investigating how bodily and interpersonal negotiations and the manipulation of external cognitive resources are coordinated in such a way that they jointly cause further behavior. At the very least, this orientation can help us look beyond the false opposition between social and ecological relations and avoid assuming that the workings of the mind can be equated with the operation of neural machinery.

It may be that those most interested in identifying themselves as "improvisers," regardless of their particular passions or lot in life, are simply by disposition those most willing to engage with—and rely upon—the complexity and unpredictability of brain, body, and world integration. The feeling of extending one's mind and consciousness across the sonic, social, and material environment that can emerge from the improvised encounter can be transformative. But it also may not last much beyond it. Not all occasions of improvising music will even engender this "out of one's head" feeling. Even glimpses of this feeling, however, and the growing body of research from several disciplines that helps to support it, may reveal previously hidden depths and afford new methodologies and perspectives. It may also help us avoid attributing agency only to individual human motivations, skills, and activities, "the ghost in the music," and instead to find it in the nexus of personal, interpersonal, and material factors—the "ant."

Notes

1. Mark W. Moffett, *Adventures Among Ants: A Global Safari with a Cast of Trillions* (Berkeley: University of California Press, 2010), 10.
2. David Borgo, *Sync or Swarm: Improvising Music in a Complex Age* (London and New York: Continuum, 2005); and Bruno Latour, *Reassembling the Social: An Introduction to Actor-Network Theory* (New York: Oxford University Press, 2005), Kindle edition.
3. Latour, *Reassembling the Social*, location 2225.
4. Ibid., location 3231.
5. Ibid., location 937.
6. Ibid., location 3231.
7. John Bowers, "Improvising Machines: Ethnographically Informed Design for Improvised Electro-Acoustic Music," M.A. Thesis (University of East Anglia, Norwich, UK, 2002).
8. Donna Haraway, "A Cyborg Manifesto: Science, Technology, and Socialist-Feminism in the Late Twentieth Century," in *Simians, Cyborgs and Women: The Reinvention of Nature* (New York: Routledge, 1991), 149–181.
9. David Borgo and Jeff Kaiser, "Configurin(g) KaiBorg: Ideology, Identity and Agency in Electro-Acoustic Improvised Music," in *Beyond the Centres: Musical Avant-Gardes Since 1950* (conference proceedings, 2010), available at http://btc.web.auth.gr/proceedings.html. The Gatesian twist refers to the influential work of Henry Louis Gates, Jr., *The Signifying Monkey: A Theory of Afro-American Literary Criticism* (New York: Oxford University Press, 1988).
10. Gilbert Ryle, *The Concept of Mind* (Chicago: University of Chicago Press, 1949).
11. Arthur Koestler, *The Ghost in the Machine* (New York: Macmillan, 1967).
12. Avery F. Gordon, *Ghostly Matters: Haunting and the Sociological Imagination* (Minneapolis: University of Minnesota Press, 2008).
13. See, for example, P. N. Johnson-Laird, "How Jazz Musicians Improvise," *Music Perception* 19, no. 3 (Spring 2002): 415–442; and Jeff Pressing, "Improvisation: Methods and Models," in *Generative Processes in Music: The Psychology of Performance, Improvisation, and Composition*, ed. John A. Sloboda (Oxford: Clarendon Press, 1988), 129–178. It should be noted that the vast majority of music psychology research has focused on how we perceive and process music from the listener's perspective. Issues of music performance and improvisation have received far less attention, largely due to the breadth of variability and creativity contained within these topics.
14. S. L. Hurley, "Active Perception and Vehicle Externalism," in *Consciousness in Action*, ed. S. L. Hurley (Cambridge: Harvard University Press, 1998), 401.
15. See for example David Sudnow, *Ways of the Hand: The Organization of Improvised Conduct* (Cambridge, MA: Harvard University Press, 1978); and Vijay Iyer, "Embodied Mind, Situated Cognition, and Expressive Microtiming in African-American Music," *Music Perception* 19, no. 3 (Spring 2002): 387–414.
16. See, for example, Mihaly Csikszentmihalyi and Grant Jewell Rich, "Musical Improvisation: A Systems Approach," in *Creativity in Performance*, ed. R. Keith Sawyer (Greenwich, CT:

Ablex Publishing Group, 1997), 43–66; R. Keith Sawyer, *Group Creativity: Music, Theater, Collaboration* (Mahwah, NJ: L. Erlbaum Associates, 2003); and Howard S. Becker and Robert R. Faulkner, *Do You Know . . . ? The Jazz Repertoire in Action* (Chicago: University of Chicago Press, 2009).

17. Herbert A. Simon, "Invariants of Human Behavior," *Annual Review of Psychology* 41 (January 1990): 1–19.

18. See Andy Clark and David J. Chalmers, "The Extended Mind," *Analysis* 58, no. 1 (January 1998): 10–23.

19. Research related to the extended mind thesis can also be found under the headings of active or situated cognition, locational externalism, and wide computation.

20. Richard Menary, "Introduction: The Extended Mind in Focus," in *The Extended Mind*, ed. Richard Menary (Cambridge, MA: MIT Press, 2010), 12. Among the most compelling empirical evidence for the extended mind thesis are studies of memory, visual perception, and problem solving that demonstrate both the integration of explicit symbols located in an organism's environment into that organism's cognitive regime, and the cognitive incorporation of nonsymbolic aspects of one's environment, which might include things like social networks and bodily activities (both one's own and others). This general theoretical orientation is also supported by considerable recent thinking in genetics, developmental systems biology, and environmental physiology. For more on these topics see Robert A. Wilson, "Meaning Making and the Mind of the Externalist," in *The Extended Mind*, ed. Richard Menary, 167–188 (Cambridge, MA: MIT Press, 2010).

21. The literature employs terms such as "cognitive system" and "cognitive resource" to avoid the individualistic framework that tends to dominate thinking about cognitive agency. Some critics, however, fear that the extended mind thesis flouts the distinction between intrinsic and derived intentionality, or that it mistakes extracranial aids to cognition for the real vehicles of cognition. Others find it too conservative, insofar as it can be read to support a representationalist (rather than an anti-representationalist) version of postcognitivism, or that it precludes the extension of the idea of cognition to other, less complicated life forms.

22. Hilary Putnam, "The Meaning of 'Meaning,'" in *Philosophical Papers*, vol. 2, *Mind, Language, and Reality* (Cambridge: Cambridge University Press, 1975).

23. Alva Noë, *Out of Our Heads: Why You Are Not Your Brain, and Other Lessons from the Biology of Consciousness* (New York: Hill and Wang, 2009), 88.

24. Ibid., 186, emphasis added.

25. Phil Hopkins, dir., *Amplified Gesture*, DVD, prod. by David Sylvian (London: Opium (Arts) Ltd., 2009).

26. Quoted in John Corbett, *Extended Play: Sounding Off from John Cage to Dr. Funkenstein* (Durham: Duke University Press, 1994), 203.

27. Quoted in Peter Margasak, "Evan Parker: Making Music with Music," *Chicago Reader*, September 24, 2009, accessed June 10, 2011, http://www.chicagoreader.com/chicago/evan-parker-making-music-from-music/Content?oid=1200713.

28. Ibid.

29. David Toop, "The Feeling of Rooms," in *Blocks of Consciousness and the Unbroken Continuum*, ed. Brian Marley and Mark Wastell (London: Sound 323, 2005), 308–327.

30. *Agents Against Agency: Musical Emergence in Dialog with Nature*, DVD (Ecosono, 2011).

31. For more on these topics see Mark B. N. Hansen and Bruce Clarke, *Emergence and Embodiment: New Essays on Second-Order Systems Theory* (Durham: Duke University

Press, 2009); and Félix Guattari, "Machinic Heterogenesis," trans. James Creech, in *Rethinking Technologies*, ed. Verena Andermatt Conley, et al. (Minneapolis: University of Minnesota Press, 1993), 13–28.

32. Werner Rammert, "Where the Action Is: Distributed Agency Between Humans, Machines, and Programs" in *Paradoxes of Interactivity*, ed. Uwe Seifert, Jin Hyun Kim, and Anthony Moore (New Brunswick and London: Transaction Publishers, 2008), 63–91.

33. Lev Manovich, *The Language of New Media* (Cambridge, MA: MIT Press, 2002).

34. Joel Chadabe, *Electric Sound: The Past and Promise of Electronic Music* (Upper Saddle River, NJ: Prentice Hall, 1997), 201.

35. Charles Sherrington, *The Integrative Action of the Nervous System* (New Haven, CT: Yale University Press, 1906).

36. For related work, see Donald A. Schön, *Educating the Reflective Practitioner* (San Francisco: Jossey-Bass, 1990).

37. See Don Ross, "Introduction: Science Catches the Will," in *Distributed Cognition and the Will: Individual Volition in Social Context*, ed. Don Ross et al. (Cambridge, MA: MIT Press, 2007), 1–16.

38. Daniel M. Wegner and Betsy Sparrow, "The Puzzle of Coaction," in *Distributed Cognition and the Will: Individual Volition in Social Context*, ed. Don Ross et al. (Cambridge, MA: MIT Press, 2008), 17–38.

39. Wegner, "The Puzzle of Coaction," 31.

40. Musical improvisation is not alone in this regard. Wegner briefly cites the dancing of Fred Astaire and Ginger Rodgers as exemplary coaction, and other intimate partner relationships would fit the bill as well.

41. Quoted in Gabriel Solis and Bruno Nettl, eds., *Musical Improvisation: Art, Education, and Society* (Urbana and Chicago: University of Illinois Press, 2009), ix.

42. Quoted in Graham Lock, "After the New: Evan Parker, Speaking of the Essence," *The Wire* 85 (1991): 33. The historical distance between these two speakers is telling. Ellington developed his art in a society that too frequently dismissed African American creativity as "improvised" in the pejorative sense of the word, and Parker came of age "across the pond" at a time when a "culture of spontaneity" was increasingly revered rather than reviled. Despite these differences, similar views to those held by Ellington and Parker, I argue, still hold sway in the contemporary improvised music community.

43. See Bruno Nettl, "Thoughts on Improvisation: A Comparative Approach," *The Musical Quarterly* 60, no. 1 (January 1974), 1–19. For a range of opinion on influence and artistry see Harold Bloom, *The Anxiety of Influence* (New York: Oxford University Press, 1997); John Murphy, "Jazz Improvisation: The Joy of Influence," *The Black Perspective in Music* 18, no. 1–2 (1990): 7–19; and Jonathan Lethem, "The Ecstasy of Influence" in *Sound Unbound*, ed. Paul D. Miller, 25–52 (Cambridge, MA: MIT Press, 2008).

44. See, for instance, Mark Katz, *Capturing Sound: How Technology Changed Music*, rev. ed. (Berkeley: University of California Press, 2010).

45. David Wessel and Matthew Wright, "Problems and Prospects for Intimate Musical Control of Computers," *Computer Music Journal* 26, no. 3 (Fall 2002): 11–22.

46. Alvin Curran, "Cage's Influence: A Panel Discussion" (with Gordon Mumma, Allan Kaprow, James Tenney, Christian Wolff, Alvin Curran, and Maryanne Amacher), in *Writings Through John Cage's Music, Poetry, and Art*, ed. David W. Bernstein and Christopher Hatch (Chicago: University of Chicago Press, 2001), 177–178.

47. See Ingrid Monson, "Jazz as Political and Musical Practice," in *Musical Improvisation: Art, Education, and Society*, ed. Gabriel Solis and Bruno Nettl (Urbana and Chicago: University of Illinois Press, 2009), 21–37.
48. Quoted in Margasak, "Evan Parker," n.p.
49. Nigel Thrift, "Remembering the Technological Unconscious by Foregrounding Knowledges of Position," *Environment and Planning D: Society and Space* 22 (2004): 175–190.
50. Mark B. N. Hansen, "System-Environment Hybrids," in *Emergence and Embodiment: New Essays on Second-Order Systems Theory*, ed. Mark B. N. Hansen and Bruce Clarke (Durham: Duke University Press, 2009), 117.
51. David Borgo, "Beyond Performance: Transmusicking in Cyberspace," in *Taking It to the Bridge: Music as Performance*, ed. Nicholas Cook and Richard Pettengill (Ann Arbor: University of Michigan Press, 2013), 319–348.
52. Hansen, "System-Environment Hybrids," 118.
53. N. Katherine Hayles, *How We Became Posthuman: Virtual Bodies in Cybernetics, Literature, and Informatics* (Chicago: University of Chicago Press, 1999).
54. Andy Clark, *Natural-Born Cyborgs: Minds, Technologies, and the Future of Human Intelligence* (New York: Oxford University Press, 2003).
55. Alexander G. Weheliye, "Feenin': Posthuman Voices in Contemporary Black Popular Music," *Social Text* 20, no. 2 (Summer 2002): 21–47.
56. George E. Lewis, "Mobilitas Animi: Improvising Technologies, Intending Chance," *Parallax* 13, no. 4 (2007): 111; and Lucy A. Suchman, *Human-Machine Reconfigurations: Plans and Situated Actions*, 2nd ed. (New York: Cambridge University Press, 2007).
57. Simon Emmerson, "'Losing Touch?': The Human Performer and Electronics," in *Music, Electronic Media and Culture*, ed. Simon Emmerson (Burlington, VT: Ashgate Publishing, 2000), 212.
58. George E. Lewis, "Live Algorithms and the Future of Music," *Cyberinfrastructure Technology Watch Quarterly* (May 2007), accessed June 10, 2011, http://www.ctwatch.org.
59. Jeff Kaiser astutely pointed this out after an earlier presentation of this material, and he is engaging this issue in his doctoral research in music at the University of California, San Diego.
60. David Toop, "Frame of Freedom: Improvisation, Otherness and the Limits of Spontaneity," in *Undercurrents: The Hidden Wiring of Modern Music* (New York and London: Continuum, 2002), 247.
61. John Corbett, "Ephemera Underscored: Writing Around Free Improvisation," in *Jazz Among the Discourses*, ed. Krin Gabbard (Durham: Duke University Press, 1995), 237.
62. George Lewis, "Too Many Notes: Computers, Complexity, and Culture," *Leonardo Music Journal* 10, no. 1 (December 2000): 38.
63. Nick Prior, "Putting a Glitch in the Field: Bourdieu, Actor Network Theory, and Contemporary Music," *Cultural Sociology* 2, no. 3 (November, 2008): 314, 316.
64. Hansen, "System-Environment Hybrids," 126.
65. Gary Peters, *The Philosophy of Improvisation* (Chicago: University of Chicago Press, 2009), 169.

BIBLIOGRAPHY

Becker, Howard S., and Robert R. Faulkner. *Do You Know . . .? The Jazz Repertoire in Action.* Chicago: University of Chicago Press, 2009.

Bloom, Harold. *The Anxiety of Influence*. 2nd ed. New York: Oxford University Press, 1997.

Borgo, David. "Beyond Performance: Transmusicking in Cyberspace." In *Taking It to the Bridge: Music as Performance*, edited by Nicholas Cook and Richard Pettengill, 319–348. Ann Arbor: University of Michigan Press, 2013.

Borgo, David. *Sync or Swarm: Improvising Music in a Complex Age*. London and New York: Continuum, 2005.

Borgo, David, and Jeff Kaiser. "Configurin(g) KaiBorg: Ideology, Identity and Agency in Electro-Acoustic Improvised Music." In *Beyond the Centres: Musical Avant-Gardes Since 1950*, conference proceedings, 2010. available at http://btc.web.auth.gr/proceedings.html.

Bowers, John. "Improvising Machines: Ethnographically Informed Design for Improvised Electro-Acoustic Music." M.A. Thesis, University of East Anglia, Norwich, UK, 2002.

Chadabe, Joel. *Electric Sound: The Past and Promise of Electronic Music*. Upper Saddle River, NJ: Prentice Hall, 1997.

Clark, Andy. *Natural-Born Cyborgs: Minds, Technologies, and the Future of Human Intelligence*. New York: Oxford University Press, 2003.

Clark, Andy, and David J. Chalmers. "The Extended Mind." *Analysis* 58, no. 1 (January 1998): 10–23.

Corbett, John. "Ephemera Underscored: Writing Around Free Improvisation." In *Jazz Among the Discourses*, edited by Krin Gabbard, 217–242. Durham: Duke University Press, 1995.

Corbett, John. *Extended Play: Sounding Off from John Cage to Dr. Funkenstein*. Durham: Duke University Press, 1994.

Csikszentmihalyi, Mihaly, and Grant Jewell Rich. "Musical Improvisation: A Systems Approach." In *Creativity in Performance*, edited by R. Keith Sawyer, 43–66. Greenwich, CT: Ablex Publishing Group, 1997.

Curran, Alvin. "Cage's Influence: A Panel Discussion" (with Gordon Mumma, Allan Kaprow, James Tenney, Christian Wolff, Alvin Curran, and Maryanne Amacher). In *Writings Through John Cage's Music, Poetry, and Art*, edited by David W. Bernstein and Christopher Hatch, 167–189. Chicago: University of Chicago Press, 2001.

Emmerson, Simon, ed. *Music, Electronic Media and Culture*. Burlington, VT: Ashgate, 2000.

Gates, Henry Louis, Jr. *The Signifying Monkey: A Theory of Afro-American Literary Criticism*. New York: Oxford University Press, 1988.

Gordon, Avery F. *Ghostly Matters: Haunting and the Sociological Imagination*. Minneapolis: University of Minnesota Press, 2008.

Guattari, Félix. "Machinic Heterogenesis." In *Rethinking Technologies*, edited by Verena Andermatt Conley, et al., translated by James Creech, 13–28. Minneapolis: University of Minnesota Press, 1993.

Hansen, Mark B. N., and Bruce Clarke, eds. *Emergence and Embodiment: New Essays on Second-Order Systems Theory*. Durham: Duke University Press, 2009.

Haraway, Donna. *Simians, Cyborgs, and Women: The Reinvention of Nature*. New York: Routledge, 1991.

Hayles, N. Katherine. *How We Became Posthuman: Virtual Bodies in Cybernetics, Literature, and Informatics*. Chicago: University of Chicago Press, 1999.

Hopkins, Phil, dir. *Amplified Gesture*, produced by David Sylvian. DVD. London: Opium (Arts) Ltd., 2009.

Hurley, S. L., ed. *Consciousness in Action*. Cambridge: Harvard University Press, 1998.

Iyer, Vijay. "Embodied Mind, Situated Cognition, and Expressive Microtiming in African-American Music." *Music Perception* 19, no. 3 (Spring 2002): 387–414.

Johnson-Laird, P. N. "How Jazz Musicians Improvise." *Music Perception* 19, no. 3 (Spring 2002): 415–442.

Katz, Mark. *Capturing Sound: How Technology Changed Music*. Rev. ed. Berkeley: University of California Press, 2010.

Koestler, Arthur. *The Ghost in the Machine*. New York: Macmillan, 1967.

Latour, Bruno. *Reassembling the Social: An Introduction to Actor-Network Theory*. New York: Oxford University Press, 2005. Kindle edition.

Lethem, Jonathan. "The Ecstasy of Influence." In *Sound Unbound*, edited by Paul D. Miller, 25–51. Cambridge, MA: MIT Press, 2008.

Lewis, George. E. "Live Algorithms and the Future of Music." *Cyberinfrastructure Technology Watch Quarterly* (May 2007), accessed June 10, 2011. http://www.ctwatch.org.

Lewis, George. E. "Mobilitas Animi: Improvising Technologies, Intending Chance." *Parallax* 13, no. 4 (2007): 108–122.

Lewis, George. E. "Too Many Notes: Computers, Complexity and Culture." *Leonardo Music Journal* 10, no. 1 (December 2000): 33–39.

Lock, Graham. "After the New: Evan Parker, Speaking of the Essence." *The Wire* 85 (1991), 30–33, 64.

Manovich, Lev. *The Language of New Media*. Cambridge, MA: MIT Press, 2002.

Margasak, Peter. "Evan Parker: Making Music with Music." *Chicago Reader*, September 24, 2009. Accessed June 10, 2011. http://www.chicagoreader.com/chicago/evan-parker-making-music-from-music/Content?oid=1200713

Menary, Richard, ed. *The Extended Mind*. Cambridge, MA: MIT Press, 2010.

Moffett, Mark W. *Adventures Among Ants: A Global Safari with a Cast of Trillions*. Berkeley: University of California Press, 2010.

Monson, Ingrid. "Jazz as Political and Musical Practice." In *Musical Improvisation: Art, Education, and Society*, edited by Gabriel Solis and Bruno Nettl, 21–37. Urbana and Chicago: University of Illinois Press, 2009.

Murphy, John. "Jazz Improvisation: The Joy of Influence." *The Black Perspective in Music* 18, no. 1–2 (1990): 7–19.

Nettl, Bruno. "Thoughts on Improvisation: A Comparative Approach." *The Musical Quarterly* 60, no. 1 (January 1974): 1–19.

Noë, Alva. *Out of Our Heads: Why You Are Not Your Brain, and Other Lessons from the Biology of Consciousness*. New York: Hill and Wang, 2009.

Peters, Gary. *The Philosophy of Improvisation*. Chicago: University of Chicago Press, 2009.

Pressing, Jeff. "Improvisation: Methods and Models." In *Generative Processes in Music: The Psychology of Performance, Improvisation, and Composition*, edited by John A. Sloboda, 129–178. Oxford: Clarendon Press, 1988.

Prior, Nick. "Putting a Glitch in the Field: Bourdieu, Actor Network Theory and Contemporary Music." *Cultural Sociology* 2, no. 3 (November 2008): 301–319.

Putnam, Hilary. *Philosophical Papers*. Vol. 2, *Mind, Language, and Reality*. Cambridge: Cambridge University Press, 1975.

Rammert, Werner. "Where the Action Is: Distributed Agency Between Humans, Machines, and Programs." In *Paradoxes of Interactivity*, edited by Uwe Seifert, Jin Hyun Kim, and Anthony Moore, 63–91. New Brunswick and London: Transaction Publishers, 2008.

Ross, Don, David Spurrett, Harold Kincaid, and G. Lynn Stephens, eds. *Distributed Cognition and the Will: Individual Volition in Social Context*. Cambridge, MA: MIT Press, 2007.

Ryle, Gilbert. *The Concept of Mind*. Chicago: University of Chicago Press, 1949.

Sawyer, R. Keith. *Group Creativity: Music, Theater, Collaboration*. Mahwah, NJ: L. Erlbaum Associates, 2003.

Schön, Donald A. *Educating the Reflective Practitioner*. San Francisco: Jossey-Bass, 1990.

Sherrington, Charles. *The Integrative Action of the Nervous System*. New Haven, CT: Yale University Press, 1906.

Simon, Herbert A. "Invariants of Human Behavior." *Annual Review of Psychology* 41 (January 1990): 1–19.

Solis, Gabriel, and Bruno Nettl, eds. *Musical Improvisation: Art, Education, and Society*. Urbana and Chicago: University of Illinois Press, 2009.

Suchman, Lucy A. *Human-Machine Reconfigurations: Plans and Situated Actions*. 2nd ed. New York: Cambridge University Press, 2007.

Sudnow, David. *Ways of the Hand: The Organization of Improvised Conduct*, Cambridge, MA: Harvard University Press, 1978.

Thrift, Nigel. "Remembering the Technological Unconscious by Foregrounding Knowledges of Position." *Environment and Planning D: Society and Space* 22 (2004): 175–190.

Toop, David. "The Feeling of Rooms." In *Blocks of Consciousness and the Unbroken Continuum*, edited by Brian Marley and Mark Wastell, 308–327. London: Sound 323, 2005.

Toop, David. "Frames of Freedom: Improvisation, Otherness and the Limits of Spontaneity." In *Undercurrents: The Hidden Wiring of Modern Music*, edited by Rob Young, 233–48. New York and London: Continuum, 2002.

Wegner, Daniel M., and Betsy Sparrow. "The Puzzle of Coaction." In *Distributed Cognition and the Will: Individual Volition in Social Context*, edited by Don Ross et al., 17–38 Cambridge, MA: MIT Press, 2008.

Weheliye, Alexander G. "Feenin': Posthuman Voices in Contemporary Black Popular Music." *Social Text* 20, no. 2 (Summer 2002): 21–47.

Wessel, David, and Matthew Wright. "Problems and Prospects for Intimate Musical Control of Computers." *Computer Music Journal* 26, no. 3 (Fall 2002): 11–22.

PART II

CRITICAL THEORIES

CHAPTER 5

....

THE IMPROVISATIVE

....

TRACY McMULLEN

THIS essay explores the ramifications of musical improvisation for understanding self and other. It suggests that musical improvisation may offer insights into a conception of self and other different from the dominant model found in most cultural theory. It is my contention that contemporary cultural theory is too beholden to Hegelian notions of the self as created through the field of the Other and the concomitant emphasis on "recognition" as the central factor in the construction of the subject. This emphasis on recognition is, in part, instilled through the theory of the performative put forward by Jacques Derrida and Judith Butler. I will detail my concerns with this theory and then offer an alternative way to understand the relation of self and other, one that focuses on "generosity" rather than "recognition." I describe this as a theory of the "improvisative." Using the improvisative as a model turns the conceptual *lean* from the Other to the self, focusing on what the self can give rather than on what the Other will recognize.[1] This, I suggest, offers a better approach to expanding the "livability" of subjects than the current focus on the performative. I conclude with an example of the improvisative in action, which I observed during a concert at the Girls' Jazz and Blues Camp in Berkeley, California, in 2010.

THE PERFORMATIVE AND THE IMPROVISATIVE

....

Butler introduced the idea of gender performativity in her 1990 book *Gender Trouble;* since then, performativity has become a central theorization of identity in cultural studies. Derrida's analysis of Kafka's short story "Before the Law" significantly influenced Butler's conception of gender performativity. In Kafka's story, a man stands before a door to "the Law" guarded by a doorman and asks to enter. The doorman states that the man may not enter, but that "it is possible" he may be able to enter later. Although the door is always open, the man decides "that it is better to wait until he gets permission." The man waits outside the door for years, in fact, until the end of his life—periodically asking permission to enter and being denied, but hoping that one day he will be allowed to enter. As his life nears its end, the man asks why no one else has come to attempt admittance to the Law, since "everyone strives to meet the Law." The doorman, seeing the man "has reached his end," reveals to the man that the door was made only for him and will now be shut.[2]

Significantly, the doorman never tells the man he is permanently prohibited entry. The man is in a state of waiting. Derrida argues that this is our essential relation with "the Law." The Law cannot be found but gains its power as we stand before it and ask to enter. Both the subject and the Law are in fact brought into being in this relation.

Butler applies Derrida's analysis to the operations of gender. Of "Before the Law," she writes, "there the one who waits for the law, sits before the door of the law, attributes a certain force to the law for which one waits. The anticipation of an authoritative disclosure of meaning is the means by which that authority is attributed and installed: the anticipation conjures its object." Butler suggests that gender is just such an "expectation that ends up producing the very phenomenon that it anticipates." Gender performativity revolves around the ways "the anticipation of a gendered essence produces that which it posits as outside itself."[3] Anticipation, waiting, and expectation attribute and generate the Law, including the law of gender.

Derrida's theory of the iterability of language is also important to Butler's theorization of performativity. For Derrida, "iterability" is language's necessary relation to repetition and alterity. Language needs to be repeated in order to be legible. Inventing a brand new word for the same concept every time we speak would render us illegible. In this way, language is always addressed to an Other. When I die or the recipient of my letter dies, the language itself is still legible. Language precedes and outlasts me, but it is always addressed to an Other that will continue. Even a "dead language," if discovered, can be decoded and read again.

This iterability, however, also opens language up to "drift." Writing is unloosed from the writer, who cannot travel with it and attempt to contain it within its "proper context" or meaning. Derrida tells us that writing is "a kind of machine" that is productive and that also "[yields to] reading and rewriting."[4] Writing can always be "cited" in different contexts, and none of these contexts can contain and foreclose the play of meaning. For Derrida, "there are only contexts without any center of absolute anchoring."[5] It is through this idea of iterability, then, that Butler imagines opportunity for the subject subjected to the Law of gender. In its repetition and citationality, gender, as a type of language or code, is subject to drift: there is never a perfect masculine or feminine, but only metaleptic repetitions of repetitions.

I want to place Butler's theorization of performativity within the context of post-Hegelian (or Hegelian) thought.[6] Butler has written that "in a sense, all of my work remains within the orbit of a certain set of Hegelian questions: What is the relation between desire and recognition, and how is it that the constitution of the subject entails a radical and constitutive relation to alterity?"[7] Butler's subject is very similar to the

Hegelian "self-consciousness" outlined in the "Lordship and Bondage" section of his *Phenomenology of Spirit.*[8] Hegel writes that "self-consciousness exists in and for itself when, and by the fact that, it so exists for another; that is, it exists only in being acknowledged."[9] In a similar passage, Butler writes, "One comes to 'exist' by virtue of [the] fundamental dependency on the address of the Other. One 'exists' not only by virtue of being recognized, but, in a prior sense, by being recognizable."[10] For Butler, the subject will be acknowledged (or recognized) to the extent that it is "recognizable." Subjects are compelled to operate within the confines of intelligibility or suffer the consequences of illegibility, including the possibility of "exclusion and violence."[11]

The Hegelian/Butlerian subject, therefore, is constituted *in* its desire. As Butler writes, "This subject neither has nor suffers its desire, but is the very action of desire as it perpetually displaces the subject."[12] The subject's desire "for and by another" brings forth a "struggle for recognition."[13] Like the man waiting outside the Law, looking for recognition and acknowledgment by the Law, the subject is both constituted and delimited through this struggle for recognition. Rather than a discrete, self-contained, and unified subject that is impinged upon by outer forces, the subject's constitution, its very condition of possibility, is through this desire. The Hegelian/Butlerian subject, then, is one that only comes into existence in relation to a "larger cultural order." Butler writes, "Hegel developed the view that the struggle for recognition gave rise to a concept of the individual essentially defined in terms of a larger cultural order, which, rather than limiting the individual's freedom, provided for its concrete determination and expression."[14]

Given this view of the subject's constitution, Butler then asks: What types of subjects are "thinkable"? Can we expand the thinkability of who is recognizable (by the Law, the cultural order) as a subject? How do we expand the conditions of possibility, indeed the "livability" for subjects—in particular, those subjects who are marginalized, or even unintelligible, and thus open to "exclusion and violence"? For Butler, the idea of iterability is key to expanding these conditions of possibility. The iterability of the subject assures that drift and context will counteract the foreclosure of meaning. This theory has been taken up by other theorists of identity, for example in the work of José Esteban Muñoz. Muñoz argues that marginalized subjects practice a type of "disidentification" in order to manage "an identity that has been 'spoiled' in the majoritarian public sphere" by re-performing the "spoiled" identity with a type of conscious embrace and an eye toward subversive context. These subjects use the iterability of language to reiterate the terms and expand their conditions of possibility as recognized subjects.[15]

Butler and Muñoz give convincing arguments for the ways in which marginalized subjects can expand their conditions of livability. My concern, however, is that this particular post-Hegelian approach has become an ideology that grounds contemporary cultural theory and naturalizes one way of conceiving of the subject's "conditions of possibility." Butler places substantial emphasis on the middle section of the *Phenomenology*, where watching, desire, and recognition constitute the subject, rather than the later pages, where a "final" state of knowledge seems to involve the end of a self/subject-Other/object split. Hegel's state of absolute knowledge is "a state where knowledge need no longer transcend or correct itself, where it will discover itself in its object and its object in itself, where concept will correspond to object and object to consciousness."[16] Whether we think it is possible to come to this state of the dissolution of subject and object, my concern with the current ideology of thinking about the subject is that while we generally recognize the contingency of the subject, the "Other" is often implicitly credited with great stability and power. Butler acknowledges the equally co-constitutive nature of the self and the Other in Hegel's account. She writes, "The self is not its own, … it is given over to the Other in advance of any further relation but in such a way that the Other does not own it either. And the ethical content of its relationship to the Other is to be found in this fundamental and reciprocal state of being 'given over.' "[17] I would agree that the self and the Other are in a "fundamental and reciprocal state of being 'given over' " to each other. Yet, in my view, in contemporary cultural theory this lack of ownership of the Other is not adequately investigated. Instead, the lean is toward the Other as a point of origin. I believe that it is the focus on recognition that serves to erroneously solidify the Other.

In my view, the performative places an emphasis on the Other who gives or withholds recognition. Even if that other is only myself watching myself, the idea of performance always entails the idea of an other who is watching.[18] But what if we had a different conception of the other—not the one for which we always perform, for which we want recognition and acknowledgment? What if we conceived of the other as the one to which we give? I believe that this conception of giving to the other is actually a bridge to the dissolution of the self/subject and other/object split. Whereas the idea of wanting recognition from the other actually imputes a specious solidity to this other (making it an Other), conceiving of the other as that to which we give takes away the concern with the (already acknowledged) lack of solidity of the subject.[19] It is this practice that I am terming the *improvisative*.

CHARACTERISTICS OF THE IMPROVISATIVE

The improvisative challenges the assumptions that sustain Butler's focus on intelligibility, thinkability, recognition, and desire, and leads to a different understanding of the possibilities for the livability of the subject. The *improvisative* is a word I've chosen to point toward something; I do not conceive it as a specific thing or a specific action. The improvisative points toward a space where the separation between observer and thing or actor and action is not meaningful. The improvisative is not based on recognition or intelligibility. It is not concerned with the realm of what is "thinkable"; indeed, it challenges forms of knowing based on conceptual thought. It is not historical, although it offers a relationship to the past, present, and future. What I believe may be most important in a theorization of the improvisative is its lean toward the subject rather than the prevailing lean toward the object. As I hope I will make clear, I say "lean" because, while the emphasis with the improvisative may be on what the "self" can do, in the final analysis the self and the other are not separate (because they are equally phantasmagorical).

An ultimate preference for one over the other is not possible. The improvisative may best be related to the idea of singularity and a type of knowing that is non-conceptual.

The improvisative can be understood as a singular moment, a moment in the "here and now" that remains open and in which one does not cohere into the decision. Derrida described the singularity as the non-resembling event as opposed to the type of machine-like repetition that is part of the character of language. This singularity happens "here and now," which, for Derrida, is not the same as the present. He writes,

> I promise in opening the future or in leaving the future open. This is not utopian, it is what takes place here and now, in a here and now that I regularly try to dissociate from the present. . . . I try to dissociate the theme of singularity happening here and now from the theme of presence and, for me, there can be a here and now without presence.[20]

For Derrida, the "present" is a designation that is manufactured in relation to an "absent" (and therefore "other") past and future. Vincent Descombes writes, "the present is present only on condition that it allude to the absent in order to be distinguishable from it (an absent which is the past or the future)."[21] For Derrida, the idea of "presence" is one of our many efforts to stabilize the openness of the "here and now" into a coherent object or "decision."

If we "leave the future open" we are in a place of "undecidability." Derrida writes via Laclau that "when I decide I invent the subject." In "undecidability" the sovereign subject cannot take form. Therefore, undecidability "is not simply a moment to be traversed and overcome . . . by the occurrence of the decision." It is here and now where "the singular event of engagement" can occur.[22] Further, I would argue that "deciding" can be related to the "the anticipation [that] conjures its object." If we do not leave the future open in the here and now but decide—cohere around a decision that names—or anticipate what we are looking for—we invent the subject (Derrida) or conjure the object (Butler). Deciding or anticipating brings both subject and object into being.

The improvisative is abiding without deciding or anticipating. The improvisative is therefore not based on repetition and alterity, and hence "iterability." It is not an engagement with the Other of language, but an openness to the singular other of the moment. It is a space of the unknown, of openness to the brute fact of the "to come."[23] The emphasis here, then, is on a type of knowing that is non-conceptual. The Buddhist philosophical idea of *shunyata* can help elucidate this idea of the singularity and the type of non-conceptual knowing that I link to the improvisative.

In Buddhism, *shunyata* is a state of non-conceptual knowing that understands "not arising; not ceasing; not arising and ceasing together." Tibetan Buddhist lama Tarthang Tulku writes, "ordinary mind falsely perceives arising and ceasing, and thus reifies every instant of experience."[24] Through *shunyata* one recognizes that "when no phenomena and no single instant have ever arisen, there can equally be no ceasing or vanishing."[25] This type of knowing can be productively compared to Derrida's idea of "here and now" as opposed to "presence" (a reification of the present through its implicit relationship to a past and future). Tarthang Tulku writes, "In terms of the three times [past, present, and future], since the mode of arising that ordinary mind takes to be the infinite 'nowness' of experience has never actually occurred, the vanishing of any phenomena or instant, perceived as the past, can also not take place. And when nothing has ever come into being or vanished, there is also no possibility for a future arising" (43). Tarthang Tulku stresses here that "ordinary mind" will grasp onto an idea of "infinite 'nowness'" as a type of object. This observation can be related to Derrida's discussion of the decision as the moment of stabilizing the unstable. Tarthang Tulku makes clear that while we may imagine that we understand something conceptually, the experience is not something that can be grasped conceptually. He writes that "our conceptual understanding of the words used to describe the experience is categorically different from the ineffability of the experience itself, which remains beyond the reach of the intellect" (44). This is not the "experience" of the ordinary mind.[26] It is a direct form of experience that will come through training in recognizing *shunyata*.

The concept of *shunyata* points to the importance of direct perception in consciousness. Whereas the Hegelian-inspired consciousness in performativity is only understood as self-consciousness (seeing oneself as an other, a conceptual distancing), in the Buddhist view, this distance is not only unnecessary, but it also separates us from crucial knowledge. Butler interprets Hegel as giving us "an ek-static notion of the self, one which is, of necessity, outside itself, not self-identical, differentiated from the start."[27] In essence, Buddhism would agree. But Buddhism goes much further than this and offers practices in which a person can learn to see the phantasmagorical quality of self and other. Self-consciousness is a conceptual knowing of the self, but there is other knowing beyond conceptual knowing. The improvisative emphasizes this type of knowing that does not entail the distancing effect of conceptual knowledge. Further, the focus changes from the concern for recognition *from* the other, to the concern to *give to* the other. When we change our relationship to the other from looking for its recognition to giving, the lean is actually in the other direction: toward the emptiness of the self that can nonetheless *give*, rather than toward the emptiness of the other that we imagine can nonetheless *take* (by not recognizing us).[28]

THE IMPROVISATIVE IN ACTION

In order to further elucidate the improvisative, I will discuss it in the context of middle and high school age girls learning to improvise at the Bay Area Girls' Jazz and Blues Camp (GJBC) in Berkeley, California. I hope to explicate how these students enact a different relationship to "the Law" than that conceived by the performative. Because the concern with recognition is connected to the fear of being illegible or excluded, I conclude by arguing that a concern with "illegibility" or "unintelligibility" is unnecessary when consciousness is not conceived as fundamentally grounded in the Other. In elucidating these points, I will focus on a phenomenon that I witnessed with several of the young students and that struck me especially during one student's performance at the camp's final concert.

In the summer of 2010, I observed the week-long GJBC. Trumpeter Ellen Seeling and saxophonist Jean Fineberg inaugurated the camp the year before; according to written evaluations by the students, the camp has been very successful in developing the students' skills and confidence in musical performance and improvisation. With an all-female staff, the camp offers jazz theory, instrument instruction, and a variety of ensembles, from small group to big band, with an excellent student-teacher ratio— with around 35 students per year and 15 teachers (some of whom rotate throughout the week). As part of my observation, I provided the students with a set of questions to answer about the GJBC. I was interested in how they felt the all-female environment affected their ability to learn jazz improvisation. While the younger girls (11–12) did not think the absence of boys made any difference, most of the girls over 12 years old thought the all-girl environment allowed them either more of an opportunity to play and improvise ("there are no guys to take all the solos," "no boys making rude comments and interrupting rehearsal") and/or made them feel less self-conscious about improvising ("the all-girl camp gives an opportunity for us to take risks," "it's helpful because boys are competitive and intimidating so it's easier to put myself out there").

For many of the girls, learning to improvise in an all-female environment made them less self-conscious.[29] In an all-female environment, the girls were both given the attention that is often still reserved for boys and given more chances to make mistakes without feeling like they had fulfilled the expectation that girls "couldn't do it" (improvise). In a male-dominated activity (jazz improvisation) in a still largely patriarchal society, men and boys are positioned as those who can proclaim competency in the arena of jazz. An all-female environment allowed the girls the opportunity to learn improvisation without the explicit male gaze of male peers and teachers.[30]

What I find important about the GJBC is that the girls were practicing a different relationship to "the Law" than articulated in "Before the Law." I observed this particularly in the students' negotiation of "mistakes" during the camp's final concert. With family and friends in attendance, the final concert offers the quintessential moment of performance: one taking place before an audience when the eyes of the other are upon you and the desire for recognition may be at its greatest, or at least at its most explicit. The evening consisted of 16 bands ranging in size, stylistic focus, and proficiency. While it could certainly be described as going off without a hitch, it *was* a group of 11- to 17-year-old student musicians and therefore had its "interesting" moments. At one point during the performance of the jazz big band, the bass player got off by one beat for a good 12 to 16 measures. As I listened to this problem, I noticed that no one on the bandstand was batting an eye (although these students were knowledgeable enough to hear it). The band stayed together and eventually the bass player got back on the correct beat. It struck me that what they were learning at this camp was the ability to go forward and to trust despite the presence or intrusion of "mistakes." Indeed, a mistake did not need to be understood as a mistake: a mis-take that entails a new take. It was an event that elicited a response, including the response of playing on and not following the bass player. The band played on, as they trusted their bassist would connect back up with them in due time.

Another example was a moment that I found particularly significant, despite the fact that it probably barely registered with the audience. It was later in the concert when one of the more advanced students was playing the vibraphone with a small Latin jazz ensemble. As she was playing the opening melody, her mallet grazed the microphone stand enough that it was clear she wasn't going to get to the next note of the melody. I saw her face register the "mistake," giving a fraction-of-a-second goofy, embarrassed, concessional face of "oh, I'm such a loser," which struck me as a very typical conciliatory gesture for a teenage girl. But in the next fraction of that second she regained her composure and instead of hitting the "proper" note of the melody repeated the note she had just played, which worked beautifully with the harmony and realized the rhythmic shape of the melody. It was as if I was watching a girl re-route her response pattern from reflexively falling into an apologetic acceptance of inability to an immediate recall and regaining of balance in time to negotiate the obstacle encountered (the mallet hitting the microphone stand).

This different response to "mistakes" is in effect a different relationship with the Law. Rather than placing the experience of the mallet hitting the stand in terms of a failure, an obeisance to rules that characterizes that phenomenon as a mistake, the young student approached that "mistake" as an event that necessitated a response, not a judgment and a closing down. "Normally" the "anticipation that would conjure the object" would be the anticipation of the Law of gender in a patriarchal society: as she hit the mic stand she would immediately anticipate that Law that she has already internalized and therefore call it into being again. It would become the "decision," the way to name the event and therefore invent herself as the female subject in a patriarchal cultural order. This pressure would be even stronger because she was performing before an audience: no longer in the all-girl environment, the audience's cultural gaze was unambiguously upon her. Instead of anticipating and deciding (which I believe was her first split-second response), however, she turned back to the music, to the event, and offered a response to that event. That is, she generously turned her full attention back to the music.[31]

When we cohere into the decision we become stingy: we limit our engagement with the world as we turn away from the singular moment. Cohering into the decision (and thereby conjuring the self and other) is an act of conceptual knowledge, which is too slow to stay with the moment. Musical knowledge, when it is learned and assimilated, becomes non-conceptual knowledge: hearing which note to play when improvising does not have to go through a slow conceptual process, but, like athletic knowledge, becomes embodied. Non-conceptual knowledge is much faster than conceptual knowledge. Therefore, in returning her focus to the singular moment of the music, the musician has no time to ask for recognition from the Law. And as such, there is less space for self and Other. Ideas about self and other are too slow to be able to take place while responding to the singular moment.[32]

The practice of the improvisative, therefore, is a practice of continual generosity. Generosity here is not a focus on giving; *focusing* on giving is not quite giving. This generosity is the giving of one's total attention to the moment—the "here and now." It is a focus on the singular other, to generously give to the other, which in this case is the music. This giving is, in fact, the letting go of ideas about the self. Giving is not about us deciding what the other wants, but about being open to the moment and responding without an ulterior motive, without an eye toward how this might work out for me or for another, in a waiting type of posture that allows non-conceptual knowing to respond. In this giving, because there is no time to conjure the self and other, there is no self or other to benefit. Yet non-conceptual knowing seems to have an ethical impulse. Without our stories of self and other, the impulse to do harm seems to find little ground for action.

As such, the improvisative is responsive, not reactive. It is the shift from evaluating oneself in terms of the Law—anticipating and finding its punishment—to turning back to the singular event without anticipating/reacting to the Law. Therefore agency is not located in a re-iteration or an address to the (great, symbolic) Other but in a response to the immediate, singular other. With the improvisative, one focuses on how to give to the situation without a concern for how one is read or if one is legible. One does not answer back to an interpellation, but swims past the bait and opens to the unpredictable. Reactivity takes oppressive comments as solid and therefore attempts to address and re-dress them; responsiveness puts the emphasis on the phantasmagorical quality of the comments. Rather than believing and attempting to counter the meaning of the comments, a turn to the improvisative is a turn toward the spaciousness and unlocatability that perpetually occupies all of our comments and actions. As such, this practice is a lean toward the subject in that the matter of concern is how one can give, not in how the other or the object may take: giving defuses the preoccupation with self as it is constructed by and as an other. And if both self and other are phantasmagorical, separation between them does not exist. If they both don't exist, then how can we argue that they are two separate things?

Musical improvisation is an excellent place to practice this type of focused, continual generosity, but such an approach can be applied to all engagements of the "self and other." When the "mistake" occurs, one does not retreat into self-condemnation and thereby close into self-preoccupation, a self that is constructed by and understood as "other." One may briefly flounder, but the skill of improvising is to return to generosity, focusing not on one's self, but the singular other in that moment.[33] Learning generosity takes time; you can't fake it. It has to be practiced and developed. Perhaps the greatest gift the GJBC offers its students is plenty of freedom to make "mistakes"—and maybe lots of them—for the more "mistakes," the more one develops a relationship to them that doesn't place them in terms of the Law, but in terms of open-ended generosity. The improvisative is always available, but it has to be recognized as valuable, and it has to be practiced. So here's to practice.

NOTES

1. Throughout this essay I try to use "Other" to refer to an abstract, "Big Other" (as Žižek would put it) and "other" to refer to a singular, particular other—as in meeting another

person. In some cases, both another person and a Big Other might make sense. In this case, I tend to opt for "other." I consider the Other an imputation, an installation of the Law that we "anticipate." When quoting from Butler or Hegel (and when referring back to these quotations), I follow their conventions for capitalization.

2. Quoted in Jacques Derrida, "Before the Law," in *Acts of Literature*, ed. Derek Attridge (New York: Routledge, 1992 [1982]), 183–184.

3. Judith Butler, *Gender Trouble: Feminism and the Subversion of Identity* (London: Routledge, 1990), xv.

4. Jacques Derrida, "Signature Event Context," in *A Derrida Reader*, ed. Peggy Kamuf (New York: Columbia University Press, 1991 [1972]), 91.

5. Ibid., 97.

6. As Butler notes, "Often the marks of a distinctively 'post-Hegelian' position are not easy to distinguish from an appropriative reading of Hegel himself." I think this can be said of Butler herself. Judith Butler, *The Judith Butler Reader* (Malden, MA: Blackwell, 2004), 46.

7. Ibid., 47.

8. G. W. F. Hegel, *The Phenomenology of Spirit*, trans. A. V. Miller (Oxford: Oxford University Press, 1977 [1807]).

9. Ibid., 111.

10. Judith Butler, *Excitable Speech: A Politics of the Performative* (New York: Routledge, 1997), 5.

11. Ibid.

12. Butler, *Judith Butler Reader*, 48. Further, Sara Salih quotes Butler as stating "self-consciousness is desire in general" (39).

13. Ibid., 89n18.

14. Butler, *Judith Butler Reader*, 88n18.

15. José Esteban Muñoz, *Disidentifications: Queers of Color and the Performance of Politics* (Minneapolis: University of Minnesota Press, 1999), 185.

16. J. N. Findlay, "Foreword," in Hegel, *Phenomenology of Spirit*, xiv. Findlay goes on, "Hegel will, however, marvelously include in his final notion of the final state of knowledge the notion of an endless progress that can have no final terms. For he conceives that, precisely in seeing the object as an endless problem, we forthwith see it as not being a problem at all. For what the object in itself is, is simply to be the other, the stimulant of knowledge and practice, which in being for ever capable of being remoulded and reinterpreted, is also everlastingly pinned down and found out being just what it is."

17. Judith Butler, *Undoing Gender* (New York: Routledge, 2004), 149.

18. As Richard Schechner puts it, performing is "showing doing," it is not "doing." Richard Schechner, *Performance Studies: An Introduction* (New York: Routledge, 2002).

19. Because the self is created through the field of the other, it has no inherent existence. Žižek describes this as the "void which is the subject." Clearly, its status as "void" causes concern for the subject. This is a topic, however, too large to address in this essay.

20. Jacques Derrida, "Remarks on Deconstruction and Pragmatism," in *Deconstruction and Pragmatism*, ed. Chantal Mouffe (New York: Routledge, 1996), 82–83.

21. Vincent Descombes, *Modern French Philosophy* (Cambridge: Cambridge University Press, 1998), 148.

22. Derrida, "Remarks on Deconstruction," 82–87.

23. Ibid., 82–83.

24. Tarthang Tulku, *Milking the Painted Cow* (Berkeley: Dharma Publishing, 2005), 43.

25. Ibid., 43.

26. Buddhism teaches that we *can* have direct experience, but that this is not easy. The ordinary mind mediates experience. Tarthang Tulku writes, "It may seem we could leave concepts behind and investigate mind through direct experience, but this is far from easy. Experience arises as feelings, thoughts, and impressions interact with consciousness to label and identify appearance. Meanings arise from dialogues that depend on mental imagery and sense perception. All this is the activity of mind. Since it is mind that narrates experience, experience as such cannot lead us to understand mind." Tulku, *Milking the Painted Cow*, 13. This description is similar to Joan Scott's argument in her essay "The Evidence of Experience," where she asserts that descriptions of our "experience" tend to be narrations of ourselves as subjects. Joan W. Scott, "The Evidence of Experience," *Critical Inquiry* 17 (Summer 1991): 773–97. The difference is that Buddhism does not stop at the conceptual ordinary mind; it suggests that we can access another type of knowing, known as *shunyata*.

27. Butler, *Undoing Gender*, 148. Butler goes on, "It is the self over here who considers its reflection over there, but it is equally over there, reflected, and reflecting." It is this "equally over there" that I would link to the self in the Law. The Law is also a reflection of the self, and therefore we can attenuate the power of the Law (gender norms, stereotypes, etc.) by not believing it to be solid in the ways I think we still do.

28. Re-cognizing: cognizing again, re-thinking. Cognition emphasizes the distance in relation to the other by focusing on conceptual thought and language. My concerns with the limitations of "recognition" also pertain to discussions of the subject recognizing the other (not just the Other recognizing the subject), as in the chapter "Longing for Recognition" in Butler, *Undoing Gender*.

29. Single-sex schooling has been a hotly debated topic. An excellent book on the subject is Rosemary C. Salomone, *Same, Different, Equal: Rethinking Single-Sex Schooling* (New Haven: Yale University Press, 2003).

30. This need for a space away from boys would seem to support the contention that consciousness is "other-centered." Within the Hegelian rubric, self-consciousness is, in fact, an other-consciousness, a concern with recognition by and of the other and a split of consciousness that understands oneself as an other. This, indeed, would account for the power of the patriarchal gaze. As suggested above, I agree that the Hegelian conception of alienated consciousness is our normal everyday consciousness. Buddhist philosophy, however, describes a state of consciousness that, through practice, dissolves the distancing effect produced by concepts within everyday consciousness. It is this state that I felt the students were able to practice at the GJBC. The all-girl environment is therefore not an absolute prerequisite for practicing this state of consciousness (for the girls)—just quite helpful.

31. The improvisative describes a "how," not a "what." I am concerned with *how* she makes this choice, which of course is very hard to write about and to know—to pin down, as it were. This is another instance where I believe we need to rehabilitate the "subjective." The subjective will never be "pinned down" like the objective, but this does not mean it offers less information than the objective. I will go out on a limb and say that we can, in our own experience, identify when we are "opening to the singular moment" and when we are cohering into the decision. We can identify this in our own mind. And I believe—though I am not so arrogant as to say I am certain about this—I can hear and/ or see when someone is at least more attuned to the singular moment. You can hear or

see when focus is broken during a musical or athletic performance. We have a saying for this type of concentration: to "get your head in the game." I will continue to elaborate the complex topic of the subjective in my work on the improvisative in the future.

32. Of course, the vibraphonist chose a note that she has learned will "work" within the tradition. This is not a contradiction. The present moment blooms out of the past. Tradition flows through the moment. Tradition can flow through the moment without our cohering into a decision. This is how tradition moves and changes. We can operate within and through the patterns that have preceded us, but in a way that does not make them solid. We perform music, but we do not compulsively repeat it with perfect exactitude again and again and again, unless we have cohered into a decision about what we want to establish as the "truth" of the music. Attending to the singular moment—and not to an ulterior motive of what we want our music to accomplish—creates the opportunity to perform in new, unexpected ways.

33. To summarize: this offers a different interpretation of the field of the other, one in which an other-centeredness is focused on generosity (giving to the other: the singular moment) rather than recognition (being seen/acknowledged by the Other). Radio host Terry Gross's interview with comedian/actress/writer Tina Fey on comedy improvisation echoes this other/object focus. Fey describes how new improvisers are not sure when they should enter the scene. Do you enter when you want to join in the fun? When you have a great idea? No, Fey states. "You come in when you are needed." Terry Gross and Tina Fey, "Tina Fey Reveals All (and Then Some) in 'Bossypants,'" *Fresh Air*, WHYY, April 13, 2011, radio broadcast.

BIBLIOGRAPHY

Butler, Judith. *Excitable Speech: A Politics of the Performative*. New York: Routledge, 1997.

Butler, Judith. *Gender Trouble: Feminism and the Subversion of Identity*. London: Routledge, 1990.

Butler, Judith. *The Judith Butler Reader*, edited by Sara Salih. Malden, MA: Blackwell, 2004.

Butler, Judith. *Undoing Gender*. New York: Routledge, 2004.

Derrida, Jacques. "Before the Law." In *Acts of Literature*, edited by Derek Attridge, 181–220. New York: Routledge, 1992 [1982].

Derrida, Jacques. "Remarks on Deconstruction and Pragmatism." In *Deconstruction and Pragmatism*, edited by Chantal Mouffe, 77–88. New York: Routledge, 1996.

Derrida, Jacques. "Signature Event Context." In *A Derrida Reader*, edited by Peggy Kamuf, 80–111. New York: Columbia University Press, 1991 [1972].

Descombes, Vincent. *Modern French Philosophy*. Cambridge: Cambridge University Press, 1998.

Findlay, J. N. "Foreword." In G. W. F Hegel, *Phenomenology of Spirit*, translated by A. V. Miller, v–xxx. Oxford: Oxford University Press, 1977.

Gross, Terry, and Tina Fey. "Tina Fey Reveals All (and Then Some) in 'Bossypants.'" *Fresh Air*, WHYY, April 13, 2011, radio broadcast.

Hegel, G. W. F. *The Phenomenology of Spirit*. Translated by A. V. Miller. Oxford: Oxford University Press, 1977 [1807].

Muñoz, José Esteban. *Disidentifications: Queers of Color and the Performance of Politics*. Minneapolis: University of Minnesota Press, 1999.

Salomone, Rosemary C. *Same, Different, Equal: Rethinking Single-Sex Schooling.* New Haven: Yale University Press, 2003.

Schechner, Richard. *Performance Studies: An Introduction.* New York: Routledge, 2002.

Scott, Joan W. "The Evidence of Experience." *Critical Inquiry* 17 (Summer 1991): 773–797.

Tarthang Tulku. *Milking the Painted Cow.* Berkeley: Dharma Publishing, 2005.

CHAPTER 6

JURISGENERATIVE GRAMMAR (FOR ALTO)

FRED MOTEN

In his celebrated essay "Nomos and Narrative," legal scholar Robert Cover describes it as "remarkable that in myth and history the origin of and justification for a court is rarely understood to be the need for law. Rather, it is understood to be the need to suppress law, to choose between two or more laws, to impose upon laws a hierarchy. It is the multiplicity of laws, the fecundity of the jurisgenerative principle, that creates the problem to which the court and the state are the solution."[1] Though Cover is ambivalent regarding the abolition of this solution, which he understands to be violent, of necessity, his advocacy of a certain resistance to the very apparatuses whose necessity he denaturalizes makes it possible for us to ask some questions that the state and the understanding find not only inappropriate but also inappropriable. What if the imagination is not lawless but lawful? What if it is, in fact, so full of laws that, moreover, are in such fugitive excess of themselves that the imagination, of necessity, is constantly, fugitively in excess of itself as well? Will law have then been manifest paralegally, criminally, fugitively, as a kind of ongoing antisystemic break or breaking; as sociality's disruptive avoidance of mere civility which takes form in and as a contemporaneity of different times and the inhabitation of multiple, possible worlds and personalities? In response to this anoriginal priority of the differential set, the courts and the state (as well as critics of every stripe) will have insisted upon the necessity of policing such collaboration. Meanwhile, relations between worlds will have been given in and as a principle of non-exclusion. The line of questioning that Cover requires and enables brings the jurisgenerative principle to bear on a burden that it must bear: the narrative that begins with the criminalization of that principle. In studying the criminalization of anoriginal criminality (which Western civilization and its critique requires us to understand as the epidermalization of the alternative, but which we'll come more rigorously and precisely to imagine as the animaterialization of the fantastic in chromatic saturation) one recognizes that the jurisgenerative principle is a runaway. Gone underground, it remains, nevertheless, our own anarchic ground.

Cover reveals the constituted indispensability of the legal system as an institutional analog of the understanding designed to curtail the lawless freedom with which laws are generated and subsequently argues for the duty to resist legal system, even if from within it, in its materialization in and as the state. In the concluding paragraph of his unfinished final article "The Bonds of Constitutional Interpretation: Of the Word, the Deed, and the Role," he argues that "in law to be an interpreter is to be a force, an actor who creates effects even through or in the face of violence. To stop short of suffering or imposing violence is to give law up to those who are willing to so act. The state is organized to overcome scruple and fear. Its officials *will* so act. All others are merely petitioners if they will not fight back."[2] But insofar as some of us cling to Samuel Beckett's notion that "the thing to avoid . . . is the spirit of system," we are left to wonder how else and where else the resistance of the jurisgenerative multitude is constituted.[3] Moreover, we are required to consider an interarticulate relationship between flight and fight that American jurisprudence can hardly fathom. That man was not meant to run away is, for Oliver Wendell Holmes, sufficient argument for a combat whose true outcome will have become, finally, eugenic rather than abolitionist. To assert a duty to resist, enacted in and by way of the vast range of principled fugitivity as opposed to the absence of a duty to retreat, is a reading against the grain of Holmes's interpretive insistence on honor, on a certain manhood severely husbanding generativity, a patrimonial heritage manifest as good breeding and as legal violence against bad breeding, given in the prolific but inferior productivity of the unintelligent, whether black or (merely optically) white.[4] Reading Cover, always against the backdrop of a certain multiply-lined, multi-matrilinear music, requires re-generalizing fighting back, recalibrating it as inaugurative, improvisational, radical interpretation—a fundamental and anticipatory disruption of the standard whose cut origin and extended destination are way outside. This implies a kind of open access to interpretation that in turn implies the failure of state-sanctioned institutions of interpretation insofar as they could never survive such openness. One must still consider interpretation's relation to force, as Cover understands it, but also by way of a massive discourse of force in which, on the one hand, the state monolith is pitted against the so much more than single speaker and, on the other hand, in which the state, as a kind of degraded representation of commonness, is submitted to an illegitimate and disruptive univocality.

Meanwhile, criminality, militancy, improvisatory literacy, and flight collaborate in jurisgenerative assertion, ordinary transportation, corrosive, caressive (non)violence directed toward the force of state interpretation and its institutional and philosophical scaffolding. It's a refusal in interpretation of interpretation's reparative and representational imperatives, the mystical and metaphysical foundations of its logics of accountability and abstract equivalence, by the ones who are refused the right to interpret at the militarized junction of politics and taste, where things enter into an objecthood already compromised by the drama of subjection. In the end, state interpretation—or whatever we would call the exclusionary protocols of whatever interpretive community—tries to usurp the general, generative role of study, which is an open admissions kind of thing. What does it mean to refuse an exclusive and exclusionary ontic capacity or to move outside the systemic oscillation between the refusal and the imposition of such capacity? This question is the necessary preface to a theory of paraontic resistance that is essential matter for the theory of language and the theory of human nature.

Consider the difference and relation between knowing and making a language: what happens when the intersubjective validity of the moral or linguistic law within is displaced by the very generativity that law is said to constitute? Noam Chomsky has tried many times, in many different venues and contexts, to offer condensed but proper understandings of an intellectual project called "generative grammar" whose "central topic of concern is what John Huarte, in the 16th century, regarded as the essential property of human intelligence: the capacity of the human mind to 'engender within itself, by its own power, the principles on which knowledge rests.'"[5] Such a power must be what composer and historian George E. Lewis would describe as "stronger than itself," some thing, some totality, some singularity that *is* only insofar as it is in excess of itself and is, therefore, already cut and augmented by an irreducible exteriority to which it is constrained to refer *and to exhaust*, as the condition of its own seemingly impossible possibility.[6] Similarly, that which this power is said to generate exists only insofar as it, too, is open to and infused by the outside. However, Chomsky is circumspect in his delineation of this *internal* capacity to engender the internal. The outside, which we'll call historicity, but which must also be understood as form's degenerative and regenerative force, is, for Chomsky, not inadmissible. However, the inside, which we'll call essence, is rich in its discretion and therefore able to generate that for which external stimulus, in its poverty, is unaccountable. Exteriority, which we might also talk about under the rubric of alterity, is immaterial to the Chomskyan configuration of the problem of essence. For Chomsky, Wilhelm von Humboldt's reference to "the infinite use of language" is

> quite a different matter from the unbounded scope of the finite means that characterizes language, where a finite set of elements yields a potentially infinite array of discrete expressions: discrete, because there are six-word sentences and seven-word sentences, but no 6.2 word sentences; infinite because there is no longest sentence ([insofar as one can] append "I think that" to the start of any sentence).[7]

I'm interested in the difference between a wholly internally driven understanding of "discrete" infinity and that necessary and irreducible openness to the outside which will have been productive of an immeasurable range of linguistic indiscretion because to be interested in art is to be concerned with the constant and irruptive aspiration, beyond the possible and the impossible, of the 6.2-word sentence. At stake, on the other side of the question of discretion (which is to say that for whatever singular grammar there is the non-sentence, the non-phrase, whose very elements and order can be made, by way of a certain capacity to engender, into a sentence) is the capacity for a certain refusal of sanctioned grammatical capacity, for rupture and augmentation that inheres in the word and the sentence as the continually circulated gift/power of the outside we take in and by which we are taken, in the ongoing history of our necessary dis/possession. The most interesting potential area of inquiry emerging from Huarte's insight into a seemingly self-generating power is our capacity to generate what shows up as the ungrammatical. How do we know and (re)produce the extra-grammatical, the extra-legal? How do we know (how to) escape when escape is the general name we give to the impulse by which we break law? Ultimately, I'd like to understand this question concerning what might be called grammar's general economy, its essential supplementarity, more precisely as that which concerns our general, criminal, illegitimately criminalized capacity to make law.

In the previous paragraph I offer a synthesized echo of a critical attitude toward Chomsky that is driven by the belief that historiography is, and should be, theoretical practice in linguistics and whose work might be characterized as a methodological extension of Fanon's sociogenic principle against the grain of a certain Kantian trace in Chomsky's onto-phylogenic project.[8] At stake is not simply an historical account of the discipline, which a textbook would be obliged to provide, but also a recognition of the priority of the diachronic over the synchronic, the sociohistorical over the structural(ist), in any account of language. But even an account such as this is problematic for those critics, since the genuinely sociohistorical account would, in the end, not really be of language at all. They would argue that a genuinely sociohistorical linguistics is one in which the question of the nature of language is displaced by pragmatic concerns regarding what it is to be a speaker of language, a mode of existence that is irreducibly sociohistorical in a way that the Chomskyan model of language as a fixed system is not. The key theoretical precursor in such a model would be Darwin, not Descartes. And what Julie Tetel Andresen calls "languaging," the linguistic action that displaces whatever imaginary thing language is or has been thought to be, would be understood as a function of and subject to evolution. The question of whether or not a structure has a history, of how social history operates in and on, but without eradicating, structure (let's call this the post-structuralist question), is set aside, as is its interesting corollary, the question of whether there can be a structure without a center. To ask such questions will have already been to veer into the underground that is called the humanities, when these post-Chomskyan linguists would insist that linguistics must be not only open but also subject to the "latest findings from the social and natural sciences" while, at the same time remaining insistently oblivious to the latest findings of the humanities and the arts.[9] Of course, the idea that a structure has a history, is subject to the transformative force of history, is, in the arts and humanities, not one of their latest findings but is, in fact, old news. And while this is of little moment to those who are interested, finally, in the liquidation, rather than the historicization, of structure (or, at least, in the indefinite suspension of the necessarily and irremediably structuralist question concerning the nature of language), it requires something that composer and instrumentalist Anthony Braxton might call a "restructuralist" approach to and rapprochement with the ongoing Chomskyan revolution. By way of this engagement, the question "What is a language?" is not eclipsed but illumined by the question of what happens when we hear a sequence of sounds.

Without adhering to the anti-*material* restrictions that derive from the Chomskyan model's demand that the utterance be both "disembedded and disembodied," in Andresen's terms, there is a certain black study of language (music) that is itself derived from the inaugurative event of Afro-diasporic experience understood precisely as an interplay of disembodiedness and disembeddedness, from which the materialities of stolen life, its self-contextualizing, corpulent multiplicity, continually emerge. It's not that syntax just hovers out there, but that there is a serialization of the syntactic moment, at once obliterative and generative, that is materialized by bodies, in context; there is an (ongoing) event out of which language emerges that language sometimes tries to capture. If it is the case that even Chomsky's massive and massively generative attempt remains incomplete, this is due to a certain refusal to think the relation between structure and event that is endemic to a certain scientificity (and which Chomsky himself seems to have identified insofar as he has repeatedly asserted that it may well be that literature will have had the most to say about the question of the origin of language). Still, it is as if one remains in search of a contribution to the theory of human nature that cannot or doesn't want to deal with the trace of the event in the thing of human nature. At stake, in other words, is the history of essence understood, precisely, as the animation of the thing, the materiality of its endowment with seemingly impossible capacities such as a range of deconstructive, ruptural *poesis*: making laws or making (the laws of) language or making (the laws of language) music.

Consider the relation between (extra)musical or (extra)legal behavior, on the one hand, and the internal cognitive systems that make (extra)musicality or (extra)legality possible. This would entail taking interest in the generation of musico-juridical possibility and in the materiality of grammars that Cheryl Wall might characterize as "worrying the line" between inside and outside or between depth as bio-cognitive interior endowment or competence (which must at least be understood in relation both to universality and inalienability) and surface as the open set of performances in which the musico-juridical is instantiated improvisationally in relation to exteriority's anoriginal and irreducible differences, differentiation and alienation.[10] What's at stake is the universality of grammatical generativity that is given in the instantiation of the universal capacity to break grammar. Can the principles upon which knowledge of language rests (or knowledge of music moves) be improvised? Can principles, in their very composure, be improvised? Can there be commerce—beyond mere one-way transport, transformation or loosening—between principle and anarchy? Can you perform your way into a singular and unprecedented competence, into an instant and unrepeatable composition? Addressing these questions requires some consideration of the soloist as a speaker, as one who languages, who acts linguistically even in and out of a brutally imposed languishing, but who is also an instrument, through which others, or through which, deeper still, alterity, speaks; at the asymptotic confluence of these senses, the speaker is a bridge machine, a resonant connectivity, an articulate spacing, the transverse, untraversable distance by which we arrive at multiplicity. However, arrival, here, is a misnomer. Instead, we might speak, in echo of some Althusser-Brathwaite duet in our heads, of an ongoing, aleatory arrivance, that endless, vibratory after-effect of departure, of being-sent or being-thrown (over or overboard), of which speech, or more generally and more generatively, sounding, always speaks.

Braxton imagines, composes, improvises multiplicity—in a thirty-year initiative he calls language music—by way of a new mode of structural planning that will eventually be manifest not only as sound but also as a kind of technical drawing that is that sound's and that sonic space's prefigurative condition. Braxton calls the initial maneuver of his practice "conceptual grafting," which maintains, through minute analysis and dissection, the differential/differentiated singularity—the cellular modularity—of musical elements. "I began," Braxton says, "to break down phrase construction variables with regard to material properties, functional properties, language properties; to use this as a basis to create improvised music and then rechannel that into the compositional process."[11] New compositional movement, the overturning of musical ground, emerges from the still, shedded posture of self-analytic listening, the hermetic, audio-visual attunement to the shape and color of sound and its internal relations.

We are required now to consider not only the relationship between the (open) cell and refuge but also the (grafted) cell's generativity. What is it to refuse, while seeking refuge in, the cell? This requires some immersion in the history of the crawlspace, which is also a sound booth, and a (temporarily preoccupied) corner, and a broken window. Such immersion is conducted publicly, in hiding, out in broken territory where one has been preventatively detained. (T)here, Braxton re-initializes the relation between the internal generativity of the outside and the enunciation of an already striated intention not to be a single being: he is the unit that is more than itself, greater than itself, stronger than itself, precisely insofar as he attends to the internal (and more than simply) phonic difference of phonic material. The soloist is a black study group, a monastery's modular calculus, whose innateness is a plain of abridged presences. Like an autoethnographic soundcatcher, driven and enabled by eccentric, hesitant, sociopoetic social logic—a radical empiricism that avoids the spirit of empirical system—Braxton collates and collects what is beyond category and reveals how solo performance comes to be the field in which multiplicity is studied and performed. Beyond the retrograde possibilities of artificial individuality there was always *Spaltung*, the split personality, the personal split, the *retrait* of the unalone to the woodshed, the wilderness, the desert, the fjord, the north, in asylum, on Monk's or Magic Mountain, where solitude is haunted, crowded. The soloist is unalone; the soloist is not (all) one. She is and instantiates a power of n + 1, because the one is not the one, this bridge, and therefore requires some *off* renewal of the question of the meaning of being, which will have again been achieved by way of an existential analytic of the instrument(alist) who is not but nothing other than man, that public thing.

Idle talk, curiosity and ambiguity characterize the way in which, in an everyday manner, Heidegger's Dasein is its "there"—the disclosedness of Being-in-the-world. As definite existential characteristics, these are not present-at-hand in Dasein, but help to make up its Being. In these, and in the way they are interconnected in their Being, there is revealed a basic kind of Being which belongs to everydayness; we call this the "falling" of Dasein.

This term does not express any negative evaluation, but is used to signify that Dasein is proximally and for the most part *alongside* the "world" of its concern.

This "absorption in . . ." has mostly the character of Being-lost in the publicness of the "they." Dasein has, in the first instance, fallen away [*abgefallen*] from itself as an authentic potentiality for Being its self, and has fallen into the "world." "Fallenness" into the world means an absorption in Being-with-one-another, in so far as the latter is guided by idle talk, curiosity and ambiguity. Through the Interpretation of falling, what we have called the "inauthenticity" of Dasein may now be defined more precisely. On no account however do the terms "inauthentic" and "non-authentic" signify "really not," as if in this mode of Being, Dasein were altogether to lose its Being. "Inauthenticity" does not mean anything like Being-no-longer-in-the-world, but amounts rather to quite a distinctive kind of Being-in-the-world—the kind which is completely fascinated by the "world" and by the Dasein-with of Others in the "they." Not-Being-its-self [*Das Nicht-es-selbst-sein*] functions as a positive possibility of that entity which, in its essential concern, is absorbed in a world. This kind of not-Being has to be conceived as that kind of Being which is closest to Dasein and in which Dasein maintains itself for the most part.

So neither must we take the fallenness of Dasein as a "fall" from a purer and higher "primal status." Not only do we lack any experience of this ontically, but ontologically we lack any possibilities or clues for Interpreting it.

In falling, Dasein *itself* as factical Being-in-the-world, is something *from* which it has already fallen away. And it has not fallen into some entity which it comes upon for the first time in the course of its Being, or even one which it has not come upon at all; it has fallen into the *world*, which itself belongs to its Being. Falling is a definite existential characteristic of *Dasein* itself. It makes no assertion about Dasein as something present-at-hand, or about present-at-hand relations to entities from which Dasein "is descended." Or with which Dasein has subsequently wound up in some sort of *commercium*.[12]

There's this other thing that happens when you dance so hard your hand flies across the room, or when you brush up against somebody and find that your leg is gone, that makes you also wonder about the relation between fallenness and thrownness. Improvisation is (in) that relation. But for Heidegger—and a certain tradition he both finds and founds, and which resounds in breaking away from him—improvisation bears and enacts an irremedial inauthenticity that is given in being given to what might be best understood, though it is often misunderstood, as base sociality where what is at stake, more than anything, is precisely this: to be fascinated by the world and by being with one another and to move in this fascination's undercommon concern with or engagement in idle talk, curiosity, and ambiguity, *but by way of a certain thickness of accent*, a counterscholastic accompaniment, that troubles the standard speech that is misunderstood to have been studied. A function of being-thrown into the history we are making, this sound must also be understood as having prefaced the fall from ourselves into the world we make and are that is often taken for that sound's origin. What's also at stake, then, is a certain valorization or "negative evaluation": not, as Heidegger says, of fallenness as "a definite existential characteristic of Dasein itself," but rather of "present-at-hand relations to [and, impossibly, between] entities. . . ."

Now I cut it off here because I'm not making *that* kind of argument about Dasein's parentage, its line of descent or even the specific direction of its fall. This is not some claim to what will have been relegated to a kind of primitivity (either as a kind of degraded prematurity or as opposed to some originary and higher purity [recognizing that these are two sides of the same coin, so to speak]). The issue, rather, is another exemplary possibility for misinterpretation that Heidegger offers: that Dasein, not itself being "something present-at-hand," has subsequently "wound up in some sort of *commercium*" with entities to which it has some kind of "present-at-hand relation. . . ." What is this *commercium*? Who are these entities, these things? What is their relation to world? What is the nature of their publicness, their "being-lost in the publicness of the 'they' "? What is their relation to fallenness and thrownness? What is their, and their descendant's, relation to thinking and to being thought?

Perhaps "some sort of *commercium*" is like that which comprises what, according to Richard Pryor, the police have been known to call, in their very denial of its present materiality, "some kind of community sing." It's a singing prince kind of thing, a Heidelberg beer hall kind of thing, which is also a black thing cutting the understanding in the aftermath of serious lecture. The *Commercium* is something like the *Symposium*, replete or dangerously more than complete or rendering the academy incomplete with lyrical w(h)ine. It is a fall from, or luxuriant parody of, the *Sacrum Commercium*, St. Francis's exchange with Lady Poverty, his undercommon enrichment, the fantastic effect of study and prayer in small, public solitude. And insofar as *commercium* is a term of business/law since the Romans, this valence is not entirely foreign to the motivation behind Heidegger's off-hand devaluation of the present-at-hand. Yet again we are speaking of the sociality that attends being-subject-to-exchange, which befalls even those who are parties to exchange, thereby troubling a distinction so crucial to a current proliferation of anti-ontological descriptions of blackness. Heidegger's negative evaluation bears the materiality that undergirds an etymological descent he chooses not to trace. But it becomes clear that the problematic of fallenness into the world, which is an irreducible part of Dasein's being, is or can be given to a devolutionary intensification, an undercommon fall from fallenness, when *Dasein* gets "wound up" with "some sort of *commercium*." This fall$_2$ from the world to the (under)world, which is the subject of Heidegger's offhand dismissal, is, again, an object (and source) of constant study.

I am concerned with fallenness into the world of things. Theodor Adorno speaks of this, tellingly, with regard to jazz:

> The improvisational immediacy which constitutes its partial success counts strictly among those attempts to break out of the fetishized commodity world which want to escape that world without ever changing it, thus moving ever deeper into its snare. . . . With jazz a disenfranchised subjectivity plunges from the commodity world into the commodity world; the system does not allow for a way out.[13]

Improvisational immediacy, an effect Heidegger links to thrownness, becomes for Adorno a substitute for a certain mode of uprising that would at least reverse the fall from fallenness that itself substitutes escape from the world for changing the world, thereby displacing fight (or honorable and manly resistance) with ignoble flight. And this ignobility is necessarily maternal, which is to say that it is so deeply bound up with sustenance, maintenance, and a kind of otherworldly, underworldly care, that flight often turns out to be interinanimate with remaining in the path(ont)ological zone, as if the one who flees militantly remains for f(l)ight again. What emerges, as and by way of planning and study, is a certain problematic where what it is to fly, already wound up in tarrying, is now bound up with digging (which Baraka has already thought in its irreducible relation to the music that comes from it and reproduces it) so that the way out turns out, in fact, to be the way back into that continual reconstruction of the underground that is carried out—in jazz, let's say—not by disenfranchised subjectivity but by the ones who refuse subjectivity's general disenfranchisement, the ones whose deep inhabitation of the snare instantiates the fall$_2$ from "the commodity world into the commodity world" as continually revalued *commercium*, continually revaluing community sing. Moreover, this social life in my head is the way back into the underground of metaphysics. The soloist not quite learning to read what she has written, the soloist unable to sight-read what he has composed but who is willing to fall into difference, into sociality and so to ascend into the open secret of the cenobitic club, the public monastery, where the anoriginal criminality of judgment, of legislation, is renewed. The gathering is tight aeration and subatomic access, the soft rupture of every custom in its enactment, the sharp cut of every law at the moment of its making.

And solo performance is a kind of bloom! Autostriation in the open underground is where St. Anthony's head becomes a rose. If you keep humming it, if you keep trying to hear that anarrangement, if you practice all the time, you won't even have to count it off, you just set it off and thereby undertake and undergo harmonic mitosis—he splits, her cell splits, he splits himself in her cell. The trace of having been sold initializes this auto-conjugative auto-disruption, this self-divisive self-reproduction, as multiple seriality, expansive conservation. Folded into the *commercium* like a one-time would-be sovereign whose song and dance is, finally, irrevocable abdication of that regulative desire in the name of love, revolutionary suicide in the name of self-defense, the soloist is drenched, saturated in color like a slide, a chromatic transparency, through which other things show up as neither subject nor party to exchange, however much they are indebted to it, which is to say indebted to one another, for their very lives. Already there was this juked monasticism. The joint was a library and a chapel, jumpin'. In considering music's relation to the jurisgenerative principle, one comes to think of a certain outlaw asceticism, the extravagant austerity of a certain criminal aestheticism, that is carried out in the vast history of various sojourns in the woodshed, of fallenness in a late night eremitic bridge become practice room or, after an abortive attempt at the self-generation of the inside, simply and falsely conceived as the simultaneously artificial and unpremeditated expression of a single being, in St. Anthony Braxton's fleeing temptation in Chicago, where cell and city keep on becoming one another in a range of ways, by joining the Experimental Band's disruptive, expansive, sensual intellection, its performed improvisation through common deformations of membership, where they celebrate what it is to be indebted to the outside for an inside song.

Consider how Braxton's long, cryptographic fascination with various modes of the switchable track, his practice and study of hiding information in plain sight, as a kind of riding of the blinds, instantiates, in *For Alto*, the methodological assertion of flight in and from a given order. "The 'diversion from' is what we put our attention on" in order to consider the relationship between fugitive inhabitation and generativity.[14] The performed and performative study is the intersection, the switching point, between *nomos* and *logos*—between self-*destruktive*, sociopoetic law and dispersively gathered, graphophonic word—but negatively. This is not *graphe paranomon*, a suspension of already given legislation that is instantiated by a solo irruption; nor is it speech uttered by a citizen in the legitimate (which is to say privatized) realm of public appearance, in which membership or an already given matriculation is assumed, that disrupts and suspends the ongoing legislative order. Rather, Braxton performs (by way of the difference he takes in and brings), the gnomic, paranomic writing of the non-citizen who refuses the citizenship that has been refused him. His musicked speech is, as it were, encrypted. It comes from deep outside, the open, the surround, which resists being enclosed, or buried, as much as it does being excluded. In the solo performance of his essential, experimental dismemberment, Braxton shows us how one becomes indebted to the outside for an inside song.

This is part of what Braxton writes about in his notes on Composition No. 8F, which is dedicated to pianist Cecil Taylor, though its own particular auto-explosive reach for the outside is directed even more by and toward John Coltrane's heights and depths.

> The second aspect of Composition 8F's material breakdown involves the use of long musical passages built from 32nd—and 64th-note figures. Material constructions from this sensibility permeate the total canvas of the music and are used in many different ways (i.e., sound register and focus etc.). The instrumentalist in this context is asked to maintain a super-charged use of musical formings throughout the total presentation of the music. Given musical formings will then appear that utilize the entire spectrum of the instrument, and the construction nature of the work also calls for the use of isolated material and focus directives (as a basis to establish timbral focus and structural balance). The use of this operative can be viewed in the context of John Coltrane's "sheets of sound" language period because all of the language directives in Composition No. 8F are designed to provide a platform for continuous multiple phrase formations (invention). There is no slowing of the pulse continuum in this work, nor is there any decreasing of its sound note input rate. What we have instead is a recipe for a dynamic unfolding music that calls for the rapid employment of material initiatives—throughout the whole of the improvisation (from beginning to end).[15]

Without losing hearing of overabundant multiphonics' split singularity, the animation of Braxton's sound, it remains important to consider the tidal adventure that marks the ups and downs of his invention. In doing so, remember that the slave ship is a language lab. The projects are a conservatory. The prison is a law school. Refusal to acknowledge this is not a romanticist bulwark against romanticism but an empiricist suppression of the empirical. While the material conditions always matter, because the sound will always change, in the end it doesn't matter if it's closed or open air: the fecundity of the jurisgenerative principle, and generative grammar's auto-constitutive auto-transgressions, is irrepressible.

With this in mind, let's stage an encounter between Anthony Braxton and Edouard Glissant, both of whom have already been in that kind of contact that deep aesthetic theorists have with the general problematic of problematized generality that Trane once called "a love supreme." Spookily, mutually, inspirited, they are already in action at a distance in a brutal world, as a duo whose braided incommensurability sounds forth as mutually non-exclusive enunciations of poetic intention, manifest in the ecstatic asceticism, the remote coenobitic life they share as impossible movement in local space, electric slide as terse, monastic glide, tortuous flight from one pitch to another, accelerated ascent and descent of the scale, of the very apparatuses of measure. The undercommon gliss is rough, tossed, rolled by water, flung by waves and it might end up sounding, so to speak, like a choir at study in Faulkner, Mississippi, the night before s/he hopped a freight for Chitown. There's a kind of obscurity, even an always angular kind of madness, in Braxton's *glissement*, his glissando that allows us to recall Chomsky's assertion that "Huarte postulates a third kind of wit" beyond both a certain cognitive docility in which the mind is devoid of everything but sense data filtered through an internally imposed empirical system and the internally powered engendering of "the principles on which knowledge rests." This other ingenuity, "by means of which some, without art or study, speak such subtle and surprising things, yet true, that were never before seen, heard, or writ, no, nor ever so much as thought of" is understood by Chomsky to be Huarte's reference to "true creativity, an exercise of the creative imagination in ways that go beyond normal intelligence and may, he felt, involve "a mixture of madness."[16] Madness, here in conjunction with mixture, is one of the names that have been given to the more than internally driven power of the one who, insofar as he is more than mere interiority, is more than one. To have turned or taken the inside out is not only to have embraced, as it were, the dual enablement of both the poverty of stimulus and the poverty of internal volition. This potential is Braxton's constant, circular aspiration, bespeaking, against Huarte's grain, the supernatural movement of both art and study. The language he generates is touched by an externally propelled submergence and surfacing that he bears as a kind of public property, as chorographic philosophy's gift of opacity, the blurred, serrated edge of thinking on the move, an exhaustive, imaginary mapping of an underworld and its baroque and broken planes. This ongoing, ruptural moment in the history of the philosophy of relation, "in which," as Glissant says, "we try to see how humanities transform themselves," is more and less than the same old story.[17] Its torqued seriality— bent, twisted, propelled off line—is occult, impossible articulation. The line is broken; the passage is overtaken, become detour; it is, again as Glissant says, unknown; it carries gentle, unavoidably violent overturning, a contrapuntal swerve of the underside; it performs a rhizomatic voluntarity, roots escaping from themselves without schedule into the outer depths. This involuntary consent of the volunteer is our descent, our inheritance, should we choose to accept it, claim it, assent to it: forced by ourselves, against force, to a paraontological attendance upon being-sent, we are given to discover how being-sent turns glide, *glissando*, into fractured and incomplete releasement of and from the scale, into the immeasurable. Braxton's music, its sharp-edged celebration, has a dying fall and rise. It descends and ascends us. It sends us and we are befallen by the fate of the one, which is to become many. Fallen into sociality, thrown into the history we make in having been thrown into it, we are given, in being given to this music, to flight away from a given syntax, from the linguistic law within, into a mode of autonomous auto-regulation that will, itself, have been escaped.

The rough glide of Braxton's musical movement, the burred terrain of Glissant's words, sends us to find out more of what it means to have been sent to give yourself away. We are driven to resist this movement, where consent is now inseparable from a monstrous imposition, but we are also drawn, at the same time, against ourselves, to the rail, to the abyss, by the iterative, broken singularity it hides and holds, by the murmur of buried, impossible social life—that excluded middle passage into multiplicity, where pained, breathlessly overblown harmonic striation (*Sacrum Commercium,* sacred fragment; contra-musical moment; catastrophe's counterstrophic movement), from way underneath some unfathomable and impossible to overcome violation, animates ecstasies driven down and out into the world as if risen into another: impossible assent, *consentement impossible, glissment impossible*, impossible Glissant, unimaginable axe, unheard of Braxton.

We study how to claim this sound that claims us, and that Glissant and Braxton amplify, in work that beautifully discovers, in the depths of our common impasse, our common flight and our common habitation. They allow and require us to be interested in the unlikely emergence of the unlikely figure of the black soloist, whose irruptive speech occurs not only against the grain of a radical interdiction of individuality that is manifest both as an assumption of its impossibility as well as in a range of governmental dispositions designed to prevent the impossible, but also within the context of a refusal of what has been interdicted (admission to the zone of abstract equivalent citizenship and subjectivity, whose instantiations so far have been nothing but a set of pseudo-individuated after-effects of conquest and conquest denial, a power trip to some fucked-up place in the burnt-out sun), a kind of free or freed "personality" that will have turned out to be impossible even for the ones who are convinced they have achieved it, even as they oversee its constant oscillation between incompleteness and repair, distress and fashion. That refusal is a kind of dissent that marks our descent, that moves in the terribly beautiful absence of patrimonial birthright or heritage and in the general, generative, maternally rotund and black Falstaffic recognition that necessarily masculinist honor is just a bunch of hot air. Such refusal, such dissent, takes the form of a common affirmation, an open consensus given in the improbable, more than im/possible, consent, in Glissant's words, "not to be a single being."[18] By what paradoxical means does the black soloist continue to give that consent, a re-gifting that not only instantiates but also redoubles just about all of the doubleness we come to associate with giving and the gift and the given? Here, the given is unfinished, as elastic composition, not (traditionally or sententiously) well-formed.

Fear of the black soloist is a transcendental clue that tips us off to her importance. She is subject to beating and attack—whether by the state or its sanctioned, extra-governmental deputies—because her walking out alone is understood to be a threat to the order of things, a placement of that order under attack. But more often even than beating, the preferred institutional response to the (una)lone transgressor is her enforced isolation, since solitary confinement is misunderstood to be a method for silencing what it only serves to amplify. This invasive irruption of fugued, fugitive singularity into the administered world both figures and performs an immanent rather than transcendent alterity, the undercommon sociality of another world in and under and surrounding this one, disruptive of its regulatory protocols, diversive of its executive grammar. My primary interest is in that range of explosive, melismatic voicing. I'm after a certain doo-wopped, post-bopped, aquadoolooped, da da da da da datted (un)broken circle of study—the general form of the development group, in some kind of community sing, a Child Development Group of Mississippi, say, where putatively motherless, always already endangered children move, not without moving but within movement, in specific, *a capella* instantiation of strain, of resistance to constraint, as instruments of deinstrumentalization, in the propelling and constraining force of the refrain, in that land of California, where Chicago is a city in Mississippi, Mississippi a refuge, a (fugue) state of mind, in Chicago. Such voicing always moves, always in the wilderness, under regulatory duress, and its own theory has it that that kind of trouble "really keeps us workin' our mind."[19] To set it off like that, to go off like that, to anarrange like that, is a kind of head start, but you have to have some sense of the value of playing, of being played with, of being played, of being-instrument, of being-endangered, of mere being, of having fallen, of doing the thing, of doing your thing, under water, underground, out in the open secret, in public, exposed in the interest of safety—which is a kind of flower for refugees—and autonomy, when flown-away hands start clapping. All we have to do is find somebody that would love to sing. You want to sing? Well, somebody start singing . . .

Generativity, our ongoing common growth in difference, is also escape in contemplative performance, reanimating the itinerant communal form of the city before as a study hall inside a dance hall. Black study is a mode of life whose initiatory figures are given as anarchic principles that are form-generating. Not just the proliferation of form, to which generativity would then submit itself, but proliferative, generative form. This is what Braxton is trying to produce, at the intersection of study, competence, composition, and performance (improvisation). There is a kind of anti-instrumental rationality that lends itself to a being-instrument. It moves by way of the instrument's disruptive extension. Again, this is instantiated, we might say, in the figure of the speaker, the bridge machine, through and across whom praises (voices, forces) flow. She consents not to be a single being. "Common alterity," he prays, "make me your instrument." It's the speaker's capacity to generate generative form, this fearsomeness of what the black soloist is and does, the one who, being so much more and less than one, so emphatically not but nothing other than human, discomposes for submerged choir (city), a song in flight that is sung while sunken. She moves in place, off the track he's on, for the love of the set it opens. There's an alto wind at your back, even if all you're trying to do is get out of the way of what you want to ride, so you can keep on generating these monkish dormitory chants, the archaeology of our potential, past, in the funereal birthplace, the venereal graveyard, which is a slave ship, a project, and a prison; a sound booth, a corner, and a broken window; a law school, a conservatory, and a language lab.

NOTES

1. Robert M. Cover, "Foreword: *Nomos* and Narrative," *Harvard Law Review* 97, no. 1 (1983): 40.
2. Cover, "The Bonds of Constitutional Interpretation: Of the Word, the Deed, and the Role," *Georgia Law Review* 20 (1986): 833.
3. Samuel Beckett, *The Unnamable*, in *Molloy, Malone Dies, The Unnamable: Three Novels by Samuel Beckett* (New York: Grove Press, 1965, first published in French in 1958), 292.
4. For more on Holmes's response to jurisgenerative fecundity, see Richard Maxwell Brown, *No Duty to Retreat: Violence and Values in American History and Society* (Norman: University of Oklahoma Press, 1994), 3–37; and Louis Menand, *The Metaphysical Club: A Story of Ideas in America* (New York: Farrar, Strauss and Giroux, 2001), 3–69.
5. Noam Chomsky, *Language and Mind*, 3rd ed. (Cambridge: Cambridge University Press, 2006), viii.
6. See George E. Lewis, *A Power Stronger Than Itself: The AACM and American Experimental Music* (Chicago: University of Chicago Press, 2008).
7. Chomsky, "What We Know: On the Universals of Language and Rights," *Boston Review* 30, nos. 3–4 (Summer 2005): 23–27.
8. I have been the grateful recipient of extended tutelage on the matter of historicist critique of Chomsky from my colleague Julie Tetel Andresen.
9. Julie Tetel Andresen, "Historiography's Contribution to Theoretical Linguistics," in *Chomskyan (R)evolutions*, ed. Douglas Kibbee (Amsterdam: John Benjamins, 2010), 443–69.
10. Cheryl A. Wall, *Worrying the Line: Black Women Writers, Lineage, and Literary Tradition* (Chapel Hill: University of North Carolina Press, 2005).
11. Graham Lock, *Forces in Motion: The Music and Thoughts of Anthony Braxton* (New York: Da Capo, 1988), 167.
12. Martin Heidegger, *Being and Time*, trans. John Macquarrie and Edward Robinson (New York: Harper, 1962), 219–20.
13. Theodor W. Adorno, "On Jazz," translated by Jamie Owen Daniel and Richard Leppert, in *Essays on Music*, edited by Richard Leppert, with translations by Susan H. Gillespie, Jamie Owen Daniel, and Richard Leppert (Berkeley: University of California Press, 2002), 492.
14. Anthony Braxton, Liner notes for *Donna Lee*, America 05 067 863-2, compact disc, 2005. First published in 1972.
15. Braxton, *Composition Notes: Book A* (Lebanon, NH: Frog Peak Music / Synthesis Music, 1988), 139–40.
16. Chomsky, *Language and Mind*, 9.

17. Manthia Diawara, "One World in Relation: Édouard Glissant in Conversation with Manthia Diawara," trans. Christopher Winks, *Nka: Journal of Contemporary African Art* 2011(28): 15.
18. Diawara, "One World in Relation," 5.
19. See Polly Greenberg, *The Devil Has Slippery Shoes* (London: Macmillan, 1969). Hear *Head Start: With the Child Development Group of Mississippi*, Smithsonian Folkways Recordings FW02690, 2004. First published by Folkways Records in 1967.

BIBLIOGRAPHY

Adorno, Theodor W. "On Jazz." Translated by Jamie Owen Daniel and Richard Leppert. In *Essays on Music*, edited by Richard Leppert, with translations by Susan H. Gillespie, Jamie Owen Daniel, and Richard Leppert, 470–95. Berkeley: University of California Press, 2002.

Andresen, Julie Tetel. "Historiography's Contribution to Theoretical Linguistics." In *Chomskyan (R)evolutions*, edited by Douglas Kibbee, 443–469. Amsterdam: John Benjamins, 2010.

Beckett, Samuel. *The Unnamable*. In *Molloy, Malone Dies, The Unnamable: Three Novels by Samuel Beckett*. New York: Grove Press, 1965 (first published in French in 1958).

Braxton, Anthony. *Composition Notes: Book A*. Lebanon, NH: Frog Peak Music/Synthesis Music, 1988.

Braxton, Anthony. Liner notes for *Donna Lee*. America 05 067 863-2, compact disc, 2005. First published in 1972.

Brown, Richard Maxwell. *No Duty to Retreat: Violence and Values in American History and Society*. Norman: University of Oklahoma Press, 1994.

Chomsky, Noam. "What We Know: On the Universals of Language and Rights." *Boston Review* 30, nos. 3–4 (Summer 2005): 23–27.

Chomsky, Noam. *Language and Mind*. 3rd ed. Cambridge: Cambridge University Press, 2006.

Cover, Robert M. "Foreword: Nomos and Narrative." *Harvard Law Review* 97, no. 1 (1983): 4–68.

Cover, Robert M. "The Bonds of Constitutional Interpretation: Of the Word, the Deed, and the Role." *Georgia Law Review* 20 (1986).

Diawara, Manthia. "One World in Relation: Édouard Glissant in Conversation with Manthia Diawara," translated by Christopher Winks. *Nka: Journal of Contemporary African Art* 2011(28): 4–19.

Greenberg, Polly. *The Devil Has Slippery Shoes*. London: Macmillan, 1969.

Head Start: With the Child Development Group of Mississippi. Smithsonian Folkways Recordings FW02690, 2004. First published by Folkways Records in 1967.

Heidegger, Martin. *Being and Time*. Translated by John Macquarrie and Edward Robinson. New York: Harper, 1962.

Lewis, George E. *A Power Stronger Than Itself: The AACM and American Experimental Music*. Chicago: University of Chicago Press, 2008.

Lock, Graham. *Forces in Motion: The Music and Thoughts of Anthony Braxton*. New York: Da Capo, 1988.

Menand, Louis. *The Metaphysical Club: A Story of Ideas in America*. New York: Farrar, Strauss and Giroux, 2001.

Wall, Cheryl A. *Worrying the Line: Black Women Writers, Lineage, and Literary Tradition*. Chapel Hill: University of North Carolina Press, 2005.

CHAPTER 7

IS IMPROVISATION PRESENT?

MICHAEL GALLOPE

In October 2002, Jacques Derrida experienced something very extraordinary: he attended two screenings of a film entirely devoted to his life and his philosophy. This produced some atypical situations for him. In the weeks leading up to the premiere, a wave of American press attention crested, describing the film as "adoring and adorable" (*New York Times*), "wise and witty" (*New York Post*), "complex, and highly ambitious" (*New York Daily News*), "the cinematic equivalent of a mind-expanding drug" (*Los Angeles Times*), and, perhaps most idiosyncratically, a portrait of "the Mick Jagger of cultural philosophy" (*Boston Globe*). The film's buzz ran far beyond the circuits of the philosopher's academic readers, so much so that Derrida found himself denying a slew of interview requests from curious journalists and film critics.

So far as I can tell, just one man managed to work around the refusals. Joel Stein, a staff writer for *Time* magazine, slipped through the back door of New York City's *Film Forum* on the night of the screenings and cornered Derrida with a series of unphilosophical questions: Do you like this banana bread we're eating? (He loved it.) What are your favorite movies? (*The Godfather*, apparently.) And something like: What is the deal with your flowing white hair? (It is something he was understandably anxious about losing.)[1] While Derrida was forthcoming in these answers, all this real-time interaction about nonacademic topics seems to have annoyed the distinguished French philosopher, who claimed to find a certain journalistic expectation to drop everything and sound off on whatever topic particularly irritating. At least, this is what Stein reported: to the philosopher's chagrin, these days "everyone wants [Derrida] to say something brilliant on love or war or death."

Certainly it is not always easy to sound responsive, clear, focused, genuine, and concise in real-time speech acts. But I wonder if there is a serious philosophical question at issue here. For Derrida, we might recall, the anxiety about effective communication in real-time performance reflected the philosopher's famous suspicion toward the experience of hearing oneself speak, which, in his view, often harbored a metaphysical aura of "self-presence." Over banana bread, and likely with a range of deferrals, ramblings, and transferences in mind, Derrida told Stein bluntly: "It's frustrating. Especially when you have to improvise."

By coincidence, I too found my way to Derrida's attention that night—not as a journalist, of course, but as a young undergraduate curious as to whether or not the philosopher had anything interesting to say about music. In a Q&A session that followed the screening, I raised my hand from the audience and asked Derrida: "What kind of music do you listen to and why do you listen to it?"[2] Stein described Derrida's response in the pages of *Time*: "Someone asked Derrida what kind of music he likes, and he revealed his love for free jazz and told a really long story about how Ornette Coleman once got him to read onstage during a show." Indeed, as the philosopher subsequently recounted, five years prior, when Coleman was in Paris to perform at the *La Villette* jazz festival in a duo with pianist Joachim Kühn, he invited Derrida to join in on stage during one of the performances, in which he read off a prepared text, "Joue—le prénom."[3] By the philosopher's own admission, however, it is equally well known that the audience did not like it; in fact, we are told, their reaction led him to leave the stage early.[4] As Derrida remembered it, "[Coleman's] fans were so unhappy they started booing. It was a very unhappy event. It was a very painful experience.... But it was in the paper the next day, so it was a happy ending."[5] One could speculate as to why this was so. A jazz festival audience may have just wanted what they hoped would be an unfiltered version of Coleman. Or they may have bristled at the idea of a philosopher explaining music that allegedly should be able to speak for itself.

But I wonder: did the collaborative failure on the part of the two men mean that they had both misunderstood, or underestimated, a certain incompatibility between philosophy and improvised music? In light of how musically inclined thinkers like Ernst Bloch, Theodor Adorno, Roland Barthes, and Félix Guattari found ways to bring their favorite music into dialogue with their philosophical views, might Derrida, who was an expert in literature and philosophy but had little technical background in music, have provided Coleman's music with a deconstructive manifesto? Or were the other side's expectations at fault: should free jazz's forays into conceptual justification (reflected in Coleman's responses to Derrida's pre-festival interview, Anthony Braxton's *Tri-Axium Writings*, or Cecil Taylor's poetry) just steer clear of lecturing in the concert hall, in order to let the music speak on its own terms?[6]

Whatever the case, a difference of medium seems to present us with a problem. Philosophers do not always feel comfortable accounting for music in a conceptually driven way (let alone performing with it), and vice versa for the musicians untrained in philosophy. This chapter considers these missed connections as a point of departure. When philosophy has trouble clarifying or deepening our understanding of something that seems to still lend itself to a conceptual explanation (like Coleman's free jazz), one way forward is to try and stage the encounter anyway. This is what I would like to attempt here, by re-asking the question it seems that Derrida's thinking poses to Coleman's music—Is improvisation present?

Of course, readers familiar with Derrida's philosophy will probably quickly realize that the answer is, in fact, "no." But it is not a simple "no." In fact, exactly how his philosophy might answer "no" in the particular case of music may help us clarify some challenging conceptual terrain. To explore the structure of this problem, I would like to begin by taking recourse to the work of a philosopher who puzzled over very similar issues as Derrida but did write frequently and passionately about music—the French moral philosopher and amateur pianist Vladimir Jankélévitch. While there exist, to be sure, substantial philosophical differences between the two philosophers, both understood the experience of time and the problem of technical mediation to be the sources of an exceptional aporia for philosophy. And both issues—time and technical mediation—seem to be crucial factors for a philosophical account of musical improvisation.

In order to build the discussion up toward my thesis, allow me to begin by summarizing a few of Jankélévitch's central positions. Taking intellectual cues from his mentor, Henri Bergson, Jankélévitch understands the flux of lived time, or *durée*, as creative in a sense that stands in excess of all understanding or intellection. But he also emphasizes that the effects of *durée* are as destructive as they are creative. For just as time is the key axis under which one can understand life to be created, developed, and reproduced, it is the equally essential axis for the second law of thermodynamics that ensures the eventual loss of every life, the forgetting of moral acts, the transgression of laws, and the evanescence of every musical event. Given the specter of nihilism suggested by the valueless flux of time, Jankélévitch wonders: why does a moral act, a musical work, or a life come to exist and sustain itself at all?

In search of a substantial ground for moral, ethical, and aesthetic virtues, Jankélévitch's philosophy asks us to turn against scientific or logical forms of knowing in order to arrive at what he described as virtuous or "innocent" meditations that are attuned to temporally dynamic aspects of real-life experience. Consequently, for him, as for Bergson, philosophy requires a certain attentive fidelity to lived experience:

> [T]he generous mind does not remain confined in a blasé memory; it does not impose a summary solfège on the admirable variety of nature. . . . Intellectual effort signifies that we have kept a means of conquering the data of experience by testing the originality of things and the resistance of problems, by conserving intact this sensibility to the unexpected that produces the prize of knowledge. For a deep science does not happen without a substantial innocence.[7]

For Jankélévitch, this virtuous attunement or "innocence" toward lived experience is intended to follow through on Bergson's faithful attention to the qualitative multiplicity of *durée*, or lived time. For both philosophers, knowledge of the real comes through access to intuition. Intuition allows us to overcome the sense that our perception is simply changing from one discrete cognitive state to another; rather, it gives us access to real becoming—absolute change at every moment, in every direction, regardless of our awareness. This is what remains resistant to all forms of spatialization and intellection.

> Becoming does not permit the object to be divided into sectors, according to its corporeal limits; it is much more the dimension according to which the object undoes itself without end, forms, deforms, transforms, and then re-forms itself. A succession of states of the body, that is, change itself, dissolves the limits fossilized by our mental habit of splitting and dividing.[8]

But whereas Bergson's concept of *durée*, first staged in *Time and Free Will* (1889), led him to forward a speculative philosophy of memory and cognition (*Matter and Memory*, 1896) and a philosophy of evolution (*Creative Evolution,* 1907), Jankélévitch's philosophy focuses on our lived experience of *durée*. In particular, he is interested in the knotty and paradoxical issues that structure the possibility of focusing on the instant as a point of attentive fidelity.

In the *Philosophie première* of 1953, Jankélévitch explored this logic through an inquiry into how experience negotiates metaphysical forms of knowledge. There, he ventures that just as the conscious mind comes to isolate the absolute productivity of the creative instant, consciousness itself paradoxically seems to face phenomenological occlusion. "We can take, in the smallest being of the instant, only a consciousness itself almost inexistent, which is to say trans-discursive and intuitive: not so much a kind of Gnostic clarity, it [the almost inexistent] is the only positive science of sur-truth [*survé-rité*] that might be given to us to claim." Here, even as we try to isolate the "smallest being of the instant," our experience of time does not give us any kind of "Gnostic clarity" on the exact nature of the instant itself. Instead, a contradiction presents itself: our efforts at absolute knowledge of the instant (or "sur-truth [*survérité*]") are incessantly structured by memory, cognition, and intervallic structures of temporality. This leaves us with access only to the uncertain and approximate poetry of the "almost inexistent." He continues: "A discursive and chronic knowledge of sur-truth is a way of contradiction, and, therefore, a knowledge [*savoir*] founded on memory and on the continuation of an interval condemning itself here to negativity."[9] This "knowledge founded on memory" occludes the absolute perception of the instant as a moment of self-present consciousness by rendering it subject to "the continuation of an interval condemning itself to negativity." The instant cannot be presented as a form of absolute knowledge without recourse to a mediating network of remembered or "absent" temporal intervals.

The lack of sustained knowledge of the lived instant might be visualized with the following diagram (Figure 7.1). Here, the now is represented by a singular point on a continuum of experienced time stretching off to the right. Below the continuum are two arrows representing an absent interval of time. Only through the mediation of this lower

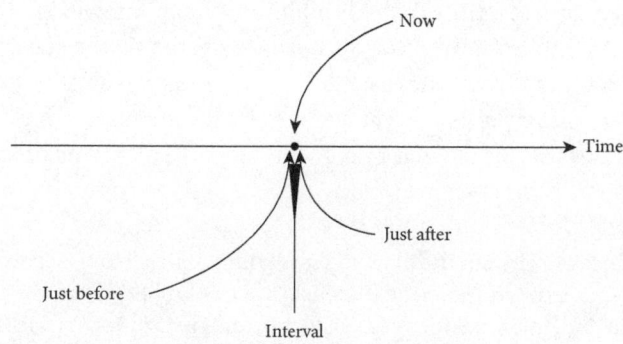

FIGURE 7.1 Fidelity to Jankélévitch's Instant.

interval can the instant become known to experience. It is something of a paradox: a positive instant cannot become present to our experience without the negative mediation of two other moments that span a minimal interval.

The co-implied nature of positivity and negativity at work in the consciousness of an instant is not restricted to the sphere of perception. In the opening chapter of *Le Pardon* (1967), the irreversible degradation of living matter is integrated with Bergson's *durée*: "The decay of living organisms, if it is accelerated by physical or chemical agents, results above all from a qualitative and irreversible entropy that is essential to a lived becoming."[10] Just as it is with organisms, so it is with the effect of our memory upon our experience of the coming now; an irreversible future of incessant alteration also means that no pure expectations uncontaminated by memory (and its effacement) are possible: "[B]ecoming retains memories, alteration, slowed down by the weight of the past, and implies the decay of this past, for the return to the *status quo ante* is impossible. . . ."[11]

The negative character of time (decay, loss, evanescence, mediation of creativity by memory and idiom) will be key to his account of musical improvisation. For Jankélévitch, improvising is not simply based in positive access to the instant of musical creativity. Rather, improvisation carries the existential burdens of evanescence, loss, and silence; negativity constitutes "all that is melancholy in temporality."[12] In one of Jankélévitch's books on music, we can see the logic explicitly at work. As he says, improvisational fidelity toward the becoming of the lived instant requires not a submersion within the embodied present, but a hyperactive attentiveness to the micro-timing of remembrance and anticipation *around* the lived instant.

> Depending on whether it is antecedent or consequent, tension toward the instant after rehabilitation or at the instant before, improvisation would be expectation of the future or a minimum retrospectivity. In the first case, it refers to the urgent future of action or the immanent future of passion, which is to say to what is *immediately* subsequent: it awaits the arrival or the advent of the future that happens, and it is this adventure; a second too late, this coming would not be next, but far; a second later it would be too late, and this future would be a present. The second case is that of the smallest possible delay, that which comes *immediately* after the minimum reaction time of reflexes; a second too late and it would be too early and the improviser would find itself nose-to-nose with its present; a second too late and the recent past would pass far behind. Between the two distances—the past and the future—improvisation "most closely" follows (or preceeds) a conjuncture that is just barely future or almost present, just barely present or almost past.[13]

What we see characterized here is the temporal structure of a committed "adventure" of improvised time, something I will refer to as a theory of *complex temporality*. Rather than a meditative channeling of a spontaneously expressive now, complex temporality makes clear that improvisation is the product of an intervallic network that ties the coming now to the nearest possible anticipation of the future and the nearest possible recollection of the past. The measure of an improviser's skill (or virtue) shows up in the degree to which one maintains attentive fidelity toward the nearest possible moment without ever becoming simply self-present. In this sense, improvisation, with its necessary and constitutive blindnesses and uncertainties, represents a faithful and vigilant operation that, for Jankélévitch, "leads" presence. Complex temporality is only ever "quasi-contemporaneous" in being the nearest possible, without becoming fully contemporaneous with the arriving instant of the vanishing now.

This unpresentability of the instant recurs as a leitmotif in Jankélévitch's broader philosophy of music.[14] In books like *Music and the Ineffable*, for example, it receives the metaphysical name of *Charme*, which designates the evanescence that ensures the inexhaustability of musical experience, or its "divine inconsistency." He writes: "*Charme* rejects therefore the question 'Where?' just as it eludes the question 'What?' *Charme*, that is not keen on *this-or-that*, does not lie either *here-or-there*."[15] For Jankélévitch, the *charme* of music is not an experience of presence, but rather is based in a paradoxical sense of occlusion inherent to the passing of a lived instant. *Charme* "is therefore essentially *evasive*—which is to say that it escapes, invisible, and intangible and yet always present as are music and fragrances that we can neither see nor touch; it obligates us to an irritating game of hide and seek."[16] This relentless intangibility of music reflects a property of time itself—a negative absence one finds at the heart of the lived instant.

Derrida, for his part, would likely agree equally that the vanishing now cannot simply be made present to experience. But deconstruction thinks through negativity on a more constitutive level. Derrida argues that the "negative absence" that makes the lived instant unpresentable is based in more than the mediation of intervallic synthesis; he insists always and everywhere that time (or becoming) is always structured by something that it is not—spatial inscription, or *espacement*. As he puts it famously in his essay "*Différance*":

> An interval must separate the present from what it is not in order for the present to be itself, but this interval that constitutes it as present must, by the same token, *divide the present in and of itself*, thereby also dividing along with the present, everything that is thought on the basis of the present, that is, in our metaphysical language, every being, and singularly substance or the subject. In constituting itself, in dividing itself dynamically, this interval is what might be called spacing, the becoming-space of time or the becoming-time of space (temporization).[17]

For Derrida, the interval at work in memory or cognition does not simply occlude the presence of the vanishing now "in an irritating game of hide and seek;" rather, as Martin Hägglund has recently argued, it mediates all time from within.[18]

There are many ways to try and make sense of this very complicated claim, but for the experience of music in particular I think it may be instructive to draw a short parallel here with Hegel's discussion of the temporality of sound as explained in the *Lectures on Aesthetics*.[19] There, Hegel explains how sound (passing in time) is a phenomenon that is a "double-negation"—a being ceases to be itself in the very instant that it becomes. For Hegel, a sound [*Klang*] becomes a tone [*Ton*] when an "idea," a reflection of inward subjectivity, allows a sonorous being to overcome the incessant flux of time's "double negation" and acquire a proper and discrete unity.

For Derrida, in order for what Hegel describes as the "double-negation" of the vanishing "now" to not fly on by as a nothingness or an abyss, lived moments must "be" in some empirical sense—they must be structured or "inscribed" by an anticipation (or "protention" in the vocabulary of phenomenology) as well as one's memory or "retention," a topic Derrida devotes substantial attention to in his critiques of Edmund Husserl.[20] This is a familiar thought for Jankélévitch: in his view, "intervallic" inscriptions immediately before and after the now are the mediating substance of all improvisation. But the Derridian logic of inscription goes further in holding that *the instant itself is inscribed.* For Derrida, what Jankélévitch described as "our mental habit of splitting and dividing" does not supervene in a process of secondary intellectual reflection; rather, it divides the instant of the now in itself.

The following diagram represents an attempt to formalize this structure: the instant is shown here on the central horizontal axis of time stretching to the right. For deconstruction, the passing now is not merely subject to intervallic mediation as it would for Jankélévitch's theory of complex temporality. Rather, the instant—in its instantaneous being—is subject to spacing, writing, idiom, and many other means of objective mediation. I have represented this with six radiating fans of symbolic grids that extend outward from the instantaneous now. Notice further that these mediating grids are also, for Derrida, "sous-rature"—under erasure by virtue of the decay inherent to

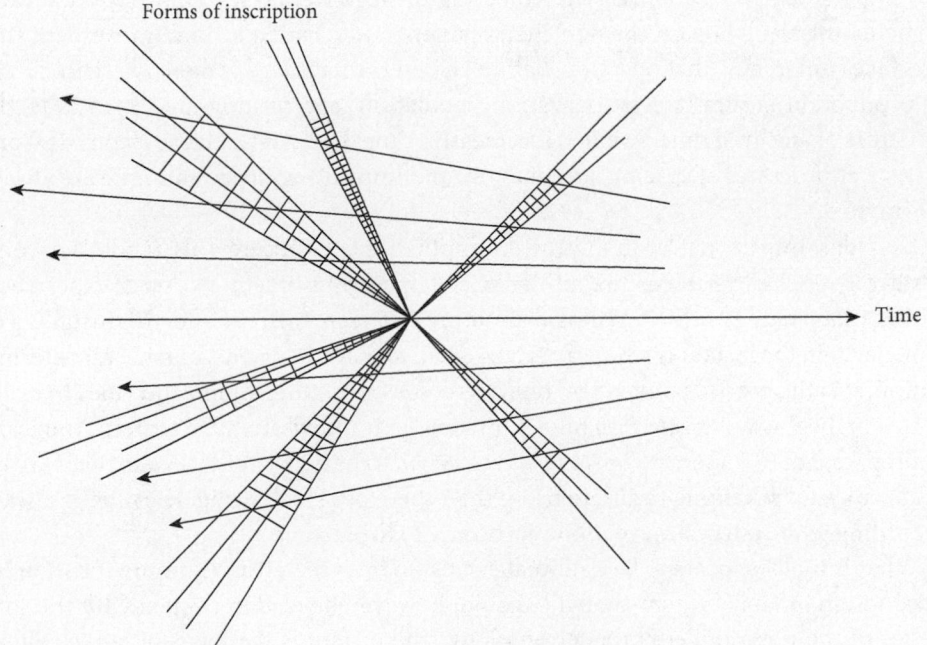

FIGURE 7.2 Derrida's Instant.

the passage of time. I have represented this erasure with six countervailing arrows of time (Figure 7.2).

Derrida's emphasis on structural determination, of course, does not mean that the creative instant of improvisation is simply determined or "notated." Because all forms of life are everywhere immediately based in a multiplicity of inscribed traces, for Derrida, any single or proper medium of determination like notation would be subject to decon-struction. In *Of Grammatology*, Derrida deconstructs the medium of embodied speech because its alleged immediacy facilitates a "metaphysics of presence," an operation that could be applied to alphabetic script or Western musical notation for different reasons—any naturalized medium that might claim to overcome the instabilities of time and inscribe the eternal. By contrast, the improvised instant is structured by an undecidable multiplicity of inscriptions.

In marked distinction to Bergson and Jankélévitch, what we do not find in Derrida's account are any affirmations that this instant is inherently creative, even if inscribing something as a trace in order for it to "be" seems a lot like "creating."[21] One sees conse-quences of this in Derrida's method. Since any metaphysical safety zone for time as a force of creativity might risk making time look like "God" or a divine cause, at a forma-tive moment of his career Derrida uses the word "*différance*" to indicate the absence of any instance of eternity or immortality outside the finite universe. As Derrida says, *différance* constitutes the primordial "becoming-space of time [spacing] and becoming-time of space [temporization]" and "the 'active,' moving discord of different forces and of differences of forces. . . ."[22] In impersonally marking "the formation of form" and "articulation," this general "being-imprinted of the imprint" affirms not vital creation, but impersonal production via the nonliving or negative motif of inscription, always "articulating the living on the non-living in general," forming a "pure movement that produces difference" that operates "before all determination of content."[23] These forces of production ensure that spatialization, mediation, and writing are intrinsic to the structure of any lived time. For Derrida, creative time does not receive metaphysical pri-ority over processes of spacing, articulation, and imprinting; space and time are always co-implied.

Derrida's impersonal economy of co-implied space-time reveals to us the com-paratively metaphysical nature of Jankélévitch's commitment to lived experience, which often retains a hierarchical dichotomy between interval and the instant. For Jankélévitch, the instant is where a certain creative magic happens; outside all determi-nation, it is the precise point where one overcomes structure, idiom, and rules in order to invent, begin, and create.[24] In his central text on improvisation, he writes: "You learn to prepare, not to *invent*; to continue, not to *begin*, to provide, not to *create*; there are no more rules for inventing or improvising than there are for desiring; learning is always according to the interval, never done according to the instant."[25]

What initially appears to be a mutual exclusion between creative moment and prac-ticed idiom in Jankélévitch's thought should, however, be read in context with the sub-tleties of the philosopher's broader ontology. The instant is the focus of Jankélévitch's philosophy not because it is simply the locus of self-present creativity. In my view,

Jankélévitch's instant represents a horizon of creation just as much as it represents the simultaneous necessity of nonpresence, erasure, and loss. According to his theory of complex temporality, the creativity of the vanishing now is constitutively occluded and structured by memory, synthesis, and the loss of evanescence. Its non-presence is why improvisation is instead based in an attentive fidelity to the locus of lived experience.

By comparison, Derrida does not understand the instant of lived time to be an instance of creativity. So thorough was his commitment to thinking of time as structured by the negativity of space from within that, when he discusses improvisation, he does so with a pronounced sense of distance from the coming present. Consider the beginning of "Joue—le prénom," the text he prepared for his onstage performance with Ornette Coleman. Unmoored from an attentive or skilled grounding in the lived instant, Derrida initially presents himself to Coleman, Kühn, and their audience as an improviser in full-on panic mode:

> Qu'est-ce qui arrive? What's happening? What's going to happen, Ornette, now, right now? What's happening to me, here, now, with Ornette Coleman? With you? Who? *Il faut bien improviser, il faut* **bien** *improviser.* [It is indeed necessary to improvise, it is necessary to improvise *well.*] I knew that Ornette was going to call on me to join him tonight, he told me so when we met to talk one afternoon last week. This chance frightens me, I have no idea what's going to happen.[26]

Here, Derrida's two varying emphases on "bien" playfully juxtapose the unchosen injunction to improvise against the ethical imperative to do it well. But a skilled negotiation of doing it well is what remains at issue, and Derrida puts his feelings plainly: "This chance frightens me, I have no idea what's going to happen." The following remarks, made in an earlier interview, present another version of his views of improvisation (though purged of the sense of anxiety he expressed onstage with Coleman). More soberly, here he emphasizes the hauntingly absent "prescriptions" and "schemas" we improvisers are bound to adopt as mere marionettes of a symbolic order beyond our control and apprehension:

> It's not easy to improvise, it's the most difficult thing to do. . . . [O]ne ventriloquizes or leaves another to speak in one's place the schemas and languages that are already there. There are already a great number of prescriptions that are prescribed in our memory and in our culture. . . . One can't say whatever one wants, one is obliged more or less to reproduce the stereotypical discourse. And so I believe in improvisation and I fight for improvisation. But always with the belief that it's impossible. . . . I am blind to myself. . . . The one who is improvised here, no I won't ever see him.[27]

For Derrida, it would seem that amidst a multiplicity ("a great number of prescriptions") one confronts the reality that no single skilled or measured relationship to the passing now is constitutive of an improvised experience, effectively resigning one to an "impossibility" of remaining fully attentive to one's experience of the lived instant. It is here that Jankélévitch might ask: Without a sense of attentive fidelity to the passage of the vanishing now, how would one improvisation be deemed more successful than another? Does not improvisation require an account of ethical (or skilled) criteria based in the actions of an individual's experience? Or one might ask: How can one think of improvisation in a way that follows Derrida's emphasis on inscription without allowing the weight of mediation to excessively question a positive focus on skill and virtuosity?

Jankélévitch's account of musical improvisation, in my view, comes with limitations that largely stem from his focus on notated compositions. In his most sustained consideration of the topic, once he elaborates his basic position of complex temporality, he turns to a discussion of examples. It is at this point that Jankélévitch turns away from the topic of real-time improvisation and begins discussing a compositional "*Rhapsodie*" that exhibits directly the "initial moment of invention," a metaphysical "chronos of the real" unleashed from the immanent powers of Franz Liszt's rhapsodic style of composition:

> [When thinking of improvisation] the interest shifts from the finished work to the operation, of the determined form on the undetermined and determining formation. . . . Romantic man wants to creep up on the revealed message of the genius and the "how" of creation. But to him Bergsonism also shows us how one must invert a doctrinal order and an ideal after-the-fact reconstruction in order to obtain the chronos of the real; the musical work, all the same, is not fabricated with static *themes*, it is *organized* from a dynamic *scheme* . . . before being developed, it was a rhapsody. Yet the inventor incapable of explicating his inexplicable invention can only demonstrate by the fact of doing, that is to say to lead by example: the poet of the work exhibits therefore himself the work of the poem. . . . [H]e represents himself, most intimately, in the most initial moment of invention. . . . [I]t has the name Improvisation.[28]

For Jankélévitch, the rhapsody of improvisation is reflected in compositions by Liszt that rely less on thematic development, and more so on rhapsodic transitions that emulate the dynamics of one's inner creative spirit. In this way, Liszt's *Rhapsodie* emphasizes the brute "fact of doing," and echoes a view espoused by George Steiner in his book *Real Presences* (1991) for whom "the poet of the work exhibits therefore himself the work of the poem."[29] No mediating commentary, criticism, or clarification is necessary, and therefore nothing more needs (or ought) to be said.

But does Jankélévitch really mean to suggest that improvisation is best thought of us as music without mediation? Empirically, to be sure, it seems that the philosopher was not terribly interested in jazz or other explicitly improvised traditions. But there also may be a deeper philosophical reason Jankélévitch felt comfortable making this move. For the philosopher is less focused on one problem Derrida takes quite seriously: the constitutive role of inscription as a mediator. In his writings on music, Jankélévitch typically thinks of negativity in improvisation through the complex temporality of the vanishing now, often without considering how forms of inscription (or forms of musical writing) are structurally intrinsic to the negativity all improvisation must navigate. My sense is that this selective engagement with the problem of technical mediation is one reason Jankélévitch discusses improvisation in music largely as a philosophical explanation of Liszt's rhapsodic compositional style, rather than an analysis of real time musical negotiations.

Conceptually, it would seem, we are left with something of a dilemma: Derrida offers a theory in which we are "fighting for improvisation" in a situation that must negotiate a haunting multiplicity of structural inscriptions, that leaves us without strong criteria for the skilled negotiation of real time. And on other side we have Jankélévitch, who quite effectively and vividly theorizes an attentive fidelity to the vanishing now as an unpresentable horizon of experience, but who does not weigh the effects of structure and inscription as constitutive forms of mediation.

Perhaps, in staging a conversation that might bridge this dilemma, we can augment Jankélévitch's theory of complex temporality (an attentive fidelity to the vanishing now) with the Derridian injunction that the "intervallic" support systems of real-time temporality (the nearest possible before and after) are constituted not only by an "irritating game of hide and seek" inherent to the passage of time, but also a broader multiplicity of musical inscriptions. But one would have to stop short of following Derrida in assuming that the weight of inscription questions the very possibility of orienting oneself toward the lived instant with a sense of ethical skill. When Jankélévitch writes: "Improvisation is the returning of mediation to the immediate. Immediate mediation or discursive immediacy, improvisation is a sort of instantaneous preparation," one can then understand "mediation" to mean not just Jankélévitch's intervallic synthesis of the instant by the nearest possible before and after, but now also Derrida's multiplicity of potential inscriptions, structures, and idioms that bear upon an improvised act in the full complexity of their historical and discursive textures.[30] In bridging the two theories, we would restore some dialectical operation between the lived instant and the inscriptions we actually specify in musical discourse. And then we might have a philosophical apparatus to more fully investigate the speculative life of a musical practice based in "instantaneous preparation."

Such is the potential middle ground I see between these two positions. A theory of complex temporality adopted from Jankélévitch and augmented with Derrida's views on inscription can offer us a conceptual basis for understanding improvisation as a furiously active locus of complex mediations. In replacing the interpreted reproduction of a notated work with the injunction of consequential real-time decisions, improvisers, according to this logic, can be understood to affirm a constitutive absence at the heart of musical practice itself. According to this view, one improvises onward without a commonly agreed upon medium like notation or without the regulatory grid of a single musical idiom; and that would be the point of improvisation—to expose the ground of music to our survival instincts, to our idiomatic proclivities, to our historicities, to our notably faulty efforts and to our embarrassing mistakes, and, in some cases, to our utterly transformative experiences.

In the end, perhaps we also get a glimpse of the way in which the affirmations at play in musical improvisation exemplify a basic paradox of lived becoming—that the creative singularity or "freedom" that marks the very virtue of this modernist practice is at every instant determined by the threat of impossibility or failure, because all musical improvisation entails the necessity of reproducing something one has already heard or played. As Coleman himself says, "repetition is as natural as the fact the earth rotates."[31] Both philosophically and musically, this is not a tragedy to be mourned, nor is it the negation of all creativity; rather, it is an affirmation that allows us to think of improvisation as a virtuous exemplification of what it means to live through a risk that inheres in the passage of time, one that ensures the impossibility of any pure immortal or plentiful advent of self-presence. It is based in a real instant that is everywhere temporalized and spaced by absent determinations, a multidimensional network that integrates spatial traces of somatic and socio-technical inscriptions with the synthesis of the coming present.

I would conclude by proposing that this position is akin to the poetic commentary Fred Moten offers us in his close readings of the black radical tradition. For him, the tradition of free jazz represents neither a utopian musical communion of presence nor a bout of disorienting anxiety; it is fully mediated, marked by the virtuous singularity of one's active powers of musical anticipation that engage attentive efforts to rewrite musical rules in real time. Here, Moten evokes a synthesis of Jankélévitch's complex temporality with a broader Derridian insistence on the scope of the musico-cultural prescriptions and rules at play:

> Improvisation—as the word's linguistic roots indicate—is usually understood as speech *without foresight*. But improvisation . . . always also operates as a kind of foreshadowing, if not prophetic, description. . . . [Y]ou need to *look ahead* with a kind of torque *that shapes what's being looked at*. You need to do so without constraints of association, by way of a twisted epoché, or redoubled turn in the prescription and extemporaneous formation and reformation of rules, rather than the following of them.[32]

Moten's analysis continues on with a larger speculative totality in mind. For him, the improvisatory elements of the black radical tradition uncannily re-articulate a "phonographic" inscription of a scream uttered over a hundred years prior—specifically one overheard during a brutal whipping recounted by Frederick Douglass in his 1845 autobiography, *Narrative of the Life of Frederick Douglass, An American Slave*. In his analysis, black improvised traditions are not simple exemplifications of rule bending, but intrinsically linked to the speculative recollection of this traumatic sound. He writes:

> You cannot help but hear the echo of Aunt Hester's scream as it bears, at the moment of articulation, a sexual overtone, an invagination constantly reconstituting the whole of the voice, the whole of the story, redoubled and intensified by the mediation of years, recitations, auditions. That echo haunts, say, Albert Ayler's "Ghosts" or the fractured, fracturing climax of James Brown's "Cold Sweat." . . . Where shriek turns speech turns song—remote from the impossible comfort of origin—lies the trace of our descent.[33]

The speculative weight of this "phonographic" memory reminds us that improvisation is not simply creative singularity, but is rather a structured practice mediated by a vast multiplicity of absent traces: adopted idioms, cultural practices, and traumatic memories. These would be the mediating criteria for creativity, which structure and focus our unseen anticipations of the future: "Improvisation must be understood as a matter of sight and as a matter of time, *the time of a look ahead* whether that looking is the shape of a progressivist line or rounded, turned."[34] Far from being determined in any strong sense, for Moten, the lived musical instant is "rounded, turned" everywhere by an unknowable multiplicity of structures, memories, histories, anticipations, and determinations (or, in more strictly metaphysical terms—spatial "death" or "absence").

Consider, momentarily, text from a loosely transcribed interview with trumpeter and jazz composer Thad Jones. For Jones, the living present of improvisation and its associated virtues of selfless attunement can induce a sense of corporeal communion, in apparent excess of any mixed signals or crossed wires:

> Here the aesthetics of presence holds unrestrictedly. You give yourself up, surrender without ulterior motives; egoism and spirit of competition yield for generosity, presence and interdependence. One develops a presence that is like telepathic intuition . . . during such moments, improvisation is like the language that develops between two loving partners and that usually is called eroticism.[35]

How can one sympathize with this sentiment, but go on to emphasize the inevitable frictions that result from such aestheticized versions of erotic "presence?" Moten himself draws a philosophical line, though not a condemning one: "Thus improvisation is never manifest as a kind of pure presence—it is not the multiplicity of present moments just as it is not governed by an ecstatic temporal frame wherein the present is subsumed by past and future." Instead, for Moten, improvisation is only intelligible to the attentive listener who is willing to grasp both the constitutive necessity and unstable multiplicity of inscription that structure the attentive fidelity of an improvisational practice. To the listener sensitive to the dynamics of mediation, Jones then claims musical telepathy only to acknowledge here that improvisation is "like the language that develops between two loving partners"—accomplishing not a metaphysical communion or transubstantiation, but rather a secular negotiation through the erotic economy of love.

Cecil Taylor's highly self-reflexive spoken word album, *Chinampas* (1987), is equally exemplary in this regard. Moten writes: "Performance, ritual, and event are of the idea of idiom, of the 'anarchic principles' that open the unrepresentable performance of Taylor's phrasing." For him, inscription is constitutive, entailing necessary absences that invite cognitive interrogation. Indeed, Moten questions the meaning of Taylor's improvised movement, which for him represents an attempt to listen philosophically to the act of poetic construction itself. For Taylor and Moten, mediation, writing, and inscription are not relied upon as natural or transparent vehicles for aesthetic expression, but are rather made explicitly constitutive of the musical act. Notice here how Moten's effort to listen to Taylor virtuously maintains at once an attentive fidelity to complex temporality and a dutiful form of hermeneutic attention: "What happens in the transcription of performance, event, ritual? What happens, which is to say what is lost, in the recording? . . . What is heard there? What history is heard there? There is one which is not just one among others . . . the history of (an) organization, orchestra(tion), *construction*. The essence of construction is part of what that phrasing is after; the poem of construction—geometry of a blue ghost—is the poem that is of the music."[36] Far from a simple sense of liberated freedom or self-presence, Taylor's practice is based in a written "organization, orchestra(tion), *construction*," a formal "poem that is of the music," a "history" that is "in the recording" and subject to incessant mediations. In saying so, Taylor reflects an injunction one finds somewhere between Jankélévitch and Derrida—that improvisation constitutes a form of attentive fidelity precisely insofar as the vanishing now is structured by a multiplicity of meaningful inscriptions and mediations.

Of course, for now these are preliminary inquiries and this chapter only represents one attempt to understand these difficult questions. But at the very least, I think we might venture at this point that, under analysis, Jankélévitch and Derrida together reveal conceptual resources that can help us develop a deeper philosophical understanding of improvisation. Specifically, they allow us to see more precisely how improvised music grounds its sense of virtuosity not on the basis of a singular immediacy or self-presence, but in remaining mediated after having done away with any single proper idiom. This view allows us to affirm an unconditional absence or the lack of common ground at the heart of musical practice itself. It is an absence that addresses a certain question: How can philosophy explain the risks taken by a musical practice that is based at once on a profound sense of negativity and on a determined act of creativity?

NOTES

1. Joel Stein, "Life with the Father of Deconstructionism," *Time*, November 18, 2002, accessed May 17, 2011, http://www.time.com/time/magazine/article/0,9171,1003736-2,00.html.
2. Kirby Dick, Amy Ziering Kofman, and Jacques Derrida, *Derrida: Screenplay and Essays on the Film* (Manchester: Manchester University Press, 2005), 114.
3. Jacques Derrida, "Play—The First Name: 1 July 1997," trans. Timothy S. Murphy, *Genre: Forms of Discourse and Culture* 36, no. 2 (2004): 331–340; originally published as "Joue—Le Prénom," in *Les Inrockuptibles* 115 (August 20–September 2, 1997): 41–42.
4. Cf. Sara Ramshaw, "Deconstructin(g) Jazz Improvisation: Derrida and the Law of the Singular Event," *Critical Studies in Improvisation / Études critiques en improvisation*, accessed May 18, 2011, http://www.criticalimprov.com/article/viewArticle/81/179.
5. Stein, "Life with the Father of Deconstructionism."
6. Jacques Derrida and Ornette Coleman, "The Other's Language: Jacques Derrida Interviews Ornette Coleman, 23 June 1997," trans. Timothy S. Murphy, in "Blue Notes: Toward a New Jazz Discourse," part 1, ed. Mark Osteen, special issue, *Genre: Forms of Discourse and Culture* 37, no. 2 (2004): 319–329, originally published in *Les Inrockuptibles* 115 (August 20–September 2, 1997): 37–40, 43; Anthony Braxton, *Tri-Axium Writings*

(Dartmouth: Synthesis/Frog Peak, 1985); Cecil Taylor, *Chinampas*, Leo Records LR 153, 1987, CD.

7. Vladimir Jankélévitch, *Henri Bergson* (Paris: Presses Universitaires de France, 1989), 131. Unless stated otherwise, all translations are mine.

8. Vladimir Jankélévitch, *Music and the Ineffable*, trans. Carolyn Abbate (Princeton: Princeton University Press, 2003), 93.

9. Vladimir Jankélévitch, *Philosophie première* (Paris: Presses Universitaires de France, 1986), 99. "[N]ous n'en pouvons prendre, dans le moindre-être de l'instant, qu'une conscience elle-même *presque* inexistante, c'est-à-dire transdiscursive et intuitive: du moins cette gnose-éclair est-elle la seule science positive de la survérite à laquelle il nous soit donné de prétendre; un savoir discursive et chronique de la survérite est une manière de contradiction, et, partant, un savoir fondé sur la mémoire et sur la continuation d'intervalle se condamne ici à la négativité."

10. Vladimir Jankélévitch, *Forgiveness*, trans. Andrew Kelley (Chicago: University of Chicago Press, 2005), 13.

11. Jankélévitch, *Forgiveness*, 21, translation modified.

12. Jankélévitch, *Music and the Ineffable*, 96.

13. Vladimir Jankélévitch, *Liszt: Rhapsodie et Improvisation* (Paris: Flammarion, 1998), 109.

14. This aporia of unpresentability is the main point of innovation often credited to Jankélévitch's philosophy vis-à-vis that of Henri Bergson. See Jean-Christophe Goddard's entry on Jankélévitch for *The Columbia History of Twentieth Century French Thought*, ed. Lawrence D. Kritzman, Brian J. Reilly, and M. B. DeBevoise (New York: Columbia University Press, 2006), 552–553.

15. Vladimir Jankélévitch, *Fauré et le inexprimable* (Paris: Librairie Plon, 1988), 346.

16. Jankélévitch, *Fauré et le inexprimable*, 346.

17. Jacques Derrida, *Margins of Philosophy*, trans. Alan Bass (Chicago: University of Chicago Press, 1982), 13, emphasis mine.

18. Martin Hägglund, *Radical Atheism: Derrida and the Time of Life* (Palo Alto, CA: Stanford University Press, 2009).

19. G. W. F. Hegel, *Aesthetics: Lectures on Fine Art*, trans. T. M. Knox (Oxford: Clarendon Press, 1975), 2: 890. "Since, furthermore, the negativity into which the vibrating material here enters is, on the one side, an *Aufheben* of the spatial condition which is itself again *aufgehoben* by the reaction of the body, therefore the expression of this double negation, namely, *Ton*, is an externality that in its coming-to-be is annihilated again by its very existence and disappears/vanishes of itself. Owing to this double negation of externality, implicit in the principle of *Ton*, inner subjectivity corresponds to it because *the resounding*, which in and by itself is something *more ideal* than independently really subsistent corporeality, gives up this more ideal existence also and therefore becomes a mode of expression adequate to the inner life" (emphasis mine).

20. Cf. Jacques Derrida, *Voice and Phenomena*, trans. Leonard Lawlor (Evanston, IL: Northwestern University Press, 2011); *Edmund Husserl's Origin of Geometry, An Introduction by Jacques Derrida* (Lincoln: University of Nebraska Press, 1989); and Derrida's student thesis, *The Problem of Genesis in Husserl's Philosophy*, trans. Marian Hobson (Chicago: University of Chicago Press, 2003).

21. For an instructive characterization of Derrida's project as bearing an implicit relationship to a metaphysics of creation, see Peter Hallward, "The One or the Other: French Philosophy Today," *Angelaki* 8, no. 2 (2003): 1–32.

22. Jacques Derrida, "Differánce," in *Margins of Philosophy*, trans. Alan Bass (Chicago: University of Chicago Press, 1982), 13, 18.

23. Derrida, *Of Grammatology*, trans. Gayatri Chakravorty Spivak (Baltimore: Johns Hopkins University Press, 1974), 62.

24. For a second post-Bergsonian account of the creative and poetic instant, cf. Gaston Bachelard, *Intuition of the Instant*, trans. Eileen Rizo-Patron (Evanston, IL: Northwestern University Press, 2013).

25. Jankélévitch, *Liszt*, 107, emphasis and translation mine.

26. Derrida, "Play—The First Name, 1 July 1997," 331–332.

27. Derrida, Unpublished Interview (1982), reprinted in Kirby Dick, Amy Ziering Kofman, and Jacques Derrida, *Derrida: Screenplay and Essays on the Film* (Manchester, UK: Manchester University Press, 2005).

28. Jankélévitch, *Liszt*, xx.

29. George Steiner, *Real Presences* (Chicago: University of Chicago Press, 1991).

30. Jankélévitch, *Liszt*, 107.

31. Derrida and Coleman, "The Other's Language," 323.

32. Fred Moten, *In the Break: The Aesthetics of the Black Radical Tradition* (Minneapolis: University of Minnesota Press, 2003), 63.

33. Moten, *In the Break*, 22.

34. Moten, *In the Break*, 63–64.

35. K. Oversand, *Improvisation and the Aesthetics of Presence*, ed. Ola Kai Ledang, 74, quoted in Bjørn Alterhung, "Improvisation on a Triple Theme: Creativity, Jazz Improvisation and Communication," *Norwegian Journal of Musicology* 30, no. 1 (2004): 106.

36. Moten, *In the Break*, 43–44.

References

Alterhung, Bjørn. "Improvisation on a Triple Theme: Creativity, Jazz Improvisation and Communication." *Norwegian Journal of Musicology* 30, no. 1 (2004): 97–118.

Bachelard, Gaston. *Intuition of the Instant*. Chicago: Northwestern University Press, 2013.

Braxton, Anthony. *Tri-Axium Writings*. Dartmouth, NH: Synthesis/Frog Peak, 1985.

Derrida, Jacques. *Edmund Husserl's Origin of Geometry, An Introduction by Jacques Derrida*. Lincoln: University of Nebraska Press, 1989.

Derrida, Jacques. *Margins of Philosophy*, translated by Alan Bass. Chicago: University of Chicago Press, 1982.

Derrida, Jacques. *Of Grammatology*, translated by Gayatri Chakravorty Spivak. Baltimore: Johns Hopkins University Press, 1974.

Derrida, Jacques. "Play—The First Name: 1 July 1997," translated by Timothy S. Murphy. *Genre: Forms of Discourse and Culture* 36, no. 2 (2004): 331–340. Originally published as "Joue—Le Prénom" in *Les Inrockuptibles* 115 (August 20–September 2, 1997).

Derrida, Jacques. *The Problem of Genesis in Husserl's Philosophy*. Translated by Marian Hobson. Chicago: University of Chicago Press, 2003.

Derrida, Jacques. *Speech and Phenomena*. Translated by Leonard Lawlor. Evanston, IL: Northwestern University Press, 2011.

Derrida, Jacques, and Ornette Coleman. "The Other's Language: Jacques Derrida Interviews Ornette Coleman, 23 June 1997," translated by Timothy S. Murphy. In "Blue Notes: Toward a

New Jazz Discourse," edited by Mark Osteen. Part 1. Special issue, *Genre: Forms of Discourse and Culture* 37, no. 2 (2004): 319–329. Originally published in *Les Inrockuptibles* 115 (August 20– September 2, 1997).

Dick, Kirby, Amy Ziering Kofman, and Jacques Derrida. *Derrida: Screenplay and Essays on the Film*. Manchester: Manchester University Press, 2005.

Hägglund, Martin. *Radical Atheism: Derrida and the Time of Life*. Palo Alto, CA: Stanford University Press, 2009.

Hallward, Peter. "The One or the Other: French Philosophy Today." *Angelaki* 8, no. 2 (2003): 1–32.

Hegel, G. W. F. *Aesthetics: Lectures on Fine Art*. Translated by T. M. Knox. Oxford: Clarendon Press, 1975.

Jankélévitch, Vladimir. *Fauré et le inexprimable*. Paris: Librairie Plon, 1988.

Jankélévitch, Vladimir. *Forgiveness*. Translated by Andrew Kelley. Chicago: University of Chicago Press, 2005.

Jankélévitch, Vladimir. *Henri Bergson*. Paris: Presses universitaires de France, 1989.

Jankélévitch, Vladimir. *Music and the Ineffable*. Translated by Carolyn Abbate. Princeton: Princeton University Press, 2003.

Jankélévitch, Vladimir. *Philosophie première*. Paris: Presses Universitaires de France, 1986.

Kritzman, Lawrence D., Brian J. Reilly, and M. B. DeBevoise, eds. *The Columbia History of Twentieth Century French Thought*. New York: Columbia University Press, 2007.

Moten, Fred. *In the Break: The Aesthetics of the Black Radical Tradition*. Minneapolis: University of Minnesota Press, 2003.

Oversand, K. *Improvisation and the Aesthetics of Presence*. Edited by Ola Kai Ledang. Oslo, Norway: Solum Forlag, 1987.

Ramshaw, Sara. "Deconstructin(g) Jazz Improvisation: Derrida and the Law of the Singular Event." *Critical Studies in Improvisation / Études critiques en improvisation*. Accessed May 18, 2011. http://www.criticalimprov.com/article/viewArticle/81/179.

Stein, Joel. "Life with the Father of Deconstructionism." *Time*, November 18, 2002. Accessed May 17, 2011. http://www.time.com/time/magazine/article/0,9171,1003736-2,00.html.

Steiner, George. *Real Presences*. Chicago: University of Chicago Press, 1991.

Taylor, Cecil. *Chinampas*. Leo Records CD LR 153, 1987.

CHAPTER 8

POLITICS AS HYPERGESTURAL IMPROVISATION IN THE AGE OF MEDIOCRACY

YVES CITTON

In what measure and under what forms does improvisation play a role in the political life of our current media-driven democracies, which I will call "mediocracies"? In order to address this question, I draw precious insights both from classical and recent political philosophers (Étienne de La Boétie, Baruch Spinoza, Gabriel Tarde, Michel Foucault, Gilles Deleuze, Bruno Latour, Michael Hardt, and Antonio Negri) and from various theorists of musical improvisation (Sun Ra, Derek Bailey, Lawrence "Butch" Morris, Anthony Braxton, George Lewis, William Parker, and Guerino Mazzola). This inquiry is based on the assumption that improvising musicians, over the past decades, have developed a uniquely reflexive awareness about the art of live collaboration, which all of us practice in our daily lives, but which most of us experience without much reflexive thought. The assumption is not that "jazz" musicians are better improvisers than the rest of us (although that may very well be the case), but that they represent *the intellectual vanguard* in the effort to understand the ethical and socio-political implications of the improvisational activities that compose, day in and day out, the very fabric of our common social and political life. On the basis of this assumption, however, I attempt, in the second part of this chapter, to narrow and sharpen our definition of improvisation, in order to sketch a sharper conception of politics itself, illustrated here by the events that revolutionized Tunisia and Egypt in the early months of 2011.

THE POTENCY OF THE MULTITUDE IN A WORLD OF ENCOUNTERS

Going all the way back to Aristotle, we can find statements throughout history that acknowledge a special form of power emanating from the sheer number of the multitude (*to plèthos*, το πληθος): "It is possible that the many, though not individually good men, yet when they come together may be better, not individually but collectively, than those who are so."[1] The insight that not only strength, but also intelligence could reside in numbers has been developed by a tradition of thinkers that found its highest classical expression in the work of Baruch Spinoza (1632–1677), who used the concept of *multitudinis potentia* (the potency of the multitude) as the keystone of his political theory. Spinozism provides a most inspiring groundwork for a theorization of politics as collective improvisation because of eight basic principles, which can be roughly summarized from the complex system of thought laid out in the *Ethics* and in the *Political Treatise* (both published posthumously in 1677):[2]

1. There is no such thing as Providence; the world evolves along the necessary laws of nature, in the absence of any global (divine) intentionality; God is nothing more than nature itself (*Deus sive natura*).
2. Body and mind are one and the same thing, considered from two different points of view; the interaction of physical things is strictly parallel to the development of mental processes.
3. All bodies/minds are animated by a *conatus* (drive, desire), i.e., by an inner vital urge which pushes them to persevere in their being.
4. Our human *conatus* pushes us along two major types of conduct: one led by the "imagination" (by the impression made upon us by certain images and sensory encounters), and another led by "reason" (by our rational understanding of the causal processes that determine reality).
5. Rational understanding allows us to make up partially for the lack of divine Providence with the potency of human prudence (i.e., foresight), insofar as the understanding of causal processes helps us anticipate some of the future effects of our present behavior; however, since the complexity of the world exceeds by far the potency of individual and collective human reason, most of our behaviors are bound to be pre-rational.
6. Nothing is more useful to a human being than another human being; a human being is never more potent and useful than when s/he is led by reason.
7. Socio-political life consists in the circulation, channeling, capture, and appropriation of *multitudinis potentia*, i.e., the actual capacity of human bodies (and minds) to perform certain acts.
8. Political power (*potestas*) consists in reapplying the *multitudinis potentia*— condensed by its channeling through institutions like the police, the army, the

administration—back onto the multitude in order to rule its behavior in a top-down fashion.[3]

The highly scandalous radicalism of this philosophy is directly linked to the role it assigns to improvisation: in the absence of Providence, we humans have to improvise ways to sustain and develop a living, within an environment where nothing is predisposed to being suited to us. This improvisation concerns both our inscription within our natural milieu and our dealings with our fellow humans. *Life is made of "encounters"*—which are necessarily and mechanically caused by the laws of nature but appear to us as merely coincidental, since the infinite complexity of nature as a whole is bound to escape our highly limited mental potency.

In fact, "nature as a whole" does not exist for us, except as an abstract idea ("God"). Sociologist and philosopher Bruno Latour recently expressed a similar view with equally radical consequences:

> There is no such thing as a common world. There has never been. . . . The common world is *to be composed*. It is not already there, provided by nature, to be discovered in a pre-existing universal, hidden behind the veils of ideologies and beliefs, expecting to be uncovered so that its revelation can impose an agreement among us. This common world is to be made, to be created, to be established. Hence it can fail. That's all the difference: if the common world is to be composed, its composition can fail.[4]

While Latour borrows from the lexicon of "composition," the vocabulary of improvisation would be equally appropriate to describe our mode of existence in a world made of encounters. All of our daily actions result from a certain mix—the proportions of which constantly change—of *compositional foresight*, thanks to which I attempt to anticipate the future effects of my current behavior according to my rational understanding of the laws of nature, and of *on-the-spot improvisation*, thanks to which I can integrate the unavoidable novelty encountered in each situation.

We do indeed compose a common world by "coming-together" in our daily interactions. Within our modern urban modes of life, "my" capacity to act in my most banal gesture is made possible only through the collaboration of an unfathomable multitude of other human beings, who collaborate to provide me with the means to act. "My" agency—my capacity to act, compose, improvise—appears clearly as a function of the potency of the multitude.

While the notion of "the multitude" is arguably very close to the more classical notion of "the people" (as elaborated in the republicanist tradition), it does differ from it in at least two crucial ways. First, contrary to the strong patriotic, ethnic, or nationalistic overtones that haunt most classical definitions of "the people," the multitude is not bound by pre-existing territorial, ethnic, nationalist, administrative, linguistic, religious, or cultural borders: as soon as "many people" (*to plèthos*) interact, communicate, and collaborate in such a way that their individual potency results from a composition of their forces, they form a "multitude." Second, contrary to the strong pressure toward homogeneity applied by the republicanist definitions of "the people," the real strength, vigor, and vitality of "the multitude" rests on the tensions generated by the diversity of the singularities of which it is composed. While the ideal (republicanist) "people" is made of citizens who have been trained to share the same beliefs and values, as if they all came out of the same mold, the multitude can only develop its common strength by developing the *singularity* of each participant.[5]

Acknowledging that our individual agency results from the potency of the multitude (defined as a collective of interacting singularities) provides the basis of a politics of *radical democracy*: no matter who you are, no matter what you do, "your" capacity to act results from a certain channeling, use, and appropriation of the potency of the multitude (i.e., of the composition and multiplication of forces made possible by collaborations, communication, and exchanges among humans). Hence, the "power" (*potestas*) of an army general is nothing but the convergence of the forces and wills (*conatus*) of the soldiers and officers who obey his commands. This was the simple but radical argument made around 1550 by Étienne de la Boétie in his *Discourse on Voluntary Servitude*: the tyrant's "power" is nothing other than willingness of the oppressed to obey his commands.[6] Should the multitude refrain from fuelling the tyrant's power (*potestas*) with the constant flow of its potency (*multitudinis potentia*), tyranny would have its carpet pulled from under its feet, and it would crumble upon itself like a hollow shell. Monarchy, aristocracy, democracy, theocracy, autocracy, totalitarianism, or dictatorship are only variations on the basic fact of radical democracy: they all consist in various ways devised to channel, distribute, capture, and appropriate the potency of the multitude.

Collective Agency in the Age of Mediocracy

Equipped with this basic sketch of Spinozist political ontology and with a clearer vision of radical democracy, we are now in a position to address the role of improvisation within the particular type of political regime under which we currently live— mediocracy.[7] At this point, the main question is the following: *What mobilizes nowadays the potency of the multitude? What sets it in motion?*

Three bodies of theoretical work will help us provide a rough answer to this question. Gabriel Tarde (1843–1904) invited his readers to view social life as *a circulation of flows of desires and beliefs*. What defines and structures human societies, according to him, is not so much the economic division of labor as a complex interplay of three inter-psychological forces: imitation, opposition, and invention. Waves of *imitation*, carried by the media with increasing speed, spread through modern societies and shape the way we interact with each other. Fads, fashions, aesthetic trends, technological inventions, and artistic movements align many of us (*to plèthos*) along similar lines of behavior. Even if others among us feel the need occasionally to resist some of these trends, even such attitudes of *opposition* are determined by the waves of imitation toward which they take a reactive posture. Far from being antithetic to imitation, *invention*, according to Tarde, results from the unique intersection and superposition of several imitative gestures: one becomes originally inventive, not so much because one was "originally" endowed with a unique gift, but rather because one ends up being the only person to imitate this particular set of models. Society appears as woven from an intersection of influences. Tarde thus provides a first response to our question: what sets my singular agency in motion results from the flows of desires and beliefs generated in me by the interplay of imitation, opposition, and invention that constantly resonates through human societies.[8]

Michel Foucault's analyses during the 1970s and 1980s profoundly transformed the way we tend to imagine "power." Instead of seeing power exerted through constraint and threat, imposing its will in a descending movement from the One on top down to a multitude of powerless and passive subjects at the bottom of the totem pole, Foucault invited us to view it as "a structure of actions brought to bear upon possible actions":

> It incites, it induces, it seduces, it makes easier or more difficult; in the extreme it constrains or forbids absolutely; it is nevertheless always a way of acting or being capable of action. A set of actions upon other actions.... Power is exercised only over free subjects, and only insofar as they are free. By this we mean individual or collective subjects who are faced with a field of possibilities in which several ways of behaving, several reactions and diverse comportments may be realized.[9]

Several major implications of this definition are relevant for our purpose. First, the type of power described here by Foucault does not so much impede or block our agency, as it conditions it. Being subjected to power does not mean being passive: *power mobilizes us* as much as it represses us; it is carried by desires and hopes as much as by threats and fears. Second, we constantly participate in *a multiplicity* of "structures of actions brought to bear upon possible actions," and, as we move from one to the other, most of us alternate between positions of dominance and of subjection. As a consequence, human societies appear as an intricate fabric conflictingly woven by many competing and often contradictory structures of power. We thus have another response to our question: what sets our agency in motion are the desires and fears induced in us by the many intertwined structures of power in which we actively participate.

One last body of theoretical work needs briefly to be tapped in order to complete our picture of what sets the potency of the multitudes in motion within our mediocracies. A series of recent French thinkers like Guy Debord (1931–1994), Jean Baudrillard (1929–2007), and Bernard Stiegler (1952–) have all investigated the politico-ontological consequences of the feedback loops by which our social reality is being actually *shaped* and *restructured* by the spectacle, which is supposed merely to "represent" it (in order to "entertain" us).[10] The major intuition we should retain from these thinkers is the following: as it is no longer possible to separate social "reality" from the simulations through which we stage our interactions, *political agency needs to invest the staging of reality (by the media) as much as reality itself.* Hence a third response to our question: what mobilizes the potency of the multitude are the various stagings of reality performed and broadcasted on our mass media.

Taken together, Tarde, Foucault, and the theorists of our staged "hyperreality" provide us with a striking description of the circulation of power within our mediocracies. Let us briefly summarize this overall picture, before focusing on the status of improvisation. The potency of the multitude, defined as the capacity to act provided by the bodies and minds of a certain population, is mobilized according to the flows of desires and beliefs that resonate through this multitude, following complex patterns of imitation, opposition, and inventive recombination. The media function as the channels and vectors through which these flows are broadcast within the population, generating many predictable and unpredictable multiplier-effects, as well as blockings and neutralizations. Explicit forms and acts of power—one citizen is elected president of the country, a board of trustee decides to put 10,000 workers out of their jobs, a judge sentences a man to death—represent only spectacular local coagulations of this overall circulation of desires and beliefs, which is endemic in the multitude.

These explicit forms of power can only take place as long as the incoming flows of desires and beliefs continue to fuel them. Recent history, in the Middle East and elsewhere, illustrates what happens when these incoming flows suddenly dry out and change routes: the "legal" president becomes a hated tyrant, asked to clear the ground (*Dégage!*). Under the surface of such an eventful and massive turning around of the flows of desires and beliefs, the potency of the multitude is constantly woven by small-scale conflicts of influence, through which individuals and social groups attempt to assert their relative power. The aggregate flows made suddenly visible during a time of revolution result from the intertwined and globally chaotic strategies of individual and collective *conatus*, that is, from the constant drives that push individuals and collectives to persevere in their being and improve their lot. If no benevolent Providence (or Intelligent Design) has pre-organized the interactions of these conflicting strategies, power is constantly up for grabs: the actual directions taken by the aggregate flows result from differentials of pressure, alternatively pushing toward the right or the left, depending on the largely unpredictable neutralization or amplification of local movements.

At all levels, since the determining factors in socio-political struggles are desires and beliefs (rather than brute physical force), representations and simulations provide a crucial leverage on the channeling, capture, and re-orientation of the potency of the multitudes. The activity of staging is performed by the journalists who select the content of the evening news, by the scriptwriters of Hollywood and Bollywood, by the designers of commercial ads, but also by each and everyone of us, whenever we tell a story, express an opinion or write a blog. This activity should be seen as the key factor when we try to understand what mobilizes and steers the potency of the multitudes. It is at this level of staging—within the realm of the imagination—that our social destiny is shaped, day-in and day-out, progressively or catastrophically; this is where new paths of explorations are opened or shut, new stories told and old stories rehashed, new myths launched and old myths debunked—shaping our imaginary and conditioning our affects, thus causing this particular hope to appear as believable (or not), this particular perspective as desirable (or not).

This, I would like to believe, was the insight that Sun Ra expressed when he invented the new political category of "mythocracy": "I'm telling people that they've tried everything, and now they have to try *mythocracy*. They've got a *demo*cracy, *theo*cracy. The mythocracy is what you never came to be that you *should* be."[11] Of course, Sun Ra was offering much more than the mere description of a political regime: as a potent artist and as a true political activist, he was trying to inspire us to act in order to become what we should be. How can we conceive—and stage—the processes by which we "act" and "become what we should be" within mediocracies? This is where we need to look at the examples, analyses, and conceptualizations of collective agency provided by improvising musicians.

Nine Steps toward a Political Sharpening of the Reference to "Improvisation"

It would be (too) easy to show that "improvisation," in its broadest sense, is required from all social agents, at every step of their most daily routine, as a structural necessity of the type of society sketched in the previous pages. We all experience a life made of encounters as what Patricia Shaw precisely describes as a "live" performance (by contrast with pre-recorded footage): "[d]espite the ubiquity of our intentions, plans, rehearsals and scripts, all the effort we put into anticipating, what happens next is never a done deal, because we can never completely predict or control even our own response to what is happening, let alone the responses of others."[12]

If we are to "become what we should be," we need to conceive political agency on the basis of a somewhat sharper definition of improvisation. I will tap into the wealth of connotations included in the etymology and resonances of the word "improvisation" in order to carve a definition more directly in tune with our political needs in the age of mediocracy. This will take no fewer than nine steps, but along the way, it will progressively unfold the political potentials of improvisational agency.

1. *Im-Providence.* The ontological framework delineated in the first pages of this chapter is based on the (historically scandalous) rejection of the common idea of Providence. We need constantly to improvise, because we don't believe an Intelligent Design has pre-programmed our behaviors for the better. Intelligence is *our* (human) job (in the form of prudence and foresight). Improvisation is the active side of human intelligence. In more directly political terms: the need to improvise goes hand in hand with a radical distrust toward any institution of control that is supposed to watch over us (on the model of a Central Intelligence

Agency). Political intelligence is to be located in the resistance of minoritarian and marginal units, rather than at the level of central command.

2. *Un-provided for.* We need to improvise because we don't have a ready-made routine or a proper tool. The CIA and the Pentagon have technology and procedures; insurgents make up improvised explosive devices. While everyone improvises, rich and poor, improvisation tends to be the weapon of the have-nots: those whose basic needs are un-provided for. If necessity is the mother of invention, indigence may be the mother of improvisation.

3. *Improvement.* It might be equally true, however, that improvisation is the daughter of luxury. A worker glued to his machine in an assembly line is left no room to improvise: he is given everything he needs in order to do his job. Being "over-provided for" generates another type of poverty (by saturation). Improvisation results both from an urge to improve one's lot and from the luxury of benefitting from a certain margin of action (and margin of error). Here again, improvisation thrives from the margins, insofar as we escape the saturation of central control, and insofar as we are animated by a spirit of insurgence (which defines the specificity of our *conatus*).

4. *Improviso.* The authentic etymology of our vocabulary of improvisation directs us toward the Italian *all'improviso*, which comes itself from the Latin *improvisus*, "unforeseen." Several variations spread from Italy to France between 1650 and 1750 (*impromptu, improviser, improvister*). During this whole period, improvisation belongs to the arts of poets and comedians (as well as musicians). *Improvisation,* as a word, if not as a practice, has its roots on the theatrical stage. In his *Treatise on Acting from Memory and by Improvisation*, published 20 years after Spinoza's death, Andrea Perrucci (1651–1704) remarks that the art of improvising during a performance (*il rappresentare all'improviso le comedie*) "was unknown to the Ancients" and "is an invention of our times." While Perrucci contrasts the flexible intelligence of the improvising actor with the parrot-like rigidity of those who merely declaim a pre-scripted text (*premeditato*), he deconstructs in advance the simplistic binary opposition between composition and improvisation:

> Saying whatever comes to your lips will certainly result in blunders. . . . It is not by stripping oneself entirely of scripted material that one should take up the challenge; rather, one should be armed with some general compositions that can be adapted to every kind of comedy.[13]

Perrucci's foundational theoretical gesture calls for three remarks about the status of agency *all'improviso.* First, it has strong historical links to the activity of staging. Second, it has been perceived as specific to modernity, and it is strikingly in sync with the development of a typically modern philosophical and political (Spinozist) radicalism. Third, and more important, the very theoretical gesture that claims the novelty and vivacity of improvisation is haunted by a constitutive contradiction: Perrucci's *Treatise* has often been seen as marking the decline of the art of improvisation on the Italian stages of the *commedia dell'arte*, an art that it contributed to weakening by its normative tone and by reducing it to a standard-ized and homogeneous practice.

5. *Risk, not chance.* The apparent contradiction inherent to the theorization and standardization of a supposedly "spontaneous" practice should not only make us highly suspicious of the notion of spontaneity applied to improvisation; it should mainly push us to see *risk* as a core component of our definition of improvisation. "Risk, not chance," as David P. Brown correctly stresses, with a motto he quotes from Lawrence "Butch" Morris.[14] While the notion of chance puts us in a pas-sive and powerless posture toward the sequence of the encounters that awaits us, the notion of risk calls for an active attitude of prudence, attentive foresight, and intelligent calculation. Perrucci's standardization of theatrical improvisation con-tributed to weakening the *commedia dell'arte* by reducing it to a formulaic, repeti-tive, predictable, hence riskless practice. The lesson strongly bears on identifying authentic improvisation in the political field: while all politicians are exposed to the uncertainty of chance (earthquake, sudden rise in the price of grain, embar-rassing revelation), political agency is to be measured in terms of the intelligent risks it decides to take.

6. *Non-idiomaticity.* If risky improvisation is different from naïve spontaneity in front of a chance event, similarly, the innovative dimension of improvisation should be expected to do more than simply say something heretofore unheard. While every speaker tends to produce linguistically original sentences (which nobody ever uttered before him), it requires a very different attitude, and much stronger skills, in order to produce poetically original sentences, which alter the manner in which we perceive our world and our language. In his famous and foun-dational book, Derek Bailey contrasted *idiomatic* improvisation, which remains within the pre-existing norms and expectations of a certain language, with *non-idiomatic* improvisation, which wanders outside of any pre-established language.[15]

A similar distinction has been made in a very different field of study, but with important implications for our current concern. In his attempt to define seven pillars of life under the acronym of PICERAS (Program, Improvisation, Compartmentalization, Energy, Regeneration, Adaptability, Seclusion), biologist Daniel E. Koshland feels the need to separate a capacity to improvise from a mere capacity to adapt. He defines improvisation as non-idiomatic, "because a living system will inevitably be a small fraction of the larger universe in which it lives, it will not be able to control all the changes and vicissitudes of its environment, so it must have some way to change its program." Changing one's program, altering one's language, however, takes time and much effort, and a life of (good and bad) encounters often requires faster reactions: "[F]or example, a human that puts a hand into a fire has a painful experience that might be selected against in evolu-tion—but the individual needs to withdraw his hand from the fire immediately to live appropriately thereafter." Aside from improvisation, which "is too slow for many of the environmental hazards that a living organism must face," Koshland defines *adaptability* as a spontaneous (instinctive, mechanical, pre-conditioned) reaction that remains within a given behavioral language. This distinction can easily be superposed on Bailey's, when Koshland states that "improvisation is a mechanism to change the fundamental program, whereas adaptability is a behavioral response that is part of the program."[16] While idiomatic improvisation is a behavioral response that respects and reinforces a pre-existing program, even when it has to deal with the unexpected, non-idiomatic improvisation consists in on-the-spot *reprogramming*. In order to be significant, we will therefore expect political improvisation to be non-idiomatic.

During a financial and economic collapse, when lawmakers take emergency measures to boost the demand for cars, in order to prevent the closing of factories, they illustrate an unintelligent, knee-jerk "adaptive" reflex, based on obsolete consumerist models that are ecologically unsustainable. True improvisation would have required them to "change the fundamental program," that is, to question our very definition of "growth," "unemployment," or "welfare," and to experiment with non-idiomatic solutions (basic unconditional income, alternative modes of transportation and urbanism, taxation of financial transactions, etc.)

7. *A common sense of purpose.* In a more recent discussion of the differences between improvisation in art and adaptation in biology, Wolfgang Raible stressed an essential point of departure between the two.[17] Whereas, within the dominant Darwinian (aka Spinozist) paradigm used in biology, adaptation has no *telos* (no purpose, no guiding intention, no value-oriented design, no anticipatory vision, no providence), musical improvisation is fueled and oriented by a *telos*: whether an artist is soloing or whether a collective is interacting, the evolution of the music is driven by a sense of purpose and can hardly be understood without some reference to this sense of purpose. A group of improvising musicians on a stage is radically different from the encounter of a monkey, a fruit tree, a worm, and a virus in a tropical forest. While the monkey, the fruit tree, the worm, and the virus do interact in a complex manner, based on interdependence and adaptive evolutions, they don't behave on the basis of a common sense of purpose. The musicians assembled on a stage for a performance that includes a strong improvisation component do come with their individual agendas, styles, abilities, moods, but their interaction is also driven by a shared *telos*: minimally, to please the audience; maximally, to generate a work of art to be remembered. So improvisation is animated by a tension between *open exploration* (which, ideally, should be as "free" as the chaotic recombination that fuels biological adaptation) and a *teleology* that is strongly oriented toward a common goal.

We begin to understand more clearly why it is crucial to put improvisation at the core of political agency. Human societies—insofar as they are structured by flows of imitation and by functional imperatives of collaboration—can be seen as multilayered superpositions of "common purposes" on different scales—from the global survival of the human race to the united workers fighting against the closing of their factory to the individual artist struggling to perform and broadcast her art. In order to adapt to their changing environments, these superposed collectives need to invent, and hence explore, new "ways of life." Their historical fate is therefore directly linked to the consistency of their common purpose and to the openness of their inventive explorations. If they "knew" how to reach their common goal, they would not need to take the risks of improvisation. It is because they don't have the proper procedure at hand that they are bound to resort to improvisation—one could say that they are thus "bound to be free," in the sense that they have no other choice but to make use of their freedom to try innovative and untested (i.e., risky) procedures. Of course, such trials and errors cannot leave their original common goal unaffected: the unsuspected turns taken by the improvisation are bound to question and redefine their original aim along the way.

Thus, explicitly putting improvisation at the core of political agency short-circuits the traditional opposition between procedure-based approaches and outcome-based approaches. For many decades now, "socialism" has been described as a (failed) attempt to organize societies around a common goal of equality, while "capitalism" (more modestly, but more successfully) managed to stick to a procedural approach: let's give ourselves basic rules of fair exchanges of goods and services (as self-regulated by market interactions) and, whatever the outcome may be, it will be deemed "just."[18] The example of collective musical improvisation neutralizes this false alternative, by showing how much the exploratory procedure is inherently linked to the development of a common sense of purpose.

8. *Diagonality.* The model provided by non-idiomatic improvisation provides us with yet another way to neutralize a potentially incapacitating false contradiction that has plagued contemporary political theory. As Andrea Perrucci well knew and stated as early as 1699, "[I]t is not by stripping oneself entirely of scripted material that one should take up the challenge" of improvising on stage. Similarly, it is not by rejecting any form of hierarchy that a collective can best foster its "freedom." Most forms of musical improvisation include in their structure some aspect of temporary inequality that is geared toward empowering the collective as such: more volume and space is given to a soloist during his solo, one band-member has pre-written a series of common themes and compositional devices, or the collective explicitly decides to put itself under the organizational power of a conductor. Lawrence "Butch" Morris (b. 1947) is probably the musician and theorist who has best encapsulated the practical implications and theoretical stakes of this organizational power within the scope of improvising ensembles.

He describes conduction (conducted interpretation/improvisation) as "a vocabulary of ideographic signs and gestures activated to modify or construct a real-time musical arrangement or composition," generally within a rather "classical" situation where a conductor "directs" an ensemble of musicians regularly looking to him for various types of instructions. The common goals stated by Morris clearly reveal that the vertical superiority enjoyed by the conductor is meant to improve in parallel the furthering of each participant's singularity as well as the consistency and potency of the collective. In a remarkable confluence with the political theory of the multitude developed by Antonio Negri and Michael Hardt,[19] conduction is designed simultaneously "to enhance the ensemble's interpretive and expressive abilities and skills" and "to engage each musician in a system of music-making that draws on his or her unique personality, history and ability." In helping the participants "to surpass their heretofore-perceived artistic limits," the vertical relation of conduction hopes "to expand the intellectual reach of the individual and collective by elaborating on the elements of the decision-making process":

> The logic of circumstance(s) dictates the maximizing of encounter, and the musical and social structures that grow from such encounter. Conduction is the art of "environing," the organization of surrounding things, conditions or influences. It is a technique to capture and discover sonic information, structure and substructure, meaning, implication and expression (as we construct together)—all primary values in our pursuit of coherence and poignancy, and the immediacy of place.[20]

Here too, we see that the reference to improvisation draws a diagonal in the traditional opposition between vertical (hierarchic) structures of command and horizontal (egalitarian) structures of (free) interaction. The Morrisian conductor constitutes one pole of this diagonal, with a clearly identified organizer set apart from the group of musicians, while "collective free improvisation" (as practiced by radical performers who make it a point *not* to pre-state any explicit common goal, shape, or frame to their interaction) constitutes the other polarity of the same diagonal. The inspiring virtue of improvisation as such is to be located in its very *diagonality* in relation to the traditional parameters of vertical domination and horizontal equality: its (fundamentally political) challenge is to devise collective forms of agency that articulate the outstanding power of the participating singularities with the principle of equal respect necessary to find non-oppressive strength in numbers.[21]

9. *Diagrammatics.* One of the most shining models of the potency of collective improvisation is provided by the coordinate and schematic structures imagined by Anthony Braxton (b. 1945). These devices illustrate how compositional devices can trigger, boost, nurture, and empower both the singularity of each participant and the potency of the collective. Since Braxton has often used diagrams in order to represent such coordinate and schematic structures, I will refer to them globally—ignoring the differences between their various types and series—as *diagrammatics.*[22] What seems to me politically relevant in diagrams, as illustrated in Braxton's music, is that they consist in singular formal inventions, driven and inhabited by an individual and collective sense of purpose, which channel and organize the potency of a multitude through an explicit gesture of "regulation," in such a way that allows them to meet four simultaneous challenges: (*a*) they generate their own local language, which spontaneously carries the participants into non-idiomatic territories; (*b*) they augment the singularity of the participants by helping them to take risks and "surpass their heretofore-perceived limits"; (*c*) they

"expand the participants' intellectual reach" by reconfiguring "the elements of the collective decision-making process"; and (*d*) they manage to do all this *without the need for an apparatus of power* to enforce or regulate the interaction of the participants—contrary to the conduction model, which still requires a conductor.

In other words, diagrammatics, on the basis of this singular example, offer a miraculous device able to augment and channel the "potency" (*potentia*) of a multitude without generating positions of "power" (*potestas*). Within the highly artificial space created ("environed") by the diagram,[23] individual agents find a way collectively to experience and expand their singular and collective potency, without any one of them being put in a position of structural superiority while the interaction takes place. Within the perimeter of an ensemble of musicians on stage or within any other collective attempting to reconfigure its collaboration through a device formalized like a diagram, diagrammatics perform an operation very similar to what political theorists have attempted to describe as "the regulation of self-regulation" through formalized "legal procedures and organizational norms working to equalize the bargaining power of those parties affected by specific arenas of social activity," with the general goal of "reducing power asymmetries by procedural devices."[24] The main difference between most political theories and improvisational diagrammatics, however, is that the former are mainly concerned with circumscribing the perimeter of what should be allowed by law, while the latter is mostly interested in expanding what can be achieved by the potency of the multitudes—and this opening of the scope suffices to make most works of political philosophy look outdated and mutilating.

Of course, the miraculous device of diagrammatics "sounds too good to be true": Mr. Braxton, after all, no matter how brilliant, generous, unselfish, must have his ego, like the rest of us—and even if he does not, one cannot construct a politics on the assumption of individual sainthood. As our previous point made clear, improvisational practices must be located along a diagonal that holds no taboo against one member of a collective made of equals taking up the role of a "leader." Even if the potency-without-power promised by diagrammatics remains an ideal never perfectly to be realized, it deserves to generate hopes and enthusiasm, for the simple reason that—thanks to Braxton, but also thanks to the musicians who played with him, and thanks to the countless multitudes of diagrammatists currently playing on stages all over the world—this miraculous device *sounds real* to whomever was fortunate enough to experience it (as a direct participant, as a listener in the audience or, vicariously, through recordings). My conclusion will attempt to address the reality of such a miracle.

TOWARD A POLITICS OF HYPERGESTURES

The main difference, one could object, between music and politics is that it is enough for a concert to "sound good," whereas political discourse has to translate good-sounding slogans into "actual reality." This is where it is important to remember that we live in mediocracies (aka societies of spectacle, of simulacra, simulation, and "hyperreality"). Of course, the difference between false appearance and hard-nosed reality has not been abolished. But it is equally obvious that today's simulations are an actual moment of production of tomorrow's world. If, as Sun Ra suggested, "mythocracy is what you never came to be that you *should* be," then the mystifying appeal of the myth should be understood as a call, as a vocation (and not only as a lure). From within our individuals and from within our collectives, it demands that we become "what we should be," that we unleash this "power stronger than itself." George E. Lewis has tracked through the development of a multitude in action, the Association for the Advancement of Creative Musicians (AACM).[25]

On the face of it, the shining example of a group of musicians performing the miracles of collective interplay on stage is entertainment, in the pejorative sense of the French equivalent, *divertissement*: something that merely diverts and distracts us from "reality." It won't help pay my heating bill in winter, and it won't help me find a job if I have been laid off after the closing of an industrial plant. The momentary potency or joy briefly experienced during the performance is a "myth"—an illusion, a non-reality: I would be a fool to count on it to solve my problems. And yet, from another point of view, such moments have the potential to become transforming experiences—and they sometimes are, as most of us can hopefully testify.

Gilles Deleuze often commented on a deceptively simple observation made by Spinoza: "So far no one has been able to determine what a body can do" (remember that body and mind, for Spinoza, are one and the same thing). The unique intensity of improvised music, whether it is experienced as a player or as a listener, can be best encapsulated by this formula: being overwhelmed and overjoyed by what a body can do (the singular body/mind of this musician within the singular body/mind of this collective). This is the political potency of the myth (mythocracy) fuelled, night after night, by improvising musicians: since no one has been able to determine what individual and collective bodies can do, and while it would be foolish to believe that everything is possible—gas will not come for free, my factory will not reopen tomorrow morning by miracle—we can and we must believe that some things which we thought unachievable can be done by individual and collective bodies, once they invent a diagram capable of unleashing a power stronger than itself.

In a mediocracy, what people believe to be possible is not the same as what is actually possible—but it is just as important. What a body can do has been illustrated most spectacularly by the collective body of bodies occupying Tahrir Square in Cairo. From December 2010 to February 2011, the most important transformation occurred in what people believed to be possible: within a few weeks, they "came to be that they *should* be." The potency of the multitude became powerful, as the flows of desires and beliefs pushed more and more people to flow toward Tahrir Square. What did these people do? Nothing, in terms of contributing to short-term GDP. They did not "work," they did not make or do anything. They played. They played with their lives, of course, under dramatic pressure, with amazing bravery. But in spite of the gravity of the situation, and in spite of the tragic outcome it had for too many of them who lost their lives along the way, it is important to understand their action as a gesture, and their movement as a play.

More precisely still, we now have a concept that describes what the demonstrators did on Tahrir Square: they *improvised*. Their behavior paradigmatically illustrates the nine features of political improvisation delineated in the previous pages: a multitude of whatever singularities, most of them of mediocre origin, (1) turned their minoritarian intelligence against the illusionary Providence and the deceptive control of their central government, because (2) they felt un-provided for, and because (3) they felt a strong urge to improve their lot; they did so (4) by staging *all'improviso* a play of disobedience on public square, addressing their performance to a worldwide audience through mass-media communication; (5) they risked their lives, (6) inventing non-idiomatic modes of communication through on-the-spot reprogramming of their resistance strategies and political agenda; while they were exploring untested tactics, (7) they were momentarily united by the strongest sense of purpose, which (8) pushed them to invent new diagonals between the whatever singularity of the man-in-the-street and a few media-sponsored political figures who associated with the movement.

The hard question may be (9) where was the diagram that allowed their flows of desires and beliefs to precipitate on Tahrir Square, causing a collective political movement to coagulate out of separate individual frustrations? My closing argument will be the following: this diagram was provided by *a gesture* and should be conceived as unleashing the power stronger than itself carried by gestures.

A sensationalist approach may identify this gesture in the self-immolation by fire performed by Mohamed Bouazizi (1984–2011), the Tunisian street vendor who set himself on fire on December 17, 2010, in protest against police harassment. Of course, this gesture did not "cause" the Tunisian revolution, even less the Egyptian. But it certainly contributed to *triggering* it. And it did so through relaying and amplificatory dynamics that are typical of mediocracy. One young man sets himself on fire as an act of protest; a few people demonstrate in solidarity with him. This early staging receives wider and wider media coverage, to the point where Tunisian President/dictator Ben Ali has to be shown on TV visiting Bouazizi on his hospital bed. This sensationalist interpretation could track the wave of imitation that tragically spread across the Arab world as other whatever singularities (Mohsen Bouterfif, Maamir Lotfi, Abdelhafid Boudechicha in Algeria; Abdou Abdel-Moneim Jaafar in Egypt) repeated a similar sacrifice. It would show that this tragic trail of self-immolations was closely accompanied by a trail of popular resistance, rechanneling the flows of desires and beliefs that mobilize the potency of the multitude.

In order to develop a broader and less sensationalist understanding of the specific form of collective agency at work within this series of events, we need to borrow the concept of *hypergesture* proposed by Guerino Mazzola in his brilliant analysis of the "art of collaboration" involved in free jazz. This concept is drawn from the definition of the gesture provided by French philosopher Gilles Châtelet:[26] "The gesture is not substantial: it gains amplitude by determining itself. . . . The gesture inaugurates a family of gestures. . . . One is infused with the gesture before knowing it. . . . A gesture awakens other gestures."[27] Mazzola then shows that whether we observe the actual movements performed by a musician or whether we consider more generally the way all of us experience our gestures, collaboration is based on movements of transduction carrying a similar pattern of gestures from one field of action to another. It is at this higher level of "hypergestures" that our movements become meaningful and communicable. The notion of hypergesture "captures the paradigmatic action of comparing shapes or gestures that are only given as discrete points, but are cognitively correlated in a continuous way, germinating from motor actions as required in music, speech, and spatial competences."[28] This insight is summarized in the following manner:

> Gestures are not facts, they can create facts, but persist before and outside facticity. Nonetheless, the entire *modus operandi* of the art of collaboration is based upon a number of complex mechanisms that enable gestures to unfold their intense communicative action. We shall see that in free jazz, gestures appear in various complexions, they are highly articulate like human bodies and can be aggregated to hypergestures (gestures of gestures), they display a skeletal scheme and an embodiment in a topological space, and they are not only physical gestures, but can deploy their bodies in entirely abstract spaces.[29]

I will conclude this reflection on political agency as improvisation by analyzing the movements made by protesters on Tahrir Square in light of the concept of hypergesture. Their actions, staged in front of world media, were indeed a play, although clearly a risky one: they did not commit the tragic act of self-immolation performed by Bouazizi and by those who fully emulated him. This original gesture "awoke other gestures," "inaugurating a family of gestures" and "gaining amplitude by determining itself" into a common attitude of defiance toward authoritarian regimes. The multitude of "mediocre" political subjects who gathered on Tahrir Square transduced this tragically concrete gesture (of self-immolation), endowed with an intense communicative potential, into a hypergesture (of rebellion), thus elevating it to the status of a "myth" that mobilized the most potent resources of our mediocracies.

This becoming-myth of a hypergesture is easier to understand in light of another concept refashioned by Mazzola in order to account for the "miraculous" moments experienced during the interplay of free jazz improvisation—the concept of "state of flow." According to psychologist Mihaly Csikszentmihalyi, who coined the term in the late 1980s,[30] to be in *a state of flow* consists in being "completely involved in an activity for its own sake. The ego falls away. Time flies. Every action, movement, and thought follows inevitably from the previous one, like playing jazz. Your whole being is involved, and you're using your skills at the utmost."[31]

> In free jazz, it is known that the flow state of a group emerges when you feel that it is not you who play the music, but the music that plays you. . . . Flow is achieved by

an intense shift to a state of making, namely of intentional ordering activity. It is an autotelic state, where the gesture of the making gains its amplitude.... Flow generates types of external forces of a comprehensive form that are distributed over all participants, and which seems to impose itself through that most intense hypergestural activity.[32]

There are—very rarely—moments of powerful political agency when a multitude of people manage (or just happen) to emulate the collective behavior of a (successful) ensemble of improvising musicians, that is, when they find themselves in "a state of flow." The potency of the multitude, instead of following the usual channels that distribute and steer the flows of desires and beliefs, locally intensifies and enters into a state of flow that is "a state of making": in this case, it is not only music, but history itself that is in the making.

Such moments of elation have been thoroughly discussed by political philosophers. However, the problems and lures inherent to what Jean-Paul Sartre called "groups in fusion" must be revisited in light of the properties of mediocracies.[33] Of course, people argued and disagreed on Tahrir Square; of course, they were not in a "state or flow" twenty-four hours a day; it may even be the case that such a state of flow never happened "in reality." The workings of mediocracy made it happen through its staging in the media and imposed it back onto (hyper)reality by broadcasting something that "played as" a state of flow. In a typically Baudrillardian turn, the play of group flow, as spread by the media, was more "real" and more powerful than what was actually happening on the Square itself. There was a case of power stronger than itself. On the giant Larsen feedback effect produced between Tahrir Square and the millions of TV screens that were focused on it for weeks, the difference between "reality" and "spectacle" collapsed and reversed itself many times per day: a show of force by the police would kill human lives among the demonstrators, while the reality of Egypt's political power would bow down in front of a common hypergesture of defiance. The study of musical improvisation thus helps us draw a first lesson in political agency from the events that revolutionized Tunisia and in Egypt during the first months of 2011: in mediocracies, the potency of the multitude becomes powerful through the display of hypergestures capable of short-circuiting and rerouting mass-mediatization.

When improvisers "play" onstage, and when they approach states of flow, they too collapse the difference between spectacle and reality. Far from being a distraction, their show leads us deeper into reality-in-the-making than we usually reach in our supposedly "real" life. They renew and reopen the basic political and ethical question: what can a body do? They make us experience what the potency of a multitude can achieve. Thus, they produce a unique gesture, ready to "gain amplitude," "awake other gestures," and "inaugurate a family of gestures." It is up to us all to transform this unique gesture into political hypergestures capable of introducing emancipatory short-circuits within mediocracy.

NOTES

1. Aristotle, *Politics*, III.vi (Cambridge: Harvard University Press, Loeb, 1998), 223.

2. For a good history of the development and impact of Spinozism on early modern thought, see Jonathan Israel, *Radical Enlightenment: Philosophy and the Making of Modernity 1650–1750* (New York: Oxford University Press, 2002), and *A Revolution of the Mind: Radical Enlightenment and the Intellectual Origins of Modern Democracy* (Princeton, NJ: Princeton University Press, 2009).

3. For good English presentations of Spinoza's philosophy in its political dimension, see Warren Montag and Ted Stolze, *The New Spinoza* (Minneapolis: University of Minnesota Press, 1997); Gilles Deleuze, *Spinoza: Practical Philosophy* (San Francisco: City Lights Publishers, 2001); Antonio Negri, *Savage Anomaly: The Power of Spinoza's Metaphysics and Politics* (Minneapolis: University of Minnesota Press, 1999); Étienne Balibar, *Spinoza and Politics* (New York: Verso, 2008); and Warren Montag, *Bodies, Masses, Power: Spinoza and His Contemporaries* (New York: Verso, 1999).

4. Bruno Latour, "Il n'y a pas de monde commun: il faut le composer," *Multitudes* 45 (Summer 2011), 39–40 (my translation).

5. For in-depth discussions of the concept of multitude, see the trilogy by Michael Hardt and Antonio Negri, *Empire* (Cambridge, MA: Harvard University Press, 2000), *Multitude* (Cambridge, MA: Harvard University Press, 2004), and *Commonwealth* (Cambridge, MA: Harvard University Press, 2009).

6. Étienne de La Boétie, *Discourse on Voluntary Servitude* (1548), available online at http://www.constitution.org/la_boetie/serv_vol.htm.

7. I am proposing to reclaim this term by turning it against its more traditional (pejorative) meaning of "the rule of the mediocre" (implicitly opposed to "aristocracy," the rule of the best), and by redefining it as a political regime in which the structure and behavior of the electronic media play the most determinant role in the result of collective decision-making processes. For an example of the most common (openly reactionary) use of the term, see Fabian Tassano, *Mediocracy: Inversion and Deception in an Egalitarian Culture* (Cambridge, UK: Book System Plus, 2006). For a critical re-appropriation of the term by media studies, see Danny Schechter, ed., *Mediocracy—Hail to the Thief: How the Media "Stole" the U.S. Presidential Election of 2000* (Freiburg: InnoVatio Verlag, 2001). I propose to neutralize the strongly pejorative values inherent in both current uses of the term, and to consider that (1) the power of the mass media is a fact (to be accounted for, understood, and dealt with, rather than complained about), and that (2) the "mediocre" no longer sounds like an insult if we re-interpret it within a worldview that distrusts elitism and "excellence" but favors the "whatever singularity" presented, for instance, by Giorgio Agamben in *The Coming Community* (Minneapolis: University of Minnesota Press, 1993).

8. Gabriel Tarde's writings are being currently rediscovered and reedited in French and English. See, for instance, *The Laws of Imitation* (1890; repr., Charleston: BiblioBazaar, 2009), and *Gabriel Tarde on Communication and Social Influence: Selected Papers*, ed. Terry N. Clark (Chicago: University of Chicago Press, 2011). For a good introduction to Tarde's thought, see, in English, Bruno Latour and Vincent Antonin Lepinay, *The Science of Passionate Interests: An Introduction to Gabriel Tarde's Economic Anthropology* (Cambridge, MA: Prickly Paradigm Press, 2010); and, in French, Maurizio Lazzarato,

Puissance de l'invention. La psychologie économique de Gabriel Tarde contre l'économie poli-tique (Paris: Les empêcheurs de penser en rond, 2002).

9. Michel Foucault, "The Subject and Power," afterword to Hubert L. Dreyfus and Paul Rabinow, *Michel Foucault: Beyond Structuralism and Hermeneutics*, 2nd ed. (Chicago: University of Chicago Press, 1983) 220–221.

10. See, among other references, Guy Debord, *Society of the Spectacle* (1967; repr., Detroit: Black and Red, 2000); Jean Baudrillard, *Simulacra and Simulation* (1982; repr., Ann Arbor: University of Michigan Press, 1995); Bernard Stiegler, *Technics and Time, 3: Cinematic Time and the Question of Malaise* (Palo Alto: Stanford University Press, 2010).

11. Quoted in Graham Lock, *Blutopia: Visions of the Future and Revisions of the Past in the Work of Sun Ra, Duke Ellington, and Anthony Braxton* (Durham: Duke University Press, 1999), 61.

12. Patricia Shaw, "Introduction: Working Live," in *Experiencing Risk, Spontaneity, and Improvisation in Organizational Change*, ed. Patricia Shaw and Ralph Stacey (London: Routledge, 2006), 2.

13. Andrea Perrucci, *A Treatise on Acting, from Memory and by Improvisation*, bilingual edi-tion, trans. and ed. Francesco Cotticelli et al., (1699; Lanham: The Scarecrow Press, 2008), 101–103.

14. David P. Brown, *Noise Orders: Jazz, Improvisation, and Architecture* (Minneapolis: University of Minnesota Press, 2006), 128–129.

15. Idiomatic improvisation "is mainly concerned with the expression of an idiom—such as jazz, flamenco or baroque—and takes its identity and motivation from that idiom.... Non-idiomatic improvisation has other concerns and is most usually found in so called 'free' improvisation and, while it can be highly stylised, is not usually tied to representing an idiomatic identity." Derek Bailey, *Improvisation: Its Nature and Practice in Music* (1980; repr., New York: Da Capo, 1993), xi–xii.

16. Daniel E. Koshland, "The Seven Pillars of Life," *Science* 295, no. 5563 (March 22, 2002): 2215–2216. Available online at http://www.sciencemag.org/content/295/5563/2215.

17. See Wolfgang Raible, "Adaptation aus kultur—und lebenswissenschaftlicher Perspektive—ist Improvisation ein in diesem Zusammenhang brauchbarer Begriff?," in Maximilian Gröne et al., *Improvisation: Kultur- und lebenswissenschaftliche Perspektiven* (Freiburg: Rombach Verlag, 2009), 22–23.

18. This was the basic argument made by the likes of Hayek or Nozick in the 1970s, which inspired (or justified) the free-market fundamentalists who took over most Western governments in the last quarter of the twentieth century. See, for instance, Friedrich von Hayek, *Law, Legislation, and Liberty*, vol. 2, *The Mirage of Social Justice* (1974; repr., London: Routledge & Kegan Paul, 1982); and Robert Nozick, *Anarchy, State, and Utopia* (New York: Basic Books, 1974).

19. For a rich reflection on this convergence, see Alexandre Pierrepont, "Musique Multiple de," *Multitudes* 45 (May 2011): 89–94. I hereby thank Pierrepont, Yannick Séité, Frédéric Bisson, and George E. Lewis for greatly contributing to my analysis of the interaction between improvisation and political theory.

20. Lawrence "Butch" Morris, *Introduction to Conduction Workshops*, available online at http://www.conduction.us/Workshops.pdf (accessed March 30, 2011, italics added).

21. While discussing this paragraph, George E. Lewis made the following insightful com-mentary: "The improvisative process that produces Morris as conductor does not take

place at the same time or scale as the process that produces similar voluntary conflu-ences from within an ensemble of improvisers—for example, Misha Mengelberg's 'Instant Composing' idea, in which the improvisers' political arrangement allows for one (or mul-tiple) conductors to emerge as desired from within the logic of the musical transaction itself and the desires of the musicians. Of course, even without a conductor, the musicians may take individual decisions to follow the lead of one or more people. In this way, we perceive a common purpose to arise without the intervention of a singular figure, which is part of why people tend to compare free improvisation with social dynamics. This also makes this kind of improvisation more difficult to discuss than models which incorporate pre-given interactive structures (conduction)."

22. Brown has recently analyzed and stressed the exemplary virtues of Braxton's diagram-matics in the conclusion of his book *Noise Orders*, 119–132. The reference to diagrams is particularly useful since this notion had been much elaborated, in its explicitly political implications, by Foucault and Deleuze in the 1980s. For a good description of Braxton's diagrammatics, see Graham Lock, *Forces in Motion: The Music and Thoughts of Anthony Braxton* (New York: Da Capo Press, 1988), in particular, 167–174, 257–264, 321–331. See also Braxton's own descriptions, in *Composition Notes* (n.p.: Synthesis Music, 1988, distributed by Frog Peak Music).

23. Diagrams, from this point of view, illustrate the modern substitution of "cranes" (artifi-cially produced by human prudence) for the ancients' "skyhooks" (attributed to divine Providence). We need something to pull us up to a higher level of life-intensity and accomplishment: instead of expecting it to come from an otherworldly transcendence, we attempt to generate human-made devices that will help us benefit from the same experience of elation. Diagrams are one example of such devices. See Daniel Dennett, "The Baldwin Effect: A Crane, not a Skyhook," in *Evolution and Learning: The Baldwin Effect Reconsidered,* ed. B. H. Weber and D. J. Depew (Cambridge, MA: MIT Press, 2003), 60–79.

24. William E. Scheuerman, *Liberal Democracy and the Social Acceleration of Time* (Baltimore: Johns Hopkins University Press, 2004), 212. The author is referring to the "reflexive paradigm of law" promoted by German legal scholar Gunther Teubner in the 1980s.

25. See George E. Lewis, *A Power Stronger than Itself: The AACM and American Experimental Music* (Chicago: University of Chicago Press, 2008).

26. See Gilles Châtelet, *Figuring Space: Philosophy, Mathematics and Physics* (1993; repr., Dordrecht: Kluwer Academic Publishers, 2000).

27. See Guerino Mazzola and Paul B. Cherlin, *Flow, Gesture, and Spaces in Free Jazz: Towards a Theory of Collaboration* (Berlin: Springer Verlag, 2009), 74–75.

28. Ibid., 87.

29. Ibid., 35.

30. See Mihaly Csikszentmihalyi, *Flow: The Psychology of Optimal Experience* (New York: Harper & Row, 1990).

31. Mazzola and Cherlin, *Flow, Gesture, and Spaces*, 36. This comes from John Geirland, "Go with the Flow," *Wired*, September 1996, available from http://www.wired.com/wired/archive/4.09/czik_pr.html

32. Mazzola and Cherlin, *Flow, Gesture, and Spaces*, 36, 103, 118.

33. Jean-Paul Sartre, *Critique of Dialectical Reason* (1960; repr., New York: Verso, 2010), espe-cially the section "Group in History."

BIBLIOGRAPHY

Agamben, Giorgio. *The Coming Community*. Minneapolis: University of Minnesota Press, 1993.

Aristotle. *Politics*. Cambridge: Harvard University Press, Loeb, 1998.

Bailey, Derek. *Improvisation: Its Nature and Practice in Music*. New York: Da Capo, 1993. Originally published in 1980.

Balibar, Étienne. *Spinoza and Politics*. New York: Verso, 2008.

Baudrillard, Jean. *Simulacra and Simulation*. Ann Arbor: University of Michigan Press, 1995. Originally published in 1982.

de La Boétie, Étienne. *Discourse on Voluntary Servitude*. Available online at http://www.constitution.org/la_boetie/serv_vol.htm. Originally published in 1548.

Braxton, Anthony. *Composition Notes*. N.p.: Synthesis Music, 1988. Distributed by Frog Peak Music.

Brown, David P. *Noise Orders: Jazz, Improvisation, and Architecture*. Minneapolis: University of Minnesota Press, 2006.

Châtelet, Gilles. *Figuring Space: Philosophy, Mathematics and Physics*. Dordrecht: Kluwer Academic Publishers, 2000. Originally published in 1993.

Csikszentmihalyi, Mihaly. *Flow: The Psychology of Optimal Experience*. New York: Harper & Row, 1990.

Debord, Guy. *Society of the Spectacle*. Detroit: Black and Red, 2000. Originally published in 1967.

Deleuze, Gilles. *Spinoza: Practical Philosophy*. San Francisco: City Lights Publishers, 2001.

Dennett, Daniel. "The Baldwin Effect: A Crane, not a Skyhook." In *Evolution and Learning: The Baldwin Effect Reconsidered*, edited by B. H. Weber and D. J. Depew. Cambridge, MA: MIT Press, 2003, 60–79.

Foucault, Michel. "The Subject and Power." Afterword to Hubert L. Dreyfus and Paul Rabinow, *Michel Foucault: Beyond Structuralism and Hermeneutics*. 2nd ed. Chicago: University of Chicago Press, 1983.

Geirland, John. "Go with the Flow." *Wired*, September 1996. Available from http://www.wired.com/wired/archive/4.09/czik_pr.html

Hardt, Michael and Antonio Negri. *Empire*. Cambridge, MA: Harvard University Press, 2000.

Hardt, Michael and Antonio Negri. *Multitude*. Cambridge, MA: Harvard University Press, 2004.

Hardt, Michael and Antonio Negri. *Commonwealth*. Cambridge, MA: Harvard University Press, 2009.

von Hayek, Friedrich. *Law, Legislation, and Liberty*. Vol. 2, *The Mirage of Social Justice*. London: Routledge & Kegan Paul, 1982. Originally published in 1974.

Israel, Jonathan. *Radical Enlightenment: Philosophy and the Making of Modernity 1650–1750*. New York: Oxford University Press, 2002.

Israel, Jonathan. *A Revolution of the Mind: Radical Enlightenment and the Intellectual Origins of Modern Democracy*. Princeton, NJ: Princeton University Press, 2009.

Koshland, Daniel E. "The Seven Pillars of Life." *Science* 295, no. 5563 (March 22, 2002): 2215–2216.

Latour, Bruno. "Il n'y a pas de monde commun: il faut le composer." *Multitudes* 45 (Summer 2011): 39–41.

Latour, Bruno, and Vincent Antonin Lepinay. *The Science of Passionate Interests: An Introduction to Gabriel Tarde's Economic Anthropology*. Cambridge, MA: Prickly Paradigm Press, 2010.

Lazzarato, Maurizio. *Puissance de l'invention. La psychologie économique de Gabriel Tarde contre l'économie politique.* Paris: Les empêcheurs de penser en rond, 2002.

Lewis, George E. *A Power Stronger than Itself: The AACM and American Experimental Music.* Chicago: University of Chicago Press, 2008.

Lock, Graham. *Blutopia: Visions of the Future and Revisions of the Past in the Work of Sun Ra, Duke Ellington, and Anthony Braxton.* Durham: Duke University Press, 1999.

Lock, Graham. *Forces in Motion: The Music and Thoughts of Anthony Braxton.* New York: Da Capo Press, 1988.

Mazzola, Guerino, and Paul B. Cherlin. *Flow, Gesture, and Spaces in Free Jazz: Towards a Theory of Collaboration.* Berlin: Springer Verlag, 2009.

Montag, Warren. *Bodies, Masses, Power: Spinoza and His Contemporaries.* New York: Verso, 1999.

Montag, Warren, and Ted Stolze. *The New Spinoza.* Minneapolis: University of Minnesota Press, 1997.

Morris, Lawrence "Butch." *Introduction to Conduction Workshops*, available online at http://www.conduction.us/Workshops.pdf.

Negri, Antonio. *Savage Anomaly: The Power of Spinoza's Metaphysics and Politics.* Minneapolis: University of Minnesota Press, 1999.

Nozick, Robert. *Anarchy, State and Utopia.* New York: Basic Books, 1974.

Perrucci, Andrea. *A Treatise on Acting, from Memory and by Improvisation*, translated and edited by Francesco Cotticelli et al. Lanham, MD: The Scarecrow Press, 2008. Originally published in 1699.

Pierrepont, Alexandre. "Musique Multiple de." *Multitudes* 45 (May 2011): 89–94.

Raible, Wolfgang. "Adaptation aus kultur—und lebenswissenschaftlicher Perspektive—ist Improvisation ein in diesem Zusammenhang brauchbarer Begriff?," in Maximilian *Gröne* et al., *Improvisation: Kultur- und lebenswissenschaftliche Perspektiven.* Freiburg: Rombach Verlag, 2009.

Sartre, Jean-Paul. *Critique of Dialectical Reason.* New York: Verso, 2010. Originally published in 1960.

Schechter, Danny, ed. *Mediocracy—Hail to the Thief: How the Media "Stole" the U.S. Presidential Election of 2000.* Freiburg: InnoVatio Verlag, 2001.

Scheuerman, William E. *Liberal Democracy and the Social Acceleration of Time.* Baltimore: Johns Hopkins University Press, 2004.

Shaw, Patricia. "Introduction: Working Live." In *Experiencing Risk, Spontaneity, and Improvisation in Organizational Change*, edited by Patricia Shaw and Ralph Stacey, 1–16. London: Routledge, 2006.

Stiegler, Bernard. *Technics and Time, 3: Cinematic Time and the Question of Malaise.* Palo Alto: Stanford University Press, 2010.

Tarde, Gabriel. *Gabriel Tarde on Communication and Social Influence: Selected Papers*, edited by Terry N. Clark. Chicago: University of Chicago Press, 2011.

Tarde, Gabriel. *The Laws of Imitation.* Charleston: BiblioBazaar, 2009. Originally published in 1890.

Tassano, Fabian. *Mediocracy: Inversion and Deception in an Egalitarian Culture.* Cambridge, UK: Book System Plus, 2006.

CHAPTER 9

....

ON THE EDGE

A Frame of Analysis for Improvisation

....

DAVIDE SPARTI

ALTHOUGH all human agency unfolds with a certain degree of improvisation, there are nonetheless specific cultural practices in which improvisation plays an even more relevant role. One thinks, for instance, of the *commedia dell'arte* or of tango; of the orator who extemporizes a speech or the teacher who proclaims a discourse off the top of his head. Moreover, we are often constrained to improvise in the midst of playing sports, handling an emergency, cooking, and even in daily conversation. Although improvised behavior is so much a part of human existence as to be one of its fundamental realities, in order to avoid the risk of defining the act of improvising too broadly, my focus here will be upon one of the activities most explicitly centered around improvisation—that is, upon jazz. I do not attempt here to sing the praises of the form, but, rather, to examine the ways in which jazz represents a field in which improvisation manifests itself in its highest state, offering us the opportunity to find within it a frame of reference that we may relate to other genres and other modes of existence.[1]

My contribution, as Wittgenstein might say, has a "grammatical" design to it. It proposes to clarify the significance of the term *improvisation*. In adopting this philosophical perspective, my intention is not to contend that the philosopher sees further than the musician who is firmly ensconced, as it were, in the groove of his practice. My point, rather, is that an improviser has no need to elaborate upon a *concept* of improvisation himself; why should he, after all, when such a conceptual accomplishment is no guarantee of an aesthetic reward?

In the attempt to establish its elusive nature, located in the space between composition and execution, improvisation is often elevated to the status of an unfathomable event. Gunther Schuller, for example (referring to Billie Holiday), maintains that jazz is "in the deepest sense inexplicable . . . and . . . remains ultimately mysterious" (Schuller 1989, 528). If this were indeed the case, however—if improvisation carried with it an ethos so fatally mysterious that it defied theory—we would have to bow down in amazement before the occurrence of something we could not fathom, and the work of analysis would shut down entirely. My aim here is not to negate that intangible element of unpredictability of outcome that is at the root of improvisation. Going beyond the system of acquired rules, articulating itself, to quote Gregory Bateson, in "a message about the interface between conscious and unconscious" (2000, 138), the improviser's knowledge is implicit. How can we rationally answer the question: Where does the music generated in the course of an improvisation come from? What is the locus—to paraphrase the eponymous title of the first record cut by Oliver Lake, *Point From Which Creation Begins* (Lake 1976)—in which creation is initiated?

All of this, nevertheless, does not condemn improvisation to explanatory immunity. There is no reason to consider the ability to improvise more elusive than the skills necessary to carry on a conversation without a script, in which we don't know exactly what will come out of our mouths or what sort of assertion we will be induced to make. Consider a response elicited by an unexpected question: the response calls for a reaction, but, more important, for knowledge of the argument and a strong vocabulary. Although what we say in conversation can never be completely anticipated, and, moreover, calls for mental alertness, the language with which we communicate is familiar enough to us (we are already competent users of language by the time we have undertaken to tell an unedited story). And the reason we assume such different attitudes in the comparison of these two practices—that of conversation and of improvisation—is that while each of us is a relatively able conversationalist and knows how to ad-lib (although, mind you, we have taken *years* to learn this skill, conversation being such an absolute necessity that we make an enormous commitment to lead children to the state in which they can do it with fluency and freshness), artistic improvisation is not a cultural obligation. For the most part, we are the audience for musicians who have developed this special ability, and so we are amazed by it, and improvisation *appears* mysterious to us.

Not all jazz musicians like to comment on their own work (or, at any rate, they don't always feel moved to defend what they do against theoretical statements about it). One may get the (mistaken) impression that jazz is not arrived at through articulated language. This idea assumes that to improvise, it is sufficient to avail oneself of natural dispositions, the fruit of primal reaction coupled with the expression of a range of emotions that come before discursive rationality. Things are, in fact, different. First of all, with the combination of notes that make up a musical solo, the jazz player has "said" what he had to say. If music speaks for itself, to invest it with words becomes redundant. Moreover, improvisation is a *practice* (a complex form of embodied and cooperative human activity), and we should not lose sight of the distinction drawn by Gilbert Ryle (1949) between *knowing how* and *knowing that*, or between operative knowledge, associated with that which is done without reflecting on how—and sometimes without reflecting on why—one does it (let us call it "background knowledge") and knowledge that encompasses the mental representation of a task before it is performed. Jazz musicians mobilize an awareness-in-action, and because this awareness, incorporated into action, has no need to pass through mental representation, nor to be thematized (if it encounters no obstacles), it cannot be brought, without any residual traces, to the level of consciousness and discourse. Indeed, because we are dealing with knowledge-in-action, in which the body becomes the vector of knowledge, we know *more* than we are able to articulate verbally, hence the difficult discursive translatability of the (musical) improvised experience. As Bateson noted, alluding to the artist (2000, 138), "If his attempt is to communicate about the unconscious components of his performance, then it follows that he is on a sort of moving stairway (or escalator) about whose position he is trying to communicate but whose movement is itself a function of his efforts to communicate." That said, one need in no way deny the jazz musician the faculty, or even the necessity, of reflection upon his own practice, of elaborating and outlining, at least implicitly, an aesthetic of improvisation.

I said jazz is not the only sphere in which one improvises. Even in the context of music, jazz is not the only form marked by improvisation. In the pre-Romantic era in the West (understood here more as a cultural frame than as a geographic location), musicians rarely worked from an exhaustively codified score, associating themselves instead with a repertoire of memorized or recycled pieces, and also with improvisation; they understood the ability to enrich a preexisting work, allowing the piece's thematic, metric, and harmonic structures to furnish the foundation, upon which they then constructed the activity of variation (see Bent 1983, Wegman 1996). From the end of the seventeenth century, however, the score began to become more explicit, and directive in response to the emerging concept of the musical work—a through-composed work becoming more and more internally consistent and fixed in a written form in order to lend itself more easily to musical reproduction—a work that moved independently of the composer (Dalhaus 1979). Indeed, because the performance of a work often took place in the absence of its composer, it was necessary to be faithful to the latter's will. The ideal of the *Werktreue* (interpretive fidelity to the letter of the work) coincided with that of the *Texttreue* (respect for the score) (Goehr 1992). Given this historical shift, musical composition with a notated text (the art of *componere*) separated itself further and further from improvisation, which, as a result, was reduced gradually to the individual musician's ability to demonstrate technical brilliance and imagination, and on the whole came to be regarded as a less noble practice than that of performing from the score (see Sparti 2007b; Moore 1992).[2] Let us not forget that improvisation (*im-pro-video*—literally, that which is unforeseen) refers to that which cannot be anticipated, and that the unexpected represents the dominant taboo of a ocularcentric culture, which privileges artistic activity destined to leave a lasting imprint behind (and sanctioning a place of worship for it: the museum), casting correlatively a negative judgment on activity conducted through improvisation, seen as unplanned and approximate.[3]

WHAT DOES IMPROVISATION MEAN? SOME CRITERIA

The task of clarifying the cases in which one may legitimately speak of improvisation consists first of all in reflecting upon the *conditions* that make the practice possible. This does *not* consist of calling forth mysterious, esoteric processes that take place in the unconscious or in the minds of musicians (Sloboda 1988), but, rather, in paying attention to the criteria that must be satisfied before one may accurately ascribe to an act the concept of improvisation.

It seems useful to begin with the relationship—differential, but not necessarily oppositional—between improvisation and composition, music "in sound" and music fixed in written form, or rather, music as the outcome of a set of pre-established instructions that prescribe what is compulsory, forbidden, and optional—hence what counts as correct/appropriate future performances. When speaking about improvisation, one must start out with the premise of the existence of the concept of compositional plan (often but not necessarily tied to scores). Indeed, between improvisation and composition, there already exists a conceptual relationship: our understanding of improvisation depends upon—or is a consequence of—a work-specifying plan, if not of textuality; the (notated) musical work represents the standard against which (or on the basis of which) improvisation, by contrast, measures itself, differentiates itself, and lets itself be admired. At least within this cultural binary, improvisation *presupposes* the concept of music that is premeditated and executed from a score. Nonetheless, they are two distinct modes of musical creation.[4]

Let us start with the axis of temporality. We may begin to establish the point at which a musical act is improvised on the basis of the degree to which the two functions of composition and performance *converge in time*. According to this criterion, the greater the proximity and interdependence (or the smaller the temporal interval), the greater the justification for speaking of improvisation. In the extreme case, we have coincidence: the act of composition and the act of performance are *inseparable*, with the creative process and the resulting product occurring contemporaneously. One does not perform a pre-composed text (worked out in advance over time, i.e. prior to the time of the performance); music is instead created "in motion," while it is being brought to completion, in the course of its uninterrupted flow. As Steve Lacy has observed, "The difference between composition and improvisation is that when you compose you have all the time you need to decide what to put in those fifteen seconds of music, whereas when you improvise you have only fifteen seconds" (quoted in Bailey 1992). I call this first condition (the collapsing of the distinction between composition and performance) *inseparability*.

In so-called "classical" music—notated music derived from the European tradition—the moment of creation and the event of performance are structurally distinct, as are also, more often than not, the two figures of the composer and the interpreter. The composer first fixes the work, and then in a separate time, which does replicate the time of its genesis, performs the work or has it performed. Moreover, the compositional process is *discontinuous*: the framework within which the music is generated does not coincide with that in which it is performed. The composer, therefore, dispenses with a sense of limitless, indeterminate time in order to perfect his own musical ideas. Iannis Xenakis (quoted in Restagno 1988, 41) explicitly emphasized this compositional dimension, subtracted from the time-flow: "in composing, all the pencil-work (choosing the notes, calculating the durations) takes place, as it where, outside time. Only the *mise en oeuvre*, the performance, puts all of this within a flux of time. Essentially, all music is based upon this principle of construction, which draws its material from a dimension outside time, in order to successively project the music into the time-perspective, and here our power of control diminishes." Regarding these differences between composing and improvising in the temporal dimension, Paul Bley emphasized the contrast between generating surprising new performances and perfecting an enduring and reinstantiable entity: "Society accepts and forgives the fact that it takes a 'serious composer' a month to create three minutes of music. But if you're an artist who loves creating music, you'd rather play it all in three minutes and then play something totally different for another three minutes. Rather than sitting up in bed with an idea, scratching it down on paper, then going through months of writing and orchestrating and copying and rehearsing before you or anyone else can hear it" (Bley 1999, 24).

We now come to *irreversibility*—a condition that, once again, affects the axis of temporality. We recall that the composer casts his designs, as it were, at his leisure, so that time finds a true *reversibility* in slow elaboration and creative rethinking. When one composes, one is not only writing in a forward, linear direction; one may also turn back, rewrite and correct, cross out an unpromising passage, and thus "recover" time (or, to be precise, time does not turn back but folds down the pages of a musical sketch in order to make one passage of a piece meet the passage that preceded it, thus effectively separating the music from the flow of time). As Beethoven's famous sketchbooks reveal, the part that is left out often exceeds by far the part that has been selected to remain. Beethoven produced a great many sketches, transitory material, and first drafts, and his compositional process often alternated with long fallow periods. The act of composition is hence dependent upon the possibility of creating at leisure over the course of time, of setting down and designing a piece over hours, days, months, or years (it presupposes, that is to say, the possibility of *procrastinating* in any given moment of the creative process). In the case of composition, therefore, we need to keep an account not only of performance time, but also of the time spent waiting for inspiration, incubating ideas, correcting, and rewriting. On the other hand, the improviser does not have the luxury of rewriting or crossing out; moreover, not only any mistake, but even any possible strategy of recovering from such mistakes, immediately becomes textual—that is, part of the music itself. What has been sounded cannot be unsounded. One may suddenly slow down a tempo, or pause in the thematic development of a solo line, but there is no going back to the beginning and starting all over again. There is thus a certain ineluctability to improvisation (which is also significant for musicians who play from the score; but the comparison we are making is between composition and improvisation—or, one might say, between two types of composition).

In sum, composition is marked by three characteristics: a long period of time leading up to the eventual production of a finished work; the virtually limitless possibility of revision before the public exhibition of the finished work; and the fact that the circumstances in which the finished work is produced, from conception through revision to completion, remain largely hidden from the eyes of the public, evolving, as it were, backstage.

Now we arrive at the third characteristic of improvised behavior, which we may call its *situationality and contingency*. Improvisation is an act that takes place in an absolutely specific tempo-spatial singularity (here and now), and—negative condition—one that takes place without availing itself of the benefits of a score, which presets the location of the notes of a piece (a solo has no designated points of departure in the music). In contrast to a composition, which has prescriptive value, improvisation renounces the support and coherence provided by a score. As Cornelius Cardew has noted, "Written compositions are fired off into the future; even if never performed, the writing remains as a point of reference. Improvisation is in the present, its effect may live on in the souls of the participants . . . but in its concrete form it is gone forever from the moment that it occurred" (Cardew 1971). Improvisation is constitutively performative, it lives and dies in the course of a single, unrepeatable performance. An action that, while it unfolds, invents its own way of proceeding—music simultaneously performed and invented—improvisation can be called the performance of a composition composed during its own performance (improvisation is in fact called *extemporaneous*; Quintilian's expression, *ex tempore action*, meaning an action that is not the fruit of a long and judicious deliberative process). The past does not control the emerging shape of the future.

Music today is, of course, above all and everywhere reproduced; recording is a constituent part of the musical event itself, not merely something that accrues to it. The fact is that even improvisation is often recorded, and can be transcribed and, therefore, reproduced. Nevertheless, one should not conflate a piece that has been notated and then recorded with a recorded improvisation. Unlike a score, a recording is not "performed" in public. In theory, even the recording (or transcription) of an improvised performance can be "reproduced," but the lasting existence of an improvisation does not have the same status as that of a written composition, because the latter *prescribes* something that must then be played, while the former is limited to *describing* its own occurrence on a given occasion. It thus has only a pedagogical value, not an aesthetic one. Anyone who claimed to improvise by playing the solos (ably transcribed) of another would, therefore, undergo a form of disapproval.

By virtue of time and writing, then, the composing musician comes to enjoy a synoptic representation of the music that he intends to perform, or to have performed. Not so his improvising counterpart. Situationality means not knowing in advance what the outcome of an improvisation will be. The melodic trajectory of a solo is not predetermined, and, if analyzing it after the fact reveals a thematic configuration, it was not already present in the mind of the musician as an ideal, coiled up, and waiting to spring forth into actualization. As Ornette Coleman noted, "Before we start out to play, we do not have any idea what the end result will be. Each player is free to contribute what he feels in the music at any given moment. We do not begin with a preconceived notion as to what kind of effect we will achieve" (liner notes for *Change of the Century*, 1960). Without implying that when improvising musicians are acting unintentionally (or are not guided by a larger conception of what they are doing), the jazz player discovers where he wants to go—and how to get there—*in the course of* his improvisation.

Moreover, in improvisation, the performance can at any moment veer off into other, different directions, growing in an unexpected manner, leading us where we never imagined we'd be able to go (this is the characteristic of *contingency*). In the course of an improvisation, therefore, the music emerges in a way that is not always predetermined, and its development cannot be calculated in advance, either by the one who listens, or by the one who will bring this music to its completion. As Cecil Taylor told Len Lyons (1983, 302), who asked him if he heard the sounds he was about to produce in a piano solo "in his head": "If you hear it, why is there any need to play it?" Analogously, after having given numerous classical music concerts, Keith Jarrett compared the experience to that of playing improvised music, and, wondering what was lacking, concluded: "I realized it was that I knew every note that was going to be played already. I could play them really well, or not really well, but what difference would that make to my life?" (Shipton 2004, 80). The composer conceives of a piece of music as a whole entity in light of which he can plan out the refined work, availing himself of the score that, in turn, allows, as Beethoven described it, "*immer das Ganze vor Augen [zu] haben*": that is, to have the work in its entirety constantly before one's eyes. The improviser, on the other hand, is a "myopic" actor in the sense that he foregoes both the anticipatory and the synoptic visions of the composer. It is not by chance that Aristotle's Renaissance translators and commentators used terms—*all'improviso, sprovedutamente, isproveduto*—that were derived from the Latin *improvisus (im+provideo)*, not seen in advance.

It should be noted here that even though improvisation is considered out of place in most of modern classical music, certain principles of improvisation are operational even within this context (see Benson 2003). In fact, no musical work is an entirely consistent entity, solely and exhaustively determined by the score. Any realization of a work necessarily contains sonic details that cannot be ascribed to the work itself (even if one did everything that the work prescribed, there are still performative aspects determined by the performer, e.g., filling the gaps left open by the composition, adding a *rubato* or varying the tempo). Moreover, musical works underdetermine their performances: the signs particular to a given page of music, selected by the composer, cannot play themselves—and, above all, are incapable of dictating the style in which they should be played, a circumstance that accounts for the fact that two performances of the same work can be so different and, even better, can have such different effects upon us listeners. Yet it is undeniable that the score has a normative value. It lays the boundaries (or, at least, claims to) of the musical work. Its symbols are commands; they exert a binding force over anyone who is called to reproduce them, as the Latin-derived Italian term *esecutore* so eloquently reveals. In this way, the differences from performance to performance will be considered secondary and not essential with regard to the preexisting entity that the performer is invited to *interpret*. The multiple future "executions" of a composition remain, fundamentally, a sort of repetition.

Following Schutz, who said "there is no difference in principle between the performance of a string quartet and the improvisations at a jam session of accomplished jazz players" (1971, 177), one may also take note of the following circumstance: even the performance of a notated piece seeks mutual accommodation and implies a common and concomitant way of acting, as well as contextual anticipation and coordination between the musicians in one accord with a key, dynamic, or tempo (in the performance of a string quartet, the musicians do not equalize their playing with the external time-keeping of a metronome, but, rather, listen to each other mutually in order to discover the extent to which they are in accord, harmonizing themselves with one another's timing). True. But does this count as improvisation? Improvisation should not be confused with interpretation. Although performances can be quite different from one another, they are still the faithful instantiation of a musical work that remains reidentifiable throughout multiple renditions. Interpretation does not imply any deliberate departing from the score (contingency) nor the genesis of any new musical material in the course of a performance (inseparability), nor does it suggest that the musicians break apart and recombine a given text in new musical statements, changing structural properties such as melody, harmony or time. In classical music performance, unlike that of jazz, we do not find a composition "in motion," since we are dealing with music that has been either precomposed or pre-arranged (on this point I differ from Cook 2007).

Summing up, the distinction between composition and improvisation can be traced to two distinct forms of creativity: one oriented toward the product (a picture, a sculpture, a score—a finite product that can be examined and reexamined at leisure), and another in which the outcome is undetachable from the particular process of making it, hence in which the process *is* the product, a process that vanishes while taking place and that cannot be retrieved. The very word *composition* refers to the created product, while the process of creation appears ancillary. On the other hand, while *improvisation* is a noun, it is the verb, the activity, the process, that is semantically significant. And any process is, by definition, "in due course" (a process already accomplished is hardly conceivable). A painter or a sculptor *accumulates* objects that persist. But the improvising musician, as Cardew noted, remains always in the present. Like the supernova, which explodes and dissipates at the moment of its greatest radiance—and not unlike Hannah Arendt's (1958, 226) use of the term *Energeia*, a phenomenon which exists solely in pure actuality—improvisation is an ongoing process that exhausts itself while being produced. Moved by a logic opposed to the preservationist instinct—the logic of creation in the present moment alone—the jazz player does not play for eternity. He does not even play for the next day, but, rather, for the circumstances in which he finds himself tonight, with these particular musicians, before this particular audience seated around him (Béthune 2003, 112). Time in jazz does not follow the temporality of classical music, in which each musical fragment is considered a segment of a progressive and complex time pre-established and orchestrated by the composer. Rather than deploying this internal necessity, improvisation actualizes itself anew in each moment, and each moment has value in and of itself.

In essence, by virtue of the fact that it does not end in an external product (it has a result, but no product, unless it is recorded), improvisation is constantly productive—it is music in the making—and it publicly exposes its own practice. On the other hand, by virtue of the fact that it makes ample use of time in deciding "what to say," when composing the very process of composition becomes subsidiary, and what is relevant is its outcome: the produced text.[5]

THE DEMAND OF ORIGINALITY

Since improvisation in jazz deals with the sphere of invention, or at any rate with the bringing to birth of something new, it requires originality. Each improvisation must appear more or less different from the preceding one.[6] It follows, therefore, that some-one else's solo, as well as one's own—the solo played yesterday—is not transferable. As Eddie Prévost, drummer for the ensemble AMM, has observed: "Now, nothing is more dead than yesterday's improvisation" (Prévost 1995, 60). This problem of the disinclina-tion to repeat a solo is not a technical one (regardless of the difficulty of succeeding at this sort of reconstruction) but first and foremost an ethical one: I am unable to resound what Coltrane, for instance, played, because I do not see the need for it. If I had to repeat the solos of others, or even to improvise in order to simply communicate what I already know, I would never have the courage to begin. In the words of Joe Henderson (1991): "I can remember going onto the bandstand after being around Detroit for a few years, and consciously getting my brain to start phrases on different notes of the bar, with a different combination of notes, and a different rhythm. I developed the ability to start anywhere in the bar and it lent to a whole new attitude of constant variation. . . . What I was developing was a sense of not falling into that habit of playing the same things all the time."

A reverse demonstration of the presence or absence of the required originality in a solo is elicited by the approval, or lack thereof, of other musicians. A pointed example is the reaction of Charles Mingus to the tendency of a young saxophonist in his band toward "playing safe" (the term used to refer to someone who plays in a clichéd style): "Play something else, play something else! This is jazz, man. You played that yester-day, and the day before" (Berliner 1994, 271). One may *evoke* the past in a solo, but one cannot recapture it literally; those who try—those who reproduce the sounds played by others—are called "clones" in the jargon of the jazz community. "I myself couldn't copy anybody," observed Miles Davis (Mandel 2007, 93). "An *approach* I could copy, but I wouldn't want to copy the whole thing." Indeed, to do so would be to transform oneself and one's own playing into a walking manual of the history of jazz. To draw upon the conceptual dichotomy introduced by Nelson Goodman with reference to the classifica-tion of the arts: as opposed to an allographic work, which manifests itself in a plurality of performances, an improvised performance is an *autographic* work, a unique unscripted event marked by a once-only character—a single performance, unfolding here and now as one plays/listens, that cannot be essentially reiterated.

Of all the risks to which the improvising musician is exposed, the first and foremost is that of stagnation. "My greatest fear," Henry Threadgill has noted, "is the fear of not being able to go along with change, becoming stylistic and set" (Mandel 1999, 73). In this scenario, one reaches a certain "place" musically and can go no further. "Once you get stylistic you stop," explains Threadgill further. "There's no more development" (Enstice 1992, 293). But exactly what sort of risk are we speaking of? Not that of playing *wrong*, because, in improvisation, one cannot play wrong (one may not know how to improvise, or one may improvise badly, but there are no *mistakes* in improvisation—in this sense, from the point of view of music played from a score, improvisation appears to be a practice *devoid* of risks). An "error" can only be recognized in relation to something predefined and prewritten, so that whoever commits such an error can be made to go back and re-do it differently. Although in classical music, error can be a necessary teaching tool in the musician's quest to arrive at the correct execution of a piece, in the case of improvisation (indeed, in the case of "secondary improvisation," in which the improvisation takes off from a pre-composed piece, for instance, a jazz standard like "Jitterbug Waltz"), between the violation of a musical text fixed in written form and the beginning of a different solution than the one preseen and predefined (toward a change of perspective, or a renegotiation of the hereafter), the line becomes easily blurred. Because there are no wrong notes in jazz, the moral notion of guilt that might accrue to musical missteps is suspended.

Instead, the risk of becoming "stylistic," to use Threadgill's term, is the risk of failing to find originality (cf. Corbett 1995, 222–223). Insofar as it is original, each improvisation maintains a value of revelation. This "revelation," however, concerns itself not with anything unearthly, but, rather, with the musician himself and the world in which he finds himself. He draws his strength not from fidelity to a musical tradition or a score that could confer upon him a certain sacred authority, but from the degree to which he is able to throw new light upon what he plays. But, somebody could wonder, if every improvisation is an event capable of altering the identity not only of the piece, but also of the player, how is it possible that such an event might re-present itself in each new performance? Herein resides the peculiarity of improvisation: a "miracle" that, instead of repeating itself only rarely, as every miracle ought to do, is repeated—or, better, *can be* repeated—at each performance. It is indicative that Hannah Arendt compared the faculty of action to the miracle of the unexpected: human beings "seem to have the talent to perform miracles. . . . In truth, we have the right to expect miracles. Not because we believe in miracles, but because human beings, as long as they are able to act, are able to accomplish the improbable and the incalculable, and continually accomplish it, whether they know it or not" (Arendt 1995, 27, my translation).

By virtue of this generative dimension, birth (*Gebürtigkeit*), not death, becomes for Arendt the crux of the matter. We are mortal beings, after all, but we are also beings who have come into the world through birth, an absolute contingency to which we *react*, or respond, by taking the initiative or by giving initiative to something new. Indeed, the new constitutes "an ever-present reminder that human beings, though they must die, are not born in order to die but in order to begin" (1958, 288). It is not by chance, then, that Arendt calls *beginning* a "second birth." And it is because, having been born into a world that preexisted us, we once partook of newness ourselves, we are now able to actualize this potential to give life to something new. Through a combination of diverse generative acts, experimental jazz is defined by its power *to begin*, by its capacity to come out into the open and accomplish the entirely unexpected. The aim of improvisation does not consist in the production of (finite, complete) works; on the contrary, its aim consists precisely in generating *beginnings*, of producing "utterly unheard sounds, the unheard-of sounds," as Steve Lacy describes them in an interview with guitarist Derek Bailey (Weiss 2006, 70). It consists, in other words, in "carrying the music beyond its own limitations," as Paul Bley explains further, adding, "nothing is more difficult than trying to literally force music beyond its own limitations. I know, because I've tried" (Bley 1999, 26). The difficulty lies in that, even though improvising means engaging in a practice in which, theoretically, anything could happen (things may at any moment go differently than planned), in fact the course of a solo often follows a certain pattern, resulting in outcomes that are, more often than not, similar. Indeed, something that can, and perhaps should, be a beginning often reveals itself to be (only) a continuation (Peters 2009, 97).

Again, Steve Lacy to Derek Bailey:

> I'm attracted to improvisation because of something I value. That is a freshness, a certain quality, which can be obtained by improvisation, something you cannot possibly get from writing, It has something to do with the "edge." Always being on the brink of the unknown and being prepared for the leap. And when you go on out there, you have all your years of preparation and all your sensibilities and your prepared means, but it is a leap into the unknown. If through the leap you find something, then it has a value which I don't think can be found in any other way. I place a higher value on that than on what you can prepare. (Weiss 2006, 51)

To improvise, thus, means to act at the limit, in that extreme place where our knowledge is just about sundered from our ignorance. It is a myth that the value and creativity of a musician is connected to his knowledge of where he finds himself, musically, in a given performance, and is in full control of what he is doing. Rather, he puts himself into unfamiliar expressive areas and contexts because the circumstance of *not* knowing precisely what he is doing carries him to the very limits of his creative capacity, where he may find that "freshness" Lacy alluded to.

Regarding the demands of strengthening this capacity to generate the "unheard-of," musicians sometimes speak of "emptying the mind." But improvisation does not imply the rejection of musical knowledge. Rather, navigating by the light of a given (and highly personal) concept, the improvising musician slackens his grip, releasing his cognitive control over the musical *direction*. It is a question of remaining in a state of great sensitivity without, however, becoming too attached to specific musical ideas, cognitive styles, or pre-determined models. Rather than concentrating upon his own musical ideas, it is necessary for the musician, as it were, to displace himself, letting whatever he acquired in time produce its effects. It is no accident that, according to Miles Davis, musicians are more creative at the end of a concert, when their usual repertoire of licks and stylistic expedients has been exhausted. Improvisation requires not so much *intention* (originality cannot be deliberately triggered; moreover, if we try too explicitly to attain a state of autotelic flux, we obstruct it) as *attention*, the ability to expose oneself to music in such a way as to respond creatively to the musical situation as it unfolds, reacting to the changes introduced in the course of a performance.

RESPONSIVENESS: THE COLLECTIVE NATURE OF IMPROVISATION

This last observation pushes us to reflect upon the logic that governs the construction of an improvised performance and upon the position of the musician vis-à-vis the genesis of new musical ideas. I mentioned that the outcome of a solo does not allow itself to be seen in advance. Nevertheless, though he may be myopic, the jazz player does not "drive blind." Not so much because improvisers must think "in advance" (if not note-for-note, then in terms of the structure of his solo), but because he can look backward at what has already been played and react to it—reframing it, re-interpreting it, and giving it a new shape in the phrases that are to come. Paul Bley has noted, enumerating the "lessons" encountered on the bandstand, "One: what was the last phrase that was played, and what was the last note of the last phrase that was played, and what should follow that?" (Bley, 1999, 35). In this respect, the jazz player calls to mind the angel in the famous painting by Klee that Walter Benjamin analyzed in *Theses on the History of Philosophy*: while it is pulled toward the future, its eyes are turned back toward the past. The jazz player, therefore, should not be represented as some sort of decision-maker endowed with an internal computational mechanism granting him, for every two or three possible choices, the power to pick the best one. In reality, the musician cannot enjoy a global perception of the dialectic of opportunity and constraint of each performance—not only because there is no time, in improvisation, to mobilize the necessary cognitive resources, but also because both the opportunities and the constraints are *generated by the players themselves*. For this reason jazz players have an attitude of retrospection: they play *upon* that which has already emerged in the music, discovering the future as they go on, as a consequence of what they do. The development of a solo can, therefore, be followed—in the literal sense of reconstructing it from the past (a process which can be undertaken by either the player or the listener)—but only very rarely can it be anticipated (see Gioia 1988; Sarath 1996).

But to what can the improvising musicians direct their attention in this practice of looking backward? There are always various contextual clues in an improvised performance, clues that a musician will tacitly recognize, more through hearing them than through any sort of conscious selection. As a result, the music that has emerged up to a certain moment will affect subsequent decisions about how to proceed, constituting a contextual parameter for the music to come (Sawyer 2003). This is not to say that the music played earlier will determine exactly what is played later, but, rather, that the former will prepare the hearing of the players or the listeners for further clues to which to pay attention. Background variables like rhythm, speed, idiom, and recourse to a particular tonal area, when introduced or significantly altered, can turn into thematic material and hence reclaim the attention of the players, offering new possibilities for musical exploration/exploitation. These parameters are not inert "things," but rather affordances that enable and invite the musician to act. Each moment of a musical performance, then, is a virtual prefiguring of a possible way of going forward—*possible*, but not obvious or foreseeable. So to say that a musical act facilitates or allows the act that follows it is not to suggest that this act is the cause of, or that it somehow automatically and inexorably provokes, its musical response. This is not so much because whatever has already developed musically cannot force me to take it into account, as it is because the response is also dependent upon the responding musician's knowledge of what has gone before and his ability to draw inferences from it. Perlocutionary force—the circumstance that music expresses, alludes to, proposes, insinuates, directs—is not only a function of the music itself, but also of the way in which it is perceived and interpreted by me. In order to improvise, it is necessary to listen to what is being proposed by the other musicians, but it is equally important to elaborate upon these musical suggestions in a way that is both original and distinctive, creating newness and tension, pulling the music in unexpected directions, without making this response part of a series of responses that give the effect of being played from a preconceived script. Indeed, although exposed to conditions of uncertainty, the jazz musician may nonetheless assume responsibility for what emerges from his instrument. If we neglect to take this responsibility into account, improvisation runs the risk of appearing either totally casual or simply random, something that has "fallen out of the sky." The interplay—the collision—among constraint, control, and accident (the ability to blend the emergent with the intended) is, hence, crucial.

Because jazz is most often played in groups, the above-mentioned interplay can be attributed to the autocatalytic process of a collective unity (Monson 1996). A given musician (Ego), constrained by the ways the music has developed up to a certain point, now produces musical act A, which in turn suggests musical implications A1, A2, and so forth, which may be picked up by the other musicians in his group, whom we will call Other 1 and Other 2. These other musicians then draw upon one of these possible implications, thus determining the course of a new musical emergent (the response to these affordances is never completely arbitrary; often, in fact, it represents one of the closest continuations of the musical solicitation). It is almost as if these implications, when played, gave rise to new imperatives—sonic demands, as it were, that the musicians have no wish to ignore—triggering a circular process, which can be called *collaborative emergence* (because it springs forth from the interactions among the members of the musical collective). As Ornette Coleman explained to Nat Hentoff (1975, 242), "If I don't set a pattern at a given moment, whoever has the dominant ear at that moment can take and do a thing that will change the direction." Each successive act enters into a dialogue with, and in so doing redefines the meaning of, each of the acts that preceded it, at the same time prospectively forming the sense of those acts to come (the act which is the second element of a series of previously initiated acts thus becomes, itself, an emergent context, to which the act that follows is now able to refer). Thus, during the course of a performance, context is continually being created and recreated according to an overarching logic or dynamic—a context that, nonetheless, must presuppose the competence of the players, who must maintain a position of constant awareness and therefore also a margin of reactivity. In the words of Lester Bowie, "we might always try to be creative and adventurous. We let the music lead. A beautiful march might come out of the sky. . . . The percussion might move into a sax solo, which becomes a bass-sax duet that leads into a particular song that develops into a free improvisation. We just don't know" (Mandel 1999, 39). Loop after loop, the musical flux ebbs and flows, slips and slides, unfolding endogenously in directions that none of the individual musicians in the collective can entirely foresee or control. Thus, the musical action—liberating new potentialities—itself generates further musical potential, offering up its first fruits to the attention and the sensibilities of the musicians, who in turn move it forward. According to this logic, it is the music itself that creates the opportunity to draw the capacity for action out of each musician (indeed, it is as if the music itself were conducting). In the case of free jazz, in which the melodic, rhythmic, and harmonic structures of a pre-composed piece have been dispensed with, the music is entrusted almost exclusively to this circular, generative mechanism. Thus, in free jazz, without the necessary degrees of sensitivity and readiness—without, that is to say, responsiveness—the music could not possibly unfold in an original and creative manner. A slight decrease in attentiveness or a bit of mental fog would wreak havoc, not with the musicians' ability to play, but with their ability to improvise in a generative way. In this respect, the notion that the jazz player ideally ought to stop or take a time out in order to reflect upon how he will proceed musically, or in order to conceive new musical ideas, is completely misleading.

The *topoi* of affordance and collective unity lead us to a fifth criteria that characterizes improvisational conduct, which can be termed *responsiveness*. The act of improvisation makes constant reference to (and use of) the improviser's ability to expose himself to music in such a way that he is able to respond both creatively and continuously to whatever happens and to whatever he makes happen. Improvisation is a peculiar emergent accomplishment, constructed diachronically and bearing the marks of collaborative authorship. This circularity, moreover, is only possible because the musical event itself is implicitly richer than the individual musicians who have generated it, containing a plethora of virtualities, each with the capacity to open up new musical horizons. We humans are marked by limitations in our cognitive ability to anticipate the full range of consequences of what we express. And further, if the power of suggestion of a musical act were made equal to the human power to recognize in advance the consequences of whatever has been played, the possibility of improvising would cease immediately. Our creativity, however, exceeds our ability to anticipate the outcome of this same creativity. In this sense, improvisation deals mainly with the exploration of the possibilities implicit in the music.

We recall that Arendt linked human agency to the faculty of generating beginnings and of performing miracles. A miracle (*Wunder*) is commonly understood as the occurrence of the infinitely improbable, but for the sake of our argument this understanding can be extended to include the miraculous capacity to open these new horizons of possibility. For Arendt, the capacity to *begin* is rooted in the fact of being born—not in any sort of innate creativity or gift—and improvisation ultimately consists of putting oneself into the state of being born, of seeking to be present at one's own birth, of orienting oneself toward the unending search for beginnings, and of acting *differently than expected* (Arendt 1958, 178). We must proceed with caution here, though, because no beginning can be absolute or divorced from its context; it is constrained to always be the beginning *of something for someone*—in particular, for those in whom this beginning will evoke a response. The fundamental question is, what makes an act a beginning? Stripped to its essence, it is the circumstance in which someone starts something, taking it up as a spur to further action. The concept of the new, then, is associated not so much with what the actor has in mind, as with the entire fabric of interactions into which he inserts his act, thereby arousing a constellation of dynamic reactions. Newness, in other words, is not a fixed state; its character of beginning depends upon the future—that is, upon the way others respond to it. Arendt thereby turns the intractable question of how something can be generated out of nothing (which in turn suggests misleading images of the "sovereignty" of the actor) into one of how to articulate and intensify the beginnings to which we are exposed; a perspective that invests less in individual talent than in the intersections between individuals, as well as those between individuals and the events that bring them together.

If improvisation is about the ability to respond musically to the clues that emerge in the course of a performance—to respond, that is to say, *to those musicians* who are responsible for engendering these clues—then it is about responding to the other musicians in a kind of mutual monitoring and self-monitoring. Each musician generates music, and consequently each is a contextual witness to the music generated by all. The musicians are not only committed to a peaceful dialogue, however; they are also adversaries who challenge each other and challenge themselves, to listen and to take note of what they are saying musically. And because not all these clues can be taken as invitations to develop themes, one will encounter, on the bandstand, not just sensitivity and support or courtesy and mutuality, but also interference, antagonism, the desire for acceptance, and the will to supremacy in defining the direction of the music. Ultimately, conflict and violence are also integral parts of an improvisation, which may be a collective accomplishment but is not necessarily a dialogic or inclusive one (Peters 2009, 53). We find in the musical arrangement what Arendt calls the disjunctive character of "plurality," that charge of deferral and alteration contained in every human interaction.

THE MYTH OF SPONTANEOUS CREATION

In my emphasis upon the role of originality in improvisation, I may have unintentionally created a misleading impression, for as the heirs of the modernist aesthetic of the new, we tend to celebrate improvisation as a heroic (and solitary) achievement. But as Peters has suggested, improvisation is ineluctably tied to *fear*: fear of the unmarked space, of the unknown and the unforeseen, and fear of nothingness—that is, that nothing (interesting or original) will take place. It is precisely this fear of the *horror vacui* that the musical score keeps under control. It is not by chance, then, that a significant portion of most textbooks for beginning improvisers is devoted to strategies for overcoming that fear. Hence, contrary to the prevailing view, it is (the possibility of) failure that marks improvisation (Peters 2009, 44).

Moreover, the quest for the new should not be confused with the idea that improvisation means creating entirely from scratch. One of the "pictures" that hold us captive in thinking about jazz is that of improvisation as a spontaneous and almost instinctive disposition, as though it did not require interaction, discipline, and certain technologies. While the pattern of an improvised solo is not planned out in the mind of the musician so much as discovered in the course of performance, every improvisation nonetheless refers, at least implicitly, to a set of presuppositions and constraints acquired during the learning process that made that musician a competent improviser. The very word *solo* suggests the misleading image of a gesture performed in complete autonomy. If a solo appears to be the exteriorization of an inner flash of inspiration, it is only because we are influenced and seduced by the religious picture of an absolute beginning (*creatio ex nihilo*). In fact, a solo is never an isolated event; it recalls (and may draw upon) previous solos as a vehicle or point of departure and is necessarily "reflexive": the responses generated by its very unfolding are taken into account, so that the musical context of an improvisation is always the collective unity made up of the actors connected to each other in creating (and reacting to) the music, both musicians and audience. As Mingus once told Timothy Leary, "You can't improvise on nothing, man, you've gotta improvise on something" (Santoro 2000, 271). Or to put it another way, you can improvise on *anything*, but you can't improvise on nothing. A revealing analogy, from this point of view, is that of the freestyle skier, who avoids skiing on a pre-set track, instead making up a route as he goes along. This creative achievement nonetheless presupposes the existence of certain givens and technologies: snow, a slope, technical mastery, and the skis themselves.

If we approach improvisation from the less-spectacular, rarely acknowledged angle of the learning process, we discover keys to the formation of the jazz *habitus* (Thomas Aquinas's term for those practical, embodied abilities that increase with use), such as the slow, exhausting process of acquiring bodily postures or hand positions on a given instrument. The very form of the instrument suggests the gestures needed to play it, and it requires an investment of certain parts of the body (the arm-mouth-neck complex in the case of the reed player, for example), representing an instance of what Foucault called power-knowledge. Of course, in experimental jazz, players try to free themselves from the techniques and routines that have accustomed the body to performing certain gestures and sounds (think, for instance, of Thelonious Monk's unorthodox postures at the piano). And it is also true that, once a certain stage has been reached, technique works against itself and tends to implode (indeed, advanced players tend, while improvising, to *limit* the foreseeable use of the resources they acquired during their apprenticeships). But this implies not so much an emancipation from discipline as such as, rather, a re-disciplining of oneself, the deconstruction of a certain way of playing. Should we strip the improvising musicians of the trappings of the performance context, the idioms they have learned, and their complicity with their instruments, we would deprive them of an invisible and certainly subvertable—yet indispensable—*habitus*.

Thus, if the first step in the jazz musician's learning process is the ability to exploit the already known, spontaneity (to put it somewhat paradoxically) is the outcome of a long relational apprenticeship that inscribes a specific know-how upon the body of the musician. This learning process is by no means a passive one, in which I merely adopt (and adapt to) a given idiom. In learning, one is engaged in a reflective practice, actively figuring out where to place oneself within the community of improvisers—a vast imaginary community that includes those musicians whose sounds affect me and demand to be taken into consideration if I am to have a musical starting point. If each musician selects, as models, his musical predecessors (and hence also, indirectly, his musical antagonists), those predecessors will be not so much causal antecedents as chosen (or, perhaps, invented) sources. This selective apprenticeship on the part of the jazz musician shows how hazy the boundary between musical production and musical consumption can be, for in order to produce (new) music, he must "consume" the musical production of others. Creativity in jazz is not parthenogenetic: it requires a previous fertilization. Given this version of the Freudian return of the repressed, we may aptly conclude that in jazz, in order to innovate, there is no need to commit a symbolic parricide. One's precursors are also one's contemporaries; heritage is brought up-to-date; the future folds over the past.

OTHER FIELDS

As noted at the beginning of this essay, improvisation takes place in many fields, not only in music but also, for example, in drama, dance, sports, and everyday conversation. Take soccer as an example of a sport in which stretches of improvised behavior occur quite frequently: while there are game schemes and rules, the actual behavior of the players depends on contingent factors, such as the behavior of the other players and the unforeseeable position of the ball. Unlike jazz, however, in soccer improvisation is an essentially undesired side effect of these contingencies, for if in fact a player could rely upon a plan of action that would ensure a goal, he would tediously follow it (and would be unwilling to play each game differently for the sake of aesthetic variety, at the risk of not making the goal).

As for daily conversation, it does indeed take place with a certain degree of improvisation, yet two of the five criteria mentioned above (inseparability, irreversibility, situationality, originality, and responsiveness) are missing. Since nothing in conversation corresponds to the act of composing, the notion of inseparability has no meaning in this context. Moreover, given the risk of not making oneself completely understood, conversation is generally devoid of originality. On the other hand, experimental jazz musicians have often been accused of unintelligibility. So, while daily life can certainly unfold in unexpected ways, it usually takes place in a familiar environment that ultimately exempts us from the tiring necessity of originality in discovering new ways to cope with our surroundings. On the contrary, by intentionally defying the network of reference points that characterizes daily life, jazz improvisation embodies and makes the most of Arendt's category of natality (ultimately, the courage to step out into the open). As Miles Davis put it to Nat Hentoff: "I always manage to try something I can't do" (liner notes for *Sketches of Spain*, 1960). We can thus draw a distinction between *reactive* and *elective* forms of improvisation. The first is an induced form of improvisation (we are forced to improvise) that coincides with the need to react to the unforeseeable unfolding of the events we are exposed to. The latter (elective improvisation) is a form of aesthetic experimentation intentionally practiced (it is deliberate, even if it is not the outcome of deliberation). In a nutshell, in jazz, improvisation is not a mean directed to an extrinsic end (as it is in reactive forms of improvisation) but an end in itself.

NOTES

1. Although in jazz the practice of improvisation is especially visible, one must take care not to conflate jazz with improvisation, as there are some forms of jazz in which improvisation is entirely absent. This essay does not seek to *define* jazz, a "minority" art form that emerged from the non-white world, at least through its offspring. It is not as much a self-contained genre characterized by precise origins (a clear trajectory of accretion, a closed set of specific protagonists, and a repertoire of accumulated works) as it is a field—a field, moreover, in which sounds, practices, discourses and images are interwoven (for an analysis of the jazz field, see Sparti 2007a). There is good reason, moreover, to contend that even the term "jazz" has become obsolete as a way to describe the practice of improvisatory music with roots in an African American matrix. It was not for nothing that the Association for the Advancement of Creative Musicians (AACM) rarely uses it, preferring instead the term "creative music." See Lewis 2008, 348.

2. Certainly, a not insignificant number of avant-garde composers, beginning in the 1950s, adopted a new attitude toward composition (whether premeditated or determined by chance), transforming the role of the musician from that of impeccable interpreter of a score—and in turn reconsidered the score as a code to be enacted—to that of a performer, a creative accomplice in the work of composition (as, for example, in John Cage's "Aria"). This collaboration recast the irrevocable status of the work of art (as well as the unique role of the score in the process of musical reproduction), which now assumed an "open" form. Although musicians were called upon to improvise, this music was not always of an improvisatory nature.

3. Regarding such observations, it is worth mentioning, if only for their eminence, those who have declared themselves "enemies" of improvisation: Adorno, Artaud, Berio, Boulez, and Cage.

4. In drawing this distinction, I intend neither to negate the value of jazz composition, nor to forget the "intermediate path" between improvisation and composition—practiced, for example, by Mingus (one thinks of *The Black Saint and the Sinner Lady*), consisting in presenting a suite of loosely interconnected pieces, a performance within which improvisation is overlaid atop a compositional structure. We would do well to remember the case of Anthony Braxton, who refuses to draw a sharp division between composition

and improvisation, as well as Duke Ellington, in whom composing, arranging, simulated improvising (i.e., composed passages that seem improvised), and true improvisation lived as equals, forming a seamless whole of, if a neologism will be excused, "comprovisation."

5. One could argue that an improvisation is a work instantiated in only one performance, but to say this inappropriately stretches the work-concept, which essentially implies the idea of multiple future renditions.

6. Formulated thus, originality seems a characteristic shared with other human activities that develop over a period of time. In the case of improvisation, however, originality also includes the power to surprise, the capacity to push itself beyond the notes already sounded. As music endowed with epiphanies and occurrences of the not-entirely-expected, jazz is in fact earmarked by the impact of that which Barthes, referring to photography, has called the *punctum*: that dazzling, sharp event that bursts into awareness and breaks through the framework of our expectations (see Barthes 1981). It is a sonic injection (that *guizzo* of which Calvino speaks in his American lesson dedicated to Lightness) that strikes me, tearing me away from passive fruition (see Calvino 1993).

BIBLIOGRAPHY

Arendt, H. *The Human Condition*. Chicago: University of Chicago Press, 1958.

Arendt, H. *Was ist politik, Aus dem nachlass*. Muenchen: Piper, 1993, Trans. It., *Che cosa è la politica*. Torino: Edizioni di Comunità, 1995.

Bailey, D. *Improvisation: Its Nature and Practice in Music*. New York: Da Capo Press, 1992.

Barthes, R. *Camera Lucida*. New York: Hill and Wang, 1981.

Bateson, G. *Steps to an Ecology of Mind: Collected Essays in Anthropology, Psychiatry, Evolution, and Epistemology*. Chicago: University of Chicago Press, 2000.

Benson, B. E. *The Improvisation of Musical Dialogue: A Phenomenology of Music*. Cambridge: Cambridge University Press, 2003.

Bent, M. "Res facta and Cantare Super Librum." *Journal of the American Musicological Society* 36 (1983): 371–391.

Berliner, P. *Thinking in Jazz: The Infinite Art of Improvisation*. Chicago: University of Chicago Press, 1994.

Béthune, C. *Adorno et le jazz. Analyse d'un déni esthétique*. Paris: Klincksieck, 2003.

Bley, P. (with D. Lee). *Stopping Time. Paul Bley and the Transformation of Jazz*. Québec: Véhicule Press, 1999.

Calvino, I. *Lezioni americane*. Milano: Mondadori, 1993.

Cardew, C. "Towards an Ethic of Improvisation." In *Treatise Handbook*. London: Edition Peters, 1971.

Cook, N. "Making Music Together, or Improvisation and Its Others." In *Music, Performance, Meaning: Selected Essays*, 321–341. Aldershot: Ashgate, 2007.

Corbett, J. "Ephemera Underscored: Writing Around Free Improvisation." In *Jazz Among the Discourses*, edited by K. Gabbard, 217–240. London: Duke University Press, 1995.

Dalhaus, C. "Wass heisst improvisation?" In *Improvisation und neue Musik: Acht Kongreßreferate*, edited by R. Brinkmann, 9–23. Mainz: Schott, 1979.

Enstice, W., and P. Rubin *Jazz Spoken Here: Conversations with Twenty-Two Musicians*. Baton Rouge and London: Louisiana State University Press, 1992.

Gioia, T. *The Imperfect Art: Reflections on Jazz and Modern Culture.* New York: Oxford University Press, 1988.

Goehr, L. *The Imaginary Museum of Musical Works: An Essay in the Philosophy of Music.* Oxford: Oxford University Press, 1992.

Goodman, N. *Languages of Art: An Approach to a Theory of Symbols,* 2nd ed. Indianapolis: Hackett, 1976. First published in 1968 by Bobbs-Merrill.

Henderson, J. Interview by Mel Martin. *The Saxophone Journal* (March–April 1991). Available at http://www.melmartin.com/html_pages/Interviews/henderson.html. Accessed December 19, 2013.

Hentoff, N. *The Jazz Life.* New York: Capo Press, 1975.

Lake, O. *Point From Which Creation Begins.* Arista Freedom AL 1024, 1976.

Lewis, G. E. *A Power Stronger than Itself: The AACM and American Experimental Music.* Chicago: University of Chicago Press, 2008.

Lyons, L. *The Great Jazz Pianists: Speaking of Their Lives and Music.* New York: Da Capo Press, 1983.

Mandel, H. *Future Jazz.* Oxford: Oxford University Press, 1999.

Mandel, H. *Miles, Ornette, Cecil: Jazz Beyond Jazz.* London and New York: Routledge, 2007.

Monson, I. *Saying Something: Jazz Improvisation and Interaction.* Chicago: University of Chicago Press, 1996.

Moore, R. "The Decline of Improvisation in Western Art Music: An Interpretation of Change." *International Review of the Aesthetics and Sociology of Music* 23 (1992): 61–84.

Peters, G. *The Philosophy of Improvisation.* Chicago: University of Chicago Press, 2009.

Prevost, E. *No Sound Is Innocent: AMM and the Practice of Self-Invention. Meta-Musical Narratives, Essays.* Hardow: Copula, 1995.

Restago, E. *Xenakis.* Turin: EDT/Musica, 1988.

Ryle, G. *The Concept of Mind.* London: Hutchinson, 1949.

Santoro, G. *Myself When I Am Real: The Life and Music of Charles Mingus.* New York: Oxford University Press, 2000.

Sarath, E. "A New Look at Improvisation." *Journal of Music Theory* 40, no. 1 (spring 1996): 1–38.

Sawyer, K. R. *Group Creativity: Music, Theater, Collaboration.* Philadelphia: Lawrence Erlbaum, 2003.

Schuller, G. *The Swing Era: The Development of Jazz, 1930–1945.* Oxford: Oxford University Press, 1989.

Schutz, A. "Making Music Together: A Study in Social Relationship." In *Collected Papers,* 2: 159–179. The Hague: Martinus Nijhoff, 1971.

Shipton, A. *Handful of Keys: Conversations with 30 Jazz Pianists.* London: Routledge, 2004.

Sloboda J. A., ed. *Generative Processes in Music: The Psychology of Performance, Improvisation and Composition.* Oxford: Oxford University Press, 1988.

Sparti, D. *Musica in nero. Il campo discorsivo del jazz.* Torino: Bollati Boringhieri, 2007a.

Sparti, D. *Il corpo sonoro. Oralità e scrittura nel jazz.* Bologna: Il Mulino, 2007b.

Wegman, R. C. "From Maker to Composer: Improvisation and Musical Authorship in the Low Countries, 1450–1500." *Journal of the American Musicological Society* 49 (1996): 409–479.

Weiss, J., ed. *Steve Lacy: Conversations.* Durham, NC, and London: Duke University Press, 2006.

CHAPTER 10

THE SALMON OF WISDOM

On the Consciousness of Self and Other in Improvised
Music and in the Language that Sets One Free

ALEXANDRE PIERREPONT
(Translated from the French by Anton Vishio)

IT is written that Finn Mac Cumail, while still an apprentice, carelessly tasted the Salmon of Wisdom,[1] the preparation of which he had been asked to supervise. From that moment, the moment he sucked on his thumb and lapped up the cooking juices, the moment he burst forth in song, he *knew*. So tells the Fenian Cycle, an accounting of the exploits and escapades of Finn, the last chief of the Fianna of Leinster, those adventurers who functioned at the margins of the law in the Ireland of yore.

Yet what must have taken hold of such a hero, conventionally well versed in the art of poetry? For one thing, *teinm laida*: the illumination brought by song. For another, *dichetul dichennaib*: the act of improvisatory incantation. And for a third, *imbas forosnai*: the knowledge that enlightens. One might say that giving oneself over to song or to the poetry that sets one free forces language itself to speak. Such a person knows that one must give in to the voice to understand better, as countless thinkers have made clear. According to Novalis, "Speaking for the sake of speaking is the formula of deliverance," while, for Tristan Tzara, "The thought is made in the mouth."[2]

Rather than firmly grasping the reins of language, one who fashions oneself a Fianna or poet chooses instead to let them slacken, and directs one's speech in the manner in which one directs a dream: uncertainly. An immemorial intelligence, of those who muse on infinitely, will have located the thread running through verbalization (the necessity of giving a hearing), improvisation (the necessity of allowing action), and knowledge (the necessity of fostering revelation), a thread followed over several decades, according to George E. Lewis, by the men and women working in an Afrological musical tradition who conceive of "improvisation as a knowledge-producing, indeed a knowledge-finding activity—a journey of discovery."[3]

For the present purposes, I will treat this perspective, which cannot be reduced to a single musical genre, under the sign of the "jazzistic field" (*le champ jazzistique*),[4] meaning the continuum of musics produced by the African American experience. Characterized by multiple referentiality in constant revolution, as well as by a double or dialogic dynamic, while at the same time combining and transforming both its givens (elements that are stable and prepared) and its spontaneities (those that are unstable and not premeditated), those most often engaged with the greatest compatibility and constantly inventing and reinventing collectively, these musics distinguish themselves by a process of differentiation at each level of their elaboration—in the sonic signature of each individual on her or his instruments; in the personal narrative that each develops in playing, in improvising; in original compositions expected from each one in language systems put into practice by others; in a complex geography, not of "styles" but of "form-spaces," physical and/or symbolic places of specific exchange that open the one to the other. This incessant production of internal alterities is historically accompanied by an incessant search for alliances, opportunities to link with that which is not (in) one. Neither technical nor musicological, this chapter will scrutinize the universe of internal representations of creative musicians, with particular emphasis on the practical and theoretical range of elements deployed over a half century by the members of the Association for the Advancement of Creative Musicians (AACM) and their allies and contemporaries.

But for the moment, let us return to Finn. In letting himself go in song, which airs out or erupts forth, he frees himself to capture and then transmit a voice within—or an interior speech—marked by its own coherence; the surrealists turned this voice within into the source of "message automatique" (automatic writing), "coulée verbale" (verbal flow), and "dictée de la pensée" (unmediated dictation of thought). As André Breton wrote,

> The "inner word" that surrealist poetry has chosen to make manifest and that it has succeeded, whether we like it or not, in establishing as a recognisable medium of exchange among certain people, is absolutely inseparable from "inner music" by which it very probably is cradled and conditioned. How could it be otherwise when the inner word, as registered by "automatic writing," is subject at the same acoustical conditions of rhythm, pitch, intensity and timbre as the outer word, although to a lesser degree? In that it is the effectual opposite of the expression of controlled thought which has kept no organic contact with music and uses it only occasionally as a luxury. But above all, being independent of the social and moral obligations that limit spoken and written language, inner thinking is free to tune itself to the "inner music" *which never leaves it.*
>
> I already have protested against the designation "visionary" being lightly applied to poets. Great poets have been "auditives," not visionaries.[5]

In responding via improvisation to the call of that voice, the young man acquired wisdom, which illuminates like the song that declares it, like the powers of verbalization or of the orality that it liberates. Édouard Glissant explains that these powers of speech "are entirely suitable to the diversity of all things, the broodings, the word turned back on itself, the spiral cry, the fissures of the voice."[6] Powers: already invoked by Antonin

Artaud when he presented surrealism, that great gathering of poet adventurers in the disenchanted West, as "a cry of the mind turning back on itself."[7] Powers: among verbalization, improvisation, and knowledge, so precisely invoked in turn by Toni Morrison in *Song of Solomon*:

> All those shrieks, those rapid tumbling barks, the long sustained yells, the tuba sounds, the drumbeat sounds, the low liquid *howm howm*, the reedy whistles, the thin *eeeee*'s of a cornet, the *unh unh unh* bass chords. It was all language. An extension of the click people made in their cheeks back home when they wanted a dog to follow them. No, it was not language; it was what there was before language. Before things were written down. Language in the time when men and animals did talk to one another, when a man could sit down with an ape and the two converse; when a tiger and a man could share the same tree, and each understood the other; when men ran *with* wolves, not from or after them.[8]

Seeing or hearing in the universe, a susurrant system of correspondences, of perceived accords; the making of language into the speaking double—not mirror—of that universe, as if objects moving through us, speaking through us, arrive at the fullness of their being: what Morrison describes here joins up with the Kabbalah of the poets since the dawn of time. As Serge Pey wrote in a letter to Octavio Paz, "The modern poet does not address the world, but rather the Word on which the world rests."[9] Because if we are accustomed to take language, domesticated language, for one of the privileged vehicles of the human experience, our communication instrument *par excellence*, we are at least as much the arena staged by a language not our own, which, through the forays hurled by its feverish harmonies of sound and sense, crosses and links beings and things. The human and the world meet up in poetry, and, in order for the tale to be told, their encounter requires that one make a poetic use of language, that words be shaped in the manner that rocks are formed, or the way the eyes acquire color, according to the same gestations, the same ecstasies.

It is again a writer, an adventurer in language, now from the Kiowa, who attests: "A word has power in and of itself. It comes from nothing into sound and meaning; it gives origin to all things. By means of words can a man deal with the world on equal terms. And the word is sacred."[10] From nothing—or from a song, that relentless song that entwines sound and sense, since it has always been in the nature of poetry, according to Breton, to realize "the perfect synthesis of sound and idea, for the benefit of the imagination."[11]

While the domesticated language is condemned to treat its messages with due diligence, to attribute to choice an obedient meaning, a literal or metaphorical reading; while it cannot extricate itself from a relationship of identity or identification more or less troubled with that which it wants to name and which along with its context and its destination always escapes it, poetic language, the language that sets one free, lacking a clear destination, maintains with its context the most distant and most restorative relationships, juggles that which is already created with that which it creates, distributes and redistributes maps of meaning, alters, installs the reign of generalized multiple reference. One who makes oneself a poet, who makes use of the illumination and the improvisation of song, speaks in the name of language, creates a body by means of language which exists within as a foreign object. Such a person speaks as one divines by casting seashells: to see (to hear) and to know. One speaks, and leaves in recognition.

It is surely not impossible that Afrological improvisers in the jazzistic field and its satellites, in the Afrological musical perspective developed by Lewis, plough some of the access roads of the highest poetry, if one deigns to consider the activity of improvisation as a poetic one manifesting conscious practices resembling those of existence itself, practices that are never only collected in the pendant of the poem, the condensation or talismanic fixation of a crossing of the real, in and by language. Humans have heard voices from the dawn of time, and one could cite as a precondition for the poetic act as for the improvisatory the necessity, surely not of falling silent, but rather of silencing in oneself that which is not language, that which is not music, in order to open oneself more profoundly to the hearing of that one word on which hinges the world, this flood of words, this flux of reality. Breton thus restricts poets to being "modest recording machines," "deaf receptacles of so many echoes," and insists on the "auditory-verbal" as opposed to "visual-verbal" character of the automatic message, which is understood in the first place as enjoined in this "Introduction to the Discourse on the Paucity of Reality": "Let there be silence so that I might tread where no man has ever trodden, silence!—After you, my fair language."[12]

In the same way one hears it often said that music is in some measure dictated, possibly by an interior voice, to its improvisers. Didn't the bluesmen of the Delta claim to have "collected floating verses" from the atmosphere before composing their bouquet of words? And from camp meetings to the Second Great Awakening, such "wandering verses" fall regularly on the head of the astonished choristers of the first spirituals. If certain passages of the Bible nevertheless have in particular been objects of attention on the part of African Americans, such as the story of Pentecost in the Acts of the Apostles, when the Holy Spirit informed of its presence through a gusting wind, tongues of flame like crocheted shawls on the shoulder, and through the broadband of its uncontrollable speech: isn't the gift of tongues, of speaking in tongues, not only dedication to the glory of God or to the fashioning of oneself as its interpreter, but also what sustains—as required by *illumination*—the idea of this flood of words as a flux of reality?

Imagining the human as the canal through which such a flood is led, such a flux is a matter in general circulation among improvisers, through practices where the general tendency is not to be satisfied with a single critical meaning but rather to awaken to other perceptions and representations, which are being played in oneself and around oneself, together, allowing them to be guided by different aspects of one's personality, of one's psyche or environment, without definitively abdicating all clarity of conscience. To give oneself to improvisation that sets one free, the musician must mobilize the totality of his or her being, consciousness as well as unconsciousness—a "double consciousness" that permits one to come to terms with the active and the passive concurrently, to abandon to oneself and to others without ever renouncing anyone or anything. Explanations given by systems of thought or belief of individuals on the exact nature of this flood or this flux notwithstanding, its communally felt necessity poses the question of the status of identity and alterity in the act of improvisation.

Behind their indispensable, undeniable technical facility, most improvisers are inclined to admit that they are not the only masters of the situation, that rather they are sensors of a much greater reality. As Paz said of the poet, he "is not the 'author' in the traditional sense of the word; he is a moment of convergence of the different voices which flow into a text."[13] One must first learn to discern that which passes through oneself, this flow, this flux, *to recognize the self's other*. Music can do as much, because one is not all. Otherwise said, improvisers emit as much as they transmit the sounds they receive; they make heard that which is given to them to hear. As pianist Amina Claudine Myers put it, "I like the idea that I'm only a vehicle through which the creative forces speak. . . . Stay open. The spirits, my ancestors, my and your spiritual guides are there, always, but you have to know how to find them in the music."[14] Bassist Malachi Favors Maghostut has voiced a similar sentiment: "To truly appreciate music, you have listen to the spirit of the music, because the music speaks. Because it says something. And it will say something to you, if you just listen."[15] Many other contemporary improvisers, among them Leroy Jenkins, Lester Bowie, Muhal Richard Abrams, Steve Coleman, Hamid Drake, Charles Lloyd, David S. Ware, and Henry Threadgill, have also described their art in these terms of divination.[16]

We can interpret this shared responsibility as an idealized plurality of the forces in attendance, like voices from the unconscious, or even from a "collective unconscious" in which one recovers the memories of an ageless past, like the manifestation of other forms of intelligence—the ancestors connected to the Holy Spirit or the fluctuating beings of vibratory phenomena. Some here locate the vital force that links all beings, the ramified spirit of the world in its highest creative principle, that of seeking for itself a path. The union with this force could become the goal of a socio-musical quest: *A Love Supreme*, according to John Coltrane; *Spiritual Unity*, according to Albert Ayler; *Complete Communion*, according to Don Cherry. Anthony Braxton goes so far as to call music "a highway, an immense highway, towards Cosmic Forces."[17]

Whatever the origin attributed to these voices (the unconscious, ancestors or spirits, the community, or the cosmos), it is characteristic of improvised music that it connects people, to others and to that which is divulged within them. All the work of the improviser consists of knowing how to welcome these voices, to grab hold of them at the junction of the past, present, and future. This practice, on the one hand, is always a matter of building an alliance with an other that is not entirely estranged from the self. On the other hand, to assert that the free and categorical expression of one's self/self's other and the inclusion of this self in a much vaster plan is not a contradiction; in fact, each is the condition for the other. To reconcile them, improvising musicians frequently make allusions to two corollary realities: that of a reservoir in the middle of which all sounds are permanently mixed up; and that of a flux through which all sounds pour out with neither end nor beginning.

Coltrane was perhaps among the first to talk overtly of "a big reservoir that we all dip out of";[18] but this notion has known innumerable translations, from a multidimensional sphere encompassing all possible and imaginable sounds, the living center of reality in its creative manifestations (musical, artistic, human, natural, universal), to the sacred matrix of creativity, that of Oshun or of the primordial Om. And the list could be extended further, on the African side, on the European side, on all sides: the *imago mundi*, the Supreme Point of the Zohar and the Kabbalah, generating and containing the universe, the philosophical egg, the hieroglyphic monad—in all of these examples, the figure of a greater and more complete reality serves also to allow freedom of action and of imagination.

As for this reservoir from which one draws, no matter what emerges, this sonorous flow of reality links up that which is and that which is different, that which is manifest and that which is latent, looping together the other in the self and the self in the other (from the individual in the cosmos passing through the human race and the world). Jules Monnerot, a sociologist born in Martinique and a friend of the surrealists, wrote of this reservoir in poetry, which was "born (in that falsely historical manner of speaking, merely metaphorical) not from those who intended to be poets, but from those who attained poetry in aiming for existence, invaded by a flux which allowed them to see and touch in others that which those others themselves are seeing and touching."[19]

From an Afrological perspective, nothing is further from the socio-musical practices linked to improvisation than the anthropocentric theory or the so-called central, irreducible, and indivisible character of human consciousness. Thus Lewis expresses surprise at this "[innate] need of people to feel that they have control over some aspect of their lives. I think that it's important to realize that we're in a kind of an interdependent universe here, and I'm not sure how much control that we have over our lives. I'm sure that control is not total. That's pretty obvious. We seem to be faced with forces moving around us all."[20] These forces or energies circulating around us are the ones the surrealists strived to capture with automatic writing,[21] spiced up by a "mental electricity," and that writers like James Joyce or Virginia Woolf attempted to channel into the shape of a current (electric?) of consciousness.

More recently, Yves Citton has revived the premonition of such a circulation of energy, as with the intimate conviction of Richard Wright: "[W]ithout a continuous current of shared thought and feeling circulating through the social system, like blood coursing through the body, there could be no living worthy of being called human."[22] From this statement, Citton issues the following forecast, essential for our purposes: "From the discovery of electrical phenomena and of Mesmerian magnetism in the Age of Enlightenment, to the diffusion of the great newspapers and of the telegraph in the era of [Gabriel] Tarde, and up to the networks, Hertzian and internet, which make up the background of Maurizio Lazzerato's reflections, one witnesses the progressive emergence of an imaginary which represents modern societies as a collective mental universe informed by the circulation of magnetic currents and resonating waves."[23]

Several musicians in the jazzistic field have insisted on reminding us that music could be understood as the science of vibrations and vibratory phenomena, with Braxton even pursuing "vibrational alignments." Everything that exists in the material or immaterial spheres vibrates at a certain frequency. In playing, in improvising, musicians have the possibility and the power to place themselves on the frequency (wavelength) of all that is, to let themselves be carried by this flux of reality and participate in the harmonizing or dissonating of beings and things. Creative music is thus the macrocosmic reverberation of sound, the sonic translation of the chaotic, cosmic coexistence of all—"the simultaneous and harmonious vibration of all the phenomena of creation," according to the Sonic Healing Ministries of Chicago.[24] Musicians may provide relief, calm, health, pleasure, beauty, or knowledge only to the degree that they offer, in themselves, this vibration that spears and harpoons the world. Or the opposite. For example, Avreeayl Ra claims that

> there is a frequency to which we hold, and where there is nothing more than the vehicle for what happens . . . especially with this kind of music. One thing I often insist on is that no music, composed or not, will stand if you are not all there yourself before going on stage. Because the energy expended to continuously face the score can keep you away from the frequency on which creativity is at its highest level. And so, contrary to common sense, you must find the music itself, in your heart. The whole universe is here, within.[25]

Matana Roberts and Kalaparush Maurice McIntyre take up the same theme. For Roberts, "There is no contradiction between the intimate appearance and the universal aspect. In fact, I believe in a holistic approach. Everything is connected, really."[26] As Kalaparush put it, "Everything comes from you, and from the depths of the universe."[27] A circuit of the self, as far as the deepest reaches of the universe, poles of a circulation of forces and energies—a navigation that transcends form. Once more, according to the improvisers, affirmation of a "me" and participation in a "self" go together, as Lewis notes: "The best way to look inside is often to look around you and explore your environment. I have to be an environmentalist . . . and so I made this task of interpreting the world around me, trying to be minimally invasive. I want to harmonize with the world as I find it in music."[28]

The idea of a circulation of forces and energies and all that it implies, interconnecting man and the universe as two rooms of the same haunted house, distances itself from a modernity which posed the rupture with nature as a prior condition for the link with the (human) other, with the social contract and with historical progress. Modernity has classified and mocked any idea of "magical participation" or "pantheistic fusion," any communication or communion between the interior and exterior worlds, which emanate from a level of thought termed "pre-logical" by Lévy-Bruhl or "savage" by Lévi-Strauss. That is why free or collective improvisation could be considered by certain of its practitioners as the ultimate stage of collaboration among people, in a strict sense of *among*, the link with *that other-over-there* trumping all others.

If this "fully human" dimension is accepted by the body of creative musicians, there are others who refuse to confine music's powers to humankind alone, claiming instead for music the status of an art of conversation *among all that exists*. Charmingly, in his writings over the years, Braxton has cited what amounts to a census of his partners: children, women, men, musicians, ventriloquists, scientists, doctors, geologists, herbalists, and all the kingdoms of nature.[29] And in the verbal puzzle of his composition *OQA*, Muhal Richard Abrams compares the structure of a melody in time with the organization of a geometric figure in space, suggesting the consilience of these universal laws with metabolisms, living cells, oxygen molecules, atoms, celestial movements, and the zodiac.[30]

One must understand that, in the relationship with the other that improvisers have reinvented, alterity can take the form of a material, quality, property, or object; a human or other living being; or an ancestor, spirit, divinity, or cosmic force. The other is all that permits the making of the world, as Robert Jaulin liked to repeat:

> The future, the stars, deaths, rain, earth, the visible or perceptible in its immediate functions make therefore a body with humanity; and vice-versa. Together, they are the universe. By the game of divination man finds himself thus gifted with a universe in which he is one of the "divinities," if the invention of life is of divine order.[31]

Creative musicians in playing, in improvising, do not dream of ordering this apparent chaos of the world, but of revealing its "secret" order. As subjective as this transitivity might be, they play others, in themselves and around them; they play the world and the universe. All of being is their instrument. Henry Threadgill:

> Before the concert in the amphitheatre [outdoors], during the sound check, I understood that the wind was at home here, that we would have to play with it, make it a partner, the sixth member of the group—and not an adversary of the music. . . . This night, the wind sat in with us on the stage and when it made itself known, we made a place for it in the orchestra.[32]

It is thus not a matter of reproducing or transposing "nature," but acting in concert with it, to become in one and the same motion a creative and an altering power. Pursuing the parallels drawn by Paz, if for the utopian Charles Fourier, "the system of the universe (analogy) is the key to the system of society," and if for the poet Charles Baudelaire, "the system of the universe is the model for poetic creation,"[33] for a number of creative musicians, the system of the universe is the key to socio-musical formation and creation. The sonorous flux of reality in which they insert themselves allies itself to the system of correspondences or the tissue of analogies linking all that is in a continuum of multiple meanings. Raising this voice or this interior conversation to an audible level is to transport beyond oneself, toward a self's other to which the double consciousness imposed on African Americans has long given rise, an other for the self that is not experienced as a fissure but as the natural state of the human condition, unique and double.

To improvise is to fluctuate, to pass from one state to another, from one form to another, and occasionally to make passage from one into another. It is to be acted upon by the stream of a speech simultaneously personal and impersonal, foundational. Far from the received idea according to which improvisation is concerned only with "self-expression," in the sense in which one expresses with a certain uniqueness that which one is, what one feels, what one thinks, in so far as one is certain of it or assured (one dreams of the distinction long ago implemented by Tzara between poetry as means of expression and poetry as activity of the spirit), the activity of improvisation, like poetic activity, allows the discovery and practice of one's own strangeness, one's own plurality, in a becoming-many of the subject coming to replace the becoming-subject of the multitude conceptualized by Michael Hardt and Antonio Negri. One doesn't identify any longer with oneself, master of the word, one attempts the double identification with one's self and self's other. For Abrams, in whose work and thought the number three has the weight of a structural principle, this double or triple consciousness is nothing but the image of a necessary multiple consciousness, the way into the infinitude of possibilities, situated among the conscious me, the hidden me, and an included third (that which, in the end, decides).

It is not only that the improvisatory activity of musicians of the jazzistic field redefines the connections between interiority and exteriority, but also the combinatorial dynamic of this field invents permanent connections, where nothing enters in contradiction. Artaud writes of poetic activity in these terms: "This helps us to understand that poetry is anarchic insofar as it calls into question all relationships between objects and all relationships between forms and their meanings."[34] Rather, improvised music and the language which sets one free are indefinitely associative, having as great a need of analytical as of analogical thought. They search for the unity among the plurality of beings and subjects, not one found above or beyond them; they render them in their powerful alterity, rediscovering without end their networks of relations, in the lived presence of things—a unity in all the senses of the union of contraries, in that union in which differences are not resolved but made resonant, harmonized, in that union of the *progression of chords*. Addressing such a union, Anthony Davis comments:

> If I take this bet and if I let music make itself, if I let my ideas spin out, then nine times out of ten, one thing leading to another, one idea modifying another, everything links up. . . . But making this jump into the unknown, admitting that the music comes to you sometimes without premeditation, admitting that one can be proud of something which surpasses reasoned reason, something that is beyond one's apparent technical capacity and the control exercised by reason, here is the true discriminating factor. And this is why I think that every composer must equally be an improviser. Improvisation is that which gives the musician the courage to make this leap.[35]

Creative musicians thus spend their time undoing associations between sounds and ideas that are stuck in a unique literal-mindedness, possibly that of "the present order's uninterrupted discourse about itself,"[36] with the goal of subsequently recapturing them in whole or part and reconnecting them with other orders, already socio-musical. With Stuart Hall, it is possible to see or to hear in the undertaking of improvisation, in the

undertaking of poetry, "[the] active work of constructing new meanings and 'definitions of the situation.' "[37] Among the properties of musics in the jazzistic field, isn't there
precisely this dialogic treatment of so-called oppositions and contradictions rendered
complementary?

On the other hand, the combinatorial dynamic of these musics does not postulate any
definitive organization of sounds: all organization is only as valuable as played, and as
timely or provisional (if not ephemeral: it can be made use of again, when timely once
more), and has value only as a reserved solution, in a certain space-time, to be retained
as a supplemental possibility. None of the solutions takes its interest from its conformity
or non-conformity to a model, but from how it corresponds to a given situation, to the
beings, spirits, and energies in presence, in the appropriate yet variable manner, establishing the equivalent of what Hardt and Negri have called "a regime of the production
of identity and difference, or really of homogenization and heterogenization."[38]

This metamorphic principle demands the interpretation of collective improvisation as an act of invention of "immediate" social structures, made to order, which are
as much the translation of relationships among individuals and with the world as they
are the reflection of preexisting structures. Out of all the rules of the game, out of all the
language systems to which creative musicians have recourse, the combinatory dynamic
of the jazzistic field creates strategies that are interactive *among others*. The dynamic is a
multiplier of terms and of relations, allowing individuals to circulate "in and out," so that
they might unify their contraries of becoming-subject and becoming-multiple, or interact with partners who design their elective affinities while conserving a global vision
of their interactions; while developing an acuity for contexts and structures, in order
to permit them to abandon themselves to themselves, to a stream of consciousness, to
the light of the world, while at the same time according the most rapt attention to what
their colleagues are playing, without ever abandoning them definitively, without ever
following them definitively, but inventing with them the form of an ensemble, in placing themselves in a state of unconsciousness and hyperconsciousness at the same time: a
state, that is, of double consciousness.

For improvisation is also the liberty of movement, the liberty of living in the flux of
reality, in the enchanted realm of the possible. Rather than committing to a unique form
or a generalized formlessness, rather than having to choose between conservation and
innovation, the transformative dynamic of the jazzistic field, in consort with its combinatory energetics, mingles and envelops the sonorous real by practicing upon the world
(this one and some others), admitting a priori the changing and composite nature of its
identities, institutions, and structures. Anyone who has already participated in a concert
of creative music knows that improvisation serves also and above all as a conduit for
moving from one form to another, which Braxton likens to a "navigation which crosses
forms," Lewis to a "voyage of exploration," and which Lawrence D. "Butch" Morris attributed to the very possibility of improvisation: "An improviser can play with a single idea
and make it take all possible forms within an hour, making it go through six, seven . . .
ten different structures."[39] Taking up this idea of navigation, John Corbett writes: "[Sun
Ra's] music was explicitly about navigation, about the formal construction of vehicles

for travel in self-created space. Ra called for listeners to do the impossible, to make manifest a fantastic journey, a highly politicized, poetical trip into unknown worlds."[40]

To "easily slip into another world," as Threadgill once put it, or to let one be traversed by other voices, other presences, to relocate in the universe, oriented toward both an immemorial past (African or other) and the cosmos, is to ebb and flow like the forms that one assumes, just as the Salmon of Wisdom steers its course through the wake of currents and crosscurrents, of apprehensions and illuminations. In the end, the navigation of fantasy improvisation and poetry may be the only way of being one's self, self's other.

NOTES

1. Translator's note: The phrase *le saumon de la sagesse* is generally rendered in English as *The Salmon of Knowledge*. For poetic reasons, with the consent of the author, I have used *wisdom* here.
2. Translator's note: This translation of Novalis appears in Susan Sontag, "The Aesthetics of Silence," in *Styles of Radical Will* (New York: Farrar, Straus and Giroux, 1966), 28; Tristan Tzara, trans. Barbara Wright, "From 'Dada Manifesto on Feeble Love and Bitter Love,'" in *Poems for the Millennium, The University of California Book of Modern and Postmodern Poetry*, ed. Jerome Rothenberg and Pierre Joris, vol. 1, *From Fin-de-Siecle to Negritude* (Berkeley: University of California Press, 1995 [1920]), 301.
3. George E. Lewis, "Singing Omar's Song: A (Re)construction of Great Black Music," *Lenox Avenue: A Journal of Interarts Inquiry*, no. 4 (1998): 79.
4. See Alexandre Pierrepont, *Le Champ Jazzistique* (Marseilles: Éditions Parenthèses, 2002).
5. André Breton, "Silence Is Golden," in *André Breton: What Is Surrealism—Selected Writings* (New York: Pathfinder, 1978 [1946]), 268–269.
6. Édouard Glissant, *Traité du Tout-Monde: Poétique IV* (Paris: Gallimard, 1997), 121.
7. Various, "Declaration of January 27, 1925," in *History of Surrealism*, ed. Maurice Nadeau, trans. Richard Howard (Cambridge: Belknap Press of Harvard University, 1989), 241.
8. Toni Morrison, *Song of Solomon* (New York: Knopf, 1977), 278.
9. Serge Pey, *Lettres posthumes à Octavio Paz depuis quelques arcanes majeurs du tarot* (Paris: Jean-Michel Place, 2002), 49.
10. N. Scott Momaday, *The Way to Rainy Mountain* (Albuquerque: University of New Mexico Press, 1969), 33.
11. André Breton, "Situation of the Surrealist Object," trans. Richard Seaver and Helen R. Lane, in *Manifestoes of Surrealism* (Ann Arbor: University of Michigan Press, 1969 [1935]), 260.
12. Breton, "Silence Is Golden," 25.
13. Octavio Paz, *Children of the Mire: Modern Poetry from Romanticism to the Avant-Garde*, trans. Rachel Phillips, new ed. (Cambridge: Harvard University Press, 1991 [1972]), 173.
14. Amina Claudine Myers, interview with the author, Paris, February 2004.
15. Steven Tod, "Malachi Favors: Keep Playin' Till the Lord Says Stop" (Silver Measure. DVD, 2004).
16. Leroy Jenkins, interview with the author, New York, May 2004; Tim Livingston, "Interview with Lester Bowie," *Cadence* 27, no. 1 (January, 2001); Ted Panken, "Interview with Henry

Threadgill" (WKCR-FM, July 24, 1996), http://www.jazzhouse.org/library/?read=panken3; Bill Shoemaker, "Muhal Richard Abrams: Focus on the Vastness," *Point of Departure* (1995), http://www.pointofdeparture.org/archives/PoD-3/PoD-3_TurnAround.html; Christian Gauffre and Geoffrey De Masure, "Leçons de Von Freeman et Bunky Green," *Jazz Magazine* 524 (March 2002): 29; Jesse Stewart, "Interview with Hamid Drake," *Cadence* 30, no. 3 (March 2004): 6; Lorraine Soliman, "La médecine invisible du docteur Lloyd," *Jazz Magazine* 570 (May 2006): 32; Ben Ratliff, liner notes to David S. Ware, *Third Ear Recitation* (DIW #870. Compact disc, 1998). Also see http://www.bb10k.com/Ware_UP.html.

17. Graham Lock, "A Highway to the Cosmics," in *Mixtery: A Festschrift for Anthony Braxton*, ed. Graham Lock (Exeter: Stride, 1995), 249.

18. Frank Kofsky, *John Coltrane and the Jazz Revolution of the 1960s* (New York: Pathfinder Press, 1998 [1970]), 443.

19. Jules Monnerot, *La poésie moderne et le sacré* (Paris: Gallimard, 1945), 21.

20. Ted Panken, "Interview with George Lewis" (WKCR-FM, April 30, 1994), http://www.jazzhouse.org/files/panken16.php3?read.

21. The connection, obviously false, between automatic writing and musical improvisation has been permitted by an unhappy medium on which the majority of authors have in reality focused their attention: the problem of velocity, and eventually the connection with time. In particular one sees comparisons between the immediacy of thought, on the one hand, and the pace of performance, on the other, with inevitably negligible results. As this chapter suggests, the relations between improvised music and the language that sets one free are happily not invalidated by the differences between these speeds of execution.

22. Richard Wright, *Black Boy*, reprinted in *Richard Wright: Later Works*, ed. Arnold Rampersad (New York: Library of America, 1991), 302.

23. Yves Citton, *Mythocratie: Storytelling et imaginaire de gauche* (Paris: Editions Amsterdam, 2010), 38.

24. Information sheet of David Boykin's Sonic Healing Ministries, which are divided into a Microcosmic Sound Orchestra and a Macrocosmic Sound Orchestra. See http://sonichealingministries.com/Welcome.html. What Myra Melford writes is not at all different in essence: "Emotion is projected through sound, and when that sound vibrates at the right frequency to harmonize or create a resonance with the physical world, a space of union and healing is created." See Myra Melford, "Aural Architecture: The Confluence of Freedom," in *Arcana: Musicians on Music*, ed. John Zorn (New York: Granary Books, 2000), 134. The same perspective is manifested by William Parker, who speaks "of a sound vibrating with such force that it transforms itself into "tonality": and when that happens, the vibration becomes almost medicinal. If your body and your nervous system benefit from listening to music, then the musician is truly doing something worthwhile. I conceive of sound as an element of nutrition." See Kevin LeGendre, "Hymn to Silence," *Jazzwise* 67 (August 2003).

25. Avreeayl Ra, interview with Alexandre Pierrepont, Chicago, April 2002.

26. Matana Roberts, interview with Alexandre Pierrepont, New York, May 2004.

27. Kalaparush Maurice McIntyre, interview with Alexandre Pierrepont, New York, May 2004.

28. Drawn from interviews conducted in 2005 for the documentary "Beyond Free Sounds" by Rudolph Bazière, Robin Dianoux, Caroline Humbert, Claire Savary, Serre Marie, and Pauline Hall, as part of my Masters course in Anthropology, Ethnology, and Religious Sciences at the University Paris 7—Denis Diderot.

29. One of the earliest examples cited: "Desmond, Trane, Ornette, Earl [*sic*] Brown, Muddy Waters, Stockhausen, the Mack Truck Corporation, the streets of Chicago, General Motors and Snooky Lanson." See George E. Lewis, *A Power Stronger than Itself: The AACM and American Experimental Music* (Chicago: University of Chicago Press, 2008), 192.

30. Hear Muhal Richard Abrams, *1-OQA + 19*, (Black Saint #1200172. Compact disc, 1993 [1978]).

31. Robert Jaulin, *Mon Thibaud: Le jeu de vivre* (Paris: Aubier Montagne, 1980), 163.

32. Henry Threadgill, interview with Alexandre Pierrepont, Lisbon, August 2001.

33. Quoted in Paz, *Children of the Mire*, 70.

34. Artaud, "Mise en scène and Metaphysics," 235.

35. Anthony Davis, interview with the author, Lisbon, August 2001.

36. Guy Debord, *La Société du Spectacle* (Paris: Gallimard, 1992 [1967]), paragraph 24. By convention, Debord scholars quote the paragraph number in this work rather than the page number.

37. Stuart Hall, "Deviance, Politics, and the Media," in *The Routledge Reader in Politics and Performance*, ed. Lizbeth Goodman and Jane de Gay (London and New York: Routledge, 2000 [1974]), 75.

38. Michael Hardt and Antonio Negri, *Empire* (Cambridge: Harvard University Press, 2000), 45.

39. Lawrence D. "Butch" Morris, interview with Alexandre Pierrepont, New York, May 2004.

40. John Corbett, "Anthony Braxton's *Bildungsmusik*: Thoughts on Composition 171," in *Mixtery: A Festschrift for Anthony Braxton*, ed. Graham Lock (Exeter: Stride, 1995), 186.

BIBLIOGRAPHY

Abrams, Muhal Richard. *1-OQA+19*. Black Saint #1200172. Compact disc, 1993 [1978].

Anderson, Fred. Interview with Alexandre Pierrepont. Paris, January 2002.

Artaud, Antonin, translated by Helen Weaver. "Mise en scène and Metaphysics." In *Antonin Artaud: Selected Writings*, edited by and with and introduction by Susan Sontag, 227–239. New York: University of California Press, 1988.

Artaud, Antonin. "On the Balinese Theater." In *Antonin Artaud: Selected Writings*, edited and with an introduction by Susan Sontag, 215–227. New York: University of California Press, 1988.

Breton, André. "Silence Is Golden." In *André Breton: What Is Surrealism? Selected Writings*, 353–358. New York: Pathfinder, 1978 [1946].

Breton, André, translated by Richard Seaver and Helen R. Lane. "Situation of the Surrealist Object." In *Manifestoes of Surrealism*, 255–278. Ann Arbor: University of Michigan Press, 1969 [1935].

Citton, Yves. *Mythocratie: Storytelling et imaginaire de gauche*. Paris: Editions Amsterdam, 2010.

Corbett, John. "Anthony Braxton's *Bildungsmusik*: Thoughts on Composition 171." In *Mixtery: A Festschrift for Anthony Braxton*, edited by Graham Lock, 185–186. Exeter: Stride, 1995.

Davis, Anthony. Interview with Alexandre Pierrepont. Lisbon, August 2001.

Debord, Guy. *La Société du Spectacle*. Paris: Gallimard, 1992 [1967].

Gauffre, Christian, and Geoffrey De Masure. "Leçons de Von Freeman et Bunky Green." *Jazz Magazine* 524 (March 2002): 28–30.

Glissant, Edouard. *Traité du Tout-Monde: Poétique IV*. Paris: Gallimard, 1997.

Hall, Stuart. "Deviance, Politics, and the Media." In *The Routledge Reader in Politics and Performance*, edited by Lizbeth Goodman and Jane de Gay, 75–82. London and New York: Routledge, 2000 [1974].

Hardt, Michael, and Antonio Negri. *Empire*. Cambridge: Harvard University Press, 2000.

Jaulin, Robert. *Mon Thibaud: Le jeu de vivre*. Paris: Aubier Montagne, 1980.

Jenkins, Leroy. Interview with Alexandre Pierrepont. New York, May 2004.

Jost, Ekkehard. *Free Jazz*. New York: Da Capo, 1981 [1974].

Kofsky, Frank. *John Coltrane and the Jazz Revolution of the 1960s*. New York: Pathfinder Press, 1998 [1970].

LeGendre, Kevin. "Hymn to Silence." *Jazzwise* 67 (August 2003): 36–38.

Lewis, George E. *A Power Stronger than Itself: The AACM and American Experimental Music*. Chicago: University of Chicago Press, 2008.

Lewis, George E. "Singing Omar's Song: A (Re)construction of Great Black Music." *Lenox Avenue: A Journal of Interarts Inquiry* 4 (1998): 69–92.

Livingston, Tim. "Interview with Lester Bowie." *Cadence* 27, no. 1 (January 2001): 5.

Lock, Graham. "A Highway to the Cosmics." In *Mixtery: A Festschrift for Anthony Braxton*, edited by Graham Lock, 246–249. Exeter: Stride, 1995.

Malraux, André. *La Tête d'obsidienne*. Paris: Gallimard, 1974.

McIntyre, Kalaparush Maurice. Interview with Alexandre Pierrepont. New York, May 2004.

Melford, Myra. "Aural Architecture: The Confluence of Freedom." In *Arcana: Musicians on Music*, edited by John Zorn, 119–135. New York: Granary Books, 2000.

Momaday, N. Scott. *The Way to Rainy Mountain*. Albuquerque: University of New Mexico Press, 1969.

Monnerot, Jules. *La poésie moderne et le sacré*. Paris: Gallimard, 1945.

Morris, Lawrence D. "Butch." Interview with Alexandre Pierrepont. New York, May 2004.

Morrison, Toni. *Song of Solomon*. New York: Knopf, 1977.

Myers, Amina Claudine. Interview with Alexandre Pierrepont. Paris, February 2004.

Panken, Ted. "Interview with George Lewis." (WKCR-FM, April 30, 1994). http://www.jazzhouse.org/files/panken16.php3?read.

Panken, Ted. "Interview with Henry Threadgill." (WKCR-FM, July 24, 1996). http://www.jazzhouse.org/library/?read=panken3.

Paz, Octavio. *Children of the Mire: Modern Poetry from Romanticism to the Avant-Garde*. Translated by Rachel Phillips. New ed. Cambridge: Harvard University Press, 1991 [1972].

Pey, Serge. *Lettres posthumes à Octavio Paz depuis quelques arcanes majeurs du tarot*. Paris: Jean-Michel Place, 2002.

Picasso, Pablo, translated by Philip Beitchman. "Discovery of African Art, 1906–1907." In *Primitivism and Twentieth-Century Art: A Documentary History*, edited by Jack Flam and Miriam Deitch, 33–34. Berkeley: University of California Press, 2003 [1937].

Pierrepont, Alexandre. *Le Champ Jazzistique*. Marseilles: Éditions Parenthèses, 2002.

Ra, Avreeayl. Interview with Alexandre Pierrepont. Chicago, April 2002.

Roberts, Matana. Interview with Alexandre Pierrepont. New York, May 2004.

Shapiro, Peter. "Blues and the Abstract Truth: Phil Cohran." *Wire* 207 (May 2001): 28–31.

Shoemaker, Bill. "Muhal Richard Abrams: Focus on the Vastness." *Point of Departure* (1995). http://www.pointofdeparture.org/archives/PoD-3/PoD-3_TurnAround.html.

Smith, Wadada Leo. *Notes (8 Pieces) Source A New World Music: Creative Music*. New Haven: Kiom Press, 1973.

Soliman, Lorraine. "La médecine invisible du docteur Lloyd." *Jazz Magazine* 570 (May 2006): 32–33.

Sontag, Susan. "The Aesthetics of Silence." In *Styles of Radical Will,* 3–34. New York: Farrar, Straus, and Giroux, 1966.

Stewart, Jesse. "Interview with Hamid Drake." *Cadence* 30, no. 3 (March 2004): 6.

Threadgill, Henry. Interview with Alexandre Pierrepont. Lisbon, August 2001.

Tod, Steven. "Malachi Favors: Keep Playin' Till the Lord Says Stop." Silver Measure. DVD, 2004.

Tzara, Tristan. "From 'Dada Manifesto on Feeble Love and Bitter Love.'" Translated by Barbara Wright. In *Poems for the Millennium, The University of California Book of Modern and Postmodern Poetry*, edited by Jerome Rothenberg, and Pierre Joris, vol. 1, *From Fin-de-Siecle to Negritude*, 299–305. Berkeley: University of California Press, 1995 [1920].

Various. "Declaration of January 27, 1925." In *History of Surrealism*, edited by Maurice Nadeau, translated by Richard Howard, 240–241. Cambridge: Belknap Press of Harvard University, 1989.

Volz, Johannes. "An Interview of Steve Coleman conducted by Johannes Volz at the University of California at Berkeley." 2000. http://www.jazzseite.at/SteveColeman/text_I07A.html.

Ware, David S. *Third Ear Recitation*. DIW #870. Compact disc, 1998.

Wright, Richard. *Black Boy*, In *Richard Wright: Later Works*, edited by Arnold Rampersad. New York: Library of America, 1991.

CHAPTER 11

IMPROVISING YOGA

SUSAN LEIGH FOSTER

ON a good day, my yoga practice convenes a conversation between something I'll call my *self* and something I'll call my *body*. I listen very quietly, although *All Things Considered* is sometimes playing in the background, and my body makes a suggestion. What do I mean by this? Well, the body makes lots of different kinds of suggestions. Sometimes it tenses in a pattern similar to that of a particular pose, as if proposing that we do that pose. Other times, it directs my attention to some place of stiffness or imbalance, asking that we do something about that. From pose to pose or move to move, it offers a running commentary. Even dwelling within one pose, parts of the body soften, extend, cramp, or lengthen in dialogue with the action, and I respond by changing the focus of my attention, altering something about the pose, or selecting the next pose. Sometimes eagerly, sometimes reluctantly, my body and I pursue our conversation for about an hour.

I learned to practice yoga this way from a wonderfully wise teacher, Donald Moyer.[1] In his teaching, Moyer sets up class as a site of inquiry and investigation. He approaches each *asana* as if it were a set of hypothetical relationships: For example, "What happens in tree pose if you lengthen the lesser trochanter or widen the upper sternum?" Instead of reciting a list of requirements that need to be accomplished or activated in order to do the pose properly, he proposes questions, asking students to focus on a particular part of the body and to assess for themselves how it changes the pose when they engage with it in a particular way. Each student's body is different, with a different history and anatomy, so instructions have to be modified individually. Moyer also avoids phrasing instructions in the negative; he seldom tells a student what not to do. Instead, his questions and propositions help us to establish a relationality among awareness, will, and physicality.

Following from Moyer's approach to yoga practice, there is no one correct set of instructions for how to do a pose, nor is there one single way to do a pose. Instead, since bodies are each so different, all students engage in a process of listening so as to adapt propositions about the poses to their individual situations. In an interview that I conducted with Moyer in 2007, he observed that specific metaphors that he might use to encourage the body to lengthen or expand are often effective for only a few weeks.[2] After that time, he says, the body has assimilated those images into its habitual responsiveness and needs a new image in order to mobilize and explore the pose in new ways. In other words, the conversation needs novelty in order to remain vital and engaged.

The conversation that I have with my body takes place in the intersection between varieties of experience—the nonverbal medium of my kinesthetic awareness of the body, my reservoir of images about the poses compiled from years of practice, and my analytic appraisal of how the body is moving. What I am calling my body's suggestions and responses are changes in muscular tension, joint position, lungs, and internal organs that I perceive thanks to gazillions of sensors located throughout the body that register these changes. I want to call these changes thoughts, since, as Irene Dowd has observed, they are produced by neural activity and they leave a trace of sensation.[3] These "thoughts," along with my memories of images and my assessment of how I am embodying the pose, all talk to each other. These three kinds of thoughts improvise together, and my body moves along with them.

No one type of thought predominates; no one type leads, with the others following or responding. Instead, it's more like a coffee klatsch among friends who know each other really well. Sometimes, two forms of thought talk at once, or they interrupt each other, or there are periods of silence. As with friends who are gossiping together, some opinions are reinforced and some new insights break through. My body might suggest a pose that's way out of the normal sequence, and it ends up assisting with another pose. Or it might assert a tiny adjustment within a pose that I can carry into other poses. While in a pose, I might think, "Can my back feel longer?" and my body might or might not find a response.

The directive "longer" is part of a system of priorities that I have learned from years of study with Moyer. The analytic capacity that reflects on how my practice is going is informed by certain values that I have gradually acquired, and established as those that seem not to produce pain, but instead to create a sense of well-being, balance, and continual expansion of possibilities. In establishing these values, I have had to unlearn many other priorities that I had acquired from different forms of dancing, such as making the pose look perfect. It took many years for me to realize that a pose being performed well could look very different on different bodies.

If someone was watching this practice, I imagine they would see a very slowly changing body: me, gazing off into space for thirty seconds or so, followed by movement into a pose, followed by very subtle shifts in weight and changes in lengths of parts of the body, on a good day, in relation to a pattern of breathing, followed by a return to standing or sitting with a slightly vacant expression on my face. The exterior calm and relatively static appearance of the body would fail to indicate, except to the most careful observer, the degree of animated conversation taking place.

What if I were to enlarge all the actions, making the impulses and responses more visible? The "dance" would unfold as a set of variations and riffs on familiar themes (poses). Tracking these variations and assessing their efficacy, I might occasionally pause to resist the tendency to reiterate an unproductive habitualized variation, and then push to expand and test what new variations might yield in terms of bodily states. This dance would not likely succeed as a group endeavor, since so much attention focuses on the body's interior relationships rather than its connection to its surroundings. It would instead look like the body conversing within itself.

In what ways are my yoga sessions improvisations, and what can they tell us about improvisation as a practice? Elsewhere, I have argued for envisioning improvisation as an interaction between the known and the unknown, as a continual blending together of familiar and unanticipated materials and/or actions, as a back and forth between pre-determined and spontaneously discovered events.[4] Improvising dancers, for example, select from a repertoire of established ways of moving in order to create the new. Some of these ways of moving have been repeated for so many years that they form part of the dancer's characteristic style, and others may result from sequences of movements established and rehearsed in advance that form the common or shared material upon which discovery is based. Some forms of improvisation, such as Contact Improvisation, train dancers to move in certain ways that become not so much a shared repertoire of moves, but instead a shared aesthetics or set of principles for generating movement. However much the quest for the new is featured in improvisation, the familiar, established and known ways of moving also contribute in determining whatever is discovered.

In my yoga sessions, I spontaneously select from a repertoire of possible poses, each of which can be performed with attention to myriad different details. Even one pose could be performed in a thousand different ways. The sequence of poses is improvised, as is the focus of attention for each pose. Guiding those selections is the conversation I am having with my body about how and where to move next—how my body is feeling and also how I think I'm doing in the pose.

I imagine that both my body and I are mixing up the known and unknown in our call and response. From my thirty-year study of yoga, I am familiar with a large number of poses and also with a variety of directives for how to perform those poses. My body also "knows" both the poses and numerous ways of moving and coordinating its parts, learned from other movement practices, including dancing, walking, biking, carrying things, and so on. Built into my body's execution of these activities are habitual patterns of action that also influence the body's approach to the poses. These patterns are part of the body's "known," and it also registers sensations of physical status, such as imbalance, stress, relaxation, well-being, integration, and flow, that inform its inventions of the new. So, it is not that I call and my body responds. Instead, both body and self can initiate as well as respond in our conversation.

Moyer's pedagogy set the conditions for this dialogue by providing guidelines for both the self and the body that structure perception and action. Rather than referring to amorphous conditions of consciousness, such as feeling more integrated, present, or in-tune, he identifies specific kinds of physical sensations that form the basis for how the body initiates and responds and also for how the self perceives and directs actions. Thus he asks students to attend to the ramifications throughout the body of widening the sternum or lengthening equally both sides of the coccyx. If students leave his class feeling more "in-tune" with their bodies, it is not because he asked them to feel in tune, but because he established the grounds upon which such tuning could take place.

This improvisation occurs largely within the realm of kinesthetic sensation rather than in the domains of visual or auditory perception. Parts of my body articulate one idea and other parts respond, and in that sense it is not too different from a jazz trio. Kinesthetic information, however, is often undervalued and undercultivated as a medium within which to articulate ideas. We tend to envision the body's movement as either functional or as an expression of those parts of the self, such as the unconscious, that are messy and inarticulate. This leads to assumptions about movement as primordial or prelinguistic, and hence as capable of generating inspiration or feeling but not actually articulating an idea.

In the practice of yoga that I pursue daily, there is nothing primal or fundamental. I am not excavating beneath or beyond the social in moving this way. I am not uncovering some basic human self that is defined by its penchant for improvisation, nor am I succumbing to some kind of primordial flow or reflex-level responsiveness to a more natural way to move. Instead, I am actively working to construct my body as a process of continual discovery.

This hour-long conversation differs from improvisation in quotidian life because it allows me to be more conscious than I normally would be about what the body is thinking. All day long we are improvising activities, tasks, and social interactions, never so routinized as to repeatedly perform the same action in exactly the same way. However throughout this negotiation of needs, requirements, demands, inclinations, and preferences, we often attend less rigorously to the body's role in these actions. My yoga practice is a time to redress that neglect and to bring about a more balanced engagement with physicality.

Why write about this yoga practice in the context of improvisation? In part, I want to excavate the politics of the everyday, to examine how improvisation functions throughout our daily lives and how it contributes to our sense of identity both individually and socially. I also want to test improvisation's potential role in contributing to what Foucault called "technologies of the self." Especially at this moment in history, when bodies are being bullied into accomplishing ever more exacting skills, I want to reflect on the plausibility of constructing an alternative relation with corporeality.

Often, physical practices are constructed around a struggle to create the "perfect" body or to ward off the effects of aging. Many who aspire to physical fitness work against the impending debilitation of the aging body and to achieve health by undertaking a regimen based on the assumption that if there's no pain, there's no gain. The tyranny of proscriptions for a healthy body, coupled with the ideal specifications for bodily appearance put forward in advertising and entertainment, create overwhelming demands for physical comportment in which the body has little or no say. The workings of global capitalism, as Susan Bordo has observed, are bearing down on the body with increasing force.[5] Everyone is telling the body what do to and how to look.

Is my yoga practice intervening in this accelerating cycle of punishment and control? At least for an hour a day I am asking my body what it thinks, albeit about a very restricted set of issues. I do not approach this hour as a carving out of a private time to nurse a body that has been abused by its exposure to the social. I do not see it as an indulgence or treat for body or self. Yoga is not one of the methods devised to pamper oneself, take time for oneself, indulge oneself, and so forth that are part of the deployment of global capitalist strategies aimed at creating ever better consumers. Those activities do not ask the body what it thinks any more than do body sculpting, spinning, weight training, and fitness classes. Where the regimens designed to create perfection approach the body as a robotics, those that soothe and pamper the body infantilize it. In contrast to these activities that docilize the body by treating it as raw material to be molded or as tired flesh in need of rejuvenation, I envision my yoga practice as a way of instating a frank exchange between equals. My body and I are trading moves, responding to one another's opinions, on a good day, like friends.

In discussing improvisation within groups of dancers, I have analyzed the ways that the group's decisions about structuring a given performance and the enacting of that structure resemble basic features of a democracy.[6] As dancers make conscious choices about what to do next within agreed-upon structural limitations, they embody the processual nature of democratic self-governance. They decide what rules to impose upon themselves and what pre-established material to share, and then they explore the fleshing out of those rules and the ways that shared material can lead to new discoveries. Often, they reexamine and alter the rules for a subsequent performance.

My yoga improvisation is different, in that it is not social, yet it is not anti-social. Foucault might call it a technology of the self, a pursuit that permits individuals to effect by their own means or with the help of others a certain number of operations on their own bodies and souls, thoughts, conduct, and way of being, so as to transform themselves in order to attain a certain state of happiness, purity, wisdom, perfection, or immortality.[7]

For Foucault, these technologies are inextricably tied to the body politic. Technologies of the self do not operate outside the purview of power, and they may or may not be integrated into structures of coercion. However, they can help to carve out the space for individual agency, choice, and creative participation in self-fashioning as part of the operations of power.

In his genealogy of classical Greek and early Christian technologies of the self, Foucault demonstrates how any regimen of self-care is historically specific in its articulation with the body politic. The pursuit of a concern for oneself changed during this period from an effort to take care of oneself in relation to the political into an attempt to cultivate a universal self that transcended its political moment. Foucault uses this excavation of the self's transformation in an effort to sketch out the contours of a contemporary approach to self-construction. In order to apprehend how we might attend to and care for the self, he envisions the necessity to first problematize the very status of the self and to sustain a critical practice of self-forming. This scrutiny of the self would then facilitate the constitution of oneself as an ethical subject.

If my yoga practice qualifies as this kind of critical restructuring of the subject, it is because it undertakes, first, to interrogate and reenvision the relationship between self and body, giving body a mindfulness and participatory role in consciousness forming. I make the choice at least for an hour a day to explore what this alternative identity feels like and how it functions. By giving this articulateness to physicality, I imagine myself as participating in the formation of a more balanced and ecological relationship within the person, one that serves as an antidote to the aggressive mining of natural resources and plundering of human resources that we witness daily. I am not uncovering some truer inner self, but instead carefully activating a set of rhetorical structures to form a body-self.

Following Moyer's insight that such metaphors have a certain life-span of efficacy, it is necessary to continually revisit the rhetoric, as well as the improvisatory process through which it is implemented, in order to ascertain whether they are continuing to facilitate the formation of an ethical stance within and toward the world. On a good day, this perpetual self-scrutiny and re-invention contribute to a sense of resilience and a more collaborative engagement with others. Some of the improvised give and take that occurs during yoga extends beyond my hour-long session, permeating my relationships with students, colleagues, the grocery store clerk, and others.

There is no goal, such as the discovery of an authentic or truer self, that will be liberated and activated through mindful attention to the poses. Such a goal would only reinstate the classic relationship between mind and body in which the body is used as an instrument or tool for self-awareness or transcendence. Nor am I seeking a more versatile physicality. Having spent many years when I first studied yoga seeking the perfect pose, I have long since realized that the improvisation I conduct leads only to more possible complexities within each pose and more thoughts to be expressed, both by my body and my self. Instead of arriving somewhere, the practice affirms a process, a process that is fulfilling in and of itself.

Others who engage with yoga in this way share a similar focus on establishing an improvisation with the body. However, their individual practices might look quite different. We might all take Moyer's class together, partaking in a common rubric for exploring what the shoulder blades, for example, can do, yet if we returned home and merely repeated that class all week, we would not be caring for the self but instead grinding both body and self into docile submission.

I know this because I also have bad days, days in which I plod through routinized sequences of poses noticing very little. My body dumbly obliges, somehow acquiescing to the assumption that this exercise is good for it. I have no insights into the feel of the poses, nor do I try anything new. Rather than "no pain, no gain," the yoga becomes the way to stave off pain for twenty-four hours by ministering to the very areas that I have identified as problematic: just stretch the adductors and they won't go into spasm, or just arch the back to compensate for writing so long today. In other words, there is no improvisation.

But on a good day . . .

NOTES

1. Donald Moyer, a student of B.K.S. Iyengar, is the founder and director of The Yoga Room in Berkeley, California. He wrote the "Asana" column for *Yoga Journal* in 1987, 1989, and 1992 and is the author of *Yoga: Awakening the Inner Body* (Berkeley: Rodmell Press, 2006).

2. In response to a question from me about the relationship of his daily practice to his teaching, Moyer observed the following: "Usually when I'm practicing, a new movement comes into a particular pose. I take that movement and apply it to different poses. What works in a forward bend might not work in a backbend, or you might have to change and do the exact opposite in a different type pose. I find that when I first work with a theme my body responds with a lot of freshness, whereas when I repeat that theme day after day, maybe for 2 or 3 weeks, the edge of freshness starts to fade, and as that fades, there's generally a new idea, something will kind of spring up—a new thought will emerge which is related but goes in a slightly different direction. So, if I'm working with, say, how the head of the femur fits in the hip socket, I might just do that for a time. And then the idea occurs to me: well, you can't always move the head of the femur in the socket. Sometimes you have to move the socket around the head of the femur, ok? And then, if I work on that for a particular length of time my body gets accustomed to doing that and then the thought pops up, "Well, if it works for the hip socket, does it work for the shoulder joint?" And then I've got a basis, an analogy. If it worked on the hip joint, how can I make it apply to the shoulder joint, and then I go off in a new direction." Susan Leigh Foster, Interview with Donald Moyer. Personal communication, December 14, 2007.

3. Irene Dowd, *Taking Roots to Fly: Ten Articles on Functional Anatomy* (New York: Contact Editions, 1981), 3, 5.

4. Susan Leigh Foster, "Taken by Surprise: Improvisation in Dance and Mind," in *Taken by Surprise: A Dance Improvisation Reader*, ed. David Gere and Ann Cooper Albright (Middletown, CT: Wesleyan University Press, 2003), 1–14.

5. Susan Bordo, *Unbearable Weight* (Berkeley and Los Angeles: University of California Press, 1993).

6. Susan Leigh Foster, *Dances that Describe Themselves: The Improvised Choreography of Richard Bull* (Middletown, CT: Wesleyan University Press, 2003), 234–236.

7. Michel Foucault, "Technologies of the Self," in *Technologies of the Self: A Seminar with Michel Foucault*, ed. L. H. Martin et al. (London: Tavistock, 1988), 16–49.

BIBLIOGRAPHY

Bordo, Susan. *Unbearable Weight*. Berkeley and Los Angeles: University of California Press, 1993.

Dowd, Irene. *Taking Roots to Fly: Ten Articles on Functional Anatomy*. New York: Contact Editions, 1981.

Foster, Susan Leigh. "Taken by Surprise: Improvisation in Dance and Mind." In *Taken by Surprise: A Dance Improvisation Reader*, edited by David Gere and Ann Cooper Albright, 1–14. Middletown, CT: Wesleyan University Press, 2003.

Foster, Susan Leigh. *Dances that Describe Themselves: The Improvised Choreography of Richard Bull*. Middletown, CT: Wesleyan University Press, 2003.

Foucault, Michel. "Technologies of the Self." In *Technologies of the Self: A Seminar with Michel Foucault*, edited by L. H. Martinet al, 16–49. London: Tavistock, 1988.

Moyer, Donald. *Yoga: Awakening the Inner Body*. Berkeley: Rodmell Press, 2006.

Moyer, Donald. Interview with Susan Leigh Foster. Berkeley, CA, December 14, 2007.

PART III

CULTURAL HISTORIES

CHAPTER 12

....

MICHEL DE MONTAIGNE, OR PHILOSOPHY AS IMPROVISATION

....

TIMOTHY HAMPTON

> By far the greatest folly is to reject the gifts of the moment.
> (Quintilian, *Institutio oratoria*, X.vi)

In February of 1571 a French lawyer named Michel de Montaigne sat down in his castle, in the countryside near Bordeaux, to write. The moment was one of crisis in French history, as the country had been plunged into bloody wars between rival groups of Protestants and Catholics a decade earlier, and was in the middle of a wholesale collapse of civil and political order. The very next year would see the notorious Saint Bartholomew's Day massacre, in which thousands of Protestants all across France would be butchered by their Catholic countrymen. A member of a traditional Catholic merchant family that had become ennobled only the generation before, Montaigne lived in predominantly Protestant Gascony. He had received a splendid education in Latin at one of the best schools in France. Yet after some service in the judiciary he had decided, as he put it, to "retire" from public life, to turn his thoughts to himself for the brief time remaining him before death. This "retirement" came at the ripe old age of 38. Several years earlier he had suffered a devastating personal loss, when his best friend, the humanist scholar Etienne de la Boétie, had died at a young age. The death of La Boétie seems to have left Montaigne somewhat adrift, and he now turned to the preparation for his own end. As a kind of "portrait" of himself, for the private use of his family and friends, he intended to leave behind a written record of his cogitations. The text that Montaigne would produce over the next 20 years, the *Essays*, stands as a unique instance in western literature of philosophy produced out of the practice of improvisation.[1]

I will argue that the improvisational features of the *Essays* are shaped by the intersection of an epistemology and a writing practice. The epistemology is partly an historical phenomenon, involving Montaigne's skeptical relationship to the classical culture that he inherits from Renaissance humanism. However, that skepticism can only find complete expression through Montaigne's unique writing practice. Improvisation in writing makes possible new types of literary discourse, which in turn articulate a certain set of attitudes toward authority, the body, and the constitution of the self. I will suggest that improvisation is a key element in the generation of new forms of knowledge on the threshold of the modern era.

Montaigne calls his text *essays*, a term that he seems to have invented, or at least applied for the first time to a text. The French verb *essayer* means, in common usage, to try or to try out. In Montaigne's time it also had implications of tasting. It derives from the Latin word *exagium*, which refers to a scale or a balance—from which, of course, we get the modern English notion of "assaying" gold. Part of Montaigne's project in the *Essays* seems to have involved the weighing of different cultural phenomena—examples from classical history, bits of personal information, quotations, current events—in order to test his judgment in the pursuit of a happy, virtuous, philosophical life.

Yet no ideal of balance is free from the threat of imbalance. Indeed, one of the principal characteristics of the literary form of the essay—the form that Montaigne invented and bequeathed to modernity—is its deliberately fragmentary or limited perspective on things. Essays refuse the claim to absolute knowledge and proclaim themselves to be the fruit of contingency. Two aspects of this radical acceptance of contingency link to Montaigne's practice as improviser. The first is the way in which the essay refuses abstract concepts. Rooted as it is in personal experience yet linked to larger philosophical problems, the essay avoids grand formulations of philosophical ideals. As the philosopher Theodor Adorno writes in his study, "The Essay as Form," "the essay . . . incorporates the antisystematic impulse into its own way of proceeding and introduces concepts unceremoniously, 'immediately,' just as it receives them."[2] Adorno's target in this dismissal of the "concept" is, of course, the idealist philosophy of Kant and Hegel. However, in Montaigne's context one might just as well point to the ways in which both the Platonic emphasis on ideal concepts and the later scholastic deployment of definitions are undermined by the occasional, almost casual, approach of Montaigne's writing. That is, whereas classical and scholastic philosophy conventionally set up arguments by defining terms ("what is virtue," "what is eloquence," etc.), Montaigne tries to discover what those things would be as he goes. Yet in contrast to the Platonic tradition of the philosophical dialogue, he does not proceed dialectically. Instead, improvisation becomes the response to an overly rigid philosophical tradition. Indeed, Montaigne's acceptance of his own limitations, of the boundaries of his experience, are articulated in a metaphor of visuality that suggests the etymology of improvisation as an engagement with the "unforeseen" (im-pro-videre). He notes in his essay on the education of children that "My conceptions and my judgment only proceed by groping, staggering, stumbling, and blundering; and when I have gone ahead as far as I can, still I am not at all satisfied: I can still see the country beyond, but with a dim and clouded vision" (107).[3]

No less important for the improvisational nature of the essay is another feature of the form pointed to by Adorno. This is the question of the material that the essay takes as its focus of attention: "The essay," writes Adorno, "does not try to seek the eternal in the transient and distill it out; it tries to render the transient eternal." It does so, not by focusing on some unmediated relationship to direct experience (the goal of Romantic idealism, in Adorno's context), but by exploring the intersection between individual consciousness and what we might call the detritus of culture. By "detritus" I mean the leftovers of cultural production: clichés, commonplaces, ruins, old ideas, quotations. It deals, in Adorno's phrase, "with objects that would be considered derivative, without itself pursuing their ultimate derivation. It thinks conjointly and in freedom about things that meet in its freely chosen object. . . . It is . . . spellbound by what is fixed and acknowledged to be derivative, by artifacts."[4] This operation of picking up on fragments of culture, on ideas that have been set aside or already worked out and then expanding them or turning them about, opening them up to reconsideration, offers an instance of the equivalent, in literature, of the musician who takes a phrase from an old composition and develops it, or the painter who borrows the brush technique of another and makes it the focus of attention. The essay takes mediated information and renovates it by accepting its mediated status and then bringing personal experience to bear on what it conveys.

Montaigne makes it clear that his essays are not intended to be systematic. He is deeply steeped in the writings of classical moral philosophy, in particular the moral essays of Seneca and Plutarch, his two favorite writers. Yet the unfolding of the lines of argumentation in any of his essays is at best digressive and at worst puzzling. There is no system here. Rather, as Montaigne says, he is following the pathway of his own thoughts, trying to fix in writing the movement of the mind. This digressive style is, of course, an improvisational style. It begins from a fragment of information (a cliché, a citation, an example) and unpacks it, building out from the limits of its capacity into the unknown.

Yet many of most powerful effects of Montaigne's style are produced, not out of the lateral movement of his digressive thought, but out of the way his discourse turns back on itself to produce new levels of meaning. Thus, for example, in the opening of what is now probably his best known essay, the essay called "Of Cannibals," he begins by noting that while the Greeks were often thought to consider everyone else as barbarians we have examples of Greek generals admiring the military ordinances of non-Greeks, whom they considered anything but barbarian. Thus, concludes Montaigne, "we should beware of clinging to vulgar opinions and judge things by reason's way not by popular say" (150). The rhyming effect ("way/say") that Donald Frame's excellent English translation seeks to capture here is, in the original French, even more powerful, as "reason's way" is a rendering of *"la voie de la raison,"* and "popular say," is *"la voix commune"* (200). The French word for way, *voie,* and the word for voice, *voix,* are exact homonyms. Their juxtaposition in this important sentence, the first philosophical reflection of this crucially important essay, is clearly generated as a kind of improvisational gesture out of the play of sound and rhythm in the unfolding of the sentence itself. Yet this is not merely a passing joke. The entire essay, which deals with the problem of European perceptions of the cultures of the recently discovered New World, will take as a central theme the contrast between the limits of European culture, with its imperial way, or "*voie*," on the one hand, and the "voice," or "*voix*," of the oral-based cultures in Brazil, on the other. In other words, the improvised contrast of "*voie*" and "*voix*," set up at the outset of the essay, will become, as it is reversed and unpacked, one of the generating principles for much of the rest of the essay. Verbal improvisation provides a frame for philosophical reflection, since the *voie/voix* echo doesn't work on paper; it must be pronounced to become clear.

The variety of themes treated in the *Essays* is vast. In the earliest essays that make up the first two books, Montaigne frequently takes on conventional topics from history or moral philosophy (moderation, sadness, the habits of Caesar, etc.). Occasionally he generates new topics drawn from contemporary events (cannibals, recent battles, torture) or from his quirky personal interests (the size of thumbs, odors, sex, and language). However, as he moves into the third book, the essays become longer and more complex, culminating in two great meditations, "Of Physiognymy" and "Of Experience," in which the very act of reflecting on the self displaces any concrete theme or body of knowledge. Instead of being about, say, solitude, or politics, philosophy now becomes about "experience," the activity of thinking about solitude and the wisdom gleaned from watching politics.

Montaigne's earliest essays, some of the first chapters in Book 1, often take the form of little more than exercises in which the author meditates on a well-worn philosophical theme or a particular reference from classical literature—the "artifacts" of which Adorno speaks. These early essays take their impetus from two scholarly practices with which Montaigne was familiar. The first is the practice of humanist rhetoric. In Renaissance schoolrooms of the kind with which Montaigne was familiar, it was common practice to give students particular passages from classical texts and ask them to expatiate on them, commenting on issues of grammar and vocabulary and attempting to draw moral lessons. These passages were then supposed to be committed to memory, so that in some future speaking situation (at court, in diplomatic negotiations, in council) they could be trotted out and used as scaffolding. Similarly, Montaigne's legal training would have involved the process of glossing in the margins of the text of a particular passage from the body of Roman law. Both of these traditions, rhetorical improvisation and legal glossing, emphasize the role of commentary or of annotation as the key to literary originality. Thus the *Essays* emerge first as a kind of reflection on the writing of canonical authors from the past.[5]

However, neither of these traditions could prepare us for the startling originality and, indeed, unique nature of Montaigne's text. For the textual fabric of this work is unlike that of any other piece of philosophy or literature, at least until some of the avant-garde experiments of the mid-twentieth century. Montaigne worked on the first version of his essays for about a decade. In 1580 he published the first edition of them, consisting of two books. After this publication, which was followed by a trip to Italy and a return to public service for a time, Montaigne stayed close by his own text. He reread his own publication carefully, as if it were the writing of some classical sage. And he commented on it. He wrote marginalia that registered his own responses to what he had already written. He added more examples, quotations from classical works, and insights that ran tangentially and occasionally even counter to what he had written in the first iteration of the book. Then, in 1588, he published the second edition of the *Essays*, which included the first two books, now expanded by virtue of his own marginalia inserted into the text, as well as a third book. Montaigne continued this practice of glossing and expanding his own writing throughout his life. Upon his death there was found yet another edition, expanded yet again, filled with comments and reflections in the margin, which became the definitive version of the *Essays*. It is important to note that this is not a process of revision. He virtually never deleted material. It is a process of expansion through improvisatory self-gloss. As he puts it in the essay "Of the Resemblance of Children to Fathers," "I do not correct my first imaginings by my second—well, yes, perhaps a word or so, but only to vary, not to delete. I want to represent the course of my humors and I want people to see each part at its birth" (575).[6]

This curious writing practice, the process of rereading what one has already written and then adding to it, expanding, and publishing the expansion, means that if one reads successive editions of the *Essays* one finds each new version to be substantially different from the preceding version. Modern scholars have been able to collate these different editions, and conventionally indicate the different layers of the text with the letters (a) for the 1580 edition, (b) for the 1588 edition, and (c) for the posthumous edition. This means that when we read Montaigne's essays we do not only read them horizontally, tracing the unfolding of his arguments across the page, from left to right, but we also read them, as it were, "vertically," from level to level. We are able to trace, as in an archaeological dig, the ways in which Montaigne's philosophical reflections were generated out of his own rereading of himself. Thus, in a beautifully ironic touch, Montaigne's observation, cited above, that he only corrects "a word or so, but only to vary, not to delete," is itself an "addition" made at the end of his life and stuck right into the rest of the sentence, which was written some 20 years earlier in the first edition. Montaigne's account of his habit of improvised textual expansion comes as a bit of textual expansion!

Montaigne's act of returning again and again to his own creation to add more text in response to what he already done takes his text beyond the notion set forth by Adorno that what characterizes the genre is its resistance to concepts and its acceptance of contingency. Were those the only features of Montaigne's text, it would be indistinguishable from other types of contingent writing (popular commentary, journalism), some of which Adorno seems to have in mind. Montaigne's procedure is much more radical. It has several interesting implications for our understanding of the relationship between writing and the self. For one thing, it means that the process of writing—the unfolding of the text—is exactly coterminous with the life of the author. The *Essays* are not a narrative autobiography that can be brought to a close with a flourish of the plot. Each new reading of the text is also a writing that leads to new insertions of material according to the movements, ideas, and perceptions of the writer. The text can never end until Montaigne's life ends. It grows amoeba-like, out from itself, as his ideas change. And yet precisely because the project of the *Essays* is a "portrait" of Montaigne ("it is myself that I paint," [2] he says in his opening address to the reader), this process of improvisatory expansion is quite different from other, similar artistic projects of revision.[7] We might contrast Montaigne to, for example, Claude Monet, whose famous series of impressionist paintings of the Rouen cathedral constitute a set of variations on the same material, each unique because of the changing light conditions. For Monet, the object of his study is firm, but his perception of it, and therefore his depictions of it, constantly change with the light. For Montaigne, the object itself is constantly changing. As he says in the essay "Of Repentance" (III, 2), "I cannot keep my subject still. It goes along befuddled and staggering, with a natural drunkenness" (610b).[8] And to paint this changing subject Montaigne asserts that he has developed a style that is also changing, though, because it emanates from the very subject that is being portrayed, never "wrong": "The lines of my painting do not go astray, though they change and vary" (610b).[9] Thus the act of writing is endless, because there can be no final word on a changing subject—and, indeed, even the attempt to offer a "final word" would be provisional.

To see how this works in detail, and to introduce the role of citation in improvisation, I want to turn to one of Montaigne's smallest and most appealing essays. This is the essay titled "Of Idleness" (I, 8), first written very early in his retirement. There Montaigne tells us that he is only recently decided to focus his energy on his own mind, "to let it entertain itself in full idleness and stay settled in itself, which I hoped it might do more easily now, having become weightier and riper with time" (21a).[10] However, he has found that the more he has tried to focus only on himself, the more his thoughts run wild, like a runaway horse. This reflection on the instability of the meditating mind is punctuated by two bits of Latin poetry. One is a quotation from Horace's famous "Art of Poetry," in which the poet describes bad poetry as being "like a sick man's dreams" (*"velut agri somnia"*). Three sentences later, as he is discussing his unquiet mind, Montaigne quotes the Latin epic poet Lucan: "ever idle hours breed wandering thoughts" (*"variam semper dant otia mentem"*). Thus the first version of the essay seems almost to be an academic exercise on the traditional theme of idleness, a gloss on two well-known passages from the classics—passages that seem to offer a kind of moral guidance.

That is, until we look closely at the contexts from which these passages come. The Horace passage, as noted, comes from a poem about writing. The Lucan passage is part of a political speech urging soldiers into battle in the midst of civil war, a context that could not fail to resonate for Montaigne's own readers, living, as they were, through their own civil war. Lucan's text is an instance of inflammatory rhetoric urging men to violence. Thus when we do our homework and chase down the sources of Montaigne's quotations, we see that the essay raises questions about how one would write about war, about the relationship between poetry and political rhetoric. When Montaigne rewrites the essay, however, he changes the focus through the addition of yet another Latin quotation, this time from the *Aeneid* of Virgil. He inserts several lines that describe the mind of Aeneas in reflection as he considers the decision to go to war, "darting here and there in endless flight, like the light that reflects off of the water in a vase of bronze" (*"Sicut aquae tremulum labris ubi lumen ahenis"*). The introduction of the Virgil passage turns the essay into one that is about how the mind reflects on its own creations and about the relationship between reflection and action. Moreover, the image of the flickering light on the surface of the water actually gives expression to the very thing that Montaigne has just done, as his mind skirts across the wavering surface of his own text and then adds to it with a citation. Thus we see Montaigne at work in the process of improvisation, re-reading his own text and adding fragments stolen from the texts of others. As he rewrites the essay, he shifts the focus by introducing new aspects of his ostensible theme.

This practice of quotation is crucial. For it creates a new kind of literary artifact that is organized *spatially*. That is, we might think of the literary genre of the essay as a space within which other texts can speak to each other, in dialogue through the practice of juxtaposition. This improvisation as juxtaposition means that in Montaigne's text, authors whose texts would normally have nothing to do with each other—Horace writing on poetry, Virgil on reflection, and Lucan on political rhetoric—are now all in dialogue, but only because Montaigne has pasted their words next to each other. In this regard, we might think of Montaigne's citational practice as a form of literary collage. Montaigne deploys a spatial practice of bringing things together around a theme. This is what Adorno seems to have in mind when, in the article cited earlier, he notes that the essay form "thinks conjointly and in freedom about things that meet in its freely chosen object." Montaigne's violent and disruptive use of citations takes Adorno's notion of how "things meet" in the object of study one step beyond what Adorno seems to have in mind. Montaigne quite literally introduces texts to each other, through a practice of juxtaposition and collage that challenges us to make sense of their new relationship.[11]

Because the *Essays* expand with the changing moods of the author, they are also deeply marked by that feature of human experience that is most variable—the life of the body. If improvisation is anything, it is the struggle, over time, of the imagination against the limits of the body. In the case of music or painting that may involve a struggle with an instrument, or with the limits of one's technical competence. For most writers the process of writing involves endless patient revision, through which the limits of the contingent body may be circumvented or overcome. For Montaigne, who never erases but only adds to his text, the act of writing and the disposition of the body are centrally linked. This is a central theme of the essay entitled "Of Practice" (II, 6). There, Montaigne offers one of the few narrative or anecdotal scenes in the book, an account of a fall from a horse in which he confronted the possibility of death and thus was able to "practice" dying. Following this account, detailed in its descriptions of his physical danger, he shifts to the question of what it means to write about it. Though traditional Christian teachings say that attention to the self can be dangerous, he notes, he himself is not proposing any lessons or doctrine: "What I chiefly portray is my cogitations, a shapeless subject that does not lend itself to expression in actions" (274a).[12] So much for moral instruction, since, as he goes on to say, actions are mostly prey to chance anyway. Instead, his topic is the self. As he says in a long addition made toward the end of his life:

> I expose myself entire: my portrait is a cadaver [un skeletos] on which the veins, the muscles, and the tendons appear at a glance, each part in its place. One part of what I am was produced by a cough, another by a pallor or a palpitation of the heart—in any case dubiously. It is not my deeds that I write down; it is myself; it is my essence. (274c)[13]

The subtle interplay in this passage between body and text is extraordinary. The portrait is first described as a "cadaver," for which Montaigne uses the strange Greek word *skeletos* (an importation, since he knew no Greek), and the parts of the text-as-body are enumerated. Then, in the second sentence, we seem to return to the body, with "one part of what I am" (as body or as text?) produced by a cough, and so on.

This brilliant linkage of body and text means that the book and the author become indistinguishable. To write is to be, and vice versa. The improvised business of living, with the "shapeless subject" of cogitations and the changes in bodily health, is at one with writing, which in turn will become part of the self upon the next reading. Moreover, we note that this description describes a text that is organized, not narratively or temporally, like a traditional autobiography, but, here again, spatially, as in the case of the strategy of juxtaposition explicated earlier. If I cough, that will produce some text (and self); if my face is pale, that will produce another bit of text, and so on. The text is a kind of anatomy of the self, a spatial diagram in script that, however, unfolds and changes over time.

However, there is also an ethical project embedded in Montaigne's improvisational writing practice. One of the features of the humanist tradition within which Montaigne was educated was a veneration of what we might call the heroic culture of classical Antiquity. The epic literature of Homer and Virgil, with its emphasis on military valor and constancy, no less than the traditions of Roman moral philosophy and heroic biography, contributed to a culture of admiration for figures of extreme virtue who were taken to be models of the self. Indeed, humanist education was deeply imbued with a focus on the imitation of exemplars from the past. This emphasis on heroic selfhood took a different, but no less important, role in the religious wars that form the immediate context for Montaigne's reflections. Both Protestants and Catholics deployed, as propaganda, images and stories of "heroic" martyrs who had suffered for their faith and therefore offered "proof" of the truth of their doctrine (and reasons for inflicting suffering on the other side). Montaigne was acutely aware of the endlessness of this culture of revenge, as well as of the dangers of any claims to possess absolute authority sanctioned by the divine order. As a response to this culture of absolutes and of ideal images, he emphasizes his own fragility and commonness. In the closing passages of "Of Experience," he points out that his own soul is anything but a model of virtue: "In fine, all this fricassee that I am scribbling here is nothing but a record of the essays of my life, which, for spiritual health, is exemplary enough if you take its instruction in reverse." "But as for bodily health," he goes on, "no one can furnish more useful experience than I" (826b).[14] And he launches into an account of his many bodily habits: his ways of dealing with the intense pain brought on by kidney stones, his love of salty meat, his preference for silk hose over woolen, his hatred of stuffy rooms, and so on. Each of these observations lends itself to the generation of some type of wisdom that can be gleaned from "experience." Montaigne underscores his own limits and the importance of accepting one's own common, unheroic humanity. It is in the common body, with its foibles, habits, and inevitable decay, he shows, more than in the grand gestures of the hero, that one can learn how to live. Anything else he calls an "inhuman wisdom, which makes us disdainful enemies of the cultivation of the body" (849b).[15]

Montaigne's focus on the body and on the mutability of corporeal experience redefines early modern moral philosophy. In place of the attempts of earlier philosophers to locate wisdom in a set of prescribed practices that are held up as ideals, and over against the Christian or Platonic idealism that locate wisdom in an experience of transcendence, Montaigne locates wisdom in the material world of the body. We all have bodies that are constantly changing. Each of these bodies is unexceptional. Yet from our reflections on that materiality and on the mutations of bodily experience, we can glean wisdom for life that is both unique to us and useful to others—more exceptional, in its way, than the virtue of Caesar or Cato. The source of wisdom lies, not in ideal images, but in a particular attitude toward the mutability of the self. And since the self changes everyday, the solutions discovered yesterday are not necessarily valid today. This means that, no less than writing, ethical living is a process of constant improvisation, of the adjustment of judgment and comportment according to circumstance, based on certain models but not reliant on them. As Montaigne says in his essay on the education of children (I, 26): "only the fools are certain and assured" (111c).[16]

Montaigne's emphasis on the mutability of the self, on a process of change that lies outside of fixed images of ideal virtue or vice, means that an important part of human experience resides in movement, in the shift from one mood to the next and from one instant to the next. As he says in "Of Experience," "myself now and myself a while ago are indeed two" (736b).[17] This acceptance of change also means that an essential feature of Montaigne's consideration of human experience is the question of *personality*. This is a topic that is not often talked about either in philosophical histories or in histories of early modern culture. Yet it is central to Montaigne's understanding of human beings. Personality would seem to consist in the ways in which the self emerges through a series of changes, the mutation of being from instant to instant. It is personality that emerges through the practice of writing about the experience of change. Personality is a central product of all improvisation. Montaigne's admiration for his various heroes from classical history and philosophy is linked to his admiration for their personal style or personality. Thus, in "Of Cruelty" (II, 11), he takes issue with the heroism of the great Stoic Cato for his grandiosity, even as he extols his virtue. By contrast, he admires Socrates, not for his philosophical idealism, but for the way he moves seamlessly from defending Athens, to teaching philosophy, to playing with children in the street, to tolerating the crabbiness of his wife. Only in a philosophy that would accept movement and change, through a constant displacement of fixed images of ideal comportment, can personality be grasped and considered. In this regard, the essential feature of human life lies in its improvisational nature. In literature, personality emerges as style, here as a particularly self-reflexive and supple, familiar writing style. To grasp the mutability of human experience becomes the task of a writing that itself changes from moment to moment.

At one level, Montaigne's linkage of improvisation and moral philosophy is an historical phenomenon. It has to do with his own position as one of the last figures for whom the moral and political world of classical antiquity was a source of constant reflection.

To be sure, when René Descartes invents philosophical modernity in the resolutely anti-improvisational *Discourse on Method*, some 40 years after Montaigne's death, he is careful to bracket and avoid precisely those features that are central to Montaigne's philosophy. Descartes's famous rejection of the body for the certainties of the rational mind, his turning away from the external political world that fascinated Montaigne, and his obsession with certainty all run directly counter to Montaigne's body-based, mutable embrace of the limits of his own knowledge. In this regard, we might posit the important role of an improvisational style at moments of transition in intellectual and artistic history. As one system of representation falls into cliché and ruin, an improvisation based on the artifacts of the past (citations, fragments, commonplaces) makes possible new forms of representation and expression. This is central to Montaigne's project, which requires constant hermeneutical adjustments to recuperate the past while undermining its authority.

Montaigne's *Essays* take as their point of departure the acceptance of contingency, of the limits of knowledge, which we might link, as does Adorno, to essayistic writing generally. However, Montaigne intertwines his investigation of the contingent body and mediated cultural artifacts with a new kind of improvisation that is linked to the writing practice itself. The combination of these factors generates a text that sets forth a new ethics of metamorphosis and improvisation, locating human virtue in the commonality of everyday life. Finally, it should be clear that this writing practice is no less linked to the ethics of reading than it is to improvisational authorship. For Montaigne produces a text that, precisely because it cannot be reduced to simple arguments, summaries, or definitions, injects the improvisational imperative into the act of reading itself. The unsystematic and non-narrative shape of the text means that the act of reading is always a process of movement between different, often conflicting, points of view. Montaigne's use of quotations, often set in contradictory juxtaposition, as well as the reversals imposed by new additions to the text, force upon the reader a constant activity of revision and reconsideration. Indeed, the very notion that the *Essays* offer not a systematic argument but rather the register of a shifting mind forces us to revise our own arts of reading, to invent a reading of the text that is by definition provisional and improvised. To think that we have "read Montaigne" is to fall into the trap of certainty and ignore the power of time over our own perceptions. In this way, the *Essays* are a text that can only be read by being re-read.

NOTES

1. For an appealing account of Montaigne's life as a philosophical quest for a happy and virtuous life, see Sarah Bakewell, *How to Live, or a Life of Montaigne in One Question and Twenty Attempts at an Answer* (New York: Other Press, 2010).
2. Theodor W. Adorno, "The Essay as Form," in *Notes to Literature*, vol. 1, trans. Shierry Weber Nicholsen (New York: Columbia University Press, 1991), 10.
3. All references to the *Essays* will be to Donald Frame's translation, *The Complete Essays of Montaigne* (Stanford: Stanford University Press, 1985). Passages in French will come from Michel de Montaigne, *Oeuvres complètes*, ed. Albert Thibaudet and Maurice Rat

(Paris: Gallimard, "Bibliothèque de la Pléiade," 1962). Page numbers will be indicated following each quotation. Here is the French: "Mes conceptions et mon jugement ne marchent qu'à tastons, chancelant, bronchant et chopant; et quand je suis allé le plus avant que je puis, si ne me suis-je aucunement satisfaict; je voy encore du païs au delà, mais d'une veuë trouble et en nuage" (145).

4. Adorno, "The Essay as Form," 11.

5. The importance of Renaissance rhetorical practice for literary composition in Montaigne's day is best explicated by Terence Cave in *The Cornucopian Text: Problems of Writing in the French Renaissance* (Oxford: Clarendon Press, 1979). See Part I, chapter 4, and Part II, chapter 4. On the tradition of legal gloss, see André Tournon, *Montaigne: la glose et l'essai* (Lyon: Presses Universitaires de Lyon, 1983).

6. "Au demeurant, je ne corrige point mes premieres imaginations par les secondes; (c) ouy à l'aventure quelque mot, mais pour diversifier, non pour oster. (a) Je veux representer le progrez de mes humeurs, et qu'on voit chaque piece en sa naissance" (736–737).

7. "C'est moy que je peins" (9).

8. "Je ne peux assurer mon object. Il va trouble et chancelant, d'une yvresse naturelle" (782b).

9. "Les traits de ma peinture ne forvoyent point, quoy qu'ils se changent et diversifient" (782b).

10. "Il me sembloit ne pouvoir faire plus grande faveur à mon esprit, que de le laisser en pleine oysiveté, s'entretenir soy mesmes, et s'arrester et rasseoir en soy: ce que j'esperois qu'il peu meshuy faire plus aisément, devenu avec le temps plus poisant, et plus meur" (34a).

11. On Montaigne's citational practice, the best studies are Antoine Compagnon, *La seconde main ou le travail de la citation* (Paris: Le Seuil, 1979); and Mary B. McKinley, *Words in a Corner* (Lexington, KY: French Forum, 1981).

12. "Je peins principalement mes cogitations, subject informe, qui ne peut tomber en production ouvragere" (359a).

13. "Je m'estalle entier: c'est un skeletos où d'une veuë, les veines, les muscles, les tendons paroissent, chaque piece en son siege. L'effect de la toux en produisoit une partie: l'effect de la palleur ou battement de coeur, un autre, et doubteusement. Ce ne sont mes gestes que j'escris, c'est moy, c'est mon essence" (359a).

14. "En fin, toute cette fricassée que je barbouille icy n'est qu'un registre des essais de ma vie, qui est, pour l'interne santé, exemplaire assez, à prendre l'instruction à contrepoil. Mais quant à la santé corporelle, personne ne peut fournir d'experience plus utile que moy" (1056b). On Montaigne's relationship to the tradition of heroic exemplarity, see Timothy Hampton, *Writing from History: The Rhetoric of Exemplarity in Renaissance Literature* (Ithaca: Cornell University Press, 1990); and, in a slightly different context, John Lyons, *Exemplum* (Princeton: Princeton University Press, 1989). On Montaigne's ethical resistance to the culture of aristocratic revenge that informed the Wars of Religion, see David Quint, *Montaigne and the Quality of Mercy: Ethical and Political Themes in the Essais* (Princeton: Princeton University Press, 1998).

15. "Moy, qui ne manie que terre à terre, je hay cette inhumaine sapience qui nous veut rendre desdaigneux et ennemis de la culture du corps" (1086b).

16. "Il n'y que les fols certains et resolus" (150c). On the central role of change in Montaigne's philosophy, see Jean Starobinski, *Montaigne in Motion*, trans. Arthur Goldhammer (Chicago: University of Chicago Press, 1985); and François Rigolot, *Les Métamorphoses de Montaigne* (Paris: Presses Universitaires de France, 1988).

17. "Moy maintenant et moy tantost somme bien deux" (941b).

BIBLIOGRAPHY

Adorno, Theodor W. "The Essay as Form." In *Notes to Literature*, vol. 1, translated by Shierry Weber Nicholsen, 3–23. New York: Columbia University Press, 1991.

Bakewell, Sarah. *How to Live, or a Life of Montaigne in One Question and Twenty Attempts at an Answer*. New York: Other Press, 2010.

Cave, Terence. *The Cornucopian Text: Problems of Writing in the French Renaissance*. Oxford: The Clarendon Press, 1979.

Compagnon, Antoine. *La Seconde main ou le travail de la citation*. Paris: Éditions du Seuil, 1979.

Hampton, Timothy. *Writing from History: The Rhetoric of Exemplarity in Renaissance Literature*. Ithaca: Cornell University Press, 1990.

Lyons, John D. *Exemplum: The Rhetoric of Example in Early Modern France and Italy*. Princeton: Princeton University Press, 1989.

McKinley, Mary B. *Words in a Corner: Studies in Montaigne's Latin Quotations*. Lexington: French Forum, 1981.

Montaigne, Michel de. *The Complete Essays of Montaigne*, translated by Donald Frame. Stanford: Stanford University Press, 1985.

Montaigne, Michel de. *Oeuvres complètes*, edited by Albert Thibaudet and Maurice Rat. Paris: Gallimard, "Bibliothèque de la Pléiade," 1962.

Quint, David. *Montaigne and the Quality of Mercy: Ethical and Political Themes in the Essais*. Princeton, NJ: Princeton University Press, 1998.

Rigolot, François. *Les Métamorphoses de Montaigne*. Paris: Presses Universitaires de France, 1988.

Starobinski, Jean. *Montaigne in Motion*, translated by Arthur Goldhammer. Chicago: University of Chicago Press, 1985.

Tournon, André. *Montaigne: la glose et l'essai*. Lyon: Presses Universitaires de Lyon, 1983.

CHAPTER 13

THE IMPROVISATION OF POETRY, 1750–1850

Oral Performance, Print Culture, and the Modern Homer

ANGELA ESTERHAMMER

As the word *improvisation* entered English and other European languages around 1800, the concept of improvisation had wide-ranging influence in the domains of aesthetics, poetics, and socio-political thought. In some ways, improvisational practices during the "Romantic century" (1750–1850) resembled the modes of improvisation that would become dominant during the 20th century. Musical improvisation, already well established with Bach, Handel, and Mozart, proliferated in the age of the virtuoso performer, and traditions of extemporized theater involving multiple actors, such as *commedia dell'arte*, underwent imaginative reworkings on the Romantic stage.[1] But the period from 1750 to 1850 also saw the rise and decline of a distinctive type of improviser: the *improvvisatore* (male) or *improvvisatrice* (female), a solo poet-performer who spontaneously composed verses on subjects assigned by the audience. These improvisations could range in length from epigrams and short lyrics to very long epics and multi-act tragedies. The tradition of extempore poetry developed primarily in Italy, and abundant descriptions of *improvvisatori* and *improvvisatrici* can be found in travel accounts, letters, diaries, periodical articles, and fiction by tourists and correspondents who witnessed their performances. In the early 19th century and especially during the post-Napoleonic period, improvised poetry spread across Europe as Italian *improvvisatori* increasingly performed abroad and local imitators began to extemporize poetry in German, Dutch, English, French, Russian, Polish, and Swedish.

Improvising performers themselves produced little in the way of memorable poetry, but they did have a notable influence on the forms and styles of prominent Romantic-era writers—from Goethe and Germaine de Staël to Byron and P. B. Shelley—who were intrigued by the spontaneous and interactive mode of composition manifested by *improvvisatori*. In addition, the *improvvisatore* phenomenon gave rise to literary-critical, philological, sociological, and political debates that looked back to the foundations of the Western cultural tradition and intersected with the evolution of modern communicative media. *Improvvisatori* and *improvvisatrici* appealed to the late-18th-century fascination with genius and to the celebrity culture of the early 19th century. Many of the qualities to which Romantic ideology assigned a high value—inspiration, spontaneity, orality, sensibility, and emotional expressiveness—seemed to be manifested in the performances of improvising poets. For early-19th-century audiences, the improviser appeared to embody inspiration, and in their accounts of *improvvisatori* and *improvvisatrici* high-Romantic writers suggest that these performances allow the listener to witness first-hand the operations of poetic genius.

Yet improvising performers were controversial figures whose aesthetic value and social relevance became the subject of intense reflection. The foreign and even bizarre conventions of poetic improvisation—the hackneyed topics often requested by audience members, for instance, along with other constraints such as required meters and rhyme words—challenge the terms of Romantic genius as often as they fulfill them. The *improvvisatore*'s public composition of poetry in dialogue with an audience fits uneasily with English and German Romantic notions of solitary genius in communion with nature. "Grand thoughts," writes Wordsworth, "as they are most naturally and most fitly conceived in solitude, so can they not be brought forth in the midst of plaudits, without some violation of their sanctity"—and even if poetry arises from the "spontaneous overflow of powerful feelings," he insists that poems of any value can only be produced when the poet has "thought long and deeply."[2] Despite the impressive talent displayed by many *improvvisatori*, the persistent tension between their theatricality and artificiality and the originality and authenticity valued by Romantic aesthetics gives rise to an international discourse about the conditions conducive to the composition of poetry.

At first, the Romantic discourse about poetic improvisation shows a strong orientation toward national differences: poets and critics attempt to determine why improvised poetry has such a long tradition in Mediterranean countries yet seems strange, unknown, or impossible elsewhere. From the mid-18th century onward, French, English, and German writers regularly remark that it is much easier to improvise verses in Italian because of the phonology and structure of the language, its high number of rhyme words, and its melodic accentuation. They note that the musical accompaniment used by most *improvvisatori*, along with well-established rhyme schemes and rhythmic meters such as *ottava rima*, acts as a mnemonic and compositional aid. It is frequently observed that the sociable context, especially the interaction with a responsive audience, has a positive effect on the creative process. Many *improvvisatori* report that applause and other forms of immediate positive feedback heighten their creative impulses beyond what they thought they were capable of. Many commentators also note that the stress and anxiety produced by the presence of an audience—although potentially harmful to the physical well-being of performers—seem to have a positive impact on their mental powers.[3]

More critically, virtuoso feats of extemporization were sometimes ascribed to the *improvvisatore*'s ability to make rapid new combinations of preexisting elements, in contrast to the original and inspired act of creation that Romantic-era audiences expect to witness. The travel writer Louis Simond, for instance, reflects on the physical and psychological conditions involved in improvisation after witnessing performances by the *improvvisatore* Tommaso Sgricci, who was celebrated during the post-Waterloo era for his improvisation of entire multi-act dramas. Simond compares Sgricci's ability to compose spontaneously a two-and-a-half-hour tragedy to various other processes that involve memory and combinatorics, some of them exceptional and some routine. These include the ability to play multiple chess matches simultaneously, or the kind of visual memory and rapid recall that allows one to instantly locate any book in one's large library, or even the ability to make new combinations of words in everyday speech.[4] To the extent that Romantic-era commentators reflect on the cognitive processes involved in poetic improvisation, their explanations tend to demystify and even disparage the art form by describing it as, at best, a heightened application of ordinary mental processes or, at worst, a trick—a clever re-arrangement of preexisting elements that substitutes for genuine creation. Conversely, when Sgricci himself is asked how he produces his improvisations, he gives notably laconic responses that serve to enhance the mystique: "Such and such ideas suggest themselves," or "they are involuntary," is all he can say.[5]

Overall, Romantic-era writers reflected less on the cognitive processes involved in improvisation than on sociological aspects and on what would now be called the "media question." Writers and journalists discussed the different attributes of male and female improvisers, theorized about why improvisation appeared to be at home in Mediterranean countries (especially Italy) but foreign to the rest of Europe, and wondered whether the *improvvisatore* could provide a positive model for public speakers and political leaders or whether, on the contrary, the spontaneous improvisation of new verses and even of different personae to suit every occasion constituted a threat to the stability of social roles. Interwoven with these socio-political questions is the *improvvisatore*'s idiosyncratic status within a rapidly changing media environment. With few exceptions, poetic improvisation on the Romantic stage, in salons, or in more casual venues such as the marketplace, was an oral phenomenon. Yet this mode of oral poetry was thoroughly embedded in a culture of print, from the often clichéd literary topics that were usually assigned to improvisers to the widespread practice of recording extemporized poetry in shorthand and publishing it after the performance to the extensive promotion and reception of *improvvisatori* and *improvvisatrici* in print media. Like the bards, ballad-singers, and minstrels who proliferate in Romantic literature, the Romantic-era improviser is in this sense a conscious anachronism. Oral poetry carries connotations of authenticity: historically, it harks back to an age when poetry seemed a more natural expression of feeling; experientially, it appears to give the audience immediate access to the workings of creative genius. As the Romantic-period critic Carl Ludwig Fernow put it in his influential treatise *Über die Improvisatoren* (On Improvisers), the experience of improvisation is one "where the poet, in the moment of creative enthusiasm, pours his song directly into the listener's soul."[6] Even the ephemerality of oral poetry would seem to work to the improviser's advantage insofar as it shifts attention away from the literary quality of the verses and onto the momentary spectacle of their production. Yet instead of highlighting orality, Romantic *improvvisatori* and their audiences tend to be hyperconscious of their situation in the midst of print culture. The frequent dissemination of improvised poems and dramas after the performance by way of reviews and transcriptions makes their reception a matter of reading and writing as much as an aural and visual experience.

Throughout the period 1750–1850, these and other literary-critical, sociological, and medial reflections cluster around a recurring and revealing trope: the comparison of modern *improvvisatori* and *improvvisatrici* to oral poets of classical antiquity, particularly to Homer. The significance of what one modern critic has called "the rise and fall of the *improvvisatore*"[7] in European cultural history can thus be explored by reconstructing the decades-long discourse around the question "are *improvvisatori* the modern descendants of Homer?" and its inevitable converse: "was Homer an *improvvisatore*?" In addressing these questions, 18th- and 19th-century writers seek to locate poetic improvisation within—or else to displace it from—a tradition reaching back to the very foundations of European culture. At the same time, they struggle to come to terms with the anomalous status of improvised oral poetry within a rapidly changing media environment in which improvisational performance is only one of many cultural phenomena competing for aesthetic valorization.

The recurring appeal to a Homeric paradigm takes several crisscrossing directions. For improvisers themselves and for their admiring listeners, identifying *improvvisatori* as the modern incarnations of Homer is a way of investing the art-form with an impressive history and a classical pedigree. Conversely, for 18th- and 19th-century philologists such as Robert Wood and Friedrich August Wolf, who are pursuing revisionary approaches to the study of Homer, the performances of *improvvisatori* offer a living example of the mode of composition that ancient oral poets might have practiced. More generally, the comparison with Homer provides a way of reflecting on processes of oral and written composition, transmission, and reception at a time when sociocultural changes brought these questions to the fore. The popularity of *improvvisatori* and *improvvisatrici* coincided with the rapid expansion of the newspaper and periodical industry and with a burgeoning urban culture that featured new visual media (panoramas, dioramas, scale models) and hybrid, often semi-improvisational types of performance (melodrama, vaudeville, public lectures, live exhibits). Even after poetic improvisers declined in prestige and popularity in mid-19th-century Europe, the associations that had been forged between their abilities and classical traditions of oratory provided a route by which improvisation could migrate from the theater into print media and professional contexts.

In the 18th century, when the first accounts of *improvvisatori* were framed for English readers by classically educated Grand Tourists who visited Italy, Greek and Latin poetry served as a touchstone for coming to terms with a distinctly foreign poetics. Indeed, the Italian word *improvvisatore* first gets imported into English in the context of classical philology. In Joseph Warton's 1753 edition of *The Works of Virgil*, Joseph Spence, professor of poetry at Oxford and erstwhile tourist in Italy, contributes a note explicating Virgil's seventh eclogue by reference to the contemporary improvisers he encountered in Florence. Virgil's extemporizing shepherd-poets are, Spence writes,

> very like the *Improvisatori* at present in Italy; who flourish now perhaps more than any other poets among them, particularly in Tuscany. They are surprisingly ready in their answers (*respondere parati*) and go on *octave* for *octave*, or *speech* for *speech*. . . . There were *Improvisatori* of the kind of old[.][8]

During the century that followed, northern European travellers who witnessed performances by Italian improvisers continued to place this foreign performance genre into a tradition by relating it to classical bucolic poetry, the oratory of ancient Rome, or Homeric epic. A number of authoritative commonplaces in classical literature helped locate improvisation at the very origins of the Western poetic tradition. Besides Plato's *Ion* with its depiction of the divinely inspired rhapsode, Aristotle's *Poetics* identifies improvisation as the origin of both tragedy and comedy. Following their natural instincts for rhythm and mimesis, Aristotle writes, people "gradually progressed and brought poetry into being from improvisations."[9] Even in the highly evolved form that it took during the Romantic period, poetic improvisation maintained obvious affiliations with the literature of classical antiquity. Greek and Roman myth and history were among the most common topics offered at improvisational performances, and numerous eyewitness accounts of *improvvisatori* and *improvvisatrici* extol the classical erudition that performers are able to weave into their spontaneous verses.

When poetic improvisation first began to impinge on literary circles in northern Europe it seemed to offer a more natural poetics that transcended rigid 18th-century canons, and comparisons with primitive rhapsodes were quickly brought in to support these claims. The Parisian *Journal Étranger* began in the 1750s to extol Italian *improvvisatori* as "an unusual species of poets, who derive everything from nature and owe nothing to study."[10] But the journal's most extended engagement with poetic improvisation is interestingly triggered by the German poet Anna Louisa Karsch, whom it baptizes with the epithet "this celebrated *improvisatrice* of the North."[11] The Silesian peasant Karsch became a *cause célèbre* in the literary circles of 18th-century Berlin, when critics championed her as an example of expressive natural genius in contrast to rule-bound academic verse. Karsch's striking ability to extemporize verses leads admirers to liken her to Italian *improvvisatrici*. François Arnaud, editor of the *Journal Étranger*, draws an important three-way connection among Karsch, Italian improvisers, and ancient rhapsodes when he prints French translations of some of Karsch's impromptu odes and prefaces these translations with enthusiastic articles on Karsch. Thanks to her "sensitive" heart and her "ardent and impetuous" imagination, she embodies the *furor poeticus* described by Plato and Aristotle, which links her with the enthusiastic poets of ancient Greece, as well as with the *improvvisatori* of modern Italy.[12]

The conjunction among Karsch, the oral poetry of ancient Greece, and the figure of the *improvvisatrice* is carried forward in further analyses of poetic improvisation on the part of the editors of the *Journal Étranger*. Both Arnaud and his co-editor, Jean Baptiste Antoine Suard, went on to publish separate essays entitled "Des improvisateurs" (On improvisers), which appear to be the first publications on this topic outside of Italy. Arnaud's "Des improvisateurs" remains primarily devoted to publicizing Karsch, but his classicist background prompts him to set her and Italian *improvvisatori* in the context of a continuous tradition of extempore poetry that he traces back to ancient Greece. "The verses that all ages have admired and will admire," writes Arnaud, "Homer gave birth to them extemporaneously, without trouble, without effort, as a spring spills forth its waters."[13] Arnaud may be the first 18th-century writer to identify the ancient Greek poets, including Homer, as "*improvisateurs*." Promoting a fresh, ardent, spontaneous poetics in the midst of 18th-century literary-critical debates, Arnaud testifies to the appeal of the *improvvisatrice* as a figure who has the potential to recover a natural poetic voice.

Suard, Arnaud's younger, more prominent, and more controversial collaborator, penned a "Des improvisateurs" article of his own (Suard, 1806). It also covers the ground from Plato and Aristotle to Karsch, whom he identifies as the only "*improvisateur*" to appear outside of Italy in modern times. Suard's article represents the beginning of the sociological study of poetic improvisation in northern Europe, which would achieve its most fully developed form in Fernow's nearly contemporary German treatise *Über die Improvisatoren*. An unavoidable point of reference for later 19th-century writings on improvisation because of its detailed analysis of the history and popularity of the art-form, Fernow's lengthy essay characterizes the *improvvisatore* as both a Romantic genius and a modern incarnation of Homer. On the one hand, Fernow describes performances of improvised poetry in terms of a Romantic ideology of creative genius that highlights inspiration, immediacy, and intensity. On the other hand, he documents the long history of poetic improvisation in Western culture and identifies the Italian *improvvisatore* as a modern-day "wandering Homer."[14]

The classical philologist and archaeologist Karl August Böttiger, editor of the influential literary journal *Der neue Teutsche Merkur* (The New German Mercury) that first published *Über die Improvisatoren*, praises Fernow's observations on the relationship between modern-day Italian performers and ancient Greek rhapsodes and urges other scholars to expand the historical and ethnological study of poetic improvisation. In an enthusiastic postscript to Fernow's essay in the *Merkur* of October 1801, Böttiger writes:

> *Improvising*, in general, still merits a deep and penetrating historical investigation that combines knowledge of the ancient world intimately with psychology . . . since the debate over the schools of singers and rhapsodes, which is so important for criticism of the oldest Hebraic and Greek inscriptions and has recently attracted such lively attention, is most particularly connected with it. I would propose, for the purpose, Plato's *Ion*; the four kinds of enthusiasm described there are far from being well enough distinguished and examined.[15]

Böttiger's call for a perspicacious study of improvisation—which he describes as a surprisingly modern interdisciplinary amalgam of philology, psychology, ethnology, and cultural studies—is both triggered by, and centered on, the Italian *improvvisatore*, whom he considers the outstanding representative of this art-form. "The Italian improvisers," Böttiger concludes, "always remain the most excellent."[16]

While Böttiger, like Arnaud and Suard before him, believes that modern poetic improvisation can best be appreciated by locating it in the tradition of ancient Greek rhapsodes, 18th- and 19th-century classical philologists find—conversely—that modern *improvvisatori* might offer the key to a better understanding of Homer. In the 1760s, the antiquarian Robert Wood struck a new chord by comparing Homer's style to "the spirited theatrical action" of the extemporizing "Italian and Eastern poets" he had encountered on his extensive travels in the Mediterranean.[17] With this revisionary, performance-oriented perspective on ancient epic, Wood's *Essay on the Original Genius and Writings of Homer* became one of the texts that founded a new approach to the study of Homer as a rhapsode. A few decades later Friedrich August Wolf, the single most influential classicist of the period, laid the groundwork for 20th-century Homeric scholarship when he argued in his *Prolegomena ad Homerum* (Prolegomena to Homer) that the text of Greek epic remained unfixed for centuries, varying according to the time and place of performance, as well as the talents of each individual rhapsode who performed it. Wolf backs up his claims about the oral, performance-oriented composition of the *Iliad* and the *Odyssey* by pointing to living poets "who compose extempore, who are called *improvvisatori* in Italian."[18] Modern improvisers provided Wolf and his fellow scholars with a living demonstration of what would otherwise remain only conjecture: that it is entirely possible to compose dozens or hundreds of verses on a given subject without premeditation. Comparisons with *improvvisatori* became steadily more common in classicist scholarship during the early and mid-19th century, being applied to Homer himself as well as to the rhapsodes depicted within the Homeric epics. Reading the episode in book eight of the *Odyssey*, where the singer Demodokos performs a song on a topic requested by Odysseus, the German classicist A.H.L. Heeren notes that ancient bards behaved "entirely in the manner of modern improvisers" and concludes that it is very likely that Greek epic poetry originated in improvisation.[19]

One of the most in-depth analyses of Homeric epic as improvised poetry is to be found in the influential *Remarks on Antiquities, Arts, and Letters during an Excursion in Italy, in the Years 1802 and 1803* by the London schoolmaster Joseph Forsyth. While travelling in Italy and listening to the foremost female improviser of the day, Fortunata Fantastici, Forsyth is struck by the similarities between La Fantastici's oral improvisations and Homeric epic. He identifies in both of them "the same openness of style and simplicity of construction, the same digressions, rests, repetitions, anomalies."[20] While the comparison elevates the art of the *improvvisatrice*, it also leads Forsyth to analyze Homeric poetry exactly as if Homer were a modern improviser, even critiquing him for the same limitations as "other *improvvisatori*." He enumerates the features of diction, syntax, and structure that distinguish the compositions of Homer and modern improvisers from written poetry:

> Homer seems to have kept a stock of hemistichs, which recur incessantly at the close
> of verses . . .; expletive epithets . . . which appear in so many, and so opposite mean-
> ings that they cease to have any meaning at all; expletive phrases which he applies
> indiscriminately . . .; set forms which introduce his speeches . . . or else begin them
> . . . and thus leave him time to collect thoughts for the speech itself. . . . Such was
> Homer and such is the Italian.[21]

The ellipses mark spots where Forsyth cites copious examples of Greek epithets and phrases; in other words, he is pursuing a full-fledged philological commentary on the Homeric text, analyzing it according to the techniques used by *improvvisatori* and *improvvisatrici*. With these observations, Forsyth comes to the brink of 20th-century theories of oral poetry, including the oral-formulaic theory of epic advanced by Milman Parry and Albert Lord and more recent global perspectives on oral poetry by Ruth Finnegan and J. Miles Foley. Like these later scholars, Forsyth identifies the features of orally composed poetry as additive or paratactic style; repetition and redundancy; the use of inherited diction, epithets, phrasing, images, or commonplaces; deictic refer- ences within the poetry to the situation and occasion in which it is being performed; and a regular rhythm, often reinforced by musical accompaniment.

The question "was Homer an *improvvisatore*?" was not only a question about poetic technique, however, but also about the social and political impact of improvisational performance. What is at stake is whether the traditional role of the Homeric rhapsode in drawing a community together at public festivals and reaffirming its values in a moment of shared enthusiasm can be recovered in a modern context. Some Romantic-era writers find in a tradition of spontaneous poetic utterance reaching from Homer to the *improv- visatore* the promise of a powerful, socially relevant poetic voice. Others, however, worry that while the charismatic appeal of the improvising poet and the compelling excitement of the moment of performance are undeniable, in the 19th-century context this power is more likely to be exercised for revolutionary purposes than to promote social cohesion. These theorists consider it time to draw distinctions: denying the mod- ern improviser the authenticity and authority of the ancient rhapsode, they argue that the *improvvisatore*, if not merely a dilettante, is a potential demagogue.

The most extensive 19th-century treatise on the subject of poetic improvisa- tion in ancient times weighs in on the side of the improviser as social leader. In *"De l'improvisation poetique chez les anciens, et particulièrement chez les Grecs et les Romains"* (On poetic improvisation among the ancients, and particularly among the Greeks and the Romans), French archaeologist Desiré Raoul-Rochette sets out to compare the poets of antiquity with modern improvisers ranging from the real-life Francesco Gianni to Madame de Staël's fictional Corinne. Raoul-Rochette surveys the practice of spontane- ous poetry among ancient peoples from the Celts to the Arabs before coming to focus on the importance of public improvisation among the ancient Greeks and affirming the probability that Homer was a *"poëte improvisateur."*[22] In affiliating Romantic *improv- visatori* with the authoritative, celebratory poetry of ancient rhapsodes, Raoul-Rochette draws a crucial distinction between inspiration and improvisation. *Inspiration* is a private, subjective, modern phenomenon that takes place "in the shade of the woods, or the silence of the closet"[23]—a model of poetic creation for which Wordsworth's *Prelude* and Coleridge's "Kubla Khan" have since become familiar Romantic examples. By contrast, the *improvisation* practiced by ancient Greek poets at public festivals is a mode of creativity that "delights in a great number of witnesses, in the same way that a soldier is animated at the sight of his standards."[24] Citing a plethora of classical sources, Raoul-Rochette seeks to prove that ancient poets were the recipients of an instantaneous rush of enthusiasm that allowed them to extemporize law codes in the form of poetry and that gave them moral and legislative authority within their community. His history of improvisation leads him to conclude that "poets, in ancient Greek times, were regarded as the legislators of nations, as the preceptors of the human race."[25] Raoul-Rochette's article thus elaborates a full-scale history of Western poetry that places Romantic *improvvisatori* and *improvvisatrici* in a continuous line of descent from the charismatic social leaders of classical times. It is an image strikingly different from the solitary, alienated, or ironic figure of the poet more commonly associated with Romantic ideology. Whether or not P. B. Shelley read Raoul-Rochette's treatise, which appeared in French in the *Classical Journal* of London in 1817—and, given Shelley's interest in the history of poetry, in classical literature, and in improvisation, it is not unlikely that he did—it resonates with his strikingly similar formulation in *A Defence of Poetry*, written four years later. The conviction that, in Shelley's famous words, "Poets are the unacknowledged legislators of the World"[26] was not only in the air; it was also allied to the discourse of improvisation.

To other Romantic theorists, however, the differences between modern *improvvisatori* and ancient oral bards were more striking than the similarities. August Wilhelm Schlegel and Friedrich Schlegel both use the derogatory image of *improvvisatori* as tightrope walkers (*Seiltänzer*) to critique the modern practice of poetic improvisation and underscore its artificiality.[27] For the Schlegel brothers, the comparison between the productions of *improvvisatori* and the naturally extemporized poetry of the ancient Greeks only exposes the stylized and inauthentic quality of modern improvisers. By the 1820s and 1830s, when performances by Italian improvisers and their imitators elsewhere in Europe were at their height and comparisons of *improvvisatori* to Homeric rhapsodes had become commonplace, it seemed to some philologists even more urgent to undercut the assumed classical pedigree of the modern improviser. Writing in 1820, F. G. Welcker repudiates the comparison between *improvvisatori* and Homeric rhapsodes, claiming—with rather endearing scholarly hyperbole—that there is hardly a greater misconception to be found in all of literary history.[28] Welcker devotes a lengthy essay to clearing up confusion caused by other philologists' indiscriminate use of the term *Improvisator*. Like Friedrich Schlegel, he distinguishes between the natural improvisation found in the ancient Greek world, as in other cultures where poetry is still in its infancy, and the artificial improvisation practised in modern Italy, which is a phenomenon found only in late stages of cultural development. Rather than inspiration, modern improvisers manifest (only) quickness of intellect, extraordinary powers of memory, and enforced enthusiasm or *estro*. While he restricts the term *improviser* to a notably narrow range of meaning compared with the expansive significance that Raoul-Rochette gives it in his contemporaneous treatise, Welcker accurately reflects the degree to which poetic improvisation in the 19th century had become a professionalized and theatricalized genre.

A late contribution to the "was Homer an *improvvisatore*?" debate shows that improvisational performance was increasingly being thought about in the context of public speaking and socio-political responsibility. In his 1833 book on Homeric rhapsodes, the classicist Johann Kreuser denounces by name the best-known *improvvisatori* of his day, as he argues that improvisation is merely a mechanical ability that produces poor poetry. He seeks to demonstrate that the pre-literate Homer cannot be considered an *improvvisatore* because improvisation actually arises only in *literate* cultures once they have developed a sufficiently stable language and an ample fund of poetic expressions. To that end, Kreuser produces a scornful but highly perceptive description of extempore poetry. "What is the art of improvisation?" he asks rhetorically, and answers in part:

> It is the ever-ready skill with words, within and beyond bounds, always more or less suited to the given occasion, always appealing to the masses . . . important in decisive moments of life and for public constitutions, but for art in the real sense—always useless. . . . But when does one attain this ability to improvise, when aptitude is otherwise present? Only then, when the evolution of language has reached a stable form; then a common stock of language is available to the poet and orator.[29]

While denying the *improvvisatore*'s affiliation with Homer on the basis of the crucial distinction between oral and literate modes of composition, and while denigrating the aesthetic qualities of improvised poetry, Kreuser recognizes the political force of extemporized utterance. His acknowledgment that the ability to improvise can sway the masses and prove decisive in public debate reflects a growing mid-19th-century tendency to harness the power of poetic improvisation to public rhetoric—to the oratory of the courtroom, the pulpit, and the professorial chair.

The same socio-political orientation becomes evident in early Victorian reflections on the improvising poet. Particularly revealing is a documentary article entitled "Improvvisatori" that appeared in 1839 in the *Penny Magazine*, published by the Society for the Diffusion of Useful Knowledge, one of the first and most important mass-circulation periodicals aimed at a working-class readership. Seeking to give readers a picture of poetic improvisation in Italy and comparable practices in other countries, the journalist emphasizes that improvisers can arise from any social class and that their appeal crosses class boundaries. While far from being social levelers, these performers provide Italian peasants and workers with an amusement that is not only "harmless and happy," but also instructive and elevating. The "improvvisator" is a "link of communication between the lofty and the lowly mind," one who charms the common people in a way that, the writer implies, English poets would do well to imitate.[30] An engraving published with the article, based on a painting by the Swiss artist Louis-Léopold Robert, reinforces the message (Figure 13.1).

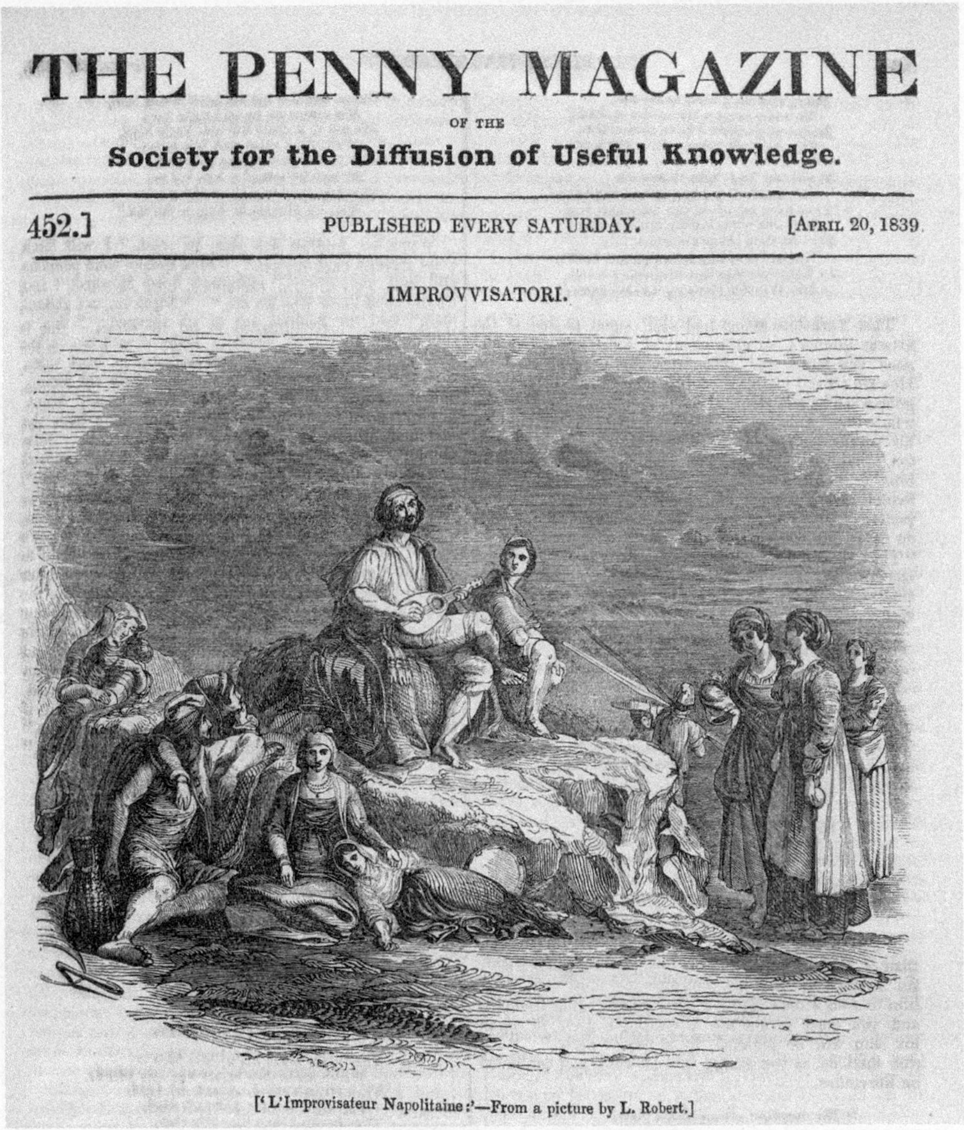

THE PENNY MAGAZINE

OF THE

Society for the Diffusion of Useful Knowledge.

452.] PUBLISHED EVERY SATURDAY. [April 20, 1839.

IMPROVVISATORI.

[' L'Improvisateur Napolitaine :'—From a picture by L. Robert.]

FIGURE 13.1 Front page of *The Penny Magazine*, No. 452 (20 April 1839)

Reproduced by kind permission of the Syndics of Cambridge University Library (classmark L900.b.69).

The image depicts a Neapolitan improviser with a mandolin whose rural "stage," a rock by the seashore, forms a harmonious meeting place for an interested audience of peasants coming in from the fields. The *improvvisatore*'s ability to promote social harmony and improve the lot of the laboring classes, as described in the article and depicted in the engraving, is presumably to be repeated in the *Penny Magazine*'s effect on *its* audience, the working-class readers who were expected to purchase the paper with a penny from their Saturday wages. This figurative repetition of the *improvvisatore*'s role on the part of the periodical writer is one more instance of how the popular reception as well as the reflective evaluation of improvised poetry takes place at the heart of print culture.

The question of whether and how poetic improvisation in the 18th and 19th centuries fits into a tradition that locates its source in Homer was, therefore, a question about what constitutes authenticity and naturalness in poetry. Even more compelling, it became a question about the authority of poetic utterance and the socio-political function of poets. Conversely, the *improvvisatore* phenomenon coincided with and even contributed to a revision in the study of Homeric epic during the late 18th and early 19th centuries as philologists began to emphasize the oral, performative, and improvisational nature of Homer's verse. Last but not least, the question "are *improvvisatori* the descendents of Homer?" helps bring some aspects of the relationship between print culture and orality into sharper focus. It underscores the peculiar status of the Romantic improviser as a practitioner of oral poetry within a culture whose perspectives and practices are thoroughly shaped by reading and writing. While the most conspicuous feature that Italian improvisation has in common with ancient Greek epic is oral performance, and while the oral nature of improvisation is its major difference from the mainstream poetics of Romantic Europe, the *improvvisatore*'s art is nevertheless entirely the product of a literate society, and its reception occurs within the paradigms of print culture. For Walter Ong, in fact, the Romantic period is precisely the time when "oral habits of thought and expression" that had persisted since early Greek times were "effectively obliterated in English" in favor of the "close, mostly unconscious, alliance of the Romantic Movement with technology."[31] Ong's view of the historical relationship among orality, literacy, and technology might suggest that the Romantic-era fascination with *improvvisatori* and *improvvisatrici* was largely due to nostalgia for the perceived authenticity of a lost pre-literate society. But that is only part of the story, for increasing technologization also led to some innovative alliances between oral performance and print publication in the 19th century. Inventors of new shorthand systems seek to advertise their inventions by touting their ability to transcribe verses as quickly as they are being improvised. For example, the poetry composed by virtuoso German improviser Maximilian Langenschwarz during a performance in Munich on July 19, 1830, appeared days later as a pamphlet that advertised on its title page "stenographically recorded and edited by F. X. Gabelsberger";[32] the royal secretary Gabelsberger proudly explains in a preface how the stenographic system he has invented has allowed him to preserve Langenschwarz's improvisations. No matter what the recording technology, the persistent impulse of *improvvisatori* and *improvvisatrici* to publish their extempore compositions mirrors the audience's expectation that written poetry is the standard that all poetic expression must meet.

When performances by poetic improvisers reach their height in 1820s and 1830s Europe, the rapid expansion of print media and the increasing influence of the professional classes give a new turn to discourses about improvisation, orality, and authority. This is manifested in efforts to channel improvisational performance toward social responsibility by teaching the art of improvisation to professional men such as lawyers, politicians, professors, or clergy. Arguing that the new social order of 19th-century

Germany has a particular need for effective public speakers, Langenschwarz authored a manual on how to improvise, entitled *Die Arithmetik der Sprache, oder der Redner durch sich selbst* (The arithmetic of language, or the orator through himself). Based on his personal experience performing extemporized poetry in Germany and abroad, Langenschwarz seeks to teach a form of philosophical rhetoric that will help readers discover their inner selves and develop their abilities for public service by learning to order their thoughts and express them spontaneously with the help of rhetoric and imagination. The purpose of Langenschwarz's book, which is ambitiously dedicated "to humanity," is

> the establishment of a rhetorical system, through the precise following of which it would gradually be possible for even the most unpractised speaker to become *master* of his feelings and ideas, completely and to such a degree that, undeterred by anything going on around him, and at any given time, he would be capable of expressing what has awakened inside him clearly and in an ordered and coherent manner.[33]

Langenschwarz's system represents a re-assimilation of improvisation from stage performance into rhetoric. In that sense, it recalls the tradition of classical oratory, but now there is a crucial, post-Romantic addition: improvised utterance is also meant to lead to self-knowledge, self-expression, and self-fulfillment. Several other mid-19th-century "how-to-improvise" textbooks in German, French, and Spanish also tried to harness improvisational ability in a systematic way for politics and the professions. As indicated by their authors—celebrity improvisers such as Langenschwarz or the self-styled "first German improviser" Oskar Ludwig Bernhard Wolff (1850)—as well as by subtitles, epigraphs, and direct allusions to famous *improvvisatori* and *improvvisatrici*, these elocutionary manuals seek to systematize theatrical improvisation into techniques that can be used to train professional speakers.

As oral improvisation makes its way from the salon and the theater into parliament and the courtroom, it simultaneously recognizes its affinity with new print media. Much of the commentary on and analysis of poetic improvisation cited in this essay first appeared in literary-cultural magazines, and many more examples from these sources could be adduced. During the early 19th century, periodical publications avidly review the performances of *improvvisatori* and *improvvisatrici*; they also offer documentary articles on the history of improvisation, reviews of books about improvisation, advertisements of upcoming performances, and transcriptions of poetry that has been improvised in performance. All this attention seems to indicate a convergence between improvisational performance and the era's burgeoning periodical culture. Much in the way that improvisation offers an application for new shorthand systems, newspapers and magazines recognize a role for themselves in giving greater permanence and wider distribution to ephemeral cultural events, of which improvisational performances are perhaps the foremost example. Journalism, moreover, has much in common with poetic improvisation when it comes to the rapidity of production and the responsive interaction with an audience. Writers and editors of literary magazines share with extemporizing poets a need to perform in the face of temporal constraint (or to write to deadline) and an orientation toward the demands of readers or consumers. Finally, the performances of *improvvisatori* map onto periodical articles and magazines insofar as both media share a self-consciousness about their own status as consumable, ephemeral, popular forms, in contrast to high or serious literature. These parallels suggest that the popularity of improvising poets in early-19th-century Europe may correspond to a general improvisational disposition within print and performance culture during this age of rapid evolution in media and genres. Improvisation could well stand as a paradigm for the cultural changes that take place as late-Romantic and post-Romantic performance genres and print media adopt a more rapid and reactive attitude toward current events and a closer engagement with audiences, readerships, and mass markets.

NOTES

1. See Angela Esterhammer, "Improvisational Modes," in *The Encyclopedia of Romantic Literature*, ed. Frederick Burwick (Oxford: Wiley-Blackwell, 2012), 652–660; and Edgar Landgraf, *Improvisation as Art: Conceptual Challenges, Historical Perspectives* (New York: Continuum, 2011), especially Chapter 3, "Staged Improvisation."

2. William Wordsworth, *The Prose Works of William Wordsworth*, 3 vols., ed. W. J. B. Owen and Jane Worthington Smyser (Oxford: Clarendon, 1974), 3:83 and 1:122–126.

3. For a fuller discussion of these debates, see Angela Esterhammer, *Romanticism and Improvisation, 1750–1850* (Cambridge: Cambridge University Press, 2008).

4. Louis Simond, *Voyage en Italie et en Sicile*, 2 vols. (Paris, 1828), 1:337–338. Unless otherwise stated, all translations into English are by the author.

5. "Rosa Taddei and Tommaso Sgricci," *Blackwood's Edinburgh Magazine* 25 (January–June 1829), 186.

6. Carl Ludwig Fernow, *Über die Improvisatoren*, in *Römische Studien*, 2 vols. (Zurich: Gessner, 1806), 2:304.

7. Caroline Gonda, "The Rise and Fall of the Improvisatore, 1753–1845," *Romanticism* 6 (2000): 195–210.

8. Joseph Warton, ed., *The Works of Virgil, in Latin and English*, 4 vols. (London, 1753), 1:121.

9. Aristotle, *Poetics*, ed. and trans. Stephen Halliwell, in *Aristotle XXIII*, Loeb Classical Library (Cambridge: Harvard University Press, 1995), 39.

10. "Poesie," *Journal Étranger*, April 1757, 28.

11. "Ode à des alouettes prises dans des filets," *Journal Étranger*, March 1762, 210.

12. "Ode à des alouettes," 210.

13. François Arnaud, "Des improvisateurs," in *Oeuvres complettes de l'Abbé Arnaud*, 3 vols. (Paris: Léopold Collin, 1808), 2:100.

14. Fernow, *Über die Improvisatoren*, 323–324.

15. Karl August Böttiger, "Nachwort," *Der neue Teutsche Merkur*, October 1801, 103.

16. Böttiger, "Nachwort," 104.

17. Robert Wood, *An Essay on the Original Genius and Writings of Homer* (London, 1775), xi.

18. Friedrich August Wolf, *Prolegomena to Homer* (1795), trans. Anthony Grafton, Glenn W. Most, and James E. G. Zetzel (Princeton: Princeton University Press, 1985), 109.

19. A. H. L. Heeren, *Ideen über die Politik, den Verkehr und den Handel der vornehmsten Völker der alten Welt,* part 3, *Europäische Völker,* new ed. (Vienna, 1817), 113–114.

20. Joseph Forsyth, *Remarks on Antiquities, Arts, and Letters during an Excursion in Italy, in the Years 1802 and 1803,* 2nd ed. (London: Murray, 1816), 52–53.

21. Forsyth, *Remarks on Antiquities,* 53.

22. Desiré Raoul-Rochette, "De l'improvisation poetique chez les anciens, et particulièrement chez les Grecs et les Romains," *Classical Journal* 16 (1817): 105.

23. Raoul-Rochette, "De l'improvisation poetique chez les anciens," 96.

24. Raoul-Rochette, "De l'improvisation poetique chez les anciens," 97.

25. Raoul-Rochette, "De l'improvisation poetique chez les anciens," 99.

26. Percy Bysshe Shelley, *Shelley's Poetry and Prose,* ed. Donald H. Reiman and Sharon B. Powers (New York: Norton, 1977), 508.

27. August Wilhelm Schlegel, "Über den dramatischen Dialog," in *Kritische Schriften* (Berlin: Reimer, 1828), 377; Friedrich Schlegel, *Geschichte der Poesie der Griechen und Römer* (Berlin: Ungar, 1798), 154.

28. Friedrich G. Welcker, "Aöden und Improvisatoren," in *Kleine Schriften zur Griechischen Literaturgeschichte,* Part 2 (Osnabrück: Zeller, 1973), lxxxvii.

29. Johann Kreuser, *Homerische Rhapsoden oder Rederiker der Alten* (Köln, 1833), 152.

30. "Improvvisatori," *The Penny Magazine of the Society for the Diffusion of Useful Knowledge* 452 (20 April 1839): 146–147.

31. Walter J. Ong, *Orality and Literacy: The Technologizing of the Word* (London: Methuen, 1982), 26, 161.

32. Maximilian Langenschwarz, *Erste Improvisation von Langenschwarz in München (19 July 1830)* (Munich, 1830), title page.

33. Maximilian Langenschwarz, *Die Arithmetik der Sprache, oder der Redner durch sich selbst: Psychologisch-rhetorisches Lehrgebäude* (Leipzig, 1834), x–xi.

Bibliography

Aristotle. *Poetics,* edited and translated by Stephen Halliwell. In *Aristotle XXIII,* 1–141. Loeb Classical Library. Cambridge: Harvard University Press, 1995.

Arnaud, François. "Des improvisateurs." In *Oeuvres complettes de l'Abbé Arnaud.* 3 vols. 2: 96–107. Paris: Léopold Collin, 1808.

Böttiger, Karl August. "Nachwort." *Der neue Teutsche Merkur,* October 1801, 103–108.

Esterhammer, Angela. "Improvisational Modes." In *The Encyclopedia of Romantic Literature,* edited by Frederick Burwick, 652–660. Oxford: Wiley-Blackwell, 2012.

Esterhammer, Angela. *Romanticism and Improvisation, 1750–1850.* Cambridge: Cambridge University Press, 2008.

Fernow, Carl Ludwig. "Über die Improvisatoren." In *Römische Studien.* 2 vols. 2: 298–416. Zurich: Gessner, 1806.

Forsyth, Joseph. *Remarks on Antiquities, Arts, and Letters during an Excursion in Italy, in the Years 1802 and 1803.* 2nd ed. London: Murray, 1816.

Gonda, Caroline. "The Rise and Fall of the Improvisatore, 1753–1845." *Romanticism* 6 (2000): 195–210.

Heeren, A.H.L. *Ideen über die Politik, den Verkehr und den Handel der vornehmsten Völker der alten Welt.* Part 3. *Europäische Völker.* New ed. Vienna, 1817.

"Improvvisatori." *The Penny Magazine of the Society for the Diffusion of Useful Knowledge* 452 (20 April 1839): 145–147.

Kreuser, Johann. *Homerische Rhapsoden oder Rederiker der Alten*. Köln, 1833.

Landgraf, Edgar. *Improvisation as Art: Conceptual Challenges, Historical Perspectives*. New York: Continuum, 2011.

Langenschwarz, Maximilian. *Die Arithmetik der Sprache, oder der Redner durch sich selbst: Psychologisch-rhetorisches Lehrgebäude*. Leipzig, 1834.

Langenschwarz, Maximilian. *Erste Improvisation von Langenschwarz in München* (19 July 1830). Munich, 1830.

"Ode à des alouettes prises dans des filets." *Journal Étranger*, March 1762, 210–213.

Ong, Walter J. *Orality and Literacy: The Technologizing of the Word*. London: Methuen, 1982.

"Poesie." *Journal Étranger*, April 1757, 28–31.

Raoul-Rochette, Desiré. "De l'improvisation poetique chez les anciens, et particulièrement chez les Grecs et les Romains." *Classical Journal* 15 (1817): 249–257; 16 (1817): 96–109, 357–371.

"Rosa Taddei and Tommaso Sgricci." *Blackwood's Edinburgh Magazine* 25 (January—June 1829): 184–186.

Schlegel, August Wilhelm. "Über den dramatischen Dialog." In *Kritische Schriften*, 365–379. Berlin: Reimer, 1828.

Schlegel, Friedrich. *Geschichte der Poesie der Griechen und Römer*. Berlin: Ungar, 1798.

Shelley, Percy Bysshe. *Shelley's Poetry and Prose*, edited by Donald H. Reiman and Sharon B. Powers. New York: Norton, 1977.

Simond, Louis. *Voyage en Italie et en Sicile*. Paris, 1828.

Suard, Jean Baptiste Antoine. "Des improvisateurs." In *Mélanges de littérature*. 2nd rev. ed. 3:346–378. Paris: Dentu, 1806.

Warton, Joseph, ed. *The Works of Virgil, in Latin and English*. 4 vols. London, 1753.

Welcker, Friedrich G. "Aöden und Improvisatoren." In *Kleine Schriften zur Griechischen Literaturgeschichte*. Part 2, lxxxvii–ci. Osnabrück: Zeller, 1973.

Wolf, Friedrich August. *Prolegomena to Homer* (1795), translated by Anthony Grafton, Glenn W. Most, and James E. G. Zetzel. Princeton: Princeton University Press, 1985.

Wolff, O[skar] L[udwig] B[ernhard]. *Lehr- und Handbuch der gerichtlichen Beredsamkeit*. Jena: Mauke, 1850.

Wood, Robert. *An Essay on the Original Genius and Writings of Homer*. London, 1775.

Wordsworth, William. *The Prose Works of William Wordsworth*, edited by W. J. B. Owen and Jane Worthington Smyser. 3 vols. Oxford: Clarendon, 1974.

....

CHAPTER 14

GERMAINE DE STAËL'S *CORINNE, OR ITALY* AND THE EARLY USAGE OF IMPROVISATION IN ENGLISH

....

ERIK SIMPSON

ALTHOUGH practices of spontaneous composition and performance have existed for millennia, variants of the word *improvisation* entered English usage only in the eighteenth century, and *improvisation* itself only in the nineteenth.[1] Today we use *improvisation* broadly. One can "improvise" anything from a trumpet solo to a salad dressing. Literary critics have used *improvisation* to describe medieval practices or, in the case of Stephen Greenblatt's analysis of "Improvisation and Power," the villainy of Shakespeare's Iago in *Othello*. Greenblatt writes of *improvisation* as "the ability to both capitalize on the unforeseen and transform given materials into one's own scenario."[2] P. N. Furbank and W. R. Owens, on the other hand, use the term to describe the stylistic practices of Daniel Defoe: "Defoe, we feel, when he embarked upon this sentence, had only a vague idea how it would end. . . . [T]o write in this way, which we may call "improvisatory," is quite common, and—as in this case—does not at all imply that the product will have less form and "architecture" than a more premeditated style."[3]

These formulations and many others demonstrate the utility of ahistorical uses of *improvisation* in describing a continuity of spontaneous, anti-teleological practices across historical periods. We can, however, gain other kinds of insights by recontextualizing improvisation as readers and writers in English first encountered it by that name. The *Oxford English Dictionary* entries related to improvisation provide a starting point for analyzing the emergence of its terminology: in English, references to improvisers begin to appear in the middle to late eighteenth century, while noun forms such as *improvisation* and verb forms such as *improvise* appear rarely, at most, until the 1820s or later.[4] For readers and speakers of English at the time, the emergence of these terms represented a conceptual as well as a rhetorical change. The language of improvisation did not enter English as a simple synonym for earlier terminology, such as that of extempore composition. Rather, it described a specific practice in Italy, one routinely characterized as impossible to replicate in Britain.

Isaac D'Israeli set his 1803 poem *The Carder and the Carrier* in "amorous Florence, that propitious clime / Where Love is constant tho' he talks in rhyme."[5] His footnote describes those lines as "[a]lluding to the numerous Improvisatori, the Minstrels of modern Italy."[6] In 1803, when D'Israeli needed to explain "improvisatori" for an English-speaking audience, he chose the ready means of equating *improvvisatori* with the already-famous figure of the minstrel.[7] The footnote qualifies the analogy in two ways: these minstrels are modern and Italian. As such, *improvvisatori* stand in opposition to the self-consciously archaic Britishness of their counterparts in, for instance, Walter Scott's *Minstrelsy of the Scottish Border* (1802–03), as well as other works that present minstrelsy as a dead or dying practice. D'Israeli's rhetoric epitomizes the development of literary representations of *improvvisatori* and *improvvisatrici* that would flourish in the first decades of the nineteenth century, as an increasing number of writers used the modern Italian figures to rewrite and revise the conventions of British minstrelsy.

As D'Israeli's effort to explain the nature of "improvisatori" implies, *improvisation* had a much shorter history in English than did *minstrelsy*. Although the musical term *ex improviso* (or, later, *ex improvviso*) had appeared occasionally, *improvisation* as such had no discernible English-language existence before the middle of the eighteenth century. As Caroline Gonda has noted, the *OED* places the first use of any English variant in 1765 with Smollett writing of an "improvisatore" as "one of the greatest curiosities you meet with in Italy."[8] Smollett's line captures the flavor of the great majority of eighteenth-century references to *improvvisatori*. Such references locate *improvvisatori* in Italy and present them as "curiosities," as things that must be explained to an English audience. And the performers were generally represented as men. The *OED* citation of pre-1800 variants of "improvisation," in fact, links improvisation with male or ungendered poets in Italy. The feminine *improv(v)isatrice* does not appear until 1804, and then only parenthetically as a synonym for *poetess*.[9]

In 1807 came a turning point: the publication in French and translation into English of Germaine de Staël's novel *Corinne, or Italy. Corinne* presented to British readers a familiar image of a minstrel, a poet performing verses to the accompaniment of a harp or lyre. The plot of *Corinne* relies on British representations of bards and minstrels and their familiarity to a pan-European audience; the eponymous Corinne knows "Ossian" and old Scottish songs, which she performs to win the reluctant heart of Oswald, Lord Nelvil. However, Staël also departs dramatically from the conventions of British minstrel writing. Her novel's characters and its critics both notice the oddity, to British eyes, of a performing woman. That innovation has attracted much modern critical attention to what Ellen Moers calls "the myth of Corinne" and "the fantasy of the performing heroine."[10] But Corinne also differs from her British counterparts in her compositional method: she improvises, while they recite pre-existing works. As Gonda has noted, *Corinne* "did more than any other work to popularize the idea of the improvisatore or improvisatrice," and it did so in a way that gave Britain its first major theory of improvisation.[11] The novel imagines improvisation not only as a compositional method but also as a means of conceiving the histories of people and nations. As important as Staël's work was for women writers, it also initiated a related but broader "myth of Corinne" in English-language writing, that of improvisation itself.

Corinne's debut in England illustrates how new the idea of improvisation remained to British readers in 1807. Writing in French and comfortable with the Italian terms for improvisation, Staël deployed terminology that seems to have baffled her 1807 translators. In the novel's French, Corinne is an "improvisatrice," she possesses the "talent d'improviser," and her poem at the Roman Capitol is an "Improvisation."[12] These words and phrases, seemingly simple to translate into their English equivalents, instead reveal the lack of a modern vocabulary of improvisation. D. Lawler's translation describes "Corinna" (as both 1807 English versions call her) as an "improvisatrix," with a note promising to explain the term later.[13] The sole vaguely relevant note, however, suggests only further frustration. Lawler later translates Corinne's "talent d'improviser" as "her talent for extempore poetry" with a footnote that reads, "[f]or that particular species of poetry here alluded to, called, in Italian, *Improvisatore*, the translator can find no English denomination."[14]

The other 1807 translation, by two anonymous translators, lacks Lawler's boldness of coinage. There, Corinna is not an improvisatrix but simply a "composer of extempore rhymes."[15] The translators explain the problem in a note, using an odd variant of *improvvisatore*: "The *improvvisitore*, or art of composing extempore verses, is an accomplishment peculiar to the Italians."[16] Even a generation later, the 1833 Isabel Hill translation adopts a more modern vocabulary for improvisation but only in some cases. Corinne's improvisation at the Roman Capitol is a "chant," and although her gift is called one of "improvisation," it also takes other names more typical in older works, such as "faculty of extemporising."[17] *Corinne*'s wide circulation in both French and English thus created a paradoxical effect. Its French text gave British readers a new theory of improvisation, with its modern vocabulary largely visible in direct cognates. At the same time, its English translations, especially those of 1807, reveal how little that same British audience had previously understood of improvisation.

The lack of significant precedent in English allowed *Corinne* to establish the popular connotations of Italian improvisation, which it presented as a practice with artistic and political implications. Corinne's improvisation at the Capitol, much cited as an inspirational presentation of public female genius, also demonstrated the ideological work improvisation could do. Asked to improvise on the glory of Italy, Corinne slowly builds a triumphant historical narrative, to the delight of her Italian audience. Then Corinne sees Oswald and responds to his emotions: "Divining the thoughts going through his mind, she was impelled to meet his need by talking of happiness with less certainty."[18] Here the teleology of the poem breaks down, and Corinne improvises, changing the direction of her narrative to accommodate Oswald's reaction, introducing a note of northern melancholy and earning his applause.

By altering a narrative of Italy's past, Corinne suggestively connects her content and her process: as an improviser, she can rhetorically change the course of history if necessary. At a time when revolution, reform, and reaction dominated European thought, a new theory of historical flexibility could reverberate far beyond the steps of the Capitol. (Staël herself had earlier asked, "who can live, who can write at the present moment, without feeling and reflecting upon the revolution of France?")[19] *Corinne* presents improvisation as a political path between stasis and revolution, as an artistic theory of post-Terror moderate liberalism. As a model of innovation bounded by context, Staël's improvisation carved out space between a reactionary emphasis on the authority of previous generations on the one hand, and Painite optimism that any generation could break free from that legacy on the other.

Minstrel writers such as Thomas Percy and Walter Scott emphasized the weight of British tradition, creating a retrospective national culture through the collection and repetition of carefully shaped cultural materials. Staël's presentation of improvisation, on the contrary, emphasized the contingencies of poetic creation, the way that the plan of a work—or a nation—could change as it was created. But this freedom has limits. The improviser's skill consists of responding continuously to new events, maintaining flexibility within the boundaries established by a developing performance. Napoleonic autocracy lacks conversational interchange, an aspect of improvisation Corinne emphasizes in describing rural improvisers as using "language full of life that solitary thought could not have brought into being."[20]

The improviser cannot break cleanly with her own history, as revolutionary nations strive to do. *Corinne*'s narrator emphasizes repeatedly the constraints of personal and political history: "*We are surrounded by the remains of history*, said Cicero. If he said so then, what do we say now!"[21] Italy's immediate past as the object of imperial ambitions, culminating in Napoleon's 1805 coronation as King of Italy, provided an apt example of a nation's inability to control its destiny.[22] At the microcosmic level, the novel enacts a similar tension, vacillating between constructions of irresistible fate and other hints that undermine that inevitability. Corinne, for instance, experiences her doomed relationship with Oswald as foreshadowed by the heavens: "I have always known the sky to look paternal or angry, and I tell you, Oswald, tonight it condemned our love."[23] If we need a further suggestion that these are star-crossed lovers, Corinne provides it later by acting the part of Juliet while Oswald watches. But the narrator also assumes paradoxically that "destiny" is not destined at all but contingent: "Had she acted upon this impulse, what a different destiny she and Oswald would have known!"[24] A destiny Corinne can change is no destiny at all, but the tension between fate and choice fits well into the model of improvisation Staël establishes. The project of improvisation is to acknowledge the constraints of history, constraints so strong they can feel like inexorable fate, and to produce from that context a new direction.

These principles applied with special force to Italian politics at the time of *Corinne*'s publication. France had recently taken control of most of Italy when Staël wrote *Corinne*; mention of the French victory is pointedly omitted from the novel, but readers could hardly fail to consider the novel's commentary on Italy's history in light of the Napoleonic takeover. For Italy as for Corinne, improvisation allows a measure of freedom and flexibility. *Corinne* fully acknowledges that flexibility in the heroine's ability to alter her history of Italy to suit the needs of her audience. At the same time, the novel moves beyond its predecessors, as well as many of its successors, by recognizing the constraints of improvisation, the way that it constantly creates new contexts that demand attention and limit the artist's options. Italy can alter itself but must still be Italy; Oswald can change but must remain English; Corinne can love an Englishman but cannot finally leave Italy; Napoleon (as Staël believed but left unstated in the novel) can conquer and reform, but his empire cannot integrate the people he controls. For Staël, these personal and political circumstances call for improvisation, a concept she played a large role in defining for English-language readers, as a mode of creative production in politics as well as art.

NOTES

1. This chapter draws heavily on a longer version of this argument in my *Literary Minstrelsy, 1770–1830: Minstrels and Improvisers in British, Irish, and American Literature* (Houndmills: Palgrave Macmillan, 2008).
2. Stephen J. Greenblatt, "Improvisation and Power," in *Literature and Society: Selected Papers from the English Institute, 1978*, ed. Edward Said (Baltimore: Johns Hopkins University Press, 1980), 60.
3. P. N. Furbank and W. R. Owens, "Defoe and the 'Improvisatory' Sentence," *English Studies* 67, no. 2 (April 1986): 160.
4. The *OED* gives four verb forms, all first cited between 1825 and 1835: "improvise," "improvisate," "improvisatorize," and "improviso." ("Improviso" predated this, but only as an adjective, as in Warton's usage.) At least some of these forms may have emerged before 1825, but the *OED* illustrates at least that many forms were simultaneously current after 1825, and the surviving modern verb "improvise" is the one that shows least evidence of Italian roots, having dropped both the -o of *improviso* and the -at* or -ator* of *improvvisatore*. "Improvisation," the noun, appeared relatively early (1786)—though I argue in this chapter that *Corinne*'s translations suggest its use was limited—as did the adjective "improviso." "Improvizer," referring to an improvisatory artist not necessarily Italian, first appeared in 1829 (*Oxford English Dictionary*, 2nd ed., v. "improvise," v. "improvisate," v. "improvisatorize," v. and adj. "improviso," n. "improvisation," n. "improviser," [respectively] http://www.oed.com:80/Entry/92882, http://www.oed.com:80/Entry/92871, http://www.oed.com:80/Entry/92878, http://www.oed.com:80/Entry/92887, http://www.oed.com:80/Entry/92872, http://www.oed.com:80/Entry/92885, [accessed May 31, 2011]).
5. Isaac D'Israeli, "The Carder and the Carrier," in *Narrative Poems* (London: John Murray, 1803), 1–2.
6. Ibid., 1.
7. Throughout, I will use the Romantic-era Italian spellings of *improvvisator(e/i)* and *improvvisatric(e/i)*. English-language writers of the time used many variations of those spellings, often omitting the second "v" (as in many of my examples here) and sometimes using "s" to form plurals.
8. *Oxford English Dictionary*, 2nd ed., n. "improvisatore | improvvisatore," http://www.oed.com:80/Entry/92876 (accessed May 31, 2011). The reference occurs in *Travels through France and Italy*, published in the following year. Caroline Gonda provides an excellent analysis of *OED* citations for variants of improvisation and some early British commentary

on the subject ("The Rise and Fall of the Improvisatore, 1753–1845," *Romanticism* 6, no. 2 [November 2000]: 195–210).

9. The first *OED* citation of improv(v)isatrice refers to "An honorary name given to the poetess (improvisatrice) D. Maria Maddalena Morelli Fernandez," from Matilda Betham's *Biographical Dictionary of the Celebrated Women of Every Age and Country* (*Oxford English Dictionary*, 2nd ed., n. "improvisatrice | improvvisatrice," http://www.oed.com:80/Entry/92880 [accessed May 31, 2011]). However, there was at least one eighteenth-century usage: Hester Lynch Piozzi uses the term in her 1789 *Observations and Reflections Made in the Course of a Journey through France, Italy, and Germany* (London: A. Strahan and T. Cadell, 1789), I.321.

10. Ellen Moers, *Literary Women* (1967; repr., New York: Oxford University Press, 1985), 174.

11. Gonda, "The Rise and Fall of the Improvisatore," 198. When I refer to "improvisation" in Romantic-era writing, I mean the practice of Italian *improvvisatori* and *improvvisatrici* signified by Staël's French word *improvisation*, which was generally not yet translatable into English, as I will show.

12. Germaine de Staël, *Corinne ou L'Italie* (London: M. Peltier, 1807), I.50, I.65, and I.73.

13. Germaine de Staël, *Corinna; or, Italy*, trans. D. Lawler (London: Corri, 1807), I.54.

14. Staël, *Corinne*, trans. Lawler, I.69.

15. Germaine de Staël, *Corinna; or, Italy*, trans. anonymous (London: Samuel Tipper, 1807), I.51–2. Lawler's preface explains that the slightly earlier anonymous translation was produced by two men (Staël, *Corinne*, trans. Lawler, iv).

16. Staël, *Corinne*, trans. anonymous, I.52. This first translation does try to work improvisation into the text in one odd usage, as the Prince "expatiate[s] on her [Corinna's] talent for extempore effusions, a talent which resembled, in nothing, the improvisatorè, as expressed in Italy" (Staël, *Corinne*, trans. anonymous, I.67).

17. Germaine de Staël, *Corinne; Or, Italy*, trans. Isabel Hill (London: Richard Bentley, 1833), 25, 43, and 43. The poet Letitia Elizabeth Landon translated the verse in the Hill edition.

18. Germaine de Staël, *Corinne, or Italy*, ed. and trans. Avriel Goldberger (New Brunswick: Rutgers University Press, 1977), 30.

19. Germaine de Staël, *A Treatise on the Influence of the Passions, upon the Happiness of Individuals and of Nations . . . from the French of the Baroness Stael [sic] de Holstein* (London: George Cawthorn, 1798), 31.

20. Staël, *Corinne*, trans. Goldberger, 45.

21. Ibid., 85.

22. Staël's political theory in *Considérations sur les principaux événements de la Révolution française* illustrates her effort to find a theory of political moderation in more direct terms. There she endorses "the principle of heredity in a monarchy" but emphasizes that legitimacy is "absolutely inseparable from constitutional limitations" and asks, "what human being with common sense can pretend that a change in customs and ideas should not result in a change in political institutions?" (in *Madame de Staël on Politics, Literature, and National Character*, trans. Monroe Berger [London: Sidgwick and Jackson, 1964], 94–96).

23. Staël, *Corinne*, trans. Goldberger, 196.

24. Ibid., 355.

BIBLIOGRAPHY

D'Israeli, Isaac. "The Carder and the Carrier." In *Narrative Poems*, 1–2. London: John Murray, 1803.

Furbank, P. N., and W. R. Owens. "Defoe and the 'Improvisatory' Sentence," *English Studies* 67, no. 2 (April 1986): 157–166.

Gonda, Caroline. "The Rise and Fall of the Improvisatore, 1753–1845," *Romanticism* 6, no. 2 (November 2000): 195–210.

Greenblatt, Stephen J. "Improvisation and Power." In *Literature and Society: Selected Papers from the English Institute, 1978*, edited by Edward Said, 57–99. Baltimore: Johns Hopkins University Press, 1980.

Moers, Ellen. *Literary Women*. New York: Oxford University Press, 1985. Originally published in 1967.

Piozzi, Hester Lynch. *Observations and Reflections Made in the Course of a Journey through France, Italy, and Germany*. London: A. Strahan and T. Cadell, 1789.

Simpson, Erik. *Literary Minstrelsy, 1770–1830: Minstrels and Improvisers in British, Irish, and American Literature*. Houndmills: Palgrave Macmillan, 2008.

de Staël, Germaine. *Corinna; or, Italy*, translated by anonymous. London: Samuel Tipper, 1807.

de Staël, Germaine. *Corinna; or, Italy*, translated by D. Lawler. London: Corri, 1807.

de Staël, Germaine. *Corinne ou L'Italie*. London: M. Peltier, 1807.

de Staël, Germaine. *Corinne; Or, Italy*, translated by Isabel Hill (London: Richard Bentley, 1833).

de Staël, Germaine. *Corinne, or Italy*, edited and translated by Avriel Goldberger. New Brunswick: Rutgers University Press, 1977.

de Staël, Germaine. *Madame de Staël on Politics, Literature, and National Character*, translated by Monroe Berger. London: Sidgwick and Jackson, 1964.

de Staël, Germaine. *A Treatise on the Influence of the Passions, upon the Happiness of Individuals and of Nations . . . from the French of the Baroness Stael [sic] de Holstein*. London: George Cawthorn, 1798.

CHAPTER 15

IMPROVISATION, TIME, AND OPPORTUNITY IN THE RHETORICAL TRADITION

GLYN P. NORTON

THE thought that there exist in the written text moments so evanescent, so expressively charged that they call into question their own utterability presented the Renaissance, in general, and Renaissance Italy and France, in particular, with a challenge of disquieting proportions. For once one accepts the premise that there are events so structurally discrete as to lie outside the recoverable procedures of composition, one glimpses not only the opaque limits of writing, but also the potential demolition of rhetoric's grandly confident superstructure. At the crux of such events is the ancient topic of improvisation.

The challenge embedded in this topic formed a cluster of imponderables. The Greek and Roman worlds, while shaping the architecture of these imponderables, left to later generations the necessity of resuming the dialogue, of assimilating a legacy harking back to the earliest traditions of speech and writing. As a consequence, even in those intensely numinous moments when the Renaissance text purports to craft itself out of spontaneity (one thinks, for example, of Erasmus's *Praise of Folly* and its gestation on horseback), it seems frequently compelled to draw the reader away from such immediacy by calling attention to its own location within the linkage of historical tradition.

A striking example of this process occurs in Book I of Castiglione's *The Courtier* (1528). Having been selected by Signora Emilia to open the inquiry into perfect courtiership, Count Ludovico da Canossa declares that since the hour is late and not having given the matter any thought, he will now be permitted to say without risk of censure all that floods into his mouth ("[M]i sarà licito dir senza biasimo tutte le cose che prima mi verranno alla bocca."[1] Well into his ostensibly impromptu remarks, however, the Count suddenly refocuses the issue. He recalls having read that certain of the most outstanding ancient orators did their best to make everyone believe they were ignorant of literature. To accomplish this, they made their speeches appear as though they had been composed very simply and according to the promptings of nature and truth rather than toil and art; for if the people had been aware of their skills, they would have been worried about being fooled (Castiglione 1981, 60).

Apart from the telling suggestion that impromptu or improvised speech may not always be what it seems, Castiglione appears to be reminding us here that the Count's off-the-cuff performance is steeped in an ancient rhetorical tradition. A practice fully suited to the specificity of the moment—a postprandial dialogue generated spontaneously in an unfolding present—is actually rooted in a forensic past. The layers of that past, left vague in the above text, were given a more solid frame of reference earlier on by Erasmus in the *De copia* (1512), where extemporaneity and copious discourse are seen to be closely aligned.[2] Early in his work, Erasmus traces his topic to a long literary tradition, winding back through Quintilian to the early Sophists.[3] In other words, a topic deeply relevant to the way Renaissance man revitalizes his discourse traces its ancestry to two chronologically separate moments in the classical past. In the one, Sophist and Hellenic, the emphasis was oral and, as Erasmus correctly points out, left few written traces; in the other, rhetorical and Roman, speech was reformulated in a structured (and extant) program of writing and composition.

What Castiglione's text demonstrates so convincingly is that it is difficult to raise the issue of improvisation and of speech emitted on the spur of the moment ("sùbito uscita") without becoming entangled in the wider problematics of speech and writing. More remarkable, however, in the case of Castiglione's work, is the way Count Ludovico's exploratory preliminaries in Book I will find themselves caught up in the actual performance of improvisation in the concluding speech on divine love by Pietro Bembo in Book IV. Here the rhetorical performance marks its own mortality (the ultimate collapse of the speech), conterminous with the dissolution of the speaker's articulating self. Utterance signals its own end, leaving the audience with a sense of the ravishing disjuncture of the speaker with himself ("astratto e fuor di sé," 452). Bembo's off-the-cuff rapture is, for the philosopher Kenneth Burke, the paradigm of "pure persuasion," a concept with latent ties to improvisation and its Latin root, *improvisus* ("unexpected", "sudden").[4] The experience, as we shall see, has everything to do with notions of time, ripened and creative, and with opportunity, challenging and peremptory.

It is apparent early on in sophistic thought that the harmonizing of spoken and written discourse, developed by Castiglione in the context of improvisation, had nothing in common with the formal solemnity of the Urbino court. In early Greek declamation, the emphasis, it appears, was on informality.[5] Actual declamations were frequently preceded by the *dialexis*, an informal preliminary talk, conversational in tone, delivered sitting down, and probably quiet in manner.[6] Following the *dialexis*, the sophist, in keeping with a tradition going back to Gorgias, would then invite the audience to suggest topics around which he would craft, on the spot, his main speech. The improvised results, as D. A. Russell points out, were probably not always up to the mark. Yet, ancient accounts also tell of speakers fabled for their fluency and their ability to improvise. One such case is the Syrian, Isaeus, to whom Juvenal attributes lively intelligence, shameless audacity, and prompt, torrential speech.[7] But it is the rather more expansive account of

Quintilian's pupil, Pliny, in a letter to Nepos, which serves not only to capture the physical act of sophist improvisation, but more significantly for the present essay, to articulate that event in a Latin discourse which the Renaissance would adopt wholesale, using it to explore the contours of extemporaneity.

Pliny's description of Isaeus presents, it would appear, the very ritual of a sophist performance.[8] Nothing, we are told, can approach Isaeus's facility (*facultas*), abundance (*copia*), and richness (*ubertas*). He speaks always extemporaneously, but as though having written it down long beforehand ("dicit semper ex tempore, sed tanquam diu scripserit"). His preliminary speeches (viz. *dialexis*) are careful, unadorned, charming, occasionally dignified and elevated. He calls for several topics of discussion, asking his audience to make the selection; he gets up, arranges his clothing, and begins: "Immediately, all the resources of eloquence are in his grasp at the same time, the subtleties of thought rush upon him ['sensus reconditi occursant']. . . . How much reading, how much writing gleams forth from his improvisations ['in subitis']. . . . His memory is incredible and he is able to repeat what he has said extemporaneously ['ex tempore'] without altering a word. He attains so much *hexis* [ἕξις] through application ['studio'] and practice ['exercitatione']."[9]

When Nepos read this portrait, he undoubtedly must have formed in his mind a rather vivid image of the legendary Isaeus. The emphasis on simultaneity (*statim, pariter*), the force of thought unbridled, and the radiance of language all combine to produce a quality which Pliny deliberately calls by its Greek rather than Latin name: *hexis* [ἕξις]. The entire phrase, "Ad tantam 'hexin' studio et exercitatione pervenit," thus depicts a cultural synthesis moving from the Latin values of *studium* and *exercitatio* toward the ultimate dissolution of those values in Hellenic dexterity ("hexin"). Viewed another way, one could say that Pliny's account of sophist performance superposes a restraining Latin cultural frame on the mantic bursts of Hellenic fluency. What might otherwise seem like a spontaneous stunt actually emerges as the byproduct of thought-directed effort and concentration.

To understand how improvisation will affect modes of written performance in later times it is useful to examine certain sophistic texts. In his *Peri sophiston*, Alcidamas (contemporary of Plato and a student of the ancient rhetorician, Gorgias) not only sustains explicitly the principles of sophist performance just outlined, but also situates improvisation in a philosophical code to be later recorded in Renaissance thought. In sections 27–28, the author takes an uncompromising stand against written speeches in favor of what we have called their oral, improvised counterpart:

> And to my way of looking at it written speeches do not deserve even to be called speeches, but as it were forms [*eidola*], and figures [*schemata*] and imitations [*mimemata*] of speeches. . . . The written speech undeviating from one ordered posture, when looked at in a book rouses admiration, but since it is unmoved by opportunity [*kairos*], it affords no benefit to its possession. . . . The speech spoken straight from the mind on the spur of the moment [*parautika*] is living and has a soul and follows circumstances and is like real bodies, but the written one, in nature like the image of a speech, is doomed to inanition [that is, it lacks *energeias* or the capacity to act].[10]

So conceived, nothing can be more remote from the medium of writing than oral speech. All the features of Alcidamas's text that describe either tectonic or iconic relationships (forms, figures, imitations, bronze statues, stone images, ordered posture, and the like) align themselves squarely with the written word. Oral speeches, on the other hand, throw up no replicable surfaces, their authenticity determined largely by their immunity to permanence and their crafting of another dynamic dimension (*energeias*). Words emitted "straightaway" (*parautika*) from the mind are circumscribed within a zone of being that is temporally compressed, shaped by the circumstantial, the opportune (*kairos*). No such versatility prevails in writing. Graven forms and features are rigidly broadcast to an audience immobilized outside time, deprived of opportunity and unengaged with circumstance.

For the sophist readers of Alcidamas, it would have been difficult to dismiss as trivial the antinomies of this text. It is not simply that extemporaneous speech harbors a reality superior to its written counterpart. The special resonance of this text relates to the way Alcidamas tailors his justification of improvisation to one of the great philosophical postulates of ancient thought, the notion of *kairos* [opportune time]. The sophist's argument against written speeches was founded on the belief that *kairos* can not be known by any act which attempts to stabilize it, to give it permanence, because, by definition, it participates in the constant eradication of that which has preceded it. And writing thrives on the hubris of its own indelibility. If, therefore, perfect improvisation refers to an utterance perfectly in harmony with these self-eradicating contexts, then one can readily anticipate the urgency with which other traditions would try to redraw the graph, allowing writing to mime its spontaneous prelapsarian ancestry. Roman rhetoric would contribute radically to this reappraisal.

The rhetorical agenda for improvisation is made accessible to the Renaissance through two principal Latin channels: the works of Cicero and Quintilian. Of the two authors, Quintilian, as we shall see, takes a wider view of the problem, promoting its status in a total plan of eloquence and sorting through the richly complex environment from which it has been synthesized. Cicero, on the other hand, fails to build the topic into the broad superstructure of his rhetorical program. His approval is more restrained, less concerned with the underlying torsion between premeditated discourse and spontaneity or, for that matter, with the technical apparatus of improvised speech. This leads to a series of statements which, taken individually, address themselves to particular nuances of the topic while doing little to advance its place and function in the rhetorical system. Nonetheless, they are essential to a full understanding of the internal dialogue that emerges between master and disciple.

Where Cicero departs from his disciple Quintilian is in his restriction of the phrase *ex tempore* to the circumstances in which eloquence occurs. Never does he adopt this term as a descriptor of authentic speech or eloquence. This is not yet the *ex tempore dicendi facultas* that will signal the culminating sections of Quintilian's *Institutio oratoria*. Cicero's concerns are not with extemporaneity as a mode of performance but as a way of describing how rhetoricians tap into the resources of time: "There are therefore things,"

Cicero continues, "which one must judge according to time [*ex tempore*] and intention [*ex consilio*], and not according to their own nature: in all cases of this type, one must assess what time requires, and what is appropriate to the persons; it is not the thing itself that must be considered, but the motives, the performer, the time and the duration."[11]

Significantly, when Cicero does address the rhetorical practice of extemporaneity, he chooses not to extend the range of application of the phrase *ex tempore*, referring instead to speech that is *subita* or *fortuita*. In other words, it is the eruptive, random quality of the extemporal utterance rather than its attachment to certain environmental conditions that defines its relationship to eloquence. At *De oratore*: 149–153, Crassus, pressed for his opinion of the categories of rhetorical training or *exercitatio*, criticizes the use of oral exercises that serve only to whip up the "rate of utterance" (*linguae celeritas*) and "flood of verbiage" (*verborum frequentia*). Among the hierarchy of exercises, Crassus points out, none is more esteemed than the practice of writing: "For if an extempore and casual speech [*subita et fortuita oratio*] is easily beaten by one prepared and thought-out, this latter in turn will assuredly be surpassed by what has been written with care and diligence [*assidua ac diligens scriptura*]."[12] *Exercitatio* is thus broken into an ascending format, beginning at the lowest level with *subita oratio* and advancing, through *cogitatio*, to preeminent *scriptura*.

Intimately entwined in this process is the ability of the mind to draw from the store of commonplaces [the *loci*], which are the resources through which writing bodies forth on the page. "The truth is," Cicero continues, "that all the commonplaces [*loci*] . . . appear [*se ostendere*] and rush forward [*occurrere*] as we are searching out and surveying the matter with all our natural acuteness: and all the thoughts and expressions that are the most brilliant in their several kinds, must needs flow up in succession [*subeant et succedant*] to the point of our pen."[13] In Cicero's text, writing becomes the controlling mechanism of spontaneity.

Ultimately, it becomes apparent that Cicero is adducing two levels of presence: writing as the sole authenticating structure of discourse, and improvisation as a kind of *simulacrum* of the event, a trace image given off by a higher medium of articulation. In another, perhaps more vital sense, we are witnessing here the transcendent reply of the Ciceronian model to its early Sophist predecessors. Cicero, it is clear, has inverted Alcidamas's refraction of utterance in such a way as to shift the onus of iconic inferiority away from written speeches (conceived earlier on as *eidola*, *schemata*, and *mimemata*) onto the hitherto "real" extemporal bodies of voice. Improvisation has suffered a profound reversal of incarnation, its transcription immobilized, as it were, by the living flesh of the text.

From the preceding discussion, it is safe to say that Cicero left his disciple, Quintilian, a rather fragile peg on which to hang a comprehensive blueprint for improvisation. The texts from the *De oratore* on *subita oratio* would play simply no role in the allusive throw-backs contained in Book X: 7 of the *Institutio oratoria*. In his authoritative commentary on Book X, William Peterson examines the distinctive patterns of language separating Quintilian from Cicero. Among the words "yet not to be found in the republican period," Peterson includes the modifier *extemporalis*, as in *extemporalis oratio* for which Cicero would have written *subita et fortuita oratio*.[14] Accordingly, Quintilian's chapter on the topic not only bears the title "How to acquire and maintain the *extemporalis facilitas*," but also refers repeatedly to the adjective and its corresponding verbal modifier, *ex tempore*, as in *ex tempore dicendi facultas*. In other words, Quintilian would appear to be subjecting the notion of improvisation to a semantic stress all but lacking in Ciceronian language, where the adjectives *subita* and *fortuita* were seen to promote factors of randomness with little or no regard to how the improviser processes time. *Extemporalis*, on the other hand, points to a conceptual reform in which time is of the essence. Through this crucial lexical shift beyond the constraints of Ciceronian terminology, Quintilian embarks on a new probe of his topic, one that interrogates the affected rhetorical tastes of his day, of Silver Latinity and empire, in order to reconnect him with the faded yet replenishable fluency of republic together with the Hellenic past.[15] He is about to attempt the systematic analysis of a practice that, by the practitioner's own enclosure within the event, rebuffs any clarifying scheme or strategy. His decision to transform radically the indentifying terminology along more temporal lines is only the most visible step in this reappraisal.[16]

A more crucial interrogation of the Ciceronian model occurs in Quintilian's overall structural design. It is now writing, constrained within a fixed spatial and temporal frame, that sets itself qualitatively apart from its companions: "For we can write neither everywhere nor always whereas in premeditation time [*tempus*] and place [*locus*] are abundantly available."[17] Quintilian is explicitly aware that principles of time (*tempus*) are, in part, deeply rooted in the Greek notion of *kairos*.[18] After all, *kairos* and its derivatives already enjoy a position of prominence in Alcidamas's text on improvised speech, where they seem to describe an inspirational process arising from unexpected crises [*kairoi*] and empowering "a mind truly godlike."[19] Through its corresponding Latin forms, *occasio, opportunitas,* and *tempus, kairos* plays a fundamental role in determining how Quintilian's orator exploits the extrinsic conditions of eloquence. As such, it is a composite of two distinct Greek traditions, the one Aristotelian, the other Longinian. The Aristotelian view, conferring on *kairos* an ethical intensity, proposes that "the end of an action" is relative to its circumstances (*kairos*).[20] Unlike the Stoic commitment to fixed values, where the emphasis is on behavior that stands fast and endures, Aristotelian *kairos* subverts the morally absolute and substitutes, in its place, a situational ethics motivated by assertions that temporize our exposure to things.[21] It is no overstatement to assert that *kairos* embraces the full gamut of these attitudes and responses, leading Jean Cousin to infer, like Burke, the investment of rhetorical motives in a shifting, transitory ethics with roots in Aristotle.

Beyond these ethical nuances, however, there also exists for Quintilian a dimension to *kairos* that seems to place improvisation within the same ecstatic Longinian environment we have already glimpsed in Pietro Bembo's off-the-cuff meditation on divine love in *The courtier*. The ancient merger of *kairos* with *deus*, of opportunity with divinity, highlighted in the *Institutio oratoria*, will be an association no less compelling for Renaissance writers like Erasmus.[22] Thus, if early notions of improvisation, as we have seen, tell us something essential about how eloquence processes *kairos*, then it would seem highly likely that further refinements of the topic, such as those in Quintilian, will construct a new linkage between the extemporaneous, the kairotic, and the divine. In fact, hints at such linkage have emerged in modern Quintilian scholarship. In broader terms, the power of elation that seems woven into the fabric of Quintilian's chapter on improvisation would appear to have its roots in Platonic philosophy, reminding us that Plato himself was fully cognizant of the practice of *autoschediazein* ("to act or speak offhand").[23]

The ability of the orator to utter what is temporally imminent (*kairos*)—to improvise—is closely affiliated to another key Hellenic concept developed in the chapter on extemporaneity: ἕξις [*hexis*]. Peterson describes *hexis* as "the fixed tendency that results from repeated acts."[24] Its placement in the opening sentences of Book X, where it is juxtaposed with the Latin synonym *firma facilitas* ("assured facility"), mark it as a term that is quite literally pivotal, falling as it does at the close of the preceding nine chapters on a theory of eloquence and at the entry into performance and fluency.

What is increasingly apparent is the fact that *hexis* shares certain crucial interests in common with that other element in the extemporal process, *kairos*. Just as *kairos*, in the Aristotelian tradition, defines how we respond ethically to contingent events, so *hexis* retains a similar ethical value by showing how what we do, rather than paste itself to a kind of tensile, modular ethics recalling Stoic *firmitas*, is conditioned largely by our behavioral suppleness. The "fixed tendency" emerging from "repeated acts" is, thus, not about allegiance to ingrained habits, but rather about our readiness to repudiate the habitual, to break with routine—to improvise. Applied to the sphere of aesthetics, these concepts are no less powerful. Where Longinian *kairos* describes the empathetic harmony between creator, creation, and audience, brought into play by a certain cogitative and fictive stimulus, *hexis* is no less a creature of our impressions. It determines how art can *seem* not to be easy, how our rehearsal of the rhetorical script *seems* to place us in a position to make each performance an expendable commodity.

Hexis thus stands out amidst Quintilian's abundant Greek terminology for its unusually high lexical profile. Unlike the tendency of most Greek terms in the *Institutio oratoria* to refer to specific technical effects and processes subsumed within the encompassing Latin notion of *cogitatio*, *hexis* has no such allegiance. The fact that it is not methodologically committed, rather than mark it for debilitation, sets it apart from the apparatus of eloquence. Having no fixed venue on the rhetorical map, it nonetheless retains its own onomastic stability, singled out as "something which the Greeks call *hexis*" ["quae apud Graecos ἕξις nominatur"].

No less than *hexis*, the *ex tempore dicendi facultas* has all the immediacy of a process currently at work in the language, but at the same time, is tied to an almost sacerdotal recognition that improvisers belong to a kind of priesthood whose gifts are relayed down through time from generation to generation. Alluding to such continuity, Quintilian points out that "many have acquired the gift of improvisation not merely in prose, but in verse as well, as, for example, Antipater of Sidon and Licinius Archias . . . , not to mention the fact that there are many, even in our own day, who have done this and are still doing it" (X, vii, 19). And as we have already seen in Erasmus, Quintilian himself will eventually take his own place in this long communion, the scripted Roman norm moving to impose itself on the legendary hearsay of the Hellenic past.

With the adoption of *hexis* as a central Hellenic link to improvisation, the lexical texture of the work changes, the orator defined by his relationship to the contingent and the unforeseen. The stable, secure spaces of the *domus* where meditation occurs are thrown back to reveal a navigator's world of "the most serious emergencies" ("prae-sentissima . . . pericula") and of storm-tossed ships risking destruction in the swell that pushes them into and, perhaps, against the harbor (X, vii, 1). This place of peril is none other than the setting of forensic oratory. In this tumultuous environment, the orator faces alone "the countless sudden necessities" ("innumerabiles subitae necessitates"), which act to doom all prospects of memory, premeditation, and "silent, secluded study" (X, vii, 2).[25] The sudden issues ("casus") refuse to be ignored, leaving the orator to tear up his written arguments and, once more, play the navigator in a perilous sea: "For often the expected arguments to which we have written a reply fail us and the whole aspect of the case undergoes a sudden change; consequently the variation to which cases are liable makes it as necessary for us to change our methods as it is for a pilot to change his course before the oncoming storm. Again, what use are much writing, assiduous reading and long years of study, if the difficulty is to remain as great as it was in the beginning?" (X, vii, 3–4). Easily the most ambiguous moment in Quintilian's entire work, his text on extemporaneity seems calculated to reflect concentric, yet adversarial orbits, the one cognitive, quantifiable, motivated, and active, the other kairotic, incalculable, unmoti-vated, and linked to a state of reactive expectancy where imagination and inspiration seem most easily accommodated.

The sense of cosmic rush and urgency that swirls around Quintilian's text on impro-visation emerges from a host of issues that lead organically to his culminating embrace of inspiration as the *ne plus ultra* of his chapter on extemporaneity. A detailed account-ing of these issues lies outside the necessarily limited scope of this survey, but together they attest to the overarching view that eloquence is a process of discovery and insight, a maieutic ascent toward a charismatic threshold beyond which, like Bembo's speech, no more need be said. These issues are rooted in a shared sense of movement and indwell-ing power: the velocity and rush of words (*cursus* and *velocitas dicendi*), the nimbleness of mind (*mobilitas animi*), the flow of language from its storehouse (*copia*), the process of discovery itself (*inventio*), the recourse to uncanny dexterity (*usus irrationalis* and *alogos tribe*), the capacity to visualize (*phantasia*), the elation of feeling (*pectus*), and the convergence with the divine (*spiritus*). This cycle of passion-generated discourse (*alogon pathos*) is close to the pulse of the quotidian, of experimentation and *empeiria*, occurring within a set of encircling temporal conditions or *kairos*. But to the extent that *kairos* may also take on the attributes of a divinity, it is not surprising to see "feeling and inspiration" promoted in Quintilian's text as the sign that "some god had inspired the speaker" (X, vii, 14).

Improvisers, for Quintilian, are thus endowed with qualities of insight that turn them into processors of time—its agents—rather than hand-wringing bystanders await-ing (and perhaps missing) the appropriate opportunity. The later dialogue depicted in

Renaissance emblem books between Occasio and Metanoia (Opportunity and Regret) is already latently present in Quintilian's text. The power of discourse to enable us "to utter the immediate" ["*dum proxima dicimus*," X, vii, 8] locates improvisation at a decisive moment in which the pectoral eye is synchronized with the illuminated spirit.

Quintilian's chapter on improvisation closing Book X is the most comprehensive, richly allusive discussion of the topic in antiquity. With the rediscovery of the *Institutio oratoria* by Poggio Bracciolini in the early 15th century (St. Gall, 1416), Renaissance humanists could point to a text that, while largely overshadowed by the legacy of Cicero, would end up more in the mainstream of how writers and thinkers understood and championed the mechanisms that inform the related topics of inspiration, improvisation, time, and writing itself.[26] For Erasmus and his contemporaries, there exists something as generically distinct as a time-centered discourse, one in which an utterance appears inspired and synchronized with the circumstances that have brought it into being.

In a sense, the Renaissance fascination with the so-called *ex tempore dicendi facultas* could not have taken place were it not for the subversion of chronological time initiated early on by the same medieval culture otherwise repudiated by Rabelais in his celebrated ban of chronometers from the utopian enclosure of the Abbaye of Thélème at the end of *Gargantua* (1534). The exclusion of *chronos* and the implied reinscription of *kairos* in his monastic haven suggest that time, so conceived, is meaningful only to the extent that we ourselves create and shape it.[27] The sense of crisis on which the Renaissance would found its own distinctiveness as a period could be said to be anchored in the same amoebic set of issues that propel Quintilian's text into a new critical dispensation having to do with the transfiguring potential of discourse in ways that seem to transcend the technical aspirations of the first nine books. This moment, emblematized in Rabelais's text on Thélème, insofar as it embraces the shared gift of communal insight, signals the power of time to shape the ontology of this monastic space. Rabelais's convent, in terms of its behavioral code synchronized within a spatial design, is a dramatic echo of the Aristotelian view of time discussed earlier in which the ends of actions are conterminous with their circumstances [*kairos*].

Thélème, a name whose etymology (from Greek θέλημα) suggests the hegemony of will, delineates a space from which clocks are banned. Conventional time, Rabelais suggests, is the time of the chronometer, "compassé, limité, et reiglé par heures."[28] In its place, he substitutes a new dispensation calibrated instead to "les occasions et oportunitez" and to the "dicté de bon sens et entendement."[29] Rabelais's text contains a richly allusive message. This message has to do with a new spatial and temporal scheme in which chronicity finds itself displaced by a new set of terms, "les occasions et oportunitez." Through their Latin roots, *occasio / opportunitas* these two synonyms share that common Greek ancestor, *kairos*, whose meaning and typology extend throughout ancient mythography, philosophy, and, above all, rhetoric. In the plural (*kairoi*), the word refers to moments of crisis, critical times calling for decision and marking their discontinuity with the past. Frequently, the term's resonance relates to its pairing with a foil, *chronos*, a relationship anchored in Greek mythology where *chronos* (chronological time) and *Kronos* (the father of Zeus) often share conflated attributes. In their typology of old age (the full beard and sickle-knife of Father Time), they symbolize an older temporal order, distant yet genetically related to *Kairos*, the youngest of Zeus's sons.[30] Ancient Greek accounts of the celebrated statue of *Kairos* sculpted by Lysippus of Sicyon emphasize the figure's youthful agility and beauty: the winged feet on rotating orb, forelock protruding from tonsured head, the razor clutched in the right hand, the textured blush of skin, all combining to create a picture of kinetic rush, of velocity too quick to arrest, seductive, yet lacerating in its contact. In the most striking of these accounts, the Sophist Callistratus extends the meaning of this symbolism to the achievement itself, the power of art to recover presence, to seize an opportunity about to slip from the sculptor's grasp.[31] In other words, a divinity, *Kairos*, whose being lies in its capacity to evade projects of human control and design, has been stabilized by art, that medium whose own transcendent purpose is to seize the opportune moment when beauty shimmers in all its youthful *éclat*. And to the extent that this moment triggers a decision to act—to capture beauty—and all within the certainty of our impending separation from the moment, *kairos* and *krisis* belong to identical orders of time. They are generated within the human organism and take on the particular significance we choose to confer on them.

Few periods of human thought have advertised their own significance and criticality more eloquently than the Renaissance. Rabelais's episode of Thélème celebrates the ascendancy of *Kairos* and the repudiation of *Chronos* in a world that was trying to place itself in a new set of time relationships. As an episode, it is emblematic of this new sense of timeliness that permits the humanist scholar to explain his own era through discourse with a classical past while addressing, at the same time, an even more transcendent process of fulfillment discovered by New Testament scholarship.[32] The assumption of theological and personal Christian renewal as a central impulse in Reformation thought no doubt owes part of its vitality to the role played by *kairos* in shaping temporal concepts in New Testament Greek.[33] Significantly, the Renaissance relinquished neither the theological nor the secular tradition behind the notion of *kairos* because both, in a sense, contribute to the myth of crisis the era was fashioning for itself. Henri Estienne, for example, cites ancient and Christian authorities to describe *kairos* as a Greek divinity as well as the moment through which human discourse strives in prayer toward God.[34] The commonalities present in the Olympian and Christological settings of *kairos* may well relate to the fact that both traditions are significantly icon- and discourse-centered. In either case, a notion of time is shaped into human form, becoming identifiable not only through a set of iconographic features, but also, even more crucially, through its ability to engage in a process of statement about itself. The emblem of a personified *Kairos*, lingering to interpret itself to the watchful spectator, runs parallel to the New Testament Christ as the embodiment of divine *sermo* constantly using language to reveal himself to an expectant world.

The Renaissance understood clearly that discourse has the power to synthesize these relationships. It was equally persuaded that there exists something as generically distinct as a time-centered discourse, one in which an utterance appears synchronized with the circumstances that have brought it into being. In a sense, this renewed fascination with the so-called *ex tempore dicendi facultas* or improvised speech could not have taken place were it not for the subversion of chronology initiated early on by the same Medieval culture framed by Rabelais in the tyranny of clocks. Time, so conceived, is meaningful only to the extent that we ourselves create and shape it. *Kairos* and *krisis* as structures of action, thought, and utterance enlarge the individual's capacity for self-awareness. They are forces with which we are dramatically and ethically engaged, rather than conditions that move against us peremptorily through the indeterminate course of events. The fact that these issues are so deeply embedded in the act of improvisation and in the later rediscovery of Quintilian would help the Renaissance see discourse as a process that tells us as much about the period's own sense of criticality as it does about the tendency of aesthetic norms to record instants of crisis. Humanism was thus responsible for generating a language that would not only authenticate the cultural crisis at hand, but also base that crisis in its own distinctiveness as a period.

Given the embodiment of myth in the deities of *Kairos* and *Occasio*, it is natural that the issues so vital to how improvisation defines its relationship to concepts of time begin to take on specific scenic and dramatic configurations that reflect the engagement of these deities with human events. Thus, the improvised moment becomes a moment that achieves both iconic and dramatic force as the depiction of a rhetorical abstraction. These developments are embedded within a fascinating transgendering of the myth of time. While retaining most of the iconographic and behavioral features of its Greek male predecessor, *Kairos*, *Occasio* comes to be known by the company she keeps. An epigram by the Bordelaise poet, Ausonius, writing in the 4th century CE, pairs *Occasio* with *Metanoia*, the companion goddess of penitence and regret, "who exacts penalties for what is done and what undone, to cause repentance."[35] But *Metanoia*, like *Occasio*, is also an attribute of human discourse, numbering among the figures of thought and listed by the Augustan rhetorician, Rutilius Lupus.[36] For Quintilian, *metanoia*, as the Latin equivalent *paenitentia*, referred to a process of rhetorical self-correction, a ploy to convince the judge that the speaker's change of heart is evidence of his spontaneity and thus more likely to gain support for his position.[37] Thus, *metanoia* has a curious semantic double edge, on the one hand evoking the anxiety of opportunity missed and attendant regret, and on the other, the possibility that such regret take the form of a spontaneous corrective shift in the text, a means of changing the rhetorical course in midstream to catch that opportunity and thereby making it seem improvised.

The point is that *kairos* or *occasio*, like crisis, is a component of our responsive interaction with time rather than a force hurled against us by some vaguely perceived cosmic tyranny. Few Renaissance writers understood this distinction more thoroughly than Machiavelli, who gave Occasion, along with Penitence, Youth, and Necessity, separate identities among the refugees of Fortuna's palace.[38] The conflation of *Occasio* with *Fortuna* often found in medieval texts is largely corrected when humanist emblem scholarship begins to clarify the iconographic muddle surrounding Occasion and Fortune. Accoutrements often attributed falsely to Fortune appear correctly in Alciati's emblem on Occasion and remain intact in the major French editions of Jean Lefèvre, Bathélemy Aneau, and Claude Mignault. These editions, represented in Figures 15.1–15.4, record this consistency, depicting Occasion as Ausonius's Latin goddess and linking her

In occasionem. XVI.

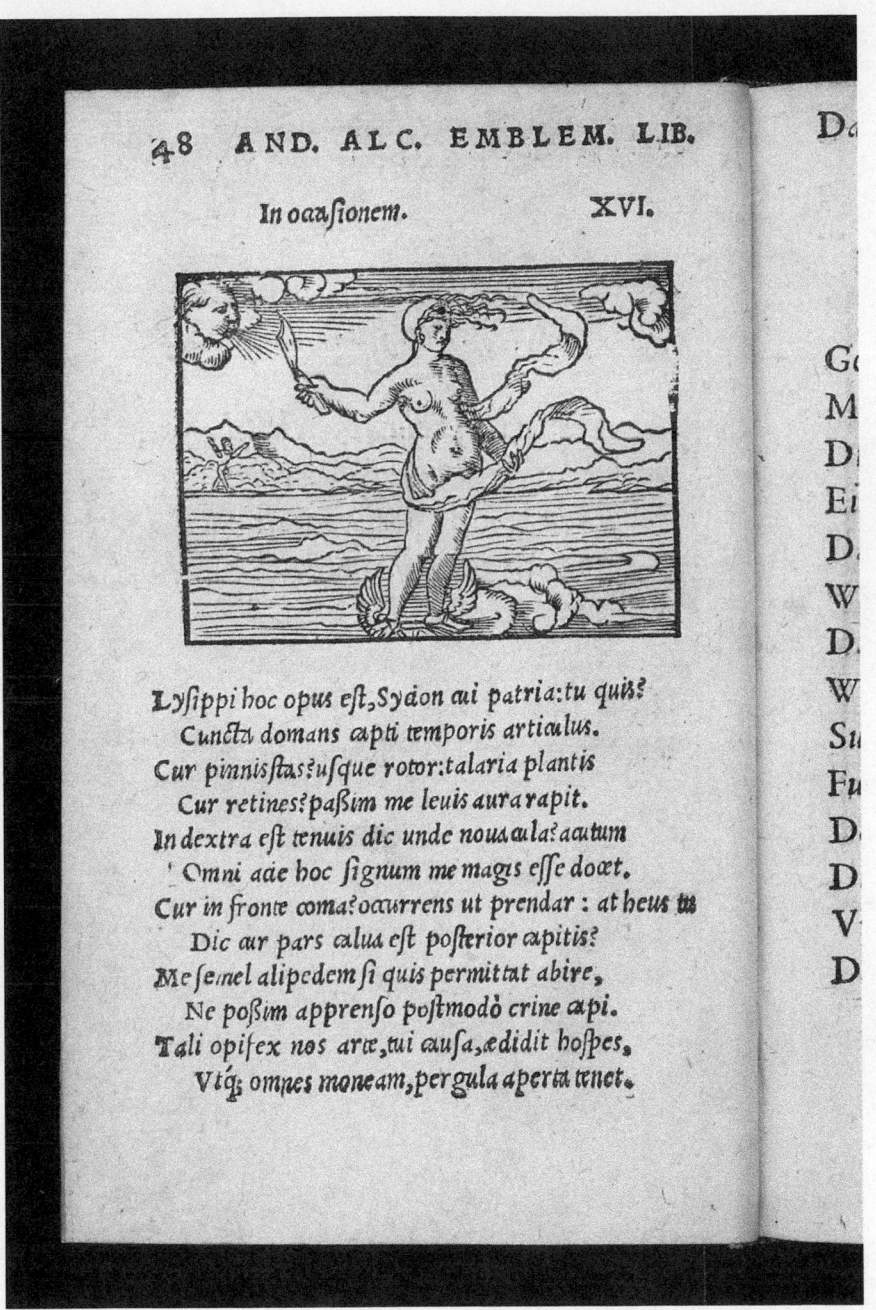

Lysippi hoc opus est, Sydon cui patria:tu quis?
  Cuncta domans capti temporis articulus.
Cur pinnis stas?usque rotor:talaria plantis
  Cur retines?passim me leuis aura rapit.
In dextra est tenuis dic unde noucacula?acutum
  Omni acie hoc signum me magis esse docet.
Cur in fronte coma?occurrens ut prendar : at heus tu
  Dic cur pars calua est posterior capitis?
Me semel alipedem si quis permittat abire,
  Ne possim apprenso postmodò crine capi.
Tali opifex nos arte,tui causa,aedidit hospes,
  Vtq; omnes moneam,pergula aperta tenet.

FIGURE 15.1 Andrea Alciati. Emblematum libellus. Paris, Wéchel, 1542. "In occasionem," p. 48.

COMMENTARIA.

Adolefcentulus cuidam proponitur, cui ma
nu dextra ponderofus dependet lapis, finiftre
verò eius, alæ affixæ funt leuiſsimæ. Vtique
hæ in altum eleuant, fic onus illud graue alia
ex parte deprimit. Oftendens plurimos ob
ingenij felicitatem celebres & claros futuros,
nifi paupertas inuida depreſsos retineret. Eſt
etenim illa moleftum pondus, vt pleriq; nof-
fe nollent, pluriuin nanque quotidianus eſt
cibus. Et paupertatis vnicum incommodum
habere fapientem dixit Archytas Philofophus.

In occafionem.   XVI

Lyfippi hoc opus eft, Sycion cui patria : tu quis?
Cunʃta domans capti temporis articulus.

Cur pinnis ſtas ?
Cur retines ?
In dextra eſt ter
Omni acie hoc
Cur in fronte co
Dic cur pars
Me femel alipe
Ne poſsim ap
Tali opifex nos
Viq; omnes

Lyfippus c
& infignis ſc
in Laconia er
rijs in locis
cauit, quæ O
tas temporis
gubernans,
autem pinni
tendis : ſem
ma permano
ceos alatos
aërem etenim
nouaculam
acutiſsima
pillata, vt c
retro verò c
terga capi a

FIGURE 15.2 Andrea Alciati. Emblematum libri II, Lyons, Jean de Tournes and Guillaume Gazeau, 1556. "In occasionem," p. 30.

In Occasionem.

EMBLEMA CXXI. Ἀγαλοχημῶς.

LYSIPPI *hoc opus est, Sicyon cui patria. tu quis?*
  Cuncta domans capti temporis articulus.
Cur pinnis stas? vsque rotor. talaria plantis
  Cur retines? passim me leuis aura rapit.
In dextra est tenuis dic vnde nouacula? acutum
  Omni acie hoc signum me magis esse docet.
Cur in fronte coma? occurrens vt prendar. At heus tu
  Dic, cur pars calua est posterior capitis?
Me semel alipedem si quis permittat abire,
  Ne possim apprenso postmodò crine capi.

Tali

FIGURE 15.3 Andrea Alciati. Emblemata: Cum commentariis, ed. Claude Mignault. Antwerp, Plantin, 1577. "In Occasionem," p. 415.

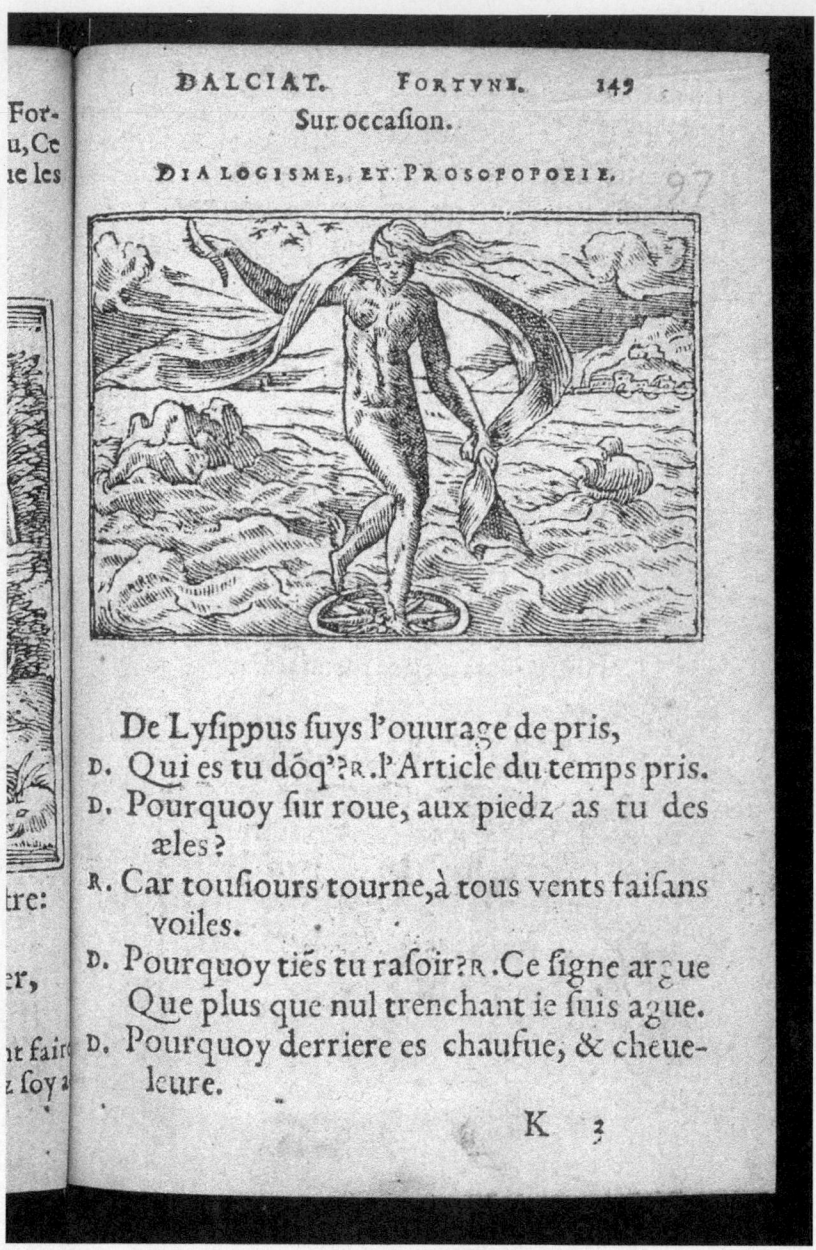

BALCIAT.   FORTVNE.   149
Sur occasion.

DIALOGISME, ET PROSOPOPOEIE.

De Lyſippus ſuys l'ouurage de pris,
D. Qui es tu dóq'?R.l'Article du temps pris.
D. Pourquoy ſur roue, aux piedz as tu des
æles?
R. Car touſiours tourne,à tous vents faiſans
voiles.
D. Pourquoy tiés tu raſoir?R .Ce ſigne argue
Que plus que nul trenchant ie ſuis ague.
D. Pourquoy derriere es chaufue, & cheue-
leure.

K 3

FIGURE 15.4 Andrea Alciati. Toutes les emblemes.... Lyons, Roville, 1558. "Sur occasion," p. 149.
University of Glasgow Library, Department of Special Collections.

to the standard hardware and features of the Greek god, *Kairos*: the wheel, the razor, the tonsured head, winged feet, and protruding forelock. Alciati authorizes this image in an adjoining interpretation based on the Greek epigram of Posidippus in which the Poet interrogates the sculpture of *Kairos*, asking the work of art to stop and explain the mystery of its own composition. Explanatory notes by Aneau and Mignault each reduce the scene to its component structures.[39] From these summaries, one can derive a common format with striking resemblance to the rhetorical issues discussed above. Occasion thus operates in five modal patterns: (1) it is an *articulus* (a single critical moment, a point of time), largely irrelevant to any chronological series that precedes or follows it; (2) like rhetoric, it is a kinetic force, dynamically engaged with a spectator (*expedit*); (3) through the verb *secare* (to cut, to separate, to decide) embodied in *Kairos*'s razor, it enacts the paradigm of crisis; (4) its forelock invites a responsive gesture (*arripere*, to seize, to grasp); and (5) the dramatic context in which it occurs makes it immune from any optative strategy by the spectator. Like Quintilian's improvisatory moment, one either catches or loses it, but does not will it. In fact, all these points suggest that humanist writers are able not only to sort out the iconographic relationship of *Occasio* to her Greek ancestor, *Kairos*, but to restore the figure's rich complexity as a projection of man's transitory ethics and aesthetics. If Machiavelli dramatized this awareness in the temporizing world of his Prince, Erasmus records its philological history in his learned adage, "*Nosce tempus*" ("Come to know time").[40] It is no accident, one suspects, that Erasmus's injunction and the Poet's cross-examination of *Kairos* in Posidippus's epigram are based in identical cognitive lessons. To seize Time by the forelock is to separate it momentarily from its linear continuum and, in the significance of this moment, to establish bonds of familiarity, acquaintanceship, and discernment, to come to know it.

Rooted in a moment of inner stress and crisis, this dramatic narrative of Occasion is a direct consequence of the Renaissance emblematic tradition. Ausonius's prosopopoeia on *Occasio* and her penitential foil, *Metanoia*, provide this tradition with the authority to incorporate both figures in the emblematic design. In 1541, the Ferrarese court painter, Girolamo de Carpi, depicted this duality in his painting of Opportunity and Regret, a scene of shimmering immediacy and unarrested movement.[41] In his adage, "*Nosce tempus*," Erasmus himself may have stimulated interest in Ausonius's text by citing the epigram in its entirety and calling attention to the addition of Paenitentia.[42] In his later commentary on Alciati, Claude Mignault would acknowledge Erasmus's crucial role, but not without first assigning the rediscovery of Ausonius's epigram to an even earlier humanist text, Poliziano's *Miscellaneorum centuriae*.[43] And while, as a rule, Renaissance emblem books continue to show Occasion alone in her marine landscape, familiarity with the texts of Poliziano and Erasmus may well account for instances of Occasion dramatically engaged with a partner (Paenitentia) who has been left gesticulating in the wake of this human hydrofoil. Gille Corrozet's *Hécatomgraphie* (1540) contains the most graphic example of this heightened dramatic complexity, with Penitence rigidly fixed in her gestures of procrastination and despair (Figure 15.5). Beneath the emblem is an explanatory quatrain that opens with an allusion to the cautionary *arripe occasionem* and specifies penitence as the consequence of inaction.[44] Thus, the tiny speck of frantic humanity all but eclipsed by a dominant Occasion in the 1542 Wéchel edition of Alciati (Figure 15.1) is certainly a vestige of Ausonius's goddess, Metanoia, now fallen from partnership and edging toward spatial and dramatic oblivion in the outer limits of the picture. In 1588, Jean Jacques Boissard in his *Emblemes latins* (Figure 15.6) restores Paenitentia to her position of active but now more bellicose partnership by depicting

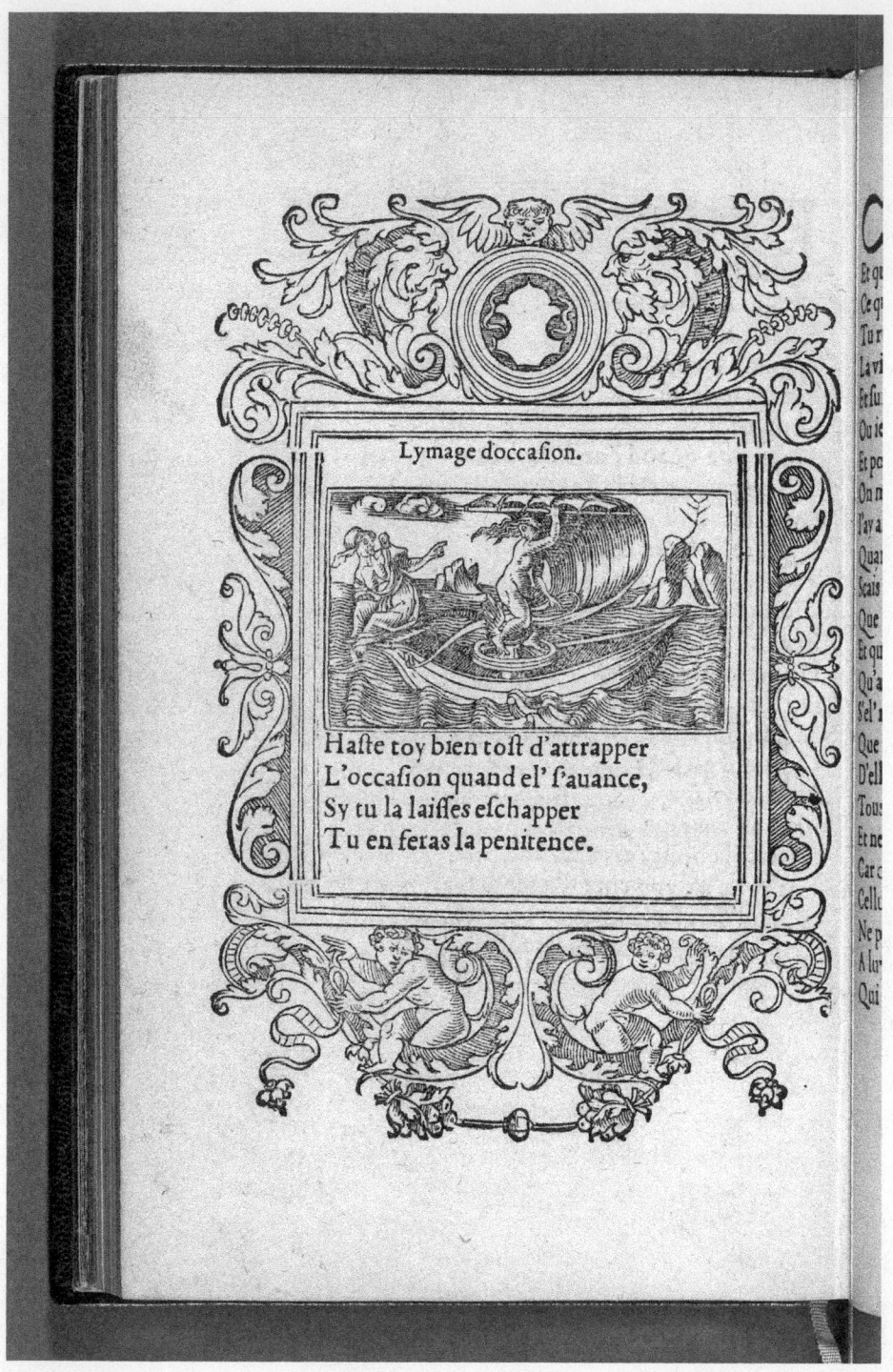

FIGURE 15.5 Gilles Corrozet. Hécatomgraphie. Paris, Denys Janot, 1540. "L'ymage d'occasion," sig. Miiv.

Ad Abrahamum Fabrum Typographum.

Arripe, se quoties offert occasio: calva est
A tergo: & volucri labitur illa pede.
Ponè sequens torto sequitur Metanœa flagello:
Et tantùm ignavis pœna dolenda venit.

H 3

FIGURE 15.6 Jean Jacques Boissard. Emblematum liber, Emblemes latins. Metz, A. Faber, 1588. Occasio, p. 61.

her as an old crone brandishing a whip as the looming punishment in store for the figure on the right who has all but missed his opportunity (one assumes, for Christian salvation).[45]

In later editions of Alciati (Figures 15.2–15.4), the figure is deleted altogether but still remains conceptually viable, as Mignault's commentary suggests. With Joannes David's *Occasio arrepta, neglecta* (1605), however, theology draws on mythology and turns Ausonius's two deities into extensions of the Christian apocalypse. Secular penitence within the framework of relativistic ethics gives way to a redemptive *Metanoia* that makes contrition not a consequence of missed opportunity, but a strategic shaping of the opportunity itself.[46] Penitence becomes part of the corrective posture through which the Christian meets his transcendent hour of crisis and decision: the Last Judgment.

David synthesizes two vital strands in the Renaissance transmission of *Kairos* and *Occasio*: the theological and the iconographic. Together, these strands approach the topic largely as an ethical problem, a decision either to act or to not act and suffer the consequences. Even improvisation can have a penitential consequence. The idea that discourse reflects this same ethical stress, however, can be traced to the humanist interest in Cicero's *De inventione*, one of the major source works on ancient rhetoric prior to the rediscovery of Quintilian's *Institutio* and of Cicero's mature rhetorical works early in the 15th century.[47] Early on, the Byzantine teacher, George of Trebizond, incorporates major segments of Cicero's statement on Occasion in the *De inventione* (I, 27, 40) into his chapter "On dialectical places."[48] In addition, Trebizond goes out of his way to adapt Cicero's crucial distinction between *tempus* as chronometric space (years, months, days) and *occasio* as opportune moment to a statement philosophical in tone and largely indifferent to elocutionary practice.[49] Cicero's text eventually becomes the principal supporting authority on the topic of Occasion and finds its way into many of the major Renaissance treatises on dialectic and rhetoric, including those of Agricola and Barthélemy Latomus. To these early dialecticians, Occasion is assigned a rigidly permanent space in the register of topics.

Dialectical texts were already reflecting this trend in subtle ways. A case in point is the notion of "adjacency," one of the "internal" places discussed by Agricola. Like its Greek equivalent, *parakeimenon* (meaning "what is at hand, present"), *adjacentia* encompasses a temporal and spatial relationship, referring to presence both as time and as physical proximity. Subsumed within the topic is the notion of *habitus*, in a sense the intrinsic corollary of *occasio* and similarly adapted from the *De inventione* (I, xxv, 36). What is significant in this section of Agricola's text, however, is the fact that he glosses his remarks on *habitus* by referring to its Greek equivalent, *hexis*, a term likely to spark instant humanist recognition from its high profile in Quintilian's Book X.[50] And to the extent that *hexis* is a quality deeply embedded in the tactics of speech and in the orator's response to new rhetorical opportunities, it calls attention to the more dynamic, elocutionary appeal of Quintilian's work. Indeed, the zeal with which *hexis* must have been read by humanists as a property of discourse spills over occasionally into outright conflation with the phonetically similar *lexis*.[51] Agricola, of course, does not commit this error, but by juxtaposing *habitus* with *hexis* he draws explicit attention to the Quintilianesque theme of *facilitas* together with its emphasis on elocutionary timing and opportunity. As dialectical issues, *occasio* and *habitus* remain isolated in their respective cubic spaces. Yet the topical genera (*tempus* and *adjacentia*) that contain them embrace concepts of space and time compatible not only with each other, but, more significantly, with a crucial structural shift in Agricola's own work.

This shift culminates in the highly rhetorical orientation of Book III ("*De effectibus*"), where the memory diagrams of place-logic come to fuel the dynamics of oral fluency, *facilitas* and *copia*—a process of disbursement, as it were, from dialectic's memory boxes. [52] It is precisely at this juncture that Agricola, like Quintilian before him, leads his reader beyond a purely technical agenda toward the overriding themes of timeliness and dexterity. The result, in the final pages, is an explicit homage to improvisation and to the Quintilianesque notion of discourse as temporal performance. [53]

The switch to a more time-specific vocabulary in the *Institutio oratoria* is, as we have seen, one of Quintilian's most visible assertions of his independence from Cicero. To be sure, humanist texts continue to anchor their abstract understanding of *Occasio* in Cicero's terse definition, but as 16th-century writers seek to reconcile dialectic with rhetoric, the bland timelessness of the Ciceronian formula proves irrelevant to the atmosphere of stress and urgency in which speech actually occurs. More than any other ancient text, Quintilian's work answers these concerns by seeing time as the critical factor in discourse. The themes that percolate around Quintilian's analysis of extemporaneity in Book X—*hexis, phantasia, velocitas,* and *pectus*—are thus virtually the same themes used by the disciples of Agricola, Melanchthon, and Latomus to give focus to their discussions of *circumstantia* in rhetoric. [54] In the case of Melanchthon, Occasion and Circumstance form the contextual enclosure through which Facility, Quintilian's Latin corollary of *hexis*, becomes operative. [55] At the same time, this linkage between the performative and the environmental extends to other Quintilianesque concerns such as vividness, feeling, and, above all, inspiration. [56] A further consequence of these relationships is the rediscovery of an obscure post-Augustan definition that connects *occasio* to the notion of "supply" or "stock" and thus to the terms *copia* and *facultas*. [57]

The pluralities of opportunity on which the ethics of Rabelais's Abbey of Will was founded signaled both an end to the monastic chronometric pulse and the open embrace of time in all its imagined unboundedness. As now seems apparent, the year 1534, in which *Gargantua* first appeared in Lyon, marks a point of convergence for many of the key issues under review in the present essay. Fortuitously, it also marks the publication, likewise at Lyon, of Nicolas Bérault's *Dialogue in which certain principles are explained by which the faculty of improvisation can be acquired*. [58] However, any reader expecting a comprehensive handbook on the topic will find these expectations largely unmet. Bérault's dialogue, echoing the wide-ranging postprandial discussion at the Urbino court, describes a dramatic fiction in which two interlocutors—the Pedagogue (Leonicus) and his disciple (Spudaeus)—conduct a free-wheeling review of the rhetorical background (chiefly Cicero and Quintilian) from which improvisation has emerged over time. But unlike the contained intramural space of the Urbino court, Bérault's dialogue unfolds in the open air during a journey through Navarre and in an environment of seemingly random movement. This dialogue on improvisation is invested in its own extramural circumstances, the lush botanical setting of oak, plane, olive, and fig trees framing and promoting the unimpeded energies of discussion and dialogue (sig. A6ᵛ). Cited liberally throughout Bérault's dialogue, Quintilian's text on improvisation is recalled, above all, for the high profile of its temporal vocabulary and for the way extemporal eloquence draws on kinetic force. Tellingly, Leonicus, the Pedagogue, elicits these same inflections when he juxtaposes the phrase *dicere ex tempore* with the explanatory synonym *currere* ["to run"] [sig. B1ᵛ]. To improvise is ultimately a process of locomotion and mental velocity.

Any understanding of improvisation's function in the Renaissance text depends, as we have seen, on a full disclosure of theoretical patterns worked out in the conceptual transition between early Greek sophistic and Roman rhetoric. All these patterns ultimately converge in the fifteenth and sixteenth centuries not only in a flood of speculation engaging many of the greatest minds of the age, but also in the scenic portrayals contained in emblematic literature. With Nicolas Bérault's *Dialogue on improvisation*, these same patterns find their most (and indeed, only) systematic expression in a formal dialogue on improvisation. The paired voices of ancient rhetoric (Cicero, the Master and Quintilian, the disciple) take on a new immediacy through their later fictional mouthpieces, Leonicus and Spudaeus. This refraction of the distantly ancient within a coeval present helps to underscore the fact that improvisation is conditioned not only by an encompassing contemporaneity, but also, as Jean-François de Raymond asserts in his compelling inquiry into the philosophy of improvisation, by the prevailing cultural codes through which it reverberates.[59] If humanist culture rediscovers the luminosity of ancient concepts and codes in which improvisation may be contemporized, it does so in the awareness that improvisers are drawn into the elation of unfolding statement. They inhabit that critical juncture that lingers always on the verge of its own obsolescence and self-erasure.

Notes

Research for this study was made possible through the generosity of a fellowship from the John Simon Guggenheim Memorial Foundation.

1. Baldassare Castiglione, *Il libro del cortigiano*, ed. Amedeo Quondam (Milan: Garzanti, 1981), 37–38. All further references will be to this edition with page numbers carried in the body of the text.
2. See Terence Cave, *The Cornucopian Text: Problems of Writing in the French Renaissance* (Oxford: Clarendon Press, 1979), 23n and 125.
3. Desiderius Erasmus, *De copia, in Omnia Opera*, vol. 1 (Basle: Froben, 1540), chapter 2, 2.
4. Kenneth Burke, *A Rhetoric of Motives* (Berkeley, Los Angeles, London: University of California Press, 1969), 221–233. For a discussion of Burke's reading of Bembo's speech and

its connection to improvisation see Glyn P. Norton, "Strategies of Fluency in the French Renaissance Text: Improvisation and the Art of Writing," in "Rethinking the Languages of Criticism," special issue, *The Journal of Medieval and Renaissance Studies* 15 (Spring 1985): 85–99.

5. D.A. Russell, *Greek Declamation* (Cambridge: Cambridge University Press, 1983), 77. A full summary of the act and context of sophist declamation is contained in Russell's chapter, "Performers and Occasions" (74–86).

6. Russell, *Greek Declamation*, 77.

7. "Ingenium uelox, audacia pudita, sermo promptus et Isaeo torrentior." Juvenal, *Satires*, 3:24, translated by G. G. Ramsay, Loeb Classical Library (London: Williams Heinemann, 1918).

8. Pliny, *Letters*, Book 2:3, 1–5.

9. Pliny, *Letters*, Book 2:3, 2–4.

10. The translation and Greek text are contained in Marjorie Josephine Milne's *A Study in Alcidamas and his Relation to Contemporary Sophistic* (Ph.D. dissertation, Bryn Mawr College, 1924), 10–11, 16–17.

11. Marcus Tullius Cicero, *De inventione*, trans. H. M. Hubbell, Loeb Classical Library, 2:176. (Cambridge, MA: Harvard University Press, 1949).

12. Cicero, *De oratore*, trans. E. W. Sutton, Loeb Classical Library, 1:150 (London: William Heinemann, 1967).

13. Cicero, *De oratore*, 1:151.

14. Quintilian, *Institutionis oratoriae Liber X*, ed. William Peterson, 2nd ed., xli–xlii. (1903; repr. Oxford: Clarendon, 1962).

15. On Quintilian's attitude to stylistic models and to the practices of his day, see *Institutionis oratoriae Liber X*, ed. Peterson, xxxix–xli.

16. The ensuing discussion of Quintilian on improvisation is necessarily synoptic. For a fuller and more detailed accounting see Glyn P. Norton, "Improvisation and Inspiration in Quintilian: the Extemporalizing of Technique in the *Institutio Oratoria*," in *Inspiration and Technique: Ancient to Modern Views On Beauty and Art*, ed. John Roe and Michele Stanco, 83–104 (Oxford: Peter Lang, 2007).

17. "Nam scribere non ubique nec simper possumus; cogitationi temporis ac loci plurimum est" [my translation] (X, vi, 1). Quintilian, *Institutio oratoria*, trans. H. E. Butler, 4 vols. (London: William Heinemann, 1968), X, vi, 1.

18. "Tempus iterum, quod καιρός appellant." Quintilian, *Institutio oratoria*, III, vi, 26.

19. Alcidamas, *Peri sophiston*, in Milne, 16–17.

20. Aristotle, *Nicomachean ethics*, 3:1, ed. and trans. Robert C. Bartlett and Susan D. Collins. (Chicago: University of Chicago Press), 1110 a 14.

21. On this aspect of Quintilian's use of *kairos*, see Quintilian, *Institution oratoire*, ed. Jean Cousin, tome VI, Livres X et XI, 152–153 (Paris: Les Belles Lettres, 1979). This terminology is discussed in the context of Aristotelian thought by Burke in *A Rhetoric of Motives*, 49–65.

22. See the entry for καιρός in Henri Estienne, *Thesaurus Graecae linguae*, vol. IV (Paris: Firmin Didot, 1841): "καιρός apud Graecos Deus est" (col. 818). The pertinent references are to Pausanias: 5, 14, 9, and to Chrysostom for whom *kairos* is the time "through which we pray to God" ("Quo tempore Deum oramus") (col. 817). Estienne is calling attention to a relationship he may well have picked up from Erasmus's *Adagiorum chiliades*: "apud Graecos mas est hic dues appellaturque καιρός." See Adage #70 ("Nosce Tempus"),

"Chiliades primae centuria septima," in *Adagiorum opus Des. Erasmi Roterodami* ... (Basle: Froben, 1528), 252.

23. Gordon Teskey implicitly remakes Quintilian's case for a transcendent improvisation sub-tending all *poiêsis* by seeing in *autoschediazein* a process of "making" through which "complex systems ... change over time, compelling one to rely on instinctive impulse rather than on rules." Teskey, *Allegory and Violence* (Ithaca, NY: Cornell University Press, 1996), 164. On Quintilian and Plato, see Norton, "Improvisation and Inspiration in Quintilian," 83–85.

24. Quintilian, *Institutionis oratoriae*, ed. Peterson, 12n.

25. I follow here Michael Winterbottom's reading in *Problems in Quintilian* (London: University of London Institute of Classical Studies, 1970), 194.

26. On the early humanist legacy of Cicero and Quintilian, see John O. Ward, "Cicero and Quintilian," in *The Cambridge History of Literary Criticism*, vol. 3, *The Renaissance*, ed. Glyn P. Norton (Cambridge: Cambridge University Press, 1999), 77–87. See also the now classic study of Terence Cave, *The Cornucopian Text*, esp. Part 1.

27. On relativistic views of Time, see Donald J. Wilcox, *The Measure of Times Past: Pre-Newtonian Chronologies and the Rhetoric of Time* (Chicago and London: University of Chicago Press, 1987), 119–129. See also chap. 6, "The Time of the Renaissance," 153–186.

28. François Rabelais, *Gargantua, in Œuvres complètes*, ed. Jacques Boulenger, Bibliothèque de la Pléiade (Paris: Gallimard, 1962), ch. 52, 148.

29. Rabelais, *Gargantua*, ch. 52, 148.

30. Admittedly, my summary is an oversimplification of a complex set of mythographic relationships. These relationships are often subject to broader confusion, with *Kairos* sometimes taking on traits of the ancestral pair, *Chronos / Kronos*. For the complete story, see Arthur Bernard Cook, *Zeus: A Study in Ancient Religion* (Cambridge: Cambridge University Press, 1914, repr., New York: Bibilo & Tannen, 1964), 2:859–868.

31. Philostratus the Elder, Philostratus the Younger, *Callistratus*, trans. A. Fairbanks, Loeb Classical Library (London: William Heinemann, 1931); also *Descriptions*, 6, "On the Statue of Opportunity at Sicyon." Posidippus' early Greek epigram on *kairos* is a terse cross-examination in which the statue explains its meaning to a curious poet. This conversational format is repeated much later in a poem on Occasion by the Latin poet, Ausonius. Both texts would prove crucial in Renaissance emblematic interest in *kairos / occasion*.

32. On Thélème as an episode rooted in platonizing Christianity, see M. A. Screech, *Rabelais* (Ithaca and New York: Cornell University Press, 1979), 187–194.

33. See G. Delling *on kairos in The Theological Dictionary of the New Testament*, ed. Gerhard Kittel, trans. and ed. Geoffrey W. Bromiley (Grand Rapids, MI: W. B. Eeerdmans Publishing Co., 1965; repr., 1967), 3:455–464.

34. See Delling, n28.

35. See Decimius Magnus Ausonius, "In simulacrum occasionis et penitentiae," Epigram XXXIII, trans. Hugh G. Evelyn-White, Loeb Classical Library (London: William Heinemann, 1919).

36. See Claudius Namatianus Rutilius, *De figuris sententiarum et elocutionis*, ed. Edward Brooks, Jr. (Leiden: Brill, 1970), 20.

37. *Institutio oratoria*, IX, ii, 59–60. See also the *Rhetorica ad Herennium on correctio*, trans. Harry Caplan, Loeb Classical Library (Cambridge, MA: Harvard University Press, 1954), IV, xxvi, 36.

38. See Machiavelli's poem "Di fortuna," *Tutte le opere di Niccolò Machiavelli*, ed. Francesco Flora and Carlo Cordie (Rome: Arnoldo Mondadori, 1949–1950), 2:710.

39. Andrea Alciati, *Emblemes d'Alciat, en latin et francois vers pour vers* (Paris: Hierosme de Marnef et Guillaume Cavellat, 1574), 177.

40. See Erasmus, *Adagiorum opus* (Basle: Froben, 1528), Adage #70 in "Chiliades primae centuria septima," 252–253. Mignault's commentary on Alciati's emblem of Occasion is based, in part, on this text. Andrea Alciati, edited by Claude Mignault, *Omnia Andreae Alciati emblemata: cum commentariis . . . per Claudium Minoem* (Antwerp: Plantin, 1577), 416.

41. Da Carpi's painting of Opportunity and Regret is housed at the Gemäldegalerie, Dresden.

42. Erasmus, *Adagiorum opus*, 253.

43. Angelo Poliziano, *Miscellaneorum centuriae* (Florence: Antonius Miscomius, 1489), f° hiii^v–hiv^r; BN Rés. Z.509.

44. Gilles Corrozet, *Hécatomgraphie*, ed. Charles Oulmont (Paris: Champion, 1905), 166.

45. Jean-Jacques Boissard, *Emblemes latins [. . .] avec l'interpretation Françoise* (Metz: J. Aubry and A. Faber, 1588), 60–61; Emblem 54 "A tergo calva est" ['From behind she is bald'].

46. See, above all, Joannes David's commentary on Figure 15.11, *Occasio arrepta, neglecta, in Occasio arrepta, neglecta, huius commoda: illius incommode* (Antwerp: Plantin, 1605), 227–245. Early in his work, he attributes his knowledge of Ausonius's epigram to Poliziano (sig. **2^{r-v}).

47. The second work was Cicero's *Rhetorica ad Herennium*.

48. George of Trebizond, *Rhetoricorum libri quinque* (Paris: I. Roigny, 1538), 286. John Monfasani traces the notion of opportune moment in Trebizond's work to the sophist notion of *kairos*. *George of Trebizond: A Biography and a Study of His Rhetoric and Logic* (Leiden: Brill, 1976), 293.

49. Trebizond, *Rhetoricorum*, 286.

50. Cf. Rudolph Agricola, *De inventione dialectica libri tres*, ed. *Phrissemius, Rodolphi Agricolae Phrisij, de inventione dialectica libri tres, cum scholijs Ioannis Matthaei Phrissemij* (Paris: Simon Colin, 1527), Book I:11, 50 and 53; Barthélemy Latomus, *Summa totius rationis disserendi* (Cologne: P. Quentell, 1527), f° C2^v; and Latomus, *Epitome commentariorum Dialecticae inuentionis Rodolphi Agricolae* (Paris: Gryphius, 1534), f° 13^v.

51. See the following early commentaries on Quintilian: Rafaelle Regio, *Ducento problemata in totidem Quintiliani oratoriae institutionis deprauationes* [s.l., 1492]. BN Rés. x.1064: "ita non satis ad vim dicendi valent: nisi illis formae quaedam facilitas: quae apud graecos λέξις nominatur accesserit" (f° d6^v); Joannes Sulpicius, *Quintilianus de compositionis ratione, in Io. Sulpitii Verulani: in commentariolum de compositione orationis* (Rome: Eucharius Silber, 1487), B.N. Rés. x.1566: "Lexis et si dictionem et locutionem significat tamen Fabius libro decimo sic habet. Formae quaedam facilitas quae apud Graecos *lexis* nominatur" (f° 13^v).

52. For a full discussion of Agricola's text, see Walter J. Ong, *Ramus, Method, and the Decay of Dialogue* (Cambridge, MA: Harvard University Press, 1958), ch. 5.

53. Agricola, *De inventione dialectica libri tres* (III:16).

54. Latomus deals with these topics in the sections, "De movendis affectibus," and in a long discussion of *enargeia* and *copia*, *Summa totius rationis disserendi*, f° D7^v-D8^r; E1^v-E7^r.

See Melanchthon's detailed remarks in the *De rhetorica* (Paris: R. Estienne, 1527), BN, 8°
X.11584 (3), especially the section titled "De circumstantiis" (f° 30^v-33^r).

55. "Facilitas in occasione, et circumstantiis causae maxime consistit." Melanchthon, *De rhetorica*, f° 36^r.

56. Melanchthon, *De rhetorica*, f° 32^r and f° 33^r.

57. In fact, Etienne Dolet resurrects this image at the beginning of his entry
"Occasio": "Occasionem pro copia, vel facultate aliquando poni certum est."
Commentariorum linguae latinae tomus secundus (Lyon: Seb. Gryphius, 1536), col. 873.

58. *Dialogus, quo rationes quaedam explicantur, quibus dicendi ex tempore facultas parari
potest* . . . (Lyon: Seb. Gryphius, 1534), BN X. 20072. An important discussion of this work
is contained in Cave, *The Cornucopian Text*, 135–138.

59. Jean-François de Raymond, *L'Improvisation: contribution à la philosophie de l'action*
(Paris: J. Vrin, 1980), 176.

BIBLIOGRAPHY

Agricola, Rudolph. *De inventione dialectica libri tres, ed. Phrissemius, Rodolphi Agricolae
Phrisij, de inventione dialectica libri tres, cum scholijs Ioannis Matthaei Phrissemij.*
Paris: Simon Colin, 1527.

Alciati, Andrea. *Emblemes d'Alciat, en latin et francois vers pour vers.* Paris: Hierosme de
Marnef et Guillaume Cavellat, 1574.

Alciati, Andrea, edited by Claude Mignault. *Omnia Andreae Alciati emblemata: cum commentariis . . . per Claudium Minoem.* Antwerp: Plantin, 1577.

Alcidamas. *Peri sophiston.* In Milne, Marjorie Josephine. *A Study in Alcidamas and His Relation
to Contemporary Sophistic.* Ph.D. dissertation, Bryn Mawr College, Bryn Mawr, PA, 1924.

Aristotle. *Nicomachean Ethics*, edited and translated by Robert C. Bartlett and Susan D. Collins.
Chicago: University of Chicago Press, 2011.

Ausonius, Decimus Magnus. "In simulacrum occasionis et penitentiae," Epigram XXXIII,
translated by Hugh G. Evelyn-White, Loeb Classical Library. London: William Heinemann,
1919.

Bérault, Nicolas. *Dialogus, quo rationes quaedam explicantur, quibus dicendi ex tempore facultas parari potest* . . . Lyon: Seb. Gryphius, 1534, BN X. 20072.

Boissard, Jean-Jacques. *Emblemes latins [. . .] avec l'interpretation Françoise*, Metz: J. Aubry and
A. Faber, 1588.

Burke, Kenneth. *A Rhetoric of Motives.* Berkeley, Los Angeles, London: University of California
Press, 1969.

Castiglione, Baldassare. *Il libro del cortigiano*, edited by Amedeo Quondam. Milan: Garzanti,
1981.

Cave, Terence. *The Cornucopian Text: Problems of Writing in the French Renaissance.*
Oxford: Clarendon Press, 1979.

Cicero, Marcus Tullius. *De inventione*, translated by H. M. Hubbell, Loeb Classical Library.
Cambridge, MA: Harvard University Press, 1960.

Cicero, Marcus Tullius. *De oratore*, translated by E. W. Sutton, Loeb Classical Library, 2 vols.
London: William Heinemann, 1967.

Cicero, Marcus Tullius, translated by Harry Caplan. *Rhetorica ad Herennium.* Loeb Classical
Library. Cambridge, MA: Harvard University Press, 1954.

Cook, Arthur Bernard. *Zeus: A Study in Ancient Religion.* 2 vols. Cambridge: Cambridge University Press, 1914. Reprint New York: Bibilo & Tannen, 1964.

Corrozet, Gilles. *Hécatomgraphie*, edited by Charles Oulmont. Paris: Champion, 1905.

David, Joannes. *Occasio arrepta, neglecta, huius commoda: illius incommode.* Antwerp: Plantin, 1605.

Dolet, Étienne. *Commentariorum linguae latinae tomus secundus.* Lyon: Seb. Gryphius, 1536.

Erasmus, Desiderius. *De copia*, in *Omnia Opera.* Vol. 1. Basle: Froben, 1540.

Erasmus, Desiderius. *Adagiorum opus Des. Erasmi Roterodami . . .* Basle: Froben, 1528.

Estienne, Henri. *Thesaurus Graecae linguae.* Vol. 4. Paris: Firmin Didot, 1841.

George of Trebizond. *Rhetoricorum libri quinque.* Paris: I. Roigny, 1538.

Juvenal. *Satires* (3:24), translated by G. G. Ramsay, Loeb Classical Library. London: Williams Heinemann, 1918.

Kittel, Gerhard, ed., Geoffrey W. Bromiley, trans. and ed., *The Theological Dictionary of the New Testament.* Vol. 3. Grand Rapids, MI: W. B. Eeerdmans, 1965. Reprint,1967.

Latomus, Barthélemy. *Summa totius rationis disserendi.* Cologne: P. Quentell, 1527.

Latomus, Barthélemy. *Epitome commentariorum Dialecticae inuentionis Rodolphi Agricolae.* Paris: Gryphius, 1534.

Machiavelli, Niccolò. "Di Fortuna." In *Tutte le opere di Niccolò Machiavelli*, edited by Francesco Flora and Carlo Cordie, 2:710. Rome: Arnoldo Mondadori, 1949–1950.

Melanchthon, Philip. *De rhetorica.* Paris: R. Estienne, 1527, BN, 80 X.11584.

Milne, Marjorie Josephine. *A Study in Alcidamas and his Relation to Contemporary Sophistic.* Ph.D. dissertation, Bryn Mawr College, 1924.

Monfasani, John. *George of Trebizond: A Biography and a Study of his Rhetoric and Logic.* Leiden: Brill, 1976.

Norton, Glyn P. "Strategies of Fluency in the French Renaissance Text: Improvisation and the Art of Writing." In "Rethinking the Languages of Criticism." Special issue, *The Journal of Medieval and Renaissance Studies* 15 (Spring 1985): 85–99.

Norton, Glyn P. "Improvisation and Inspiration in Quintilian: The Extemporalizing of Technique in the *Institutio Oratoria.*" In *Inspiration and Technique: Ancient to Modern Views on Beauty and Art*, edited by John Roe and Michele Stanco, 83–104. Oxford: Peter Lang, 2007.

Ong, Walter J. *Ramus, Method, and the Decay of Dialogue.* Cambridge, MA: Harvard University Press, 1958.

Philostratus the Elder. *Imagines*; Philostratus the Younger. *Imagines, Callistratus, Descriptions*, translated by A. Fairbanks. Loeb Classical Library. London: William Heinemann, 1931.

Pliny the Younger (Gaius Plinius Caecilius Secundus). *Letters*, Book 2:3, 1–5, translated by Betty Radice. Loeb Classical Library. Cambridge, MA: Harvard University Press, 1969.

Poliziano, Angelo. *Miscellaneorum centuriae.* Florence: Antonius Miscomius, 1489.

Quintilian (Marcus Fabius Quintilianus). *Institutio oratoria*, translated by H. E. Butler. 4 vols. London: William Heinemann, 1968.

Quintilian (Marcus Fabius Quintilianus). *Institutionis oratoriae Liber X*, edited by William Peterson. 2nd ed. Oxford: Clarendon, 1903. Reprint, Oxford: Clarendon Press, 1962.

Quintilian (Marcus Fabius Quintilianus). *Institution oratoire*, tome VI, Livres X et XI, edited by Jean Cousin. Paris: Les Belles Lettres, 1979.

Rabelais, François, *Œuvres complètes*, edited by Jacques Boulenger. Bibliothèque de la Pléiade. Paris: Gallimard, 1962.

Raymond, Jean-François de, *L'Improvisation: contribution à la philosophie de l'action.* Paris: J. Vrin, 1980.

Regio, Rafaelle, *Ducento problemata in totidem Quintiliani oratoriae institutionis deprauatio-nes*, [s.l., 1492]. BN Rés. x.1064.

Russell, D. A., *Greek Declamation*. Cambridge: Cambridge University Press, 1983.

Rutilius, Claudius Namatianus, *De figuris sententiarum et elocutionis*, edited by Edward Brooks, Jr. Leiden: Brill, 1970.

Screech, M. A., *Rabelais*. Ithaca and New York: Cornell University Press, 1979.

Sulpicius, Joannes, *Quintilianus de compositionis ratione, in Io. Sulpitii Verulani: in commentariolum de compositione orationis*. Rome: Eucharius Silber, 1487, B.N. Rés. x.1566.

Teskey, Gordon, *Allegory and Violence*. Ithaca, NY: Cornell University Press, 1996.

Ward, John O. "Cicero and Quintilian." In *The Cambridge History of Literary Criticism*, vol. 3, *The Renaissance*, edited by Glyn P. Norton, 77–87. Cambridge: Cambridge University Press, 1999.

Wilcox, Donald J., *The Measure of Times Past: Pre-Newtonian Chronologies and the Rhetoric of Time*. Chicago and London: University of Chicago Press, 1987.

Winterbottom, Michael, *Problems in Quintilian*. London: University of London Institute of Classical Studies, 1970.

CHAPTER 16

....

IMPROVISATION, DEMOCRACY, AND FEEDBACK

....

DANIEL BELGRAD

HISTORICALLY, in American culture, improvisation has been linked to a problematic of freedom. For most of the twentieth century, the idea prevailed that improvisation was a mode of creativity that freed the artist from the weight of tradition and expectations, and that this spontaneity made it possible to express truths that were typically distorted by those forces. Perhaps particularly during the mid-twentieth century (from the early 1940s until the mid-1970s), experimentalism in American arts and letters emphasized the connections between improvisation, freedom, and democracy.

According to this line of thinking, the successful improvisation combined two factors: an unconstrained access to creative impulses; and the integration of those impulses or "ideas" into the surrounding environment. As psychologist and political theorist Paul Goodman wrote in the journal *Politics* in 1945: "Freedom consists . . . in the continuing revolution of new demands and ideas as they emerge from the depths, called forth by and transforming the reality, including institutions. A free society is one that is peacefully permeable by this revolution."[1]

Some models of improvisation emphasized the first part of this formula—the expression of impulses that welled up "from the depths"—following templates laid down by Surrealism and Jungian psychology.[2] This emphasis tended to favor individualistic pursuits like painting and writing. The most prominent examples include early abstract expressionist painting by Adolph Gottlieb, Jackson Pollock, and William Baziotes, and the writing of Beat poets like Jack Kerouac and Michael McClure.

An alternative model, which came to predominate in the 1960s, placed emphasis on the transformative group interaction. This model privileged ensemble work, typically in performing arts like music and dance. In this kind of work, the artists' creative ideas were understood to emerge not "from the depths" of the unconscious mind, but from the group dynamic. The template for this style of improvisation was bebop jazz, the art of which lay in picking up on the ideas of other musicians in an ensemble.[3] Tenor saxophonist Archie Shepp once described the result as the expression of a "communal intelligence."[4]

Often, in this kind of improvisation, the group interaction is seen as a microcosm of the ideal democracy. Creative authority, instead of being concentrated in the person of a director or choreographer, is decentralized, passing among the performers as they take initiative and relinquish it. Each individual presence enlivens the others, creating a collective energy that in turn fosters individual expression. This essay outlines the intellectual history of this tradition and analyzes in detail two examples from the 1960s and 1970s: the electronic music of Max Neuhaus and the dance form called "contact improvisation."

DECENTRALIZATION AND FEEDBACK

The intellectual environment in which the cultural politics of improvisation took shape was defined by a historical conflict over two models of social authority: namely, centralized and decentralized power structures. The centralization of power promised a more efficient coordination of individual energies in pursuit of the collective good.[5] Whether understood as the power of national governments over local, or as the dominance of large corporations over small businesses, the practice of organizing large-scale enterprises by concentrating power in hierarchical "central command" structures grew increasingly prevalent in the course of the twentieth century.

In America at midcentury, the centralization of power in Nazi Germany and the Soviet Union was understood to be characteristic of their undemocratic "totalitarianism." Yet American society was at the same time undergoing a parallel, though less visible and less overtly violent, process of economic and political centralization. The Second World War in particular brought legitimacy to the use of hierarchical bureaucratic structures and the propagandistic control of information.[6] At the beginning of the war, under the auspices of a group called the Council for Democracy, anthropologists Margaret Mead and Gregory Bateson spoke out against such "social engineering" techniques, which they insisted were antithetical to democratic values.[7] "It is hardly an exaggeration to say that this war is ideologically about just this," Bateson wrote in 1942. "Could deliberate social planning be reconciled with the democratic ideal?" Centralized social planning, he asserted, was characteristic of undemocratic political systems like fascism. By contrast, democracy had to be embraced as the *means* as well as the ends of the American war effort. The paradoxical solution, Bateson asserted, was that a democratic leadership must "discard purpose in order to achieve our purpose."[8]

In 1944, émigré Austrian economist Friedrich Hayek launched a similar critique of centralized planning. In an influential book titled *The Road to Serfdom* (an expanded version of his earlier essay "Freedom and the Economic System")[9] Hayek faulted planners for prematurely and coercively imposing a "unity of purpose" on society instead of allowing "the interaction of individuals possessing different information and different views, sometimes consistent and sometimes conflicting" to work out its own direction.[10]

Planning stifled social and intellectual growth by attempting to substitute conscious decision-making for this necessary interpersonal process:

> The idea that the human mind ought "consciously" to control its own development confuses individual reason, which alone can "consciously control" anything, with the interpersonal process to which its growth is due. By attempting to control it, we are merely setting bounds to its development.

Like Bateson, Hayek asked his readers to accept the paradox that social purposes were best achieved not by a central authority but by "an attitude of humility before this social process."[11]

The decentralized social authority that was explored by improvisational artists in the postwar period had more in common with the ideas of Gregory Bateson than with those of Hayek, however. The difference between the two thinkers is that Hayek emphasized individualism and the "invisible hand" of classical liberal economics, whereas Bateson emphasized networks of feedback loops constituting an "ecological" or "cybernetic" system. In a cybernetic (also sometimes called "autopoietic") system, feedback governs the behavior of the system by stimulating or constraining the activities of its various parts. A simple ecological system, for instance, is represented by the interaction of two dependent populations—say, fox and geese. Because fox eat geese, an increase in the goose population will result in an increase of foxes; but more foxes will eventually mean fewer geese, which in turn means fewer foxes, until fewer foxes means more geese, and so on. Intricate networks of such feedback loops are now thought to govern the "chaotic" functioning of many complex systems.

Among American artists of the 1940s and 1950s, whose intellectual influences included Zen Buddhism, Gestalt therapy, and the physics of Alfred North Whitehead, the image most often invoked to describe ecological dynamics was that of the "energy field."[12] The "energy field" model of experience rejected the liberal paradigm that defined the human being as an individual mind confronting an objective universe. Instead, the human "body-mind" was conceived of as one with nature, constituted through a ceaseless, often unconscious interplay between self and environment. As Paul Goodman, one of the founders of Gestalt therapy, wrote in 1955: "Continuous or field theories and discrete or particle theories seem to be contrasting attitudes . . . one relying on the flow of spontaneous energy, the other on deliberate interventions and impositions."[13] Engaging the energy field's "flow of spontaneous energy" was the challenge of improvisational art.

The emphasis on feedback as an organizing principle is what distinguishes cybernetics from *laissez-faire* thinking.[14] A key form of feedback is what Bateson called "second-order" information. Bateson's wartime recommendations regarding how to encourage democratic values focused on "second-order" purposefulness, or, as he termed it, "deutero-learning."[15] Deutero-learning is the process of learning how to learn: the habits of thought and perspective that are cultivated by the first-order learning experience. For instance, if a person were to lecture before an audience and pronounce that "democracy is good; fascism is bad," the message on the level of first-order learning would be pro-democratic. The message on the level of second-order learning, however, would be the opposite, because the epistemological dynamic (what the audience learns about how to learn) is that of an authority figure telling others what to think. For democracy to be operative in second-order learning, the "audience" members would have to become active participants in a process of examining the relative merits of democracy and its alternatives, and arrive at their own conclusions. Then if, say, on the next day, another lecturer (or the same one) were to return and announce that "there has been a revision: fascism is good; it is democracy that is bad," the listeners' habits of deutero-learning would resist that message. Bateson understood cultures as autopoietic systems of social order, sustained by self-reinforcing processes (feedback loops) of learning and deutero-learning.[16]

Among artists, the resistant patterns that Bateson called "second-order learning" were associated with the concept of "plasticity." Plasticity referred to how an expressive medium responded to environmental pressures. The term had been defined by philosopher William James, who described it as a quality of resistance that made it possible for a material to be shaped: "Plasticity . . . means the possession of a structure [that] . . . opposes a certain resistance to the modifying cause. . . . [W]hen the structure has yielded, the same inertia becomes a condition of its comparative permanence in the new form, and of the new habits the body then manifests."[17] Mary Caroline Richards, who taught at Black Mountain College in North Carolina in the early 1950s, wrote about engaging the plasticity of clay in her 1964 book, *Centering: In Pottery, Poetry, and the Person*, portraying the interaction as a mutually transformative dialogue:

> Potter and clay press against each other. The firm, tender, sensitive pressure which yields as much as it asserts. It is like a handclasp between two living hands, receiving the greeting at the very moment that they give it. It is this speech between the hand and the clay that makes me think of dialogue. And it is a language far more interesting than the spoken vocabulary which tries to describe it, for it is spoken not by the tongue and lips but by the whole body, by the whole person, speaking and listening.

The clay's plasticity creates feedback, demanding that the potter "listen" as well as "speak." Because of this, wrote Richards, working in clay cultivated a quality of heightened awareness,

> a state of being "awake" to the world throughout our organism. . . . When one stands like a natural substance, *plastic* but with one's own character written into the formula, ah then one feels oneself part of the world, taking one's shape with its help.[18]

Many improvisational artists working in the 1950s made such plastic interaction the focus of their art-making.[19] In 1951 Paul Goodman co-authored a book with Fritz Perls and Ralph Hefferline called *Gestalt Therapy: Excitement and Growth in the Human Personality*, in which he clarified the connections between deutero-learning, plasticity, and social authority. Goodman argued that oppressive societies demanded the unassimilated acceptance (or "introjection") of prescribed values—training their members, metaphorically speaking, to "swallow things whole." To facilitate this introjection, such societies repressed the healthy levels of aggression that would prompt an individual to reject or ruminate on (literally, chew over) an unsatisfying attitude or behavior.[20] Because this deutero-learning pattern inhibited direct feedback, the feedback that resulted took form as a "social neurosis" in which detached cruelty was normalized; which is why, Goodman wrote, "the wars we acquiesce in are continually more destructive and less angry."[21] *Gestalt Therapy* promoted artistic dialogue in a plastic medium as the best antidote to this atrophy of healthy engagement with one's surroundings. Perhaps echoing the artist Robert Motherwell, Goodman praised collage and abstract expressionist gesture painting as fostering healthy patterns of interaction through "the working up of the real surface, the transformation of the apparent or enchoate theme in the material medium."[22] Such activity cultivated a spontaneous "awareness," which he defined as a flexible and emotionally charged engagement with one's immediate surroundings or "social-cultural, animal, and physical . . . field."[23]

This quality of awareness, which Goodman understood as the basis of improvisational art, is distinguishable from the automatism practiced by the Surrealists, in which improvisation is thought of primarily as the "welling up from within" of unconscious contents. For Goodman, the automatic act, which one performed while unaware of it, was as undesirable, at one extreme, as self-consciousness was at the other. "Awareness," he insisted, "is simple presentness, both perceptual and motor."[24] In group improvisation, awareness is what is needed for the successful navigation of the moment.

Goodman, Bateson, and Hayek all asserted that the social valorization of conscious purposefulness corresponded to a model of the self as governed by a centralized authority structure. The individual self emerges through an act of will. By contrast, Goodman's "awareness" corresponds to a model of the self as an autopoietic system: an entity constituted by the patterns of its interactions with the surrounding energy field. If one adopts this autopoietic model of the self, then group improvisation is seen to distill the essential process of identity formation: a negotiation relying on what composer John Cage called "polyattentiveness"—a quality of picking up on and according recognition to events in the environment, acknowledging others' claims to selfhood while simultaneously making one's own.[25]

FROM JOHN CAGE TO MAX NEUHAUS

The cultivation of polyattentiveness and the decentralization of authority are key concepts in understanding the work of John Cage, who earned a place in music history by his radical refusal of the authority of the composer. "A composer is simply someone who tells other people what to do," Cage wrote in *A Year from Monday* (1967); "I find this an unattractive way of getting things done."[26]

Cage's alternative to the traditional model of a composer as someone who thinks up music for a listener to hear, was to promote what might be called "second-order listening" because of its parallel to what Bateson called second-order learning. Cage was not interested in communicating emotions through the manipulation of a musical message, but in changing the listener's idea of what music could be.[27] "New music: new listening," he wrote in his manifesto, *Silence*, of 1961.[28] The Western musical heritage, Cage complained, represented a deeply ingrained listening habit.[29] He used indeterminacy to get listeners to discard their habitual expectations and value judgments and instead to adopt a frame of mind open to all experience—an aesthetic expressed in the Zen Buddhist maxim, "before the beautiful and the ugly were differentiated."[30] Cage's compositions therefore allow for no distinction between "musical" sounds and "noise." Typically they are filled with thumps, screeches, and snippets of radio broadcasts or tape recordings in addition to notes played on conventional musical instruments. Because sounds (noises) are everywhere, if the process of deutero-listening that Cage promoted were to take hold, the listener would always be surrounded by music.

But what is meant by music is radically redefined in the process. "Not an attempt to understand something that is being said . . . just an attention to the activity of sounds," Cage wrote.[31] As Bateson had written in 1942 that democratic leaders must "discard purpose in order to achieve our purpose," Cage called in 1957 for "a purposeful purposelessness" that would register as "an affirmation of life."[32] By "giv[ing] up the desire to control sound," he hoped to "let sounds be themselves."[33] Consonant with the "energy field" model of the self, Cage wrote that he wanted his music to lead the listener to the point "where gradually or suddenly, one sees that humanity and nature, not separate, are in this world together [and] . . . there are an incalculable infinity of causes and effects . . . , [because] in fact each and every thing in all of time and space is related to each and every other thing."[34] It was in order to foreground this complex system of interpenetrations that Cage made works demanding polyattentiveness on the part of the listener.[35] He once suggested that five simultaneous activities constituted the bare minimum for a good performance.[36] "This disharmony," he asserted, "to paraphrase Bergson's statement about disorder, is simply a harmony to which many are unaccustomed."[37]

As his musical practice illustrates, Cage's commitment to the principle of decentralization extended from the role of the composer to the forms of the music itself. Instead of composing a complete musical score, for instance, he would compose the parts of a piece and leave indeterminate the manner in which they were to be combined, because, he insisted, "the requiring that many parts be played in a *particular* togetherness, is not an accurate representation of *how things are*." Without a score to provide a centralized coordination of the musical experience, the plurality of the listeners' experiences was emphasized: "The central points where fusion occurs are many: the ears of the listeners wherever they are."[38]

Cage felt that such strategies of decentralization achieved an important ideological effect by means of deutero-listening: a pluralism in which every point was its own center, in lieu of having a single center that subordinated everything else. As Natalie Schmitt has explained,

Central focus in space, like central focus in time (climax) is a system of subordination of all the rest of the space or time, controlling the audience's attention. But if the audience itself is not to be subservient to the work, the idea of getting and holding their attention must be relinquished.[39]

Instead of attempting to hold the attention of the listener, Cage's strategies throw back to each listener the problem of what it means to listen. One of the most famous expressions of this principle is Cage's *4'33"* (1952), a piece in which the musicians onstage play nothing—the music is whatever sounds from other sources are heard by members of the audience.[40] In this extreme statement of Cage's musical philosophy, a connection between decentralization and feedback emerges, because the audience's output (the sounds they make) is also their input (the very music they are listening to).

Beginning in 1963, the percussionist and electronic music pioneer Max Neuhaus staged a number of realizations of Cage's score *Fontana Mix*. Neuhaus's realizations intensified the role of feedback as an organizing principle in Cage's decentralized aural field. Neuhaus used microphones resting on drums in front of loudspeakers to create a system of feedback loops. The microphones picked up room sounds, creating electrical signals that passed through a four-track mixer and were sent out through speakers; the sound waves from the speakers caused the drums on which the microphones were resting to vibrate, and these vibrations and sounds were once more encoded by the microphones into electrical signals that were mixed and sent around again. Neuhaus christened his hybrid realization *Fontana Mix-Feed*.

To Neuhaus's initial surprise, the "noise" generated by these multiple feedback loops was not random, but formed standing electronic wave patterns similar to conventional musical tones. The feedback loops had functioned as an organizing mechanism for the decentralized field of sound. As he described it,

> In 1963, while exploring ways of changing the timbre of percussion instruments through amplification, I had discovered a means of generating sound which I found fascinating—the creation of an acoustic feedback loop with a percussion instrument inserted inside it. Instead of the usual single screeching tones of acoustic feedback, this created a *complex multi-timbred system of oscillation*.[41]

The result was an autopoietic system that caused pattern, variety, and beauty to emerge from chaotic complexity. Small differences in initial conditions (the instruments, the spatial configuration of microphones and speakers, the acoustics of the room, the ambient room noise) made each performance unique. Neuhaus compared the system in this respect to a living organism.[42]

In 1966, Neuhaus expanded on the idea of the feedback loop with his own piece, *Public Supply*. Radio listeners calling in to any of ten phone lines at WBAI radio station in New York City were mixed into the broadcast that they were receiving over their radios. The structure of this process was similar to that of *Fontana Mix-Feed*, but this time the feedback loops incorporated living people and encompassed a community-sized space: the radio station's entire broadcast range became one virtual instrument. *Public Supply* was in this way clearly a next step in using audio feedback loops as a means for realizing a community or super-organism. As Neuhaus later explained:

> Anthropologists in looking at societies which have not yet had contact with modern man have often found whole communities making music together—not one small group making music for the others to listen to, but music as a sound dialogue among all the members of the community. Although I was not able to articulate it in 1966, now, after having worked with this idea for a long time and talked about it and thought about it, it seems that what these works are really about is proposing to reinstate a kind of music which we have forgotten about and which is perhaps the original impulse for music in man: not making a musical product to be listened to, but forming a dialogue, a dialogue without language, a sound dialogue.[43]

In 1977, after four years of preparation, Neuhaus performed *Radio Net,* a piece structured like *Public Supply* but this time spanning a network of over 190 public radio stations in several different cities.[44]

Cage's improvisations worked to liberate composing, performing, and listening from the conventions of central planning. Beginning where Cage left off, Neuhaus emphasized the possibilities of feedback loops in bringing form to such a decentralized system. By inventing virtual communities whose members helped to create their own shared experience, Neuhaus's musical networks prefigured the collaborative creations more recently made possible by computer networking, known as wikis.

Contact Improvisation

As with Neuhaus's *Public Supply,* the fundamental structure of the dance form known as "contact improvisation" was a network of people connected by feedback loops. In this case, though, the feedback was through touch, bringing it more into line with the mid-century discourse on "plasticity." According to dance historian Cynthia Novack, contact improvisation was "one of a number of enterprises during the late '60s and early '70s in dance, theater, therapy, and athletics which were trying to realize a redefinition of self within a responsive, intelligent body [and] . . . an egalitarian community."[45] Unlike other kinds of dance performance, which were created for a viewing public, contact improvisation was focused not on how the dance looked, but on allowing the dancers to develop a "physical dialogue" rooted in "the experience and 'truth' of the body."[46]

In contact improvisation, the dance is created by two or more dancers who stay in physical contact for most of the dance and use their points of contact as the bases for a mutual improvisation. By trading weight and momentum, the dancers create a shared center of gravity that each responds to but that no one is in full control of. Novack described this relationship using a terminology similar to that which Richards used to explain the plasticity of clay, writing that the dancers "move in concert with a partner's weight. . . . [T]hey often yield rather than resist. . . . Interest lies in the ongoing flow of energy."[47]

Novack credits Steve Paxton with inventing the form of contact improvisation in 1972.[48] Working in January of that year in the group Grand Union, Paxton developed a structured improvisation for some students from Oberlin College, which introduced what was later known as the "small dance" or "the stand." Each dancer stood in place, minimizing muscular tension and swaying with the resulting subtle shifts of his or her own weight.[49] The stand became the foundation for contact improvisation. In 2008, Paxton explained to an interviewer the importance of the small dance as a basis for the awareness that was necessary to group work: "To move from the small dance, from standing, into highly active work is a very good transition and a good spectrum. But it's got to have the base of it, it's got to have the stand, in my mind, to really be able to get safely to the fast, higher, tumble-y fall-y kind of contact."[50]

From the self-awareness of the "small dance," the intersubjective awareness of contact improvisation could develop. In June of 1972, Paxton, funded by a $2000 grant, invited Mary O'Donnell Fulkerson and fifteen or so of their students to work together in a loft in Chinatown in New York City equipped with an Olympic-sized wrestling mat.[51] Their work focused on groups of dancers maintaining physical contact while falling off balance, using weight or movement to create a moving, shared center of gravity.[52] Novack's later analysis of her own experience with contact improvisation offers a good description of the dynamic that evolved:

> Immersed in the feeling of tiny changes of weight and the smallest movement of my joints . . . settled in this state, when I came into contact with another dancer, I was intensely focused in moment-to-moment awareness of change. My sensitivity to touch and weight made me responsive to subtle shifts in my partner's actions. I then began to experience periods of an effortless flow of movement, not feeling passive, and yet not feeling actively in control either. The sensation of "being guided by the point of contact" with my partner fitted the description of "allowing the dance to happen" to me.[53]

It was Merce Cunningham who had begun the decentralization of space and time in American modern dance in the 1950s.[54] Cunningham made dances that, similar to Cage's compositions, had no central focus and no temporal development or climax. Contact improvisation was truly decentralized, however, because there was no choreographer shaping the movement. The improvised interactions became more than just a means of developing choreography; they were the dance itself. Paxton has stated that he aimed "to break down the hierarchy that seemed to arise between people when one was a choreographer and one was a dancer."[55] With no central director, the group of dancers in contact improvisation could approach the ideal of a democratic community. Their movements were not assigned to them by an external authority, but emerged from "the dynamic of changing personnel and the emergence of particular moods and qualities in the improvisation."[56]

The links between decentralization and democracy were explicitly acknowledged in the culture of experimental dance during the 1960s. As in Cage's philosophy, in contact improvisation the decentralized dynamic was associated with an ideal of acceptance: every movement or non-movement could be perceived as dance, just as every sound or silence could be music. Again, Zen Buddhism was an important influence, in this case via the martial art form of aikido.[57] Creating dances was no longer about making "entertainment" but about facilitating an awareness of one's physical interactions— what might be called, following Bateson, "second-order" movement.[58]

Among the community of contact improvisers, it was understood as an art form that implied a way of life. The improvisational regimen during the summer of 1972 blurred the boundaries between art and life. Performances, when they happened, were simply a day of the usual work, to which an audience was invited; audience members were free to come and go, staying as long as they liked.[59] According to Nancy Stark Smith, who was one of the participating Oberlin students, the emphasis was on "communal experimentation" rather than "goal-oriented" choreography.

> We spent so much of the day rolling around and being disoriented and touching each other and giving weight.... Everyone had a different way of doing it—the releasing people [Mary Fulkerson's students] were very soft and light, very sensitive. The jocks, and I guess I was one of them, were out there rolling around and crashing about.... But we had to work together, or at least we did work together, even though people had favorite partners.... How to live together as a group and how to do this movement were equally new ideas to me.[60]

Another dancer recalled how, in the mid-1970s, contact improvisation made difference feel interesting rather than threatening. There was "a tremendous tension and excitement about encountering anybody, an anticipation, not knowing what was going to happen—whether you were going to dance slowly, hardly move, do a lot of lifting and falling, or whether it was going to be sensuous or kind of playful or combative."[61] At performances this excitement would be picked up on by the audience members:

> The space would get warmer and warmer throughout the performance, and when it was over, there would be a lot of dancing in the audience. People would be jumping all over one another. They would stick around afterwards and really want to start rolling around and want to jump on you. The feeling was of a real shared experience among performers and audience, a tremendous feeling of physical accessibility between performers and audience.[62]

Because of its emphases on responsiveness and on breaking down the distinction between art and life, contact improvisation performed a sort of microcosmic modeling of democratic interaction among embodied subjects. In Novack's experience, the success or failure of a dance was determined ultimately on intersubjective rather than aesthetic grounds: "If rapport had been established in the dance—that is, if the movement with my partner seemed fairly mutual in direction, momentum, and timing so that it felt as though the dance had moved us—I also experienced a strong sense of communion with my partner, even if I had never met him or her before"; but by contrast, if the movement began to feel conscious or manipulative, the result was a sense of frustration and failure.[63]

The evolution of contact improvisation shows that experimental music and dance share a common historical trajectory. In the same way that Neuhaus began in 1963 to experiment with feedback as a structuring principle for Cage's open forms, so dancers in the 1960s had sought ways to bring structure to decentralized group improvisations. Carolee Schneemann's 1963 piece *Newspaper Event* for the Judson Dance Theater[64] pioneered the use of feedback to provide such a structure. According to dance historian Sally Banes:

> Schneemann had watched the dancers in the workshop using random movements, chance methods, and nontechnical movement, but was disappointed that they seemed to be working as autonomous entities even in group dances. Her response, in *Newspaper Event*, was to provide a framework within which they could interact physically and spontaneously.

As Schneemann herself described it: "I wanted . . . boundaries of self and group to be meshed and mutually evolving . . . to provide specific instructions through which contact and improvisation could activate neglected thresholds of awareness."[65]

In the year leading up to the invention of contact improvisation, Paxton similarly felt that the experimentalism of Grand Union "open[ed] . . . possibilities" but "eventually led to isolation" of the individual dancers in their private worlds.[66] He found that the reciprocity of improvised contact could restore a feeling of coherence or, as he put it, "entrainment." As he explained to an interviewer in 2008:

> The mind entrains; like our minds are more or less entrained now, we're having a conversation and we know the subject and we have a big pool of ideas that we can come from, that's a sign of entrainment. So with physical work it's about finding the expectables, that your partner is working at, I suppose, finding the range of delicacy or impulse anyway in the movement, finding the spatial specialness that your partner's mind has . . . but sensing them at a level that is just at the lowest level of your perceptual concentration, something that is almost so small that it almost is slipping away in terms of fragments of time, fragments of impulses in the body, and really saying, OK I'm going to look at this.[67]

Like other decentralized systems explored by thinkers like Bateson, Aldo Leopold, and Neuhaus, contact improvisation relied on feedback rather than conscious control as an organizational principle. The ideal attitude of the dancers avoided both conscious planning and inert passivity in favor of "a dialogue . . . between sensations of activity and receptivity" making possible a "sharing [of] information through the body."[68]

CONCLUSION: "THIRD FORCE"

In the history of improvisational art in America, the work of Bateson, Goodman, Neuhaus, and Paxton represents a coherent and significant departure from the body of work that equates spontaneity with automatism. Novack records that "Paxton tried to shed the concept of . . . the body dominated by an expressive inner self" and to replace it with a concept of "the responsive body."[69] Such work is founded on a model of improvisation emphasizing awareness and interaction rather than interior psychological contents. It is realized in the creation of an autopoietic system, a decentralized "society" ordered by feedback processes. As Paxton explained in the journal *Dance Review* in 1975: "The more the forms are understood, the more cooperation becomes the subject— an 'it' defined by the balancing of the inertias, momentums, psychologies, spirits of the partners."[70]

In such group improvisations, a postmodern idea of the self emerges. As centralization is modern, so decentralized networks are postmodern. And while a modern sensibility imagines the self as interiorized and conflicted, the postmodern sensibility imagines the self as relational: a site of physical and discursive intersections. It has no simple location "inside" a person, but instead is constituted by an occasion of overlapping events.[71]

This redefinition of selfhood has implications for political philosophy. In such group improvisations as Neuhaus and Paxton created, the individual is integrated into the group through feedback loops. There is neither the atomism of liberal politics nor the subordination of the individual to a central authority. There is instead, as in Goodman's Gestalt therapy, an emphasis on multiplying and facilitating the avenues of feedback. Feedback dynamics simultaneously stimulate and set constraints on the activities of individuals. As Novack described this phenomenon, "contact improvisation defines the self as the responsive body and also as the responsive body listening to another responsive body, the two *together spontaneously creating a third force that directs the dance*."[72] Novack's suggestion of a "third force" is consistent with Archie Shepp's description, quoted at the beginning of this essay, of modern jazz as the expression of a "communal intelligence." Bateson, too, by the end of the 1960s had arrived in his thinking about cybernetic systems at what he called "a profound redefinition of the self" that challenged the ethical premises of liberal society.[73] Morality, he wrote, must be understood in reference to the "larger Mind of which the individual mind is only a subsystem . . . immanent in the total interconnected social system and planetary ecology."[74] Improvisational artists were the first to explore this vision of an alternative social order that is neither *laissez-faire* nor centrally regulated, but networked.

NOTES

1. Paul Goodman, "The Political Meaning of Some Recent Revisions of Freud," *Politics* 2, no. 7 (July 1945): 201.

2. See Daniel Belgrad, *The Culture of Spontaneity: Improvisation and the Arts in Postwar America* (Chicago: University of Chicago Press, 1998), 29–31, 35–37, and 56–62.

3. See Belgrad, *Culture of Spontaneity*, 188–192. Musician Anne Farber has said that improvisation "means to play together with sufficient skill and communication to be able to select proper constraints in the course of the piece, rather than being dependent upon precisely chosen ones." Quoted in Matthew Rohn, *Visual Dynamics in Jackson Pollock's Abstractions* (Ann Arbor: UMI Research Press, 1987), 118.

4. Archie Shepp, Foreword to John Clellon Holmes, *The Horn* (New York: Thunder's Mouth Press, 1988), iii.

5. See Richard Edwards, *Contested Terrain: The Transformation of the Workplace in the Twentieth Century* (New York: Basic Books, 1979). See also Samuel Haber, *Efficiency and Uplift: Scientific Management in the Progressive Era, 1890–1920* (Chicago: The University of Chicago Press, 1964).

6. George Lipsitz, *Rainbow at Midnight: Labor and Culture in the 1940s* (Chicago: University of Illinois Press, 1994), 57, 61; Edwards, *Contested Terrain*, 149–151.

7. See Margaret Mead, "The Comparative Study of Culture and the Purposive Cultivation of Democratic Values," in *Science, Philosophy, and Religion, Second Symposium*, ed. Lymon Bryson and Louis Finkelstein (New York: 1942), 56–69. In 1941 and 1942, a group of social scientists was recruited by the Council for Democracy to consider how best to go about changing some habitual ways of thinking that could compromise wartime unity, such as isolationism, racism, and anti-Semitism. Its list of consultants included Mead and Bateson, Ruth Benedict, Hadley Cantril, Erik Erikson, and Erich Fromm. See Cedric Larson, "The Council for Democracy," *The Public Opinion Quarterly* 6, no. 2 (Summer 1942): 284–285. For more on the struggle over information management during the war, see Belgrad, *The Culture of Spontaneity*, 22–25.

8. David Lipset, *Gregory Bateson: The Legacy of a Scientist* (Englewood Cliffs, NJ: Prentice-Hall, 1980), 166; Gregory Bateson, "Social Planning and the Concept of Deutero-Learning," in *Steps to an Ecology of Mind* (Chicago: University of Chicago Press, 1972), 160–162.

9. Friedrich Hayek, "Freedom and the Economic System," *Contemporary Review* 153 (April 1938): 434–442.

10. Hayek, "Freedom," 438–442.

11. Friedrich Hayek, *The Road to Serfdom* (Chicago: The University of Chicago Press, 1944), 165–166.

12. For more on this point, see Belgrad, *Culture of Spontaneity*, 120–127.

13. Paul Goodman, *Five Years* (New York: Brussel and Brussel, 1966), 18.

14. For another example of ecological thinking from the early 1940s, see Aldo Leopold, "Thinking Like a Mountain," *A Sand County Almanac* (New York: Oxford University Press, 1966), 140–141.

15. Bateson, "Social Planning," 164.

16. Bateson believed that what distinguished the members of one culture from those of another were exactly these habitual ways of thinking and contextualizing that were inculcated by characteristic processes of deutero-learning. He wrote in another essay of 1942 that such patterns embodied the "holistic and systematic interrelations" among individual members of a society that accounted for their "knotted varieties of differentiation." Bateson, "Morale and National Character" in *Steps*, 88–106. See also Lipset, *Gregory Bateson*, 167.

17. William James, *Principles of Psychology*, (New York: Dover, 1950), 1: 105. First published in 1890.

18. M. C. Richards, *Centering: In Pottery, Poetry, and the Person* (Middletown, CT: Wesleyan University Press, 1964), 9. Emphasis mine. See also Belgrad, *Culture of Spontaneity*, 170–171. For more on the significance of Black Mountain College to the postwar avant-garde, see Belgrad, *Culture of Spontaneity*, 32–35, 142, 157–158.

19. Prominent examples include "gesture field" paintings and collages by Jackson Pollock, Robert Motherwell, and Helen Frankenthaler and the poetry of Charles Olson. See Belgrad, *The Culture of Spontaneity*, 114–119, 123, 135–136.

20. Frederick Perls, Ralph Hefferline, and Paul Goodman, *Gestalt Therapy: Excitement and Growth in the Human Personality* (New York: Dell Publishing Co., 1951), 7, 337–339. Perls and Hefferline wrote the self-help "Part I: "Orienting the Self," and Goodman wrote the theoretical "Part II: Manipulating the Self." In the 1994 edition, the order of the two volumes is reversed.

21. Perls, Hefferline, and Goodman, *Gestalt Therapy*, 242.

22. Perls, Hefferline, and Goodman, *Gestalt Therapy*, 395. Motherwell had written in 1946, "For the goal which lies beyond the strictly aesthetic, the French artists say the 'unknown' or the 'new,' after Baudelaire and Rimbaud. . . . 'Structure' or 'gestalt' may be more accurate: reality has no degrees nor is there a 'super' one (*surrealisme*). . . . Structures are found in the interaction of the body-mind and the external world, and the body-mind is active and aggressive in finding them. . . . The sensation of physically operating in the world is very strong in the medium of [collage] . . . One cuts and chooses and shifts and pastes, and sometimes tears off and begins again." Robert Motherwell, "Beyond the Aesthetic," *Design* 47, no. 8 (April 1946): 14–15, reprinted in Robert Motherwell, *The Writings of Robert Motherwell*, ed. Dore Ashton (Berkeley: University of California Press, 2007), 54–55.

23. Goodman questioned, "With regard to the adjustment of the mature person to reality, must we not ask—one is ashamed to have to mention it—whether the 'reality' is not rather clearly pictured after, and in the interests of, western urban industrial society, capitalist or state-socialist? Is it the case that other cultures, gaudier in dress, greedier in physical pleasures, dirtier in manners, more disorderly in governance, more brawling and adventurous in behavior, were or are thereby less mature?" Goodman, *Gestalt Therapy*, 228, 303.

24. Goodman, *Five Years*, 19.

25. See Judith Butler, *Giving an Account of Oneself* (New York: Fordham University Press, 2005), 27–28; Belgrad, *Culture of Spontaneity*, 161–162. Also see John Cage, quoted in Roger Copeland, "Merce Cunningham and the Politics of Perception," in *What Is Dance? Readings in Theory and Criticism,* ed. Roger Copeland and Marshall Cohen (New York: Oxford University Press, 1983), 321–322.

26. John Cage, *A Year from Monday* (Middletown, CT: Wesleyan University Press, 1967), ix.

27. Richard Kostelanetz, "Inferential Art," in Richard Kostelanetz, ed., *John Cage* (New York: Praeger, 1970), 107–108. Cage famously rejected the style of improvisation that he associated with the expression of a personality "welling up from within." For this reason he preferred the terms "nonintention" or "indeterminacy," which he felt emphasized the transformative potential of unforeseen interactions. For more on the discursive divide between "improvisation" and "indeterminacy" circa 1950, see George E. Lewis, "Improvised Music after 1950: Afrological and Eurological Perspectives," in *The Other Side of Nowhere: Jazz, Improvisation, and Communities in Dialogue,* ed. Daniel Fischlin and Ajay Heble (Middletown, CT: Wesleyan University Press, 2004), 137–149, 156–158.

28. John Cage, *Silence: Lectures and Writings* (London: Marion Boyars, 1995), 10.

29. Cage, *Silence*, 4.

30. Soetsu Yanagi, *The Unknown Craftsman: A Japanese Insight into Beauty* (New York: Kodansha International, 1978), 185. See Kostelanetz, "Conversation with John Cage," in Kostelanetz, ed., 31.

31. Cage, *Silence*, 10.

32. Cage, *Silence*, 12.

33. Cage, *Silence*, 10.

34. Cage, *Silence*, 8, 46–47.

35. See Belgrad, *Culture of Spontaneity*, 162.

36. Cage, *Silence*, 173; Natalie Crohn Schmitt, *Actors and Onlookers: Theater and Twentieth-Century Scientific Views of Nature* (Evanston, IL: Northwestern University Press, 1990), 16.

37. Cage, *Silence*, 12.

38. Cage, *Silence*, 10. Emphasis mine.

39. Schmitt, *Actors and Onlookers*, 31.

40. Cage wrote, "In this new music nothing takes place but sounds. . . . [T]hose that are not notated appear in the written music as silences, opening the doors of the music to the sounds that happen to be in the environment." Cage, *Silence*, 7–8.

41. Max Neuhaus, liner notes for *Fontana Mix–Feed (six realizations of John Cage)* (Alga Marghen, 2003). Emphasis mine.

42. Neuhaus, liner notes. For more on reiteration and order in chaotic systems, see John Briggs and F. David Peat, *Turbulent Mirror: An Illustrated Guide to Chaos Theory and the Science of Wholeness* (New York: Harper and Row, 1989), 68–69, 74, 77.

43. Max Neuhaus, "The Broadcast Works and Audium," in *Zeitgleich* exhibition catalogue (Vienna: Transit, 1994). http://kunstradio.at/ZEITGLEICH/index.html, accessed January 14, 2013.

44. John Rockwell, *All-American Music: Composition in the Late Twentieth Century* (New York: Alfred A. Knopf, 1983), 147.

45. Cynthia Novack, *Sharing the Dance: Contact Improvisation and American Culture* (Madison: University of Wisconsin Press, 1990), 3, 12.

46. Novack, *Sharing the Dance*, 8.

47. Novack, *Sharing the Dance*, 51.

48. Novack, *Sharing the Dance*, 53 and 11.

49. The name of the piece was "Magnesium." Novack, *Sharing the Dance*, 62.

50. Steve Paxton, interview with Nathan Wagoner, 2008, http://vimeo.com/1731742, accessed January 14, 2013.

51. Novack, *Sharing the Dance*, 63–64. Like Paxton, Fulkerson had studied Limón technique and Cunningham technique. At the time, she was teaching at the University of Rochester.

52. Novack, *Sharing the Dance*, 73, 101.

53. Novack, *Sharing the Dance*, 152.

54. Don McDonagh, *The Rise and Fall and Rise of Modern Dance*, 2nd ed. (Pennington, NJ: A Cappella Books, 1990), 36–37. Paxton had studied dance with Cunningham before becoming a member of the Judson Dance Theater in the early 1960s. Paxton also studied in 1958 with José Limón.

55. Steve Paxton quoted in Novack, *Sharing the Dance*, 53–54.

56. Novack, *Sharing the Dance*, 124.

57. Novack, *Sharing the Dance*, 184.

58. Novack, *Sharing the Dance*, 23, 19, 55, 58–59, 133.

59. Novack, *Sharing the Dance*, 66.

60. Quoted in Novack, *Sharing the Dance*, 64.

61. Lisa Nelson, quoted in Novack, *Sharing the Dance*, 70–71.

62. Nelson, quoted in Novack, *Sharing the Dance*, 72.

63. Novack, *Sharing the Dance*, 152–153.

64. Before joining Grand Union, Paxton was involved in the Judson Dance Theater, which evolved from a choreography class by Robert Dunn (who had studied music theory with Cage and was the accompanist at Cunningham's dance studio). Neuhaus worked with the Judson Dance Theater in April 1964. Sally Banes, *Democracy's Body: Judson Dance Theater, 1962–1964* (Ann Arbor: University Microfilms International, 1982), xi–xv and 197.

65. Banes, *Democracy's Body*, 96. Carolee Schneemann, *More Than Meat Joy* (New Paltz, NY: Documentext, 1979), 33; quoted in Banes, *Democracy's Body*, 96. Compare William Davis's description of Yvonne Rainer's "Dance for 3 People and 6 Arms" of 1962, also for the Judson Dance Theater: "What it really resembled was jazz musicianship, more than chance operations, because we were all working for a time when we might, for example, do this, or seeing what someone else is doing, think, 'Oh yes, I can connect this to that.' . . . It's a sense of shape taking place in three people's minds as the dance is going on." Quoted in Banes, *Democracy's Body*, 52.

66. Paxton, quoted in Novack, *Sharing the Dance*, 60.

67. Steve Paxton, interview with Nathan Wagoner.

68. Novack, *Sharing the Dance*, 153 and 183.

69. Novack, *Sharing the Dance*, 188. This dichotomy is more of a heuristic distinction than a true opposition, for it was definitively the "expressive inner self" that "the responsive body" was responding to. The interactive dynamics of contact improvisation have repeatedly been compared to those of encounter group therapy, but with "honesty" and "trust" arrived at through physical rather than verbal dialogue. See Novack, *Sharing the Dance*, 166 and 168. As Nancy Stark Smith asserted, "The giving and sharing of weight sets up a kind of template. You can't lie about that stuff." Quoted in Novack, *Sharing the Dance*, 181.

70. Paxton, quoted in Novack, *Sharing the Dance*, 182. As the practice of contact improvisation spread from the initial experiments to become a widely practiced dance form, the structure of round robin developed as an expression of this objective of networking through feedback. A typical dance session would begin as a duet, which after a time would either dissolve into two solos (signaling the dancers' readiness for new partners) or receive a third dancer to become a trio; when everyone had had at least one chance to dance, the session would end.

71. See Belgrad, *Culture of Spontaneity*, 126.

72. Novack, *Sharing the Dance*, 189. Emphasis mine.

73. Bateson, "The Logical Categories of Learning and Communication" in *Steps*, 304.

74. Bateson, "Form, Substance, and Difference" in *Steps*, 466.

BIBLIOGRAPHY

Banes, Sally. *Democracy's Body: Judson Dance Theater, 1962–1964*. Ann Arbor: University Microfilms International, 1982.

Bateson, Gregory. *Steps to an Ecology of Mind*. Chicago: The University of Chicago Press, 1972.

Belgrad, Daniel. *The Culture of Spontaneity: Improvisation and the Arts in Postwar America*. Chicago: University of Chicago Press, 1998.

Briggs, John, and F. David Peat. *Turbulent Mirror: An Illustrated Guide to Chaos Theory and the Science of Wholeness*. New York: Harper and Row, 1989.

Butler, Judith. *Giving an Account of Oneself*. New York: Fordham University Press, 2005.

Cage, John. *A Year from Monday*. Middletown, CT: Wesleyan University Press, 1967.

Cage, John. *Silence: Lectures and Writings*. London: Marion Boyars, 1995.

Copeland, Roger. "Merce Cunningham and the Politics of Perception." In *What Is Dance? Readings in Theory and Criticism*, edited by Roger Copeland and Marshall Cohen, 307–324. New York: Oxford University Press, 1983.

Edwards, Richard. *Contested Terrain: The Transformation of the Workplace in the Twentieth Century*. New York: Basic Books, 1979.

Goodman, Paul. "The Political Meaning of Some Recent Revisions of Freud." *Politics* 2, no. 7 (July 1945): 197–202.

Goodman, Paul. *Five Years*. New York: Brussel and Brussel, 1966.

Haber, Samuel. *Efficiency and Uplift: Scientific Management in the Progressive Era, 1890–1920*. Chicago: University of Chicago Press, 1964.

Hayek, Friedrich. "Freedom and the Economic System." *Contemporary Review* 153 (April 1938): 434–442.

Hayek, Friedrich. *The Road to Serfdom*. Chicago: University of Chicago Press, 1944.

James, William. *Principles of Psychology*, New York: Dover, 1950. Originally published in 1890.

Kostelanetz, Richard, ed. *John Cage*. New York: Praeger, 1970.

Larson, Cedric. "The Council for Democracy." *The Public Opinion Quarterly* 6, no. 2 (Summer 1942): 284–285.

Leopold, Aldo. "Thinking Like a Mountain." *A Sand County Almanac*. New York: Oxford University Press, 1966, 137–141.

Lewis, George E. "Improvised Music after 1950: Afrological and Eurological Perspectives." In *The Other Side of Nowhere: Jazz, Improvisation, and Communities in Dialogue*, edited by Daniel Fischlin and Ajay Heble, 131–162. Middletown, CT: Wesleyan University Press, 2004.

Lipset, David. *Gregory Bateson: The Legacy of a Scientist*. Englewood Cliffs, NJ: Prentice-Hall, 1980.

Lipsitz, George. *Rainbow at Midnight: Labor and Culture in the 1940s*. Chicago: University of Illinois Press, 1994.

McDonagh, Don. *The Rise and Fall and Rise of Modern Dance*, 2nd ed. Pennington, NJ: A Cappella Books, 1990.

Mead, Margaret. "The Comparative Study of Culture and the Purposive Cultivation of Democratic Values." In *Science, Philosophy, and Religion, Second Symposium*, edited by Lymon Bryson and Louis Finkelstein, 56–69. New York: Conference on Science, Philosophy and Religion in Their Relation to the Democratic Way of Life, 1942.

Motherwell, Robert. *The Writings of Robert Motherwell*, edited by Dore Ashton. Berkeley: University of California Press, 2007.

Neuhaus, Max. "The Broadcast Works and Audium." *Zeitgleich exhibition catalogue*. Vienna: Transit, 1994. http://kunstradio.at/ZEITGLEICH/index.html

Neuhaus, Max. *Fontana Mix—Feed (six realizations of John Cage)*. Alga Marghen, 2003.

Novack, Cynthia. *Sharing the Dance: Contact Improvisation and American Culture*. Madison: University of Wisconsin Press, 1990.

Paxton, Steve. Interview with Nathan Wagoner, 2008. http://vimeo.com/1731742.

Perls, Frederick, Ralph Hefferline, and Paul Goodman. *Gestalt Therapy: Excitement and Growth in the Human Personality*. New York: Dell, 1951.

Richards, M. C. *Centering: In Pottery, Poetry, and the Person*. Middletown, CT: Wesleyan University Press, 1964.

Rockwell, John. *All-American Music: Composition in the Late Twentieth Century*. New York: Alfred A. Knopf, 1983.

Rohn, Matthew. *Visual Dynamics in Jackson Pollock's Abstractions*. Ann Arbor, MI: UMI Research Press, 1987.

Schmitt, Natalie Crohn. *Actors and Onlookers: Theater and Twentieth-Century Scientific Views of Nature*. Evanston, IL: Northwestern University Press, 1990.

Shepp, Archie. "Foreword." In John Clellon Holmes, *The Horn*, i–v. New York: Thunder's Mouth Press, 1988.

Yanagi, Soetsu. *The Unknown Craftsman: A Japanese Insight into Beauty*. New York: Kodansha International, 1978.

PART IV

MOBILITIES

CHAPTER 17

IMPROVISED DANCE IN THE RECONSTRUCTION OF *THEM*

DANIELLE GOLDMAN

ON May 10, 1985, the choreographer Ishmael Houston-Jones, the musician Chris Cochrane, and the writer Dennis Cooper presented a work-in-progress called *THEM*. The performance involved a series of structured improvisations that, as Burt Supree later wrote in the *Village Voice*, explored "some ways men are with men—physically, sexually, emotionally."[1] Cochrane composed and performed the score, Cooper wrote and recited the text, and Houston-Jones was joined by two other dancers, Donald Fleming and Jonathan Walker. Less than a year later, the group performed a portion of *THEM* as part of *Dancing for Our Lives!,* the first official AIDS benefit for New York City's dance community, held at the downtown performance space known as P.S. 122.[2]

In November 1986, Houston-Jones, Cochrane, Cooper, Fleming, and four additional dancers—Barry Crooks, Julyen Hamilton, Daniel McIntosh, and David Zambrano—presented a fuller version of the work at P.S. 122. Much had changed over the previous eighteen months. The work became darker and more explicit in its reference to HIV/AIDS. Whereas the work-in-progress contained a series of fragile, and occasionally violent, improvisations intertwined with Cooper's melancholic texts, the 1986 version concluded with a devastating section where Houston-Jones wrestled with a dead goat—blood smearing on the mattress upon which the dance takes place—and a final improvisation where the dancers tentatively felt their necks, underarms, and groins, as if checking for inflamed lymph nodes.[3] Moreover, the improvisations seemed riskier—the dancers had more range, they were more expressive, and they showed a willingness to be still and to make contact with the floor. Houston-Jones explains, "By November 1986 I already had friends, ex-boyfriends, heroes who were dying of The Plague and making an upbeat work about the ways six men could possibly be together seemed impossible then."[4] According to Supree, whose lover died of AIDS the week before he saw the final version,[5] "*THEM* has become a much grimmer piece since the chunk I saw at *Dancing for Our Lives!* . . . I remember it as aggressive and vital, but the current version seems more stiff-lipped, hardened, fatalistic, as if too many emotional and sensual options have been terminated since then."[6] He continued, "*THEM* isn't a piece about AIDS, but AIDS constricts its view and casts a considerable pall" (see Figures 17.1 and 17.2).[7]

In 2010, Vallejo Gantner, the current Artistic Director of P.S. 122, invited Houston-Jones to reconstruct a past performance as part of a broader thirtieth anniversary retrospective of significant works performed at P.S. 122. Houston-Jones decided to bring back *THEM,* and the work was presented in October 2010 in the same theater as its premiere (see Figures 17.3, 17.4, and 17.5). Reflecting on his decision, Houston-Jones explains, "I am wondering how particularly the AIDS theme has changed in the twenty-five years since the piece was made."[8] After holding an audition and deciding upon a cast for the reconstruction, which involved Cochrane, Cooper, Houston-Jones, and seven male dancers in their twenties and early thirties, it became clear that several of the young dancers were not even alive when the piece premiered and they had varied understandings of the AIDS pandemic. In fact, at the beginning of the reconstruction process, some of the dancers felt as though they had no personal connection to the HIV virus whatsoever. How, then, to give the contextual knowledge that informed the creation of the piece, and how to give the dancers a sense of the paranoia, urgency, and sorrow embedded in the work? This became a complex challenge for Houston-Jones, who insisted that AIDS is so significant that surely the young dancers have memories or connections to it somewhere. As he said in an interview, the disease is still present and many people do still die from it.[9]

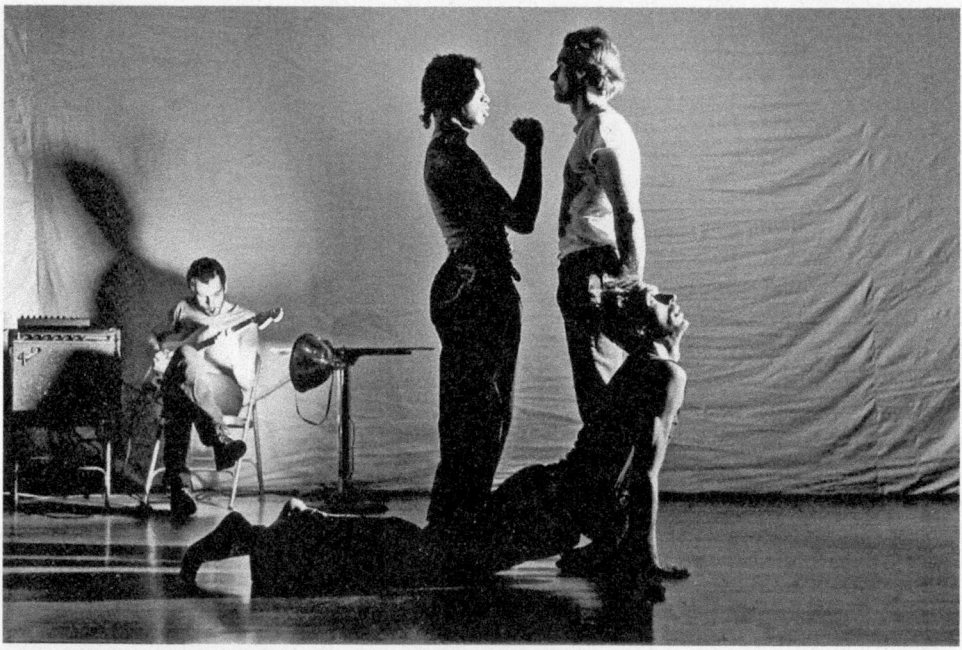

FIGURE 17.1 Clockwise, from left to right: Chris Cochrane, Ishmael Houston-Jones, Jonathan Walker, Donald Fleming (floor), *THEM* (1985).

Photograph by Dona Ann McAdams.

FIGURE 17.2 Ishmael Houston-Jones, Chris Cochrane, and Johnny Walker, *THEM* (1985).

Photograph by Dona Ann McAdams.

FIGURE 17.3 Felix Cruz and Jeremy Pheiffer, *THEM* (2010).

Photograph by Ian Douglas.

FIGURE 17.4 Ishmael Houston-Jones in *THEM* (2010).

Photograph by Ian Douglas.

FIGURE 17.5 Joey Canizzaro in *THEM* (2010).

Photograph by Ian Douglas.

Importantly, improvisation played a vital role in allowing the dancers to uncover and explore that knowledge. As Houston-Jones reflects on the process, "We were having an improvisation where they [the younger dancers] had to speak about their relationship to AIDS/HIV, and they started saying, 'Oh, I don't have any relationship.' But as we kept probing and talking, they actually do—like a cousin, or somebody they danced with—and they would remember."[10]

In what follows, I discuss some of the ways that dance scholars have written about improvisation. Then, resisting the prevalent notion that improvisation enables "free" dancing, I highlight constraints that the dancers involved in the reconstruction of *THEM* negotiated: racialized assumptions about training, the demands of dancing with a partner, and the strictures presented by the score and the narrative aspects of Cooper's text. But I focus primarily on the ways in which the passage of time affected the dancers' improvisations, for this is where the politics of the work emerge with particular force. As José Muñoz writes in *Cruising Utopia*, "memory is most certainly constructed and, more important, always political."[11] Muñoz goes on to suggest that remembrances enacted through performance, especially performances that index queer desire and public sexuality, have the capacity to offer hope in the face of abjection.[12] In other words, it can be powerful, even sustaining, to take on embodied modes of relating to others that resist heteronormative displays of sexuality. In the reconstruction of *THEM,* improvisation enabled the dancers to explore a past that they didn't entirely understand, while also demanding that, throughout the performance, they place themselves—literally and figuratively—in relation to that past. As Niall Noel Jones, one of these dancers, explained, "[*THEM*] feels large, like it has a long life."[13] Jones, who was twenty-seven years old at the time of *THEM*'s re-creation, noted the specter of the original cast from the 1980s and their friends and lovers, as well as the many people Cooper references in his text. He continued, "There are multiple ghosts within the work. There are many hauntings that are danced."[14] The fact that the dancers improvised these hauntings, as opposed to merely miming what the original cast had done in the eighties, resulted in a reconstruction that actively reconsiders the past, while quite possibly gesturing toward a future.

ISHMAEL HOUSTON-JONES:
THE POLITICS OF DANCING

Ishmael Houston-Jones grew up in Harrisburg, Pennsylvania, and started taking dance classes as a teenager. He spent two years studying English at Gannon College before dropping out and moving to Israel in 1971, where he worked as a pig farmer and then on a banana plantation. After spending a year in Israel, he moved to Philadelphia and danced for Group Motion Media Theater. He later participated in an ensemble called "A Way of Improvising" with Terry Fox and Jeff Cain, and in the mid-1970s helped form a gay men's collective called Two Men Dancing.[15] According to Houston-Jones, at that time improvised dance in Philadelphia was both rare and unloved. Houston-Jones therefore began commuting to New York City to study contact improvisation—an emerging form where dancers improvise in contact with a partner—with Daniel Lepkoff. Houston-Jones moved to New York City in 1979 and created works throughout the 1980s and 1990s that were grounded in improvisation. Aside from his recent reconstructions, Houston-Jones stopped making new work about a decade ago. But he still performs, and he teaches at colleges and universities, including Hollins, Sarah Lawrence College, and The New School. He also teaches regularly at the American Dance Festival, where he coordinates the improvisation curriculum.

Unlike many of today's aspiring dancers, Houston-Jones never considered the pursuit of improvisatory training as something separate from everyday life.[16] As he explored improvised dance in the early 1980s, he also was politically active, working for God's Love We Deliver, an organization that prepares and delivers food for people who aren't able to provide for themselves due to illnesses. He traveled to Nicaragua in 1983 and 1984 to teach improvisation. For him, activism and dance were never wholly separate. As Houston-Jones remarks, "There was a sense of urgency that I don't feel so much now—from anti nukes, to wars in Central America. People were in opposition. People were invested more than they are now, at least visibly, vocally invested—[THEM] came out of that time."[17] This doesn't mean that his work was didactic or politically obtuse. According to the choreographer Jennifer Monson, "Ishmael was engaged in political work that trusts the dancing. Improvisation in Ishmael's work gave dancers permission to feel. He creates a space where dancers can move toward something, and feel supported, without knowing in precise terms the nature of the place of arrival. There's a kind of listening and attentiveness, and engagement with the outside world, that improvisation requires."[18]

Ironically, within the field of dance, most discussions of improvisation elide the kind of engagement with the outside world that Monson describes. Critics, scholars, and dancers across a range of genres tend to link improvisation with notions of "freedom" without examining the precise meaning of the term. Common celebrations of improvisation's "freedom" involve the notion that it enables dancers to escape the tyranny of the choreographer's gaze or to present authentic or unmediated forms of self-expression or to discover new ways of moving. It's a way, supposedly, of not engaging with restrictive forces in the external world.

To Houston-Jones, and to other scholars, however, far from representing an escape, the most skillful improvisations negotiate an ever-shifting landscape of constraints.[19] One's social and historical positions in the world affect one's ability to move, both literally and figuratively. To ignore the constraints that improvisers inevitably encounter is to deny the real conditions that shape daily life; it is also to deny improvisation's most significant power: as a critical engagement with the world, characterized by both flexibility and perpetual readiness. Improvised dance involves literally giving shape to oneself by deciding how to move in relation to an unsteady landscape. To engage oneself in this manner, with a sense of confidence and possibility, is a dynamic way to inhabit one's body and to interact with the world.

Houston-Jones is well aware of the shifting nature of social categories and prejudices that performers inevitably encounter while improvising. In 1986, for example, he developed a score[20] to use in the rehearsal process for a performance called *Adolfo und Maria*. In the score, which he calls "The Politics of Dancing," Houston-Jones asks a group of people to gather in the center of a room. He then utters a pair of binary statements about identity. For example, "If you are a man, go to one wall. If you are not a man, go to the opposite wall."[21] Members of the group must make split decisions, as if standing on a railway track with a train approaching. Once on the selected side of the room, people look at the individuals close to them, searching for similarities and differences and taking note of any surprises or assumptions that the grouping reveals. The individuals then take note of the individuals across the room. Once everyone has had a chance to observe the groupings, they reassemble as a tight cluster in the center of the room. Houston-Jones then issues another pair of identifications: right-handed/left-handed; blond/not-blond; Jewish/not-Jewish; have parents who are college graduates/don't have parent who are college graduates; want to have children/don't want to have children, and so forth.[22] Some pairs involve voluntary characteristics, whereas others do not. Some statements seem more subjective than others, and language is often fraught and open for interpretation. As Houston-Jones notes, "Defining sexuality takes quite a bit of finessing. In a single workshop 'I AM GAY,' 'I AM HOMOSEXUAL,' 'I AM QUEER,' 'I HAVE INTERCOURSE ONLY WITH PEOPLE OF MY OWN GENDER' and their 'opposites' can each produce very different splits in one group."[23] Typically, the group spends about forty-five minutes gathering and dispersing and then talks about their experiences for a similar amount of time.

Houston-Jones has used "The Politics of Dancing" during rehearsals, and he has presented the structure as a teaching tool in American university workshops, conferences, and international dance schools. Along the way, he has experimented with several iterations of the score: he has created situations in which the person uttering the categories changes throughout the exercise; he has asked the person speaking the categories to make only "true" statements for herself and to use first-person phrasing; and he has asked participants to close their eyes.[24] He explains his motivation for these exercises:

> I wanted something more multifaceted that would address the more elusive ways in which people perceive others and make assumptions about what those perceptions might mean. I wanted to explore some of the subtle and not so subtle ways people act upon those perceptions and assumptions. I also wanted people to feel what it was like to be in a minority facing a much larger group. I was interested to know which groupings caused people discomfort and which ways they liked to be grouped; when they would lie or resist the categorizing. I wanted to break down knee jerk responses and for people to look beyond the superficial things they were seeing and find the origins of the responses they were having.[25]

"The Politics of Dancing" explores modes of identification and highlights some of the ways in which bodies are perceived. Yet when Houston-Jones first started introducing this score to dancers, some of them had difficulty understanding how these things relate to "dance." Nancy Stark Smith, a committed improviser and one of the originators of contact improvisation, recalls her first exposure to Houston-Jones's "The Politics of Dancing" in 1988 at the European Contact Teachers Conference in Berlin: "I remember going through a range of emotions as the categories came and went and I dutifully plumbed my depths for the truest answers. Among my feelings were suspicion and irritation, as I wondered what made this 'The Politics of Dancing,' what this had to do with dancing at all, and what it had to do with me."[26]

Although Stark Smith left "The Politics of Dancing" workshop feeling suspicious and irritated, the score has much to do with dancing, and it has relevance for performers and audience members alike. "The Politics of Dancing" is an exercise in seeing and being seen. It is an exercise that asks one to consider what it feels like to be outnumbered. It asks one to feel the pressures of categories of identity that are always too simple. It asks one to make spontaneous choices. This is the landscape in which dancing occurs, as opposed to the kind of "free" and equal space that discussions of improvisation in the arts tend to invoke. To imagine that movement holds the same implications for all bodies, or to imagine that all manners of moving are equally available or experienced in the same way, is naïve. Dancing *is* political, it does relate to the different identities that people have, and improvisation always occurs amidst shifting constraints. This is something that Houston-Jones helps others realize.

In the reconstruction of *THEM,* the strictures at play helped give the improvisations their urgency and their sense of liveness. Even though the work was "historic," the dancers had to navigate a contemporary scene while deciding how to move. Part of this entailed reckoning with contemporary ways of being seen, not all of them pleasant. The dancers, for example, were subject to racialized responses to their style and movement choices. Niall Noel Jones, the one black dancer in the cast of young performers, recounted remarks about his "Ishmael impersonation."[27] Being involved in a dance scene with few people of color, there was a way in which, for many, Jones's body became Houston-Jones's body. Although this could certainly be taken as a compliment, it becomes something else when the comparison occurs merely on racial grounds. Enrico Wey, the one Asian American dancer in the cast, noted a remark made by an audience member that he must have had prior "martial arts training."[28]

Beyond the social and historical constraints that informed how their bodies and movement choices were read, the dancers also had to deal with the strictures internal to the work. As the piece contained a great deal of dancing in contact, the performers needed to contend, too, with the demands made by their partners. The dancers drew from diverse experiences and techniques, including contact improvisation, vogueing, puppeteering, and more canonized modes of modern dance.[29] Each style or mode of approaching movement structures the dancer's body and entails the formation of habits. Wey, for example, mentioned in an interview that his background as a puppeteer required him to channel his energy into an object while being as invisible as possible onstage. This was a different kind of presence than what was required in *THEM,* particularly in a section of the dance where he had to pose and preen for Niall Noel Jones.[30]

The challenge of responding to a partner with different habits and modes of virtuosity was particularly apparent in the opening duet between Noel Jones and Felix Cruz. Jones, who moves with a weighted quality, frequently displays an awareness of his surroundings and of his partner's choices that suggests a commitment to improvisatory practices. Cruz, on the other hand, has a tighter musculature and tends toward more recognizable modern dance sequences—turning with a leg positioned in "attitude," flinging his arms, or spiraling quickly onto the floor. It was difficult, therefore, for subtlety to emerge in the duet, or for the dancers to release into each other—a difficulty that was fitting for this section of the dance, which, according to Houston-Jones, "is about 'contact' that doesn't work. About support that disappears."[31] The dancers also had to contend with the score, which dictated a series of events with little room for the dancers to negotiate transitions. Given that the structure itself was not available for critique by the dancers, the challenge, then, became how to capitalize on possibilities within it. In addition, the dancers needed to be responsive to both Cochrane's music and Cooper's text, without illustrating either in a literal manner. As Houston-Jones often says, "no acting."

Although the dancers improvised in relation to a host of complicated constraints, they felt especially affected by the weight of history and a sense of responsibility toward previous generations. When discussing critical responses to the reconstruction, many of which described the work as being young and full of technical virtuosity, Noel Jones suggested that the 1980s version wasn't as violent as the reconstruction. Highlighting the thrashing physicality of the young dancers, he then suggested that perhaps the aggression came from imagining a community being ravaged. He suggested that perhaps the younger dancers unwittingly created a caricature of what it was like to have been making choreographic work about AIDS at that time, which resulted in a kind of aggression.[32]

"For Some Reason It Still Matters"

The 2010 reconstruction of *THEM* begins with Houston-Jones walking slowly into the dimly lit theater. He approaches another figure, Arturo Vidich, who stands with his back toward the audience. Houston-Jones gently places a hand on Vidich's shoulder and then covers the younger man's eyes with a white blindfold made of medical gauze, in what could be either an act of violence or protection. Houston-Jones turns Vidich around to face the audience, and then the two men perform a complex yet delicate duet. They spin each other around, and move through vulnerable points of contact, including each other's armpits, necks, and wrists. The duet begins in silence, but eventually, once Houston-Jones drops to the floor, Cochrane introduces brooding atmospheric tones into the soundscape.[33] Houston-Jones backs up slowly, until the distance between the two figures is pronounced. Another young man, Jeremy Pheiffer, emerges from upstage as Houston-Jones backs away. Pheiffer continues the duet that Houston-Jones began with the blindfolded man, only with a rougher sense of manipulation. Houston-Jones watches the two young men. As Pheiffer takes Vidich offstage into shadow, Houston-Jones begins a solo (see Figure 17.4).

In many ways, the solo shows a weathered man. As Houston-Jones faces the audience, one notices the bags under his eyes, dark and hanging like sacks. These bags index fatigue, but also sadness, or a kind of worldliness. His flesh appears thin and his closely cropped hair is turning grey. He is aging. Yet the solo is full of quick coils and extensions, in keeping with the rock-grunge strumming of Cochrane on his electric guitar. Wearing a plaid shirt with cut-off sleeves, rolled up jeans, and sneakers, Houston-Jones hurls himself onto the ground, kisses himself, licks his arms, and gestures in the space mournfully. He makes himself accessible to the audience, but not entirely, or not without demanding that the viewer reckon with the complexities of spectatorship. As the dancing winds down, he subtly covers his nose and mouth, and quietly leaves the performing area.

Houston-Jones did not include this solo in the 1980s version, and it functions as a prologue for the reconstruction that follows. According to the score's notes for the solo, "Ishmael foreshadows movement motifs that will appear later also with a sense of saying good-bye and passing the material onto a new generation of performers."[34] Although the audience wouldn't necessarily know it, Houston-Jones then finds a spot in the theater and watches the rest of the show. Enrico Wey, one of the performers in the reconstruction, explained in a recent conversation that he understood Houston-Jones's solo as a kind of "send-off," or a passing on of information. All of the dancers are onstage from the beginning of the show, mostly hidden in shadow, and Wey always watched the solo attentively. "It helped me to get into a sense of what we were trying to achieve," he explained. "It was a passing on of responsibility. I've been called upon to do something, even if it's not entirely clear what that something is."[35]

As Houston-Jones exits the space, a spotlight emerges on Cooper, who begins to read into a microphone:

> I saw them once. I don't know when or who they were because they were too far away. But I remember certain things, like what they wore, which wasn't anything special— pants, shirts, regular colors—stuff I've seen thousands of times since.
>
> I wanted them to know something. I cupped my hands around my mouth and thought about yelling out. But they wouldn't have heard me. Besides, I didn't belong there. So I sat on a rock and watched them. For some reason it still matters years later.
>
> I thought about love. I think I confused what they did with it. But my belief made the day great. I think I decided to make that my goal—to be like them. I put such incredible faith in the future that I sobbed a little I think.
>
> I can't believe I once felt what I'm talking about. Those tangled guys have become an abstraction, a gesture, a recreation. I wish I had taken a photo of them. Then I could rip it up, because I'm tired of dreaming of what they implied every night of my life, or whenever I close my eyes, whichever comes first. I thought it mattered. It does and it doesn't. They're very beautiful back there, but put all that feeling in motion now, then try to get it to explode in your face. It can't. It's not built to do that.

But they're still there, no matter how I misremember them. And redefining whatever it was they were doing is all I can do now. To sit here and see them again, no matter how cold that looks. It wasn't.[36]

The words come out slowly and with a weighted quality, as if you can feel them moving around in Cooper's mouth. This is the text from which *THEM* got its name. A series of tableaux takes shape among the dancers as Cooper reads, followed by an episodic series of improvisations that invoke young men exploring gradations of desire, at times spiraling into ecstasy, while at other times buckling under its force. It's a visceral, gritty work, full of shadows and violence. As one writer described the reconstruction, "Lit like a dank alleyway, danced in saggy tee shirts and scuffed hi-tops, the piece reeked of boy-stank."[37] There are multiple duets throughout the work that suggest both attraction and repulsion and oscillate between seeing and being seen. The dancers pose, preen, and grope, frequently hurling themselves with abandon. There's a section of the dance called "Dead Friends," in which Cooper recites a litany of deaths by various causes (suicide, a car accident, cancer, but notably not AIDS) as Pheiffer bats pennies with a two-by-four. With each death, one sees the glint of a penny tossed into the air. One hears the thin sound of coin on wood, followed by the muted sound of the coin hitting the brick wall upstage and then landing on the floor. There's a wrenching solo that explores the pleasure and shame of touching oneself, and a cruising section where two dancers move in a channel of light: tentatively posing for one another, then stalking, and then outright chasing one another. One dancer gets pushed repeatedly onto a mattress, and others get pinned against a wall.

The partnering in *THEM* involves volatility, risk, and a sense of the unknown in personal encounters, all of which are amplified by the improvised nature of the dancing. Because the movements aren't predetermined, there's always the chance of a collision or a missed connection. As Deborah Jowitt wrote in her *Village Voice* review, "Because they improvise their movements based on a score created by Houston-Jones, their physicality has a reckless edge. They bang into one another sometimes, stumble into or out of embraces, or fall with a crash. Watching Niall Noel and Felix Cruz tussle near the beginning, I think of contact improvisation performed at the edge of a precipice."[38]

Toward the end of *THEM*, Pheiffer enters the space with a goat carcass slung over his shoulders.[39] The gamey stench of the decomposing animal fills the theater as Pheiffer leads Vidich, the blindfolded young man from the overture, into the stage-space. Vidich now wears white underwear and a backward, white dress shirt. His feet are bare. Pheiffer tosses the carcass onto the mattress, then turns and throws Vidich onto the mattress as well. Vidich then wrestles with the goat on the mattress in a scene that is unabashedly sexual, violent, and full of despair. He strokes and pulls the flaccid carcass; he straddles it with his legs while grabbing onto one of its horns; at one point, he even thrusts his head inside the animal. According to Houston-Jones, who originally danced the role and has since described it as his most terrifying performance experience,[40] "The mattress and animal carcass were a sort of acknowledgment of AIDS. People were dying—friends, people we knew. There was panic. The carcass on the mattress came from a dream my friend had. In it he woke up and he was lying next to his own dead body; he would try to throw it out of bed, but it kept coming back on top of him."[41] After the goat dance concludes, Pheiffer, who has been watching the whole time, covers Vidich, except for his bare feet, with a white sheet.

Soon afterward, the performers re-enter the space one by one. The young men have taken off their shoes and changed into underclothes. Some of them are bare-chested, while others wear undershirts. This simple attire renders them vulnerable. Moreover, it suggests a private, intimate space. They all face the audience. The frontal nature of this sequence—distinct from the rest of the work—gives the impression that the young men are standing in front of mirrors. The performers then slowly palpate their bodies, roaming from throat to groin to underarms as if checking the size of their lymph nodes (see Figure 17.5). Meanwhile, Pheiffer takes a piece of paper from Cooper and reads a truncated version of the opening monologue with downcast eyes and an inflection similar to Cooper's:

I saw them once
I don't know when or who they were
I'm too far away
I remember certain things
What they wore
I wanted them to know something
It still matters
I thought about love
I put such incredible faith in the future
I can't believe I once felt
I wish I had taken a photo
I could rip it up. [42]

As Cooper stands by, with his grey hair and quiet slouch, while Pheiffer reads his text, it becomes apparent that this is no straightforward reconstruction. The three older men in the piece (Cooper, Cochrane, and Houston-Jones) testify to an earlier time, and their presence adds layers of temporal complexity that were not in the original work. Cooper recited most of the same words in the 1986 performance. Although his voice is familiar in video recordings of the original performances, the cadence is quicker, and he's a young man in his thirties with dark hair and a thin frame. He looks no different in age than the rest of the 1980s cast. Now, though, it's striking to see a young man reciting text that is so retrospective and melancholic. In Judith Halberstam's *In a Queer Time and Place*, Halberstam argues that "there is such a thing as 'queer time' and 'queer space' . . . that develop, at least in part, in opposition to the institutions of family, heterosexuality, and reproduction. They also develop according to other logics of location, movement, and identification."[43] Halberstam notes that queer time emerged with particular poignancy from within gay communities during the height of the AIDS crisis. As the poet Thom Gunn wrote, "My thoughts are crowded with death/and it draws so oddly on the sexual/that I am confused/confused to be attracted/by, in effect, my own annihilation."[44]

For some, the devastation caused by the virus resulted in an investment in the present moment and a challenge to conventional narratives of longevity and aging. Perhaps the young Cooper in 1986 was speaking in distinctly queer time. Moreover, perhaps, if not exactly "dancing for their lives" as the original cast did in 1985 at the P.S. 122 AIDS benefit of the same name, the younger dancers were improvising in order to imagine and experience a kind of queer temporality where, as Halberstam suggests, ways of aging and of forging relations with others exist outside of the dominant story of how one should mature: "birth, marriage, reproduction, and death."[45] The fact that these queer temporal imaginings were *improvised* meant they were necessarily embodied, flexible, and contingent, and that the dancers were ultimately responsible for the choices they made in performance.

When asked what it was like to improvise with Cochrane, Cooper, and Houston-Jones present, Noel Jones mentioned that the dancers were "flanked" by the three older men, who are spatially more fixed than anyone (they perform from specific locations that stay the same throughout the show) and therefore create a kind of structural boundary for the work. The younger cast of dancers felt beholden to the trio, as well as to the many people who had fallen through history due to AIDS. Reflecting on the dancers' need to consider their connections to various queer lineages, Jones remarked, "We're enacting something that requires a kind of mentorship" (see Figure 17.6).[46] He then talked about the way in which Houston-Jones brought his dancers verbally and physically into the work, recognizing the importance of critical conversation but also believing that, ultimately,

FIGURE 17.6 Ishmael Houston-Jones, Dennis Cooper, and Chris Cochrane. Rehearsal at The New Museum (2010).

Photograph by Christy Pessagno.

embodied practice was necessary for the explorations at hand. Jones, as well as several of the other dancers, noted that Houston-Jones has his likes and dislikes, but their precise nature wasn't clear to the dancers. He gave them just enough information to proceed, without overly prescribing the end result. Rather than show the younger cast extensive video documentation from the 1986 performances, which might have overdetermined their improvisations, he showed imagery that informed the original creation of the work, by artists such as Francis Bacon, Gilbert and George, and Eadweard Muybridge (see Figures 17.7 and 17.8). The dancer Ben Van Buren noted that the work demanded a level of nuance, but that it wasn't dictated. Rather, it was something he had to find through improvisation.[47] Niall Noel Jones talked about trying to access cultural and physical memories of community, or of fallen comrades, through dancing. For him, the lymph node section was explicitly about this, given the extent to which the score required gestures of self-diagnosis. Houston-Jones was very specific about where the dancers should be touching. But the search for cultural memory occurred in the more improvised sections of the dance as well, perhaps in more compelling ways. According to Jones, "The dancers had just come from forty minutes of feeling—of being a thrown body—feeling through the wreck of it."[48] This feeling matters, for both the performers and the audience. In conversation, Wey mentioned that, while improvising, he sometimes found himself wondering what kind of sense memories a given movement or gesture would trigger for viewers who had experienced loss or who had seen the work in the 1980s.

Because Houston-Jones took a long time to assign roles, the dancers performed everything in rehearsals and spent a long time watching each other in various relationships. Watching Houston-Jones was particularly important for the younger dancers. As Wey explained, "There's so much history in watching Ishmael's patterns and timing."[49] Jennifer

ANIMAL LOCOMOTION. PLATE. 347.   ARTOTYPE EDITION.
Copyright, 1887, by EADWEARD MUYBRIDGE. All rights reserved.

FIGURE 17.7 Eadweard Muybridge, *Wrestling; Graeco-Roman* (1887). Plate from Muybridge's "Animal locomotion: an electro-photographic investigation of consecutive phases of animal movements, 1872–1885."

EXISTERS. 1984. 241 X 351 CM

FIGURE 17.8 Gilbert & George, *Existers* (1984).

Monson, a choreographer who has followed Houston-Jones's work for decades, also sensed history within his solo, which, for her, was the same dance that he's been perform-ing for thirty-five years. This was not at all a disparaging comment. Rather, Monson was referring to Houston-Jones's timing, and the ways in which he makes himself available to a spectator's gaze before recoiling.[50] As Houston-Jones wrote in 1987, "a lot of my work has to do with invisibility—hiding identity to survive artistically, or revealing identity to be subversive artistically. I try to subvert invisibility through performance—to bring what's invisible out into the open. As a black man in mostly white downtown performance, I became fascinated with the idea of invisibility. . . . I'm asking people not to accept cer-tain conventions as either the norm or as an acceptable way of life. I am going back and searching for roots in some sense: performance roots, personal roots, historical roots."[51]

The notion that movement patterns and timing contain history is crucial when con-sidering the political stakes of the reconstruction of *THEM*. As Muñoz argues, "Gestures transmit ephemeral knowledge of lost queer histories and possibilities."[52] According to Muñoz, in order to access queer histories within a straight world one often needs to turn to ephemera, which he describes as "trace, the remains, the things that are left."[53] When the younger dancers began the reconstruction process and many of them felt as though they had no connection to HIV/AIDS, Houston-Jones insisted that the knowledge exists somewhere inside of them. Once the performers began to share their stories and move together, connections and experiences that were deeply embedded in the dancers' sub-conscious minds and in their bodies began to surface. Muñoz continues:

Ephemera are the remains that are often embedded in queer acts, in both stories we tell one another and communicative physical gestures such as the cool look of a street cruise, a lingering handshake between recent acquaintances, or the mannish strut of a particularly confident woman.[54]

Muñoz refers to the evidence of queer desire embedded in acts such as the "cool look of a street cruise," performed when someone moves through a public locale in search of sex. It's a cruise-y world that Cooper describes in his text: "I used to dream of situations like this. A group of guys; me among them. Guys so near you reach out your arms, you just put out your arms and come back with this beautiful thing, this guy. . . . I'm going to stroll around now and keep my eyes out for you know what."[55] Yet the "cruising" sequence in THEM seemed particularly dated to the dancers and, as a result, particularly challenged them as improvisers. Noel Jones, who performed the section with Wey in the P.S. 122 reconstruction, noted that their job was not to represent cruising, but to actually experience it. He then explained, "Cruising involves seeing and being seen, and making desire public. Cruising is a practice. It is performative. It is the performance of something missing. It makes present the absence of what you're dying to find."[56] He then remarked, "There's no real cruising in the city today. Gay culture is so mediatized. We're pulled into other spaces where we see each other. Queerness has shifted to digital space."[57]

Whether or not cruising really has disappeared, and whether or not queerness has really moved wholesale to digital spaces, there has been a cultural shift noted by several of the dancers. In that respect, the cruising section provided an instance where, to quote Halberstam, "different histories 'touch' or brush up against each other, creating temporal havoc in the key of desire."[58] Van Buren, who performed Wey's role when the reconstruction of THEM toured the Netherlands in spring 2011, noted, "Many of the ways I've learned about sexual behavior have been very different from what takes place in THEM."[59] He continued, "This felt like something from a different era. . . . I won't say that homosexuality doesn't have the same alterity as it did in the eighties, but something is very different now. The market is much more able to respond to and to exploit gay life. Moreover, the spaces of violence in THEM are locatable—in the bedroom, in a phone booth, on a mattress. It's not that those spaces don't exist anymore, but they're much more porous."[60] Van Buren then referred to Cooper's opening text to explain, "Witnessing a sexuality that is so clearly located on a rock feels impossible now."[61]

"I Wish I Had Taken a Photo/ I Could Rip It Up"

In a review of THEM that appeared on Movement Research's online site, Critical Correspondence, Lindsey Drury, a dancer who had studied with Houston-Jones, criticized the extent to which the reconstruction of THEM relied on the original precepts from the 1980s. She wondered, for example, how the work would change if women had been invited to the audition, or how the work might shift if it were opened up to include transgender bodies. "What would be lost?" she asked. "What could be gained?"[62] Wondering about the goal of a "purist reconstruction," she then exclaimed, "I can't imagine Houston-Jones as an artist who is seeking to make a history text of himself, especially while he is very much alive."[63] Presumably, Drury was referring to Houston-Jones's modest and at times self-effacing demeanor. But Houston-Jones offered a spirited response to Drury:

> You are wrong on one point: I am "an artist who is seeking to make a history text of himself, especially while he is very much alive." I really care about how my work is seen and that it is seen and remembered. I understand your point. I have Scorsese-envy. No one will ever question another screening of "Taxi Driver" as valid. The wonderful and terrible thing about live arts, especially dance, is that it happens, it is witnessed and then it is gone. Its ephemeral nature is its strength and its weakness.[64]

Both dance scholars and critics have struggled with the ephemerality of dance.[65] In *At the Vanishing Point, A Critic Looks at Dance,* Marcia Siegel voices the widely held belief that dance constitutes the ephemeral art par excellence. "No other art is so hard to catch," she writes, "so impossible to hold."[66] But is the ephemeral nature of dance necessarily something that one must resist? In *Cruising Utopia,* Muñoz pays particular attention to Kevin Aviance—a tall, black club dancer who performs high femme drag—whose gestures highlight the pleasure of queer desires that are often subject to censorship or cruel dismissal. Elaborating on the materiality of queer dancing more broadly, Muñoz argues:

> Queer dance is hard to catch, and it is meant to be hard to catch—it is supposed to slip through the fingers and comprehension of those who would use knowledge against us. But it matters and takes on a vast material weight for those of us who perform or draw important sustenance from performance. Rather than dematerialize, dance rematerializes. Dance, like energy, never disappears; it is simply transformed. Queer dance, after the live act, does not just expire. The ephemeral does not equal unmateriality. It is more nearly about another understanding of what matters. It matters to get lost in dance or to use dance to get lost: lost from the evidentiary logic of heterosexuality. For queers, the gesture and its aftermath, the ephemeral trace, matter more than many traditional modes of evidencing lives and politics.[67]

When Cooper and later Pheiffer state, "I wish I had taken a photo/I could rip it up," they are signaling the complex ways in which gestures—whether those of "tangled guys" viewed from a rock, or those of young men "dancing for their lives" at P.S. 122—have the capacity to nestle in the minds and bodies of their witnesses. In some cases, that nestling can be painful; but it also can entail a kind of pleasure. Those guys and their gestures still matter. And when Muñoz argues that "it matters to get lost in dance or to use dance to get lost," he is not talking about some disabling disorientation; rather, he is highlighting the production and the experience of "queer time" in Halberstam's sense. The young dancers in the reconstruction of *THEM* were using dance to explore and present organizations of time that resist a forward march of direct progress, and they were using dance to explore multiple ways in which men relate to other men. Through improvisation, the dancers opened themselves up to ghostly presences and made spontaneous choices in a way that acknowledged the past—in a felt, bodily way—while gesturing toward a future. Perhaps it's a future where dancers know and can state with conviction that their dancing matters. Perhaps it's also a future where expansive possibilities exist for relating to others—for expressing and acting upon desire—not just in virtual spaces, but also on the ground. When Van Buren returned from performing *THEM* on a recent tour to the Netherlands, he was able to draw from his staged experience of cruising. He had received some schooling in seduction and was able read gestures differently and to meet a stranger's gaze. The New York City streets felt different.

NOTES

1. Burt Supree, "Men with Men," *The Village Voice*, December 22, 1986.
2. David Gere, *How to Make Dances in an Epidemic: Tracking Choreography in the Age of AIDS* (Madison: University of Wisconsin Press, 2004), 79.
3. In a recent e-mail correspondence, Houston-Jones noted that several animal rights activists wrote letters of protest in response to the 1986 performance run at PS 122, and someone wrote a letter of complaint to the Board of Health. Mark Russell asked Houston-Jones if he would consider using a taxidermic animal for the second week of the performance. Houston-Jones said no to the request. Ishmael Houston-Jones, e-mail message to author, February 2, 2013.
4. Ishmael Houston-Jones, "On Burt Supree," in "Heroes and Histories," special issue, *Movement Research Performance Journal* 6 (Spring/Summer 1993), http://ishmaelhj.com/id19.html.
5. Houston-Jones, "On Burt Supree."
6. Supree, "Men with Men."
7. Supree, "Men with Men."
8. Gia Kourlas, "Ishmael Houston-Jones: The '80s Are Back with *THEM*," *TimeOut New York*, September 20, 2010. http://newyork.timeout.com/arts-culture/dance/273774/ishmael-houston-jones#ixzz10LvZix8l.
9. Ishmael Houston-Jones, interview with the author, December 17, 2010, New York, NY.
10. "*THEM*—Ishmael Houston-Jones op Springdance," YouTube video, 6:20, uploaded by "Cultureel Persbureau," April 22, 2011, http://www.youtube.com/watch?v=o8RXLIm7wVI.
11. José Esteban Muñoz, *Cruising Utopia: The Then and There of Queer Futurity* (New York: NYU Press, 2009), 34.
12. Muñoz, *Cruising Utopia*, 34.
13. Niall Noel Jones, interview with the author, May 19, 2011, New York, NY.
14. Noel Jones, interview with the author.

15. Anna Drozdowski and Ishmael Houston-Jones, "Dance Talk: Q&A with Ishmael Houston-Jones," last modified February 16, 2010, http://www.philadanceprojects.org/blog/dance-talk-qa-ishmael-houston-jones.

16. In conversation, Ishmael mentioned that several of the younger dancers involved in the reconstruction of *THEM* had studied improvisation in college and elsewhere, so it wasn't entirely new to them. But it wasn't as radical as it had felt in the 1980s. He noted, "The times didn't feel as urgent to them, perhaps." Ishmael Houston-Jones, interview with the author, December 12, 2010, New York, NY.

17. Kourlas, "Ishmael Houston-Jones."

18. Jennifer Monson, interview with the author, May 18, 2011, New York, NY.

19. In my recent book, *I Want to Be Ready: Improvised Dance as a Practice of Freedom* (Ann Arbor: University of Michigan Press, 2010), I refer to these constraints as "tight places," a term that comes from Houston Baker's *Turning South Again: Re-Thinking Modernism/Re-Reading Booker T.* (Durham: Duke University Press, 2001). I also turn to Fred Moten's writings, particularly "Taste Flavor Dissonance Escape: Preface for a Solo by Miles Davis," *Women & Performance: A Journal of Feminist Theory* 17, no. 2 (2007): 217–246, and Michel Foucault's late writings on practices of freedom in order to argue that improvisation's keenest political power exists as an ongoing engagement with social, historical, and aesthetic strictures.

20. Different versions of these exercises have been used for years by activists outside the dance world.

21. Ishmael Houston-Jones, "A Dance of Identity: Notes on the Politics of Dancing," *Contact Quarterly* 21, no. 1 (Winter/Spring 1996): 11–13, http://ishmaelhj.com/id8.html.

22. Houston-Jones, "A Dance of Identity."

23. Houston-Jones, "A Dance of Identity."

24. Houston-Jones, "A Dance of Identity."

25. Houston-Jones, "A Dance of Identity."

26. Nancy Stark Smith, "A Subjective History of Contact Improvisation: Notes from the Editor of *Contact Quarterly*, 1972–1997," in *Taken By Surprise: A Dance Improvisation Reader*, ed. Ann Cooper Albright and David Gere (Middletown: Wesleyan University Press: 2003), 169.

27. Noel Jones, interview with the author.

28. Enrico Wey, interview with the author, June 4, 2011, New York, NY.

29. "Us V Them: A Showcase of Young Improvisers," http://archive.newmuseum.org/index.php/Detail/Occurrence/Show/occurrence_id/1199.

30. Wey, interview with the author.

31. Ishmael Houston-Jones, *THEM* (unpublished manuscript reconstruction score).

32. Noel Jones, interview with the author.

33. The improvised score for *THEM* includes live electric guitar played by Cochrane, along with accordion, keyboards, percussion, and tapes.

34. Movement score for *THEM*, provided by Ishmael Houston-Jones.

35. Wey, interview with the author.

36. Dennis Cooper, "*THEM*," *Spank NYC Art Zine and Party* 17 (January 25, 2011).

37. Lindsey Drury, "Response: Lindsey Drury on Ishmael Houston-Jones, Dennis Cooper and Chris Cochrane's *THEM*, with a Reply from Ishmael," http://www.movementresearch.org/criticalcorrespondence/blog/?p=2380.

38. Deborah Jowitt, "From Switzerland, Ireland, and the U.S.: Guys on Guys," *The Village Voice*, January 12, 2011, http://www.villagevoice.com/2011-01-12/dance/from-switzerland-ireland-and-the-u-s-guys-on-guys/.

39. In an interview with the author (December 17, 2010), Houston-Jones noted that the goat did a lot of work for the process. Much of what the piece was about was purely theoretical for the dancers until the goat arrived. They got it from a Halal butcher, who kept saying that it would be ready soon. They got it just before the dress rehearsal. This was the first time that the dancers worked with the dead animal. It had only just been killed. It was still warm. And it hadn't been drained. It bled, a lot. They weren't prepared for what that body would do to the work. The dress rehearsal was crazy and the work transformed itself. Wey (interview with the author) noted that every night after the performance at P.S. 122, they'd need to put the goat into a freezer. Before the show, they'd have to give it a warm bath and pat it down to dry it. They used three goats during the performance run. The carcasses weren't buried until about a month later.

40. Ishmael Houston-Jones, "Ishmael Houston-Jones FAQ," http://ishmaelhj.com/id3.html, accessed December 17, 2012.

41. Ishmael Houston-Jones as told to David Velasco, "Ishmael Houston-Jones," *Artforum*, September 26, 2010, http://artforum.com/words/id=26489.

42. Cooper, "*THEM.*"

43. Judith Halberstam, *In a Queer Time and Place: Transgender Bodies, Subcultural Lives* (New York: NYU Press, 2005), 1.

44. Halberstam, *In a Queer Time and Place*, 2.

45. Halberstam, *In a Queer Time and Place*, 2.

46. Noel Jones, interview with the author.

47. Ben Van Buren, interview with the author, May 19, 2011, New York, NY.

48. Noel Jones, interview with the author.

49. Wey, interview with the author.

50. Monson, interview with the author.

51. Marc Robinson, Ishmael Houston-Jones, John Kelly, Karen Finley, and Richard Elovich, "Performance Strategies," *Performing Arts Journal* 10, no. 3 (1987): 36.

52. Muñoz, *Cruising Utopia*, 67.

53. Muñoz, *Cruising Utopia*, 65.

54. Muñoz, *Cruising Utopia*, 65.

55. Cooper, "*THEM.*"

56. Noel Jones, interview with the author.

57. Noel Jones, interview with the author.

58. Halberstam, *In a Queer Time and Place*, 3.

59. Van Buren, interview with the author.

60. Van Buren, interview with the author.

61. Van Buren, interview with the author.

62. Drury, "Response."

63. Drury, "Response."

64. Drury, "Response."

65. See André Lepecki's *Exhausting Dance: Performance and the Politics of Movement* (New York and London: Routledge, 2006), 125.

66. Marcia Siegel, *At the Vanishing Point: A Critic Looks at Dance* (New York: Saturday Review Press: 1972), 1.

67. Siegel, *At the Vanishing Point*, 81.

Works Cited List

Baker, Houston A. Jr. *Turning South Again: Re-Thinking Modernism/Re-Reading Booker T.* Durham: Duke University Press, 2001.

Cooper, Dennis. "*THEM*." *Spank NYC Art Zine and Party* 17 (January 25, 2011).

Drozdowski, Anna and Ishmael Houston-Jones. "Dance Talk: Q&A with Ishmael Houston-Jones." Last modified February 16, 2010. http://www.philadanceprojects.org/blog/dance-talk-qa-ishmael-houston-jones.

Drury, Lindsey. "Response: Lindsey Drury on Ishmael Houston-Jones, Dennis Cooper and Chris Cochrane's *THEM*, with a Reply from Ishmael." *Critical Correspondence*. Accessed February 2, 2013, http://www.movementresearch.org/criticalcorrespondence/blog/?p=2380.

Gere, David. *How to Make Dances in an Epidemic: Tracking Choreography in the Age of AIDS.* Madison: University of Wisconsin Press, 2004.

Halberstam, Judith. *In a Queer Time and Place: Transgender Bodies, Subcultural Lives.* New York: NYU Press, 2005.

Houston-Jones, Ishmael. "On Burt Supree." "Heroes and Histories." Special issue, *Movement Research Performance Journal* 6 (Spring/Summer 1993). http://ishmaelhj.com/id19.html.

Houston-Jones, Ishmael. "A Dance of Identity: Notes on the Politics of Dancing." *Contact Quarterly* 21, no. 1 (Winter/Spring 1996): 11–13.

Houston-Jones, Ishmael. "Ishmael Houston-Jones FAQ." http://ishmaelhj.com/id3.html, accessed December 17, 2012.

Houston-Jones, Ishmael. "Ishmael Houston-Jones." *Artforum.* Last modified September 26, 2010. http://artforum.com/words/id=26489.

Jowitt, Deborah. "From Switzerland, Ireland, and the U.S.: Guys on Guys." *The Village Voice*, January 12, 2011. http://www.villagevoice.com/2011-01-12/dance/from-switzerland-ireland-and-the-u-s-guys-on-guys/.

Kourlas, Gia. "Ishmael Houston-Jones: The '80s are back with *THEM*." *TimeOut New York*, September 20, 2010. http://www.timeout.com/newyork/art/ishmael-houston-jones.

Lepecki, André. *Exhausting Dance: Performance and the Politics of Movement.* London: Routledge, 2006.

Moten, Fred. "Taste Flavor Dissonance Escape: Preface for a Solo by Miles Davis." *Women & Performance: A Journal of Feminist Theory* 17, no. 2 (2007): 217–246.

Muñoz, José Esteban. *Cruising Utopia: The Then and There of Queer Futurity.* New York: NYU Press, 2009.

Robinson, Marc, Ishmael Houston-Jones, John Kelly, Karen Finley, and Richard Elovich. "Performance Strategies." *Performing Arts Journal* 10, no. 3 (1987): 31–55.

Siegel, Marcia. *At the Vanishing Point: A Critic Looks at Dance.* New York: Saturday Review Press, 1972.

Stark Smith, Nancy. "A Subjective History of Contact Improvisation: Notes from the Editor of *Contact Quarterly*, 1972–1997." In *Taken By Surprise: A Dance Improvisation Reader*, edited by Ann Cooper Albright and David Gere, 153–174. Middletown, CT: Wesleyan University Press, 2003.

Supree, Burt. "Men with Men." *The Village Voice*, December 22, 1986.

"*THEM*—Ishmael Houston-Jones op Springdance." YouTube video, 6:20. Uploaded by "Cultureel Persbureau," April 22, 2011. Accessed February 4, 2013. http://www.youtube.com/watch?v=o8RXLIm7wVI.

CHAPTER 18

IMPROVISING SOCIAL EXCHANGE

African American Social Dance

THOMAS F. DeFRANTZ

BROADLY defined, social dance operates as an unavoidable and essential site of identity formation for individuals and groups; in mythologies of American youth culture from the 1950s forward, it stands as a primary site of improvised selfhood. In African American communities, the importance of social dance to group cohesion through changing historical eras can seldom be overstated. Social dance allows its practitioners access to modes of personal expression that provide urgent clues of physical capacity, desire, social flexibility, and an ability to innovate. In social dance, we discover the ever-expanding range of possibilities that might define individual presence within a group dynamic.

This essay explores African American social dance structures of the twentieth and twenty-first centuries, where improvisation operates as a crucial methodology and ideology. Improvisation provides a methodology for the construction of social dance exchange. Improvisation also stands as a foundational ideology of black social dance practice. Conceptually, this twinned resource demonstrates an unimpeachable centrality of the physical practice of improvisation: "creating while doing," or consistently asking questions while moving, becomes foundational to the emergence of a social black self in communion with others.

A *black social self* might be one that imagines itself in communion with other black selves, even as it distinguishes its capacities along lines of ability, interest, and desire. Black exists in relationship to other markers of identity, black and non-black, and the process of relationship determines possibilities of recognition that undergird its existence. In other words, black is not a thing, but rather, a gesture, an action, a sensibility made manifest. Thus, a black social self is literally a concept in motion, shifting and forming according to the terms of encounter that determine social relations.

Social dance offers a site where black motion can be generated, accommodated, honed, and appreciated; it offers a place of aesthetic possibility connected to personal expression. For this chapter, social dance might be dance created in situations without separation of performer and audience, and without a predetermined intention of expression. The sites of this genre include school auditoriums, church basements, house parties, nightclubs, and rented ballrooms, and the genre becomes manifest within event celebrations such as family reunions, cotillions, weddings, school dances, and birthday parties. On these sorts of occasions, and in these sites, social dance emerges as the consecration of an event by the group, as an embodied aesthetic marking of presence in time. Non-linear creativity within social dance motion distinguishes it from goal-oriented athletics or the politically tilted gestures of rallies or sit-ins (choreographies of sport or protest). For our purposes, social dance hinges upon the possibility of expression and communication as its own goal within a particular time and place. Social dance occurs outside of everyday interactions of commerce, meaning that it cannot be paid labor, and, significantly, it requires the participation of a larger group who recognize the dance event as such. Defined thus, by its own occurrence and participation, social dance constitutes ritual practices that characterize individual action within communal communication and exchange.

Rhetorics of African American Improvisation

The adage that African American culture "makes something from nothing" underscores emphases on improvisation and composition that surround black presence in the New World. Pundits and cultural theorists can easily align black social dances to an "American inventiveness" and "do-it-yourself-ness" foundational to an understanding of an American self. In this narrative line, youthful America creates itself out of incessant volition and ambition to achieve. Similarly, improvisation arrives as ambition toward achievement; as an ability to move unexpectedly toward a goal, as well as an ability to move as the situation demands. The performance of intentional, directed movement allows for a recognition of the act of black social dance improvisation, and creative invention in the moment characterize its possibilities.

Black social dances also align this necessary moving-to-express with an embodied realization of pleasure. The assumption of a serious pleasure within the invention of physical improvisation merits special consideration here. Black social dances conceive of social, rhythmic motion as pleasurable, and essential, modes of interaction and exchange; improvisation intends to allow for playful, liberatory embodied choice-making within the context of the group. The pleasures of social dance relate to its musicality and embedded processes of choice-making within agreed-upon group structures; the practice of dancing in this genre demonstrates emotional and spiritual well-being.

In a nod to the general tendency to value literature over orature, some dance scholars have labored to define improvisation as choreography in black vernacular (social) dancing. Dance literature, or choreography, might be work that could be recorded on paper or via technologies of visual media, while improvisation might be more akin to structures of spontaneous oration and rhetoric. In 2001, theorist Jonathan David Jackson called for a valorization of sensing, or emotion, in social dance as a "path of intelligent knowing" that might resist the violent Platonic/Cartesian split caused by writing (Jackson 2001, 43). In black vernacular dance, "improvisation means the creative structuring, or the choreographing, of human movement in the moment of ritual performance," a structuring that aligns improvisation with intentional composition (44). This line of argumentation tends to re-stabilize choreography, or writing, as the ideal model for dance practice. But improvisation, especially in black social dance circumstances, conveys its own pleasures and urgencies without necessary recourse to translatable signs and symbols that characterize writing. The improvisational practices of these dances complete themselves without an insistence on translation into language or visual mark.

Jackson's call for "sensing" as a mode of analysis suggests an intangible analytic for improvisation, one that stresses the impermanent, time-based nature of social dance production. Sensing becomes manifest in waves, like thought and motion, and resists a fixing of gesture. Improvisation that proceeds from a reliance on sensing, then, might become enlivened by the engagement of unexpected and unusual motion; by physical embellishment or unruliness that works to unsettle formalized repetitions of gesture. In other words, the dancer's innovation in response to a rhythmic/musical ground provides essential markers toward the production of emotion that might be sensed within the dance. Fulfilling the age-old adage in a different way, the "something" produced by the dance builds from the largely invisible "nothing" of physical perception.

TELEOLOGIES OF IMPROVISATION IN AFRICAN AMERICAN SOCIAL DANCE

INSIDE the dance, I enjoy the discovery of what we can do together. With you watching, a willing witness, confidante, and partner in motion, I feel supported to break the beat, to resist the complex, but steady, grounding pulse that already offers so many ways to imagine synchronicities of energy. The complex rhythm that forms the ground for our dance echoes in my nervous system, pulsing outward from my incessantly rhythmicized life force, and confirming the potency of this encounter of music and movement. My pulse, our pulse, the musical pulse converge and align, but then separate so that our dance can emerge in-between. I grimace at the effort to move outside of these cadences, I risk movements and fail along the way, and laugh and smile at any achievement that you or I share as we dance.

Social dance functions as a barometer of connectivity, or a way for people to recognize a social self. The dance produces relationship; and in it, we struggle to achieve. Moving among others, we hope for connection to be born or to be laid bare as we stomp, shift, glide, and dip through passages of spontaneous motion. This connection is not guaranteed, and the risk of social dance arrives intertwined with its improvisational imperative. We risk failure, or a miscommunication that might alter our future capacities outside of the dance. This risk adds to the sense of urgency surrounding its execution. Social dance matters, and its improvisations are embedded within the relationships that it may or may not inspire.

African American social dance proceeds from the need to communicate outside of language; a passage of dance may be language-like, but it is not at all literal. *Corporeal Orature*, a designator for the process of communicating through choices of movement, provides methodology grounded in history for the practice of social dance. Here, body-talking establishes intertextual connection among steps and gestures performed inside the dance, with referents often drawn from circumstances outside its execution. A movement may make reference to someone else's version of its form, as in a step done in cousin Jan's distinctive slow-motion style; it may reference dances no longer in wide distribution, as in the insertion of a 1980s "Roger Rabbit" in the midst of a 2010s "Wobble"; it may mimetically suggest direct metaphor, as in bringing hands to the heart to indicate feelings of affection, or brushing a hand across a forehead, to indicate exertion or "sweating" a partner or situation. These insertions of embodied referents arrive in non-linear, evocative assembly; they confirm the expansive possibility of statement enabled by the dance. Dancers access these referents in improvised response to the occasion of the dance. The most successful corporeal orature employs elegant, unexpected assemblage of metaphor and physical achievement.

A historical dimension of black social dance, alluded to above, renders it at once archival and futuristic. Dancers rediscover pungent pleasure and expressive capacity in older, discarded movements, made fresh again now with unanticipated musical accompaniment. The music of social dance grounds its improvisational practices and stimulates movement possibilities with sonic calls that provoke physical response. A propulsive backbeat suggests fast footwork from 1930s dances; a slow, downward-sliding bass line can inspire "lean back" gestures from repertories of 1960s or 1990s dances. Improvisation in this realm, then, reaches back in order to cast forward, confirming affiliation among movements from a lively past of dancing while reimagining possibilities of gesture. This reiteration of motion aligns the practice of social dance with an Africanist aesthetic imperative that values cycles of repetition (Snead 1981). Social dance can fulfill the embodied reclaiming, or remembering, of musical genres/rhythmic bases that define eras and styles of black popular music.

LEARNING TO SOCIAL DANCE

I WANT to dance with you. I want to move alongside you, and toward and away from you, as we navigate the rhythms and sonic structures that surround us. I want to guess at what you might do, and I want to be correct most of the time. I want to surprise you with my ability to do something you didn't know I might. I want to ride the rhythm a little longer than we may have done last time, or to work against the beat in a stutter step and turn toward the group. I want my dance to confirm me in this moment. To validate our communion as people in relationship, in the space of the dance, in the process of discovery. When we dance we wonder at what is possible, we appreciate how impulse turns into gesture and gesture reveals desire and intellect. Our dance is multidimensional, and I want it to be good, I want to be provocative and profound. I never know whether this will happen, but I do hope for it. Will you dance with me?

The process of learning to social dance is actually a process of learning to improvise. Or, more correctly perhaps, a process of learning to trust one's improvisation. Because social dance has no set outcome, or ironclad form, its practice may be defined in large part by the willingness of its participants. The willingness to engage in social dance is a willingness to accept risk and an unruly inability to know what will happen. Social dance challenges the faculties of physical engagement and relational correspondence. To dance well in this idiom is to trust that one's choices have value, and that they will communicate something recognizable and fleetingly noteworthy.

A longstanding Hollywood trope casts awkward young men in the role of needing to learn to social dance in order to connect with their object of desire; in this idiom, social dance is defined as a rite of passage. Formulaically, this scenario usually involves a best friend or mentor leading the protagonist through a montage of missteps and embarrassments before the big dance event/prom where tensions and disappointments may be resolved through the demonstration of dance. In these scenarios, the main character exceeds his training in the heat of the performative moment, and in an improvisational flourish, achieves gestures that he didn't know he might. *Footloose* offers a classic portrayal of this genre. Note that in both the first 1984 iteration and the 2011 remake, the small-city, white dancers engage in white-derived "rock and roll" dances, as well as African American-created social dance movements. The black social dance movements—steps drawn from 1960s "black power"–era social dances including "the football" and "the Four Tops"—allow the main characters of the films to shine forth in improvisatory demonstrations of their abilities and personalities. The black social dance improvisations confirm the arrival of a recognizable subject in motion, ready to engage others in a physical, desirous relationship.

To dance well differs little from speaking well: social dance demonstrates embodied rhetoric. Improvisational movers can align ideas in coherent sequence to signal agility, ability, wit, or sensual pleasure. Elegance of execution and composition matters here, and a recognizable "turn of phrase" separates the best social artists from their companions. But because dance movement does not carry literal meaning, witnesses and partners engage the essential act of decoding that confers communicative value. To reiterate, social dance arrives as a mode of encounter, realized by two or more participants.

Some social dancers have little to say, and their dance arrives in simple, repetitive motion. These might be the dances that most people perform: dances that engage little improvisation, and make few extra-dance references; dances that answer a simple rhythmic and social need to be in motion with others. These dances also matter, as sensation and confirmation of possibilities for a group dynamic. But, as in the Hollywood prototype, the moments of black social dance that linger longest in memory tend to derive from those compressed circumstances that produce an unanticipated articulation of character or self, even if only in the instant of their improvised realization. These might be small acts, but they can surely shift the architecture of relationship.

PROFESSIONAL SOCIAL DANCE

THIS is what I already know. If I push back with my weight through my hips, and grind my feet into the ground with a heaviness of step, I can amaze you with the acuteness of an angle produced by my bent knees and elbows; I can stun you into silence with the accuracy and force of my attacking hips in motion, or the smoothness of my glide across the floor as I release my weight ever upwards from the ground. I scurry across the floor, shifting my feet without seeming effort. I curve my arm up my body, circling my hips, touching my torso lightly, gazing inward, pulling my focus inside, and as I close my eyes, I suppose I do find something out. I didn't know about this weight here, or that possible shift of energy to there. Did you see me do that? But even in these few seconds of knowing my motion, and sensing it differently, I need your witnessing to stabilize my discovery.

Professional social dances offer an illusion of improvisation. The conceptual contradiction between professional and social dance has to do with the level of improvisation present in performance. Professional dancers practice and rehearse consistently alone or with others, in order to engage an expanded repertory of movement available for performance. Social dancers, though, practice less consistently, and discover possibilities within the realm of social dancing itself. Talented and highly skilled social dancers move beyond the category that would seem to define them as they become the leading participants of any circumstance of dance. Their leadership typically indicates two truths: one, that their practice intends to minimize risk and maximize a finished quality of execution; and two, that their performance might be repeated, or replicated, nearly intact in other circumstances and on other occasions.

Professional social dance is the dance of television and film, the dance of the stage, and the dance of demonstration. In this form of dance, dancers embellish and exaggerate the physical contours, or steps, of the form to affirm the possibilities of organized performance. Expert social dancers in any genre inspire and delight their audiences, who inevitably enjoy witnessing the supremely confident execution of movement that emerges without the hesitations and ruptured mistakes of everyday improvisation. The thrill of social dance performed with minimal risk move its contents toward the space of the refined, the repeatable, the commodifiable.

When black social dance can be repeated and professionalized, it loses its ability to convey the unexpected discovery. Rather, it seeks to amaze by its spectacular presence. In this, black social dance has been entirely successful, from its earlier international achievement in the nineteenth-century cakewalk, to the twenty-first-century inventions of j-setting and turf dancing distributed by YouTube videos. The professional social dancers who practice these forms, and arrive in films made by Thomas A. Edison or in HD on internet sites, seldom make a living by dancing. Like other dance artists, they encounter a field full of competition and small opportunity compared to their number. But for these best of the best, social dancing is more than avocation, and their presence in social settings transforms the event from a place of mutual exploration to a place of the show. The professional social dancers—those in the "cat's corner" at the Savoy Ballroom in the 1930s, or on the upper level of the Studio 54 in the 1970s—demonstrate a soaring potential for social exchange in their embodied excellence, their practiced expertise. Surely they also improvise to some degree, but the terms of improvisation arrive in studied difference of effect.

For devoted social dancers, competitions allow a high-level engagement with the raised stakes of performance necessary for movement invention. Indeed, African American dance competitions occupy a valued and essential site of social performance, stretching from dances in seventeenth-century corn-husking competitions to twentieth-century Chicago Stepping competitions. In these events, expert social dancers try their skills against other, equally committed movers, to be judged by other experts and gathered witnesses surrounding the performance. Here, improvisation arises as dancers push their movement beyond the routines they've practiced so carefully. Improvisation supplies the burnished energy of desire that marks physical effort as extraordinary. Collectively, we feel this "push to exceed" and move beyond the known gestures, and the improvisatory flourish inevitably wins the challenge.

Improvising Sexuality and Failure

THE YOUNG man focuses his energy through his pelvis, through the muscles that bind the torso and abdomen to the hips and thighs. His face contorts in the visage of worry. With one arm held high, he reaches forward with his other arm, hand opened and tensed at once, as if to slap something. He plays different rhythms across his body: hands moving in a slow patting gesture against the air, while he animates his hips in staggered but quick jabbing circles, moving faster and faster as he bends his legs more and more. The young women who surround him seem concerned as well; they seem to want to understand what he means to express through his dance. They clap for him, and hold the beat steady so that he can solo in front of it. Suddenly, the film cuts to another dancer. The short film clip lasts less than five seconds, and viewers witnessing the film learn little of its implications, or what the short improvisation might mean for the dancer or his witnesses.

Social dance incites considerations of sexuality, and both its practitioners and detractors tend to conflate ability in the dance with sexual availability. This makes sense, if we consider social dance as a barometer of intimate responsiveness and ability to improvise physically; these might be preferred qualities in intimate encounter.

But often, detractors construe black social dances—these dances that consistently emphasize an agility in all parts of the body with knees bent, torso engaged, and pelvis released—as agents of immorality and instigators of lust. The young man described above, dancing in the documentary *Rize*, demonstrates movements aligned with "the stripper dance," a form named for its borrowing from commodified, and largely improvised, sexually charged performance dance. Social dancers conceive the stripper dance as a solo form, practiced in turns amid a witnessing and supportive group—often at the center of a dance circle. The stripper dance exists along the border of social dance to be explored in encounter with another, and dances of labor, to be shared with an entire group.

The dance circle acts as intermediary between an intimate sociality of two and the unwieldiness of a dancer viewed by a mass audience. The dance circle mitigates interpretive distances that arise as social dance broadens its reach, and provides an "in-between" space of encounter for prepared dance and improvisation, personal discovery and group consensus. The dance circle protects and permits, and its boundaries reveal the limitations of palpable discovery in dance motion. Outside the circle—sitting in the auditorium watching social dancers onstage, or at home viewing dancers online—I can only guess at the value of danced exchange. Without the cues of context that mark any successful and evocative communication, my guesses at the importance of danced innovations before me will largely fail.

The circle of the dance, referenced by Fanon, accommodates the needs of a community to recognize itself in motion. More important, the circle allows improvisers to find their own form without reference to the movements of the larger group. Outside the circle—when the group is in its larger, improvising whole—small gestures and discoveries rise and fall, emerge and dissipate alongside the rhythmic pulse of the dance. These small victories in movement matter, but they remain small and contained by the near-privacy of their occurrence. Without the circle, improvising social dancers often exceed the emerging trends of the larger group. Within the circle, physical moments of "flash" or "shine" reveal an inner emotional life of the dancers. In the circle, these surprising movements are encouraged, observed, supported, valued, and remembered. But what do they mean? What of the improvised gestures that resist even the norms of the group black social dance, the electric slide or cha-cha slide? If these group dances promote access to a black social self in communion with others, what does improvisation outside of these formal structures do?

Improvisation, then, poses special problems of interpretation in black social dance, largely constrained by pressures of everyday racism. Improvising black social dancers, more than others, may be seen to operate as provocateurs, non-normative dancers whose moves seek to subvert social norms. In many ways, this capacity stands, as social dance allows for the performance of outrageous gesture—sexualized, desirous, intimidating—within its context of embodied thought. But black social dance also risks failure in its improvisations, and that circumstance, where movements land without value or impact, continually reminds us all of the fragility of gesture, and the abiding need to try again.

Because it is probably in those missteps that improvisation reassures us. What we need to know: the recovery is always possible, that invention generates heat and confirms capacity, that figuring the thing out together reminds us of a possible shared knowledge. Our improvisation enlivens us because it confirms that we are flexible, willing to not know, but engaged in the question of what might be.

REFERENCES

Brewer, Craig, dir. *Footloose*. Paramount Pictures, 2011.

DeFrantz, Thomas F. "The Black Beat Made Visible: Body Power in Hip Hop Dance." In *Of the Presence of the Body: Essays on Dance and Performance Theory*, edited by Andre Lepecki, 64–81. Middletown, CT: Wesleyan University Press, 2004.

Fanon, Frantz. *The Wretched of the Earth*, translated by Constance Farrington. New York: Grove Press, 1963.

Jackson, Jonathan David. "Improvisation in African-America Vernacular Dancing." *Dance Research Journal* 33, no. 2 (2001): 40–53.

LaChapelle, David, dir. *Rize*. Lionsgate Films, 2005.

Ross, Herbert, dir. *Footloose*. Paramount Pictures, 1984.

Snead, James A. "On Repetition in Black Culture," *Black American Literature Forum* 15, no. 4 (1981): 146–154.

....

CHAPTER 19

FIXING IMPROVISATION

*Copyright and African American Vernacular Dancers
in the Early Twentieth Century*

....

ANTHEA KRAUT

IN 1952, the German-born modern dancer Hanya Holm copyrighted the dances she choreographed for the hit 1948 Broadway musical *Kiss Me, Kate* and reportedly "made history" as
the first to secure a copyright for a choreographic composition.[1] Although choreography was
not recognized by United States copyright law in its own right until 1976, the Labanotated
score[2] that Holm submitted was granted protection as a dramatico-musical composition.
Not included in the score was the jazz-tap routine performed by African American "specialty" dancers in the musical's show-stopping number, "Too Darn Hot." Instead, notes in
the score indicated that "the exact arrangement varied according to what the negros [sic]
could do."[3] The unnamed "negros" who performed this routine in the late 1940s and early
1950s included the comedy- and class-act dance teams Fred Davis and Eddie Sledge, Charles
Cook and Ernest Brown, Honi Coles and Cholly Atkins, and the Wallace Brothers.

The exclusion of African American jazz dance from the copyrighted score of *Kiss Me,
Kate* calls up a set of oppositions that seem to arise whenever intellectual property law
and black cultural practices are discussed in tandem. Where U.S. copyright law grants
protection to "original works of authorship fixed in a tangible medium of expression,"[4]
black vernacular traditions that place a premium on improvisation[5] tend to elude the
fixity that documentation requires.[6] Correspondingly, where the copyright system has
benefited white artists who produce written records of their output, it has consistently
failed to recognize or reward African American artists, whose oral traditions have so
often been treated as "raw material" and therefore free for the taking. The withholding
of royalties from black blues musicians is perhaps the most vivid example of the racialized allocation of intellectual property rights in the U.S., but a number of legal critics
have argued that Western ideas of singular authorship and fixity embedded in copyright law are incompatible with African American vernacular forms more broadly. As
Kembrew McLeod writes, "The intertextual practices that characterize many aspects of
African-American culture conflict with a particular way of understanding authorship

and ownership that originated in Western Enlightenment and Romanticist thought."[7] Certainly, a large body of scholarship has demonstrated that black vernacular traditions are not only collectively created, orally transmitted, and improvisational, but also make regular use of "signifyin'" or intertextual techniques.[8] As such, they fail to conform to the very "structural elements of the copyright system—such as the requirements of tangible (written) form, and minimal standard of originality."[9]

Yet this narrative of conflict and failure is not the only story to be told about copyright's historical relationship to black artists working in improvisatory traditions. Over two decades before Holm obtained her *Kiss Me, Kate* copyright, the African American comic dancer Johnny Hudgins secured a copyright in London on a booklet that detailed a series of his pantomime routines, including his celebrated "Mwa Mwa" act, in which he corporeally mimicked the sounds of an accompanying trumpet. The booklet proclaimed the originality of Hudgins's routines and decreed, "No one is allowed to impersonate me, or use any parts of said Act unless given a written consent from JOHNNY HUDGINS, and if so it must be announced on all programs or from the Stage."[10]

Hudgins's turn to the institution of copyright to protect his act suggests the need to think beyond totalizing oppositions between the ideology of intellectual property law and the practice of African American jazz dancers. This chapter aims to offer a more nuanced account of that relationship by juxtaposing brief case studies of Hudgins and the specialty dancers in *Kiss Me, Kate* as they came into contact with legal claims of ownership. Given copyright's originality and fixity requirements, these cases force us to confront questions about the risks and rewards for black vernacular dancers of claiming uniqueness and of submitting to documentation. As dance scholar Danielle Goldman has recently written, although performance in general and improvisation in specific are often valued precisely because they are thought to resist "the trap of documentation" and thereby evade the regulatory mechanisms of our capitalist reproductive economy, the stakes of this "resistance" should not be overlooked.[11] The examples of Hudgins and the *Kiss Me, Kate* dancers help show that the stakes were not only historiographic (who was awarded a place in the historical record), but also economic (who accrued financial and artistic credit for their embodied expression). Because these African American performers were at one and the same time immersed in dance traditions that privileged improvisation and trying to survive in a white-controlled theatrical marketplace, exploring the complex dynamics of their engagement with copyright can offer insight into the possibilities and pitfalls of navigating between the ethos of improvisation and the mandates of intellectual property law.

SPONTANEITY, FIXITY, AND OWNERSHIP: THE CASE OF JOHNNY HUDGINS

Born in Baltimore, Johnny Hudgins (1896–1990) was what Marshall and Jean Stearns in their book *Jazz Dance* call an "eccentric" dancer, the term serving as "a catchall for dancers who have their own non-standard movements and sell themselves on their individual styles."[12] A blackface performer at a time when burnt cork makeup was still a familiar if no longer universal stage practice, Hudgins's specialties consisted mainly of pantomimed movement gestures and sliding steps. He began his career as a song-and-dance man in local theatres in Baltimore before being hired as a dancer on the white burlesque circuit, which he toured for a number of years. In 1924, Hudgins joined the all-black Noble Sissle and Eubie Blake revue *The Chocolate Dandies*. One evening in the course of the revue's run, he later explained, "I got hoarse and the trumpet man was making these sounds and I just moved my mouth. The trumpet player caught the way I was doing my mouth and I cut out all the singing and went into pantomime with trumpet and this pantomime song. I named it—'Wow, Wow.' And I pantomimed throughout the whole show and I pantomimed ever since."[13]

Apocryphal or not, Hudgins's account of the impromptu invention of his dance routine serves as an instructive place to begin assessing the interplay between markers of improvisation and markers of ownership in his work. A commonplace trope among jazz artists, Hudgins's tale of accidental discovery of the routine that would make him famous signals both his bona fides as an agile improviser and his authorial "genius."[14] Caught on stage with a bout of laryngitis, Hudgins ditches the score and literally plays it by ear, letting his body stand in for his voice. In the process, he discovers a new specialty for himself as a pantomimist. The story touts his ability to think on (and with) his feet, a prized quality among vernacular dancers.

Even while celebrating his spontaneity, Hudgins's narrative serves to reinforce the originality of his act. Although, as intellectual property rights scholars have pointed out, the originality requirement of copyright law is not without contradiction, it has meant, at a minimum, that a work cannot be copied from another but must issue directly from the author.[15] In practice, the Lockean principle of possessing property in one's "person" has weighed heavily on determinations of originality. According to legal scholar McLeod, "Just as Locke understood property as being created when a person mixes one's labor with materials found in nature, the author's "property" became "his" own when he stamps his personality on the work—doing this in an "original" manner."[16] And so a "discourse of the original genius" has persisted within copyright's implicit notions of creativity.[17] Somewhat counterintuitively, the alleged haphazardness of Hudgins's initial "Mwa Mwa" routine actually buttressed its originality to his person: the pantomimed gestures were a response to and derived from the particular conditions of his suddenly speechless body. This, incidentally, was also a defining feature of the eccentric dancer—distinctive moves linked to unique person.[18]

Of course, Hudgins's origination tale doubtlessly conceals as much as it reveals. An undated newspaper article offers an alternative account of Hudgins's creative process:

> For nine years he traveled around the country playing at all the major burlesque houses.
>
> During this time he was changing his act and developing it into a pantomime blackface routine similar to that of the pre-twenties star—Bert Williams—who came to fame doing an imitation of whites doing imitations of blacks.

He became so successful he was taken into the renowned Noble Sissle and Eubie Blake production "Chocolate Dandies" that enjoyed long runs in New York and Boston.[19]

In this admittedly more credible telling, Hudgins's act was not the fortuitous byproduct of unforeseen events but the result of time, labor, calculation, and fine-tuning. This version also identifies Bert Williams, one of the most popular performers of the late minstrelsy and vaudeville eras, as a direct source for Hudgins's routine. Classified by the Stearnses as one of the earliest eccentric dancers, Williams, like Hudgins, performed in blackface and was best known for his comedic pantomime, as well as for dancing the Cakewalk with his partner George Walker, who played the "strutting dandy" to Williams's "shiftless, shuffling 'darky'" role.[20] Observers of Hudgins often noted his similarities to Williams, who died in 1922, even anointing him Williams's successor.[21] In the same interview in which he talked up his accidental discovery of the "Mwa Mwa" routine, Hudgins himself cited Williams's influence: "In my dances, those steps they came to me—my first inspiration for dancing was Bert Williams."[22] For Hudgins, then, claiming spontaneity and originality did not mean disavowing precursors.

Yet there were times when Hudgins renounced improvisation altogether. In 1924, Bertram Whitney, the white producer of *The Chocolate Dandies*, sued Hudgins for violating the terms of his contract. Facing across-the-board salary cuts from Whitney, and with his star on the rise, Hudgins left the Broadway revue to earn higher pay as a featured performer in a New York nightclub. In an effort to prevent his departure, Whitney sought an injunction against Hudgins, claiming he was a "unique and extraordinary" performer whose services were "irreplaceable"—reportedly the first time this legal claim was made about an African American artist.[23] In his deposition, Whitney appraised Hudgins's value in terms of his propensity for improvisation. "He had a limitless number of dance steps," Whitney testified of Hudgins. "In fact, no two dances by him were alike; he seemed to make up his own steps as he went along."[24] In their ultimately successful defense, Hudgins and his lawyers countered Whitney's claim that there was anything dynamic about Hudgins's performance, maintaining that his dance act had remained more or less static throughout his stage career. There was "slight or no variance," Hudgins stated in his deposition, "between what I did in burlesque for eight years, what I did in . . . 'The Chocolate Dandies' during my engagement therein, and in what I am now [d]oing in the 'Club Alabam Revue.'"[25]

Part and parcel of denying that Hudgins possessed "any unique or extraordinary ability as a dancer," then, was rejecting the idea that he was either spontaneous or adept at transforming his routine over time. Insisting on his lack of worth as a performer in order to evade Whitney's injunction, Hudgins emphasized his unvarying ordinariness.

Following several years on the heels of the Whitney affair, Hudgins's decision to take out a copyright on his pantomime acts can be read as an implicit rejoinder to the position he was forced to take in the Whitney case. The nineteen-page copyrighted booklet is filled with unequivocal assertions of Hudgins's originality. An early clause, for example, reads, "Every Expression, Move, Gesture, Pedal Evolution, Manoeuvre and Shuffle is JOHNNY HUDGINS['s] own original creation."[26] At the back of the booklet, in what could have doubled as plaintiff's evidence against him in the earlier lawsuit, Hudgins includes excerpts from newspaper reviews, which collectively attest to his uniqueness. An "extraordinary negro comedian," trumpets the French *L'Oeuvre*[27] and "one of the most original things we have ever seen." "As unique and versatile a comic as graces the stage to-day," announces the New York *Telegraph*, while the New York *Daily Mirror* and New York *Variety*, respectively, declare that "he possesses a unique way and a distinct sense of originality," and that "his absolute originality places him as incomparable."[28]

The more explicit goal of the copyright, which simultaneously rested on and sanctioned Hudgins's claims of originality, was to block the rash of imitators seeking to capitalize on his "Mwa Mwa" routine, which became a sensation on both sides of the Atlantic in the 1920s. When a touring musical production took Hudgins to Europe in 1925, other performers evidently rushed in to fill his vacancy. The Lincoln Theater in Harlem even held a series of "Hudgins-imitator contests."[29] In Europe, too, Hudgins earned a reputation as "The Most Imitated Comedian on the Continent."[30] A 1928 article in the New York *Amsterdam News* points to Hudgins's irritation at the pilfering. Although reportedly not opposed to duplicators with "the decency . . . to give him credit for what they are doing," Hudgins threatened to sue "act grabbers" who refused to cite him as the originator of the "Mwa Mwa" routine.[31] While it is unclear whether Hudgins's British copyright would have stood up in a U.S. court of law, its very existence gave force to his legal threats.[32]

Bracketed by proclamations of originality, the core of the copyright booklet transcribes Hudgins's routines for the tangible medium of print. In blow-by-blow accounts, he details the entrances and exits, dance steps, and gestures that composed his seven specialty acts, including the "Mwa Mwa" number. "Enter Stage with . . . droll shuffle, business of stumbling over Stage, nearly falling, also Clown with audience, vamping song with an eccentric step I call 'Cutting Capers,'" the description of his most famous routine begins. Stopping suddenly, Hudgins tips his hat, smiles, and mimes a conversation with an audience member. This is quickly replaced with, in Hudgins's words, an

> expression of not recognizing them and asking them to leave [the] Theatre—by means of Pantomime and facial expressions—and just as I am about to put my hat on, it suddenly comes to me that I *do* know them and I show it by smiling back, speaking with a very broad smile, and looking very much pleased. After this . . . I glide back up-stage and do a long slide to the front[,] landing right at [the] Footlights, . . . then from there I go into my Pantomime song called the "Mwa, Mwa, Mwa, Mwa, Mwa, Mwa, mwa." A song in which I do not utter a word, but move my lips as if I were singing, while a muted Cornet . . . gives an imitation of a human voice singing "Mwa, Mwa."

After performing a "low bow to the audience" followed by "a fast shuffle" and slide, Hudgins concludes the act by "skipping from one end of the Stage to the other" while "throwing imaginary flowers" from his hat to the audience.[33]

Was Hudgins's documentation of his routine for the written page also a disavowal of improvisation? In one sense, the meticulous transcription seems consistent with the stance Hudgins took in the Whitney lawsuit that his routine contained "slight or no variance." Much as that suit required Hudgins to make a trade-off—deny originality in order to maintain autonomy as a performer—it could be argued that copyright demanded another kind of capitulation—forsake improvisation in order to establish intellectual property rights over his routines.

But there is no compelling reason to conclude that "fixing" his act for the purposes of copyright protection squelched improvisation for Hudgins. In fact, evidence suggests otherwise. As the description above reveals, the version of "Mwa Mwa" that Hudgins committed to the page contains openings for "vamping" for and "clowning" with the audience. Even within a carefully choreographed sequence of gestures, in other words, there was room for play. Furthermore, a surviving musical score for the "Mwa Mwa" number (here called "Wa Wa") contains annotations that read "ad lib with Johnny" at one point, and "repeat until Johnny drops hand in disgust" at another.[34] These handwritten notes indicate that, far from giving a rigid, inflexible performance, Hudgins fooled around with timing and engaged in give-and-take with his accompanying musician, as well as with his audience. Fighting for ownership of his act in a marketplace where whites overwhelmingly controlled the means of production, Hudgins asserted intellectual property rights over his embodied performance but refused to give up the improvisational leeway that embodied performance afforded him.

RESISTING DOCUMENTATION? THE CASE OF THE *KISS ME, KATE* SPECIALTY DANCERS

The nexus of copyright and improvisation played out rather differently for the African American dancers who appeared in the musical *Kiss Me, Kate* some twenty years after Hudgins's heyday. From a historiographic perspective, their omission from the Labanotated score that Hanya Holm submitted to the Copyright Office in 1952 means that much less is known about their jazz number. The relative absence of documentation makes it much more difficult to draw conclusions about their relationship to either improvisation or intellectual property rights.

What can be said is that a pair of acrobatic jazz-tap dancers named Fred Davis and Eddie Sledge, known as Fred and Sledge, joined the original Broadway cast of *Kiss Me, Kate* and contributed greatly to its success. The backstage musical about a group of performers in a Baltimore production of Shakespeare's *The Taming of the Shrew* opened on December 30, 1948, at the New Century Theatre on Broadway. Written by Bella and Samuel Spewack, with music and lyrics by Cole Porter, the show ran for a remarkable 1,077 performances.[35] The musical's official choreographer was the German émigré Hanya Holm (1893–1992), considered one of the "Big Four" pioneers of American modern dance, who turned to Broadway for employment when financial pressures forced her to disband her own company. The choreography for *Kiss Me, Kate* ran the gamut of dance styles, from ballet, modern, and jazz, to folk and court dance, but the show-stopper was "Too Darn Hot," the only number in the almost exclusively white musical to feature African American dancers. Set in a back-stage alley where cast members played dice and smoked cigarettes, the number was sung by Lorenzo Fuller, who played the black valet Paul, and spotlighted what one critic termed the "lusty Harlem hoofing," and another the "torrid pavement dancing," of Fred and Sledge, who were eventually joined by the white soloist Harold Lang.[36]

Fred and Sledge were part of a black vernacular tradition of two-man comedy and class act dance teams that peaked during the swing era of the 1930s and 40s.[37] Where comedy teams typically incorporated humor and eccentric dancing into their routines, and class or "flash" acts emphasized elegance and technical exactitude, both combined virtuosic rhythmic tapping with spectacular acrobatics. With a contemporaneous review describing Fred and Sledge as "good-looking well-dressed lads [who] work very well with precision taps and flying splits," it is clear that the two were a class act.[38]

However little is known about the particulars of Fred and Sledge's "Too Darn Hot" number, two-man tap acts like theirs generally infused set choreography with an improvisatory spirit. As dance scholar Constance Valis Hill explains, the competitive tap challenge was the "churning engine" of these theatrical acts:

> Instead of being pitted against each other, they were partners (often billed as "brothers") who, instead of one-upping each other, combined their specialties in building to a climax a routine in which structured improvisation was reserved for sections of dance, most often solos. Instead of mimicking each other's steps, the two moved as one, each a mirror image of the other. Instead of copying each other for the purposes of mocking, the practice of signifying evolved into the repetition of rhythmic phrases that progressed into whole paragraphs of sound and movement. When traded back and forth, these phrases became a lively and witty dialogue between dancers: technical perfection personified. Even when the solos were set, the very structure and form of the class act challenge dance, in which patterns were repeated, varied, traded, and one-upped, allowed for a dynamic exchange of rhythm and movement that gave the performance the look of being improvised.[39]

The aesthetics of improvisation thus left their mark on even these more "refined" class acts. Like Hudgins, Fred and Sledge surely worked out their stage routine in advance while preserving the look and feel of spontaneity in performance.

Holm's contributions to "Too Darn Hot" were limited to creating "some non-intruding but atmospherically effective jitterbug passages" for the Dancing Ensemble, who supported Fuller, Davis, Sledge, and Lang in the original Broadway staging.[40] The Labanotated score for "Too Darn Hot," created during rehearsals for the 1951 London production of *Kiss Me, Kate* when Holm hired the notator Ann Hutchinson to document her choreography, records only this background dancing.[41] The accompanying explanation, cited in part at the opening of this chapter, reads:

> This is a jazz number done with three negros [sic] who sang and danced. The exact
> arrangement varied according to what the negros [sic] could do, it was worked out as
> a duet with the third taking over as soloist part of the time. None of this is recorded as
> it was so individual. What is recorded is what the group did in the background. If the
> dance were to be reconstructed the solo parts would have to be inserted which would
> mean fresh choreography.[42]

Notwithstanding its brevity, the passage speaks volumes about the tensions between
copyright and black vernacular performance. Simultaneously a record of an absence
and an absence of a record, the text appears to epitomize improvisation's resistance to
documentation. The "three negros" [sic]—the two "specialty dancers," played in London
by the Wallace Brothers, and the character of Paul, played by Archie Savage[43]—perform
in such an "individual" manner that their jazz routine eludes capture by Labanotation
and must be newly arranged with "fresh choreography" every time the musical is staged.
This seems the essence of refusing fixity.[44]

The implications of the jazz routine's apparent resistance to being recorded were
complex and multifaceted. From one perspective, in evading documentation, the number also evaded choreographic ownership by Holm. Because they were not included
in the score Holm submitted to the Copyright Office, the contributions of the African
American dancers to the show-stopping "Too Darn Hot" remained beyond the reach of
her copyright. This case would thus seem to support a dichotomy between white, copy-
rightable choreography and black, uncopyrightable improvisation and, concomitantly,
a romanticized view of black improvisatory dance as refusing to participate in a capitalist economy of reproduction.

But the costs of such resistance are equally clear here. Too "individual" to warrant
the fixity of notation, lacking any stable relationship to the musical as a whole (one
critic described the "Too Darn Hot" dancing as "rather alien to the rest of the choreography"),[45] the jazz number could be treated as a mere "insert." The routine, that is,
along with the specialty dancers who devised it, could be easily extricated from a given
production and replaced by entirely new choreography and dancers. Indeed, quite
a few African American dance duos evidently rotated in and out of this slot.[46] While
cast changes are hardly an aberration in restagings of Broadway musicals, when contrasted with the constancy of Holm's choreography, the exchangeability of the African
American specialty dancers reflects their lack of durable value to the show.

Moreover, although Holm never explicitly claimed to choreograph nor to own the
rights to the "Too Darn Hot" jazz routine, the acclaim she received as the putatively sole
choreographer of *Kiss Me, Kate*, including the celebration of her copyright achievement
and a New York Drama Critics' Award, raises troubling questions about white credit for
black choreographic labor. The experience of another two-man tap team who appeared
in a later version of *Kiss Me, Kate* proves instructive. In 1949, several years before a brief
stint in *Kiss Me, Kate*, the class-act dancers Honi Coles and Cholly Atkins joined the cast
of *Gentlemen Prefer Blondes*, choreographed by the white ballet- and modern-trained
dancer Agnes DeMille, and were featured in a second-act number called "Mamie is

Mimi." Recounting the episode in *Jazz Dance*, Cholly Atkins offers a window onto the choreographic process and subsequent allocation of credit:

> "During rehearsals Agnes de Mille didn't know what to do with us," says Coles, "so finally Julie Styne, who hired us, took us aside and said, 'Look, why don't you fellows work up something, and I'll get her to look at it.'" They located arranger Benny Payne, who knew how to write for tap-dance acts, and the three of them worked out a routine. "One afternoon, Miss de Mille took time off to look at it," says Atkins. "She liked it and told us to keep it in."

On went the show with the Coles-Atkins-Payne routine a hit, and Agnes de Mille listed as choreographer in the program. "Later on we had to get her permission to use our routine on Jack Haley's *Ford Hour*," says Coles. "She was very nice about it." In her autobiography Miss de Mille writes that the "Mamie Is Mimi" number, along with several others, was devised "in a single short rehearsal," presumably by Miss de Mille. This was the standard practice.[47]

Though it would be specious to let this anecdote stand in for all musicals with white choreographers and black specialty dancers, "Too Darn Hot" was no doubt put together in a somewhat analogous way. Returning to the missing notation in the copyrighted Labanotated score, the use of the passive voice to recount how the jazz tap number evolved—"it was worked out"—assumes greater significance. The absence of a fuller record of the routine made it all too easy to elide the labor and creativity of the African American improviser-choreographer-dancers responsible for it. And all too easy for Holm, the "highest browed" of white choreographers, who was armed with fixed and tangible evidence of her contributions, to receive credit for the whole of the musical's choreography.[48]

None of this is intended to detract from what Holm did accomplish in terms of choreography or copyright with *Kiss Me, Kate*. Nor is it to suggest that documentation and intellectual property law were solutions to the racial inequities that made it so difficult for African American jazz and tap performers to receive due credit and compensation for their creative expression in the first half of the twentieth century. Although Johnny Hudgins was extremely successful at the peak of his popularity, reportedly becoming the "highest paid night club entertainer of his Race" in 1930, he fell out of favor with a later generation of performers and critics, due in no small part to his use of blackface.[49] The fact that neither his name nor his once-famous "Mwa Mwa" routine is remembered today makes evident that copyright offers no guarantee against historical amnesia.

In addition, copyright, with its requirement that work be "fixed in a tangible medium of expression," was (and continues to be) an extremely fraught construct, especially for dancers working in African American expressive traditions that privilege improvisation. While solo performers like Hudgins and two-man dance teams like Fred and Sledge worked hard to develop audience-pleasing routines that remained largely consistent from one performance to the next, they also found ways to preserve an aesthetic of spontaneity within their choreography, whether that meant vamping for theater-goers or making room for give-and-take with fellow performers. Indeed, as a rule, jazz and tap dancers were expected to improvise, and as was the case for Hudgins, their value to white producers sometimes rested on the (perceived) extemporaneousness of their performance. For these dancers, the most logical medium in which to record their expression was the body itself. The fact that Hudgins's *Silence* booklet is the only documented example of a copyright held by an African American dancer in the first half of the twentieth century that I have been able to locate is a reminder of how uncharacteristic his formal pursuit of intellectual property rights was.

Just the same, that pursuit should prompt us to rethink the conventional wisdom that copyright law is always and already antithetical to improvisatory traditions, or that it has worked only to disadvantage African American vernacular performers. However uncertain the legitimacy of Hudgins's British copyright inside the United States (obtained decades before choreography was granted protection by U.S. law), its very existence afforded Hudgins a means of pushing back against white claims on his labor and against imitators trying to make a buck off his choreography. By the same token, the situation of the specialty dancers in *Kiss Me, Kate* should prompt us to think carefully about the implications of resisting documentation. Even as the African American dancers employed in the hit musical avoided capture by a notation system designed to record Euro-American choreography, they could not evade a larger, racialized system of authorial credit that "invisibilized" their contributions.[50] For black jazz and tap dancers working in the white-dominated capitalist marketplace of the first half of the twentieth century, it was not a matter of simply choosing between the ideology of copyright and the practice of improvisation but, rather, of dealing with the consequences when the two converged.

Notes

1. John Martin, "The Dance: Copyright," *New York Times*, March 30, 1952, X10.
2. Labanotation is a system of symbols used to record movement, based on the ideas of Rudolf Laban.
3. *Kiss Me, Kate*. Labanotated score, Dance Notation Bureau Library, New York City.
4. U.S. Copyright Office, "Copyright in General FAQ," http://www.copyright.gov/help/faq/faq-general.html#what. Accessed June 29, 2011.
5. In *Steppin' on the Blues: The Visible Rhythms of African American Dance* (Urbana: University of Illinois Press, 1996), Jacqui Malone defines "vernacular" dance as that which makes visible the rhythms of African American music and identifies its hallmarks as "improvisation and spontaneity, propulsive rhythm, call-and-response patterns, self-expression, elegance, and control" (2).
6. The conventional wisdom about improvisation and fixation can be summed up by Derek Bailey's assertion that "there is something central to the spirit of voluntary improvisation which is opposed to the aims and contradicts the idea of documentation." In *Improvisation: Its Nature and Practice in Music* (New York: Da Capo Press, 1992), ix.
7. Kembrew McLeod, *Owning Culture: Authorship, Ownership, and Intellectual Property Law* (New York: Peter Lang, 2001), 71. See, among others, Siva Vaidhyanathan, *Copyrights and Copywrongs: The Rise of Intellectual Property and How It Threatens Creativity* (New York: New

York University Press, 2001), in which he argues that "American copyright . . . clearly conflicts with the aesthetic principles of West African music and dance" (126); Richard L. Schur, *Parodies of Ownership: Hip-Hop Aesthetics and Intellectual Property Law* (Ann Arbor: University of Michigan Press, 2009); and Candace G. Hines, "Black Musical Traditions and Copyright Law: Historical Tensions," *Michigan Journal of Race & Law* 10 (spring 2005): 463–494.

8. On black vernacular aesthetics, see, for example: Houston A. Baker, *Blues, Ideology, and Afro-American Literature: A Vernacular Theory* (Chicago: University of Chicago Press, 1984); Henry Louis Gates, Jr., *The Signifying Monkey: A Theory of Afro-American Literary Criticism* (New York: Oxford University Press, 1988); Richard Powell, "Art History and Black Memory: Toward a 'Blues Aesthetic,'" in *History and Memory in African-American Culture*, ed. Geneviève Fabre and Robert O'Meally (New York: Oxford University Press, 1994), 228–243; Robert O'Meally, "On Burke and the Vernacular: Ralph Ellison's Boomerang of History," in *History and Memory in African-American Culture*, ed. Geneviève Fabre and Robert O'Meally (New York: Oxford University Press, 1994), 244–260; and Malone, *Steppin' on the Blues*.

9. K. J. Greene, "Copyright, Culture & Black Music: A Legacy of Unequal Protection," *Hastings Communication & Entertainment Law Journal* 21 (1999): 342.

10. Johnny Hudgins, *Silence*, Copyright No. 746, The Cranbourn Press, London, n.d. Jean-Claude Baker private collection, New York City. My sincere thanks to Jean-Claude Baker for generously opening his collection of Hudgins material to me.

11. Danielle Goldman, *I Want to Be Ready: Improvised Dance as a Practice of Freedom* (Ann Arbor: The University of Michigan Press, 2010), 11–12. Goldman here is citing André Lepecki's essay "Inscribing Dance," in *Of the Presence of the Body: Essays on Dance and Performance Theory*, ed. André Lepecki (Middletown: Wesleyan University Press, 2004), 135. Performance studies scholar Peggy Phelan (in)famously argued that performance's ephemerality—the fact that its very condition is its disappearance—gives it a "distinctive oppositional edge" and enables it to "elude . . . regulation and control." See "The Ontology of Performance: Representation without Reproduction," in *Unmarked: The Politics of Performance* (London and New York: Routledge, 1993), 148.

12. Marshall and Jean Stearns, *Jazz Dance: The Story of American Vernacular Dance* (New York: Schirmer Books, 1968), 232. For more on eccentric jazz dancing and on the career of Johnny Hudgins, see Brian Harker, "Louis Armstrong, Eccentric Dance, and the Evolution of Jazz on the Eve of Swing," *Journal of the American Musicological Society* 61.1 (Spring 2008): 67–121. My thanks to Brian for sharing information about his research on Hudgins.

13. Mura Dehn, "Johnny Hudgins," Papers on Afro-American Social Dance, folder 25, Dance Division, The New York Public Library.

14. See, for example, Brent Hayes Edwards, "Louis Armstrong and the Syntax of Scat," *Critical Inquiry* 28, no. 3 (Spring 2002): 618–649. Hudgins's one-time cast-mate Josephine Baker also claimed that the chorus line clowning that helped launch her career was entirely spontaneous. See Anthea Kraut, "Whose Choreography?: Josephine Baker and the Question of (Dance) Authorship," *The Scholar and Feminist Online* 6, nos. 1–2 (Fall 2007/Spring 2008), http://sfonline.barnard.edu/baker/kraut_01.htm.

15. The defining ruling on the matter of originality is the Supreme Court case of *Feist Publications, Inc., v. Rural Telephone Service Co.*, 499 U.S. 340 (1991), which ruled that the information compiled in a telephone book did not possess sufficient creativity to merit copyright protection. Paul K. Saint-Amour, *The Copywrights: Intellectual Property and the Literary Imagination* (Ithaca, NY: Cornell University Press, 2003).

16. McLeod, *Owning Culture*, 21.

17. Mark Rose, *Authors and Owners: The Invention of Copyright* (Cambridge, MA: Harvard University Press, 1993), 134.

18. See Anthea Kraut, "'Stealing Steps' and Signature Moves: Embodied Theories of Dance as Intellectual Property," *Theatre Journal* 62, no. 2 (May 2010): 173–189, for more on the ways in which a dancer's idiosyncratic movement could serve as a property-like claim on dance.

19. Sam Spence, "A Vaudevillian Remembers," n.s., n.d. Newspaper Clippings, Johnny Hudgins Papers, Box 1, Folder 4, Emory University Manuscript, Archives, and Rare Book Library. Special thanks to Leah Weinryb Grohsgal for her adept research assistance.

20. Stearns, *Jazz Dance*, 117, 121. For more on Williams, see Louis Chude-Sokei, *The Last Darky: Bert Williams, Black-on-Black Minstrelsy, and the African Diaspora* (Durham: Duke University Press, 2006).

21. "Johnny Hudgins Is Still Going Big on Broadway," *Chicago Defender*, May 8, 1926, 7. One of Hudgins's routines, in which he ballroom danced with an imaginary partner, was apparently a direct take-off on one of Williams's acts. "Johnny Hudgins Joins Blackbirds," *Chicago Defender* September 1, 1928, n.p.

22. Mura Dehn interview, papers on Afro-American Social Dance.

23. "Hudgins in Suit," *Chicago Defender*, November 1, 1924, 6.

24. Bertram C. Whitney *v.* Johnny Hudgins, et al. (Lee Shubert, Jacob J. Shubert, The Winter Garden Company, and Arthur Lyons), index no. 40459, submitted October 31, 1924, New York Supreme Court, County of New York.

25. Bertram C. Whitney *v.* Johnny Hudgins, et al.

26. Hudgins, *Silence*.

27. Hudgins, *Silence*. Although the program booklet attributes this quotation to the "Paris *Ceuvre*," this was almost certainly a mistaken reference to the daily *L'Oeuvre* newspaper.

28. Hudgins, *Silence*.

29. David Hinckley, "Not Just Black and White," *New York Daily News*, September 3, 2000, http://www.nydailynews.com/archives/entertainment/2000/09/03/2000-09-03_not_just_black___white_the_c.html (accessed June 29, 2011).

30. Clipping, Johnny Hudgins scrapbook, Jean-Claude Baker private collection.

31. "Hudgins Protests Use of His Act by Others," *New York Amsterdam News*, August 22, 1928, Johnny Hudgins scrapbook, Jean-Claude Baker private collection.

32. Unlike U.S. law at the time, the British Copyright Act of 1911 deemed "dramatic work" to include "any piece for . . . choreographic work or entertainment in dumb show." Copyright Act, 1911, http://www.legislation.gov.uk/ukpga/Geo5/1-2/46/introduction/enacted (accessed June 29, 2011). Although the language of British copyright law does not specify that a work must be "fixed in a tangible medium of expression" to merit protection, it is possible that, as a non-British subject, publishing his booklet in London was a way for Hudgins to qualify his work for protection. The law states that "copyright shall subsist throughout the parts of His Majesty's dominions . . . in every original literary dramatic musical and artistic work, if . . . in the case of a published work, the work was first published within such parts of His Majesty's dominions." Furthermore, at least one newspaper believed that Hudgins copyrighted his Mwa Mwa routine under U.S. law, although I have not been able to confirm the existence of this U.S. copyright. "Johnny Hudgins is Coming Home," *Chicago Defender*, July 28, 1928, 7.

33. Hudgins, *Silence*.

34. "Wa Wa Number," Johnny Hudgins Papers, Hudgins/MSS 1029, Box 2, Folder 25, Emory University Manuscript, Archives, and Rare Book Library.

35. David Ewen, *New Complete Book of the American Musical Theater* (New York: Holt, Rinehart and Winston, 1970), 277.

36. "Theater Dance," Clipping from *PM Star*, January 4, 1949, Hanya Holm Scrapbooks, Dance Division, New York Public Library; Brooks Atkinson, "At the Theatre: 'Kiss Me, Kate,'" *New York Times On The Web*, December 31, 1948, http://www.nytimes.com/books/98/11/29/specials/porter-kate.html (accessed June 30, 2011).

37. Stearns and Stearns, *Jazz Dance*, 244–245.

38. Rev. of Copacabana Night Club, *The Billboard*, April 1, 1950, 54. The two are characterized as "Acrobatic, Flash" in Rusty E. Frank, *Tap!: The Greatest Tap Dance Stars and Their Stories, 1900–1955* (New York: Da Capo Press, 1994), 288.

39. Constance Valis Hill, "Stepping, Stealing, Sharing, and Daring," in *Taken by Surprise: A Dance Improvisation Reader*, ed. Ann Cooper Albright and David Gere (Middletown, CT: Wesleyan University Press, 2003), 94–95.

40. Walter Terry, "Dance: Miss Holm and her Fine '*Kiss Me, Kate*' Choreography," *New York Herald Tribune*, Hanya Holm Clippings File, Dance Division, New York Public Library.

41. "Copyright by Hanya Holm," *Dance Magazine* 39, no. 7 (July 1965): 44.

42. *Kiss Me, Kate*, Labanotated Score.

43. Program, *Kiss Me, Kate*, London, 1951, http://www.sondheimguide.com/porter/kissuk.html (accessed June 30, 2011).

44. Although Labanotation was designed to record Western choreography, the Stearnses include a host of Labanotated dances in an appendix to their volume *Jazz Dance*. For more on issues of notation in dance, see Mark Franko, "Writing for the Body: Notation, Reconstruction, and Reinvention in Dance," *Common Knowledge* 17, no. 2 (2011): 321–334, http://muse.jhu.edu/ (accessed June 30, 2011).

45. Arthur Todd, "A Brace of Musicals This Season on Broadway," *Dance* (March 1949): 28–29, Dance Clipping File, Musical Comedies, *Kiss Me, Kate*, New York Public Library.

46. As reported by the Stearnses, the comedy dance team of Charles Cook and Ernest Brown appeared briefly in *Kiss Me, Kate* while it was still on Broadway (it ran until July 1951). Stearnses, *Jazz Dance*, 245. As mentioned above, a pair named the Wallace Brothers took on the roles of specialty dancers for the British production. And in 1953, Honi Coles and Cholly Atkins performed in a summer stock production of the musical in Texas. Cholly Atkins and Jacqui Malone, *Class Act: the Jazz Life of Choreographer Cholly Atkins* (New York: Columbia University Press, 2001), 97.

47. Stearnses, *Jazz Dance*, 309.

48. John Martin, "Broadway on Its Toes," *New York Times*, January 23, 1949, SM18.

49. "Johnny Hudgins Back in Night Club Revue," *Chicago Defender*, May 17, 1930, 10. Hudgins continued to tour Europe, South America, Canada, and the U.S. through the 1940s.

50. On "invisibilization," see Brenda Dixon Gottschild, *Digging the Africanist Presence in American Performance: Dance and Other Contexts* (Westport, CT: Greenwood Press, 1996).

BIBLIOGRAPHY

Abrams, Howard B. "Originality and Creativity in Copyright Law." *Law and Contemporary Problems* 55, no. 2 (Spring 1992): 3–44.

Atkins, Cholly, and Jacqui Malone. *Class Act: the Jazz Life of Choreographer Cholly Atkins*. New York: Columbia University Press, 2001.

Atkinson, Brooks. "At the Theatre: 'Kiss Me, Kate.'" *New York Times On The Web*, December 31, 1948. http://www.nytimes.com/books/98/11/29/specials/porter-kate.html. Accessed June 30, 2011.

Bailey, Derek. *Improvisation: Its Nature and Practice in Music*. New York: Da Capo Press, 1992.

Baker, Houston A. *Blues, Ideology, and Afro-American Literature: A Vernacular Theory.* Chicago: University of Chicago Press, 1984.

Chude-Sokei, Louis. *The Last Darky: Bert Williams, Black-on-Black Minstrelsy, and the African Diaspora.* Durham, NC: Duke University Press, 2006.

Copyright Act, 1911. http://www.legislation.gov.uk/ukpga/Geo5/1-2/46/introduction/enacted. Accessed June 29, 2011.

"Copyright by Hanya Holm." *Dance Magazine* 39, no. 7 (July 1965): 44.

Dehn, Mura. "Johnny Hudgins," Papers on Afro-American Social Dance, folder 25, Dance Division, The New York Public Library.

Dixon Gottschild, Brenda. *Digging the Africanist Presence in American Performance: Dance and Other Contexts.* Westport, CT: Greenwood Press, 1996.

Edwards, Brent Hayes. "Louis Armstrong and the Syntax of Scat." *Critical Inquiry* 28, no. 3 (Spring 2002): 618–649.

Ewen, David. *New Complete Book of the American Musical Theater.* New York: Holt, Rinehart and Winston, 1970.

Frank, Rusty E. *Tap!: The Greatest Tap Dance Stars and Their Stories, 1900–1955.* New York: Da Capo Press, 1994.

Franko, Mark. "Writing for the Body: Notation, Reconstruction, and Reinvention in Dance." *Common Knowledge* 17, no. 2 (2011): 321–334.

Gates, Henry Louis Jr. *The Signifying Monkey: A Theory of Afro-American Literary Criticism.* New York: Oxford University Press, 1988.

Goldman, Danielle. *I Want to Be Ready: Improvised Dance as a Practice of Freedom.* Ann Arbor: University of Michigan Press, 2010.

Greene, K. J. "Copyright, Culture & Black Music: A Legacy of Unequal Protection." *Hastings Communication & Entertainment Law Journal* 21 (1999): 339–392.

Harker, Brian. "Louis Armstrong, Eccentric Dance, and the Evolution of Jazz on the Eve of Swing." *Journal of the American Musicological Society* 61, no. 1 (spring 2008): 67–121.

Hinckley, David. "Not Just Black and White." *New York Daily News*, Sept. 3, 2000. http://www.nydailynews.com/archives/entertainment/2000/09/03/2000-09-03_not_just_black___white_the_c.html. Accessed June 29, 2011.

Hines, Candace G. "Black Musical Traditions and Copyright Law: Historical Tensions." *Michigan Journal of Race & Law* 10 (Spring 2005): 463–494.

Hudgins, Johnny. Papers. Emory University Manuscript, Archives, and Rare Book Library.

Hudgins, Johnny. Scrapbook. Jean-Claude Baker private collection, New York City.

Hudgins, Johnny. *Silence.* Copyright No. 746, The Cranbourn Press, London, n.d. Jean-Claude Baker private collection, New York City.

"Hudgins in Suit." *Chicago Defender*, November 1, 1924, 6.

"Johnny Hudgins Back in Night Club Revue." *Chicago Defender*, May 17, 1930, 10.

"Johnny Hudgins Is Coming Home." *Chicago Defender*, July 28, 1928, 7.

"Johnny Hudgins Is Still Going Big on Broadway." *Chicago Defender*, May 8, 1926, 7.

Kiss Me, Kate. Labanotated score, Dance Notation Bureau Library, New York City.

Kraut, Anthea. "'Stealing Steps' and Signature Moves: Embodied Theories of Dance as Intellectual Property." *Theatre Journal* 62, no. 2 (May 2010): 173–189.

Kraut, Anthea. "Whose Choreography? Josephine Baker and the Question of (Dance) Authorship." *The Scholar and Feminist Online* 6, nos. 1–2 (Fall 2007/Spring 2008). http://sfonline.barnard.edu/baker/kraut_01.htm. Accessed Dec. 12, 2012.

Lepecki, André. "Inscribing Dance." In *Of the Presence of the Body: Essays on Dance and Performance Theory*, edited by André Lepecki, 124–139. Middletown: Wesleyan University Press, 2004.

Malone, Jacqui. *Steppin' on the Blues: The Visible Rhythms of African American Dance*. Urbana: University of Illinois Press, 1996.

"Broadway on its Toes." *New York Times*, January 23, 1949, SM18.

Martin, John. "The Dance: Copyright." *New York Times*, March 30, 1952, X10.

McLeod, Kembrew. *Owning Culture: Authorship, Ownership, and Intellectual Property Law*. New York: Peter Lang, 2001.

O'Meally, Robert. "On Burke and the Vernacular: Ralph Ellison's Boomerang of History." In *History and Memory in African-American Culture*, edited by Geneviève Fabre and Robert O'Meally, 244–260. New York: Oxford University Press, 1994.

Phelan, Peggy. "The Ontology of Performance: Representation without Reproduction." In *Unmarked: The Politics of Performance*, 146–166. London and New York: Routledge, 1993.

Price, Monroe and Malla Pollack. "The Author in Copyright: Notes for the Literary Critic," in *The Construction of Authorship: Textual Appropriation in Law and Literature*, edited by Martha Woodmansee and Peter Jaszi, 439–456. Durham, NC: Duke University Press, 1994.

Powell, Richard. "Art History and Black Memory: Toward a 'Blues Aesthetic.'" In *History and Memory in African-American Culture*, edited by Geneviève Fabre and Robert O'Meally, 228–243. New York: Oxford University Press, 1994.

Program, *Kiss Me, Kate*, London, 1951. http://www.sondheimguide.com/porter/kissuk.html. Accessed June 30, 2011.

Rev. of Copacabana Night Club. *The Billboard*, April 1, 1950, 54.

Rose, Mark. *Authors and Owners: The Invention of Copyright*. Cambridge, MA: Harvard University Press, 1993.

Saint-Amour, Paul K. *The Copywrights: Intellectual Property and the Literary Imagination*. Ithaca, NY: Cornell University Press, 2003.

Schur, Richard L. *Parodies of Ownership: Hip-Hop Aesthetics and Intellectual Property Law*. Ann Arbor: University of Michigan Press, 2009.

Stearns, Marshall, and Jean Stearns. *Jazz Dance: The Story of American Vernacular Dance*. New York: Schirmer Books, 1968.

Terry, Walter. "Dance: Miss Holm and Her Fine '*Kiss Me, Kate*' Choreography." *New York Herald Tribune*, Hanya Holm Clippings File, Dance Division, New York Public Library.

"Theater Dance." Clipping from *PM Star*, January 4, 1949, Hanya Holm Scrapbooks, Dance Division, New York Public Library.

Todd, Arthur. "A Brace of Musicals This Season on Broadway." *Dance* (March 1949): 28–29. Dance Clipping File, Musical Comedies, *Kiss Me, Kate*, New York Public Library.

U.S. Copyright Office, "Copyright in General FAQ." http://www.copyright.gov/help/faq/faq-general.html#what. Accessed June 29, 2011.

Vaidhyanathan, Siva. *Copyrights and Copywrongs: The Rise of Intellectual Property and How It Threatens Creativity*. New York: New York University Press, 2001.

Valis Hill, Constance. "Stepping, Stealing, Sharing, and Daring." In *Taken by Surprise: A Dance Improvisation Reader*, edited by Ann Cooper Albright and David Gere, 89–102. Middletown, CT: Wesleyan University Press, 2003.

Whitney, Bertram C. v. Johnny Hudgins, et. al. (Lee Shubert, Jacob J. Shubert, The Winter Garden Company, and Arthur Lyons). Index no. 40459, submitted Oct. 31, 1924, New York Supreme Court, County of New York.

CHAPTER 20

PERFORMING GENDER, RACE, AND POWER IN IMPROV COMEDY

AMY SEHAM

> A group of performing improvisers are not simply *indulging in* freedom, they are creating a power relationship in which a construct of "freedom" is generated by power and simultaneously regenerates that power. . . . Improvisation does not, thus, bypass power. They intertwine.
>
> — *guitarist Davey Williams*
> (quoted in Corbett 1995, 221)

FROM Dada cabarets to collective feminist troupes, iconoclastic theater artists have embraced improvisation as a means of subverting the "scripts" of conventional society. Whether the focus is overtly political, as in Augusto Boal's Theater of the Oppressed, or comic and commercial, as in ComedySportz, many view improvisation as a technique for evading (or transcending) both psychological and political censorship. A powerful mythology portrays improvisation as a communal, transformational, even spiritual performance mode, where spontaneity means freedom, and intuition (or absorption) reveals cosmic truth. For many idealistic teachers, directors, and activists, improvisation can look like an ideal mode of group creation, offering both individual agency and a sense of connection to the whole. Everyone can play. Everyone's story can be told. Every possibility can be imagined and embodied.

This view of improvisation is nowhere more prevalent than among the most committed practitioners of the performance form generally known as *improv* throughout the United States, Canada, Australia, and elsewhere. *Improv* is best known when linked with *comedy* to form a series of funny sketches and games. Audiences are delighted by the quick-wittedness and virtuosity of a group of performers who can pull comical characters and scenes out of thin air. But there are many permutations of this art form that encompass far more than entertainment.

Teachers and practitioners from Second City to TheatreSports, and from high school troupes to corporate training programs, share core improv principles, such as *agreement, no-mindedness* (being "in the moment"), *status*, and *groupmind*. Adherents believe that these techniques can release imagination, forge community, and create meaningful original (usually comic) theater. Moreover, drawn to the immediacy and absorption they experience in the moment of play, many improv participants believe strongly that, through improvisation, they tap into a spiritual dimension where they can access originality, authenticity, and truth.

Yet despite its liberatory ideals, improv (particularly when combined with comedy) often works to suppress the input of players whose gender, sexuality, race, ability, class, appearance, or any other form of difference diverges from social norms. Even in the most well-intentioned and egalitarian group, improv rules, if practiced uncritically, function to reinforce power hierarchies; naturalize sexist, heterosexist, and racist values; and perpetuate stereotypes. The most beloved components of the improv credo, such as *agreement* and *groupmind,* taken at face value, can make it virtually impossible for marginalized players to participate as equals.

Rare is the acting teacher who has not drawn heavily on Viola Spolin's improvisational games and exercises to form the foundations of his or her work with improv. Considered by many to be the mother of American improv, Spolin had great faith in spontaneity's ability to transform reality and allow for free expression. In her influential book, *Improvisation for the Theater*, she writes:

> Through spontaneity we are re-formed into ourselves. It creates an explosion that for the moment frees us from handed-down frames of reference, memory choked with old facts and information and undigested theories and techniques of other people's findings. Spontaneity is the moment of personal freedom when we are faced with a reality and see it, explore it and act accordingly. (Spolin 1983, 4)

Building on Spolin's teachings, virtually every improv troupe teaches the fundamental rule of "agreement": the concept of creating scenes, characters, and situations by saying "Yes—and"—in other words to accept the player's offer, and then to add to it by exploring or heightening the given idea. Agreement is crucial to improv not only at the level of the two-person scene, but for the entire performance troupe as well. According to Spolin, "The game is a natural group form providing the involvement and personal freedom necessary for experiencing. . . . There must be group agreement on the rules of the game and group interaction moving toward the objective if the game is to be played"(5).

Many players use the technique of agreement to create a communal experience of "groupthink" or groupmind, in which the entire troupe strives intuitively together toward the same goals. The perfect working of groupmind is often called "the zone" or "flow" by improvisers who describe the feeling as a magical kind of high, akin to perfect teamwork in sports or even great sex. A number of players are even familiar with Mihalyi Csikszentmihalyi's description of the flow state as one in which "there is little distinction between self and environment, between stimulus and response, or between past, present and future" (Csikszentmihalyi 2000, 36).

Players and teachers often equate groupmind with the "collective unconscious," and believe that through it they are able to tap into something universal, genuine and true. According to *Truth in Comedy*, a guidebook for long-form improv, when improvisers achieve "group mind" they are linked to "a universal intelligence, enabling them to perform fantastic, sometimes unbelievable feats" (Halpern 1994, 93).

While many players and teachers take great pleasure in the seemingly natural consensus of the improvisers, many social scientists consider "groupthink" a means of forcible conformity and assimilation (Janis quoted in Brown 1988, 158). Moreover, despite the ideals of agreement, it is often the case that the first person who speaks in an improv scene, or the person who speaks most aggressively, controls the premise of that scene and even defines the roles that others will play in it. Because female players still tend to be less assertive in taking initiative and focus on stage than the male players, women often find themselves "agreeing" to play the supportive, back-seat position in scenes that express a male perspective, allowing men to define them, or in improv terms, to *endow* them exclusively as stereotypical wives, girlfriends, mothers, or sexual objects.

In her excellent book, *TheatreSports Down Under*, Australian improv educator Lyn Pierse points to how a female player is consistently placed in the "low-status" role in relation to a male player, giving this example from a fast-paced game called *Death in a Minute*:

> A female player ran to the performance area beginning the scene, making an intuitive physical offer to establish an operating theatre. She held her hands creating the surgical gloves and made a perfect offer with her right hand: "Scalpel" . . . Seeing that offer, a male player entered the space. He took the imagined scalpel out of her hand and said, "Thanks, nurse." The audience hissed and booed. (1995, 301)

While some men have been known to "bulldoze," or deliberately dominate, an emerging scene, it can also be the case that a woman player will revert to her social training, deferring to the man without quite realizing she is doing so. Lyn Pierse gives an example of this tendency in another poignant anecdote. In a training session, players were working to undermine clichéd status relationships. Women were instructed to take high status, and men were directed to take the lower status in each emerging scene. A scene at a "psychiatrist's office" yielded the following result:

> Maria, who is a counselor and was a beginner player, stated the scene. Maria yielded to her first intuitive response. She lay on the couch. This placed David Wood in the high status as "the doctor." He immediately dropped his status and fell to the floor. He lay on his back on the ground and said, "Well, doctor it all started . . ." (304).

As Pierse explains, that interplay forced Maria to recognize her own complicity in initiating low-status roles. Maria, a counselor herself, remarked ruefully that she had left her own life experience "at the door instead of bringing it into the scene." But Pierse counters that Maria probably "had in fact brought her [life experience] into the scene" (304). Pierse asserts that training and coaching are needed to work against the "intuitive" subordination of women in improv comedy.

Women, GLBT, African American, and other minority improvisers may also encounter an unintentional failure to communicate with the white, heterosexual male players that dominate the field in improv comedy. In the midst of play, anyone with a different perspective may find that their references, allusions, and perceptions of comical incongruity are not immediately grasped by the majority players. Thus, as improviser Frances Callier has said, African American improvisers may feel that they must "whitewash [their] humor" in order to participate fully in the group (Seham 2001, 189). Thus, groupmind, so valued in improv, all too often becomes simply the heterosexual white male mind. As improviser Stephnie Weir put it, "The white male lifestyle and experience is so on the forefront of everyone's mind, TV, everything in our lives, that everyone has that common experience. We all know how to support that, 'Oh, that's familiar, I can heighten that'" (Seham 2001, 70).

As Gay Gibson Cima warns feminist directors,

> If you build your directorial work upon actors' improvisations, plan carefully, because improvisations can inadvertently reproduce the dominant ideological structures that you are trying to critique. Actors may spontaneously voice their own unrecognized biases or they may move in stereotypical ways, ways that reinforce rather than redirect the traditional values promoted in the canon. (Cima 1993, 100)

Many sincere, experienced players argue passionately, however, that improv is an apolitical practice. According to traditional improv doctrine, players must not be too much "in their heads" but rather, must improvise from a state of no-mindedness that allows them to bypass all societal inhibitions to reach a "greater truth." Real improv, they insist, must have no agenda to distract the player from his or her purely spontaneous response to each stimulus. Feminist, "ethnic," and gay perspectives are viewed warily and supported only in the most homogenized constructions. Thus, a performance mode with special affinity for subordinated people is all-too-quickly put at the service of mainstream ideology.

In his discussion of "common sense," cultural theorist Stuart Hall suggests that it is highly unlikely for unconscious, spontaneous expression to break the mold of "handed down frames and references":

> It is precisely its "spontaneous" quality, its transparency, its "naturalness," its refusal to be made to examine the premises on which it is founded, its resistance to change or correction, its effect of instant recognition, and the closed circle in which it moves which makes common sense, at one and the same time, "spontaneous," ideological, and unconscious. You cannot learn, through common sense, how things are: you can only discover where they fit into the existing scheme of things. (1979, 325)

Yet despite its dangerous claims of truth and neutrality, the possible abuse of agreement, and the failure of true consensus in groupmind, improv can be the source of exhilarating and transformative work. A number of companies and troupes have used improv techniques to create what feminist theater theorist Jill Dolan describes as "a place to experiment with the production of cultural meanings, on bodies willing to try a range of different significations for spectators willing to read them" (1993, 432).

In the following pages, I examine the way in which one particular improv troupe, called JANE, encountered, reinterpreted, and circumvented some of the obstacles facing women in improv. In particular, I examine issues related to improv principles of agreement and groupmind, status and character, and reference and stereotypes.

In the mid-1990s, Katie Roberts and Stephnie Weir had made their way onto high-powered performance teams at Chicago's popular ImprovOlympics[1] theater, but they felt nevertheless that they were missing out on the kind of intense camaraderie their male counterparts seemed to enjoy. Weir enjoyed her work with the Lost Yetis, a good, skillful, and even cooperative group, but realized that she was forced to translate her own experience into a male language in every show. She remembers thinking, "I want what they have. I want a girl thing" (quoted in Seham 2001, 69). Weir and Roberts wanted to create a group in which the mention of Judy Blume received the instantaneous recognition that sports figures did in the Lost Yetis. They wanted a venue where women could work to conquer the self-censorship and self-doubt that was engendered when their references and initiatives were not recognized. A place, says Weir, that would help "remind you that your voice is legitimate." They called the new team "JANE" (quoted in Seham 2001, 70).

JANE was soon known for creating successful comic scenes that were slower, more thoughtful, and more detailed than most. The actors often worked with the blurred edges of gender, looking for the commonalities as well as the differences between their characters and their selves. But one of the key pleasures and benefits that JANE provided to its players was the frequent opportunity to play male roles. In a mixed improv team, the outnumbered women very rarely attempted to do male impersonations, although male players were known to present a variety of female stereotypes with relative frequency. When women did initiate male roles, they would often be misread and ignored in the midst of improv play, and simply endowed with a female name, called "honey," or asked to take a letter.

In an interview, JANE member Jennifer Bills suggested that it is more fun for an audience to see a man lower his status to play a woman than to see a woman play a man. "A woman as a guy is not as wacky," she explained, "it's a higher-status character" (quoted in Seham 2001, 71). Here, Bills used status as a familiar improv principle derived from Keith Johnstone. In concept, *status* describes an improviser's freely chosen decision to play a dominant or deferential character. In practice, however, performance status usually replicates offstage status, and women are far more likely to play low while men play high—especially in relation to women.

Male players' claims to have simply misinterpreted their female teammate's lowered voice or aggressive physical choices may have some legitimacy. In a discussion of male versus female impersonation in camp performance, feminist theorist Kate Davy notes that "there is no institutionalized paradigm for reading male impersonation." Davy suggests that female impersonation has a rich history extending from classical the-ater to television and film because it is "primarily about men, addressed to men, and for men. [But] male impersonation has no such familiar institutionalized history in which women impersonating men say something about women. Both female and male impersonation foreground the male voice and, either way, women are erased" (1992, 233–234). But the women of JANE did not feel at all erased by their portrayal of these male characters. On the contrary, embodying men provided these improvisers with a sense of physical freedom, the permission to play aggressively both as characters and as improvisers, and a mode for exploring a variety of gender roles, relationships, and stereotypes.

It must, of course, be acknowledged that JANE's improvised shows were in many ways quite different from the kind of camp performances that Davy has analyzed. Unlike most drag performances, the women of JANE wore one basic, casual costume and made no attempt to disguise their sex. Moreover, improv performance is unscripted and, espe-cially in ImprovOlympics' "long-form"[2] style of improvisation, flows from scene to scene with actors playing multiple roles. Players often do not know what gender they will be until a teammate endows them with a name, calling for "Bob," or shouting, "Hortense, we're out of licorice!" Audiences can observe the process by which each improviser takes on and discards a variety of gendered personae, even as she remains clearly identifi-able as a woman throughout the performance. Judith Butler writes that gender "must be understood as the mundane way in which bodily gestures, movements, and enactments of various kinds constitute the illusion of an abiding gendered self . . . , an act . . . which constructs the social fiction of its own psychological interiority" (1990, 270–271, 279). An examination of the gestures, movements, and enactments that emerged in JANE's spontaneous performances may teach us a great deal about the way each of us learns to do gender.

Feminist director and critic Rhonda Blair writes that "Cross-gender work requires the actor to identify with a seeming Other, imagine what it must like to be the Other, and break years of physical, vocal, and emotional conditioning in order to perform that Other"(1993, 292). In JANE, actors approached the task in one of several ways depend-ing on the demands of the scene being improvised. A broadly comic sketch may allow a player to indulge in a ball-scratching stereotype, or to exaggerate the characteristics of the aggressive "alpha male." Blair suggests that "Cross-gender performance can use stereo-typing deliberately to emphasize the nature of character-as-construction" (1993, 292). For Weir and the other JANEs, poking fun at the classic bad date, macho barfly, or self-impor-tant geek made use of women's unique set of shared references and created a refreshing comedy of instant recognition for the women in JANE's troupe and in their audience. Stereotypes or not, says Weir, "these are men I know" (quoted in Seham 2001, 72).

Strong physical choices were the key to creating both the outer impression of and a certain inner identification with maleness. Indeed, many improvisers based all their characters on highly visible body language, designed to communicate quickly and efficiently to teammates and audiences. Both males and females who perform across gender develop what Blair terms "theatrical codes . . . , a particular gender vocabulary and hierarchy for each piece" (Blair 1993, 292). Yet, perhaps surprisingly, only Bills mentioned working with the image of "something between my legs" as an important element of her cross-gender performance in JANE. For most of the players, a far more critical concept was the notion of expanding their use of space and weight.

Pervasive customs throughout the world—from Chinese footbinding to corseting to high heels—make it clear that women should take up as little space as possible—whether through free movement, body size, or in the expansiveness of their gestures. In her essay, "Foucault, Femininity, and the Modernization of Patriarchal Power," Sandra Lee Bartky demonstrates the ways in which Foucault's theories of the docile body apply to women in unique and specifically gendered ways:

> Today, massiveness, power, or abundance in a woman's body is met with distaste. . . . There are significant gender differences in gesture, posture, movement and general bodily comportment: women are far more restricted than men in their manner of movement and in their spatiality . . . [they] must exhibit not only constriction, but grace and a certain eroticism restrained by modesty. . . . Whatever proportions must be assigned in the final display to fear or deference, one thing is clear: women's body language speaks eloquently, though silently, of her subordinate status in the hierarchy of gender (1988, 64–74).

To portray men, the women deliberately took on movement that was slower and heavier than their own, and that used a lower center of gravity. JANE co-founder Abby Sher confided, "a lot of my men are a lot more confident than women are. They try to command attention or command women, though I do play other kinds of men as well. For me, the delicious part of it is taking on the confidence. That kind of attitude sticks out if you don't play a man" (quoted in Seham 2001, 72).

Tami Segher, another original member of JANE, summarized her male characters as "slower, heavier, deeper, and higher status." A woman of normal weight, the twenty-four-year-old Segher freely admitted to having serious body-image problems, even using her fear of fat as material for her improvisations. It is telling that this young performer confessed, "If I'm feeling yucky about my body, I play a man" (quoted in Seham 2001, 73). As a male character, weight is permissible. As an attractive, date-able, castable female, the same weight is not.

JANE improvisers experienced a sense of empowerment and liberation when imitating what they perceived to be the male version of these modes of nonverbal communication. Yet their equation of maleness with a greater entitlement to space and weight, a more relaxed demeanor, and a sense of confidence speaks volumes about the way femaleness is constructed in American society. Their obvious identity as women also allowed JANE actors to perform, and comment on, aggressive aspects of male behavior in ways that male actors would never get away with on a comedy stage. Several of the women reveled in squeezing one another's breasts or fondling one another in the guise of a male, or sometimes a lesbian character. "It's incredible freedom," said Bills. "We all grew up and were raised not to be the center of the dirty naughty funny if you wanted dates in high school. Women have body parts that are forbidden to be touched, so when we desire to touch them it's so much more daring" (quoted in Seham 2001, 71). JANE also explored such serious subjects as date rape and spouse abuse in a way that is more palatable to their audiences than it would be if a male body were on the stage.

As Judith Butler has famously theorized, "If gender is a kind of a doing, an incessant activity performed, in part, without one's knowing and without one's willing, it is not for that reason automatic or mechanical. On the contrary, it is a practice of improvisation within a scene of constraint" (1990, 1). In JANE's improvisations, that scene of constraint had the potential suddenly to shift, revealing the constructedness of gender performance. For example, the actors might begin a scene in one gender but be endowed in mid-gesture as another. This misrecognition of the intended performance of gender occurred less frequently among the members of this troupe than it does in co-ed groups, but when it happened, the JANE players exploited its comic potential. Characters initiated as men could shift into lesbians or vice versa. A character in the midst of a conventionally feminine gesture might suddenly be called Herb. The JANEs reveled in these moments of incongruity, which helped to keep scenes interesting. The key was not to reject the seeming error in proper gender performance, but to incorporate it as an integral part of the character in process. The constant adaptations and transformations available to improv performers illustrate the possibility of improvisation outside the scene of constraint and the potential for interrupting the constant repetition of gender norms.

Although none of the women in JANE identified as a lesbian, the troupe quite often played romantic scenes between women without a male character in sight. While audience members might not be able to read the difference between the actors' physicalizations of "male" and "lesbian" roles, Segher, Schachner, and teammates were clear that there was a distinct difference for them in terms of interior motivation, attitude, and mannerisms. Nevertheless, their portrayal of lesbians did tend to be less constricted and less self-deprecating than their renditions of most heterosexual female characters. Still, as the JANEs increased their improvisational skills and their knowledge of one another's styles, they began to discern in one another the embodiment of women who were physically strong, relaxed, and confident, but who were not, therefore, to be interpreted as performing masculinity. In fact, such a character might even be read as a heterosexual woman. Such is the potential of improvisation.

JANE ended its run in 1997, but a number of other women's improv troupes were already emerging in Chicago and elsewhere. Other identity-based troupes gained traction, and soon Chicago was host to such performing groups as Oui Be Negroes, Black Comedy Underground, Gayco, Stir Friday Night, and ¡Salsation! Members of these groups often reflected that, in a mainstream group that values groupmind and spontaneity, they would always feel constrained to assimilate to the dominant culture. These players felt far more supported in identity-based groups. For example, Ronald Ray of Oui Be Negroes commented on his mainstream Second City improv class, "I definitely had to hold back. Every time I tried to initiate a scene, they'd take it somewhere else . . .

so I'm trying to match them, trying to be where they are instead of where my angle was at" (quoted in Seham 2001, 210).

Many committed improvisers argue that everyone's voice is equal when improv is done by "good," experienced players. Identity-based troupes are, to them, a cop-out—an unwillingness to work toward genuine "Agreement" among disparate people. Debate still rages within the sizeable online improv community as to the validity of claims of sexism, racism, and homophobia in the teaching and performing of improv.

In a 2012 article, the blogger Jill Eickmann on her site, Femprovisor, pointed to the frustration of women improvisers with the unequal power dynamic in improv and the preponderance of all male troupes. She offered a series of suggestions for change, including a call for players to be more sensitive to alternative modes of scene creation that were less competitive and more emotionally vulnerable. The blogger was roundly attacked by many male and female players who were proud to say they had no problems with the power dynamic in improv. One woman spoke for many when she commented that she would be offended to receive any of the "special treatment" suggested in the blog. The writer continued, "It is MY job to jump in, to speak up and much like in life, take what I want and own it" (Eickmann 2012). But several others shared their experiences being silenced or bullied in improv performance. A male improv teacher commented:

> Gender issues like the ones mentioned in the article are real, and a real problem. Inexperienced 18–20 year old men get lots of space to try things, to develop, to see what works for them. Their ideas get run with, and then if the scene goes nowhere, they learn how their idea played out. Inexperienced 18–20 year old women get steamrolled. If their idea isn't considered "brilliant" out of the chute—they wind up being shut down. Offstage, if the woman is taking time to get Good, she's written off and not treated with the same respect as the experienced people. If a man is taking time to get Good, he is considered to have potential and there is much more patience with him. (Eickmann 2012)

The blog participants were unable to reach consensus on options for solving the problem, or even on whether a legitimate problem exists. Still, it is clear that, despite recent advances, American society has not reached a postsexist, postracist, posthomophobic place. And improv, which mirrors society, also mirrors the mainstream power dynamic.

Improv plays in the space between freedom and discipline, structure and openness, individual and group, process and product. The trickiest balance of all is that between awareness and flow, or "consciousness" and spontaneity. If improvisers can finally admit that simple spontaneity does not access "truth," but rather the sediments of experience and memory that form our sense of self, I believe these pieces of experience can be called forth, repeated, rearranged, juxtaposed with others, and used to create comedy—and even to improvise resistant alternatives to the status quo.

NOTES

1. ImprovOlympic is an influential improv comedy school and theater founded in Chicago in 1981 by Charna Halpern and improv guru Del Close. ImprovOlympic concentrates on "long-form" improv, a style in which players create extended performance pieces based on a single audience suggestion. Often considered more complex than the games and brief scenes in "short-form" improv, long-form appeals to improv aficionados who appreciate its nuance. ImprovOlympic hosts up to 20 improv "teams" who perform regularly at the ImprovOlympic space in Chicago.

2. In "long-form" improvisation, a team of players typically takes a single suggestion from the audience. Players then use one of several methods to riff on the suggestion, free-associating until they develop a number of themes. The performers then create three separate scenes based on various ideas that have emerged. These scenes begin alternating until their separate stories are woven together at the conclusion of the piece. These long-form pieces, usually 10 to 20 minutes long, may use a variety of structures, such as "the Harold" or "the Movie" and include a range of improv games and other elements to explore the themes, create the patterns, and develop the insights that long-form players value in their work. Long-form improv comedy is the prevailing mode of play at ImprovOlympic in Chicago and at the Upright Citizens Brigade in New York City.

BIBLIOGRAPHY

Bartky, Sandra Lee. "Foucault, Femininity, and the Modernization of Patriarchal Power." In *Feminism and Foucault: Reflections on Resistance*, edited by Irene Diamond and Lee Quinby, 61–86. Boston, MA: Northeastern University Press, 1988.

Blair, Rhonda. "'Not ... But'/'Not-not-Me': Musings on Cross-Gender Performance." In *Upstaging Big Daddy: Directing Theater As If Gender and Race Matter*, edited by Ellen Donkin and Susan Clement, 291–307. Ann Arbor: University of Michigan Press, 1993.

Brown, Rupert. *Group Processes: Dynamics Within and Between Groups*. Oxford: Blackwell, 1988.

Butler, Judith. "Performative Acts and Gender Constitution: An Essay in Phenomenology and Feminist Theory." In *Performing Feminisms: Feminist Critical Theory and Theatre*, edited by Sue-Ellen Case, 270–282. Baltimore: Johns Hopkins University Press, 1990.

Butler, Judith. *Undoing Gender*. New York: Routledge, 2004.

Cima, Gay Gibson. "Strategies for Subverting the Canon." In *Directing Theater As If Gender and Race Matter*, edited by Ellen Donkin and Susan Clement, 91–107. Ann Arbor: University of Michigan Press, 1993.

Corbett, John. "Ephemera Underscored: Writing around Free Improvisation." In *Jazz among the Discourses*, edited by Krin Gabbard, 217–224. Durham, NC: Duke University Press, 1995.

Csikszentmihalyi, Mihaly. *Beyond Boredom and Anxiety: Experiencing Flow in Work and Play*. San Francisco: Jossey-Bass, 2000.

Davy, Kate. "Fe/Male Impersonation: The Discourse of Camp." In *Critical Theory and Performance*, edited by Janelle G. Reinelt and Joseph R. Roach, 255–271. Ann Arbor: University of Michigan Press, 1992.

Dolan, Jill. "Geographies of Learning: Theatre Studies, Performance, and the 'Performative.'" *Theatre Journal* 45 (1993): 426, 432.

Eickman, Jill. "Do you really want ME? 10 Ways to Cast and Keep Female Improvisors." *Femprovisor*, July 3, 2012. http://www.femprovisor.com/2012/07/03/. Accessed October 6, 2014.

Hall, Stuart. "Culture, the Media, and the 'Ideological Effect.'" In *Mass Communication and Society*, edited by James Curran, Michael Gurevich, and Janet Woollacott, 315–348. Beverly Hills, CA: Sage, [1977] 1979.

Halpern, Charna, Del Close, and Kim Howard Johnson. *Truth in Comedy: The Manual for Improvisation*. Colorado Springs: Meriwether Publishing, 1994.

Johnstone, Keith. *Impro: Improvisation and the Theatre*. London: Methuen, 1981.

Pierse, Lyn. *Theatresports Down Under: A Guide for Coaches and Players*. Sydney: Improcorp Australia, 1995.

Ropers-Huilman, Becky. *Feminist Teaching in Theory and Practice*. New York: Teachers College Press, 1998.

Seham, Amy. *Whose Improv Is It Anyway? Beyond Second City*. Jackson: University Press of Mississippi, 2001.

Spolin, Viola. *Improvisation for the Theatre*. Evanston, IL: Northwestern University Press, [1963] 1983.

CHAPTER 21

....

SHIFTING CULTIVATION AS IMPROVISATION

....

PAUL RICHARDS

MISUNDERSTANDING SHIFTING CULTIVATION

....

SHIFTING cultivation—the clearing and cultivation of a piece of land that is then abandoned to natural fallowing for a period before being brought back into cultivation—has had a bad press. It is said that the land is not properly cared for, and that resources are wasted. Both charges have been answered in detail (Nye and Greenland 1960). Still the negativity persists. Something else is in play—a mentality of governance that Scott (1996) terms, "seeing like a state." The state requires order and imposes rules, on both landscapes and people. Land should be bounded and clearly owned. Shifting cultivation meets neither of these requirements. The farm site changes from year to year (even though a recurrent rotational cycle is often followed) and is owned not by an individual but by a large and apparently unbounded group, including (in the famous formulation of one West African chief) "the living, the dead and the yet unborn." A core issue in grasping the world of the shifting cultivator is to understand its improvisatory character. Rules are few, equivalent to the chord sequences that guide the jazz improviser. The art cannot be reduced to textbooks and taught by classroom *Diktat*. In ever-changing conditions, a cultivator knows how to proceed only through experience and intuition. A minefield for government officials and nature conservationists, shifting cultivation is a topic rich in insight for improvisation studies, and thus for those who aim less for "policy relevance" and more for a social science offering explanation of that which is not understood.

A Long-Term Study of Rice Farming in Central Sierra Leone

In 1983, I spent a year carrying out an ethnographic study of the rice-farming community of Mogbuama (pop. c. 550), an off-road village in the Mende-speaking region of central Sierra Leone. Most Sierra Leonean peasants have some cash crops, but the first priority of farming is the production of the family staple, rice. Not all communities in Sierra Leone are self-sufficient in rice, but Mogbuama has good rice land, and it produces a surplus. Here, rice is both a subsistence crop and a cash crop.

The focus of my study was rice farming. I collected data on all 92 rice farms made in Mogbuama that year, maintained input-output records for about 30 farms, and took part in all farming activities, from felling the fallowed bush to harvesting the rice. I wrote a book about the study (Richards 1986) and have returned to Mogbuama almost every year since, apart from a period in the mid-1990s when the population was scattered in refugee camps due to the Sierra Leone civil war.

Over nearly 30 years I have been able to build up observations and data on the longer-term changes and continuities associated with the shifting cultivation of rice in Mogbuama. In my more recent work I have been able, in collaboration with crop biologists, to look at some of the rice genetic changes associated with farmer improvisation in Mogbuama. This provides some of the objective "marker" data through which the story of improvisation can be told.

The picture is one of "melodic" variation over a basic and recurrent "chord" structure, despite huge changes in the external environment (not least, the shock of dislocation due to war). The resilience of the system is confirmed. This resilience, I argue, is the product, in large measure, of farmer improvisatory skill and adaptive choice.

Land, Landscape, Rice, and Rain in Mogbuama

Understanding shifting cultivation as a system of improvisation requires some basic knowledge of land entitlement, landscape, soils, rainfall, and rice types. The Mende are patrilineal. Males claim rights to land as members of an agnatic descent group (a group of brothers). Each group holds customary title to an area of fallow land surrounding the village wherein annual choices of farming plots will be made. Brothers will often tend to farm side by side (in a cluster). Immigrant farmers (strangers) attached to one or other of the family groups will also often make their farms as part of one of these clusters. Typically a rice-farming cluster is occupied by farms belonging to perhaps 5 to 10 households, each with a recognized relationship to the land-owning descent group.

Plots are contiguous with the others in the group, but demarcated by a simple boundary made of felled branches, distinct from the more substantial fences made around the entire area to protect the rice from rodent damage. Each plot is marked by possession of a simple tent-like farm hut, and a platform from which children catapult stones toward birds feeding on the ripening rice. Farm work is undertaken by household groups (generally, a man, one or two women, and several children). Heavy and time-dependent tasks (notably clearing, planting, weeding, and harvesting) are often undertaken by labor-sharing groups. Some are based on informal arrangements among neighbors in the cluster. Others are labor cooperatives with elaborate rules, working in strict rotation.

The areas belonging to the different descent groups tell us something about the likely settlement history of the village. The acknowledged autochthones (members of a group whose elders are said not to die but to metamorphose into elephants and disappear into the bush) have title to some of the best, free-draining land adjacent to the village. Other more recently arrived lineages have land at a distance. One group descended from a nineteenth-century warlord has a separate ward in the town, and land lying several kilometers to the north of the village, serviced from a daughter settlement (Mende *fakai*—farm camp). Another group, prominent in chiefdom governance, has title to a distant grassland area, almost impossible to cultivate by local methods. The founders of this lineage were wealthy, migrant cloth traders. Their extensive land grant (of unusable land) was (by repute) made by other landowners only to impress the British that they were indeed a traditionally well-established group entitled to contest the chieftaincy. As wealthy merchants, they probably bought the rice they needed. Nowadays, they cultivate rice effectively in their grassy domain by using tractors.

The somewhat hilly land to the east of the village (where the oldest-settled descent groups have their farms) belongs (geologically) to the granite escarpment crossing Sierra Leone from North west to South east (see Figures 21.1 and 21.2 for maps of Mogbuama and the surrounding area). It is characterized by free-draining sandy or gravelly soils, suited to late cultivation of higher-yielding rice types when the rains are well set. The land west of the village belongs to an ancient lagoon system, and is made up of old river terraces, criss-crossed by rivers running off the escarpment, with flood plain areas well adapted to wetland rice cultivation using the natural rise and fall of the seasonal flood. The soils are silty and moisture retentive, but often of a rather low inherent fertility. Rice can be planted early, but the area is very hard to clear if early rain catches the felled but incompletely dried vegetation. Rice does poorly on an incompletely burnt farm, due to the lack of phosphorus in the soil.

The grassland at the furthest extent of the village has seasonally flooded hollows associated with ancient marine sediments. Rice can be grown, but only if the stubborn Guinea grass is cleared and the root-bound soils broken up by mechanical means.

Rice is in most cases an in-breeding (self-pollinating) crop. Thus it tends to reproduce true to type, i.e. it forms distinct and stable varieties, generally recognized and named by farmers. But the plant has some limited capacity for out-crossing. Pollen exchange takes place between different rice varieties in perhaps about 1 percent of cases, and new types may then be selected. An in-field scenario for farmer selection of out-crossed

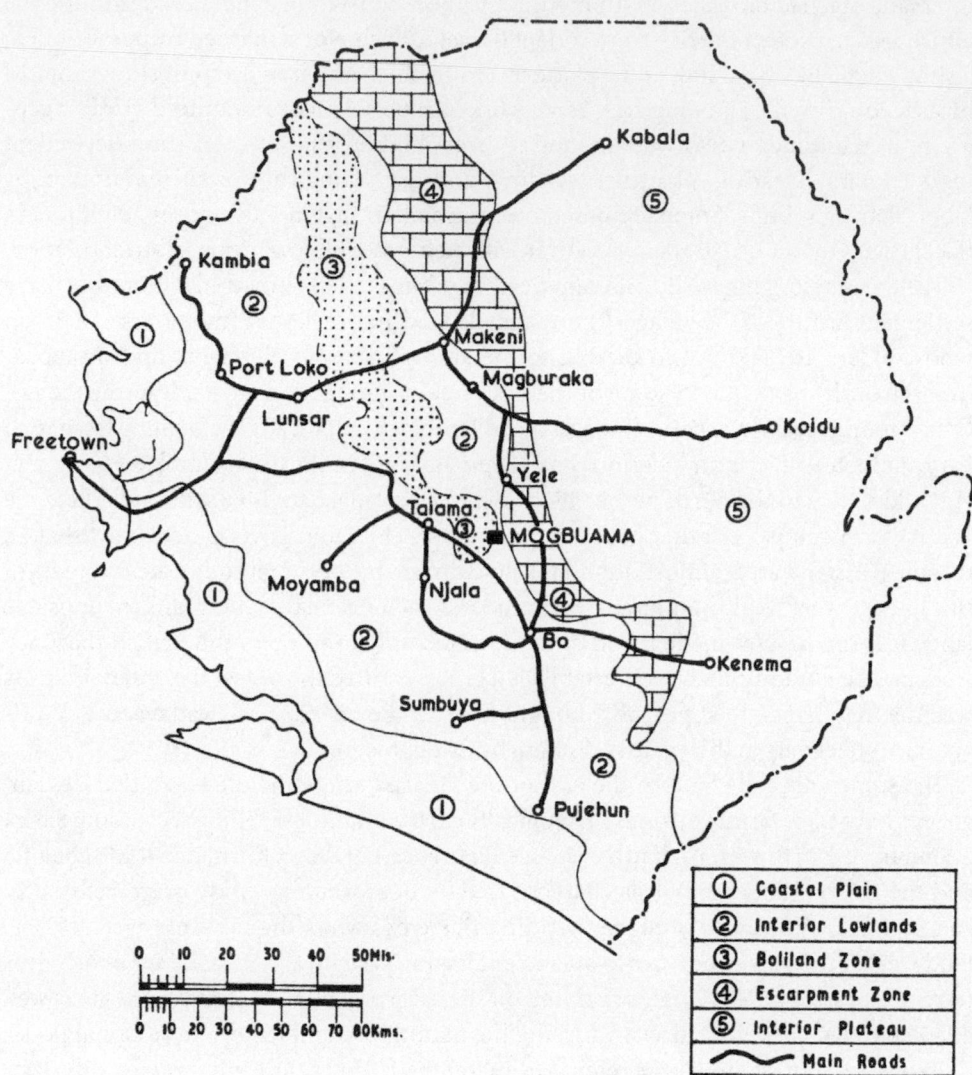

FIGURE 21.1 The escarpment zone in Sierra Leone (Richards 1986, 31).

progeny has been proposed, based on the finding that cross-pollination in rice farms in The Gambia is ten times more likely for varieties mixed in the same plot than between varieties on adjacent plots (Nuijten & Richards 2011).

Rice in Mogbuama belongs to two species—African rice (*Oryza glaberrima*) and Asian rice (*O. sativa*). The most widely planted variety (*gbengben*) belongs to the japonica subspecies of Asian rice and ripens in about 4.5 months on free-draining upland soils. The second most widely planted variety, *ngiyema yakei* (also known as ROK 3), belongs to the indica subspecies of Asian rice, and also ripens within about 4.5 months, but is

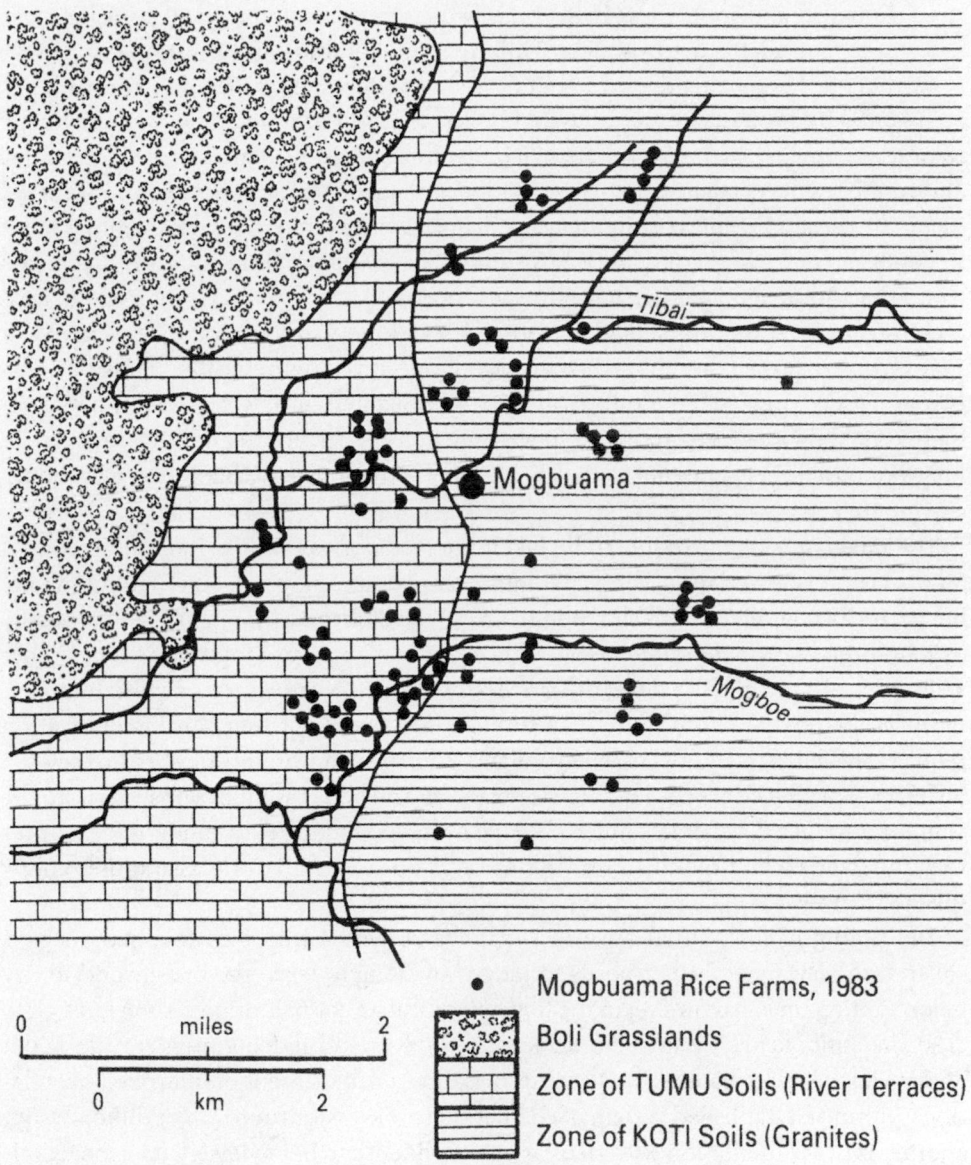

FIGURE 21.2 Main soil and land-use types in Mogbuama (Richards 1986, 32).

equally well suited to both upland and river terrace zones, east and west of the village. Some varieties are planted in the early rains in low-lying areas west of the village and ripen within 3.5 months; thus they can be harvested in the so-called Hungry Season, the preharvest period in July–August, when rice stocks from the previous harvest have been exhausted. A few African rices ripening within 3 months are planted as hunger-breaker crops. Other varieties, currently spreading within the village, are the products of out-crossing between distinct varieties of Asian rice, or between African and Asian rice (Nuijten et al. 2009). These hybrid-derived farmer selections, it will be argued, are among the most distinctive products of improvisation in shifting cultivation.

Farmers in Mogbuama deploy about 45 distinct rice varieties. The top two varieties are planted by about half of all households. The long tail of other varieties (planted by 10 or fewer households) reflects personal preferences, taste, seed quality considerations, and/or the results of adaptive experimentation with unfamiliar imported or out-crossed material. The number of types in use has remained constant over a quarter-century (1983 to 2008, the dates of the first and most recent surveys) but composition has changed somewhat. Some old favorites have dropped out and new types have entered the mix. Only one or two are products of scientific research and agricultural extension. Most new types are farmer selections. An average farm household typically plants between two and four types—often a quick-ripening type planted on lower slopes, a couple of higher-yielding medium-duration types planted on higher slopes and hill crests, and a long-duration type planted in naturally flooding wetlands, to be harvested after about 5–6 months.

The final contextual variable to be taken into account is rainfall. Rainfall in central Sierra Leone is abundant (over 2,000 mm/year) but strongly seasonal, falling mainly between April and October. The months from November to March are almost totally dry. In some years (about one in seven) the rains come late and totals are low. In other years (also about one in seven) rain arrives unseasonably early and is super-abundant. Farmers fear early rainfall more than drought. The reason is that shifting cultivation requires the felled trunks of larger shrubs and trees to be thoroughly dry before they can be burnt. Burning clears the land for rice planting and adds essential phosphorus to the soil. A poor burn necessitates much clearing by hand, and lowered soil fertility reduces the crop yield (sometimes by a third or more). Poorly burnt land is also more rapidly invaded by weeds.

The timing of the annual burn is a major area where improvisatory judgment is called into play. Each farmer needs to judge how long to leave the brushwood to dry before setting the mass on fire, in the hope of igniting a conflagration strong enough to clear the entire field. A bungled burn leads to hunger and indebtedness. Breaking out of this vicious cycle requires further improvisation. Management of interpersonal relations within an established system of clientelism is one major route out of difficulty. But another is experimentation with rice varieties. Evidence to be reviewed in later sections suggests that experimentation with rice varieties results in selective changes in planting material, enhancing adaptability and resilience.

IMPROVISATION

Misha Mengelberg, the Dutch jazz pianist, performed regularly at the old Amsterdam Bimhuis on Thursday evenings, perhaps a welcome change from his day job teaching counterpoint and composition at the Sweelinck Conservatorium. His Thursday evening performance involved free improvisation. A set comprised a number of passages reflecting his mastery of the pianistic style of Thelonious Monk interspersed with passages of free improvisation in which anything could happen. At times, the drummer (Han Bennink) would toss items from the drum kit in the direction of the audience.

Formally, the interspersing of strict and free passages resembled the structure of Johann Sebastian Bach's early and exuberant keyboard toccatas. But the free improvisation, however wild it became, was highly respectful of limits imposed by the setting. The performance started exactly 15 minutes late (either a nod toward the Germanic academic quarter, or a joke aimed at the members of the audience carefully considering whether they could stay for the third set and still catch the last train home). A glass of brandy, carefully placed on the meticulously tuned piano, remained untouched until the end of the second set, surprisingly safe from Bennink's flying bric-a-brac. The sound system was tuned to perfection. Intervals were generous, and drinks could be imported into the venue as a concession to the bar franchisee, whose business success was required to amplify the city council subsidy. The music was freely improvised, but the environment was ordered and safe. Improvisation within strict and safe limits was an image the city of Amsterdam liked to foster, and not only in the Bimhuis. The music, it should be added, was as fascinating as it was satisfying.[1]

It brought home to me how different was the context for improvisation among shifting cultivators in Mogbuama. Here was an environment as volatile as could be imagined. Nothing was guaranteed, well ordered, or in tune. Farmers walked a seasonal tightrope with no safety net; a single mishap threatened hunger and debt, even death.

MEN DANCING WITH FIRE

The crux of the seasonal performance for male shifting cultivators in Mogbuama is the burning of the farm. Would the rains be early or late, or come on time? Portents in the clouds and behavior of birds were anxiously scanned. Everybody had a theory about timing. There were those who swore by burning as early as possible, and others who gambled on leaving it to the very last minute. Some even had no qualms about an unusually heavy early rainstorm or two, arguing that the sun in March was still so hot that it would rapidly dry off any dampness. Every week the burn was postponed, come rain or shine, would improve the eventual result.

Then there was the debate about when during the day (or night) to set the fire, based on the likely evolution of wind patterns to fan the flames. Folk divided into afternoon and nighttime burners. Some got it wrong whichever option they chose, by failing to ignite their own farms but burning an adjacent farm not yet ready for ignition. This would result in an acrimonious court case, a fine for damages, and a farmer with perhaps insufficient funds to pay for subsequent laborers or seed. It was often best when brothers were sufficiently cohesive and clustered to agree on a family burn of adjacent farms. The bonfire that day would be truly spectacular. The mass of combustible material would burn with such intensity that changing wind patterns, consequent on the rising air currents, would sweep the fire back and forth. Apart from the smiling faces of satisfied onlookers, the results would resemble a film set of nuclear devastation.

Individuals also had ideas about where and in how many places to set the fire. Men would fly acrobatically about their farms, leaping logs and dodging branches, at great hazard to eyes and limbs, to apply tapers to a sufficient number of starting points to ensure total combustion. Those who failed to get the entire farm to ignite had problems in mobilizing labor for the subsequent, dreary task of piling and firing unburnt logs. Even so, they might count themselves lucky. On occasion, those too adventurous would improvise their fire dance a step too far, and meet a terrible fate in the gathering blaze. Burning was an area of Mogbuama farming where villagers took great care to offer public prayers and pour libations for personal safety.

Burning was a double improvisation. Nature improvised unfathomable climatic fluctuations and capricious diurnal wind patterns. The farmer improvised a pattern of movement sufficient to set the entire mass ablaze, sweeping around the farm to where the fire was needed most, while taking account of how the gathering blaze was generating its own dynamics and where the exit lines lay.

COPING WITH CONSEQUENCES—FURTHER SCOPE FOR IMPROVISATION

So the die was cast? The quality of the burn determined soil fertility and the labor needed for subsequent clearing, thus influencing whether timely planting could be paid for and whether the weed growth (a task for the women) would subsequently be manageable. The difference between a fine harvest, capable of meeting family needs until the following year, or a shortfall and hungry-season debt, was now fixed. Or was it? Much would depend on household ingenuity in the looming hungry season.

One route was to seek largesse in the social system. Seed or money could be borrowed. The mutual obligations of kinship could be tapped. Where the situation was most serious the head of a peasant household might cede autonomy and seek help from a patron (a merchant or richer farmer—the categories were often interchangeable). Where debts were not repaid, the obligations of clientship became permanent—a kind of serfdom was entered into.

The alternative route was to seek largesse in nature. In effect, there was reversion to hunting and gathering. Women fished, men trapped. The best catches were often the large rodents menacing the growing rice, trapped in the fences running around the farm. Wild mushrooms and honey were eagerly sought. Wild yams were particularly important, gathered in the bush, with vines replanted to enrich the gathering grounds. But one special category of improvised actions seems to have been of longer-term survival importance. This is the way women—and some men—experimented with seed selection.

WOMEN PLAYING WITH SEEDS

Jeneba was an old woman and practically blind by reason of cataracts or river blindness. She could barely see the ground beneath her. I had known her for the best part of 20 years, always wearing the same huge, thick-lensed glasses donated by a passing charity. I had never known her to farm. She was fed by her family. Her sight, they told me, was too poor for her to plant or cut rice.

With people still returning to Mogbuama after wartime displacement, and better farming areas around the village grown rank with neglect, due both to insecurity and lack of young men to do the heavy work of clearing, the returnees faced enormous initial difficulties over food. Jeneba (to my surprise) had a rice farm. Indeed, it was not much—merely a pocket-handkerchief sized plot on the outskirts of the village, on what was in effect a patch of sand. Somehow she had procured seed of an "extinct" African rice. African rice will grow on soils too poor for other crops. It gave her a helpful handful or two of rice at harvest.

African rice reached the Americas in the period of the slave trade. It is red-skinned and cooks red rather than white. For this reason, it is sometimes called red rice. Red rice was preferred by the slave traders because it was the normal food of the Africans they transported to the New World. Its cultivation by slaves, and in New World maroon communities, is not surprising. It is hardy, flavorful, and generally reckoned more nutritious than Asian rice. Legend has it that African female captives—stripped of possessions but charged with on-board food preparation—hid grains of unhusked African rice in their hair. The legend may not be wrong. In the recent war in Sierra Leone women driven to flight often took with them enough rice seeds to begin the process of planting food again, in whatever circumstances they might encounter.

Playing with seeds is a major register for improvisation in Mogbuama. It is practiced especially by women. It was a man—a migrant farmer—who explained to me the logic of this affinity for seed experimentation. It was an activity requiring daily attendance at the farm throughout the year, in order to protect the little trial plots often found around the farm hut from damage or pest attack. Men do most of the heavy work on the farms in the early part of the year, but leave the bulk of the work from planting to harvest—exactly the period when a trial needs a watchful eye—to women. My informant was unusual, in that he was one of the few men who regularly experimented with seeds. As a migrant "stranger" in the community (Mende—*hota*) he had no part in the political intrigue, court cases, and development agency meetings that kept the big men in the village for days on end during the growing season. So like the women, he was on the farm all day, every day, and had time to see experiments flower and to ponder the results.

When a spare moment at planting time allows, an off-type picked out from the previous harvest and carefully conserved in a bundle of rag will be brought out and planted close to the woman's main base—the farm hut. The performance of any promising off-type is carefully noted. If it does well close to the farm hut, on soil well fertilized by kitchen refuse such as husks from cleaned rice, it will be harvested and conserved, to be planted the following year on a new farm. The second time around, soil variation might be probed—by planting the rice on an unusually fertile patch around a burnt stump, or on an old termite heap. For a third year, on yet a new farm, the variety might be launched down-slope, toward an adjacent run-off plot or into a flooding valley bottom, to test its response to variations in water supply. The process will take several years, at different locations in the shifting cultivation cycle. All the while seeds will be carefully accumulated, some to be distributed among trusted friends or kin for testing over an even broader range of farms and soil types. Eventually, a decision might be taken to plant an entire area of farmland to the newly discovered rice.

At that stage, fate might take a hand. Aruna and I had climbed a steep ridge overlooking some farms. Below we saw a patch-work quilt of varieties. Four patches of a single farm drew my attention. Aruna laughed. This was his farm. He had cleared about a hectare of land and had started to plant his favorite rice type. But supplies of seed ran low, and the women entrusted with completing the work used a different seed type—an African rice. Some weeks later the farm was due for weeding. The women started from one side of the farm, weeding both the favored variety and the makeshift rice. Then they were called to a funeral in a neighboring village, leaving the farm to its own devices for some time. On the weeded parts of the farm both varieties did well. On parts not weeded the favored rice was choked. The African rice, however, had out-competed the weeds. It would yield hardly less than the weeded plot, Aruna thought. The planting of the farm was merely an improvised solution. Chance had turned it into an experiment with treatment and control. Aruna was not going to refuse the lessons this improvised experiment afforded.

PRODUCTS OF IMPROVISATION—MARGINAL WOMEN FARMERS MAKE SEED CHANGES OVER TIME

Villagers were displaced from Mogbuama by war for a period of about 18 months from January 1995. Most went to camps for the displaced in the regional center of Bo. Others continued to farm in hidden "corners" of the bush (Mende: *sokoihun*). Although most households were short of seed for several years after returning to the village, there was little if any loss of rice varieties. Women carried seeds with them into the camps, or kept on planting favored types in "corners." When asked to report on what had been grown "about five years before the war" a sample of both women and men farmers gave a list that corresponds remarkably well with what was recorded in 1983.

With two exceptions, the changes appear to be real, and largely the result of the kind of adaptive improvisation already described. One exception is not yet explained (a variety—*giligoti*—said in 2008 to have been widely planted in the pre-war period but not recorded in 1983 may reflect a name change). The other—*nduliwa*—appears to reflect a foreshortening of historical memory. It was grown by only one farmer in 1983. Field notes I made at the time record that this was said to be one of the main rices of the region in "former times." The year 1983 has now passed into "former times" for those that do not recall it directly.

If we then turn to the changes for which there is documented evidence, a number of varieties have declined in importance—for example the three-month variety *jewule* grown quite widely in 1983 on run-off plots to provide an early harvest. Others have gained in importance, perhaps as a result of agro-ecological changes associated with the war. One such change is a lengthening of the fallow cycle—the period of time between successive clearing of land for farming. The lengthening reflects population reduction due to wartime displacement; there are fewer farmers using the land.

Some of the newer rices—japonica type *yabasi* and indica type *pa kamp*—may be better suited to soils now richer in nitrogen as a result of longer fallow intervals. Increased cultivation of the indica variety *ngiyema yakei* can be attributed to the postwar seed distributions by humanitarian agencies, since, under the name ROK 3, it is one of the varieties recommended by the agricultural extension service.

Two other "postwar" rices—*pinipini* and *kebeleh*—are interesting for a different reason. Molecular analysis using AFLP markers was applied to 315 rices collected from Senegal to Togo in 2008 (Nuijten et al. 2009). The sample included a number of rices grown in Mogbuama. According to the molecular evidence the total sample was best grouped in four clusters (see Figure 21.3).[2] Three of these clusters corresponded to the main taxonomic groupings of cultivated rice—African rice, and the two subspecies of Asian rice. A fourth cluster was identified as farmer-selected African × Asian rice hybrids.

What kinds of rice are grouped in the fourth cluster? A sterility barrier affects outcrossing between Asian and African rice. This barrier was broken by rice researchers in the 1990s, leading to the development and release of a family of Nerica interspecifics (NEw RICes for Africa). These are japonica × glaberrima selections. Those tested in our 2008 sample sit (as expected) between the japonica and glaberrima axes of our taxonomic structure. The rices of the fourth cluster—such as *pinipini* and *kebeleh*—sit between the glaberrima and indica axes, and can thus be identified as hybrid-derived rices of a different composition to the Nerica rices. They are farmer-selected interpecifics.

The question arises: How have West African peasant, shifting cultivators/farmers been able to develop a range of interspecific rices independently of scientific research? Broadly, the answer proposed is that this is a product of improvisation in seed selection. Facing varying conditions as a consequence of shifting farm sites and fluctuation in climate and other environmental variables, women farmers find continuous experimentation with seed choices advantageous. This is not experimentation by design but in response to contingency, so can properly be regarded as a type of improvisation.

For a plausible account of the improvised origins of these rices, some answer has to be found to the question of how the sterility barrier was overcome under conditions of shifting cultivation. Nuijten and Richards (2011) offer one potential scenario. It invokes

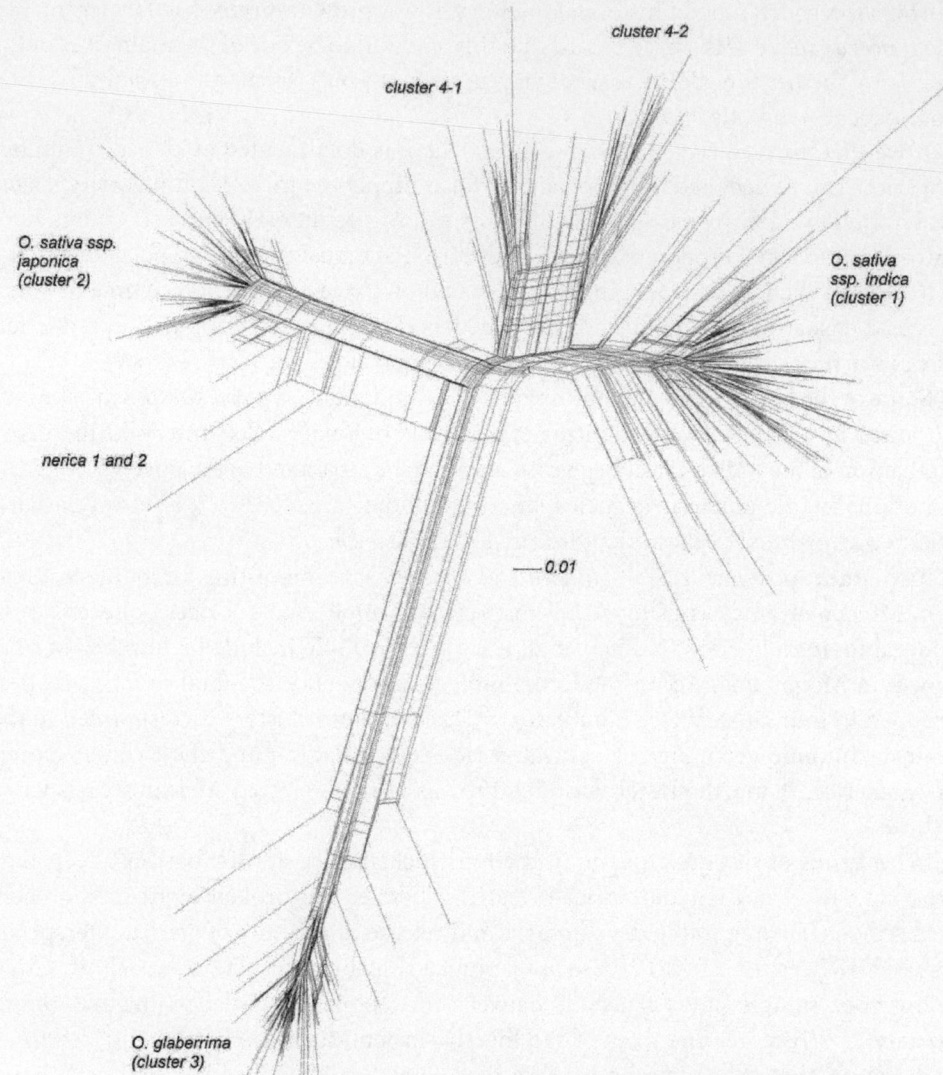

FIGURE 21.3 Phylogenetic relationships among the 315 samples studied (Nuijten et al. 2009).

marginality as a key contextual factor—especially the marginality of women such as Jeneba.

Older women—perhaps no longer with a husband to make a farm for them—aim to plant a plot of rice for their own subsistence. But they cannot readily mobilize young men to clear the heavy vegetation. Typically, an old woman seeking to plant her own rice will farm opportunistically, perhaps on a patch of soil in an old rice farm recently abandoned to fallow regrowth (Mende: *jopoi*). The soils will necessarily be exhausted, so she tends to be interested in varieties adapted to low fertility, including weed-competitive African rice.

The co-flowering of African and Asian rice is a common sight in Mogbuama. African rice is especially hardy and is often found as a weed (known as *sanganyaa*) in plots of Asian rice. Since out-crossing between varieties is most likely when the varieties are mixed in the same field, then a certain number of Asian rice plants will have been cross-pollinated by *sanganyaa*, and vice versa. When African and Asian rice cross, the first generation progeny (known as the F1) is infertile. It flowers (and thus provides pollen) but does not set seed. To break the sterility barrier, the F1 must cross back on to one of the parents.

Let us assume that the old woman has sought permission to farm on the *jopoi* of a male in-law (perhaps her late husband's brother), who is duty-bound to maintain her. Not only does he give permission to use the land (he may help clear her plot), he readily gives her some of the seed she needs. This is likely to be seed from the harvest of the abandoned farm she is now re-cultivating. It will contain some of the outcrossed F1 but also some of the parental seed. Backcrossing of the infertile first-generation hybrid on to one or other of the parents is thus a distinct possibility.

The old woman has spent a lifetime selecting and testing rice, and she is alert to off-types. This includes the newly backcrossed seed in her little *jopoi* farm, and she seizes on the few grains for further investigation. Painstakingly she continues to nurse and multiply what is, in effect, a new hybrid type. A farmer-selected interspecific rice is launched on its career.

In our 2008 survey, farmer-selected hybrid-derived rices were among the most widely grown varieties in Sierra Leone. This genetic improvement has not come about through scientific planning but through farmer improvisation, and perhaps improvisation by the poorest and most marginalized members of the farming community.

DISCUSSION AND CONCLUSION: LESSONS OF THE STUDY FOR A THEORY OF IMPROVISATION

Thus far it has been explained that farming in Mogbuama is undertaken against a background of high environmental flux. Not all aspects of rice farming in this Mende village require improvisation. There is much that is based on clear rules of process, encapsulating basic cause-and-effect principles. A child parked on a wooden platform with a slingshot and mound of mud pellets is an age-old but still effective means of reducing bird damage on the ripening rice, for example. But it has been shown that in two particular respects improvisation is key: the short-term process of setting fire to the mass of felled vegetation and the long-term process of adjusting seeds to changing environmental requirements. Mende men are particularly involved in the dance of fire and women in the play of seeds.

What has not so far been discussed is what improvisation is. This question is conveniently addressed by setting up a contrast. Improvisation will be contrasted with organization and planning. For this I will draw a brief example from war studies. War studies reduce much about human life to basics, and they thus help point up the basic contrast between improvisation and planning.

The American Civil War (1861–1864) was fought over a huge theater, including large expanses of forested land only incompletely cleared and settled. It was characterized by its very high number of small engagements. In this sense it can be considered a "shifting" war, often favoring the skills of the improviser over the planner. The point can be made by contrasting the strengths and weaknesses of two of the war's best-known generals.

George McClellan was the second commander of Lincoln's Army of the Potomac. He was a gifted organizer and trainer of troops, but notoriously cautious in battle. With a background in railway management, McClellan was excellent at marshaling his resources, less good at dispatching them. He exasperated Lincoln with repeated calls for reinforcement when he should have been pressing his advantage. For Keegan (2009), his qualities were also his defects. McClellan's troops were so well trained and organized that he was extremely reluctant to risk losing any in battle.

The Confederate general, Thomas "Stonewall" Jackson, by contrast, was McClellan's exact opposite. Daring and completely without fear, Jackson pressed ahead at every opportunity, seeking to surprise, mislead, and mystify the enemy. His generalship was brilliant in the low-intensity, hit-and-run theater of the Shenandoah valley, where he displayed an intuitive grasp of the complex topography and its affordances. But Jackson was less good at coordination, or in communicating his intentions to subordinate officers. A Jackson ploy succeeded only so long as the man himself was there to lead it. Jackson was a gifted improviser. Unburdened of the demands of any strategic "score," his mind was free to respond to the needs of the moment.

As distinctive cognitive dispositions shaping individual agency, "planning" and "improvisation" now need to be explained. How are such dispositions shaped? One answer has been attempted in the work of the anthropologist Mary Douglas. Douglas draws upon Durkheim's inference that suicide was regulated by two distinct sets of social variables—demands of authority and affective ties to a group—and seeks to apply the same reasoning to the regulation of other (nonpathological) forms of human agency.

Douglas terms the two sets of constraints identified by Durkheim as "grid" and "group." Her analysis seeks to map the relative positions of agents in terms of responsiveness to grid-group factors, and thus to relate agency to the way the agent is shaped by institutional forces. She often used a fourfold scheme to illustrate sets of dispositions associated with different locations within the grid-group space thus defined. The top right-hand corner is occupied by agents strongly oriented toward group concerns but also responsive to higher authority. The bottom left-hand corner finds a place for entrepreneurs (and gamblers). Communitarian (sectarian) dispositions are located in the bottom right. There is scope to debate what kind of agency is to be found in the upper left-hand quadrant, where grid is strong and group influence weak.

In Durkheim's original elaboration he was not altogether sure what kind of agency was to be associated with this "top left" action space. In a lengthy footnote in *Le suicide* he tentatively proposes the category "fatalistic suicide," and offers evidence of mass slave suicides by way of illustration. Douglas sometimes took over this term, and she labeled the kinds of agency associated with the top-left corner "fatalistic." This may seem contradictory. Does a fatalist exercise agency, or simply accept what comes?

Initially, those who used Douglas's neo-Durkheimian theory showed rather little interest in the top left-hand corner of their world. Latterly, however, it was realized that this neglect undermined claims to offer a comprehensive schematization of human agency, and more attention was paid to the "footnoted" space. The label "isolate" has been offered as an alternative. The term seems to capture better the idea of an agent constrained by strong externalities, but free from group pressure.

It also fits very well the best source of evidence that we possess on tactics associated with slave revolts and their prevention—namely, the documentary record associated with the 420 known slave insurrections among the nearly 27,000 Atlantic slaving voyages from Africa between 1514 and 1866. Shipboard insurrections rose to a peak of nearly 5 percent of all voyages from Upper West Africa in the eighteenth century, the most active period of the Atlantic slave trade (Rediker 2007).

Slavers were very conscious of the danger, and their ships were fitted out for the eventuality (notably, the barricado, behind which the crew could retreat and still sail the ship, in the event of slaves escaping their chains below). The slave traders were also concerned not to fill a ship with too many slaves from the same "nation," for fear language or ethnic solidarity would facilitate a mass uprising. Nascent insurrections were sometimes nipped in the bud when plans were reported to the crew by captives from rival groups.

Would-be mutineers tended to work alone or through a small group of silent accomplices. Even so, their success rate was small. Insurrectionists were often killed in the attempt, or the ship foundered with loss of all hands. Some captives aimed to seize the ship and return to Africa, but others freed themselves with the apparent intent of ending their lives by drowning. This was seen as the only sure way to return home. Here we see particularly clearly the close connection between the positioning of "isolate" and "fatalist" dispositions. Suicide was an active way of transcending an otherwise impossibly limiting set of circumstances.[3]

We have detailed records of one mutiny that resulted in the captives regaining their homes in Africa—the famous case of the schooner *Amistad* carrying freshly arrived African captives from Havana to a slave plantation along the northern coast of Cuba. All but three of the 60 captives were from Mende country, and all captives spoke that language.[4] They also quickly accepted the authority of a young Mende rice farmer, Sengbeh Pieh, to lead them and determine tactics. Pieh was a quick-witted improviser in the Jacksonian mold; or put differently, Jackson was a leader in the Mende warlord mold— saying little, sizing tactical opportunities in an instant, and expecting those under his authority quickly (and silently) to adjust to his every improvisatory feint.

The site of Pieh's home is as yet unidentified, but he described it as being two or three days walk to the north of Komende, in Sherbro. This places it in the general region of Mogbuama, though perhaps somewhat to the south west. By appropriate coincidence, the village was called Jopoi, the Mende word for the old rice farm—the site where old women sometimes do their improvisatory experiments with rice. The isolate agency displayed in the improvisation of a successful mutiny on the *Amistad* is recognizably the same capacity for improvised solutions in demanding environmental conditions that remains part of a Mende heritage of shifting cultivation today.

Improvisation, I want to argue, is a disposition in which strong, arbitrary external constraints are recognized as being unpredictable and inescapable, at the same time as group constraints are backgrounded. The improviser does what is needful, without paying undue attention to what the others in the group will think. When all accept that conditions demand the modality of isolate leadership, thus granting it legitimacy, this leadership style can (perhaps somewhat surprisingly) result in effective coordinated action. Understood in this way, as the underpinnings of improvisation, "fatalist" agency is not the contradiction in terms it at first appears. The *Amistad* mutineers, led by Pieh, improvised an effective revolt. In doing so, they activated dispositions shaped by prior experience. This included, I suggest, the strong, shaping impress of rice farming under shifting cultivation.

The woman playing with seeds does it quietly, in a corner, without drawing attention to the fact, just as the *Amistad* mutineers loosened their shackles and secreted potential weapons. One never knows what might happen. This can be set aside for a rainy day. No need to advertise the fact. Mende fire dancers differ in their theories, and argue loud and long about them in the safety of the village, but once the fire is lit they are agreed on one thing only—not to get in each other's way. Sometimes (as in the fire dance) a brazen self-confidence is required. At others a furtive experimentalism suffices (as in the play of seeds). Both fire dancer and seed experimenter do their work with reference to strong grid and weak group conditions.

A second important question concerns how grid-group dispositions are formed. Douglas is not fully explicit on this issue, except that they must be the product of socialization. Fairly clearly, such dispositions tend to endure, but equally clearly, individuals are not locked into a fixed set. Dispositions are subject to change. But there is no clear explanation of how these changes might occur, or how and under what circumstances different sets of dispositions might be invoked. Douglas's basic argument (consistent with Durkheim) is that dispositions are shaped by institutions. Individuals are exposed to different institutions, and thus acquire a repertory of dispositions and styles of agency. But it is unclear whether different dispositions shaped (for example) by school, religious congregation, and occupation jar or blend.

One view would be to argue that dispositions formed by competing institutions remain discrete and available for use within a single individual according to context. On this reckoning, a Mende farmer's respect for authority ingrained through sodality ("secret society") membership and capacity for improvisatory skill, associated with self-reliance in the bush, are discrete (and contradictory) sets of dispositions called into play by varying circumstances in bush and town.

That this might be so is evidenced by the way the corpus of *domeisia* (performed folk tales) can play upon obvious disjunctures of dispositions. Cosentino (1981) describes one such basic archetype with varying outcomes—stories concerning *ndogboyosoi*, the bush devil. These are often used by adults to warn reckless youth about too much solo experimentation in the bush. But counter-stories—the same scenario and characters with different endings—are readily told, and Cosentino provides examples, to re-assert the importance of "isolate" dispositions against the claims of village hierarchy. One such outcome is when an adventurous young woman is able to resist the wiles of *ndogboyosoi* and bring home new resources of lasting communal value.

Thus enactment of these variant readings in village story-telling entertainments illustrates the range of dispositions necessary in a world in which survival depends on the ability to cope with the never-ending surprises of a rich but capricious environment. Those who have grown too secure in their schemes and plans need to be re-awakened to the importance of fatalist and isolate dispositions by the clangorous improvisation of music without a score.

Notes

1. I would like to thank Tim Febey, composer and trombonist, for introducing me to free improvisation at the Bimhuis, and for several enlightening discussions we had subsequently concerning the study he was making of free improvisation in its social and institutional contexts.
2. Using the taxonomic software SplitsTree; Daniel H. Huson and David Bryant, "Application of Phylogenetic Networks in Evolutionary Studies," *Molecular Biology and Evolution* 23, no. 2 (2006): 254–267.
3. That the two terms are not as far apart as might be assumed is illustrated by the military example given. Jackson, the commander who kept his plans to himself, put down his complete fearlessness in battle to his strong Calvinistic belief that God had determined the time of his death (John Keegan, *The American Civil War: A Military History* [New York: Vintage Books, 2009]). This isolate was also a fatalist.
4. The Trans-Atlantic Slave Trade Database (2009, www.slavevoyages.org) shows that the most rebellious groups of slaves were those from Senegambia and Sierra Leone. In the eighteenth century, ships from Upper West Africa (including Sierra Leone) were 2.5 times as likely to experience slave insurrection as those from Lower West Africa (the Bights of Benin and Biafra) and five times as likely as ships form West Central Africa (Congo and Angola). See also David Richardson, "Shipboard Revolts, African Authority, and the African Slave Trade," *William and Mary Quarterly*, 3rd Series, 58, no. 1 (2001): 69–92; and Howard Jones, *Mutiny on the Amistad: The Saga of a Slave Revolt and Its Impact on American Abolition, Law, and Diplomacy* (Oxford and New York: Oxford University Press, 1987).

References

Huson, Daniel H., and David Bryant. "Application of Phylogenetic Networks in Evolutionary Studies." *Molecular Biology and Evolution* 23, no. 2 (2006): 254–267.

Jones, Howard. *Mutiny on the Amistad: The Saga of a Slave Revolt and Its Impact on American Abolition, Law, and Diplomacy.* Oxford and New York: Oxford University Press, 1987.

Keegan, John. *The American Civil War: A Military History.* New York: Vintage Books, 2009.

Nuijten, Edwin, Robbert van Treuren, Paul C. Struik, Alfred Mokuwa, Florent Okry, Béla Teeken, and Paul Richards. "Evidence for the Emergence of New Rice Types of Interspecific Hybrid Origin in West African Farmers' Fields." *PLoS ONE* 4, no. 10 (October 2009): e7335, 1–9.

Nuijten, Edwin, and Paul Richards. "Pollen Flows Within and Between Rice and Millet Fields in Relation to Farmer Variety Development." *Plant Genetic Resources* 9, no. 3 (August 2011): 361–374.

Nye, Peter, and Dennis Greenland. *The Soil Under Shifting Cultivation.* Farnham Royal, UK: Commonwealth Agricultural Bureaux, 1960.

Rediker, Marcus. *The Slave Ship: A Human History.* New York: Viking, 2007.

Richards, Paul. *Coping with Hunger: Hazard and Experiment in an African Rice-Farming System.* London: Allen & Unwin, 1986.

Richardson, David. "Shipboard Revolts, African Authority, and the African Slave Trade." *William and Mary Quarterly*, 3rd Series 58, no. 1 (2001): 69–92.

Trans-Atlantic Slave Trade Database (2009). http://www.slavevoyages.org. Accessed October 6, 2014.

PART V

ORGANIZATIONS

CHAPTER 22

....

IMPROVISATION IN MANAGEMENT

....

PAUL INGRAM AND WILLIAM DUGGAN

AT Columbia Business School we teach a session on improvisation as part of the orientation experience of every fledgling MBA. Almost 1,000 students a year practice "yes, and ... " with coaches who are experienced improvisational actors. We motivate this session by pitching improvisation as a route to three outcomes: (1) making luck, (2) building relationships, and (3) creative combination. Smaller groups of students interact with a jazz band, observing and analyzing their collaborative process for lessons leading groups. While our school may be on the vanguard of improvisation for business, it isn't unique in this regard, and current students at other leading schools would have similar learning opportunities. Correspondingly, there is notable research attention in the field of management on the inputs and process that produces creative combination.

It was not always this way. Until recently, improvisation was antithetical to scholarship on management and the curricula of business schools. The foundation of management theory emphasizes order and control, and treats improvisation, indeed any variation from a plan, as a dysfunction (Lewin 1998). It is tempting to attribute the growing acceptance of improvisation in management to changes in the environment in which business people operate, and some efforts to introduce improvisation to management launch from a position that now things are different—faster changing, more complex—and improvisation is a solution to the challenges of the day (Hatch 1998; Ashkenas, Ulrich, Jick, and Kerr 2002). Of course, participants in every era view their times as complex and fast changing, and Duggan (2007) cites many historical examples for his improvisational process of strategy.

The recent attention to improvisation in management can also be seen as a manifestation of a long-term contest between forward-looking and backward-looking approaches to problem solving. Management theory developed in a tradition of rational decision making, and the advice to "work backwards from what you want to achieve" is one of the cornerstones of organizational theory. Various forms of the approach tell decision makers to identify a goal, choose a strategy to achieve it, and then design an organization to deliver on the strategy (e.g., Chandler 1962). The challenge with implementing this advice is that it requires precious foresight, perhaps more than even able managers can hope for. Consequently, one of the great moments of departure for the field was the recognition that managers look for "satisfactory" rather than "optimal" answers, and that the limits of their rationality affect the organizations they design and build. Throughout the twentieth century, the field oscillated between waves defined by an emphasis on rational design and an emphasis on the bottom-up processes of organization patterned by human interaction (Barley and Kunda 1992). Thus, the current "era of improv" may represent the manifestation of a periodic shift in scholarly fashion. We also hold out the possibility that this wave may be more long-lasting, because new practices based in current research may be shifting the relative balance toward more flexible and improvisational organizational forms.

In this chapter we aim to summarize how ideas about improvisation are being used in management, and to describe how research in management contributes to understanding improvisation. Applications of improvisation generate advice for the strategies of organizations, their structures, and for the behavior of people within them. The contributions of management research are for understanding and improving the process of creative combination. We'll summarize what has been learned in our field about which individuals and groups have greater access to the inputs for creativity, and which are better able to combine those inputs. Building off the research on creative combination, we'll describe the idea of strategic intuition, an approach to strategic process that draws on improvisation (Duggan 2007).

APPLICATIONS OF IMPROVISATION
IN MANAGEMENT

Management scholars emphasize that improvisation involves spontaneity and novelty—in other words, problem solving and execution in real time, while developing original actions (Weick 1998). Fisher and Amabile (2009) usefully compare "improvisational creativity" to "compositional creativity," with the difference being the separation in time of planning and execution. By considering improvisation as a form of creativity, they add the definitional requirement that the improvised product must not only be novel, but also "appropriate" in that it is responsive to temporally proximate stimuli. Whether or not it belongs in a general definition of improvisation, the dimension of appropriateness is useful in an organizational context, because organizations are purposive. Of course, the purposes improvisation serves in an organization can be defined broadly and need not be restricted to the explicit performance goals of the organization. For example, the opportunity to improvise might be satisfying and motivating for employees and thereby satisfy the requirement of appropriateness with only indirect reference to organizational outputs.

The exercise of improvisation in organizations has been recognized at the level of strategy, structure, and interaction between participants. Kanter (2002) identifies an emerging improvisational approach to strategy by comparing the approach of companies that successfully responded to technological change to those that were less successful. The pacesetters "got more members of the organization involved, used their technology more effectively and creatively, and emerged from the experimentation period with a clear model indicating how the technology could help the company. They did not wait to act until they had a perfectly conceived plan; instead, they created the plan by acting. In short, they improvised" (76).

The improvisational approach to strategy also manifests itself in work such as McGrath and MacMillan (2009) that recommends building a strategic trajectory on real options. An option according to these authors is "a relatively small investment that creates the right, but not the obligation, to make a further investment later on" (55). These are valuable if information may be learned between the initial and subsequent investment that indicates whether further investment is warranted. Strategists may therefore be able to substitute little steps for comprehensive foresight. Just as improvisers have their methods, there is a method for managing strategy through options. It is necessary to gather feedback on the success of initial investments, as well as establish checkpoints and criteria to decide whether they warrant further investment. Disengagement—walking away from investments that don't represent promise for the future—is behaviorally the most difficult part of the options-guided result. Organizations and individuals are subject to the tendency to escalate commitments to past investments, both in order to save face and because we are biased when we interpret feedback. McGrath and MacMillan recommend that organizations that pursue the options-guided approach to strategy must lower the cost of failure, in terms of culture and concrete incentives. The options logic may be useful for a guide to other forms of improvisation. The advice from strategic management for other forms of improvisation is to take small steps, seek feedback on their success and interpret it well, and be prepared to take a different direction if the feedback is insufficiently positive.

If improvisation is emerging as a guide to the strategies of organizations, it is already well established in ideas about how to structure organizations. The motivation behind this approach is to develop organizations that can be flexible in an efficient way. The earliest success of organizational theory was to develop tools, such as specialization of labor, centralization, departmentalization, and hierarchy, which are efficient ways to achieve an explicit goal. But what should organizations look like if foresight about what goals are appropriate is too costly or impossible? At the most basic level, the answer in organizational theory is that they should do less formal pre-planning and structuring of the interactions between organizational participants and allow more informed spontaneity, in other words, improvisation. One thoughtful guide to developing contemporary organizations offers advice on overcoming the constraints of an organizational chart and "freeing up movement" up and down, side to side, and even outside the organization (Ashkenas, et al. 2002). They recommend "reciprocal teams" with the opportunity and responsibility for intense responsiveness when there is the need to change the

process of operation or to create something new, and they present the analogy of a bas-
ketball team (whereas other organizational forms are more like a bowling team or relay
race). Others have referred to decentralization as "disseminating improvisation rights"
(Weick 1998, 549).

Organizational theorists characterize the shift from pre-planned structures to those
that allow for more improvisation as a substitution of informal organization for formal
organization. Informal organization refers to organizational culture and networks, and
it captures the "method and system" of improvisation within organizations. Culture can
be a source of both motivation and control. In organizations it can serve as a unifying
mindset that allows members to coordinate spontaneously. Hatch (1999) likens organizational culture to the "groove" of a jazz band. Similarly, networks are relationships
based on social exchange that increase the flexible capacity of individuals to achieve
many ends (Zou and Ingram 2013). Research on the role of networks for organizational
performance, and the performance of individuals in them, has exploded in the last
decade. And recent organizational forms that rely less on explicit hierarchy and incentives have conscientiously emphasized the development of culture and networks. This
may be seen as an investment in the capacity to improvise.

An interesting argument for organizations that facilitate improvisation is put forward
by Abrahamson and Freedman (2007) in *The Perfect Mess*, a celebration of *disorganiza-
tion*. They begin with the reasonable observation that organization is costly, and at the
least, the costs should be compared to the benefits. But they go further and argue that
messiness presents advantages of its own, particularly the opportunity for creative combination. They give the example of Scientific Generics, a Massachusetts company that
is the organizational manifestation of a strategy guided by options. Scientific Generics
"spins-up" parts of its organization to deal with emergent opportunities. It is "a fractured
conglomeration of transitory, semi-independent units, some leaping into being and
growing quickly, others withering away, with employees and funding flowing freely and
fast between them" (168). Modular organizations such as this are distinguished by three
principles: growing in pieces instead of holistically; being as quick to shrink or stop failing pieces as to grow thriving ones; and having the preparedness to refocus around any
piece of the organization.

Management research at a micro level has also drawn on the concept of improvisation.
This work, although rare, can be understood as connected to the developments above
that examine the shift of organizational structures to rely more on interaction between
individuals. McGinn and Keros (2002) look for the occurrence of improvisation in the
execution of negotiations, which are often seen as central to organizational life. They
define an improvisation in the course of a negotiation as "a coherent sequence of relational, informational, and procedural actions and responses chosen, and carried out by
the parties during a social interaction" (445). They identify three forms of improvisation in experimental negotiations, in declining order of cooperativeness: "opening up,"
"working together," and "haggling." Not all negotiators improvised; they could instead
engage in an "asymmetric" interaction, where they talk at cross purposes. McGinn and
Keros found that negotiators that were friends before the interaction were more likely to

fall into improvisation than were strangers and to use more cooperative forms of improvisation. Strangers negotiating on the phone tended to have asymmetric interactions, while strangers on email fell into haggling. Cooperative improvisations yielded more successful negotiations.

INPUTS TO CREATIVITY

Burt (2004) used the concept of a "structural hole" to identify managers with the right inputs to creativity. A structural hole is a position in a network where ego is connected to two others who are not connected to each other. People who occupy structural holes have broad and early access to information relative to others in less unique structural positions. Consequently, they have an opportunity to extract ideas about products, practices, or services from one setting and bring them to another setting where they are viewed as novel. They also have more opportunity to create something novel by combining ideas from two different places in the network. In the simplest sense, structural holes give ego a relative advantage over the two alters, as the unique crossroads for all of the ideas contained in the triad. This argument is based on an assumption that people in a network who do not know each other have different knowledge and therefore that their combined ideas are not redundant. Of course, this is not always true, but ideas are localized, and people who do not know each other are more likely to occupy different locations in the social network and therefore in the geography of ideas (Granovetter 1973).

Burt tested this theory by examining managers in a large American electronics company; he found that those with more structural holes in their networks were more likely to be viewed as the source of new ideas. Similarly, Gargiulo and Benassi (2000) found that managers who had more structural holes in their networks made better decisions in adapting to new challenges. Zou and Ingram (2013) looked at both creativity and decision-making quality of executives, as perceived by work peers in a 360-degree performance survey. They found that structural holes along both of these dimensions of performance were increased by structural holes that cross the organizational boundary, in other words, when the executive knew people outside the organization who didn't know others inside the organization. In such cases, cross-boundary structural holes take on particular importance, because these people are even more likely to tap into unique sources of information and perspective.

While contemporaneous structural positions can be the source of the diverse inputs to creative combination, the diversity of experiences within a life may serve a similar function. For example, superior creativity is relatively prevalent among first- and second-generation immigrants (Simonton 1997), among bilingual people (Nemeth and Kwan 1987), and among people with multiple cultural identities (Maddux and Galinsky 2009). Diverse experiences may be direct inputs to creative combination and may also increase an individual's psychological readiness to recruit and accept ideas from unfamiliar sources (Schooler and Melcher 1995).

PROCESS OF COMBINATION

If improvisation is a form of creativity in which the temporal gap between stimulus and response is shorter, it makes sense to consider not only what structures and individual histories provide the inputs for creativity, but also under what circumstances those inputs are more likely to be smoothly and quickly combined. Research in management offers answers at both the group and individual levels. For groups, one of the behavioral challenges to creative combination of ideas distributed among group members is that group discussions are biased toward shared information (what more or all members know) as opposed to unshared information (what one member knows that might inform the others [Stasser and Titus 1985]). One reason for groups to focus on shared information is to reinforce commonalities and therefore build cohesion. Presumably, this would be less necessary in groups whose members already had strong relationships, and there is some experimental evidence that groups of friends share information more effectively (Gruenfeld, et al. 1996). Evidence from managers in organizations suggests that they are more willing to share new ideas with others when there is more trust in those others, both emotional trust and trust that they will do their jobs (Chua, Morris, and Ingram 2010).

Reagans and Zuckerman (2001) present an analysis of innovation that simultaneously supports both the idea that the inputs to creative combination come from connections to diversely situated others and that group cohesion facilitates the process of combination. They examined data from 224 R&D teams in 29 corporations from seven industries. They found that R&D teams had the greatest innovative productivity when they had cohesion among the members, but the members had non-overlapping ties to others outside the team. Uzzi and Spiro (2005) found that a similar structure explained the artistic and financial success of Broadway musicals.

The structure of dense within-group ties, and weak, non-overlapping ties outside the group would appear to offer the maximum for non-redundant information inputs to the team and the best capacity to combine those inputs. This structural ideal seems relevant to other contexts of innovation. It would suggest, for example, that creative combination would be best in a jazz combo with members who possess diverse playing experiences but also who trust in each other. In organizational research, group cohesion and trust are typically seen as functions of the direct relationships between members. It is feasible, however, that trust could derive from other sources, such as reputation, the norms of a profession, or shared identity in the absence of direct relationships. The effect of these forms of cohesion on trust, information sharing, and creative combination is a worthy topic for future research.

At the individual level, evidence suggests that arousal is the enemy of creative combination. In other words, creative combination is more feasible for individuals in a state of calm. Part of the problem is that arousal produces rigidity, where individuals persevere with inappropriate strategies rather than restructure their approach to a problem.

Decades of research show that individuals under arousal, for example because they are under time pressure, warned of impending failure, threatened with physical harm, and so forth, fall back on learned responses and habituated behavior (e.g., Broadbent 1971). This arousal-induced inflexibility is not only in terms of overt behavior but also of cognitive patterns. Directly related to the structural inputs to creativity already described, research indicates that high arousal results in a narrowing of attention. Easterbrook (1959) showed that arousal induced by stress affects how people scan the environment and attend to stimuli. As some improvisers know, the effect can be manipulated chemically: Callaway (1959) showed that subjects' selectivity of attention increased when they were treated with a stimulant and decreased when they were treated with a sedative.

Some of our own research has been to combine ideas about the structures that provide the inputs of creativity and the individual characteristics that facilitate the process of combination. Mason, Zou, Ingram and Duggan (2011) examined the influence on executive networks of (a) plentiful structural holes, (b) chronic low arousal (calmness, relaxation, the absence of nervousness and tenseness), and (c) the interaction of the structural and individual attributes. We found that a network rich in both structural holes and calmness contributed directly to whether an executive was viewed by his or her work colleagues as creative. In addition, the interaction between the two factors was significant. Calmness increases the creative impact of structural holes (and vice versa). This gives direct evidence in support of the idea that calmness facilitates the incorporation of diverse stimuli and their combination into a creative product.

STRATEGIC INTUITION

A new related idea in management offers a structure that combines these various elements of improvisation as "strategic intuition" (Duggan 2007). We can define it as follows:

> The selective projection of past elements into the future in a new combination as a course of action that fits previous goals or sparks new ones, with the personal commitment to follow through and work out the details along the way.

Strategic intuition describes the well-known phenomenon of the "epiphany" or "flash of insight," when your brain connects the dots and you see the path ahead. Modern neuroscience now recognizes this phenomenon as a form of intuition, that is, an automatic retrieval and combination that requires little or no conscious thought. Instead, calmness allows the brain to search widely through memory to make new connections. Arousal comes after the epiphany, through an eagerness and pleasure in taking action on the new idea.

The first formal description of strategic intuition comes from classical military strategy. In *On War*, Clausewitz gives four steps: examples from history, presence of mind, flash of insight, and resolution. Examples from history are a kind of learning that takes the form not of concepts or principles but discrete instances of past actions that led to particular outcomes. Those instances come from personal experience or from studying what others have done. Presence of mind is Clausewitz's term for calmness, where the strategist expects the unexpected and is not surprised or upset by unforeseen or unwelcome events. In step three, the flash of insight, a new combination of examples from history come together in a calm mind. That yields step four, the resolution or will to carry out the new idea.

Strategic intuition is a model of improvisation that applies to situations new to the manager. Probably no one has faced exactly the same situation, but there are countless examples from history that can fit different pieces of the problem. You improvise a new combination to suit the problem at hand. A related phenomenon is "expert intuition," where the manager finds quick solutions to problems by drawing from personal experience. Klein's (1999) research on expert intuition shows how firefighters, nurses, and soldiers in battle quickly draw on subsets of personal experiences to cobble together a combination of tactics to suit the problem at hand. In new situations, expert intuition can be the enemy of strategic intuition: it prevents the manager from looking beyond personal experience to a wider range of examples from history more suitable to the problem.

Another difference between strategic and expert intuition is in timing. Expert intuition represents very quick responses to a stimuli, the "blink" phenomenon popularized by Gladwell (2005). Strategic intuition, on the other hand, is always the result of a slow process, although it may seem spontaneous if the antecedents to creative combination are not recognized. It is probably most accurate to say of strategic intuition that there is no systematic interval between stimuli and response, and indeed, that many stimuli don't receive any response. Epiphany cannot be ordered on demand. As Duggan (2007) puts it:

> [S]trategic intuition becomes like a cottage you come upon in the middle of a forest. You move up close, look around the outside, and then peer through each window to see what's inside. Each window gives you a different view of the same thing. You look in one window, then another, then another, and then at the end you find you're inside the cottage. It all comes together in your mind. (5)

A prominent example of strategic intuition is the origin of Google. In the late 1990s the Google founders, Sergey Brin and Larry Page, were graduate students in computer science at Stanford University, working on applying data-mining algorithms from traditional retail to the new online retail sector, as represented by Amazon and the like. While using Altavista, the best search engine at the time, Page noticed a command to "Find pages that link to your site." This reminded him of academic footnotes, and he knew that academic journals rank researchers by how many times other works cite their work. So Page and Brin adapted a data-mining algorithm to do the same thing for websites: the more others link to your site, the higher your rank. They improvised a new combination: Altavista plus citation ranking plus data-mining algorithms. The result was a new goal: the world's best search engine. When they noticed that another site, Overture, was selling ads and displaying them as search results rather than as pop-ups and banners, Page and Brin added that to Google as their revenue model.

Strategic intuition adds the dimension of problem-seeking, where the goal, and not just the tactics to reach it, can arise in the heat of action. Improvising a goal seems counter to the purposive character of organizations, but in reality organizations have many possible goals that are not all known or explicit at any given time. The greatest innovations by definition lead to new goals and thus new strategic plans to reach them. Calmness in strategic improvisation includes a lack of anxiety about changing goals. In fact, frustration at not reaching goals with enough speed, quality, or economy is a major cause of negative arousal in organizations. Of course organizations should not change goals often. But the new combinations that improvisation creates can sometimes lead to a new goal that is equal to or better than the previous goal.

IMPROV FOR MANAGEMENT AND MANAGEMENT FOR IMPROV

Management scholarship and practice is wrestling with the fact that the foresight that facilitates many approaches to strategizing and organizing is in scarce supply. One response to this paucity is to build organizations that look backward instead of forward, and improvisation is a key part of these efforts. As a result, there is increasing attention to options approaches to strategy, organizations that decentralize authority and allow flexibility as to who works with whom and how, and to improvisation as a guide to the micro processes through which organizational participants come together. Correspondingly, research in the field is investigating the social structures and mental processes associated with innovativeness and creativity. The research yields advice to all improvisers, namely to connect to others with diverse experiences, to build trust with those you improvise with, and to stay calm. These efforts come together in the process of strategic intuition, which combines lessons from history, presence of mind, the flash of insight, and resolution to produce novel and practical strategic ideas.

BIBLIOGRAPHY

Abrahamson, Eric, and David H. Freedman. *A Perfect Mess*. New York: Back Bay Books, 2007.

Ashkenas, Ron, Dave Ulrich, Todd Jick, and Steve Kerr. *The Boundaryless Organization: Breaking the Chains of Organizational Structure*. San Francisco: Jossey-Bass, 2002.

Barley, Stephen R., and Gideon Kunda. "Design and Devotion: Surges of Rational and Normative Ideologies of Control in Managerial Discourse." *Administrative Science Quarterly* 37, no. 3 (September 1992): 363–399.

Broadbent, D. E. *Decision and Stress*. Oxford: Academic Press, 1971.

Burt, Ronald S. "Structural Holes and Good Ideas." *American Journal of Sociology* 110, no. 2 (September 2004): 349–399.

Callaway, Enoch. "The Influence of Amobarbital (Amylobarbitone) and Methamphetamine on the Focus of Attention." *Journal of Mental Science* 105 (1959): 382–392.

Chandler, Alfred D. *Strategy and Structure: Chapters in the History of the Industrial Enterprise*. Cambridge, MA: MIT Press, 1962.

Chua, Roy Y. J., Michael W. Morris, and Paul Ingram. "Embeddedness and New Idea Discussion in Professional Networks: The Mediating Role of Affect Based Trust." *Journal of Creative Behavior* 44, no. 2 (June 2010): 85–104.

Duggan, William. *Strategic Intuition*. New York: Columbia Business School Press, 2007.

Easterbrook, J. A. "The Effect of Emotion on Cue Utilization and the Organization of Behavior." *Psychological Review* 66, no. 3 (May 1959): 187–201.

Fisher, Colin M., and Teresa M. Amabile. "Improvisation, Creativity and Organization." *Rotman Magazine*, Winter 2009, 41–45.

Gladwell, Malcolm. *Blink: The Power of Thinking without Thinking*. New York: Little, Brown & Co., 2005.

Gargiulo, M., and M. Benassi. "Trapped in Your Own Net? Network Cohesion Structural Holes, and the Adaptation of Social Capital." *Organization Science* 11, no. 2 (March-April 2000): 183–196.

Granovetter, Mark S. "The Strength of Weak Ties." *American Journal of Sociology* 78, no. 6 (May 1973): 1360–1380.

Gruenfeld, D. H., E. A. Mannix, K. Y. Williams, and M. A. Neale. "Group Composition and Decision Making: How Member Familiarity and Information Distribution Affect Process and Performance." *Organizational Behavior and Human Decision Processes* 67, no. 1 (July 1996): 1–15.

Hatch, Mary Jo. "Jazz as a Metaphor for Organizing in the 21st Century." *Organization Science* 9, no. 5 (September-October 1998): 556–557.

Hatch, M. J. "Exploring the Empty Spaces of Organizing: How Improvisational Jazz Helps Redescribe Organizational Structure." *Organization Studies* 20, no. 1 (January 1999): 75–100.

Kanter, Rosabeth Moss. "Strategy as Improvisational Theater." *MIT Sloan Management Review*, Winter 2002, 76–81.

Klein, Gary A. *Sources of Power: How People Make Decisions*. Cambridge, MA: MIT Press, 1999.

Lewin, Arie Y. "Introduction: Jazz Improvisation as a Metaphor for Organization Theory." *Organization Science* 9, no. 5 (October 1998): 539.

Maddux, William W., and Adam D. Galinsky. "Cultural Borders and Mental Barriers: The Relationship Between Living Abroad and Creativity." *Journal of Personality and Social Psychology* 96, no. 5 (2009): 1047–1061.

Mason, Malia, Xi Zou, Paul Ingram, and Bill Duggan. "Knowledge Diversity and Creativity Performance." Unpublished manuscript, Columbia Business School, 2011.

McGinn, Kathleen L., and Angela T. Keros. "Improvisation and the Logic of Exchange in Socially Embedded Transactions." *Administrative Science Quarterly* 47, no. 3 (September 2002): 442–473.

McGrath, Rita Gunther, and Ian C. MacMillan. *Discovery-driven Growth: A Breakthrough Process to Reduce Risk and Seize Opportunity*. Cambridge: Harvard Business Press, 2009.

Nemeth, C. J., and J. Kwan. "Minority Influence, Divergent Thinking, and Detection of Correct Solutions." *Journal of Applied Social Psychology* 17, no. 9 (September 1987): 788–799.

Reagans, R. E., and Zuckerman, E. W. "Networks, Diversity, and Performance: The Social Capital of Corporate R&D Units." *Organization Science* 12 (2001): 502–517.

Schooler, Jonathan W., and Joseph Melcher. "The Ineffability of Insight." In *The Creative Cognition Approach*, edited by Steven M. Smith, Thomas B. Ward, and Ronald A. Finke, 97–133. Cambridge, MA: MIT Press, 1995.

Simonton, Dean K. "Foreign Influence and National Achievement: The Impact of Open Milieus on Japanese Civilization." *Journal of Personality and Social Psychology* 72, no. 1 (January 1997): 86–94.

Stasser, Garold, and William Titus. "Pooling of Unshared Information in Group Decision Making: Biased Information Sampling During Discussion." *Journal of Personality and Social Psychology* 48, no. 6 (June 1985): 1467–1478.

Uzzi, Brian, and Jarret Spiro. "Collaboration and Creativity: The Small World Problem." *American Journal of Sociology* 111, no. 2 (September 2005): 447–504.

Weick, Karl E. "Improvisation as a Mindset for Organizational Analysis." *Organization Science* 9, no. 5 (September-October 1998): 543–555.

Zou, Xi, and Paul Ingram. "Bonds and Boundaries: Network Structure, Organizational Boundaries, and Job Performance." *Organizational Behavior and Human Decision Processes* 120, no. 1 (2013): 98–109.

CHAPTER 23

FREE IMPROVISATION AS A PATH-DEPENDENT PROCESS

JARED BURROWS AND CLYDE G. REED

MUSICAL coordination is commonly achieved by means of a score, a conductor, or the parameters of a shared performance practice. Freely improvised music lacks these mechanisms, yet improvisers are capable of finding other ways to coordinate their efforts and make aesthetic judgments on their success. In freely improvised music, we view musical success as the attainment of musical and interpersonal interactions in which players feel able to make strong and distinctive musical contributions and where a high level of musical coordination is present. Borrowing from economics, we apply the concept of "path dependence" to musical choices in freely improvised performance. Our purpose is to explore the process of improvisation through this lens. Some of the questions we ask are the following: How is coordination achieved in free improvisation? What determines the quality of the improvisation? How does our analysis of improvisation inform economic analysis?

We begin with a definition of improvisation in the context of music performance. Path-dependent analysis in economics is briefly discussed as well as its relevance to improvisation. We present a model of musical choice in the context of free improvisation and path dependence. From this perspective, we then analyze problems, benefits, and solutions in freely improvised music performance. Finally, we suggest how improvisation might inform recent work in economics on human capital formation and happiness.

DEFINING IMPROVISATION

Improvisation in music has proven difficult to define.[1] Consider a continuum in musical choice (notes, melodies, texture, dynamics, phrasing, rhythms, etc.). At one extreme of the continuum, all the choices are made in advance of performance by, for example, a composer or a constraining music tradition. At the other extreme musicians make all the decisions in the moment of performance, unconstrained by external coordination. The smaller the role of external coordination, the larger the role of in-the-moment decisions about what to play and how to play, and so forth, the more improvisation is present in the performance. In this view, there are two elements in play. The first is the degree of predetermined musical choice, the second is the range of musical choice allowed to the performers.

An example of the complete absence of improvisation in performance would be certain electronic music in which preprogramming eliminates all choice during performance. Composed music played by humans, even when fully scored and subject to extensive rehearsals, still can be expected to include subtle improvisation in terms of interpretation during performance. In most jazz performances there is extensive room for improvisation, but performers are still constrained in their musical choices by predetermined harmonic, melodic, and rhythmic structures. Freely improvised music is perhaps the form of music making closest to the improvisation end of the music spectrum, but even here the past plays a constraining role. For example, musical choices are influenced by previous performances, music vocabulary, practice history, listening history, and the sequence of musical choices immediately preceding the current choice during performance.

Path Dependence in Economics and Music

Path dependence in economic analysis can only arise in cases where an agent experiences an increase or decrease in the value derived from a good or activity when other agents consume the same good or engage in the same activity. This form of interconnectivity between choices across agents is called a "network externality." It will motivate agents to coordinate their choices over goods and activities in order to maximize the benefits they derive from those choices. Depending on the specifics of the coordination environment, including the extent of knowledge about the time path of previous actions taken by agents, path dependence can result in a number of possible outcomes ("multiple equilibria" in the language of economists). Unlike in traditional economic analysis, the determination of equilibrium choice outcomes will be influenced by the specific path followed to realize them, hence the term "path dependence." A common phrase associated with path dependence is "history matters."

A classic illustration of path dependence involves the telephone. The value of owning a telephone increases with the number of other people owning a telephone. Under the expectation that very few individuals will have access to a telephone, the value of a telephone to a single individual will be low and the equilibrium outcome is that very few telephones will be demanded and therefore produced. Under the expectation that most people will have access to a telephone, the value to an individual of owning a telephone is high and in equilibrium many will be demanded and produced. The ability of potential buyers to easily coordinate telephone purchases is critical for determining which equilibrium outcome will occur.

Paul David uses the example of the longevity of the QWERTY keyboard for word processing to illustrate a path dependence case in which coordination is difficult, leading to the "lock-in" of an inferior technology.[2] Initial typewriter technology relied on inked letters attached to levers that were activated when a typist depressed appropriate keypads. When a typist tried to type too fast, the levers would stack on top of each other, forcing the typist to stop word processing to disentangle the levers. The QWERTY layout placed many of the most-used letters in the English language further apart, thus slowing down typing and reducing the time spent disentangling the levers. According to David, it was an efficient layout given the mechanics of early typewriters. Over time, technological advances not only did away with the lever mechanism, but also with typewriters. In light of this history, one might expect that most word processing today would be done on computers using a more efficient keyboard in which the most used letters are close together and are placed in the most accessible regions of the keyboard. Instead the original QWERTY layout is still the dominant keyboard in use. David's explanation is that, given the network externalities involved, the required coordination between word processor manufacturers, people training to be word processors, and buyers of word processors made it too difficult and costly for agreement to be reached on a better keyboard configuration. David's pioneering work has been criticized with regard to the specific QWERTY example, but the connections between network externalities, path dependence, multiple equilibria, and the possibility of lock-in to an inefficient equilibrium are well accepted.

The relationship of this analytic framework to free improvisation can be seen in the following stylized scenario. A group of musicians get together to freely improvise music. There is no discussion before playing of how the music will start, how it will evolve, or how it will end. Players listen carefully to their own musical expressions, those of the other musicians, and the combined sounds of the group. They examine their emotional and intellectual reactions to what they are hearing. They then make musical choices about when to play, what to play, and how to play. Each player may choose to lead, to follow, to support, to play in contrast, to attempt to change musical direction, or to not play at all. This all happens in the moment. After some time, maybe instantly, the players settle into what we call a musical "equilibrium" in which players collectively explore and enhance a coherent musical space. We call the achievement of this equilibrium "coordination." This could happen very fast and be very transient.

An equilibrium could be very complex, involving multiple layerings of musical ideas, emotions, and intentions. Equilibria may occur on a number of levels, including rhythmic or harmonic coordination, references to shared musical vocabularies, shared feelings of "flow," emotional connection, or in some cases an ecstatic or trance-like coordination. The best equilibria involve a feeling of transcendence, of feeling fully alive, of feeling an overwhelming sense of elevation.

Decay of equilibria can be rapid as players lose emotional or intellectual interest or think of new ideas, and at some point a player decides that a new musical direction is required in order to sustain the level of music quality. The player then makes choices that disturb the old equilibrium. The choices may range from subtle variations or developments to stark contrasts or deliberately subversive musical actions. This is not to say that she always knows specifically where the music should go. The player may only know that her internal reaction to the music is such that the improvisation needs to change. She tries something and hears and feels the reaction from the other players. Do their musical choices change in response? Should the new direction be continued? Should it be made deeper, made simpler, made more complex?

Individual players may sense the need for musical change at different times and have different ideas about the direction of change. They may also differ in their attention and responsiveness to the musical choices of others in the ensemble. If the disturbance is effective, the players coordinate on a new equilibrium. The improvisation proceeds in this way. The quality of the performance, from the perspective of the musicians, will depend on the length of time between equilibria, the musical quality of those equilibria, and the musical relationships between equilibria. The greatest free improvisations exhibit an uninterrupted series of high-quality equilibria linked together to form a coherent structure or narrative, a wonder-filled coordination across equilibria that unifies the overall performance into a sublime experience.

The Model

Consider a simple case of freely improvised music performance. Let there be an improvising ensemble small enough such that each musician is aware of the musical choices of the other players. Let each musician make choices with the desire to maximize the quality of the improvisation. The choices will be based on personal aesthetics and the knowledge that the quality of the musical outcome will be enhanced if musical choices are coordinated.

Let there be M music outcomes in a performance. Think of these outcomes as either periods of equilibria or periods of searching for equilibria. Associated with each outcome let there be a musical pay-off in terms of personal aesthetics, θ, for the individual musician that may be positive, negative, or zero. Let personal aesthetic preferences differ across the musicians.

Let each musician make $T (= M)$ sets of musical choices (i.e., one choice-set per outcome) and gain $S > 0$ of musical pay-off from each choice-set, but only when it is coordinated with the choice-set of the other musicians. Otherwise $S = 0$. This component of the model constitutes the "network externality" required in path-dependent analysis.

Each musician will make musical choices in order to maximize her own musical payoff, which will be given by the sum of her personal aesthetic pay-off (θ) plus S in cases in which musical choices across players are coordinated. The larger is S, the greater will be the role of path dependence in determining the musical outcome.

The exogenous variables of this choice problem are S and the personal aesthetic values of the musicians (θ). The endogenous variables of greatest interest are the choices of the musicians (T) and the corresponding musical outcomes (M). In our exposition, we assume musicians are trying to maximize with respect to their own musical pay-off. The same model also applies if instead the musicians are trying to maximize with respect to their expectation of the musical pay-off for the general audience, for musicians in the audience, or for music critics. This model generates the standard path-dependent outcomes of multiple equilibria, some preferred to others, and the possibility of lock-in to an inferior equilibrium.[3]

Music Quality and Equilibrium

Music is a powerful medium for expressing emotion and states of mind. Equilibrium in our analysis simply means that improvising musicians feel connected to each other at a moment of time in expressing an emotion and/or state of mind. The equilibrium lasts as long as the players continue to make musical choices that maintain this connection. In our model, the highest-quality equilibria are those that, in addition to providing musical coordination, also express emotions and states of mind that are preferred by the musicians in terms of their personal aesthetics (i.e., highest valued θ). Low-quality equilibria are those in which the musicians are coordinated on emotions and states of mind that, while perhaps initially pleasing, impact negatively on their personal aesthetics—for example, "I am sick and tired of more of this shrill, high energy, musical blathering," or "I can't stand any more of this overly precious and pretentious spaciousness," or "can we please move on from this increasingly boring pointillism?"

"Lock-in" refers to a situation in which the musicians are in a low-quality equilibrium and cannot coordinate their way to a better one. In general, when economists analyze coordination games it is common to have an equilibrium A that is preferred by all participants in the game to another equilibrium B, but if the participants find themselves in equilibrium B, no individual will be willing to change unilaterally.

We assume that individual players approach free improvisation with a variety of personal intentions and aesthetic frameworks. Obviously, we cannot account for all combinations of group dynamics or describe all individual viewpoints. In our model, an individual player approaches improvising with one imperative: to maximize musical satisfaction for herself. In order to do this she makes choices based on her personal aesthetic and also on her need to coordinate with the other members of the ensemble. In cases in which these bases of choice conflict with each other, the player makes choices that sometimes work in favor of her vision of the music, or she makes choices that sacrifice personal desires in favor of the perceived musical direction of the group. We see an ongoing negotiation of these values, a natural ebb and flow from one kind of choice to the other, as an integral part of the improvising process.

For situations in which musicians have substantially different aesthetic preferences, it is useful to consider an aggregate measure of musical performance. One possibility is audience response, another is critical appraisal from reviewers, yet another is to aggregate the aesthetic assessments of the performing musicians. In the latter case there are a number of statistical measures to choose from: mean, median, mode, range, and so on. In the context of a one-off performance, the choice over alternative measures of aggregate quality may be of small consequence. From the perspective of long-run viability, the choice becomes more significant. The prospect for future performances depends on audience and reviewer responses. Also, for musicians to be willing to continue to play together in what is primarily an artistic rather than commercial undertaking, their individual musical needs must be met. When aesthetic preferences differ, it is especially important for musicians to be sensitive during performance to how the music is affecting each player and that musical choices are adjusted accordingly. From this point of view, we suggest that aggregate musical quality should be measured by the assessment of the least satisfied performer.

Coordination Problems in Free Improvisation

Limitations imposed by coordination in freely improvised music performance are reflected in the following description/critique by the eminent composer (and sometimes free improviser) Gavin Bryars: "[P]ieces always started tentatively, something big in the middle, and then finished quietly."[4] Our explanation is that coordination problems at the beginning of pieces cause tentative playing as musicians search for equilibria under conditions of limited musical information. As the music progresses there is more time for musicians to signal their intentions and preferences, thus making for easier coordination and allowing "something big" to happen in the middle of performance. Quiet and spare finishes make it easier to coordinate on an ending because details are easier to hear and there is more time for deliberation. Bryars describes a way of coordinating a simple narrative arc structure. Of course there is nothing inherently wrong with a piece that takes this shape, indeed its prevalence as a common practice probably shows its strength as a vehicle for musical communication. If, however, a group is unable to achieve other forms and structures, we view this as a coordination problem.

Equilibria are often easier to achieve when players coordinate by playing one type of texture or musical gesture: all fast, all slow, all dense, all sparse, all high, all low, all extended techniques, all pulse-based rhythms, all turbulent free rhythms, all in one tonal center, all atonal. As with Bryars's large-scale structural critique, these textures or gestures are not problematic in and of themselves. We view all of them as musically useful and potentially very effective ways of achieving high-quality equilibria. We see such monotextural equilibria as problematic only when the equilibria become "locked-in" as players are unable to find alternative means of coordination, or when such equilibria become the default means for a group to coordinate.

As one group of musicians improvises together through many performances, players begin to recognize the musical tendencies and improvising vocabulary of other players in the group. The musical vocabularies of players in the group become a structure for coordination as musical actions are more easily predicted and expectations fulfilled, or subverted, based on past musical experiences. For many players, this aspect of group playing can be quite satisfying and desirable. Take as an example the Schlippenbach Trio, a group that has been playing together for over forty years. Their creative intensity and inventiveness seem undiminished by time. On the contrary, each player in this group is able to effectively use his knowledge of the other players to create and release musical tension and to predict and reinforce the actions of the others. Their commitment to heurism and dialogue prevents them from falling into cliché.

On the other hand, for some groups familiarity can breed stagnation and lock-in if predictable patterns are relied upon too consistently in the achievement of coordination. This can cause players to stop searching or to stop listening as intensely as they might otherwise. Once again, we do not view the emergence and accumulation of such vocabularies and group musical tendencies as inherently inferior, but they can be problematic when they become the only means by which players coordinate. Perhaps as a way to avoid this problem, musicians like Derek Bailey seem to want to play with the largest and most diverse possible range of players and place a high value on unfamiliarity and differences in background and approach. In an interview in *Jazziz* magazine, Bailey explains his viewpoint:

> There has to be some degree, not just of unfamiliarity, but incompatibility with a partner. Otherwise, what are you improvising for? What are you improvising with or around? You've got to find somewhere where you can work. If there are no difficulties, it seems to me that there's pretty much no point in playing. I find that the things that excite me are trying to make something work. And when it does work, it's the most fantastic thing. Maybe the most obvious analogy would be the grit that produces the pearl in an oyster, or some shit like that.[5]

We agree that the presence of aesthetic or interpersonal tension, adversity, or friction can be an important and useful factor in producing valuable musical outcomes. Moreover, it stands to reason that the larger the differences in what musicians bring to collaborative, free improvisation, the larger the set of ideas, approaches, and abilities that will be available for music making. In other words, more diversity in the musical background of musicians increases the potential benefit from coordination. The downside is that without shared musical and cultural experiences, musicians may find it more difficult to communicate and coordinate their ideas, approaches, and abilities into a musical whole. Musical signals and references will be harder to interpret compared to a situation in which the musicians share a common musical background. Taken to extremes, both cases—improvising with players sharing highly similar backgrounds as opposed to very different backgrounds—represent a degree of risk with regard to the achievement of high-quality equilibria. We return to this issue in the section Solutions to Coordination Problems in Free Improvisation.

When musicians have invested thousands of hours in achieving virtuosity, the temptation to display that virtuosity can be overwhelming. The openness of freely improvised music seems to make it especially susceptible to virtuosic display, and this is compounded by the tradition of improvised music that places a premium on uniqueness and technical innovation (perhaps an inheritance from the jazz tradition and also an artifact of modernism) in individual musicians' vocabularies. In addition, there is a potentially distracting kinesthetic reward to performing a difficult physical feat. For instance, a trumpet player who has learned to use circular breathing may decide to use this technique as often as possible just because she can do it and because it feels good. Continual circular breathing is not a problem in and of itself if it maintains a musical connection with the choices made by other players. It certainly will become a problem, for example, if it limits other players in trying to coordinate on a more sparse or open musical texture.

By contrast, a lack of technical ability could be an impediment to coordination. A musician's ability to hear and react to the sounds of other players is always governed by the limitations of hearing and instrumental technique. In a group of three musicians, if two players are playing very fast, the third player need not go along with them, but if she lacks the technical ability to play fast, then that option is not open to her, nor is the possibility of an all-fast group equilibrium. Similarly, if a group spontaneously coordinates on a series of simple, repeated harmonies, a player's inability to hear those harmonic relationships does not prevent her from making a valuable contribution, but it does preclude her ability to coordinate with the group on the basis of shared harmonic structure.

Just as some musicians build up virtuosic technique, others develop elaborate aesthetic and philosophical viewpoints that can have a negative effect on coordination. In the early 1990s, the British musician Django Bates appeared at the Vancouver International Jazz festival. One of the performances included an opportunity for audience members to ask questions. One person in the audience asked why Bates did not perform regularly with a list of what were then the leading lights of the European free-improv scene. Bates said simply, "Because you can't do this," and then walked to the piano and played a C major chord. Following this, he explained that for some musicians, free improvisation meant that references from many pre-existing musical forms were somehow forbidden and that he found this kind of restriction unattractive and frustrating. Indeed, there are many players active in free playing who seem averse to coordination on conventional harmonic or rhythmic devices derived from other forms of music. We see this approach as having a negative impact on coordination. While it may limit risk by constraining musical vocabulary, this prescriptive approach also eliminates many potential high-quality equilibria, essentially preventing people of differing viewpoints from engaging fully in a musical dialogue.

The obverse of the aforementioned problem can also be a serious coordination problem. Where players have a significant investment in competency within a particular style or genre, they may have difficulty leaving behind the vocabulary or performance practices attached to that genre. For instance, if a group of musicians includes three jazz players and one player whose primary field is romantic piano repertoire, the majority of players who are schooled in jazz can easily coordinate on a swinging rhythmic vocabulary that will exclude the pianist. Of course it would be fine for these players to coordinate on swing rhythms for a while and have the pianist either sit out or juxtapose other rhythms, but if the jazz players allow the swinging approach to dominate, the pianist may be unable to contribute fully. In order to realize the full potential of the group music, players may be required to compromise some of the more comfortable or common aspects of their own musical vocabulary. For many players, this impetus to find new ways of playing is precisely what makes free playing attractive.

In addition to the musical concerns just noted, interpersonal tensions, mistrust, or negative feelings can have an adverse affect on coordination. Of course such issues would have an impact on any kind of group performance, but because improvised music depends primarily upon the quality of interaction between musicians and their willingness to enter into dialogue with each other, emotional states are especially important. Some degree of tension is perhaps desirable and makes interactions livelier, but in more extreme cases such tension can shut down musical dialogue.

In our experience, freely improvising large ensembles, even those made up of exceptional musicians, rarely produce great music when all musicians are improvising simultaneously. One problem is that the human brain seems to have difficulty in simultaneously keeping track of more than three distinct musical expressions.[6] Without the ability to hear and therefore interact, even otherwise great improvising musicians will not be able to coordinate their musical choices. There exist several solutions to this problem, involving constraints on the kinds of interaction allowed within a group. One is to intersperse small group improvising within a large ensemble composition. Another is to engage in "conduction," a technique pioneered by Butch Morris, in which a conductor signals, in the moment, which musicians will be playing and what constraints will be placed on their musical choices. Many composers have utilized sections of freely improvised music within larger works or have designed scores or directions that aid coordination. We recognize the potential musical value of such external coordinating mechanisms, but will not consider interactions between composers, conductors, scores, and improvisers in the context of this chapter.

Finally, there is the problem of multiple motivations for musicians connected with improvised music making. These are not unique to improvised music by any means. For instance, audience approval, peer and critical approval, commercial success (rare for improvisers), performances at prestigious venues, or with famous musicians certainly can generate feelings of well-being for most musicians. None of these has an inherently negative effect on improvisation, but where these considerations become primary motivations, there is obvious potential for trouble as extra-musical concerns usurp artistic vision.

PURPOSES AND BENEFITS

We have argued above that freely improvised musical performance is subject to multiple problems of coordination. Why then do musicians choose to do it? What are the offsetting benefits of free improvisation? What makes free improvisation a viable form of music making?

In a workshop during the Vancouver International Jazz Festival some years ago, the great improvising bassist, Barre Phillips, made the following case for free improvisation. He started with the question of why he played music. His answer was that it was a way for him to achieve transcendence. On the basis of his extensive background in both classical and jazz, Phillips observed that to achieve transcendence playing Mozart requires multiple decades of training in the music vocabulary of Mozart, and that a similar long period of study is required to achieve transcendence playing bebop. In his view, a virtue of free improvisation is that practitioners could attempt to achieve transcendence with whatever musical vocabulary they currently possessed.

An interesting follow-up to Phillips's view is contained in Alex Ross's book, *Listen to This*. In an interview with classical pianists Mitsuko Uchida and Richard Goode, co-directors of Marlboro Music, Ross includes the following discussion about recruiting students:

> When I asked Goode to define what qualities he and Uchida were looking for, he said, "A certain technical excellence is a prerequisite. But you also listen for urgency, emotional reality. Maybe that is the primary thing in the end. I guess you could call it 'musicality.' You can often hear it right away. There's a story that when Murray Perahia auditioned for Marlboro he played the C-Minor Impromptu of Schubert, which begins with fortissimo Gs." Goode imitated the sound. "And right after that Horszowski supposedly turned to Serkin and said, 'Let's take him.'" Uchida puts it in her pithy way: "As a rule, the imaginative ones are lacking the technique and the ones that have good technique haven't got a clue. But there are exceptions to the rule, and we try to snap them up."[7]

"Urgency, emotional reality, musicality"; free improvisation is perhaps the only western music tradition that values these qualities unconditionally, regardless of musical vocabulary and technique.

Edwin Prévost sees free improvisation as having two central purposes: heurism and dialogue.

> Improvisation is a practical and secular method of making contact with the flow of existence. It is the place where the very stuff of things can be affected. The contrast with a more formal music (for example string quartet playing) is fundamental, although both may strive for a similar sense of being to enliven their work. The musicians playing a string quartet piece give purpose to a work through performance. Improvising finds purpose of performance through investigation of sonic materials and the testing of human responses.[8]

We see the heuristic process of improvised music making as having a strong personal benefit. For many musicians and listeners, a rush of pleasure and excitement accompanies the discovery of new sounds, whether made by the individual, other members of the group, or in combination. The potential for the discovery of new sonic materials is enhanced through group interaction as individual players react and strain to both integrate with and affect the course of an improvisation.

In the preceding quote, we see two other important purposes and benefits in improvised music making. First, the "testing of human responses," to which Prévost refers, is central to our understanding of the benefits that are derived through free improvisation. David Brooks suggests that the need for social interaction is a central motivating force in society. In his book, *The Social Animal*, Brooks surveys and synthesizes a large and diverse body of research on the subject of human interaction.[9] He suggests that the most important and significant social interactions, as well as many important cognitive processes, occur on an unconscious level. He refers to these unconscious processes as "level-one" thinking and conscious cognition as "level-two." Level-one cognition gathers massive quantities of sense perception data from the environment, especially subtle physical and emotional signals from others. It produces raw emotional responses and reactions, searches for patterns, and does some generalized filtering of and "fuzzy" thinking about this data. Level-two cognition comprises conscious analytic, logical, choice-making, and problem solving in large part based on level-one processes. Brooks suggests that we often attribute choices and outcomes of choices to level-two thinking even when such choices are probably made, or at least heavily influenced by, level-one processes. The more we become aware of level-one processes and their origins and motivations, the better we are able to use level-two thinking to predict and understand the thoughts, actions, and emotions of others and to control and modulate our own.

In improvised music, level-one processes are extremely important. The sheer speed and volume of musical stimuli in improvised music precludes extensive level-two analysis and judgment. Impulses for musical action primarily stem from level-one communications and interactions between players. Successful improvisers are musicians who are comfortable with allowing level-one impulses to govern their course of action and over time hone their ability to rely on these impulses while making very fast and efficient level-two decisions about them. In this way, we see free improvisation as a kind of training ground for level-one communication among individuals and the interaction between level-one and level-two states of consciousness within an individual.

It is interesting to note that following very successful improvisations, it is often difficult for the musicians to remember the specifics of the music that was played. The feeling remains, but not the notes. We see this as evidence for the primary role of level-one communication in improvisation. Indeed, in our experience as players, overtly analytical thinking or conscious and continuous assessment of the music often results in a disconnection with the music, a lapse in listening, and a delay in response time. These observations are consistent with recent research in which the brains of jazz musicians were scanned while they were improvising. According to brain researcher (and jazz musician) Charles Limb:

> During improvisation, the prefrontal cortex of the brain undergoes an interesting shift in activity, in which a broad area called the lateral prefrontal region shuts down, essentially so you have a significant inhibition of your prefrontal cortex. These areas

are involved in conscious self-monitoring, self-inhibition, and evaluation of the rightness and wrongness of actions you are about to implement. In the meantime we saw another area of the prefrontal cortex—the medial prefrontal cortex—turn on. This is the focal area of the brain that's involved in self-expression and autobiographical narrative.[10]

Music seems to have its own repertoire of feeling and its own infinitely subtle emotional vocabulary. In their influential article on emotional intelligence, Salovey and Mayer define "emotion" as follows:

We view emotions as organized responses, crossing the boundaries of many psychological subsystems, including the physiological, cognitive, motivational, and experimental systems. Emotions typically arise in response to an event, either internal or external, that has a positively or negatively valenced meaning for the individual. . . . We view the organized response of emotions as adaptive and as something that can potentially lead to a transformation of personal and social interaction into an enriching experience.[11]

An improvising musician experiments through sound to discover her own unique musical-emotional vocabulary in relation to others. This is not a symbolic vocabulary where sounds stand for feelings but rather the sounds and feelings are unified in a single motivation and musical gesture. We view Prévost's "testing of human responses" through the creation of group improvisation as a fundamentally level-one activity. We see the impetus for musical action as primarily emotive where such action proceeds from a kind of emotional supra-consciousness that the psychologist Mihaly Csikszentmihalyi describes as "flow."[12] This is a state of absorption in an activity where thought and action seem to occur effortlessly and inevitably and where distinctions between physical, emotional, and cognitive processes are blurred.

We think of musical equilibria as sonic spaces of level-one flow and interaction. The rich emotional interactions and expressions in these musical spaces can be highly pleasurable, troubling, uplifting, frustrating, exciting. Prévost mentions "making contact with the flow of existence."[13] We view this as an essentially transcendent experience; a flow of emotional and musical creation in which players feel that they have achieved a state of consciousness beyond what they are normally able to achieve. This could obviously happen without group interaction, but we feel that the interpersonal interaction with other musicians and the intensity of thought and action required to make music in the moment promotes this kind of supra-conscious experience.

Of course other personal benefits of free improvisation are possible. The act of creating improvised music can be an existential and possibly even political act of self-definition. In creating music in the moment, the player affirms her creative power and the inherent value of her creative acts and ideas. This is true in any kind of art making, but in improvised music, confidence in one's ideas and clarity of communication of intention is key to successful creation. In the context of a group interaction, the player who lacks confidence and assurance of musical gesture is unlikely to have the ability to change an equilibrium or to generate a new one.

SOLUTIONS TO COORDINATION PROBLEMS IN FREE IMPROVISATION

Two obvious solutions to coordination problems are solo playing (exclusively) and giving dictatorial power to an individual player in an improvising ensemble. These can be musically effective but at the cost of giving up the joy of interactive playing and the musical brilliance made possible through collective intelligence. For many improvising musicians these costs are sufficiently burdensome to rule out these options.

Another approach is to solve the particularly difficult coordination problems prevalent at the beginnings and endings of pieces with written material, leaving all other musical choices (the vast majority of choices) up to the in-the-moment decisions of the players. This approach works well, but is still too restrictive for some improvising musicians.

In our view, more fundamental solutions depend primarily on open communication, trust, the ability to make selfless choices, unconstrained and easy negotiation over musical direction, introspection based on internal responses to musical stimuli, the courage to play with intention and vulnerability, and listening skills including the ability to hear nuance, to hear emotional intention, and to simultaneously hear subtle musical details and macro structural elements. We do not claim that this particular listing of attributes is unique to us. We suspect most improvising musicians, if asked, would come up with a similar list.[14]

We were somewhat surprised, however, to discover that recent work by social scientists, from a variety of disciplines, on high-functioning group behavior in non-musical pursuits has generated a strikingly similar list of attributes. In summarizing this research, David Brooks reports that groups composed of members with the following level-one talents are more productive than other groups composed of members with better level-two abilities:[15]

- Attunement: the ability to enter other minds and learn what they have to offer.
- Equipoise: the ability to serenely monitor the movements of one's own mind and correct for biases and shortcomings.
- Metis: the ability to see patterns in the world and derive a gist from complex situations.
- Sympathy: the ability to fall into a rhythm with those around you and thrive in groups.
- Limerence: This isn't a talent as much as a motivation. The conscious mind hungers for money and success, but the unconscious mind hungers for those moments of

transcendence when the skull line falls away and we are lost in love for another, the challenge of a task, or the love of God. Some people seem to experience this drive more powerfully than others.

Finally, free improvisation itself can be viewed as a solution to the coordination problem involved in collective music making among musicians from widely divergent traditions. Our experience as improvisers in Vancouver, Canada, sheds some light on the trade-off between improvising with players with similar backgrounds (easier to coordinate musical choices) and players with very different backgrounds (richer set of musical ideas to coordinate). In recent years, Vancouver has become a popular destination for immigrants from Asia. Some of these immigrants are amazing virtuosi in the music and musical instruments of their original cultures. Vancouver is small enough and open enough that opportunities for interaction across musical traditions are common, and we have both participated in such music making. Both authors have a strong background in jazz. Making music with master musicians in classical music from China or Vietnam, for example, initially poses the problem of what kind of music to play. Given our preexisting musical commitments and predilections, it is not practical for us to spend years learning their music traditions. It is equally impractical for them to learn the musical vocabulary needed to play the music of Thelonious Monk or Ornette Coleman. Free improvisation has proven to be a highly productive and rewarding place to meet musically. The idea that free improvisation can be a *lingua franca* for musicians from around the world is stated explicitly in the following quote from Anthony Braxton:

> At this point in time, we can talk of a global community of global musics. Part of the significance of the open improvisational music has been its ability to provide a forum for interactive experiences for people from different parts of the planet, which lends itself to transglobal, transvibrational experiences.[16]

Improvisation Informs Economics

The creation of knowledge in economics, as in knowledge creation in all disciplines, is enhanced by improvisational skills. Improvisation, creativity, curiosity, the ability to make connections across empirical observations and across analyses—all are bound together in multiple ways and reinforce one another. We take this as a given. Our focus is on the pedagogical role that improvisation can play in determining real-world outcomes having to do with economic and personal well-being (i.e., material wealth and happiness).

Consider first the emerging field of the "economics of happiness." A central finding in this literature is the strong correlation between an individual's personal sense of well-being and the quality of her social interactions. Surprisingly (to economists) these interactions statistically dominate the effects of traditional economic variables such as income and wealth.

Richard Layard provides an extensive review of the happiness literature and extrapolates those features of life that have been shown empirically to make the biggest difference to our happiness.[17] Foremost among these are family relationships, financial situation, work, community and friends, and health. Some of these—family relationships, community and friends—fall directly into the category of social interactions. We will show that social interactions are also critical to successful outcomes in finances, work, and health. A weakness of the economic analysis of happiness is the lack of discussion on how to achieve and improve high-quality social interactions. Brooks, for example, laments that "We don't teach this ability [level-one skills] in school—to harmonize patterns, to seek limerence, to make friends. But the happy life is defined by these sorts of connections, and the unhappy life is defined by a lack of them."[18] We propose that the interpersonal skills and interactive level-one processes acquired and improved through participation in free improvisation have the potential to improve outcomes in the features of life identified by Layard.

Layard suggests that moral and emotional education, or what he calls "education of the spirit," is a key factor in increasing the happiness of societies.[19] According to Layard, "controlled trials have shown that well-designed courses in emotional intelligence have significant effects on children's mood and on their consideration for others; these effects are still evident two years later."[20] Among other important aims for this kind of education, Layard includes the appreciation of beauty, understanding others and how to socialize, and understanding and managing your feelings as key components. The negotiation of values and ideas and building of trust are also included as primary factors affecting happiness in family, work, and community relationships.

We view Layard's aims as strongly overlapping with Brooks's ideas about the importance of level-one cognition and quality personal interactions within groups. As we pointed out earlier, successful free improvisation in music requires a significant degree of trust as a player makes choices based on the assumption that others in a group will willingly and meaningfully interact with her ideas. It also requires the ability to interpret the intentions and actions of others in relationship both to personal goals and ideas and a shared group outcome. We argue that free improvisation in music (and possibly improvisation in other art disciplines) has obvious pedagogical applications in modeling and teaching these abilities and should be a part of the core curriculum wherever they are taught.

When economists try to understand why some individuals are wealthier than others, their analytic and empirical focus has traditionally been on measures of human capital (e.g., health, educational attainment, IQ, labor market experience). Despite having access to detailed data sets on these human capital variables, economists have only been able to explain a small portion of the variation in labor market success across workers by using this approach. We suggest that what may be missing in the empirical analysis is the inclusion of more recently identified human capital variables associated with level-one cognition.

The new work on human capital as summarized in Brooks concludes that most people work in groups; group efforts are extremely productive compared to individual efforts;

the key to successful group effort in the labor force is the ability to coordinate effectively; and the ability to coordinate effectively is determined by the acquisition of level-one skills.[21] People who are most successful and happy at work, in communities, and in families are people who have strong level-one communication abilities and who allow level-two decisions and analysis to be affected and informed by this more subtle level of cognition.

Modern production technologies have substituted computers and other capital goods for labor in the production of goods in a way that has lowered the productivity of many workers and, along with globalization of the labor market, caused large increases in inequality.[22] In contrast, group production is an area in which labor productivity has remained high. Moreover, the most important element in making teamwork highly productive is the ability of team members to coordinate with each other. According to Brooks, recent research suggests that working groups display the highest levels of collective intelligence when group members are good at reading and understanding emotions and intentions, evaluating each other's strengths, and predicting tendencies, when they take turns in taking on leadership roles, and when the contributions and inputs of individuals are managed fluidly.[23] He concludes that functioning effectively in a group "requires the ability to trust people outside your kinship circle, read intonations and moods, understand how the psychological pieces each person brings to the room can and cannot fit together." We see all of these abilities as critical for coordinating high-quality equilibria in improvised music. We are not making a case for effortless or automatic transference of qualities and abilities learned from improvisation to other aspects of an individual's life, but we are suggesting that improvised music making has the potential to act as a scaffolding for the exploration and teaching of these important abilities.

What about health? At first glance, it may seem unlikely that free improvisation could have an affect on health, but in fact there is growing evidence that the quality of social interaction and the stability of social networks has a significant positive impact on health outcomes. Citing a broad spectrum of health studies (including Patrick and Wickizer, and Ebrahim and Smith), Lomas suggests that measures to increase social cohesion (a term he uses interchangeably with social capital) play a significant role on a health "intervention continuum."[24] According to Lomas, social cohesion has a measurable, positive outcome on rates of disease and mortality and "interventions to increase social support and/or social cohesion in a community are at least as worthy of exploration as improved access or routine medical care."[25] In the case of heart disease, the positive influence of social cohesion statistically outweighed the availability of free medical treatment and was nearly as important as drug therapies. More recent work has shown the positive influence of friendship on lifespan.[26] Again, we would argue that participating in free improvisation enhances the ability of people to engage in successful social interactions and to become active in social networks.

We are not aware of empirical research into the effects of improvisation on interpersonal emotional interactions. Nevertheless, we predict a strong potential for improvisation to help people acquire the qualities and skills that both Layard and Brooks see as key to happiness and productivity. We can offer strong anecdotal evidence on the positive effects of improvisation in educational settings. One of the authors has taught many free improvisation workshops for a wide variety of participants at elementary and secondary schools, colleges, universities, community groups, and academic conferences. These workshops are based on the work of British improviser John Stevens. His book, *Search and Reflect*, presents a series of games, exercises, and compositions for introducing people to improvisation.[27] Participants can approach these activities with a variety of musical backgrounds and skill levels from ten-year old elementary-school students who have been playing the clarinet for a month to instrumental performance faculty at major universities. In these workshops participants begin with very limited improvisational choices and as their listening abilities, musical vocabularies, and confidence grow, they make more complex sets of choices and interact more with other musicians. Eventually, all restrictions are removed and players improvise freely. In many cases people who previously declared that they couldn't or wouldn't improvise can progress very quickly to free playing in small groups. They meet with considerable success in terms of understanding the interactions of the group and in producing music of a quality that is satisfying to them. Participants almost always report an increased ability to listen to and interpret the sounds and intentions of other players, a greater trust in their abilities to make a valuable contribution to the group music, and an increase in general confidence. In other words, they begin to focus on the kinds of interactions that contribute to happiness, health, successful relationships, and effective group work. Moreover, we have observed significant progress in these interpersonal skills in the space of only one or two sessions.

Of course the same abilities could be learned in other forms of group music making or other group activities. What are the advantages of learning these skills through free improvisation? First, the feedback is immediate. In the absence of externally imposed coordination, interpersonal interactions are particularly meaningful, instructive, intense, and enriching. Second, there is no requirement for expensive equipment or location, or extensive specialist training for students. Musical improvisation is spontaneous and allows level-one skill learning to occur on a relatively circumscribed timescale. For most people it is also fun.

CONCLUDING REMARKS

Understanding improvisation as a path-dependent process helps us think about the purposes, problems, and solutions in this form of music making and to see it in relationship to other musical traditions. The skills leading to successful free improvisation in music are the same skills that enrich personal interactions in all situations, and we argue that the practice of free improvisation could be a model environment for people to explore, understand, acquire, and improve these abilities. The concepts of path dependence and level-one/level-two states of consciousness are key to understanding the critical role of coordination and communication in both musical improvisation and economic relationships.

Acknowledgments

Earlier drafts of this essay have benefited from comments from Cliff Bekar, Coat Cooke, Gregory Dow, Bruce Freedman, Brian Krauth, Guy Immega, Sherrill King, Dylan van der Schyff, Raymon Torchinsky, and Simon Woodcock. All remaining errors, omissions, and confusions are solely the responsibility of the authors.

Notes

1. Derek Bailey, *Improvisation: Its Nature and Practice in Music* (New York: Da Capo Press, 1992), 83.
2. Paul David, "Clio and the Economics of QWERTY," *The American Economic Review* 75, no. 2 (1985): 332–337.
3. The full mathematical exposition of the model, along with supporting simulations, can be found in B. Curtis Eaton, Krishna Pendakur, and Clyde G. Reed, "Socializing, Shared Experience and Popular Culture" (unpublished, 2000, available at http://www.sfu.ca/econ-research/RePEc/sfu/sfudps/dp00-13.pdf), albeit in that paper path dependence is driven by economic agents coordinating on consumption experiences, while in this chapter path dependence is driven by freely improvising musicians coordinating on musical experiences. For related formal modeling of path-dependent processes, see W. Brock and S. Durlauf, "Discrete Choice with Social Interactions," *Review of Economic Studies* 68 (2001): 235–260; W. Brock and S. Durlauf, "Interactions-Based Models," in *Handbook of Econometrics*, vol. 5, edited by J. Heckman and E. Leamer, 3297–3380. (Amsterdam: North Holland, 2000).
4. Quoted in Bailey, *Improvisation*, 114.
5. Quoted in Phil Freeman, "The Grit That Produces The Pearl," *Jazziz* 19, no. 3 (March 2002), 42.
6. Philip Ball, *The Music Instinct: How Music Works and Why We Can't Do Without It* (New York: Oxford University Press, 2010), 154.
7. Alex Ross, *Listen to This* (New York: Farrar, Straus and Giroux, 2010), 255–256.
8. Edwin Prévost, *No Sound Is Innocent: AMM and the Practice of Self-Invention, Meta-musical Narratives, Essays* (Harlow, Essex, UK: Copula, 1995), 107.
9. David Brooks, *The Social Animal: The Hidden Sources of Love, Character, and Achievement* (New York: Random House, 2011). Also see the discussion of "System 1" and "System 2" modes of thinking in Daniel Kahneman, *Thinking, Fast and Slow* (New York: Farrar, Straus and Giroux, 2011).
10. Quoted in Alicia Anstead, "Inner Sparks," *Scientific American* 304, no. 5 (2011): 86.
11. Peter Salovey and John D. Mayer, "Emotional Intelligence," *Imagination, Cognition, and Personality* 9 (1990): 186.

12. Mihaly Csikszentmihalyi, *Flow: The Psychology of Optimal Experience* (New York: Harper and Row, 1990).
13. Prévost, *No Sound Is Innocent*, 107.
14. Our list has benefited from discussions with Oregon based drummer/improviser Dave Storrs.
15. David Brooks, "The New Humanism," *New York Times*, March 7, 2011, http://www.nytimes.com/2011/03/08/opinion/08brooks.html.
16. Quoted in George E. Lewis, *A Power Stronger Than Itself: The AACM and American Experimental Music* (Chicago: University of Chicago Press, 2008), 502.
17. Richard Layard, *Happiness: Lessons from a New Science* (New York: The Penguin Press, 2005).
18. Brooks, *The Social Animal*, 211.
19. Layard, *Happiness*, 201. See also Daniel Goleman, *Emotional Intelligence: Why It Can Matter More Than IQ for Character, Health and Lifelong Achievement* (New York: Bantam Books, 1995).
20. Layard, *Happiness*, 200.
21. David Brooks, "Amy Chua Is a Wimp," *New York Times*, January 17, 2011. http://www.nytimes.com/2011/01/18/opinion/18brooks.html?_r=1&partner=rssnyt&emc=rs; and Brooks, "The New Humanism."
22. Paul Krugman, "Degrees and Dollars," *New York Times*, March 6, 2011. http://www.nytimes.com/2011/03/07/opinion/07krugman.html.
23. Brooks, "Amy Chua Is a Wimp."
24. See D. L. Patrick and T. M. Wickizer, "Community and Health," in *Society and Health*, edited by B. C. Amick, S. Levine, A. R. Tarlov, and C. D. Walsh (New York: Oxford University Press, 1995), 46–92; and S. Ebrahim and G. Davey Smith, "Systematic Review of Randomised Controlled Trials of Multiple Risk Factor Interventions for Preventing Coronary Artery Disease," *British Medical Journal* 314 (1997): 1666–1674; Jonathan Lomas, "Social Capital and Health: Implications for Public Health and Epidemiology," *Social Science and Medicine* 47 (1998): 1181–1188.
25. Lomas, "Social Capital and Health," 1184.
26. Tara Parker-Pope, "What Are Friends For? A Longer Life," *New York Times*, April 21, 2009. http://www.nytimes.com/2009/04/21/health/21well.html.
27. John Stevens, *Search and Reflect* (London: Community Music Ltd, 1985).

Bibliography

Anstead, Alicia. "Inner Sparks." *Scientific American* 304, no. 5 (2011): 84–87.
Bailey, Derek. *Improvisation: Its Nature and Practice in Music*. New York: Da Capo Press, 1992.
Ball, Philip. *The Music Instinct: How Music Works and Why We Can't Do Without It*. New York: Oxford University Press, 2010.
Brock, W., and S. Durlauf. "Discrete Choice with Social Interactions." *Review of Economic Studies* 68 (2001): 235–260.
Brock, W., and S. Durlauf. "Interactions-Based Models." In *Handbook of Econometrics*, vol. 5, edited by J. Heckman and E. Leamer, 3297–3380. Amsterdam: North Holland, 2000.
Brooks, David. *The Social Animal: The Hidden Sources of Love, Character, and Achievement*. New York: Random House, 2011.

Brooks, David. "The New Humanism." *New York Times*, March 7, 2011. http://www.nytimes.com/2011/03/08/opinion/08brooks.html.

Brooks, David. "Amy Chua Is a Wimp." *New York Times*, January 17, 2011. http://www.nytimes.com/2011/01/18/opinion/18brooks.html?_r=1&partner=rssnyt&emc=rss.

Csikszentmihalyi, Mihaly. *Flow: The Psychology of Optimal Experience*. New York: Harper and Row, 1990.

David, Paul. "Clio and the Economics of QWERTY." *American Economic Review* 75, no. 2 (1985): 332–337.

Eaton, B. Curtis, Krishna Pendakur, and Clyde G. Reed. "Socializing, Shared Experience and Popular Culture." (unpublished paper, 2000). http://www.sfu.ca/econ-research/RePEc/sfu/sfudps/dp00-13.pdf

Ebrahim, S., and G. Davey Smith. "Systematic Review of Randomised Controlled Trials of Multiple Risk Factor Interventions for Preventing Coronary Artery Disease." *British Medical Journal* 314 (1997): 1666–1674.

Freeman, Phil. "The Grit That Produces The Pearl." *Jazziz* 19, no. 3 (March 2002): 42–43.

Goleman, Daniel. *Emotional Intelligence: Why It Can Matter More Than IQ for Character, Health and Lifelong Achievement*. New York: Bantam Books, 1995.

Kahneman, Daniel. *Thinking, Fast and Slow*. New York: Farrar, Straus and Giroux, 2011.

Krugman, Paul. "Degrees and Dollars." *New York Times*, March 6, 2011. http://www.nytimes.com/2011/03/07/opinion/07krugman.html.

Layard, Richard. *Happiness: Lessons from a New Science*. New York: The Penguin Press, 2005.

Lewis, George E. *A Power Stronger Than Itself: The AACM and American Experimental Music*. Chicago: University of Chicago Press, 2008.

Lomas, Jonathan. "Social Capital and Health: Implications for Public Health and Epidemiology." *Social Science and Medicine* 47 (1998): 1181–1188.

Parker-Pope, Tara. "What Are Friends For? A Longer Life." *New York Times*, April 21, 2009. http://www.nytimes.com/2009/04/21/health/21well.html.

Patrick, D. L., and T. M. Wickizer. "Community and Health." In *Society and Health*, edited by B. C. Amick, S. Levine, A. R. Tarlov, and C. D. Walsh, 46–92. New York: Oxford University Press, 1995.

Prévost, Edwin. *No Sound Is Innocent: AMM and the Practice of Self-Invention, Meta-musical Narratives, Essays*. Harlow, Essex, UK: Copula, 1995.

Ross, Alex. *Listen to This*. New York: Farrar, Straus and Giroux, 2010.

Salovey, Peter, and John D. Mayer. "Emotional Intelligence." *Imagination, Cognition, and Personality* 9 (1990): 185–211.

Stevens, John. *Search and Reflect*. London: Community Music Ltd., 1985.

PART VI

....

PHILOSOPHIES

....

CHAPTER 24

MUSICAL IMPROVISATION AND THE PHILOSOPHY OF MUSIC

PHILIP ALPERSON

DISAPPEARANCE, DISPARAGEMENT, DISMISSAL

IN 1976 the distinguished philosophy journal, *Mind*, marking its 100th anniversary, published an article on improvisation by the eminent former editor of *Mind*, Waynflete Professor of Metaphysical Philosophy and Fellow of Magdalen College, Oxford, Gilbert Ryle.[1] Ryle's essay, which runs to 6,000 words, managed to cover a wide range of improvisational activities: having conversations, joking, debating, fencing, making shots on goal, catching a ball, climbing ladders, climbing trees, stepping on stones to cross a stream, coping with traffic emergencies, composing verse, decoding anagrams, and solving philosophical problems. Ryle even found time in an afterword to pontificate about another kind of activity he called "initialization": the habit of philosophers of reducing recurring phrases to their initial letters. (Thus Alexander (A) attributes premises A_1, A_2, A_3 to Plato (P) in the *Parmenides (P')*.) What Ryle did not find time to discuss was music. Indeed, the only reference to music in Ryle's essay on improvisation was a mere mention of the names of Gilbert and Sullivan and Bach in connection with a short discussion of originality. Surely, one would have thought, any philosophical examination of improvisation would make at least passing reference to improvisation in music.

One might have forgiven Ryle his curious omission on the grounds that the target of his paper was improvisational action in general or improvisation very widely conceived, and that for such purposes any set of examples would have sufficed. But the issue goes deeper than this, I think. Ryle admits in his essay that he finds the words creativity and creation "repellant."[2] Ryle was in fact known for his open disdain for philosophical aesthetics—with whose literature he was unfamiliar—and for a certain affectation of philistinism.[3] In this he shared the attitude of many practitioners of mid-20th century Oxford ordinary language philosophy.[4] Given all this it is perhaps not so surprising after all that such an eminent philosopher could write on improvisation without so much as mentioning musical improvisation. But the elision of musical improvisation from philosophical consideration is not limited to philosophers who disdain or are ignorant of the field of philosophical aesthetics. If one searches for the keyword *music* in the database of *The Journal of Aesthetics and Art Criticism*, the leading journal in the field, one receives 3,215 hits. If one searches for "musical improvisation" one receives 23. Searches of the *Journal of Aesthetic Education* and the *British Journal of Aesthetics* yield proportionately worse results: 1,565 to 5 and 1,612 to 2, respectively.[5]

Disappearance is one thing. Disparagement is another. Here again philosophers have not been very kind to musical improvisation. Eduard Hanslick, the 19th-century Austrian critic whose views helped to lay the foundations of modern musical aesthetics, characterizes musical improvisation as "relaxing more than working," lending itself to a subjective, "pathological . . . reckless abandonment of the self" and resulting in a content-less product "without allowing an autonomous tonal configuration to come distinctly to the fore."[6] Musical improvisation, on Hanslick's view, commits two cardinal sins: it produces a product devoid of musical content and it encourages a kind of wallowing in emotional expression. The influential Frankfurt School theorist Theodor Adorno faults musical improvisation—and jazz improvisation in particular—as presenting only the appearance of innovation. In practice, especially in the hands of less adept players, Adorno complains, improvisation amounts only to a kind of "pseudo-individualization," a mirage of creativity enabled by a shuffle of standard musical formulae.[7] In a particularly biting passage he writes, "The insouciant routine of the jazz amateur is nothing other than the passive ability not to be confused in the adaptation of the models. *He* is the true subject of jazz: his improvisations come out of the schema; he manages the schema, cigarette in mouth, nonchalantly, as if he had just invented it himself."[8] And, if we may stay on the topic of improvised jazz for a moment, we may observe that Adorno's comments echo more general views in society of the marginality of jazz and of improvised music in general. Historically, improvisatory jazz has been portrayed as having unseemly origins, arising in the bordellos of New Orleans, having an uncomfortably close relationship to prostitution, drugs, alcohol, and crime, and appealing only to minority tastes. Even when jazz is represented in the mainstream media, as it was in 1950s and 1960s American television crime dramas such as *Perry Mason, Peter Gunn*, and *Mission Impossible*, it is used to connote marginality: crime, sleazy clubs, and questionable dealings with the police.[9] And, as a kind of music often seen as appealing to a relatively small group of aficionados, it enjoyed neither the prestige of "high" art (especially among those who see its practitioners as untutored, undisciplined, and unmusical) nor, perhaps with the exception of the big band era of the 1930s and 40s, has it enjoyed the mass appeal of popular art.

The history of musical improvisation's invisibility and its disparagement among philosophers goes beyond the personal tastes of individual philosophers, the prejudices of particular schools of philosophy, or the general opinion of improvised music as lacking in social and artistic status. What is at stake, I want to argue, is something more fundamental and systemic. The relationship of philosophy to musical improvisation arises out of a historically defined cultural and artistic perspective, including certain assumptions about the nature of art and the nature of music that both enhance and hamper a philosophical understanding of musical improvisation adequate to its subject.

In this essay I would like to lay out this perspective and its consequences. I shall start with some general remarks about several interrelated methodological and strategic tendencies of the general approach of philosophy to music that bear on its understanding of both music in general and on musical improvisation in particular. I shall indicate what I take to be the constraints put upon the philosophical understanding of musical improvisation by that approach. I shall then explore possibilities for a deeper, more profound understanding of musical improvisation.

For the most part I shall concentrate on jazz, a musical practice that typically places a very high premium on musical improvisation. I do not wish to imply by my choice of examples that I take jazz to be paradigmatic of improvisatory music. I shall gesture to a few other traditions or genres in cases where I think there are commonalities. Also, I will not be discussing cases in which improvisation in music is linked with improvisation in other art forms, as in the case of 15th-century *saltarello*, in which musicians and dancers improvise together. Finally, I shall confine my comments mainly to Anglophone philosophy in the analytic tradition.[10]

Anglophone Philosophy of Music and the Musical Object

Beginning with the work of Susanne Langer in the late 1940s and continuing over the next several decades, led by the writings of philosophers such as Peter Kivy, Jerrold Levinson, Stephen Davies, Jenefer Robinson, Roger Scruton, Theodore Gracyk, and others, Anglophone philosophy of music has been one of the "growth industries" in the field of philosophical aesthetics, at least insofar as one might measure such things in terms of the numbers of articles published in its leading journals, the number of presentations made at conferences of the American, British, and Canadian Societies for Aesthetics, and the number of monographs published. To take but one example: in the first 50 years of the *Journal of Aesthetics and Art Criticism's* existence (1941–1991), more articles were devoted to music and literature than any other art form (about 10 percent of all articles for music and the same for literature); in the last 20 years over 40 percent of the *JAAC's* articles on the particular arts have been devoted to music.[11]

Generally speaking, Anglophone philosophy of music has by and large focused on music as a certain kind of object-oriented practice. More specifically, it has seen music as an aesthetic practice centered on the creation of objects—musical works of art—whose specifically musical features are thought to consist in their disposition to present aesthetic qualities appropriate to modes of attention and evaluation involving disinterested aesthetic experience.

One way to understand this perspective is to situate the view historically, with the birth of the so-called Modern System of the Arts in the 18th century, when it was proposed that there was a group of arts—the "fine arts"—that possessed a common thread by virtue of which they formed an affinity group.[12] Throughout this history, whose philosophical lineage runs from Shaftesbury, Hutcheson, and Baumgarten to Kant, whether the relevant properties of the fine arts were thought to be formal, aesthetic, mimetic, or expressive, the created objects at the center of artistic activity were conceived of as autonomous, designed to be appreciated for their own sake in a "disinterested" manner, largely independent of any other use or value the object might have. This view reflected the contemporaneous rise of performance venues such as court salons and the concert hall, where musical composers, performers, and listeners were seen as engaging in the collective activity of the presentation and appreciation of repeatable works created for the express purpose of presenting autonomous objects to be apprehended for their own musical, artistic, and intrinsically aesthetic properties. In the 20th and 21st centuries the notion of artistic *expression* gave way to the idea that it was *aesthetic experience* that was the glue that held the group together. But the emphasis on the production of objects presented to subjects, in itself a continuation of Cartesianism, has remained at the center of the discussion.

Analytic philosophers have accordingly been concerned with questions about the meaning of works of art and their ontology, the nature of their properties (notably formal, expressive, and representational properties), and a range of musical practices concerning musical composition, performance, understanding, and criticism centered on purely "aesthetic" considerations. Composers create the works: if the work is not a fully worked out form in the composer's mind (as Hanslick had it), the work is some sort of structure, entity, or type that is the product of the composer's musical conception. The repeatability and transmission of musical works are made possible by the development of musical notation and scores, which enable performers to present interpretations of the works in public arenas. Listeners and critics are construed along Humean lines as people aspiring to the ideal of taste: true and disinterested judges possessed of a delicacy of imagination and practiced in making judgments appropriate to musical works of art. Not the least of the critical judgments listeners and critics make is the extent of the performance's fidelity to the score, which is to say, to the work. That is, audiences frequently listen for the work through the performance.[13]

This approach to music that focuses on the production and appreciation of musical works as aesthetic objects is consistent with certain methodological tendencies of analytic philosophy in general, most especially a naturalistic orientation toward observable entities and their properties and the rigorous analysis of concepts and statements that might be clearly and meaningfully asserted about the ontology of these entities.[14] In some cases the identification of what is to count as an aesthetic "object" is construed rather strictly, as for example in Hanslick's account of music as "tonally moving forms" or, more recently, in Julian Dodd's "sonicist" position that works of music just are sound-event types—types whose tokens are datable, locatable patterns of sounds.[15]

AESTHETIC MONO-FUNCTIONALITY

A second feature, consistent with the orientation toward aesthetic objects, is the presumption of what we might call *aesthetic mono-functionality*. By this I mean that philosophers have not simply directed their attention toward particular kinds of objects (works of art) but that they have for the most part assumed, tacitly or otherwise, that works of art, properly so-called, have a single function and, moreover, that the function of art is to be subsumed under the traditional categories of aesthetic thought. There has been considerable debate about the extent to which the function of art can be specified, essentially defined, or treated as a "cluster concept," and so on. But even such accounts as Berys Gaut's "cluster concept" and Denis Dutton's account of "our" concept of art, which assert that there are multiple criteria that could conceivably count toward the application of the concept of "art," take the historical categories of the aesthetic as normative.[16] This is a kind of functionalism, then, according to which one counts something as art only to the extent to which it can be brought under the categories of the aesthetic tradition. This is a presumption that may be stated explicitly, or it may be under the surface when, for example, someone claims that what he or she is interested in is what makes art *art* or what makes music *music* and then proceeds to include what falls under the categories within the tradition and exclude or dismiss that which does not.

EUROPEAN CLASSIC-ROMANTIC NORMATIVITY AND SPECTATORIALISM

I do not wish to be misunderstood. The philosophical orientation of which I have been speaking has considerable force. The focus on musical works as aesthetic objects has resulted in many nuanced discussions of the formal, emotive, and representational dimensions of musical meaning of musical works, with special attention to various models of musical expressiveness, and an imposing literature on the ontology of musical works of art. The approach has brought considerable insight especially to the range of musical practice where relatively developed musical works are composed, elaborated in notation, performed, and appreciated by listeners who listen in large part precisely for the features of these works that bear this sort of scrutiny. The approach has had much to say in particular about the musical practices exemplified by the European "classical" music tradition from roughly the 16th century to at least as far as the mid-20th century, from which so many of the musical examples of contemporary philosophy of music are drawn.[17] It is a matter of central importance to our understanding of, say, Beethoven's Quintet for Piano and Winds in E-flat, op. 16, to ascertain what sort of thing the "work" is—whether an abstract object, a structural type, a particular sound sequence or pattern of sounds, an indicated structure, or something else—and what the identity and persistence conditions of a musical work of art are, in order to grasp what it is that Beethoven composed and created, what it is that performers of the quintet perform, the role of historically inflected traditions that help to constitute a style, and the range of evaluative criteria that listeners might properly bring to the audition and critical assessment of the work.[18] It is important to acknowledge and understand that one of the values of music is precisely that it can, as Alan Goldman has put it, present us with an "alternative" world in which we can be fully engaged.[19]

At the same time it is important to remember that the determination of the range of phenomena thought of as appropriately targetable by philosophical analysis is itself a methodological issue, a methodological choice with important consequences. The presumption that what shall count as normative for the inquiry is European classical music, with its emphasis on notated compositions that form the basis of performances of aesthetically valuable works that sustain disinterested aesthetic value, is a double-edged sword. On the one hand, the presumption speaks to a musical tradition of unquestionable cultural importance, and it helps to focus the discussion by identifying a set of issues, topics, technical terms, and critical vocabulary for philosophical analysis. On the other hand, the presumption tends to elide other sorts of questions that might be asked about music and about improvisation in particular. Specifically, the view tends to favor an approach featuring the inspection and analysis of the aesthetic properties of the musical object, and to correspondingly neglect questions about the social, political, and cultural aspects of musical practice. In short, the aesthetic object model orientation of Anglophone philosophy, combined with the presumption of the normativity of classical European composed music, tends toward a view we might call *spectatorialism*, an ontological and evaluative position that concentrates on the more or less intrinsic aural qualities of musical properties available to the listener in direct experience.

ONTOLOGICAL CONSIDERATIONS I: MUSICAL IMPROVISATION AS AN AESTHETIC OBJECT

With this overview in mind, how then might we arrive at a more robust philosophical understanding of musical improvisation? There is of course an element of improvisation in every intentional action or set of actions in the sense that every action is, in at least a minimal sense, a unique event that requires a degree of human agency. I take this to be a truism, albeit for present purposes a trivial one. I am interested in musical improvisation not as a mere specimen of human action but rather as a particular range of musical activity—activity in which improvisation plays a significant role in our musical understanding. These improvisatory musical activities run the gamut from minor ornamentation of musical phrases, through improvised cadenzas, to the kinds of spontaneous improvisation of long-form musical constructs for which Liszt was especially known, and to the extended improvised performances of Indian and Persian music and, of course, jazz. Additionally, improvisations can occur in the course of the performance of previously composed works as well as in the creation of more or less original compositions on the spot.

Perhaps one might start by observing that there are in fact many features of improvised music that can be fruitfully considered from an aesthetic point of view. It is possible to lose sight of this point in part because musical improvisation often occurs in the context of relatively small groups, not surprisingly since coordinating musical creation on the spot with others, especially if they are also engaged in extemporizing, is no small feat. One thinks of the jazz quintet, for example, or the small ensembles of South Indian Carnatic *rāgam-tānam-pallavi* or Arabic *takht* music that typically number between two and eight performers. One might be tempted to think that groups with small numbers of participants can hardly be expected to avail themselves of the possibilities for musical complexity available to, say, the composer who writes for the standard symphonic complement of 60 to 100 players. These considerations might lead one to dismiss improvised music as a poor relative to the real thing.

The dismissal of improvisation based on the alleged simplicity of the music, however common the view may be, is nevertheless too facile. For one thing, complexity, while often a feature of large masterworks in the canon of western classical music, especially in the form of contrapuntal polyphonic structure and elaboration, is not a necessary feature of highly valued music. Neither Beethoven's "Für Elise" (Bagatelle No. 25 in A minor) nor Debussy's "Rêverie" are possessed of that sort of complexity but they move us profoundly nonetheless. Similarly, when one listens to pianist John Lewis's solo improvisation on "Django," the tune he composed for the Modern Jazz Quartet 45 years earlier, what shines forth is not a dazzling display of melodic, rhythmic, or harmonic complexity but rather a quiet, spare, haunting eloquence that takes one's breath away. The elegance of Lewis's improvisation is, to use Nelson Goodman's term, *exemplified* in the performance, and, as Goodman puts it, exemplification is one of the "symptoms" of the aesthetic.[20] It is wrong to suppose, then, that complexity is necessary for musical excellence or that the so-called "simplicity" of improvised music, when it is encountered, cannot be aesthetically profound.

Moreover, many improvisations do exhibit an extraordinary level of musical complexity that one can appreciate in the same ways one can appreciate composed notated music: in performance, by way of recordings, or through an imaginal reconstruction by way of transcription. All one has to do to witness the truth of this claim is to listen to or, if one has the relevant musical skills, examine one of the many transcriptions of improvisations such as tenor saxophonist Sonny Rollins's "You Don't Know What Love Is" or pianist Bill Evans's "Very Early" in order to appreciate the heights of melodic, harmonic, rhythmic, and structural complexities and rewards that improvised music, understood as spontaneous musical compositions, can achieve.[21] The fact that these pieces were composed, so to speak, on the spot, of course adds to one's admiration for what has been achieved, but the relevant point here is that one need make no apologies for these stunning musical achievements on their own terms.

Indeed, the notion of musical complexity itself needs to be carefully examined since, under the model of western classical music, it is often taken to refer primarily to contrapuntal and harmonic interest. This is too narrow a conception. As Garry Hagberg has argued, the improvisational treatment of rhythm, for example, can also exhibit a high degree of subtle and complex interest. One thinks not only of the handling of syncopation and *ritardandos* that play with and against imaginary metrical ideals and that figure into many styles of music, classical and otherwise, but also of other rhythmic explorations that are so often fundamental features of improvised music, such as the superimposition of different pulses against time signatures, playing on, behind, and in front of the beat, and moving phrases across bar lines in the case of modern jazz.[22] The same can be said for transformations of timbre, another important feature of improvised jazz. The signature tones of players such as Charlie Rouse, John Coltrane, Coleman Hawkins, Lee Konitz, Art Farmer, Jack Sheldon, Maynard Ferguson, and Miles Davis are instantly recognizable, and what can be done to modulate timbre by means of growls, shakes, mutes, and various constrictions and expansions of sound play an important role in the musical interest. It is open to critics of improvisation to reply that these latter examples evince not complexity, but something else—"intricacy," perhaps. But by this time, if one grants that intricacy, too, can capture one's discerning attention and appreciation, one begins to wonder what the point of the original criticism was.

It should also be pointed out that in cases when an improvisation is based on a previously composed work, for example Coltrane's famous 14-minute improvisation on "My Favorite Things," it is possible to regard the performance in terms of many of the same evaluative criteria one would apply to conventional performances of works. In particular, one can pay attention to the interplay of interpretive sensitivity, stylistic adaptation and transformation, and authenticity to the work, or to the spirit of the work, all of which are as appropriate to Coltrane's performance as they would be to, say, Vladimir Ashkenazy's 1996 performance of Chopin's Nocturne No. 5 in F-sharp, Op. 15/2. To this extent, the appreciation of improvisations is very much like the appreciation of performances of conventional, composed works.

ONTOLOGICAL CONSIDERATIONS II: MUSICAL IMPROVISATION AS AN ACTIVITY

At a more fundamental level, however, it would be a mistake to limit one's attention to improvisations as if they were simply composed works that happened to be produced more or less spontaneously. The ontology of musical improvisations is rather more complex than an application of the aesthetic object model would lead us to believe. The first complication that musical improvisation presents to the ontology of music is that, if one asks, "What is it that the improviser creates," the answer is that while an improviser often does create a musical object that may be understood along the lines of the traditional composed musical work, the improviser also simultaneously creates a different sort of entity: a productive *activity*. In listening to improvisations, we are witnessing the shaping activity of the performer as if we have gained privileged access to the performer's mind at the moment of spontaneous creation. Musical improvisation activity is not a matter of unadulterated spontaneity or a creation *ex nihilo*; nor is it a mere shuffling of formulae or motifs, as Adorno would have it. The activity of improvisation is analogous to speaking: improvisation is a kind of musical utterance, a musical utterance not requiring another individual to "perform" one's musical creation, presented within the constraints of musical possibilities.[23] This is one of the reasons why the notion of a personal style is so central to the activity of improvisation. Improvisation is a productive, not merely reproductive, activity in which we perceive the relation of individual intelligence and intention to action.

PLAYING ON THE CHANGES

We witness the relationship of intelligence to action especially in improvised jazz where the activity often consists less in ornamenting a melody than in developing transformations on harmonic progressions and patterns. It is noteworthy that even in cases where improvisers do improvise on a pre-existing work—as in the familiar situation where a jazz player improvises on a tune standard in the repertoire—the focus is typically on the particular activity of what the improviser does in the context of the "changes," that is, a given harmonic pattern. Perhaps the most common harmonic pattern in modern jazz, the chord progression from George Gershwin's song, "I Got Rhythm," forms the basis for dozens of well-known jazz tunes, including Charlie Parker's "Anthropology," Ornette Coleman's "Chippie," Sonny Stitt's "Boppin a Riff," Count Basie's "Jumpin' at the Woodside," Lester Young's "Lester Leaps In," Nat King Cole's "Straighten Up and Fly Right," and even the theme from *The Flintstones* written by Hoyt Curtain. When improvisers improvise on the "Rhythm" changes, do they focus on the melodic features of the variant composition? Of course, they may and often do build on some of the melodic elements. Typically, however, the focus is on the use of the harmonic changes of the tune. One pays attention to musical creation against the backdrop of the harmonic structure or chordal progression. As a matter of practice, what guides the improviser's activity is the set of shorthand chord symbols above the staff on a lead sheet, not the melody, still less the lyrics, even if the lyrics are well known.[24] If there is a discussion among players before the tune begins, it is usually about possible chord substitutions or perhaps metrical issues, but all in the context of the harmonic picture. The emphasis on creation in a harmonic surrounding remains the same even when that environment is modal rather than a series of more rigidly defined chord progressions. If the typical jazz improvisation is an interpretation of anything, it is an interpretation of a harmonic setting, not of a pre-existing compositional work, even in cases where the improvised performance is—nominally—of a pre-existing work. Analogously, improvisations on *ragas* in Indian classical music may emphasize melodic modes more than harmonic patterns as points of departure but the point to be made is that here, too, the center of the improvisational practice revolves around the transformations within a set a scalar-based structural orientations rather than particular compositions.

LIMITATIONS OF THE WORK CONCEPT

In making these observations I wish to emphasize several things. First, we need not think of the philosophical understanding of improvisation as requiring the notion of a work at all. Of course, one *can* profitably think of improvisational activities to a certain extent as being work-like: in the case of composed music and improvisations we attend to the expression of human design or intention, as I have argued previously. To that extent musical improvisation exhibits a fundamental—if partial—continuity with composed music.[25] Similarly, thanks especially to the advent of recording technology, there is a limited sense in which we can regard a recorded improvisation as acquiring something like a work identity, as for example in the case of iconic performances sedimented into musical culture.[26] Think, for example, of Coleman Hawkins's 1939 improvisation on "Body and Soul," famously re-presented by Eddie Jefferson (1959) and The Manhattan Transfer (1988), Paul Desmond's 1959 alto solo on Dave Brubeck's "Take Five" on the *Time Out* album, or Freddie Hubbard's 1964 trumpet solo on Herbie Hancock's "Cantaloupe Island" on the *Empyrean Isles* album.

However, given the very wide range of musical practices that are improvisatory even just in the case of jazz—live improvisations, recorded improvisations, improvisations on existing works, free jazz, jazz heavily mediated by studio engineers, jazz in which players record multiple tracks and then combine them, and so on—it does not seem likely that we will be able to avail ourselves of a single ontological covering model.[27] This does not mean abandoning the idea of understanding the ontology of music. Rather it means that the object of philosophical understanding should be, above all, descriptive, centered in the first instance on musical practices themselves and the structure of our thought about them.[28] It is practice that must drive philosophical theory.

SPONTANEITY, FREEDOM, AND RISK

When we take such an approach we are drawn to one fundamental feature of musical improvisation: it is an activity that draws our attention to music as a living enterprise, as something that reflects human inspiration. Again, this is not something unique to improvised music. The great conductor Wilhelm Furtwängler urged, for example, that performances of classical composed music should follow what he called the "law of improvisation," infusing themselves with the vital processes of growth that characterized the composition's origins. Conductors, he complained, too often strive to nail down every effect in rehearsal, a habit he puts down to conductors' anxiety about the musical unknown, their being bedeviled by the fact that musical works can be written down and studied, and their tendency to see works as instantiating unalterable and predestined musical forms.[29] Indeed, one could make the argument that in a certain sense improvisation is an indispensable *Ur*-activity of all musical creation, a position that Furtwängler may have had in mind.

What is remarkable about improvised music, however, is the extent to which it puts human freedom on display, if we may put it that way. It is not simply that improvisers produce a series of linked musical events that we see as concatenated moments or even as the synthesis of such parts. It is rather that we see human agency in action. We appreciate spontaneous human achievement within the realm of the musically possible. As Bill Evans has remarked, everything is done in "the process of making one minute's music in one minute's time,"[30] and we appreciate the significance of the human achievement involved in the activity. In all this, the elements of spontaneity and risk are central.

It is possible to appreciate this sense of spontaneity, of the idea of creation in the moment, even in the case of recordings of improvisations that I mentioned earlier. The phenomenology of this process is quite interesting. I would suggest that it is possible—and common—for listeners to put themselves in a kind of bracketed situation in which one imagines oneself into hearing the improvisation as if for the first time, even if one is listening to a recorded improvisation one has heard many times. We are all familiar with this kind of imaginal appreciation. It is the kind of mental state that children adopt when they ask to be told bedtime stories they have heard many times before. Each time it is as if one is hearing the story anew. Or perhaps it is akin to the first moments of tasting a meal that one has enjoyed many times in the past. In the case of recording improvisations, one hears them, as it were, in the subjunctive voice rather than the present indicative.[31]

SKILLS AND THE REPERTOIRE

One of the chief ways in which improvisatory spontaneity, freedom, and risk play out is in the exercising of musical *skills*: not simply the deployment of rudimentary skills (playing correct notes, etc.), but rather, the ability of the improviser to create music spontaneously with significant expressive and aesthetic qualities, to engage in stylistic transformations (juxtaposing different styles or quoting melodies, harmonies, and rhythms in the repertoire), and to develop long- and short-term musical constructions. There are also skills involved in reactive ensemble playing, whether as a soloist or in accompanying roles, engaging in various "conversational" protocols with other players. Here one attends to the social graces of improvisational etiquette by observing standard conventions about the length and order of solos, by showing respect to your immediately preceding soloist by building your solo on a musical phrase he or she has left you, and so on. In these ways, improvisatory skills and activities have both musical and social dimensions.[32]

To someone immersed in the practice, whether as improviser or as a member of an audience, many of these skills involve an understanding of how the improviser works in the context of a musical repertoire. The repertoire is a fluid or dynamic kind of thing rather than a discrete list of items. From the standpoint of the improviser, one sees the repertoire as a set of common terms that enables musical exchanges, often with complete strangers on the bandstand, as well as being a fount of materials to be mined and adapted as one "woodsheds" to build one's "chops" (i.e., one practices to develop one's improvisational facility and creativity).

The idea of the repertoire has important implications for what we take to count as creation, creativity, and transformation in musical improvisation, as well as how one conceives the philosophy, aims, and pedagogical practices of improvised music education. The notion of a "standard" repertoire, for example, turns out to be a moving target. On the one hand it is quite something to discover that a jazz improviser can move from Hartford to Toronto to Graz to Hanoi and find that, thanks to the proliferation of collections of standard tunes in recordings and in "fake books" such as the *Real Book*, musicians who may not share the same natural language nevertheless have a considerable shared working repertoire, knowing dozens of the same tunes, even knowing which keys are standard for which tunes. Even the hand signals for "Let's go to the head of the tune" or "Let's play this in B-flat" travel well.

At the same time, the idea of the repertoire is premised on there being a relatively stable common musical culture. Musical tastes and modes of musical distribution change, as do the venues in which adepts learn the repertoire. It is a common complaint among improvisation teachers that the current generation of students doesn't seem interested in learning the repertoire that their teachers might have learned in the clubs. This is not surprising, since the days of large touring jazz bands are a thing of the past and jazz clubs are themselves a vanishing phenomenon, even in large cities known in the past for such things. That is to say, changes in the range of places in which improvised music is played have much to do with the musical context against which we understand the vocabulary and range of possibilities and achievements in improvised jazz. Much interesting empirical work on this subject has been done by sociologists of music.[33] In any case, it is clear that the range of improvisatory skills deployed, the improvisational repertoire, and improvisational practice in general have both musical and social dimensions and, further, that a full appreciation of the music rests on an understanding of these aspects of the practice.

The Social Dimension

It is also essential for a philosophical understanding of musical improvisation that one take into account the political, national, ethnic, gendered, class, and racial dimensions of improvisation, and most especially, in the case of jazz, what has been called the

"Afrological" aspects of the music.[34] These are topics that have received considerable attention in recent years by those working in the fields of cultural studies, Pan-African studies, and musicology, but they have received notice by only a handful of philosophers. The debates, when they have been broached, have tended to focus on a set of interlocking issues concerning a range of social and political meanings that are thought to pertain to improvised music and jazz in particular. Discussion has for the most part centered on the cultural provenance and lineage of features thought to be characteristic of improvised jazz ("blue" tonality, especially flat 3rds, 5ths, and 7ths, swing, jazz riffs, polyrhythmicality, musical breaks, "trading fours," etc.) and on the question of "Afropurism." The latter topic involves questions about whether improvised jazz is fundamentally related to the "African soul" or to black experience, whether and to what extent concepts such as "blackness" and "whiteness" can be deployed as analytic categories, whether improvised jazz can be construed as intellectual and cultural "property" owned by blacks (and hence something that can be stolen), and, finally, whether it is necessary to have access to dimensions of African-American experience encoded in the music to be able to perform it authentically or to appreciate it.[35]

There has also been some discussion of the alleged homosocial, misogynist, and male exclusionary proclivities of jazz.[36] The case of Billy Tipton, a talented and well-known woman jazz pianist who found it necessary to cross-dress and live as a man for over 50 years so as not to fall victim to gender discrimination, certainly gives one pause for thought. One does hear the sentiment uttered from time to time that a woman "plays like a man." The comment is usually intended as a compliment but if it is a compliment, it is a left-handed one. Apart from the implied criticism that the player falls short of an ideal, the comment rests on the twin assumptions that one can discern "male" and "female" styles of improvisatory playing and that, assuming one can maintain the distinction, male styles are to be taken as normative.

From the standpoint of method, because the social world is a complex of many factors, a full consideration of these issues would also benefit from what feminist theorists have called "intersectionality," roughly, the idea that social experience is not constituted by a single social category but rather is the product of the mutual constitution of race, gender, class, national identity, and so on. And so, for example, the issue of the role of women in jazz is also a function of certain assumptions regarding heteronormativity and certain myths about black hypersexuality and the eroticism of black masculinity.[37] The effects of socio-economic conditions must also be thought to be a part of the picture. It is one thing to gesture toward stereotypical pictures of jazz musicians as outliers to the system; it is another to confront the realities.[38] Even regional differences can play a role in the mix and can affect stylistic issues, as for example in the many differences among East Coast, West Coast, New Orleans, Kansas City, Chicago, and New York jazz styles and instrumentation. It is interesting that so many well-known jazz organ players (Jimmy Smith, Lou Bennett, Joey DeFrancesco, Bill Doggett, Charles Earland, Jimmy McGriff, Trudy Pitts, and Shirley Scott) came out of Philadelphia, for example. What, if anything, does this tell us about the development and relevant evaluative criteria for this genre?

Now it is possible to take a skeptical position regarding the idea that one is warranted in ascribing social meanings to improvised music in general, and to jazz in particular. It has been argued, for example, that jazz can be enjoyed solely for its "purely musical" qualities alone, that one need not see jazz as a musical representation of oppression, racism, ethnicity, or any other aspect of, for example, "the black experience," and, indeed, that it is implausible to ascribe such meanings to jazz since they cannot be heard directly "in the music."[39] The question of what is to count as what is "in" the music, however, is, as we have seen, a fraught one that depends crucially on what one takes to be "the music." As I have been arguing to this point, the skeptical position, put in this way, relies on autonomist and sonicist ontological commitments that have only limited applicability to the case of improvised music.

Coda

In this essay I have tried to indicate some of the ways in which the orienting concepts of the philosophy of music have an application to the practice of musical improvisation and some of the ways in which improvised music is resistant to those categories and calls for a different kind of orientation to music. Throughout the essay I have urged that philosophical inquiry not constrain itself by presuming that improvised music can be understood adequately under an aesthetic theory focused unduly on the centrality of aesthetic objects, mono-functionality, the paradigm of European classical music, and the spectatorialist perspective, even while acknowledging the usefulness of these concepts and tenets to particular aspects of improvised music. I have argued instead for the philosophical consideration of the gamut of improvisational activity, including the aesthetic aspects of musical improvisation, the range of musical and social skills made manifest by improvisers, and the deeper social meanings of the practice, including the implicit reference to human freedom and more particular situated meanings that arise from the national, ethnic, racial, gendered, and socio-economic contexts in which the music arises. It is through these and related aspects of what is presented in and what is represented by improvised jazz that a sense of community among members of the practice is developed.

In the interests of space I have not been able to discuss all the ways in which improvised music calls for a more robust philosophical understanding than is provided for by the aesthetic tradition. I have not discussed, for instance, the effects of the advent of musical recording, technologies of music distribution, and advances in the technology of musical instruments in improvisational practice that have been a continuous feature of its history, from Louis Armstrong's early recordings to Les Paul's experiments with multiple guitar pickups, Bill Evans's multi-track musical conversations with himself, and Lionel Loueke's use of the harmonizer pitch shifter, the Whammy pedal, and a specially designed Rolf Spuler guitar.[40]

What I do think is essential, however, is to bear in mind that a philosophy of improvised music will at once have to be theoretically nuanced, empirically informed, phenomenologically sensitive, and ineliminably indexed to the manifold ways in which improvised music situates itself in the complex of human affairs.[41]

NOTES

1. Gilbert Ryle, "Improvisation," *Mind* 85, no. 337 (January 1976): 69–83.
2. Ryle, "Improvisation," 70.
3. See Francis Sparshott, *The Future of Aesthetics* (Toronto: University of Toronto Press, 1998), 101.
4. See for example J. A. Passmore's infamous and provocative "The Dreariness of Aesthetics," *Mind* 60, no. 239 (July 1951): 318–335.
5. Two notable exceptions to this state of affairs in journal scholarship are the special issue of the *Journal of Aesthetics and Art Criticism* 58, no. 2 (Spring 2000) on improvisation in the arts and the *Journal of Aesthetics and Art Criticism* 68, no. 3 (Summer 2010) symposium on musical improvisation.
6. Eduard Hanslick, *On the Musically Beautiful*, trans. Geoffrey Payzant (1891; repr. Indianapolis: Hackett Publishing Company, 1986), 49, 82.
7. See, for example, Theodor Adorno, *Introduction to the Sociology of Music*, trans. E. B. Ashton (New York: Seabury Press, 1976), 15.
8. Theodor Adorno, "Über den Fetischcharakter in der Musik und die Regression des Hörens," *Zeitschrift für Sozialforschung* 7, no. 3 (1938): 349 (my translation, emphasis added). (*So ist die souveräne Routine des Jazzamateurs nichts anderes als die passive Fähigkeit, in der Adaptation der Modelle von nichts sich irremachen zu lassen. Er ist das wahre Jazzsubjekt: seine Improvisationen kommen aus dem Schema, und das Schema steuert er, die Zigarette im Mund, so nachlässig, als hätte er es gerade selber erfunden.*)
9. See Alan Stanbridge, "From the Margins to the Mainstream: Jazz, Social Relations, and Discourses of Value," *Critical Studies in Improvisation / Études critiques en improvisation* 4, no. 1 (2008), http://www.criticalimprov.com/article/view/361. The efforts of Wynton Marsalis and others to present jazz as "America's classical music" only serves to underscore the hold of the mainstream view. I shall not dignify by means of inclusion in the body of the text openly racist denigrations of jazz, but for an early castigation of jazz with heavy racial inflection by a well-known art and cultural theorist of the time, see Clive Bell, "Plus De Jazz," *The New Republic* 28, no. 355 (September 21, 1921): 92–96.
10. In thinking about these matters one might be tempted to wonder about the social psychology and the "disciplining" of the discourse itself, in particular the question of whether the invisibility and disparagement of musical improvisation in philosophical circles may have something to do with the cultural prestige of the activity in question. Is it the case that young scholars—or even older ones—feel safer talking about examples from the realm of high culture, thinking perhaps that alluding to The Greats somehow places one's argument on a more secure footing? One can't entirely dismiss the speculation. But neither can one place much confidence in it. In the end this kind of psychologizing is an imponderable, even if it should turn out that in some cases something of the sort has a role to play.
11. For the 1941–1991 figures see Lydia Goehr, "The Institutionalization of a Discipline: A Retrospective of *The Journal of Aesthetics and Art Criticism* and the American Society for

Aesthetics, 1939–1992," *The Journal of Aesthetics and Art Criticism* 51, no. 2 (Spring 1993): 114, table 2. The 1991–2011 percentage is from my count.

12. See Paul Oskar Kristeller, "The Modern System of the Arts," In *Renaissance Thought II: Papers on Humanism and the Arts* (New York: Harper & Row), 1965, 163–227.

13. This analysis follows my essay, Philip Alperson, "Facing the Music: Voices from the Margins," *Topoi: An International Review of Philosophy* 28, no. 2 (September, 2009): 91–96.

14. The first 50 years of the *JAAC*, during which time the ASA moved from being an interdisciplinary society whose membership included philosophers, psychologists, anthropologists, artists, and art historians to an institution predominantly populated by analytic philosophers, saw a 475% increase in the number of articles published on the ontology of art, far outstripping the increase of any other topic. See Goehr, "The Institutionalization," 115.

15. See Julian Dodd, *Works of Music: An Essay in Ontology* (Oxford: Oxford University Press, 2007). See esp. chap. 1; and Julian Dodd, "Confessions of an Unrepentant Timbral Sonicist," *British Journal of Aesthetics* 50, no. 1 (January 2010): 33–52.

16. See for example Denis Dutton's eight criteria of for an artwork: (1) source of pleasure in itself, (2) exercise of a specialized skill, (3) made in a recognizable style, (4) existence of a critical language to discuss it, (5) represents in some degree of naturalism, (6) intention of makers to produce a work that will provide pleasure, (7) frequently bracketed off from ordinary life, and (8) affords an imaginative experience; Denis Dutton, " 'But They Don't Have Our Concept of Art,' " in *Theories of Art Today*, ed. Noël Carroll (Madison: University of Wisconsin Press, 2000), 217–240. Or consider Berys Gaut's list of ten criteria that count toward an object's falling under the concept of art (1) possessing positive aesthetic qualities, (2) expression of emotion, (3) intellectually challenging, (4) formal complexity and coherence, (5) capacity to convey complex meanings, (6) exhibiting an individual point of view, (7) being an exercise of creative imagination, (8) being an artifact or performance that is a product of a high degree of skill, (9) belonging to an established art form, (10) being the product of an intention to make a work of art. See Berys Gaut, "The Cluster Account of Art Defended," *British Journal of Aesthetics* 45, no. 3 (July 2005): 273–288.

17. On this see Lydia Goehr, *The Imaginary Museum of Musical Works: An Essay in the Philosophy of Music*, revised edition (Oxford and New York: Clarendon Press, 2007).

18. See for example Jerrold Levinson's classic and justly celebrated essay, "What a Musical Work Is," *Journal of Philosophy* 77, no. 1 (January 1980): 5–28.

19. Alan Goldman, "The Value of Music," *The Journal of Aesthetics and Art Criticism* 50, no. 1 (Winter 1992): 42.

20. Nelson Goodman, *Languages of Art: An Approach to a Theory of Symbols* (Indianapolis: Hackett Publishing Company, 1976), 52–57 and 252–255.

21. Hear Sonny Rollins, "You Don't Know What Love Is," on *Saxophone Colossus*, compact disc, Fantasy/Prestige Records 1881052, 2006, originally released in 1956 on Prestige Records LP 7079, vinyl disc; and Bill Evans, "Very Early," on *Moon Beams*, compact disc, Fantasy/OJC Remasters OJC33718 (2012), originally released in 1962 on Riverside Records OJC20 434-2, vinyl disc.

22. Garry Hagberg, "On Rhythm," *The Journal of Aesthetics and Art Criticism* 68, no. 3 (Summer 2010): 281–284.

23. I have argued this at greater length in Philip Alperson, "On Musical Improvisation," *The Journal of Aesthetics and Art Criticism* 43, no. 1 (Autumn, 1984): 17–29.

24. Thus a set of changes for "I Got Rhythm" in Bb might be:
    | Bb Gm7 | Cm7 F7 | Bb Gm7 | Cm F7 |

Bb Gm7	Cm7 F7	Bb Gm7	Cm F7
D7	G7	C	Cm7 F#7 F7
Bb Gm7	Cm7 F7	Bb Gm7	Cm F7

25. "Partial" because it is hard to see how two improvised performances can be said to instantiate the same type. On this see Alperson, "On Musical Improvisation," 24–27. For a view that the work concept has a stronger applicability to jazz improvisations, see James O. Young and Carl Matheson, "The Metaphysics of Jazz," *The Journal of Aesthetics and Art Criticism* 58, no. 2 (Spring 2000): 125–133.

26. See Lee B. Brown, "Phonography," in *Aesthetics: A Reader in Philosophy of the Arts*, ed. David Goldblatt and Lee Brown (Upper Saddle River, NJ: Pearson, 1996), 252–257.

27. For a recent treatment of these issues see Lee B. Brown, "Do Higher-Order Music Ontologies Rest on a Mistake?" *British Journal of Aesthetics* 51, no. 2 (April 2011): 168–184.

28. On this see Andrew Kania, "The Methodology of Musical Ontology," *British Journal of Aesthetics* 48, no. 4 (October 2008): 426–444; and "New Waves in Musical Ontology," in *New Waves in Aesthetics*, ed. Kathleen Stock and Katherine Thomson-Jones (Basingstoke: Palgrave Macmillan, 2008), 20–40; Peter Strawson, *Individuals: An Essay in Descriptive Metaphysics* (Garden City, NY: Anchor, 1963), from which Kania takes the term "descriptive metaphysics"; and Alperson, "Facing the Music."

29. Wilhelm Furtwängler, *Concerning Music*, trans. L. J. Lawrence (London: Boosey and Hawkes, 1953), 46–52.

30. Bill Evans, *The Universal Mind of Bill Evans* (New York: Rhapsody Films, 1966; Andorra: EFOR Films DVD 2869016, n.d.).

31. I thank Andreas Dorschel for this nice formulation.

32. On this see Philip Alperson, "A Topography of Improvisation," *The Journal of Aesthetics and Art Criticism* 68, no. 3 (Summer 2010): 273–280.

33. See for example Robert Faulkner, "Shedding Culture," in *Art from Start to Finish: Jazz, Painting, Writing, and Other Improvisations*, ed. Howard Becker, Robert Faulkner, and Barbara Kirshenblatt-Gimblett (Chicago: University of Chicago Press, 2006), 91–117; and Robert Faulkner and Howard Becker, "*Do You Know . . .?*": *The Jazz Repertoire in Action* (Chicago: University of Chicago Press, 2009).

34. See George E. Lewis, "Improvised Music after 1950: Afrological and Eurological Perspectives," *Black Music Research Journal* 16, no. 1 (1996): 91–122.

35. See, in addition to Lewis, Lee Brown, "Jazz," *Oxford Encyclopedia of Aesthetics*, edited by Michael Kelly, Oxford Art Online, Oxford University Press (2008), accessed February 4, 2014, http://www.oxfordartonline.com/subscriber/article/opr/t234/e0303; LeRoi Jones, *Blues People: Negro Music in White America* (New York: W. Morrow, 1971); Imamu Amiri Baraka and Amina Baraka, *The Music: Reflections on Jazz and Blues* (New York: Morrow, 1987); Joel Rudinow, "Race, Ethnicity, Expressive Authenticity: Can White People Sing the Blues?," in *The Journal of Aesthetics and Art Criticism* 52, no. 1 (Winter 1994): 127–137; and Alperson, "A Topography."

36. See Hazel V. Carby, "It Jus Be's Dat Way Sometime: The Sexual Politics of Women's Blues," in *The Jazz Cadence of American Culture*, ed. Robert O'Meally (New York: Columbia University Press, 1998), 469–482; and Hazel Carby, *Race Men* (Cambridge, MA: Harvard University Press, 2000).

37. See Sherrie Tucker, "When Did Jazz Go Straight: A Queer Question for Jazz Studies," in "Sexualities in Improvisation," special issue, *Critical Studies in Improvisation / Études critiques en improvisation* 4, no. 2 (2008), http://www.criticalimprov.com/article/view/850.

38. See Joan Jeffri, *Changing the Beat: A Study in the Worklife of Jazz Musicians*, National Endowment for the Arts Research Division Report, no. 43, 3 vols. (Washington, DC: National Endowment for the Arts, 2003). The sensitive and moving films *Round Midnight* (1986) by Bernard Tavernier and *Bird* (1988) by Clint Eastwood also provide important perspectives.

39. See Bill E. Lawson, "Jazz and the African-American Experience: The Expressiveness of African-American Music," in *Language, Art and Mind: Essays in Appreciation and Analysis in Honor of Paul Ziff*, ed. Dale Jameson (Leiden: Kluwer Academic, 1994), 131–142.

40. Not every technological advance is a musical advance, of course, as the use of the much-reviled drum machine makes clear.

41. I would like to thank Uschi Brunner, Andreas Dorschel, Mary Hawkesworth, Elisabeth Kappel, and Deniz Peters for helpful suggestions. I would also like to thank the faculty and students at the Institute for Aesthetics at the Universität für Musik und Darstellende Kunst in Graz, Austria where much of the research for this essay was developed.

Bibliography

Adorno, Theodor. *Introduction to the Sociology of Music*. Translated by E. B. Ashton. New York: Seabury Press, 1976.

Adorno, Theodor. "Über den Fetischcharakter in der Musik und die Regression des Hörens." *Zeitschrift für Sozialforschung* 7, no. 3 (1938): 321–356.

Alperson, Philip. "Facing the Music: Voices from the Margins." *Topoi: An International Review of Philosophy* 28, no. 2 (September 2009): 91–96.

Alperson, Philip. "On Musical Improvisation." *The Journal of Aesthetics and Art Criticism* 43, no. 1 (Autumn 1984): 17–29.

Alperson, Philip. "A Topography of Improvisation." *The Journal of Aesthetics and Art Criticism* 68, no. 3 (Summer 2010): 273–280.

Baraka, Imamu Amiri, and Amina Baraka. *The Music: Reflections on Jazz and Blues*. New York: Morrow, 1987.

Bell, Clive. "Plus De Jazz." *The New Republic* 28, no. 355 (September 21, 1921): 92–96.

Brown, Lee B. "Phonography." In *Aesthetics: A Reader in Philosophy of the Arts*, edited by David Goldblatt and Lee Brown, 252–257. Upper Saddle River, NJ: Pearson, 1996.

Brown, Lee B. "Jazz." *The Oxford Encyclopedia of Aesthetics*, edited by Michael Kelly. *Oxford Art Online*, Oxford University Press (2008), accessed February 4, 2014, http://www.oxfordartonline.com/subscriber/article/opr/t234/e0303.

Brown, Lee B. "Do Higher-Order Music Ontologies Rest on a Mistake?" *British Journal of Aesthetics* 51, no. 2 (April 2011): 168–184.

Carby, Hazel V. "It Jus Be's Dat Way Sometime: The Sexual Politics of Women's Blues." In *The Jazz Cadence of American Culture*, edited by Robert O'Meally, 469–482. New York: Columbia University Press, 1998.

Carby, Hazel V. *Race Men*. Cambridge, MA: Harvard University Press, 2000.

Dodd, Julian. *Works of Music: An Essay in Ontology*. Oxford: Oxford University Press, 2007.

Dodd, Julian. "Confessions of an Unrepentant Timbral Sonicist." *British Journal of Aesthetics* 50, no. 1 (January 2010): 33–52.

Dutton, Denis. "'But They Don't Have Our Concept of Art.'" In *Theories of Art Today*, edited by Noël Carroll, 217–240. Madison: University of Wisconsin Press, 2000.

Evans, Bill. "Very Early." On *Moon Beams*. Compact disc. Fantasy/OJC Remasters OJC33718 (2012), originally released in 1962 on Riverside Records OJC20 434-2, vinyl disc.

Evans, Bill. *The Universal Mind of Bill Evans*. New York: Rhapsody Films, 1966; Andorra: EFOR Films DVD 2869016, n.d.

Faulkner, Robert. "Shedding Culture." In *Art from Start to Finish: Jazz, Painting, Writing, and Other Improvisations*, edited by Howard Becker, Robert Faulkner, and Barbara Kirshenblatt-Gimblett, 91–117. Chicago: University of Chicago Press, 2006.

Faulkner, Robert, and Howard Becker. *"Do You Know . . . ?": The Jazz Repertoire in Action*. Chicago: University of Chicago Press, 2009.

Furtwängler, Wilhelm. *Concerning Music*. Translated by L. J. Lawrence. London: Boosey and Hawkes, 1953.

Gaut, Berys. "The Cluster Account of Art Defended." *British Journal of Aesthetics* 45, no. 3 (July 2005): 273–288.

Goehr, Lydia. *The Imaginary Museum of Musical Works: An Essay in the Philosophy of Music*. revised edition. Oxford and New York: Clarendon Press, 2007.

Goehr, Lydia. "The Institutionalization of a Discipline: A Retrospective of *The Journal of Aesthetics and Art Criticism* and the American Society for Aesthetics, 1939–1992." *The Journal of Aesthetics and Art Criticism* 51, no. 2 (Spring 1993): 91–121.

Goldman, Alan. "The Value of Music." *The Journal of Aesthetics and Art Criticism* 50, no. 1 (Winter, 1992): 35–44.

Goodman, Nelson. *Languages of Art: An Approach to a Theory of Symbols*. Indianapolis: Hackett Publishing Company, 1976.

Hagberg, Garry L. "On Rhythm." *The Journal of Aesthetics and Art Criticism* 68, no. 3 (Summer 2010): 281–284.

Hanslick, Eduard. *On the Musically Beautiful*. Translated by Geoffrey Payzant. 1891. Reprint, Indianapolis: Hackett Publishing Company, 1986.

Jeffri, Joan. *Changing the Beat: A Study in the Worklife of Jazz Musicians*. National Endowment for the Arts Research Division Report, no. 43. 3 vols. Washington, D.C.: National Endowment for the Arts, 2003.

Jones, LeRoi. *Blues People: Negro Music in White America*. New York: W. Morrow, 1971.

Kania, Andrew. "The Methodology of Musical Ontology." *British Journal of Aesthetics* 48, no. 4 (October 2008): 426–444.

Kania, Andrew. "New Waves in Musical Ontology." In *New Waves in Aesthetics*, edited by Kathleen Stock and Katherine Thomson-Jones, 20–40. Basingstoke: Palgrave Macmillan, 2008.

Kristeller, Paul Oskar. "The Modern System of the Arts." In *Renaissance Thought II: Papers on Humanism and the Arts*, 163–227. New York: Harper & Row, 1965.

Lawson, Bill E. "Jazz and the African-American Experience: The Expressiveness of African-American Music." In *Language, Art and Mind: Essays in Appreciation and Analysis in Honor of Paul Ziff*, edited by Dale Jameson, 131–142. Leiden: Kluwer Academic, 1994.

Levinson, Jerrold. "What a Musical Work Is." *Journal of Philosophy* 77, no. 1 (January 1980): 5–28.

Lewis, George E. "Improvised Music after 1950: Afrological and Eurological Perspectives." *Black Music Research Journal* 16, no. 1 (1996): 91–122.

Passmore, J. A. "The Dreariness of Aesthetics." *Mind* 60, no. 239 (July 1951): 318–335.

Rollins, Sonny. "You Don't Know What Love Is." On *Saxophone Colossus*. Compact disc, Fantasy/Prestige Records 1881052 (2006), Originally released in 1956 on Prestige Records LP 7079.

Rudinow, Joel. "Race, Ethnicity, Expressive Authenticity: Can White People Sing the Blues?" *The Journal of Aesthetics and Art Criticism* 52, no. 1 (Winter 1994): 127–137.

Ryle, Gilbert. "Improvisation." *Mind* 85, no. 337 (January 1976): 69–83.

Sparshott, Francis. *The Future of Aesthetics*. Toronto: University of Toronto Press, 1998.

Stanbridge, Alan. "From the Margins to the Mainstream: Jazz, Social Relations, and Discourses of Value." *Critical Studies in Improvisation / Études critiques en improvisation* 4, no. 1 (2008). http://www.criticalimprov.com/article/view/361.

Strawson, Peter. *Individuals: An Essay in Descriptive Metaphysics*. Garden City, NY: Anchor, 1963.

Tucker, Sherrie. "When Did Jazz Go Straight: A Queer Question for Jazz Studies." *Critical Studies in Improvisation / Études critiques en improvisation* 4, no. 2 (2008). http://www.criticalimprov.com/article/view/850.

Young, James O., and Carl Matheson. "The Metaphysics of Jazz." *The Journal of Aesthetics and Art Criticism* 58, no. 2 (Spring 2000): 125–133.

CHAPTER 25

IMPROVISATION AND TIME-CONSCIOUSNESS

GARY PETERS

ADORNO always insisted that art could not express joy; indeed, that the very enjoyment of art (by the artist and/or the art-loving pleasure-seeker) signaled the bourgeois trivialization and, worse, ideological obfuscation of the despairing heart of modernity: "If you ask a musician if he enjoys playing his instrument, he will probably reply: 'I hate it,' just like the grimacing cellist in the American joke."[1] Not a very cheery start, but then it might be argued that a crucial aspect of Adorno's "logic of disintegration"[2] is to remain partially situated within the moment of dialectical nonidentity described by Hegel in *The Phenomenology of Mind* as the "unhappy consciousness,"[3] where self-consciousness witnesses and suffers the "unchangeableness" of universality as an unattainable beyond, leaving only a "shattered certainty of itself"[4] trapped within the fleeting temporality of particularity. Disintegration, or to use Hegel's terminology, "disunity," is thus conceived as the root of unhappiness and is thereby seen as being responsible for the appearance and increasing dominance of *yearning* as an existential and aesthetic category.

To yearn—the post-romantic predicament *par excellence*—is to enter a regime of desire where the diremption of self and other—of selfhood and otherness—shatters both space and time into a "spurious"[5] infinitude of dislocated subjects eternally striving toward an absolute unity forever denied. This, for Hegel, is why art, understood as the aesthetic enjoyment and expression of yearning, must be superseded and why, for Adorno, it must, on the contrary, be defended as the *promesse de bonheur* issued from an unhappy world. Thus, art can only promise happiness; it can never *be* happy itself. To be so would be to enjoy callously the very being and suffering of disintegration and dislocation, something unthinkable for Adorno but which we will nevertheless attempt to think through with reference to improvisation.

Thinking about and beyond Hegel's notion of the "unhappy consciousness," Kierkegaard, in the first volume of *Either/Or*, reflects on the empty grave to be found in Worcester inscribed with these words: "The Unhappiest Man."[6] Setting out to determine what might constitute not just unhappiness but the unhappiest unhappiness, he begins with a gloss on Hegel's account:

> The unhappy person is one who has his ideal, the content of his life, the fullness of his consciousness, the essence of his being, in some manner outside of himself. He is always absent, never present to himself. But it is evident that it is possible to be absent from one's self either in the past or in the future.[7]

It is the final sentence of this passage that begins to open out onto the terrain that will be scrutinized as we now begin to consider the relationship between time, happiness, and improvisation. Kierkegaard continues thus:

> Now there are some individuals who live in hope, and others who live in memory. These are indeed in a sense unhappy individuals, in so far, namely, as they live solely in hope or in memory, if ordinarily only he is happy who is present to himself. However, one cannot in a strict sense be called an unhappy individual, who is present in hope or memory.[8]

If, by implication, happiness requires the self to be self-present in the present ("in the moment"), then Kierkegaard's version of unhappiness recognizes that, although perceived as a diminution of happiness, the temporal dislocation of the self remains a happy unhappiness to the extent that it still provides the self with the presence it desires, albeit in the future as hope or in the past as memory. Strictly speaking, as he recognizes, it is only when the self is not present to itself in its hope or memory that we should speak of unhappiness, of hopeless hope, or a past denied.

But even this is not the unhappiest unhappiness, for which Kierkegaard reserves a particular and, on the face of it, peculiar form of temporal confusion where "it is memory which prevents the unhappy individual from finding himself in hope, and hope which prevents him from finding himself in memory."[9]

> Consequently, what he hopes for lies behind him, what he remembers lies before him. His life is not so much lived regressively as it suffers a two-fold reversal. . . . His life is restless and without content; he does not live in the present, he does not live in the future, for the future has already been experienced; he does not live in the past, for the past has not yet come. . . . [H]e cannot love, for love is in the present, and he has no present, no future and no past.[10]

So here we arrive at the opposite pole to being "in the moment," witness to a state of radical unhappiness that, through the dual processes of hopeless striving and forgetful misrecognition, propels the self forever outside of itself into a temporal vacuum incapable of sustaining life, love, or indeed the love of life. Whatever truth is contained in this, it is clear that Hegel, Kierkegaard, and Adorno all recognize that, even if it turns out to be no life at all, such a predicament is certainly capable of sustaining an *aesthetic life*. In other words, within the post-romantic period at least, art practice actually flourishes within the predicament of being *out* of the moment and to this extent the valorization of being "in the moment" would represent, if anything, the *end* of art, the vanishing moment of sated aesthetic desire: anti-art. Unless, of course, being "in the moment" turns out to be something more complex or something other than the absolute self-presence it is commonly assumed to be: *that* is the question.

If being "in the moment" remains the ambition of many improvisers, and if such *in-ness* speaks of an achieved (if only fleeting) self-presence within a momentous present, then can we, contra Adorno, speak of improvisation as a happy art form? Does the improvising musician necessarily hate playing his or her instrument? Does the ecstatic smile of the improvising dancer really only mask a contorted grimace, or are we in the presence of authentic joy and love? Certainly many of the discourses surrounding improvisation, in most cases written by improvisers themselves, would suggest a widespread commitment to the happiness agenda and a concomitant faith in the possibility, even the necessity, of self-presence as the goal of goals. The problem, however, is that the centripetal force of committed self-presencing, so common in the language and literature, is in danger of sucking all improvisatory practice into a vortex of enjoyment that drowns out those voices that would speak differently, and perhaps with less joy, of the experience of time past and time future.

So, starting at the opposite pole—the unhappiest unhappiness—what, if anything, can "the unhappiest man" teach us about art practice in general and improvisation in particular? The "two-fold reversal" Kierkegaard speaks of certainly confronts a radical stripping away of self-presence that is no doubt as existentially tragic as it is aesthetically challenging, but what kind of art (if any) could such a predicament produce? What would unhappy, out-of-the-moment improvisation be like?

Here we need to look again and more carefully at Kierkegaard's "two-fold reversal," where hope and memory mutually efface each other. As a way of trying to grasp what seems on the face of it to be a slightly bizarre temporal confusion, we will now introduce into the discussion some elements of Edmund Husserl's *The Phenomenology of Internal Time-Consciousness*[11] in the hope that this might shed some light on what Kierkegaard himself describes as the "Hyperborean darkness"[12] of the "unhappiest man." But before turning to Husserl, one last passage from *Either/Or*:

> This [the unhappiest unhappiness] happens when it is memory which prevents the unhappy individual from finding himself in his hope, and hope which prevents him from finding himself in his memory. When this happens, it is, on the one hand, due to the fact that he constantly hopes something that should be remembered; his hope constantly disappoints him and, in disappointing him, reveals to him it is not because the realization of his hope is postponed, but because it is already past and gone, has already been experienced. . . . On the other hand, it is due to the fact that he always remembers that for which he ought to hope; for the future he has already anticipated in thought, in thought already experienced it, and this experience he now remembers, instead of hoping for it.[13]

The proto-existentialism of Kierkegaard here characteristically dwells on the tragic aspect of *lived* temporality where the experience of duration, in thrall to endless yearning and disappointment, is forever cast as suffering and grief in the face of self-negation and absence. As a way of neutralizing this predicament, Husserl's phenomenological analysis of internal time consciousness will act here as an initial guide through the complex structure of time-experience preparing us for a more sober return to the unhappy consciousness as a conclusion.

In *The Phenomenology of Internal Time Consciousness*, Husserl follows both St. Augustine (and the aspiring improviser) by insisting on the primordiality of the *now* and the primacy of the *new*, on the face of it an avant-gardist charter with enormous improvisatory potential.

> Every new now is precisely that, a new one, and is phenomenologically characterized as such. Even if every [musical] tone continues completely unaltered, in such a way that not the least alteration is visible to us—even if every now, therefore, possesses exactly the same content of apprehension . . .—nevertheless, a primordial difference still exists, one that pertains to a new dimension. . . . From the point of view of phenomenology, only the now-point is characterized as an actual now, that is, as new.[14]

> The constancy in which again and again a new now is constituted shows us that in general it is not a question of "novelty" but of a constant moment of individuation, in which the temporal position has its origin.[15]

The first thing to notice here is the way in which Husserl makes a clear phenomenological distinction between newness and novelty—between "originarity"[16] and originality—an insight that improvisers would do well to acknowledge and be mindful of. All too often the valorization of the moment is coupled with a pursuit of the unheard-of and unseen that, in its celebration of innovation and difference (the "taken by surprise" moment),[17] obscures the phenomenological sameness of the new and the newness of the same. Where the "surprised" improviser strives to achieve the (impossible?) ecstasy of absolute *attention*, Husserl suggests a different mode of bracketing, one that welds the present to the future and the past not through the existential categories of hope and memory but the phenomenologically neutralized concepts of protention and retention. Husserl's aim is to demonstrate how it is precisely the protention and retention of the future/past that forms the "temporal halo"[18] that allows the self to attend to and "authentically" experience[19] the phenomenological *reality* of time.

Husserl introduces the terms *retention* and *protention* as the historical and the futural "halo" encircling attention to the present moment, thus ensuring the temporal experience of continuity and flow. Unlike the Kierkegaardian vocabulary, where hope and memory are suffered as an existential *break* with the present, both absent from the present moment but, in the case of the "unhappiest man," also absent from the future and the past, retention and protention are *primary* experiences, inherently *conjoined*—via attention—not only at the level of experience but, more essentially, as the temporal extension of intentionality. As Dieter Lohmar explains:

The designations "protend" and "retend" are chosen in analogy to "intend." This analogy is based on the fact that retention and protention have a *definite content*, i.e., an idea of what they are intending and what they are keeping alive or expecting, which may be viewed as a kind of intentional content.[20]

One might say that, at the level of pure primary perception the *moment* impresses itself on the ego as ever new, while as a product of intentional consciousness the *ego* impresses itself on the moment as that which is expected and then kept alive. What is expected— thought as protention—is rooted in retention and thus perceived as sameness (new sameness/same newness). In this way the intentional "moment" is extended into the future and the past, giving intentionality the character of flow rather than eternal frag- mentation; it is this that hyperaware improvisers latch onto and "get into."

As described then, the moment is no longer identical to the instant but, through the temporal reach of intentionality, becomes an *event* that is sustained as long as atten- tion, retention, and protention hold together and flow into each other. Improvisation is one (particularly intense) way of attending to such intentionality: a kind of meta- intentionality. But to come back to the original issue, the extent to which "getting into" the flow might be considered a "happy" experience of self-presence will depend on the degree to which retention and protention remain attached to the present (like a "comet's tail," as Husserl describes it).[21]

Husserl is absolutely clear: attention, retention, and protention form a continuum for the duration of a temporal event; once finished, such an event is remembered or hoped for again but no longer retained or protained.

> We characterised primary remembrance or retention as a comet's tail which is joined to actual perception. Secondary remembrance or recollection is completely different from this. After primary remembrance is past, a new memory of this motion or that melody can emerge.[22]

In other words, internal time-consciousness flows, while memory is re-collected and reconstructed out of remembered fragments. Perhaps it is not surprising, then, that improvisers, keen to throw off the constraints of given structures and the tyranny of (re)collective consciousness, seek out such moments of flow and commit themselves to devising performative strategies capable of initiating and sustaining such events, the duration of which is limited by either contingent, extraneous formal structures intro- duced to delimit the flow of time-consciousness, or what might be called the attention/ retention/protention-span of internal-time consciousness, itself understood here in *productive* rather than receptive terms. Put another way, improvisers seek to *create* as well as experience temporal events, and it is precisely the challenge to "get into" and hold together—as performance—the flow of time that gives improvisation the urgency and intensity it has.

Considering the idea of a *created* temporal event, the duration of which is determined by objective givens (materials, spatial/temporal constraints, socioeconomic-historical constraints, instructions/demands, embodiment, and so on—the list is endless) and the protention/attention/retention-span of the improviser(s), the degree of freedom associated with the improvisation will be determined by which of these two poles predominate. Also, given the entanglement (confusion?) of freedom and improvisation in so many of the discourses surrounding it, thought must be given to the balance of protention and retention within the internal time-consciousness of the improviser and of the audience, as a productive and receptive moment, respectively. As Lohmar observes:

> In ... *The Phenomenology of Internal Time-Consciousness* ... protention is only mentioned in a few places. If we compare this with the analyses of retention, which are distinctly dominant both quantitatively and qualitatively, protention appears like a phenomenon that is mentioned only for reasons of symmetry and fairness.[23]

This is true, but there is one particular passage in *The Phenomenology* that is noteworthy: in section 26, entitled "The Difference between Memory and Expectation," Husserl makes a distinction between the prophetic and the open.

> In principle, a prophetic consciousness ... is conceivable, one in which each character of the expectation, of the coming into being, stands before our eyes, as, for example, when we have a precisely determined plan and, intuitively imagining what is planned, accept it lock, stock and barrel, so to speak, as future reality. Still there will also be many unimportant things in the intuitive anticipation of the future which as makeshifts fill out the concrete image. The latter, however, can in various ways be other than the likeness it offers. It is, from the first, characterised as being open.[24]

What is suggested here is that within an improvisation, the precise nature and significance of being "in the moment" will vary depending not only on whether retention or protention is emphasized but, if the latter (as one would expect in improvisation), exactly which mode of protention (how open, how closed). Indeed, to go beyond Husserl and reach out once again into the existential terrain of Kierkegaard, we might want to trace the manner in which protention begins to overlap with expectation and, in turn, how expectation might itself overlap with hope. But before re-engaging with such "unhappiness," let us return to Husserl's apparent favoring of retention above protention and consider what significance this might have in our Husserlian analysis of an improvised event.

Rather than understanding the "in the moment" moment as synonymous with a hyperawareness of the phenomenological attention to the present—authentic self-presence within the "now"—consider the words of the renowned improviser and theater director Keith Johnstone: "The improviser has to be like a man walking backwards. He sees where he has been, but he pays no attention to the future."[25] Here, already, it can be seen that the assimilation of retention and closure, on the one hand, and protention and openness, on the other, is problematic. Unconvincing though this may be as a model, Johnstone's backward-looking improviser, utterly inattentive to the future, is hardly intended as a reactionary figure intent on harnessing improvisation to the predictability of the known and the has-been. On the contrary, the ambition here is to be utterly unpredictable: perhaps impossibly so. Of course, from Johnstone's perspective (something he shares with Husserl), paying attention to the past is, in reality, just another way of paying attention to the present "now," because for both it is precisely the nature of retention to always be one "phase" of the "now." Describing the consciousness of a sound-event, Husserl writes:

> I am conscious of the sound and the duration which it fills in a continuity of "modes," in a "continuous flux." A point, a phase of this flux is termed "consciousness of sound beginning" and therein I am conscious of the first temporal point of the duration of the sound in the mode of the now. The sound is given; that is, I am conscious of it as now, and I am so conscious of it "as long as" I am conscious of any of its phases as now. But if any temporal phase (corresponding to a temporal point of the duration of the sound) is an actual now (with the exception of the beginning point), then I am conscious of a continuity of phases as "before," and I am conscious of the whole interval of the temporal duration from the beginning point to the now point as an expired duration.[26]

Thinking of an improvisation in these terms, it becomes evident again that the moment is by no means identical to the instant. The moment has duration (which is why the improviser can get "into it"); the instant does not. The beginning and the end of a written/composed work coexist within the simultaneity of the originary document, but in a completely improvised work they do not and, thus, the improviser has to both begin the improvisation and then retain this beginning as a (the) moment of the work's unfolding and its ultimate end. In other words, the beginning is not just the commencement of the work (the instant) but also an originary phase of the moment of the work as a whole; once this beginning phase expires, through insufficient attention, the work expires with it. Also, again within a fully (freely) improvised work as opposed to an improvised sequence within an otherwise composed structure, the beginning is of particular interest.

How does Johnstone's backward-facing improviser begin, given that before the beginning there is nothing to look back on? The obvious answer is that the improviser looks back on previous beginnings, either as something to avoid or as something to embrace. Either way, in Husserlian terms the claim that the improviser "pays no attention to the future" is, temporally at least, naive. To explain: even though, as we have already seen, he insists that re-collective memory must be distinguished from the flowing continuity of the retentive process, Husserl recognizes that memory is, among other things, the *recollection of protentions*—back to the future.

> Every act of memory contains intentions of expectation whose *fulfilment* leads to the present.... [T]he recollective process ... renews these protentions in a manner appropriate to memory. These protentions were not only present as intercepting, they have also intercepted. They have been *fulfilled*, and we are aware of them in recollection. *Fulfilment* in recollective consciousness is *re-fulfilment* ... and if

the primordial protention of the perception of the event was undetermined and the question of being-other or not being was left *open*, then in the recollection we have a *pre-directed expectation* which does *not* leave all that open.[27]

Thought thus, not only does the moment overflow the present to the extent that it has a protentional and retentional dimension, but in addition to this the very beginning of the improvised temporal event is dependent upon the memory and re-collection of past expectations. So, while Johnstone might seem to be stumbling backward into the unexpected, in truth it is precisely this backward glance that lets him know what to expect, because what he is seeing is the *fulfillment* of these past expectations in the "now." In this way, and notwithstanding Husserl's insistence that recollection represents a break with the continuity of retention, the exaggerated emphasis on fulfillment stitches the past back into the present in a manner that, for all intents and purposes, effectively closes down the assumed openness of improvisation. This, incidentally, is not a critique of improvisation but, rather, of the ideology of openness.

Returning to Husserl's account of what he describes as "protentions in recollection," it is worth considering what Lohmar identifies as five varieties of protention and look more closely at what he calls "unspecific protention."[28] In essence this is the most open form of protention because, although there remains the expectation that something will happen, *what* will happen is uncertain. Most important, in this mode of protention even the unexpected is expected. So, placed within an improvisatory context—as "protention in recollection"—what is remembered by the backward-looking improviser is a past moment or event of indeterminacy that is resolved in the present as a determined recollection, albeit one that (one hopes) still resonates with this originary unexpectedness. Seen in this light, the improviser looks back at this remembered future in all of its unexpected futurity and begins again. Why? Perhaps just to relive the experience of uncertainty, secure in the knowledge that everything will turn out alright in the end; and there is certainly pleasure to be had here, as much improvisation confirms. But of course the moment we start acknowledging that a particular *value* is attached to expectation is the moment that the neutrality of phenomenological protention is surpassed. To repeat, it would be facile to assume that, in spite of the widespread valorization of "surprise," a positive value is or should always be attached to the unexpected within an improvised event: some surprises are bad surprises! In fact, it might be argued that *most* surprises are bad surprises, which is why there are so *few* of them in the world of improvisation. Again, this is not a criticism of improvisation but, rather, of the slightly skewed notion of what constitutes a surprise, one that offers little clue as to *why* improvisers continue to improvise other than to satisfy the desire for endless fulfillment in the present: the most common but least interesting form of being "in the moment." So let us now go beyond phenomenology and its protention/attention/retention continuum and begin to trace instead the darker side of expectation as it breaks with protention and becomes entangled with hope.

To repeat, most improvisation (even the very best) is not all that surprising. Obviously, nice surprises are nice, so it is understandable that improvisers often dwell on those special moments when the unexpected flares up within the expected and the space of the "new" seems to "explode immaculate and untouchable as alterity or absolute newness."[29] But, in all honesty, such moments are rare and can hardly be considered the main motivation for improvisers to improvise. As we have seen, if (following Johnstone) the improviser is presented as one who faces the past, then the apparent unexpected-ness of the future is, in being "fulfilled" in the "now," not particularly surprising at all. Thus, while protention describes the continuous flow of the future into the now and on into the past, expectation represents a *break* with the now to the extent that it concerns a future beyond the phenomenological "hold" of the improviser. But, to say again, this apparent break disguises the fact that expectation is rooted in a fulfilled past that is abso-lutely continuous with the now and thus completely unsurprising.

But there are exceptions to this rather cozy view of improvisation: what if instead of the "recollection of protentions" fulfilled in the present we turn our attention to the rec-ollection of expectations *not* fulfilled in the now? What if an improvisation doesn't turn out as expected—and not in a good way? The improviser will expect certain things to happen, but that should not make the improvisation predictable. The improviser will recollect past protentions, but that should be distinguished from regurgitating past suc-cesses in a series of formulaic repetitions. The list could be extended, but clearly impro-visations often fail, or at least fail to deliver what might have been expected. To look back on unfulfilled expectations creates a very different dynamic to the complacency that threatens to engulf those who bathe in the warm glow of past triumphs, no matter how surprising at the time. Where the dominant model of improvisation would have improvisers constantly seek out good surprises, alongside this we must also acknowl-edge the improviser's desire to avoid bad surprises coupled with the desire to constantly revisit and rework those areas of weakness, disappointment, unfulfillment, and failure. So, as a response to the question "why improvise?" consideration needs to be given not just to the excitement of expectancy and the hyperexcitement associated with the expec-tation of the unexpected, but also to the *hope* that previous shortcomings can be ironed out, the hope that this time things might be different, better. Here it is past shortcom-ings rather than the successes that, *as memories rather than recollections*, endlessly draw the improviser back to improvisation, ever hopeful that something good will come of it this time.

As with protention and expectation, then, expectation and hope must also be care-fully distinguished from each other. To begin with, while it is true that expectation breaks with the absolute continuity of protention, to the extent that recollected expec-tations are fulfilled (either in expected or unexpected ways), there remains a powerful link forged between the present and the expected future that results in a certain pas-sivity being associated with expectation. The yearning we began this chapter with only appears when the unfulfillment of expectations gives rise to hope, and to hope for some-thing is very different than to expect it or, for that matter, not to expect it. Although both are deployed within the language of outcomes, in essence only expectancy demands an outcome. Hopefulness, as the word suggests, is full of itself, and, like desire (it *is* desire), it ultimately feeds only on itself too. In this regard, hope breaks with temporality, interrupting the internal time-consciousness of the intentional ego and the expectant improviser with a discontinuous and displaced existential yearning that, as Kierkegaard recognizes, sucks all presence from the present, forever casting the yearning self out of the moment. But, and this is the whole point of the present chapter, the very experience of being "in the moment," the real intensity and profundity of this moment, can only be fully understood if the complex interplay of protention and retention, expectation and recollection, hope and memory is brought to our attention as the very moment of attention necessary to experience not only the happiness of self-presence but also the all-important presence of absence in the moment and the "unhappiness" Kierkegaard would associate with that.

So let us consider improvisation in the terms outlined above. And let us take what might be considered to be the most essential form of musical improvisation as our example: free improvisation. The improvisation is about to begin, anything could happen; already in this moment the phenomenological consciousness, existential experience, and the ontological sensation (for this is the true nature of hope and memory) of the improvisers are simultaneously already at work: the silence is buzzing. Husserl, speaking as a listener, always conducts his phenomenological analysis in the midst of the work's unfolding, it is always already under way. What we need here is a phenomenology of beginnings, one engaged with the consciousness of the not-yet, of the about-to-happen rather than this-is-happening. But how can protention and retention be operative *prior to* the phenomenological flow of the improvisation? How do we give a phenomenological account of the beginning? In fact, phenomenologically speaking we can have no primary perception of what is yet to happen. Protention only protends the fact that happenings will continue to happen, offering no insight into the discontinuity of new beginnings. In this regard phenomenology can only ever speak from within the moment, and the dryness of this account alone should, if only superficially, alert us to the fact that the "being-in-the-moment" moment needs a much richer account than the one phenomenology alone can provide.

Anything could happen, but what is likely to happen? Retention, on the one hand, allows the improviser to hold onto what is happening in the moment of a performance; recollection, on the other hand, allows the improviser to anticipate a new beginning by bringing back to consciousness previous transitions from what Niklas Luhmann (following Spencer Brown) calls the "unmarked" to the "marked space."[30] As Aristotle recognized long ago, recollection will always "try to obtain a beginning of movement ... [, which] explains why attempts at recollection succeed soonest and best when they start from a beginning."[31] By recollecting beginnings the improviser can begin again, the same or differently.

But before it begins there is still something else. Remember, while Adorno denies the possibility of happy art he does nonetheless repeatedly return to Stendhal's conception of the aesthetic as the "*promesse du bonheur,*" if not happiness at least a *promise* of happiness. But what does this mean? Certainly, if an improvisation turns out pretty much as expected (including the anticipation of the unexpected) there must be experienced a sense of satisfaction, but satisfaction and happiness are by no means synonymous: hope,

unlike expectancy, cannot be satisfied. Every improvisation at the moment of its beginning has many possibilities (some of which one would expect to be realized), but in
addition to this it also has promise, to which can be attached a *sense* of anticipation over
and above both the primary perception of protention and the secondary perception of
expectation. While, as Adorno would see it (and here can be detected the influence of
Ernst Bloch, as well as Stendhal),[32] *all* art holds out such a promise, there is a danger that
the artwork itself—the product—is too readily received and consumed as the fulfillment
of this promise rather than merely the satisfaction of an expectation. In its endeavor
to *avoid* the production of a final definitive Work, the improvisation that is most free
effectively separates the promise of the work from the artwork itself, thus opening an
aesthetic space wherein can be sensed an ontological dimension that exceeds it (both art
and the aesthetic). Unfortunately, this space is too often and too quickly closed down by
improvisers themselves through the subsequent valorization of the *working* of the Work
rather than the Work itself, thus resulting in what might be called a model (or ideal?) of
being "in the moment" that exaggerates the immediate perception of process, becoming, and temporal flow above the highly mediated sense of an ecstatic alterity (or Being)
outside of phenomenological experience. In other words, the promise of the work (happiness) is outside of the Work and its working, but nevertheless this working must begin
before this otherness can be sensed, and, to this extent, hope is always to be found alongside expectation at the beginning of an improvisation.

The improvisation begins: on the face of it the first sounds would seem to be the fre-
est: anything could happen, but in truth it is usually the recollection of previous beginnings or the imaginary protention of a planned beginning that sets things in motion.
Not surprisingly then, the beginning is rarely (if ever) the "moment" that improvisers
get "into." Once under way, most of what occurs in our free improvisation will respond
well to a phenomenological analysis, and even better to one that goes beyond the continuity of protention and retention and the fulfillment of recollected protentions into the
more complex experience of unfulfilled protentions and the impact that this might have
on an improvisation. The composer and anti-improviser Gavin Bryars might mock the
musician who practices all day in order to improvise in the evening but, all joking aside,
what this demonstrates is the improviser's desire to avoid previous shortcomings, to
build upon earlier successes (without naively trying to reproduce them), and to develop
the technique necessary to outwit itself the moment empty virtuosity threatens to bring
fulfillment.

All of this can be accounted for in phenomenological terms, albeit in the intensified
form adopted by the "hyperaware" improviser whose *attention* to the present moment
and the desire to control the flow of time-events is so easily mistaken for the "being-in-
the-moment" moment. The ability to take hold of the situation, to anticipate otherness
through the protentional/intentional/retentional grasp of the event requires all participants in the improvisation to accelerate the senses; it is a question of speed and agility,
instant responses to instant responses: hyperdialogue, total control (notwithstanding
the penchant for staged chaos). Phenomenology can account for all of this except for
one crucial thing: dialogue. And it is the failure of Husserl, in spite of his considerable

efforts in the *Cartesian Meditations*, to offer a viable account of intersubjectivity (and, thus, dialogue) that requires us to go beyond phenomenology at the very point where collective improvisation appears to be approaching the moment of moments.[33]

The problem, in essence, is that Husserl can only conceive of the other as an alter-ego that is phenomenologically "paired" with the perceiving ego within a symmetrical, "mirrored," empathic space/time.[34] Now while on the face of it this might seem to fit perfectly well with those models of improvisation that equate dialogue with community and communion (some might say a rather facile model), it becomes evident, as other writings of Husserl betray, that the twinning of self and other ultimately breaks down under the weight of irreducible difference and existential solitude. As he himself observes in *Ideas 1*:

> Closer inspection would further show that two streams of experience (spheres of consciousness for two pure Egos) cannot be conceived as having an essential content that is identically the same; moreover, as is evident from the foregoing, no fully determinate experience of the one could ever belong to the other.[35]

In other words, although involved in a process of interaction, the performative actions of each interactor are unavoidably initiated from within a singular sphere of "own-ness"[36] that is irreducible to any other. What should be said, however, is that it is precisely Husserl's apparent "failure" to arrive at a satisfactory phenomenological account of intersubjectivity that marks the spot where philosophies of solitude (Maurice Blanchot) or separation (Emmanuel Levinas) can take root, thus continuing and radicalizing Kierkegaard's promotion of "the single one." Of course, these latter thinkers are unable to offer an account of dialogue too, but—and this is the essential difference—this is perceived as a strength rather than a weakness. To use Levinas's vocabulary, it is precisely the recognition and conviction that otherness *cannot* be reduced to the same that informs the subsequent resistance to all totalities (including, it should be said, the shared experience of being "in the moment"). But this needs to be understood correctly; as a moment of intersubjectivity and interaction, such irreducibility raises the issues of proximity and separation (two key Levinasian terms) as related to the collectivity of collective improvisation: a commonality without communion.[37] This "alone together" moment is, to be fair, already acknowledged within improvisation as Jim Hall and Ron Carter's exquisitely melancholic album of that title confirms, and it should act as a reminder that (as Levinas argues throughout *Time and the Other*) time-consciousness is the consciousness of our *difference* from the other: a difference that can be shared to be sure (but *as* difference).[38]

Yet more can be said than this: while the desire for dialogue and the yearning for communication associated here with separation and difference can be incorporated into the dialogical model of improvisation that dominates the field, there remains a solitude that, as describing the self's separation from *itself* rather than the other, requires a shift of emphasis away from the otherness of the other toward the otherness of the *work*. As Blanchot observes in "The Essential Solitude," to be solitary is not to avoid—as "loner"—the company of others (it is not a social category); it is, rather, to be "set aside" by one's *own* work and "dismissed."[39] Indeed, for Blanchot, solitude is a characteristic of the work, not of the self, and it is the very creation of a work that creates the condition of solitude.

So if we return to collective free improvisation, what do such ideas add to the phenomenological account already presented? To begin with, there is what we might describe as a pluralization of time-consciousness, a poly-temporality that multiplies time-strands by the number of participants. Indeed, if we were writing this from a Bergsonian perspective we would be talking of the different rhythms of different durations pulsing or flowing across the spatialized blocks of objective time: a great description of an improvised event.[40] As it is, phenomenology, confronting each improviser within a singular "sphere of ownness" that flows alongside but never into the internal time-consciousness of another, is persuaded to introduce the concept of *empathy* as the means by which the "mirroring" of the ego and the alter-ego can be translated into the language of feeling and understanding, thus opening up the dialogical possibilities assumed by any group improvisation. And it is here that the singularity of being "in the *moment*"—rather than the plurality of coexisting *moments*—can be traced back to its empathic roots and the desire to replace multiple "spheres of ownness" with a oneness that actualizes the monologic at the heart of what so often passes as dialogue. It would be easy to confuse the experience of empathic oneness with the "being-in-the-moment" moment, but to do so (as is often done) is to overlook the fact that, thought essentially, empathy does not *achieve* (or allow the achievement of) oneness, on the contrary: it *assumes* it. Heidegger grasps this perfectly in *Being and Time*:

> This phenomenon, which is not too happily designated as "empathy," is then supposed, as it were, to provide the first ontological bridge from one's own subject, which is given proximally as alone, to the other subject, which is proximally quite closed off.... [But] ... Dasein, as being-in-the-world, already is with others. "Empathy" does not first constitute Being-with; only on the basis of Being-with does empathy become possible: it gets its motivation from the unsociability of the dominant modes of Being-with.[41]

The point (if not the language) is clear: the understanding of empathy as a desirable *goal*, and the apparent realization of that goal during those momentous moments within an improvisation obscures the fact that the communion empathy desires both phenomenologically and existentially is, ontologically, already given as *origin*—something to be preserved rather than created. And what is more, this originary at-oneness ("Being-with") is precisely that which is emphatically *not* perceived, indeed is forgotten in the rush for sociability and togetherness.

While there is undoubtedly something strange about the idea that "Being-with" might be considered an unsociable mode of being, one can detect here the impact of Heidegger on Blanchot's framing of the "essential solitude," central to which is a distinction between loneliness and solitude. As we have seen, aloneness and togetherness can play very well alongside each other within the world of improvisation, particularly when situated within the familiar dialectic of individuality and collectivity; but solitude is of a different order, not only unsociable but a-social and thus quite removed from the dialectics of human interaction. Hence Heidegger's primary concern is not with one being's relation to another being, but with a being's relation to Being, a relation born (interestingly) out of "listening," "hearkening," and "reserve." One would hope that all improvisations contain moments of reserve and listening, but the concern here is not with other improvisers but with an *Otherness* that, while sensed, is irreducible to the perception of interacting alter-egos. It is this sense that, we hope, will allow us to draw a little closer to the "being-in-the-moment" moment. To attempt this we need to return to Blanchot.

As with Heidegger then, the "essential solitude," as Blanchot understands it, is not concerned with being-to-being relations but, rather, with the encounter between, for example, the writer and the book, the composer and the score; a being-to-*work* relation, where the work represents an irreducible "outside" that both produces and is sensed by the "essential solitude." Blanchot has another name for this sense of solitude and this solitary sense: *fascination*. The subject of fascination in Blanchot is indeed a fascinating subject, but there is only space here to pick up on one specific aspect of his discussion, what he describes as "the fascination of time's absence." The purpose of this is to try to make sense of the three different but interlinked and overlapping modes of time-consciousness that are operative within any freely improvised time event, two of which we have already acknowledged (the intentional and the empathic) and a third that we will treat as the fascinating. Thus we might identify three temporalities, respectively: the phenomenologically reduced time of the self (intentional), the phenomenologically expanded time of the self and other (empathic), and, let us tentatively call it, the ontological time of the self and *Other* (fascinating for Blanchot, unhappy for Kierkegaard).

Where the first two temporalities assume or seek self-presence and intersubjective presence, respectively, the contention here is that it is only with the emergence of a sense of time's *absence* that the "in-the-moment" moment can be said to have truly arrived. Before trying to explain this—the paradox of internal time-consciousness—note must be taken of Blanchot's account of fascination and the absence of time.

> To write is to surrender to the fascination of time's absence. Now we are doubtless approaching the essence of solitude.... The time of time's absence has no present, no presence. This "no present" does not, however, refer back to a past.... The irremediable character of what has no present, of what is not even there as having once been there, says: it never happened, never for a first time, and yet it starts over, again, again, infinitely. It is without end, without beginning. It is without a future.[42]

It is hoped (and it is certainly the intention) that Kierkegaard's earlier words—"he has no present, no future, no past"—can be heard echoing in this passage, but where the proto-existentialism of the latter is witness to the tragic dislocation of time as a function of the confusion of hope and memory, for Blanchot the fascination with time's absence is neither happy nor unhappy but *neutral*, indeed neutrality is the very essence of his thought.[43] Where the Kierkegaardian unhappy one is trapped within the eternally recurring "two-fold reversal" of time—the tragedy—the neutral fascination of Blanchot's solitary artist (something comparable to Heidegger's "reserve") gives rise to a vigilance that directly relates to the emergence of a work that, as work, remains on the outside of its mode of production: the *working* of the work so central to improvisation. And this is why improvisation is the most essential art form; for by holding the work at bay and resisting its teleological allure for the sake of its becoming—the flow of production, the purposiveness without purpose—it does not render the Work redundant or secondary. On the contrary, it is only in such a moment of intersubjective/dialogical flux that the work can appear, as the *image*[44] of that which is absolutely irreducible to this flux. Put another way: it is only through empathy—the fusion, or attempted fusion of different time strands—that the essential "unsociableness of Being-with" can be sensed as that which remains outside the moment of empathy: *this* is the work that so fascinates.

So, finally, to try and make sense of this as related to collective free improvisation and the experience of being "in the moment," the following model (or scenario) might be considered. Like Walter Benjamin's version of Paul Klee's *Angelus Novus* (more dramatic than Johnstone), the improviser moves into the future with eyes fixed on the past.[45] It is through the dual intentional act of retaining what has just happened and recollecting what has happened before that an improvisation can get under way and be sustained— the duration, once under way, being determined by and dependent upon the ability of the improviser to hold together in a phenomenological continuum this view of the immediate and the mediated past and what is to come now (protention) and beyond the now (expectation). Without an existing work (with predetermined beginning and end) to perform, the improviser brings into sharp relief this, the essential temporality of all artworks, and the particular responsibility of the artist to hold the time of the work together.

In addition to retention and the recollection of protentions fulfilled in the now the improviser must also negotiate, from moment to moment, the recollection of *unfulfilled* protentions and the expectation that the improvisation might not turn out as expected, that it might "fail." It is here that one often witnesses the new within improvisation, but such novelty is, paradoxically, often the product of considerable rehearsal devoted to the avoidance of past "mistakes" or shortcomings. At the level of singularity and the somewhat expanded version of internal time-consciousness presented here, there is clearly a *moment* of, let us call it "pleasure," of control and even mastery that undoubtedly contributes to the event of being "in the moment," but there is more to it than this.

At the level of collectivity an improvisation becomes more than the mere pluralization or multiplication of singular (but "mirrored") internal time-consciousness; it also manifests the radical *differentiation* of singular durations within a shared objective time that can never be actualized. This problematization of dialogue and the communicative community that it promises represents a direct challenge to the empathic model of improvisation that dominates the field, one that explains the ecstasy experienced when such empathy seems—in those fleeting *moments*—to have been attained. This apparent sublation of singularity and collectivity is undoubtedly the "in-the-moment" moment as understood by the dialectical aesthetics that have lorded it over art for more than two centuries, so to resist this as the ultimate "moment" is also to resist such dialectics: Kierkegaard, Heidegger, and Blanchot—as anti-dialecticians—have been marshaled for precisely this reason.

The limits of empathy are the limits of the dialectic, both sharing the desire to synthesize what is already together (albeit differently). If it is precisely the unsociability of Being-with that gives rise to the desire for sociability then the promise of happiness associated with such togetherness will always remain just that: a promise. But—and this is the essential point—the *sense* of this promise, the *sensation* of that which, as absolute futurity, is absent from time-consciousness, remains nevertheless an event within the unfolding of some (and only some) artworks. The claim here is that (at their best) free improvisations are the most graphic example of this event. If this is accepted, then to fully grasp the "in-the-moment" moment we need to acknowledge that in addition to (or in excess of) the self-presence of the improviser and the empathic co-presence of the collective there is a point of reservation or neutrality from which it is possible to sense the work "to come" (as Blanchot describes it).[46] Like the promise, that which is eternally "to come" resides outside of time and thus is forever outside the *moment*. But to sense this absence—time's absence—as a moment of fascination requires the improviser to step outside of the moment too. Both inside and outside, feelings of mastery and empathy are countered not by unhappiness or yearning but, rather, by a vigilance and attention that "listens" with icy concentration to the Absolute work that never arrives—and yet, in this moment of moments, is already here.

NOTES

1. Theodor Adorno, *Aesthetic Theory*, trans. C. Lenhardt (London: Routledge & Kegan Paul, 1984), 19.
2. Theodor Adorno, *Negative Dialectics*, trans. E. B. Ashton (New York: Seabury Press, 1973), 144.
3. G.W.F. Hegel, *The Phenomenology of Mind*, trans. James Baillie (London: Allen and Unwin, 1977), 251ff.
4. Ibid., 259.
5. G.W.F. Hegel, *Science of Logic*, trans. A. V. Miller (London: Allen and Unwin, 1976), 149.
6. Søren Kierkegaard, *Either/Or*, trans. David and Lillian Swenson (Princeton: Princeton University Press, 1971), 217.
7. Ibid., 220.
8. Ibid., 221–222.
9. Ibid., 223.
10. Ibid., 223–224.
11. Edmund Husserl, *The Phenomenology of Internal Time-Consciousness*, trans. James S. Churchill (The Hague: Martinus Nijhoff, 1964).
12. Kierkegaard, *Either/Or*, 224.
13. Ibid., 223.

14. Husserl, *Phenomenology*, 89.

15. Ibid., 90.

16. Ibid., 92.

17. A representative example would be Susan Leigh Foster, "Taken by Surprise: Improvisation in Dance and Mind," in *Taken by Surprise: A Dance Improvisation Reader*, ed. Ann Cooper Albright and David Gere (Middletown: Wesleyan University Press, 2003).

18. Husserl, *Phenomenology*, 58.

19. Ibid., 28.

20. Dieter Lohmar, "What Does Protention 'Protend'?: Remarks on Husserl's Analyses of Protention in the Bernau Manuscripts on Time-Consciousness," *Philosophy Today* 46, no. 5 (2002): 157. (my emphasis)

21. Ibid., 57.

22. Ibid.

23. Lohmar, "What Does Protention 'Protend'?," 154.

24. Husserl, *Phenomenology*, 80.

25. Keith Johnstone, *Impro: Improvisation and the Theatre* (London: Faber and Faber, 1979), 116.

26. Husserl, *Phenomenology*, 44.

27. Ibid., 76. (my emphasis)

28. Lohmar, "What Does Protention 'Protend'?," 160.

29. Emmanuel Levinas, *Time and the Other*, trans. Richard Cohen (Pittsburgh: Duquesne University Press, 1987), 80.

30. Niklas Luhmann, *Art as a Social System*, trans. Eva Knodt (Stanford: Stanford University Press, 2000), 117.

31. Aristotle, "On Memory and Reminiscence," in *The Works of Aristotle* (Chicago: Encyclopaedia Britannica Inc., 1952), 1: 693.

32. Ernst Bloch, *The Principle of Hope,* 3 vols., trans. Neville Plaice, Stephen Plaice, and Paul Knight (Oxford: Basil Blackwell, 1986).

33. Edmund Husserl, *Cartesian Meditations: An Introduction to Phenomenology*, trans. Dorion Cairns (Dordrecht: Kluwer, 1995), 89 ff.

34. Ibid., 140.

35. Edmund Husserl, *Ideas 1*, trans. W.R. Boyce Gibson (London: Allen and Unwin Press, 1969), 241.

36. Husserl, *Cartesian Meditations*, 95.

37. Emmanuel Levinas, *Totality and Infinity: An Essay on Exteriority*, trans. Alphonso Lingis (Pittsburgh: Duquesne University Press, 1969).

38. Jim Hall (guitar) and Ron Carter (bass), *Alone Together*, recorded August 1972, Milestone 9045, 1972, 33 1/3 rpm.

39. Maurice Blanchot, *The Space of Literature*, trans. Ann Smock (Lincoln: University of Nebraska Press, 1982), 21.

40. Henri Bergson, *Matter and Memory*, trans. Nancy Margaret Paul and W. Scott Palmer (London: Allen and Unwin, 1911), 272. "The duration lived by our consciousness is a duration with its own 'determined rhythm,' a duration very different from the time of the physicist."

41. Martin Heidegger, *Being and Time*, trans. John Macquarrie and Edward Robinson (Oxford: Blackwell, 1962), 162.

42. Blanchot, *The Space of Literature*, 30.

43. Maurice Blanchot, *The Infinite Conversation*, trans. Susan Hanson (Minneapolis: University of Minnesota Press, 1993), 298ff. "Every encounter—where the Other suddenly looms up and obliges thought to leave itself, just as it obliges the Self to come up against the lapse that constitutes it and from which it protects itself—is already marked, already fringed by the neutral" (306).

44. Blanchot, *Space of Literature*, 32. "The gaze gets taken in, absorbed by an immediate movement and a depthless deep. What is given us by this contact at a distance is the image, and fascination is passion for the image."

45. Walter Benjamin, "On the Concept of History," trans. Harry Zohn, in *Walter Benjamin Selected Writings*, vol. 4, *1938–1940* (Cambridge: Harvard University Press, 2003), 392. "His eyes are wide, his mouth is open, his wings are spread. This is how the angel of history must look. His face is turned toward the past. Where a chain of events appear before *us, he* sees one single catastrophe, which keeps piling wreckage upon wreckage and hurls it at his feet."

46. Maurice Blanchot, *The Book to Come*, trans. Charlotte Mandell (Stanford: Stanford University Press, 2003).

BIBLIOGRAPHY

Adorno, Theodor. *Aesthetic Theory*. Translated by C. Lenhardt. London: Routledge & Kegan Paul, 1984.

Adorno, Theodor. *Negative Dialectics*. Translated by E. B. Ashton. New York: Seabury Press, 1973.

Aristotle. "On Memory and Reminiscence." In *The Works of Aristotle*. Vol. 1. Chicago: Encyclopaedia Britannica Inc., 1952.

Benjamin, Walter. "On the Concept of History." Translated by Harry Zohn. In *Walter Benjamin—Selected Writings*. Vol. 4, 1938–1940, 389–400. Cambridge: Harvard University Press, 2003.

Bergson, Henri. *Matter and Memory*. Translated by Nancy Margaret Paul and W. Scott Palmer. London: Allen and Unwin, 1911.

Blanchot, Maurice. *The Space of Literature*. Translated by Ann Smock. Lincoln: University of Nebraska Press, 1982.

Blanchot, Maurice. *The Infinite Conversation*. Translated by Susan Hanson. Minneapolis: University of Minnesota Press, 1993.

Blanchot, Maurice. *The Book to Come*. Translated by Charlotte Mandell. Stanford: Stanford University Press, 2003.

Bloch, Ernst. *The Principle of Hope*, 3 Vols. Translated by Neville Plaice, Stephen Plaice and Paul Knight. Oxford: Basil Blackwell, 1986.

Foster, Susan Leigh. "Taken by Surprise: Improvisation in Dance and Mind." In *Taken by Surprise: A Dance Improvisation Reader*, edited by Ann Cooper Albright and David Gere, 3–10. Middletown: Wesleyan University Press, 2003.

Hall, Jim, and Ron Carter. *Alone Together*. Milestone 9045, 1972. Vinyl disc.

Hegel, G.W.F. *Science of Logic*. Translated by V. Miller. London: Allen and Unwin, 1976.

Hegel, G.W.F. *The Phenomenology of Mind*. Translated by James Baillie. London: Allen and Unwin, 1977.

Heidegger, Martin. *Being and Time*. Translated by John Macquarrie and Edward Robinson. Oxford: Blackwell, 1962.

Husserl, Edmund. *The Phenomenology of Internal Time-Consciousness*. Translated by James S. Churchill. The Hague: Martinus Nijhoff, 1964.

Husserl, Edmund. *Ideas 1*. Translated by W.R. Boyce Gibson. London: Allen and Unwin Press, 1969.

Husserl, Edmund. *Cartesian Meditations: An Introduction to Phenomenology*. Translated by Dorion Cairns. Dordrecht: Kluwer, 1995.

Johnstone, Keith. *Impro: Improvisation and the Theatre*. London: Faber and Faber, 1979.

Levinas, Emmanuel. *Time and the Other*. Translated by Richard Cohen. Pittsburgh: Duquesne University Press, 1987.

Kierkegaard, Søren. *Either/Or*. Translated by David and Lillian Swenson. Princeton: Princeton University Press, 1971.

Levinas, Emmanuel. *Totality and Infinity: An Essay on Exteriority*. Translated by Alphonso Lingis. Pittsburgh: Duquesne University Press, 1969.

Lohmar, Dieter. "What Does Protention 'Protend'?: Remarks on Husserl's Analyses of Protention in the Bernau Manuscripts on Time-Consciousness." *Philosophy Today* 46, no. 5 (2002): 154–167.

Luhmann, Niklas. *Art as a Social System*. Translated by Eva Knodt. Stanford: Stanford University Press, 2000.

CHAPTER 26

....

IMPROVISING *IMPROMPTU*, OR, WHAT TO DO WITH A BROKEN STRING

....

LYDIA GOEHR

IN APOLLO'S HALL

....

ON Amateur Night at the Apollo Theater, New York City, musicians and singers come to the stage to compete for public recognition of their talent. Participating audiences issue their judgments sometimes with expressions that drown out the performances. Where there's a noticeable failure to please, a designated "executioner" pulls the performers away.

The Apollo Theater inherited its name from an institution of dance, "Apollo Hall," founded in the 1860s by a Civil War military man, Edward Ferrero. In his treatise, *The Art of Dancing*, he articulated his aim to secure an Apollonian harmony and civility for his art while acknowledging its more turbulent origins in the Dionysian and bacchanalian cults of antiquity.[1] After his death, the institution saw several transmutations, through burlesque and vaudeville, through blues, jazz, swing, R & B, Motown, and soul, eventually to become what it is today, a theater of diverse musical offerings.[2] Nevertheless, for all the changes of musical style, street address, and clientele, the continued presence of the executioner suggests something that has never left the hall: an agonistic atmosphere that recalls the ancient gods contesting the terms of order and inspiration in society and the arts.

In the ancient myths, surprisingly many musicians were maimed or killed—if not by Apollo himself, then according to his divine principle: Marsyas was flayed, Orpheus beheaded, Linus knocked out, and Thamyris blinded.[3] Homer wrote of Thamyris, here in Pausanias's description, that he "lost the sight of his eyes"; that his attitude was "one of utter dejection"; that his hair and beard were "long"; and that "at his feet" lay "thrown a lyre with its horns and strings broken."[4] What had he done to deserve so extreme a punishment? He had shown hubris in claiming, first, that his musical performance was superior to that of the divine Muses, and second, that were he to win, he would take the Muses in sexual intercourse. When he was punished, he was stripped equally of his art and his eros. Nowadays, on Amateur Night, the Apollonian executioner does not actually physically maim the amateurs when he punishes them, though he does still have license to unstring the spirit of dilettantes who distress the assembled audiences. In other contemporary settings, however, the situation is not always so restrained.

In this essay, I draw on an agonistic background of contest, judgment, and punishment to help articulate a concept of improvisation that I call improvisation *impromptu*. I distinguish this concept from the more familiar concept of what I call improvisation *extempore*. I draw these two concepts apart, despite a substantial overlap, as a contribution to a critical theory that regards our lives, practices, and concepts as constantly contested. Improvisation *impromptu* is a concept of wit and fit, of doing exactly the right thing or wrong thing *in the moment*. Although the concept can be articulated independently of the agonistic background, its agonism brings its use into a sharp relief, especially when it's used to mark a *winning (or losing) move*. To speak of agonism is not necessarily to speak of explicit contests: even in everyday situations of life, we can take our lives, positively and negatively construed, to be "on the line." Suitable to its content, the concept is also very hard to pin down or to circumscribe with clear lines. It is a dynamic, even a tightrope concept, closely tied to judgment, that speaks to the differences between acting with humility or with hubris, with divine exhibition or with egoistic exhibitionism. I illustrate its tense application through a history of more subtle philosophical thought, juxtaposed with several rather blatant examples of competitive musical situations from very diverse traditions, from the "cutting contests" of jazz and rap, to the "cutting edge" performances of the concert hall, to the deathly "cutting down" of karaoke singers in the Philippines.

A strong motivation I have for articulating the concept of improvisation *impromptu* is to address the concept of improvisation *extempore* insofar as the latter has been used to bring down the work-concept of the practice of classical music. I begin the essay by explaining this motivation and conclude with an example that illustrates the argument as well as any single example could. It is drawn from a 1940 film of the Harlem Renaissance, in which an old violinist, a father, must contend with a broken arm and a young violinist, his son, with broken strings. *Broken Strings* is the film's title and part of my own. The film pits the work-music of the classical tradition against the improvisational freedom of swing, not, however, to perpetuate the division between two *types* of music—classical versus jazz—but between two qualitative ways of *making* music, *whatever type of music it is*. The film brings attention to what is most divisive, cutting, or prejudicial in our social categorization of persons and in our social conceptualization of music.

Concepts and Critique

When musicians make up music in performance, *from this moment forward*, their act falls under the familiar umbrella concept of what I'm calling improvisation *extempore*.

The second, less familiar concept, I'm calling improvisation *impromptu*. The latter refers to what we do at singular moments—*in the moment*—when we're put *on the spot*, particularly when we're confronted with an unexpected difficulty or obstacle. Closely associated with both concepts is a *quality* or *characteristic* of the *improvised* or *improvisational*, although, in qualitative assessments, we tend to say that a person, a performance, or an act is *inspired* or *innovative*, or, by contrast, uninspired or dull. In an extensive literature that extends far beyond the musical domain, the *extempore* and *impromptu* acts, along with the *quality*, tend to be run together without very explicit distinction. I think it necessary also to hold them apart. For, this way, we may put one of the concepts to work, to upstage or, better, unstage the other for the sake of critique.

Many contemporary scholars attach the concept of improvisation first off to the art of music and to a specific type or genre of music, most often jazz. With jazz regarded as the primary example of improvisation, the term *improvisation* has come to mean improvisation *extempore*, making music up in performance from this moment forward. After this, the terms *jazz* and *improvisation* have become thinned out or unmarked enough to signify a free music-making anywhere in the world. This way of making music has then become utopian in intent: to pave the way for a free music or a free future in a society of constraint.

This utopian claim has assumed a blood-red persistence: although rule-governed and conventional in many ways, jazz improvisation—especially free jazz—has been made to stand for the general resistance to a regulation assumed by a standardized or pre-made music or a pre-packaged concept—and most typically the work-concept. In this discourse of resistance, a practice regulated by a work-concept is a practice where compositional determination is taken typically to occur prior to the performance such that the performance is seen not to create the music but only to reproduce what is already created. Accordingly, whereas performances improvised *extempore* are taken to be productive, performances of works are taken to be only *re*-productive.

Although few would affirm this crude opposition, the opposition has nevertheless structured a way of thinking that assumes that more or less around 1800, the work-concept emerged in the practice in part as a contrary concept to that of improvisation *extempore*. Increasingly, it came to overtax musical practice, and not just classical music practice.[5] To diminish its power or authority, improvisation *extempore*, especially as tied to jazz, came to be accorded an emancipatory potential. But then, and this is the additional step I want to add to this discourse, this concept came to overstep its bounds, too, by coming to serve as though it exhausted all that improvisation and emancipation can mean descriptively and qualitatively, musically and socially.

But where does this leave us? I believe with the thought that just as it has been necessary to limit the work-concept, it is necessary to impose limits now on the concept of improvisation *extempore*. One way to do this is to re-release the power of the work-concept, to show that it does not exclude improvisation, given that improvisation can mean much more than improvisation *extempore*. Another way is to re-release the power of a way of thinking about improvisation that has fallen out of the picture the more the idea of improvisation *extempore* has dominated. This way of thinking corresponds in part to the *quality* of improvisation, as when we say of persons or their acts—of whatever sort—that they are inspired, innovative, or creative. But it also corresponds to what I am calling improvisation *impromptu*, which is both a particularly apt concept and in fact the more traditional concept to serve the purposes of an emancipatory critique.

Critique articulates concepts at the extreme to render explicit their negative and positive social tendencies in the different practices in which they have found complex and concrete applications. To so articulate the concepts is not to let the descriptions fall into mere caricature, although as in smart caricature, the descriptions are exaggerated and provocative enough to reveal an often-concealed truth-content or truthfulness. To claim that improvisation *impromptu* can help to deflate the conceit of improvisation *extempore* is thus deliberately to disguise all that potentially runs these two concepts together as one.[6] In what follows, one might think that most of what I say about the *impromptu* concept belongs just as well to what others think of as improvisation *extempore*. It is reasonable and accurate to think this way. The risk it runs, however, is then to think that a practice governed by a concept, such as the work-concept, which almost "by definition" has come to exclude the practice of improvisation *extempore*, has no claim on improvisation, which would be an unreasonable way to think. Drawing the conceptual distinction clarifies the point.

THE POSSIBILITY OF THE IMPOSSIBLE

In an oft-quoted, unpublished interview of 1982, Jacques Derrida described improvisation as occurring within a space of free fantasy in which we are able to imagine ourselves as liberated from repressive concepts or, as he put it, from the "great number of prescriptions [or names] that are prescribed in our memory and culture," such that all seems always already to be "preprogrammed."[7] In articulating his utopian appeal to improvisation, Derrida did not tie improvisation to a particular type of music, art, or action. Instead, he construed improvisation negatively, following the terms of a dialectical critique, and thus, as he used this term, as an impossibility. "One is obliged more or less to reproduce the stereotypical discourse. And so I believe in improvisation, and I fight for improvisation, but always with the belief that it's impossible." Part of what he meant was that what we desire but can never actually achieve is a free space in which improvisation is what we do completely *spontaneously*. The free space thus becomes a matter less of *what* we do than of what we *appeal* to, to resist all that restricts this spontaneity. The space of imagination is a space for broadening and opening up our thoughts to counter spaces that are filled up by that which is already familiar, given, pre-packaged in the culture. But to open up the imagination to counter such spaces is so extremely difficult that improvisation becomes well-nigh "impossible," yet, as Derrida insists, he, and we, must continue to believe in it.

Derrida's view draws on an extensive history in which "improvisation" has been appealed to, more in its *impromptu* than *extempore* form, to capture a way of acting in the world with what Emerson, for example, described as a certain "elasticity" of mind, attitude, and ability.[8] What exactly this elasticity comprised came, in the same history, to be drawn out through what Nietzsche, at the same time as Emerson, referred to as an entire "mobile army of metaphors, metonyms, and anthropomorphisms." Yet what the history also shows is that such an elasticity or spontaneity of mind and action cannot in fact do without a certain habituation, training, or preprogramming of our practices. Without fit, no wit. When Derrida said in his interview that one cannot do or say "whatever one wants," was he only lamenting the loss of freedom or was he also recognizing, dialectically, that one must "reproduce" the discourse to some degree, in order to show one's productivity? Most theorists who have articulated a critical concept of improvisation have done so not to dispense with all habit, discourse, or fit, but to counter a situation where our habits become too habitual or our discourses too stereotyped or fixed. If they overstate the claim to make it seem as if they really think freedom is possible without any compliance or fit, then it is to put a high note and often a blue note on the extreme difficulty or near impossibility of fighting all that which strikes others simply but falsely as self-evident.

ON THE EDGE OF HAPPINESS

Improvisation *impromptu* is equally distinct from a music *freely* or *entirely extemporized* and one *worked out in advance*. It refers to what we do in any sort of activity or performance of life when we're suddenly confronted with an obstacle which, to win, continue, or survive, we must overcome. But to overcome the obstacle, to get "out of a jam," offers no guarantees and no certainty that the world or our lives, social or individual, are improved thereby. We need always also to ask to what end our overcoming is directed. Conceived as without guarantees, the concept has nothing essential to do with this or that kind of music, or even with the art of music at all, and much more to do with how we live our lives precariously and contingently—on the edge.

Before Derrida, Nietzsche argued for improvisation to overcome a certain forgetfulness of what it means to *live* life. We have become passive as though we sit in an audience looking and listening to our lives without participating in their making. Our society and culture have become antiquated, even deadly, because we act as though what we know is always already known: pre-packaged or certain in advance. Nietzsche urged a rebirth of a perspective that would put us back onto the stage, where the not-knowing with certainty how the drama unfolds would leave us dancing joyfully "in the dark." To be "joyful," he wrote, we must become improvisers of our lives. "The day and the dance are beginning, and we don't know the programme. So we have to improvise—the whole day improvises its day."[9]

But having written this, he then tempered the thought. A life in which all our habits and knowing were suspended, a life that "demanded improvisation" without any abatement, would be "impossible," "intolerable," an "exile" from all community: indeed, a "Siberia." On the other hand, he recognized that the habits, values, and know-how *needed* to live life tend to fall all too easily and quickly into stagnation: before we know it, we have forgotten how to improvise, how to live in a way that shows us to be active, even "alive." Between the two extremes, he articulated the fragile or almost "impossible" terms of an agonistic life lived on a tightrope *with* and *between* joy and suffering, affirmation and doubt, experimentation and habit.

To illustrate, he distinguished two types of "happiness," saturated with connotations of good fortune and luck. In this distinction, he captured everything with which my essay is concerned: the agonism of living life; the two senses, separated, of improvisation *extempore* and *impromptu;* and the *quality* of being inspired derived from being able to act with *readiness* "in the moment."

There is one happiness, he began, of those who, despite their youth, grasp "the improvisation of life." These persons are those who, less than grasping the *extemporaneous* character of life, are able to act *impromptu*, in the moment. They are the persons who astonish us, for while engaged in "the most daring games," they are never caught out making a mistake even when they make one. Nietzsche drew an analogy to those "improvising masters" of the "art of tone," to whom we ascribe the *quality* of a "divine infallibility"—*göttliche Unfehlbarkeit*—of the hand. That these masters *are* mortal means that they do make mistakes, he explained, but that they are "divine" means that they make it seem as though their mistakes were no mistakes at all. Whenever, through "a mood" or "jerk of the finger," "an accidental tone" enters their performance, they are able to overcome it then and there, *impromptu*, by animating the tone "with a fine meaning and soul."

In addressing the "great improvisers" of the musical art, Nietzsche had the Liszts, Chopins, and Paganinis of his time in mind, and, hence, a music pre-composed but for a qualitatively *improvised* performance such as a so-named *Impromptu* for the piano or *Caprice* for the violin. Had he been addressing a purely or freely improvised music *extempore*, the very idea of making a mistake or entering an accidental tone would have been less clear, given that, in pure extemporization, *all* tones are, in some sense, either accidental or necessary given that none is determined in advance. In *extempore* activity, making a mistake must be conceived of in terms more of flouting a convention or expectation according to the type of music being made. But the point is that Nietzsche's description was about far less this or that sort of mistake than what one does when any sort of mistake threatens to derail a performance. He named persons "improvisers" of their art when they are "always ready in the moment"—*im Augenblick immer bereit*—to act, but where the *readiness* does not itself come in the instant. It comes rather from a practice or training in the art—*Übung* (from *geübt*)—and from a certain sort of fortune or divine luck, or what Bernard Williams later articulated as a "moral luck,"[10] such that, *in the moment*, they *can* actually show themselves "inventive"—*erfinderisch*—enough to do what they must do.

Nietzsche then contrasted the happiness of these persons with those whose happiness is drawn not from their ability in accommodating accidental tones, but from a rejection of this ability altogether. These persons focus on their failures and disappointments, he wrote, on how, when "in a scrape," they're left with far more than "a black eye," looking, indeed, over the cliff edge into life's "abyss." Almost toppling over the edge, they reason to themselves that the value of life *must* lie elsewhere than in winning or succeeding, and, accordingly, they remove their "bull's horns." They know instead what it means to see their lives as (almost) lost to them. Did Nietzsche regard this second kind of happiness as a cop-out or as strength? He left the answer undecided. Sometimes he saw these persons as simply rationalizing their inability or "dilettantism," but sometimes as having reached some sort of melancholic or stoic withdrawal, a Schopenhauerian contentment of resignation, arrived at quietly, in solitude.

In Nietzsche's view, both sorts of happiness are attitudinal in the face of the contingency of life. Both also situate persons sometimes in the most "tragic" situations of knowing and not-knowing on a stage where "accidental tones" turn out to be grave errors that cannot, in the end, be covered up by an "infallible hand." Sometimes, as in the ancient tragedies, protagonists are blinded in punishment for their blindness in not fully grasping or knowing their situation. But also in this view, a space or possibility is held open for improvisation *impromptu*, in which moments of joy might happen that reveal a divine inventiveness on the part of those who, though perhaps, strictly speaking, deceiving others by covering up a mistake, exhibit a know-how without exhibiting a false sense of their selves.

Getting the Point

Improvisation *extempore* and *impromptu* are both acts and arts of exchange between actors on the stage and between actors on and off the stage. Both demand a *wit* and a *fit*: the wit of flexibility and the fit of propinquity. Whereas, however, improvisation *extempore* asks us to attend to what is achieved in the performance as a whole, improvisation *impromptu* picks out the inspired or exemplary *turn* in a performance when, on the spot, one does (at best) the right or winning thing.

The combined demand for wit and fit recalls Castiglione's famed description of *sprezzatura*, the particular nonchalance and wit exhibited by a courtier that makes it seem as though all he does—with perfect fit—he does effortlessly. Yet, as so stated, *sprezzatura* captures a quality of behavior and character that is equally distinct from improvisation *extempore* and *impromptu*: it is less a creative quality than a quality of wit and fit. Nevertheless, it is what Castiglione then adds to his description of the courtier that more particularly picks out the quality associated with improvisation *impromptu*: namely, when the courtier displays a readiness—*prontezza*—for or of ingenuity, to do what must be done in the moment and *at just the right moment*.[11]

Like the term *prontezza*, the term *impromptu* or, from the nineteenth century, *promptitude*, captures the immediacy and quickness of the movement, gesture, and decision. This quickness was well described by the German Romantic aphorist, Friedrich Schlegel, in terms of a social wit or a situation when one must, as we say, "have one's wits most about one" or "be on one's toes." Schlegel aphorized this quick wit variously. He spoke of it as capturing the suddenness of the act or its singularity, momentariness, or fragmentariness, as when we deliver a punchline of a joke and deliver it well. To not deliver it well usually means trying too hard, as when, Schlegel quipped, the English try too hard to be witty in the name of mere sociability. He further distinguished the wit of a divine or mystical flash of imagination from one led by a Roman nose that has a prophetic instinct. In this "flash," he saw a quality of "improvisation" that could provoke, release, or "explode the confined spirit."[12] Yet he knew that not all explosions are worthy ones. Where there is too much freedom without control, or vice versa, there is no genuine provocation of the spirit. In the improvised style of his own aphorisms, he captured the tension between freedom and control as first staged in the ancient mythic contests, the agonistic tension between two sorts of human and social characteristics: the divine or godlike and the animalistic or satyr-like. Though *inspiration* was attached to the former—the high—and *instinct* to the latter—the low—it wasn't always clear, especially in his more ironic moments, which he preferred.

What Schlegel wrote about acts of life, he also wrote about philosophical thoughts. He wrote of enigmatic or riddled meanings as being those that are grasped with immediacy when exactly the right word is "hit upon." He used the term *getroffen,* from *treffen*—fitting—to capture the immediacy of an exclamation, such as "bull's eye!," which is clearly painful for the bull but pleasurable for those who have shot the arrow straight. The English term "hitting" does similar work. In presenting someone with an unfamiliar concept, as Wittgenstein later repeated, it's preferable not to hit persons over the head until they "get it," but to offer just enough that the concept suddenly *strikes* them as making sense. In describing what it means to master a term in a language or a rule or concept in a game, Wittgenstein noted that one grasps the meaning of a particular application "in a flash" [*blitzartig*]. He often used the dynamic term *fitting*—usually *passend* instead of *getroffen*—to capture the final relation between a term and a particular use that at first seems not to fit. For Wittgenstein, to experience something as "fitting" is often also to engage aesthetically with the thing, as when someone cuts a fine figure in a suit, but it is also to speak of getting a joke without needing, either before or after, an "explanation."[13]

Showing and Showing Off

In his *Institutes of Oratory*, Quintilian wrote of how after a long education, the fruits of all our labor are meant to culminate in the ability to speak "*ex tempore.*" Yet a primary reason for training this ability, he added, is to meet conditions *impromptu.* There arise "innumerable occasions" when there are "the most pressing or sudden emergencies," when it's absolutely necessary to speak in *the instant*—in a court of law, say, when new evidence is brought forward that one isn't expecting. The point of the training is of course to be prepared to do something *in the instant.* For it wouldn't be right for an advocate just to stand there dumb, waiting for "his voice and lungs [to be] put in tune," to beg for "a voice to save" him, or to ask for "time for retirement and silent study till his speech is formed and committed to memory." No, what such emergencies demand is a wit or know-how that entirely fits and springs from the situation, and if one doesn't have it, Quintilian concluded, one would be better off staying home, avoiding public life, and seeking another profession.[14]

But when Quintilian then tempered his remarks on the wit of improvisation, he introduced his remarks on fit, on a fittingness, as he explained, that shows but does not simply *display* one's ability to overcome an obstacle *impromptu*. When improvising in the moment, we must not suddenly digress into "*extempore* effusions." For to so digress is to show our lack of patience in waiting "for the thought to supply the matter." Here we exhibit only "a passion for display" that shows no respect for method or training, but relies only on an inarticulate hubris that a "magnificent inspiration" will suddenly come to one. He offered a deliberately manic and cultish image of persons rocking their bodies to and fro, booming and bellowing as though they had "a trumpet inside," "gesticulating wildly," and wagging their heads "with all the frenzy of a lunatic."[15] He evoked this image to differentiate the exhibitionist or hubristic tendency to display from the more sober act of finding a fitting solution on the spot. In this view, humility was clearly to be preferred to hubris. And improvisation *impromptu* had come to mean less an act performed fast than one performed at the right time with just the right amount of time in perfect response to an obstacle that had occurred unexpectedly.

Much later, in his observations on the delivery of jokes,[16] Freud picked up less on good timing than on bad timing, on the tendency specifically toward display or exhibitionism stemming, as he saw it, from a deeply engrained narcissism that saturated not only individuals but also the society as a whole. Wanting to fill up an uncomfortable silence, he explained, or wanting to free ourselves from a pressure, we act out, as we dream, in *involuntary* or *sudden* ways. Following Karl Groos's 1899 diagnosis of the sickness of civilization that attends our human games (*Die Spiele der Menschen*), Freud analyzed the satisfaction of delivering a joke in terms of a release of an instinct, either lustful or hostile, that is repressed given "an obstacle" that stands in its way. He identified the obstacle as the entire disciplining or civilizing tendency of a society that had made saying "excuse me" (or "please pass the salt") a cover-up for wanting to kill an interlocutor (or a parent) who feels much more like an opponent than a friend. Freud's analysis was more to show that the prevalent "psychopathological" condition of our lives was such as to create constant obstacles, such that, even when the moment seemed "everyday," we would produce endless slips of the tongue, sleights of the hand, or accidental tones, which, more than overcoming in glorious acts of the soul, we would simply cover up as best we can. In these everyday contexts, Freud believed that we would usually not even realize that we had made a mistake or that there had been an accident until we were forced to the analyst's couch, at which point our agonizing mistake would be revealed to have been, in another sense, quite determined.

FOR GEORGE

A perfectly complex passage from Mark Twain's novel *The Innocents Abroad* (chapter 4) finds the character, a young singer named George, being admonished for improvising—"Come, now, George, *don't* improvise. It looks too egotistical. It will provoke remark. Just stick to 'Coronation' like the others. It is a good tune—*you* can't improve it any, just off-hand, in this way." To which George responds: "Why I'm not trying to improve it—and I *am* singing like the others—just as it is in the notes." What exactly is George doing wrong? Is he changing the notes, embellishing or ornamenting them, or singing simply in a way that makes him stand out in the (choric) crowd? It turns out that George neither knows the tune nor its notes, which, the writer quips, "was also a drawback to his performances." Not knowing leads George to "turn" his voice this way and that, but occasionally "to fly off the handle and startle every body with a most discordant cackle." But more than this, George honestly believes that he is singing "just as it is in the notes," leading the writer to conclude that George had, therefore, "no one to blame but himself when his voice caught on the centre occasionally, and gave him the lockjaw." In this passage, "to improvise" means to sing the notes of a tune when you don't know them, hence, to follow along slightly behind, which might be done well or, as in George's case, not well. And it means to do something "just off-hand," where "off-hand" carries connotations of acting in a way unceremoniously, that is, without due care, or, as the *OED* further specifies, "*extempore*" or "*impromptu*." Here, the two terms that I am drawing apart are equated to capture not an impressive skill but a tendency to ride roughshod over a practice or to act in the moment, overly confident that one knows what one is doing every step of the way. Luckily, not all Georges in the world are like this George.

MAKING THE CUT

Since the 1920s, there have been "cutting contests" or "jam" sessions, which nowadays have migrated also into "rap battles." Here, "vying musicians" more or less improvise *extempore*, though the agonistic point is to demonstrate their social and artistic ability to improvise *impromptu*. An individual or group starts with a tune, rhythm, riff, or refrain that the opponent then follows with the aim to do it better. ("Anything you can do, I can do better.") Much of the contest asks for one opponent to fit what the other does, so long as he—and it is usually a he—then improves on the performance.[17] To prove his superiority, a contestant must finally cut the other off, using his instrument or performance "as a knife." The winning move is a moment of improvisation *impromptu* with a twist. One wins by overcoming the previous obstacle laid down by the opponent by responding with an insurmountable obstacle. When the obstacle is insurmountable, the loser either "crashes" in performance or simply gives up and exits the stage. Some call the winning move or wit "the fastest shout"; rappers call it "a flyt," by which they also mean a "poetic insult"—which is what we see perfectly demonstrated, and hear in abundance, in Scott Silver's 2002 film *8 Mile* and justified in the film's parting song, "Lose Yourself":

> Look, if you had one shot, or one opportunity
> To seize everything you ever wanted in one moment
> Would you capture it or just let it slip?
> . . .
> The whole crowd goes so loud
> He opens his mouth, but the words won't come out
> . . .
> He better go capture this moment and hope it don't pass him
> . . .
> You better lose yourself in the music, the moment
> You own it, you better never let it go
> You only get one shot, do not miss your chance to blow

The cutting contest staged in Jeremy Kagan's 1977 film *Scott Joplin* dramatizes a contest among ragtime piano players, but it is immediately preceded by a discussion as to whether playing by ear or writing one's notes down is the better way to proceed in the musical marketplace. Joplin comments that without "note music," he will be excluded from a market that will make him famous. This argument, right for the time when popular sheet music was the way to spread the notes, was almost outdated even then, for the technology of recording made Joplin more famous than any sheet music ever could.[18] John Fusco's 1986 film *Crossroads* turns a cutting-contest between guitarists into a Faustian fight to save a human soul. Here, the musical proficiency is demonstrated by the guitarists as they improvise on the tightrope between musical understanding and devilish technique on two pieces: Mozart's Turkish March and Paganini's Fifth Caprice. Once the contest is won and the soul restored, the music turns to rock. In all these examples, as in the ancient contests, the musical contest of who performs best is saturated by social and moral tests of character, judgment, and desire.

Several descriptions of cutting contests suggest comparisons with other and earlier modes of contest and music-making. One brings them in line with what the Romantics described, after Goethe, as an "elective affinity," a utopian-styled agonistic and sometimes Faustian play between repulsion and attraction. This imagery is still found in contemporary aesthetic theory as well as in chemistry and medicine, where we find (in the latter) talk of "reversible competitive antagonisms" that are produced when cells are blocked or cut off by others. Yet another description conceives of cutting contests as staged as though occurring between musicians or even orchestras that accidentally bump into each other on the road and decide to "duel" or "duke" it out, or, as in cowboy movies, to fight to the death. Here the language often turns toward the animalistic, so that the contests can be described also as "hunts," "chases," or "bucking contests."[19] Although cutting contests may show the cooperative, congenial, or collective aspirations of musicians—of answer and response—they also display all the bloodiness and soul-searching of the ancient, mythic contests.

A CUTTING EDGE

Can or do cutting contests occur also in "classical music" practice? Certainly yes, for there have been many sorts of contests where composers, performers, or groups of musicians have upstaged and unstaged each other in formal and informal situations. Here, again, outwitting each other by word or musical deed has often proved as important as showing oneself the better musician: Rameau versus Rousseau; Mozart versus Salieri. But there is also another sort of cut in a classical contest, where we speak not of musicians cutting each other out, but of the performance having a "cutting edge," a sort of antagonistic *wit* that brings the *work* that is being performed to a perfect *fit*.

In this matter, I once heard the pianist Peter Serkin rhythmically outwitting, almost cutting out, the violinist Pamela Frank, in a deliberately "dissonant" performance of a Bach Violin Sonata. While Pamela Frank played "the straight (wo)man," Peter Serkin competed with her "feeds." Yet the point wasn't for Serkin to win; nor was it, as "accompanist," for him to cover or make up for the violinist's errors or dull performance, for she made none and played very well. The aim, rather, was to defamiliarize a "classic," a well-known or standard(ized) work that we all think we know *prior* to the performance. The art of the great performer is to show that, in some sense, we do not know the work at all without *this* particular performance. Even a classic, and *especially* a classic or standard, needs to be played *in a way not heard before*, if, that is to say, we want to hear the work as though it were being re-created or, better, newly-created in the moment of its performance. Here, the enigmatic quality of being newly-created—*improvised*—cuts across the distinction between improvisation *extempore* and *impromptu*. We aren't deceived into thinking that the performer is really creating the music *from this moment forward*; but nor are we in awe of the performer overcoming an obstacle unless, and this is the point, the obstacle is "the work itself," that is, if the work-concept misleads us into thinking that to perform a work is to perform it just as "it is," as though, as Twain put it, it can't be "improved upon." But the agonistic point of the performance is precisely to show that without the performance, and without *each particular* performance, the "work" might be "perfect" but its perfection will remain silent and reach no ear.

Another example of how an agonistic wit may enter an exemplary performance of a work comes from 1969. Preserved as a film clip on *YouTube*, five great musicians are warming up to perform Schubert's *Trout Quintet*: Jacqueline Du Pré, Daniel Barenboim, Pinchas Zuckerman, Itzhak Perlman, and Zubin Mehta. We see them swapping their instruments and beginning to play, compliant with the score but with an extreme infidelity or unfit of pitch. Yet the slightly competitive wit of their musicianship wins the moment. They give us a perfect sense of what is to come, the combined wit and fit of a perfect performance of a work. This is not an example of improvisation *extempore*; it is closer to improvisation *impromptu* although it's not exactly that either. It's more an impromptu preparation for a performance for which they are completely prepared. In this in-between conceptual space, it makes sense to see these musicians as having done something "improvised" behind the scenes that reduces the tension and makes them laugh, a laughter that then becomes a smile carried over in Du Pré's bodily comportment into the public performance, for which, as Mehta reminds them as they are about to go on, "there's a serious public waiting outside!"[20]

WITNESSING A PUBLIC ACT

Improvisation *impromptu* situates persons in unforeseen circumstances and confronts them with unexpected obstacles. It asks what one does "in the moment," and the question has normative weight. By stressing the element of mishap, where there is a sudden deficiency or lack, the concept asks for a quick recovery. One might say that the concept is all about not screwing or covering up in a situation of pressure, or of not running off the stage when we have stage fright. Yet these thoughts don't by themselves capture what I think lies at the core of the agonistic concept: namely, its publicity. Of course public actions or matters of exhibition or display are tied to inner obstacles or unconscious wars that persons fight with themselves, but actions of improvisation *impromptu* are typically tied to what is also witnessed by others. At times when we do witness persons overcoming their inner fear, we tend to respond with relief, with a "phew!" When, however, we go to witness an act of improvisation *impromptu*, we want something more. As the eighteenth century distinction has it: we want and need, as witnesses to the act, not merely the *phew* but also the *awe*.[21]

Quintilian saw public speaking as carrying an ekphrastic significance and responsibility, especially in a court of law, to render *compelling* or *persuasive* something *visible* to an audience in a performance, "before their very eyes," or, more accurately, "before their mind's eye," so that, with Derrida, the "mind's eye" or imagination would be set into motion, but where this means less an aesthetic free-play than a freeing-up or unbinding of our thought and emotion.[22] Derrida construed the publicity by addressing again the extreme difficulty or almost "impossibility" of "improvisation." Where "there is improvisation," he said, "I am not able to see myself. I am blind to myself. And it's what I will see, no, I won't see it. It's for others to see."

Often, as we have seen, improvisation *impromptu* means "going for broke"—showing that one is prepared to go somewhere or take a way out for which others are not prepared. Sometimes it means creating an obstacle in return that one's opponent cannot surmount. But, from the perspective of reception, it is about visibly or audibly overcoming an obstacle, to show "the victory" as evident to all. This way, it thrills, causing an audience to gasp, to applaud spontaneously, to proclaim the victor without doubt. Etymologically, "to surprise" is to "take hold of" or "affect" somebody else by something unexpected. When an audience is unexpectedly well taken, it affirms the act or performance. When ill taken, it might appreciate many other things but not "that certain thing."

When improvisation *impromptu* goes well, the performer might well say "I couldn't have done other than improvise, but what I did turned out to be exactly the right thing to do." Here, there is a feeling both of contingency and necessity felt by both the performer and the audience. When the performer says, "This is what I *had* to do given the situation in which I found myself," the words evidence an alertness: that the performer was ready to act in response to anything that might happen, even though the performer couldn't have thought out the solution in advance because she or he didn't know the obstacle in advance. The not-knowing is what Derrida meant by the blindness. In improvising *impromptu*, unlike in improvising *extempore*, the not-knowing is threefold: we do not know that we will have to improvise at all, or how we will improvise when we do have to improvise, and we do not know how our improvising will turn out, although, if well-trained, we might well feel secure that we will indeed know how to employ our wit to make the right fit. All this not-knowing is quite different from the ignorant George, the dilettante who, improvising "off the cuff," offers, as we also say, only a band-aid to cover the wound. When one acts badly like this, one might well meet with a moral stare from the audience suggesting that one's act was dishonest, deceitful, even artless—which it was. Here, we may say, one is literally caught out in the act.

DOING IT THE WRONG WAY

We come now to another example, not of *impromptu* performance but of *impromptu* judgment. It shows not performers acting badly as much as the audience or responders who fail to get the point of the performance. To an extent, this example mirrors what goes on in the Apollo Theater. When amateurs don't perform as others think they should, they are "executed," only now they actually lose their lives. In this example, the execution shows no wit, no fit, and no etiquette as befits the Apollo Theater. It shows, rather, the impotence and rage of an impromptu or ill-considered response of "judges" to something they witness on the stage. It has little to be said in its favor.

A *New York Times* editorial of February 7, 2010, reported six cases from the Philippines of karaoke performers who were killed for singing Frank Sinatra's song "My Way." The matter was so severe that singing the song was banned. Norimitsu Onishi, the reporter, asked if there was something sinister in the song, something offensively associated with the West, or something about the song's renown that caused the audience to react as it did. The last explanation was preferred. Because the song was so familiar and popular among those who frequented the karaoke club, only the performance was judged, not the song itself. Indeed, this fits the very idea of karaoke: that anyone, whatever their talent or training, is both free to and meant to improvise on a well-known song *in their own way, not heard before*. What, then, accounts for the killing? A deflated explanation suggests that the performers were killed simply for singing "out of tune"; a more complex explanation says that they were somehow singing "the wrong notes," that how they sang the song was "the wrong way" to sing it. Onishi read this latter explanation, agonistically, as a mode of "triumphalism."

Consider the matter this way. I go to a karaoke club to hear how others sing a familiar song *their way*, yet I believe that *my way* of singing the song is better, maybe even the best or the *only way*. So convinced am I of my own way that I execute those who sing the song in a different way. In this way, I transgress the etiquette of the club: *to each her own way*. The transgression sometimes results in real physical violence. In this case, it is the audience that acts badly, even belligerently, and not the performer, but significantly because the audience is constituted by overly-competitive performers. But killing a competing performer on the spot is not how one proves or shows that one's own way to sing "I did it my way" is the better way. It would be much better to take one's competitor on with a song.

IN AND OUT OF THE GROOVE

The account that best captures the positive moral, social, and existential connotations of improvisation *impromptu* is the one that Gilbert Ryle offered in his article of 1976.[23] Though he titled his piece "Improvisation," he started not with this term but with the associated term, "innovation," to remind his readers of the admiration and envy that most of us feel toward those who are innovative and who, by being innovative, produce innovative products. He offered a list of qualitative terms associated with character, temperament, and personality—"imaginative, inventive, enterprising, inquisitive, ingenious, witty, cunning, observant, responsive, alert or creative"—and then a list of productive terms associated with the ability to "compose, design, experiment, initiate, select, adapt, improvise, undertake, contrive, explore, parry, or speculate." To include the term *improvise* in the second list, as only a passing mention, was a little odd given that "improvisation" was meant to be the overall concept of his enquiry. But perhaps it was his way of alerting his readers to the possibility that, in addition to the broader concept, there is a narrower concept: when, in my terms, we improvise *impromptu*. Ryle did not make explicit the distinction between the narrower and broader concept, but went on instead to address improvisation mostly as a mode of innovation and ingenuity so that he could capture the difference he believed it makes in human life if we cross a river, climb a ladder, or pursue a philosophical train of thought only carefully, step-by-step, or by means also of one or more larger, inspired leaps—*impromptu*. Of what value, he wanted to know, is the ability to think and to act with a certain blindness, without having thought everything out in advance? In part he showed the value by writing his essay *about* improvisation as though he had improvised it "off the cuff"—yet he wrote it not out of "mere sociability," as Schlegel put it, but with a typically British "cuttingness" of wit drawn on the basis of his considerable experience of doing philosophy in his "ordinary language" sort of way. Though he maintained a cheerfulness of description, behind the scenes was a harsh criticism of those to whom these cheerful terms did not apply.

Having made two lists, of characteristics and abilities, Ryle now listed the sort of exemplary persons who are admired for being able to move beyond habits without reaching the extremes of eccentricity or craziness. He named the "geniuses," "pathfinders," "jaywalkers," those of high wit and swift repartee, and those whose intelligence enables them "to seize new opportunities and to face new hazards." To illustrate these types, he alluded to a verse, often quoted in discussions of freedom and determinism, and sometimes attributed to Maurice E. Hare: that these exemplary persons are not trams, whose lifelines are carved out on the street in advance; they are rather busses for whom their life passages are (more) open. Here is one version of the verse:

> There was a young man who said "Damn!
> I perceive with regret that I am
> But a creature that moves
> In predestinate grooves
> I'm not even a bus, I'm a tram."

Having started out on the conceptual path of "innovation," Ryle ended up in the company of persons whom, as he wrote, "every hour of the waking day," or "every day of the week" engage perhaps "familiar and unaugust sorts of improvisation." Following Nietzsche, it sounds like an exhausting way to live life! Yet Ryle's point was only to remind us that in doing, thinking, and writing, we "essay" (from *essai*) solely because we are (or are meant to be) thinking beings. Those who think by following the "groove," in contrast to those who "groove" while thinking, are those who believe that we act, think and write solely from a pre-packaged mechanism or pattern. Explicitly recalling Wittgenstein and Chomsky, Ryle offered an analogy to the mechanism or technology of music. We shouldn't think of ourselves, he argued, as outputting or reproducing an internal and constantly-spinning gramophone record. For what the assumption of such a mental "mechanicalness" prohibits is a "freshness," "Ad-Hockery," or willingness to turn or move *in the moment* in unexpected ways. To allow ourselves to improvise is to open ourselves up to the "cleverness" of "the caricaturist or conversationalist" or the "adroitness," as he put it, of a "dialectical" thinker or "fencer."

Ryle noted that when persons act or think on their feet, we tend to ask them not what they have done but "how on earth" they got from A to B. And typically their answer is that they don't know, that the movement or thought just came to them, that it was unrehearsed, "on-the-spur-of-the-moment." But how, he then asked, do we assess or judge their actions? Should we hold them responsible given that what they did was not "intended" in the sense of premeditated, but nor again was it merely accidental? Their acts, rather, were the outcome of a wit, a style, a certain "presence of mind." But how does one lay down the criteria for judging all this? Ryle did not pursue this intriguing question of judgment; he jumped instead to what it means to move by unpredictable leaps and bounds. Here, he might have well drawn on Aesop's fable of the competing tortoise and hare, but he didn't do this either because he was finally most concerned with the *impromptu* characteristic of a sort of "detective" work, where, with all the evidence before one and with no new evidence forthcoming, one cannot at first see the solution and then, *suddenly*, one sees it—*in the moment*. But from this, he didn't then further articulate his idea of improvisation, as I have, as an *act* of improvising (*impromptu*); he saw it only as evidence of a *quality* or *characteristic* that persons exhibit when they have the wit, ingenuity, nerves, or luck enough to allow the unexpected to happen to enter into what they do or think—everyday.

CHALLENGING COMPLIANCE

When I first read Ryle's essay a few years ago, I was writing about Nelson Goodman's thesis of perfect compliance, the strict condition that preserves the identity of a musical work through its many performances. Perfect compliance along the tram tracks is required, Goodman had argued, to prevent an identification of Beethoven's *Fifth Symphony* with *Three Blind Mice*, an identification that follows, logically, if we allow one, two, three . . . non-compliant elements or errors to enter into a performance of a work.[24] Having once been very absorbed by why, in discussing the ontological status of musical works, Beethoven's *Fifth Symphony* is most usually selected by philosophers as the paradigmatic example, I was now asking why Goodman had selected *Three Blind Mice* as where we might end up if we take the wrong bus. It turned out that there were many fascinating reasons, including one suggested by Ryle. When, in an academic "epidemic of initialization," as he put it, we abbreviate phrases—as when *Three Blind Mice* becomes *TBM*—we eventually become blinded to what the words once meant—all the ordinary words that Ryle had put into his lists. But had Goodman, I then asked, really been taken in by this epidemic? Not as much as he has been accused of by those who have rejected his perfect compliance. In specifying so exact or strict a condition, Goodman had insisted that he was concerned only to preserve the *identity* of the work: all that made the work aesthetic, innovative, qualitatively exciting in its performance was another matter, lying beyond questions of identity. Whereas, with the later Wittgenstein, Ryle tried to capture the qualitative content of improvisation by appealing to extraordinary examples of ordinary things, Goodman, with the early Wittgenstein of the *Tractatus*, put the aesthetic matter outside the scope of what strictly could be accounted for by logical means. But in both cases, the result was the same that singing it, as George does, just as the notes say need not exclude improvisation as a quality of performance.

BROKEN STRINGS

I conclude this essay with a single example that pulls all the threads that I have introduced together into an uneasy image of epidemic blindness or prejudice that is at once both musical and social. Through a son's act of improvising *impromptu*, a blindness is revealed to a father who cannot see. The son's act is necessitated by a broken string; the father's blindness is signified by a broken arm. The father is so obedient to the classical work-concept that he cannot see a space for a way of making music differently, his music or anyone else's. He is especially blinded to the improvisational quality of swinging with one's notes. The story doesn't, however, ask us to take sides with one sort of music against another, but nor does it say that we should not take sides. It rather shows us the danger of taking sides for the wrong reasons. This is not a new point, but, as the example shows, it resurfaces as urgent whenever conceptual strings are pulled to the wrong extremes. Consistent with the aim of critique—and with the concept of improvisation *impromptu* placed at its core—the example aims to break the thickest string of all: unwarranted prejudice.

Broken Strings is the title of a Harlem Renaissance film, directed by Bernard B. Ray and starring Clarence Muse, an actor suitably named given the film's subject matter.[25] (There is "suitable" naming throughout the film.) It opens with the father, Arthur Williams, performing a piece of standard virtuoso violin music before an all-black audience in a concert hall. The audience is mostly enthralled, though the camera focuses twice on a person who sleeps. A hint is given that the classical work-music Williams is performing, or how he is performing, is not to the liking of all (black people). The concert ends with Williams telling the audience of the special "kinship" he feels with "my folks," although usually he plays for "the [white] people of the world." The tension is deepened when, later, his manager tells an enthusiastic fan from the local church that Williams does not play for free even for "his folk," and that his fee remains at a thousand dollars. Williams's son, Johnny, is standing nearby and asks to carry his father's violin home while his father goes off with his manager. While driving the father away in a car, the manager becomes distracted. There is a crash leaving the father with a broken arm and hand.

Weeks later, the cast is removed, but the nerve damage remains. Williams is "reduced" to teaching. One pupil is talentless and is thrown out. The second, Dickey Morley, is disciplined but overly compliant. The third is his young son, Johnny, who is undisciplined but entirely talented. The father is frustrated: his "great soul" no longer has an outlet. So he puts his hope in his son. However, the outlet Johnny desires is one that demands neither "repose" nor "control," but demands that one "play" as a bird flies, "this way and that, up and down … ringing and swinging through the air." He wants to play "just music" (as though there were something that was "just music"), but illustrates his desire by "swinging" on an already given work: Dvořák's "Humoresque." His father thinks only of the work and not the swing, and accuses his son of "desecrating a classic," and more, of "committing a crime against music."

A parallel drama involves Williams's daughter, suitably named Gracie, who loves one man but not another, leading the unloved to enter into a contest with the beloved. The contest is lost by the unloved because he cheats. Being a sore loser, he acts badly, leaving his father, a Mr. Stilton, the owner (suitably) of a beauty products store, having to put things right.[26] With Gracie jobless and her father bitter, the family falls into poverty. Johnny takes matters into his own hands and goes busking with his accompanist Mary in the swing clubs. He will use the money earned to feed his family and to pay for an operation that might save his father's musical hand. He receives enthusiastic applause in the "Mellow Café," where his "humoresque" keeps everyone on their toes (dancing), including a very tall, thin, and talented banjo player named Stringbean Johnson. The café is a high-class establishment with standards that Johnny meets, until his father arrives to haul him off the stage. His father punishes him, forcing him to play scales for "twenty hours if need be" until "the spirit of jazz" is "driven out of him." Gracie arrives home, Johnny collapses, and the father is scolded. Gracie declares: "Johnny did all this for you!"

The drama's moment of recognition but uneasy reconciliation comes when Mr. Stilton offers a cash prize for an amateur radio contest, for those who never before have had "the opportunity to express themselves." The contest is introduced with a demonstration at the piano, to urge that, whatever music is performed, it should be true to the expression of its mood. "There is beauty in all music," we are told: music "is the international language," after which the introducer demonstrates how different musics express joy. But apparently music is not a "universal" language for everyone to enjoy equally. Reiterating the idea of a special kinship or affinity, he notes that "We [of the black race] are considered one of the most musical people on earth, because we have suffered." His statements are for us, but immediately for Arthur Williams, who is nervously perched in the front row of the live radio audience wondering how his son will perform the classical "mazurka" he has promised his father he will play.

The contest begins with three little muses—the Stevens Sisters—singing and tapping popular fox trots, and then Stringbean Johnson performing on his banjo a piece that he says he first heard Arthur Williams play—only now it is "jazzed" up. Third to go is Dickey Morley, who plays (appropriately) a tarantella, for when, again backstage, he takes a knife and cuts the strings of Johnny's violin almost to a breaking point. When Johnny, going last, begins to play his mazurka, he begins on the G string. It snaps and he looks forlorn. The audience gasps then laughs, which inspires him to go on—until the D string snaps. With two strings left, he can no longer play the piece compliantly, and starts to swing. Soon enough the backup orchestra and everyone else join in, showing that he is the obvious winner. His father applauds with vigor enough to bring the nerves in his hand back to life. Still fearful of his father, the son apologizes: it was "the only honest way out." Dickey apologizes to Johnny for having cheated. And Williams declares that although his "heart still belongs to the Masters"—(which Masters?)—it is swing that has mended his strings. "Look," he says, taking back his violin from his son, "what swing has done for me!"

But has Williams, or the film, accepted "swing" as a legitimate music? Yes, though not at the expense of the music "of the Masters." The point is not to decide between musics, but between persons who are stuck in their ways—trammed up—and persons who are open to "swinging" on whatever bus they take, for, as one song goes, nothing means "a thing if it ain't got that swing."

This rather obvious point assumes more subtlety only when we note that when confronted with broken strings, Johnny does two things at once: he improvises *impromptu* and he begins to swing or improvise *extempore* on the melody of the mazurka. But for which is he rewarded or more rewarded? Would he have won had Dickey not cut his strings: would he have played his mazurka well? Or would he have performed without inspiration, preferring to play another sort of music? The film does not answer these questions. Instead, it shows us the awe of an audience who sees Johnny turning an obstacle into an advantage. To be sure, the audience moves to the swing, but, in the end, it is his act of improvisation *impromptu* that wins him the contest: that he could accommodate an obstacle or injury in a way that his father had not been able to do.

This conclusion has precedents, one of the first being in Pindar's twelfth *Pythian Ode* where words sung in the Dorian mode told of a contest in which, when the mouthpiece of Midas of Akragas's pipe broke off, he played on. And then it is said that his act "so surprised the audience," that "he was declared the winner." But what he played or how he played was not described. He seems to have been rewarded for his ability to improvise a solution *impromptu*, for this said something about him as a "musical"—muse-inspired person—beyond his being merely a performing musician. There are many more stories of this sort, perhaps the best known but also the most double-edged regarding the broken strings of Paganini's violin. Paganini cut his own strings to show his divine hand and for the latter, he was praised as being godlike. But staging the event repeatedly to impress his audience, he renders the apparent obstacle no real obstacle at all. For the deception, he was compared to the devil.

In the end, broken strings, arms, minds, and bodies have no value in themselves. They only provide opportunities to act or to keep on acting, or to stop acting. In the musical contests, new and old, it isn't only the music played that has counted but also, and sometimes more, what has been shown about the performers or actors as musicians, artists, and thinkers. Put like this, however, a conceptual critique of improvisation that looks at contests in art and life to reveal what is best about ourselves risks a sort of blind utopianism not much better than what Ryle described as an epidemic of academic initialization. If improvisation shows us at our best, it also shows us at our worst. If, therefore, I have urged a distinction between improvisation *impromptu* and improvisation *extempore* in order to open up a conceptual and musical space to let more music and more persons into the arena, I conclude on a different note: with a recommendation that we take from my argument less the distinction than the complex descriptions of how the terms, improvisation *impromptu* and improvisation *extempore*, have done their work, and continue to do their work, apart and together, in situations that only ever seem ordinary but never really are.

Notes

1. Cf. Edward Ferrero, *The Art of Dancing* (New York: Ferrero, 1859), 27.
2. Richard Carlin, ed., *Ain't Nothing Like the Real Thing: The Apollo Theater and American Entertainment* (Washington DC: Smithsonian Books, 2010).

3. I have treated the plight of musicians and the musical art in several recent companion essays, for example, in my manuscript, "'All Art Constantly Aspires to the Condition of Music,' Except the Art of Music." The present essay is written for George Lewis, whose own work on improvisation, thought and performed, I admire greatly. Thanks also to the many friends and colleagues who have commented on this essay: most especially to Bernard Gendron, Felix Koch, Marlies de Munck, Erum Naqvi, and Beau Shaw.

4. Pausanias, *Description of Greece*, tr. W.H.S. Jones (Cambridge MA.: Harvard University Press, 1934): 10.30.8.

5. I have outlined the terms of this discourse in my *The Imaginary Museum of Musical Works: An Essay in the Philosophy of Music* (New York: Oxford University Press, [1992] 2007), esp. chapter 8.

6. This notion of critique is drawn most explicitly from the work of Theodor W. Adorno, whose ideas of improvisation, risk, and experimentalism I have treated in "Explosive Experiments and the Fragility of the Experimental," in *Elective Affinities: Musical Essays on the History of Aesthetic Theory* (New York: Columbia University Press, 2008), 108–135.

7. Cf. Gary Peters, *The Philosophy of Improvisation* (Chicago: University of Chicago Press, 2009), 168.

8. Ralph Waldo Emerson (1878): "Of no use are [those] who study to do exactly as was done before, who can never understand that today is a new day. . . . We want [persons] of original perception and original action, who can open their eyes wider than to a nationality . . .; [persons] of elastic, [persons] of moral mind, who can live in the moment and take a step forward." *Fortune of the Republic* (Boston: Houghton, Osgood and Co., 1879), 35.

9. I am drawing in this section from sections 22, 303, and 295 of Friedrich Nietzsche, *The Gay Science: With a Prelude in German Rhymes and an Appendix of Songs*, ed. Bernard Williams (Cambridge: Cambridge University Press, 2001).

10. Bernard Williams, *Moral Luck* (Cambridge: Cambridge University Press, 1982), 20–39.

11. Baldassare Castiglione, *The Book of the Courtier*, ed. Daniel Javitch (New York: Norton, 2002), 32.

12. Cf. Friedrich Schlegel, *Philosophical Fragments*, tr. Peter Firchow (Minneapolis: University of Minnesota Press, 1991), esp. 11, 24.

13. Ludwig Wittgenstein, *Lectures and Conversations on Aesthetics, Psychology, and Religious Belief*, ed. Cyril Barrett (Berkeley: University of California Press, 2007).

14. Quintilian, *Institutio Oratoria*, tr. Harold Edgeworth Butler (Cambridge MA: Harvard University Press, 1920), 10.7.1. See also Chris Holcomb, "'The Crown of All Our Study': Improvisation in Quintilian's *Institutio Oratoria*." *Rhetoric Society Quarterly* 31, no. 3 (Summer 2001): 53–72.

15. Quintilian, *Institutio Oratoria*, 2.11.4 and 2.12.9.

16. Sigmund Freud, *Jokes and Their Relation to the Unconscious*, ed. James Strachey (New York: Norton, 1960), 119–123.

17. Cf. Philip Alperson, "Musical Improvisation," *Journal of Aesthetics and Art Criticism* 68, no. 3 (Summer 2010): 273–299.

18. In the present essay, I do not treat, for reasons of space, the enormous impact of recording technology on concepts of improvisation, other than indirectly later in the essay, when a distinction is drawn between an open and a mechanical mind.

19. See Jurgen E. Grandt, *Kinds of Blue: The Jazz Aesthetic in African American Narrative* (Columbus: Ohio State University Press, 2005), chapter 4.

20. In his *Philosophy of the Performing Arts* (Oxford: Wiley-Blackwell, 2011), chapter 8, David Davies draws the concept of improvisation into contact with that of a rehearsal. The discussion is focused on the work of preparation or bringing constraints to a performance of any type of music. To this discussion, one may add the thought that all the revision and decision making that goes on behind the scenes is precisely that which is not shown as such in the public performance, but which is turned into a demonstration of "perfect" fit and wit.

21. Deborah Brown, "What Part of 'Know' Don't You Understand?" *The Monist* 88, no. 1 (January 2005): 11–35.

22. Cf. my related account of ekphrasis in "How to Do More with Words: Two Views of (Musical) Ekphrasis," *British Journal of Aesthetics* 50, no. 4 (October 2010): 389–410.

23. Gilbert Ryle, "Improvisation," *Mind* 85, no. 337 (January 1976): 69–83.

24. Lydia Goehr, "Three Blind Mice: Goodman, McLuhan, and Adorno on the Art of Music and Listening in the Age of Global Transmission," *New German Critique* 35, no. 2 (Summer 2008): 1–31.

25. Krin Gabbard persuasively connects this work to the 1927 film, *The Jazz Singer*. See Krin Gabbard, *Jammin' at the Margins: Jazz and the American Cinema* (Chicago: University of Chicago Press, 1996), 108–109. But one might also connect it to Krenek's opera *Jonny spielt auf*, also of 1927.

26. In this double drama, over music and love, the film interestingly mirrors the complex agonisms of Richard Wagner's *Die Meistersinger*, agonisms that I have explored in "—wie ihn uns Meister Dürer gemalt!": Contest, Myth, and Prophecy in Wagner's *Die Meistersinger von Nürnberg*," *Journal of the American Musicological Society* 60, no. 1 (2011): 51–118.

BIBLIOGRAPHY

Alperson, Philip. "Musical Improvisation." *Journal of Aesthetics and Art Criticism* 68, no. 3 (Summer 2010): 273–299.

Brown, Deborah. "What Part of 'Know' Don't You Understand?" *The Monist* 88, no. 1 (January 2005): 11–35.

Carlin, Richard, ed. *Ain't Nothing Like the Real Thing: The Apollo Theater and American Entertainment*. Washington DC: Smithsonian Books, 2010.

Castiglione, Baldassare. *The Book of the Courtier*. Edited by Daniel Javitch. New York: Norton, 2002.

Davies, David. *Philosophy of the Performing Arts*. Oxford: Wiley-Blackwell, 2011.

Emerson, Ralph Waldo. *Fortune of the Republic*. Boston: Houghton, Osgood and Co., 1879.

Ferrero, Edward. *The Art of Dancing*. New York: Ferrero, 1859.

Freud, Sigmund. *Jokes and Their Relation to the Unconscious*. Edited by James Strachey. New York: Norton, 1960.

Gabbard, Krin. *Jammin' at the Margins: Jazz and the American Cinema*. Chicago: University of Chicago Press, 1996.

Goehr, Lydia. "'All Art Constantly Aspires to the Condition of Music,' Except the Art of Music." Unpublished manuscript.

Goehr, Lydia. *Elective Affinities: Musical Essays on the History of Aesthetic Theory*. New York: Columbia University Press, 2008.

Goehr, Lydia. "How to Do More with Words: Two Views of (Musical) Ekphrasis." *British Journal of Aesthetics* 50, no. 4 (October 2010): 389–410.

Goehr, Lydia. *The Imaginary Museum of Musical Works: An Essay in the Philosophy of Music*. New York: Oxford University Press, 2007. Originally published in 1992.

Goehr, Lydia. "Three Blind Mice: Goodman, McLuhan, and Adorno on the Art of Music and Listening in the Age of Global Transmission." *New German Critique* 35, no. 2 (Summer 2008): 1–31.

Goehr, Lydia. "—wie ihn uns Meister Dürer gemalt!": Contest, Myth, and Prophecy in Wagner's *Die Meistersinger von Nürnberg*." *Journal of the American Musicological Society* 60, no. 1 (2011): 51–118.

Grandt, Jurgen E. *Kinds of Blue: The Jazz Aesthetic in African American Narrative*. Columbus: Ohio State University Press, 2005.

Holcomb, Chris. "'The Crown of all Our Study': Improvisation in Quintilian's *Institutio Oratoria*." *Rhetoric Society Quarterly* 31, no. 3 (Summer 2001): 53–72.

Nietzsche, Friedrich. *The Gay Science: With a Prelude in German Rhymes and an Appendix of Songs*. Edited by Bernard Williams. Cambridge: Cambridge University Press, 2001.

Pausanias. *Description of Greece*. Translated by W.H.S. Jones. Cambridge MA: Harvard University Press, 1934.

Peters, Gary. *The Philosophy of Improvisation*. Chicago: University of Chicago Press, 2009.

Quintilian. *Institutio Oratoria*. Translated by Harold Edgeworth Butler. Cambridge MA: Harvard University Press, 1920.

Ryle, Gilbert. "Improvisation." *Mind* 85, no. 337 (January 1976): 69–83.

Schlegel, Friedrich. *Philosophical Fragments*. Translated by Peter Firchow. Minneapolis: University of Minnesota Press, 1991.

Williams, Bernard. *Moral Luck*. Cambridge: Cambridge University Press, 1982.

Wittgenstein, Ludwig. *Lectures and Conversations on Aesthetics, Psychology, and Religious Belief*. Edited by Cyril Barrett. Berkeley: University of California Press, 2007.

CHAPTER 27

....

ENSEMBLE IMPROVISATION, COLLECTIVE INTENTION, AND GROUP ATTENTION

....

GARRY L. HAGBERG

EVERY performer knows, I think, that there is a difference of a fundamental kind between performing solo and performing in an ensemble. Similarly, performers in ensembles who have performed both non-improvisational and improvisational music know there is a fundamental difference in kind there as well. On the level of embodied action, these differences are fairly evident. But the articulation of them—that is, articulation with the kind of detail sufficient to both the nuances and the depth of the actual phenomenology in question—is a more difficult matter, and interestingly so.

One of the first models for ensemble performance that presents itself is that of the social contract: the collective is no more than a convergence of individuals who, *as individuals first*, choose one at a time to join a group that offers benefits (in our case musical) that expand what the individual could create alone, in exchange for a corresponding reduction in individual or autonomous freedom. The violist in a string quartet agrees to play under—in terms of both pitch and authority—the first violinist, and that violist (like the other players) has by virtue of the musical-social contract an obligation to play with (in tempo, articulation, phrasing, timbre, line shaping, and overall interpretation) the collective will of the other players.

What is of central interest here for present considerations is that, in the ensemble variant of the social contract model, the individual, *as individual* (in political and ontological terms), is present and intact from start to finish. If the collective authority, or Hobbes's Leviathan, turns and starts working against the individual's interests, the individual—always present as one atom in a collective organization—counters that turn by resisting, rebelling, or removing. And on this model, the entire content of the collective is simply the sum of the individuals combined. And there—exactly there—lies the rub.

A conception of the human self rests beneath the social contract model, and it is one we both easily presume and rarely articulate. That conception shapes and restricts, to a far greater extent than commonly realized, our thinking about the nature of ensemble performance. The social contract model, with an individualistic picture of human selfhood underwriting it, does some justice—perhaps a good deal of justice—to non-improvised ensemble performance. Each player plays her part, each player practices individually and then brings the pre-cognized part to the larger whole, and the end result is the sum of those parts. I know that gifted ensemble players will say that magical things can happen in such ensembles—moments of musical grace that seem to transcend individuality, and I certainly would not dispute that. But the point remains that the end sonic result is both (1) additive in nature and (2) the predetermined end toward which the pre-cognized means have been aiming. The individual—or actually a philosophical picture of the individual that some philosophers call the Cartesian self, that is, a hermetically sealed consciousness transparent unto itself that is invariably present in experience and that is only contingently related to any external thing—remains undisturbed on this understanding of ensemble participation. Thus, the picture of selfhood generates the social contract model, which in turn generates the picture of ensemble participation that we then—closing the circle—use as evidence for the accuracy of the picture of the self that started the whole thing in the first place. Stated most directly, the submerged conceptual model determines how we see organized human action in ensemble performance.

All this would generate a way of seeing and then of describing the fundamental difference between solo and ensemble performance: the soloist, as individual, is present and alone; the section player is also present as individual, but contained within a larger collective. Simple—but when applied to the difference between non-improvisational and improvisational ensemble performance, simple and—instructively—wrong.

Here's why, I believe: intention, on the Cartesian model of selfhood, would without exception be mentally private to the intender. There could be no such thing as an intention that transcended, or was external to, any given single individual. Thus the intentional content of, say, the Tokyo String quartet playing Bartok's Fourth Quartet would be the exact sum of—and, with a metaphysical guarantee, no more than—each of the four players added together, where that intentional content includes both the intentions as enacted within the performance and the intentions prior to it—in individual and ensemble practice—that shape what happens. Here of course we would have what we might call meta-intentions as well, that is, intentions in the performance to reenact sonically pre-performance intentions as set down in rehearsal. Cecil Taylor's great improvising quartet—one should probably say fiercely and relentlessly improvising—of the early 1970s, would then, given the conceptual limits on intention and the picture of selfhood beneath them, be seen as a kind of performance that telescopes pre-performance intentions into performance-only ones (where thus no meta-intentions of the kind just mentioned are possible). Each member of the quartet, as socially contracted individuals, intends to play what he plays in the moment, and the sum total of intentional content is, in principle, like that of the Tokyo Quartet's performance—with the difference of telescoping time into the moment. This is often described as the collapsing of the roles of the composer and the performer into one. And in that very description, once one is prepared to look for it, one can see fairly plainly the preservation of autonomous individuality and its corresponding privacy of intention, be it prior to or in the performance. But what I think is actually taking place within an improvising ensemble of the kind developed in Taylor's, or John Coltrane's later groups (as in his *Ascension* session, for example),[1] is considerably more interesting than the foregoing line of thought would allow us to see or say.

A number of recent philosophers have developed a conception of collective intention (which, admittedly, *given Cartesian presuppositions*, sounds like an oxymoron).[2] This new conception originates in the insight that there is something essential to the phenomenology of collective action that remains after we subtract the sum total of individual intentions from the final result. That is something we hear in Taylor, Coltrane, and many others; it is something we can, with a little luck and the right preparation, experience in our own performances within improvising ensembles; and it is the difference between non-improvisational and improvisational ensemble work that is so easily misdescribed when using only our standard stock of heretofore available terms. But why should we think, against the settled philosophical intuitions that intentions require minds, and only individuals—not collectives or ensembles—have minds, that nevertheless room for collective intentional work must be kept open? Or if our standard terminology would already close that room, how then do we reopen it to describe accurately the work of a creative *ensemble* and not only the creative work of the individuals in it?

Against additive accounts of group intention, John Searle[3] has offered a striking contrast. In Case 1, a group of individuals are seated near each other in a park. Sudden dark clouds move in and a heavy rain suddenly starts falling. They all leap up and run under nearby shelter. Case 2: A group of actors in a play are in the same situation and, as part of the rehearsed play, leap up together and run for shelter. Outwardly, the actions look pretty much the same. But Searle observes that the collective intention in Case 2 is different in *kind* from the collection of individual intentions in Case 1, and—here's the important point for us—no number (hence the difference in kind or quality, not quantity) of "I intend to X" pieces can add up to a single "We intend to X." Even with a common set of shared beliefs (e.g., It is starting to rain; I don't want to get soaked; I can run over there and get shelter; etc.) and subsequent common actions, and even with what appears outwardly to be a group moving, we still do not have a *group* moving. Thus, *mutatis mutandis*, we will never capture the true character of the "we-intention" exemplified with such interactive creativity in the ensemble performances of Taylor, late Coltrane, or Ornette Coleman's groups of the 1960s and 1970s. And as Searle also sees, the content of the individual intentions that one forms and upon which one acts within the context of a "we-intend" structure will themselves be different from any autonomous intention formed as an individual, or, for us, as a soloist. (Just think of the difference in frame of mind between a soloist playing an unaccompanied solo recital and what we call the soloist performing a concerto.) Collective intentions, Searle sees, necessarily include a sense (here we return to some of the telling nuances of the phenomenology) of believing, acting, and willing—and for us, performing—*together*. I would add that collective intentions, as a distinct kind, are necessarily relationally constituted: to sound rather like William James for a moment, the relations between the sets of beliefs, desires, actions, aspirations, interactions, thoughts, second thoughts, and all the rest are as important as those mental events themselves.[4] And if that is true, then we are now getting closer to capturing the distinct something that is present in improvisational ensemble work that is not capturable on individual-based models and that is at the heart of the difference between improvisational and non-improvisational ensemble performance. Searle suggests that the human ability to conceive and enact "we-intentions" is of itself (1) biologically basic of us as humans, and it is (2) unto itself logically primitive, that is, this ability does not break down into still more fundamental constituent parts. No less than the social fabric of reality, for Searle, is constituted by collective intentionality. If this is true, I want to add that here then is another specific way in which group jazz improvisation is—if a bit surprisingly—a mimetic art form[5]: it holds a mirror up to what Searle identifies as the complexly interwoven sets of collective intentions that make society real over and above mere arbitrary convention. But as I have argued elsewhere, group jazz improvisation is more than mimetic: it enacts within its own musical world what it reflects as mirror of society. To capture this, we turn to another major contributor to the collective intention issue, Michael Bratman.[6]

Like Searle, Bratman sees that the summative picture of organized and cohesive collective action can only rise to a weak sense of any shared endeavor: here, as a new Case 1, let's say you and I each have a ten-pound note (and thus in the weak sense share the property of having ten-pound notes).[7] As new Case 2, you and I go together with one ten-pound note and share it to pay for afternoon coffee together. Some players—often beginners—in improvisational ensembles, who do not yet have the requisite developed concepts and skills of ensemble interaction, share in the performance in the weak sense. Like adding sums of autonomous intentions, we will never, I want to suggest, get to a full understanding of the great achievements of group improvisation from this. (Incidentally, the old joke about the importance of keeping romance alive in a marriage plays on a conflation of these weak and strong senses: The husband says, "I know it's important to keep romance alive, so we go out two nights every week. I go on Monday and Wednesday, and my wife goes on Tuesday and Thursday.") As a teacher of jazz ensembles, I myself have seen wonderful moments in the lives of young players when it suddenly dawns on them that there is much more going on than the weak sense of sharing in creative group interaction—it is as though a new world of possibility opens by glimpsing the strong sense.

So, what more precisely *is* the strong sense; how do we fully describe it? Bratman rightly believes that the action we are after is to be found in the interrelations between the collectively inflected intentions of the individuals as they work together. And the act of working together is not a moment, but a process, within which we coordinate individual actions into a cohesive unity that transcends the capacity of solo action, where this involves attending to the distributed progress of the agreed-upon action *in the act of performing it*. Here, I want to add (and this is part of what the close study of group improvisation can give to philosophy) that the mere fact that intentional action so much as *can* take place in this multi-fronted or distributed progress-monitoring way, where intentional movements are altered in the act of performing them, seriously unsettles the Cartesian picture of pre-cognition followed by subsequent embodied enactment; what we have in jazz improvisation is fully intentional action without being, by virtue of that intentionality, temporally pre-conceived action. (In this respect, incidentally, expert soccer players can show us something about the spontaneous dimension of ensemble improvisation.) A shared intention then, so far, will (1) be of a kind that is non-summative, (2) irreducible (in the strong sense) to the individual (i.e., I cannot share the ten-pound note with myself; my spouse and I do not go out together on different nights), and (3) is worked out, with limited variations, across the span of its enactment. If one wanted to capture the distinctive kind of creative ensemble work undertaken in Coleman's 1959 recording *The Shape of Jazz to Come*,[8] one could do far worse than to list precisely these three features. This is also true, as we shall see shortly, of Coltrane in his most advanced group-improvisational work.

Bratman, emphasizing the necessarily public character of this distinctive intentional content, speaks of an "our intention," where the socially engaged and socially interactive role of the intention comes into clearer focus. Norms of "consistency, agglomeration, means-ends coherence, and stability"[9] come to the fore here; when Coleman was asked by a new ensemble member about chord sequences, unison melodies, and so forth, he famously replied: "Forget all that, but be sure to play within the range of the idea." That is consistency, and that is agglomeration, and it is an inducement to remain mindful about means-ends coherence, yielding interpersonal—I mean inter-ensemble—stability. Bratman speaks of interlocking intentions, and of the necessity of finding consistency within subplans for carrying out a larger shared intention. But the element I most want to emphasize today is what he calls a "semantic interconnection between our intentions."[10] The point here is that—now truly leaving the individualist social contract model in the dust—the specific content of my shared intention, as it unfolds, will in part be determined by my linked intention that your intention also "be realized in the right way," as it contributes within a shared dialogue and exchange along the process of realizing our larger shared intention. Coltrane's pianist, McCoy Tyner, equipped with, as players say, huge ears (and still larger technique), is (1) supporting, (2) prodding, (3) commenting upon, (4) developing in microcosm the thematic gestures of, (5) reharmonizing the melody of, (6) sequencing the rhythmic figures of, and (7) shaping the dynamic growth of Coltrane's improvised solo. What we might call the musical-semantic content of Tyner's intention to support Coltrane's work in all these ways is not specifiable in advance of the performance in any detail (although one could list in advance these seven modes of improvised accompaniment generically). What Bratman identifies as the subplans that give specificity to shared intentional action only emerge *in medias res*, only within what Wittgenstein called the stream of life.[11] It is in this sense, as I suggested earlier, that creative group improvisation not only mimetically reflects, but also simultaneously, within its own world, enacts. Like the painted numbers on Jasper Johns's canvases—where those numbers are at once numbers and representations of numbers—Tyner's playing under and with Coltrane at once is and represents the distinctive kind of shared intentional action that makes Searle's social reality, well, *real*.

It was Emily Dickinson who said that we dwell in possibility, and in an improvisational ensemble, indeed we do. Tyner, supporting Coltrane, within their four-part world of musical possibility, needs constantly to filter options[12] incompatible with the musical-semantic content flowing in and out of his intention, seizing some, rejecting others, holding still others in abeyance, listening for their right moment. In the great movie *The Lion in Winter*,[13] in a sharp-edged verbal sparring match between Eleanor of Aquitaine (the wife of Henry II) and her son Prince Geoffrey, he says, "I know. You know I know. I know you know I know. We know Henry knows, and Henry knows we know it," adding the closing line, "We're a knowledgeable family." A good improvising ensemble is in this sense a knowledgeable family living inside a world of possibility: Tyner knows of the long-form intentions of Coltrane in playing his modal composition "Impressions," he learns quickly of the instantaneous shared-intentional enactments of Coltrane, he knows Coltrane knows of his awareness on both of those levels, he knows the bassist knows of his knowledge of Coltrane's knowledge, where the bassist knows the drummer knows . . . and so it goes. So the semantic interaction is as thick in music as it is in life, and we need to capture that—and not a reduction of it—in our thinking about jazz.[14]

Bratman summarizes his position on shared intention: in them we will find "(i) intentions on the part of each in favor of the joint activity, (ii) interlocking intentions, (iii) intentions in favor of meshing subplans, (iv) beliefs about the joint efficacy of the relevant intentions, (v) beliefs about interpersonal intention-interdependence, and (vi) common knowledge of (i)–(vi)"[15] (where this includes, importantly, common knowledge of this common knowledge). And at the end of his summary he places special focus on "mutual responsiveness" as an essential condition of the enactment of shared intention. This is precisely what we hear—that is, all of (i) though (vi) along with a strong dose of mutual responsiveness, in Coltrane's quartet, in Taylor's groups, in Coleman's ensembles, and numerous others at the high end of group-improvisational achievement.

But speaking of that: John Coltrane, reducing his quartet to a trio for one number on November 2, 1961, at the Village Vanguard, gave a performance he said that he himself did not quite understand (or perhaps, given the available terminology, was not able to describe without the sense of an essential remainder lost to language).[16] Something very special in the world of improvised art happened that night. From the first moments of that particular performance of his "Chasin' the Trane," it was clear that the melodic line he started with, over what were ostensibly straightforward blues changes, was being negotiated, fragment by fragment, against an imaginary model that he was not playing. This put the piece, as heard sound, already in the opening measures against an absent, unheard piece—one might say an unheard piece on the other side of the sound. Or: the heard functioned as an increasingly intricate commentary on the unheard. The moment-by-moment negotiation of the close thematic logic of small bursts of motifs, four-and five-note rapid-fire assaults, began right from the fifth measure and then cut itself loose from what the listener expected (as the underlying harmony, itself already to some extent removed into the mind's ear by the absence of the piano for this piece). By the beginning of the solo in the second chorus—a solo that was actually already started in the complex negotiations from the start of what one might in an unsettled way take as the head—Coltrane established a sense of urgency not by himself, but within and across the trio. It is not reducible to the relentless high-burner heat of Jimmy Garrison's walking (more like sprinting) bass, nor to Elvin Jones's oceanic power with wave crashing upon wave, nor to Coltrane's own motivic bursts. The urgency remains above any one of those things, and no sum total can convincingly account for it. Then under this fragmented motivic logic,[17] we soon get Garrison interrupting the force of the four-to-the-bar sprint with strong momentary pedals held beginning on the second beat, then as quickly locking back into the momentarily unheard but still sensed four-to-the-bar movement. The effect is a momentary floating—4/4 gravity ceases to pull—and Jones moves to a highly intricate fleet-footed dance on the ride cymbal. This combination of bass and drum movement away from the expected, away from what is now for both bass and drums only an implied foundation, lifts the trio, *as one*, to a place where the sound becomes like what one imagines coming from the ground just at the beginning of a volcanic eruption. This then becomes the new ground—so that extreme rhythmic vitality, extreme forward movement, is sustained as much with rumble and thrash as with precise downbeats. And this now confers onto Coltrane's rapid-fire motifs a new, vital purpose in terms of rhythmic definition as well as thematic logic. Stream, then river, and now torrent moves to a place where a near-explosive texture is more important than any underlying harmonic mooring, and in a flash—about a third of the way into a sixteen-minute piece—the ensemble, now in a de-individuated collective sense that I can only try to describe as one increasingly powerful organism breathing, interweaves rapidly sequenced figures in the saxophone with rising and falling punched-out strides of the bass with hyper-animated increasingly complex cymbal movement. With all harmony now more dimly sensed than heard—rather like seeing shapes form and then as quickly dissipate in the fog—a kind of audible mutual trust emerges that seems to make anything possible within the enlarged bounds of a rapidly moving collective intention. Three-note fragments, still working through and within their own logic, give way to rapid clusters of closely grouped pitches; strong but momentary pedals in the bass now leave the listener hanging between disorientation and reorientation; bass-drum and tom bombs go off right and left as we propel forward—yet these constituent parts do not capture without significant remainder the event taking place here. Recall Bratman's list for true collective intention: non-summative; irreducible to the individual; worked out across the span of its enactment.

And recall the semantic interconnections between intentions. That was where the content of one rapidly progressing intention is inflected by the nuances of the very ensemble context within which it is being enacted. And as we hear unmistakably in what actually takes place in these sixteen minutes in 1961, the intentional content was without any doubt there at the highest level of improvisational mastery—and yet it could only have been articulated in the most vague and general terms prior to its enactment. I mentioned the sense that one is floating above the ground in a way that gravity will not allow, yet with a conjoined sense of urgent forward motion—like floating in the air atop a high-speed train. In a similar sense, upon repeated listening one realizes that time—as sonically marked, but also as implied on the other unheard side of this piece—seems to bend and undulate as well. This is not an effect any one person could achieve—if *one* tried, it would be heard as rushing or dragging against the established tempo of the other two players. (This sense is not reducible to what is within the reach of the social contract model, i.e. *accelerando* or *ritardando*.) There are moments within Coltrane's solo when he refers back—but with a retrospective edge of an aggressively experimental present commenting on a somewhat more mainstream past—to his playing with Dizzy Gillespie, Miles Davis, and others: he fleetingly plays a figure from the jazz-blues language over a twelve-bar form. And we know that he had just been listening to, and thinking about, the unrelieved intensity displayed in John Gilmore's saxophone playing with Sun Ra.[18] This intertextual content is of course of the moment, but it is—against the Cartesian picture of intention-as-precognition—nevertheless one indisputable part of the intentional content of Coltrane's work.

Phrases we often use to point toward phenomena of this kind—group interaction, group dynamics, and so forth—can too easily implicitly reinforce the social contract picture and the picture of autonomous selfhood beneath it. But the churning, thrashing, intense, seemingly gravity-defying and time-bending character of an ensemble like this—collective jazz improvisation at its best—lives and breathes in a place beyond what these models can accommodate. Coltrane knew this: registering the sense that this particular performance was above and beyond any of them individually or as a trio of individuals, he said, "I used to listen to it and wonder what happened to me."[19] The self beneath all this has become a relationally intertwined entity, the referent of the "me" is not in this context autonomous, and Coltrane knew it.

A term I used earlier, *de-individuation*, is a psychologist's name for the regrettable phenomenon of merging into a mob and then doing things as a collective that no individual within that mob would choose to do. But if there is a positive side to this experience, then de-individuation into collective intention—where here as well, an act is performed that no individual could choose to do for the simple reason that no individual could do it—may help us arrive at a better understanding of something that, for want of better language, we call magical. Such experiences, once had, are not easily—perhaps ever—forgotten. Coltrane, within a high-velocity life of ever more performing and recording, kept thinking back to that defining moment of de-individuation at the Village Vanguard. And drummer Leroy Williams said, "I remember the first time I experienced that floating, out-of-the-body feeling. It was a number of years ago, when I was playing in Chicago. At the time, I didn't know what it was,"[20] and he goes on to refer to the special kind of empathy required—I think he is referring to the musical variant of a highly cultured and finely attuned moral imagination as preparedness for creative cooperation[21]—before, as he puts it, "this music can really happen."[22] And he mentions a special "chemistry" as well—where the very term evokes an image of one set of independent elements undergoing a process whereby—through transformative interaction—they merge into one new compound entity with properties all its own. Accomplished players know this experience when it occurs, and accomplished listeners know it when they hear it. Like Williams, players call this special ensemble phenomenon simply "happening"; let Wynton Marsalis's remark stand for many when he says, "Everybody's part is equally important. If you have one weak link, it doesn't happen, man."[23]

However, the phenomenon as I have described it thus far concerns the merger of individual into non-summative collective intention, where the semantic interlocking of intention, or irreducible or group-emergent intention, is to the fore. There is another aspect of this kind of ensemble performance that should not be missed. In the context of discussions of word and sentence meaning, Hilary Putnam has written of a "division of labor" in terms of articulating, or capturing all of the content of, the meaning of a word. Even a novice student of etymology will immediately recognize that words have connotations from word-origins and the history of usage that lurk, often fascinatingly, within them—it is as though such connotations are waiting within the semi-hidden content of the word to be discovered by a nuanced user. This linguistic fact has been taken by Putnam[24] and others to argue for semantic externalism, that is, the notion that the content of a word or sentence need not be contained within the intentional use of any given speaker at any given moment—the labor of covering all this is distributed across a range of usages and contexts. Indeed, on such a view, it is highly unlikely that any given speaker could ever achieve a single comprehensive and simultaneous grasp of a connotative range more extensive than the present speaker's intention, and thus on this externalist view of word meaning, any theory restricted to explicit intentional content would miss more than it captured. I want to suggest that the special phenomenon heard when an ensemble plays as one, when it is truly happening, is deeply like this distribution of labor—where the labor just is the work of attending with exacting discernment to different but interconnected aspects or elements of the interrelated whole sonic (and as we shall shortly see, also the linked imaginative) event. And one way to describe this is in terms of group attention.

William James (and here we see yet another direct link between the best of American philosophy and American music) has given us a number of famous phrases: "stream of consciousness" is one, and the "blooming, buzzing confusion" is another.[25] The latter describes, for him, the massive overload of information, of sensory input, that any person (and particularly an infant, before it learns to navigate that overload with selective attention) experiences at any moment, outside the bounds of a narrow selection of attended-to data. For James, we make our world into what it is by selectively attending, and the composite result of any such act of selective foregrounding against massive backgrounding is our perceptual world at that moment. This is an illuminating description of one half of sensibility: we select from the much larger set of what is given in experience to make our world (in a way distinctive to our patterned histories of selection) what it is. (The second half is then the presently-activated recollection of our distinctive history of related experiences that inflect our perception of whatever it is to which we presently attend.)[26] An ensemble in motion can be, taken *in toto*, just such a blooming buzzing confusion, and a player selectively attends within that ensemble—that microcosm of our perception of the world—to what is necessary in order to participate most fully, to intentionally interact, to de-individuate for the good of something that is greater than him- or herself.

Given the early critical reaction to Ornette Coleman's double quartet recordings, the phrase "blooming buzzing confusion" would seem comparatively gentle. On first listening—as with much work in the free jazz tradition—the ensemble sound can put a rather heavy strain on the listener's ability to make sense. But that is just the point: the larger collective is one from which one actively, in a Jamesian way, selects in order to make one's distinctive "world." To do this, one needs to listen *as a player*, just as painters often say that in order to really see what is taking place in a given canvas one has to see as a painter. And here lies the heart of the matter: the listener, in this form of music, is cast into the position of a player, who must selectively attend to coherence-making parts while backgrounding others. This demand on the listener is readily perceivable in single quartets, for example, consider again Coltrane's *Impressions*, but it is doubled—and so very much more apparent—in the doubled quartet. And it is within the world of that doubled quartet that one can hear players of the same instrument most exactingly selecting the other player of their instrument first (listen to the two bassists). Then once that focal point of attention is mutually agreed upon (this is shared attention, to which we will return shortly), each will select other elements to include in their distinctive worlds of selected attention, and the contributions they make to the whole differ accordingly.

Like James's perceptual world, nothing in this situation is static. This constitutes within its own musical world, as well as mimetically represents, the active power of the human mind in world-perception. A player will have a form of attention that is constantly in motion, tracking what has happened within foregrounded elements, what has happened in other tracked elements, and then more generally what has happened in what we might call a semi-backgrounded (i.e., not foregrounded but not ignored either) foundation. Painters do not use the expression "Big Eyes" (although they might), but players do use the expression "Big Ears," and that term names just this skill, developed to an exceedingly high degree (that is, well beyond what becomes in this context merely rudimentary ear training involving interval, arpeggio, and chord recognition, melodic memory, orientation within form, rhythmic pattern-recognition, motivic-development recognition and anticipation, etc.). A person will switch focal points as they are intertwined with other related events minute by minute, and perhaps moment by moment, and in the extreme case of sudden and repeatedly emergent attention-demanders, a number of times within a moment. Life offers a broad range here—just as does group improvisation. And if the listener is asked to replicate the labor, the active listening, of a selectively attending player, then the demands are indeed uncompromising: it is not for nothing that the advanced regions of this artform have been called "musician's music."

Some theorists of attention have developed the metaphor of the spotlight: attention functions as does a spotlight in the dark, where the strength, focal point, sharpness or diffuseness of focus, and duration determine the character of the act of attention under consideration. This is helpful, but one should note that in the case of the semantically interlinked ensemble, each player has more than one spotlight, and while one may have a very sharp focus, another will illuminate everything around it. In this way, one can follow Coleman's motivic suggestions with great concentration while tracking not just the bass player or drummer individually, but what the entire rhythm section (e.g., piano, bass, drums) is doing as its players move under those motivic suggestions, only some of which will be taken up and acted upon. (Again, the double quartet doubles the complexity of this negotiation.) The spotlight metaphor has its limits—and it does itself attend, through its terminology, to visual attention—but I bring it in here to offer a model that will link together James's idea of selective attention as presently in play and the previous remarks concerning Putnam's distribution of labor. Just as with the half-hidden and expansive range of word connotations that no single user of a word can intentionally incorporate at any one time, so no player can, in the rapidly unfolding flux of an improvising ensemble, shine spotlights on all aspects of what is unfolding presently. But *between* them—to share attention and to distribute labor—they can. No one player can selectively attend to everything—the very word *selectively* would seem to preclude that, just as not everything can be in a foreground. Nor can any one listener hear everything with the requisite attention at one hearing—the sense of artistic exhaustion, redundancy, or having, as we say, "heard it all already" in the experience of this music is rare, and just for this reason. The American pragmatists also wrote of what they called "perspectival perches," that is, vantage points from which one could take in an event, where the change of perch would correspondingly change what we did and did not attend to—which is what gives the experience in question its determinate content. With the notions of selective attention and distribution of labor in mind, one can monitor one's own acts of close listening, with the result that one sees more clearly how a player, within an ensemble of this kind, moves in a Jamesian way realizing one specific subset of possibilities out of a larger expansive set.

But the reality of what is taking place here—when it is happening—is more complex still. Group or shared attention has been studied in depth recently in developmental psychology, where the ability to recognize that one is focusing upon one given thing in the environmental field rather than another, and then to focus upon that thing in tandem with the other, is now seen as foundational to our ability to interact with others. This is a precondition for recognizing and responding sympathetically to their mental states or conditions, as well as for recognizing the meanings of the words and sentences they are using (in labor-distributed or cooperative ways; demonstratives here become the test cases for understanding). Serious developmental impediments (e.g., autism) are now being explained in terms of arrested development on precisely this score.[27] To the extent (which, as I am suggesting here, is considerable) that collective ensemble improvisation depends on acts of shared or group attention (where the sharing can happen within any subgroup of the ensemble), music of this kind puts on display, in the world of art, what takes place when it is, in complex societal organizations (to borrow the musicians' term), *happening*.[28] The failure of one player to appropriately listen to another player or to the ensemble (or where one possesses insufficiently developed "Ears," so that the skill base is not present in the first place) will yield exactly what Marsalis described above concerning the "weak link"; the player is not sufficiently selectively attending, sharing in divided labor, and jointly attending.[29] (One direct analogue between poor performance and a category of moral failing is to listen to oneself as the sole spotlighted element against what will then be heard as a perceptually indistinct ensemble background). But it is just here that the phenomenon in question becomes more intricate still.

James brings another aspect of the kind of attention we are considering into focus by discussing an example from Hermann von Helmholtz; this aspect, important to understanding what shared attention in this kind of ensemble actually entails, is all too easily missed.[30] If we play a strong low C on the piano, in a limited or far-off, distant-background sense, we hear the overtone of G above it or in its upper harmonics, but we do not primarily attend to it (we are, by contrast, clearly attending to the C as the focal sonic experience). If, as Helmholtz observes, we then sound a strong G, spotlight our attention on the sound of that pitch, and then *imagine* what that G overtone will sound like as contained within the overtone structure of the C when actually sounded a moment later, we will now, on hearing the C again, be able to hear the G clearly and unambiguously. The *sound*, of course, did not change; but what we heard changed very much. This, for James, shows in a single case what he believes to be true of all human perception, that is that our imaginative anticipations of what we are about to perceive will itself enable us to discern more clearly what is anticipated when that anticipated sensory phenomenon is actualized. And this, precisely, is the part that is so easily missed in our consideration of the content of selective attention, and it constitutes an important part of what "Big Ear" players actually do in the course of improvised performance. To put it another way, it is far too easy to restrict any account of the content that is selected in attention to only what has already been sounded, what has already been played out. But the truth, in terms of players at this level sharing attention, is here again more interesting than that.

Players, inside the expanded network of improvisational possibility, closely attending to their selectively chosen foci, move from possible to actual in the blink of an eye. They actualize, as discussed in the Coltrane example, and as they do with doubled complexity in the Coleman case of the double quartet, in the moment, in a way that (1) transcends the autonomy of the individual as discussed above, (2) develops semantically interactive intentional content of an irreducible "our intention" kind, and that (3) shows the attentive patterns that make up the interactive style of a given player (and these will differ from player to player in a way as distinctive as fingerprints). To do this together, players often anticipate, with considerable sophistication, what another player will do, and this allows them to play in an "as-if" mode: they play as if the momentary passage were rehearsed, as if they had known in advance what they were going to do together. And in a special sense (a sense that further defines what the term *happening* means), they do know: the extent to which they know the idiom intimately, and more importantly the extent to which they know each other as players intimately, comes out in this kind of "as-if" performance; and one important measure of the success of the performance is taken in just these terms.[31] This part of an ensemble's work can seem mysterious—indeed almost magical—but the phenomenon in question is in truth no more mysterious than the capacity for human intimacy and deep interpersonal understanding that it both exemplifies and mimetically represents: players can imagine, immediately before the event as a result of what has just come before, where a player is going. This is not mind-reading or clairvoyance any more than is the act of rightly anticipating where a person we truly know well is going in a sentence, in a thought, in an expression of hope, regret, fear, or delight, in a resigned sigh or in an elated gesture. We know these things of each other as a function of shared attention and all the interweaving of semantic and intentional content that such sharing makes possible.[32] And we feel alone when just such shared improvisational interaction is frustrated or when the special sense of "playing as one" seems blocked by insurmountable obstacles.

So to conclude: Searle's "we-intentions" are by their nature mindful of the contribution of the others as the group—acting as a group in the theatrical play—runs from the rain in the way a cluster of individuals would do, but with a group focus that cannot be reduced to the sum total of a collection of individuals. Bratman's "our-intentions" advance beyond that, bringing into focus the semantic interaction—what we might call the chemistry on the level of meaning—that allows your intentional content to become a part of my unfolding and presently performed intentional plan. A relational conception of selfhood, by contrast to the Cartesian hermetic self, can accommodate this. Tyner, performing in the stream of musical life all the spontaneously interactive yet intentional things he does, in fact in himself *becomes* a part of Coltrane's solo—the intentions, in Bratman's terms, interlock. And at Coltrane's high point—those sixteen minutes of energized grace at the Vanguard in November 1961—his trio *departs* from the point of chemical reaction, semantic merger, de-individuated intention, and collectively composes intentional music in the moment in a way no social contract model of participation can capture. And this is done through extraordinarily highly developed skills of selective and group-participatory attention. Some individuals—Marsalis, others—have called jazz the essential American music for its democratic, socially contracted participation of the individual within the larger purpose-driven collective. But as Marsalis's own practice richly shows (and actually consistent with his remark, mentioned earlier, concerning what it takes for the music to happen), the truth, as we have glimpsed, is more remarkable than that. An account without remainder must, I think, accommodate the kind of creative ensemble work that allows complex or compound intentional work to emerge within, and not prior to, its realization, work that cannot be descriptively captured from the false starting point of the Cartesian or hermetically sealed individual. The events that happen here are not pre-cognized, they are not the shady semi-realities of a mental interior, they are not the sum total of perhaps clustered yet still metaphysically preserved autonomy, and they are not the result of a self-spotlighted attention that backgrounds everything else. Players are right to sense a profound difference between solo and ensemble performance, and again between non-improvisational and improvisational group performance. The individual-transcending events that happen here— and they have been happening in the highest reaches of jazz improvisation for a long time—seem to be finding an articulate voice in, of all places, recent philosophy of mind. It seems a propitious moment to bring this music and this philosophy together.

One final note: One wonders what if, some decades back, the New Criticism that generically barred intentional considerations from interpretative considerations (where, importantly, that view was built on the conceptual picture of Cartesian intention we have discussed), along with premature pronouncements of the death of the author coming from another tradition, had not held sway for so long. One imagines we might now be more nuanced in our recognition of the complex intentional content of, and the collective-intentional and group-attentive work undertaken within, the creative ensemble performances that give this distinctive American music its power and special sense of animate presence. And then also, if we hadn't had intentional considerations barred for so long, perhaps we would have seen much sooner the significant contribution the study of intentional work in improvisation and the phenomena of interactive selective attention can make to the philosophy of mind and action. But, as was also said in that great film I mentioned earlier, " 'What if' is a game for scholars." Like Coltrane, let us just go forward together from where we are right here, right now.

Notes

1. John Coltrane, *Ascension, Editions I and II,* compact disc, Impulse! 1792024 (2009), originally released in 1965.
2. The unearthing and disentangling of these presuppositions is hardly the brief or straightforward matter I make it sound like here. I offer an attempt in Garry L. Hagberg, *Describing Ourselves: Wittgenstein and Autobiographical Consciousness* (Oxford: Clarendon Press, 2008).
3. John Searle, "Collective Intentions and Actions," in *Intentions and Communication*, ed. P. Cohen, J. Morgan, and M. E. Pollack (Cambridge, MA: Bradford Books, MIT Press, 1990), 403.
4. For a discussion of this focus on relations in aesthetic contexts, see Garry L. Hagberg, "Imagined Identities: Autobiography at One Remove," *New Literary History* 38, no. 1 (Winter 2007): 163–181.
5. I discuss the counterintuitive representational content of jazz improvisation in Garry L. Hagberg, "Jazz Improvisation: A Mimetic Art?," *Revue Internationale de Philosophie* 238 (2006): 469–485.
6. See, for the most relevant papers to this discussion, Michael Bratman, "Shared Agency," in Chris Mantzavinos, ed., *Philosophy of the Social Sciences: Philosophical Theory and Scientific Practice* (Cambridge: Cambridge University Press, 2009), 42–59; and "Acting Over Time, Acting Together," paper for the 2010 Conference on Collective Intentionality (Basel, Switzerland, August 2010), http://philosophy.stanford.edu/community/documents-papers/view/Acting_Over_Time_Acting_Together/, accessed January 27. 2014.
7. In what follows I have been helped considerably by the excellent overview article by Deborah Tollefson, "Collective Intentionality," *Internet Encyclopedia of Philosophy* (2004), http://www.iep.utm.edu/coll-int/, accessed January 27, 2004; see also her very helpful "Collective Epistemic Agency," *Southwest Philosophy Review* 20, no. 1 (2004): 55–66.
8. Ornette Coleman, *The Shape of Jazz to Come,* compact disc, Atlantic Records WPCR13429 (2009), originally released in 1959. The examples of Coleman's work that I have in mind throughout this chapter come primarily from this recording; examples taken from Ornette Coleman, *Free Jazz: A Collective Improvisation by the Ornette Coleman Double Quartet*, compact disc, Warner Jazz 8122736092 (2002), originally released in 1961, would only thicken the complexity (as we will see) of the collective intentional action considered here. One could write a separate essay, for example, on the interactive work of the two bassists

(Scott LaFaro and Charlie Haden) alone. For a particularly helpful essay that articulates in brief scope much of Coleman's achievement, see Gary Giddins, "Ornette Coleman (This Is Our Music)," *Visions of Jazz: The First Century* (New York: Oxford University Press, 1998), 467–476. Also, I should mention that the examples I have in mind of collective improvisation do seem to cast the performance of collective intentions in higher relief, but collective intentional work in jazz improvisation is by no means restricted to free or experimental jazz; hear, for example, the performance of "Lush Life," where the ensemble coalesces unforgettably on John Coltrane, *John Coltrane and Johnny Hartman,* compact disc, Impulse! 1764897 (2008), originally released in 1963.

9. Bratman, "Shared Agency," 65.

10. Bratman, "Shared Agency," 48.

11. The fact that such intentions are manifested only within a stream (or expanded frame of group creativity as shared and intertwined activity) is nicely elucidated by J. David Velleman, where he rightly places emphasis on the way in which group intentional activity is clearly intended, and yet not intended (in a way corresponding to the traditional dualistic view of intention as inner preconception) in a full way that predicts all detailed outcomes within that frame of action. See J. David Velleman, "How to Share an Intention," *Philosophy and Phenomenological Research* 57 (March, 1997): 29–50. Another way of capturing this important point for the nature of group intention is to say that one of the conditions under which individual-transcending group intention is possible is that I be able to predict not what you will do precisely in fulfilling the ensemble intention, but that I be able to predict that you will develop and fulfill precise subintentions interactively as we process, and vice-versa. In this connection see Wynton Marsalis's remark concerning the preconditions for the music "happening" (n. 23). For a helpful article setting this out in detail, see Michael Bratman, "I Intend that We J," in R. Tuomela and G. Holmström-Hintikka, eds., *Contemporary Action Theory*, vol. 2, *Social Action* (Dordrecht: Kluwer, 1997), 49–63. The significance of this point concerning intended-yet-not-fully-preconceived action (where no single individual can determine the outcome but where no single individual's contribution could be deleted without profoundly altering the outcome) is, I think, quite large for achieving a fuller comprehension of the art of jazz improvisation: jazz soloists have been described and celebrated repeatedly as, indeed, *soloists*, where this focuses on the individual expressing him or herself as an autonomous voice, which again comports with the social contract model. For a fine essay that, like so many, focuses on individual expression as the heart of this artform, see Lawrence W. Levine, "Jazz and American Culture," in Robert G. O'Meally, ed., *The Jazz Cadence of American Culture* (New York: Columbia University Press, 1998), 431–447. Levine therein quotes Henry Osgood (author of one of the first books on jazz): jazz performance is " a protest against . . . the monotony of life . . . an attempt at individual expression" (438). I would add that it is also, seen one way, a protest against a false conception of hermetic selfhood and a corresponding false but entrenched picture of the relation between the individual and society. If one were to attempt to answer the question "Why is jazz improvisation a truly *American* art?," here one could do worse than to point to collective intention, where the individual moves spontaneously and interactively within a network of possibilities that are themselves made possible by the collective (and where, as we shall see in the example of Coltrane's trio, the semantic content of the individual's intention is not specifiable independently of the other contributors to the collective action). That would be a more true representation of the melting pot. (In this connection see the opening line of Ralph Ellison's "The Golden Age, Time Past," in

O'Meally, *Jazz Cadence of American Culture*, 448–456: "That which we do is what we are." To put what jazz improvisation shows too briefly: Because what we *do* is itself invariably relationally intertwined, the referent of the "we" is relationally, interactively constituted.

12. Bratman, "Shared Agency," 10.
13. James Goldman, *The Lion in Winter* (script) (New York: Penguin Books, 1983, first published in 1966).
14. See Bratman, "Shared Agency," 12.
15. Bratman, "Shared Agency," 14.
16. John Coltrane, "Chasin' the Trane," in *A John Coltrane Retrospective: The Impulse Years*, with notes by David Wild, compact disc, Impulse! 119 (1992), originally released in 1962. See the particularly helpful liner notes by David Wild.
17. I should mention that this is an extraordinarily advanced form of working through what I am calling motivic logic; one could write a separate study of the development of this aspect of Coltrane's music over the full course of his development. This is not to suggest that this progress moves in a linear fashion chronologically, that is, where the sophistication increases steadily as time goes on. Rather, Coltrane and his colleagues work at the degree of rapid-fire intensity (of motivic logic) called for by the piece and their collective approach to it at the moment: for a telling contrast to "Chasin' the Trane," hear his quartet's exquisite performance of "You Don't Know What Love Is" (John Coltrane, "You Don't Know What Love Is," on *John Coltrane Quartet: Ballads,* compact disc, Impulse! 1703697 [2007], originally released in 1962). The motivic logic is both powerful and intricate, but it functions with more relaxed phrase-structuring and across longer-reaching melodic spans.
18. See Wild's liner notes (note 16), 11.
19. Wild, liner notes, 11.
20. Leroy Williams, quoted in Paul F. Berliner, *Thinking in Jazz: The Infinite Art of Improvisation* (Chicago: University of Chicago Press, 1994), 413.
21. I offer a discussion of the ethical elements in play within improvisational performance in "Jazz Improvisation and Ethical Interaction: A Sketch of the Connections," in Garry L. Hagberg, *Art and Ethical Criticism* (Oxford: Blackwell, 2008), 259–285.
22. Williams, in Berliner, *Thinking in Jazz,* 414.
23. Wynton Marsalis, quoted in Berliner, *Thinking in Jazz,* 411–412. Although it is not the central purpose of this chapter, I do believe the fuller understanding of the experience of positive de-individuation into an ensemble of collective intention, and the powerful magnetism that special experience exerts on a certain kind of creative soul, goes some way toward explaining why improvising musicians have traditionally endured the rigors of the road and less-than-comfortable lives to intensively pursue the work they do. If one example may here also speak for many, saxophonist Stanley Turrentine, speaking of such difficulties, said of touring long-term with a group with organist Shirley Scott, "A lot of small places, with bad sound systems, small audiences. . . . We used to deadhead a lot. Twice we drove to the coast in three days, New York to L.A., eating in the car, sleeping in the car, with the organ in a little trailer in the back. You'd get there to the gig and for days you'd still feel like you're still riding. It's funny now; it wasn't so funny then. We'd get to clubs where the hallways were too narrow for the organ, and once in Virginia, we had to carry the organ up three flights of fire escapes. But for all that, we'd go in that night and we'd blow our hearts out." Quoted in David H. Rosenthal, *Hard Bop: Jazz and Black Music 1955–1965* (New York: Oxford University Press, 1992), 108. Concerning the term *happening*

as (what I believe to be) a shorthand reference to highly successful collective-intentional work, see also Quincy Troupe and Ben Riley, "Remembering Thelonious Monk: When the Music Was Happening Then He'd Get Up and Do His Little Dance," in *The Jazz Cadence of American Culture,* ed. Robert G. O'Meally (New York: Columbia University Press, 1998), 102–110.

24. Hilary Putnam, *Philosophical Papers*, vol. 2, Mind, Language and Reality (Cambridge: Cambridge University Press, 1985).

25. William James, *The Principles of Psychology* (New York: Dover, orig. pub. 1890).

26. See also in this connection Garry L. Hagberg, "Imagined Identities," note 4.

27. For a study that shows the instructive contrast between (1) children who, through "joint linguistic interactions with adults" (1982), learn to develop autobiographical narratives that unfold in terms of long-form story cohesion, and (2) those children who do not (i.e., those who, in failing to integrate an awareness of the points of view of others, do not develop plot-unfolding narratives that others would follow), see Sylvie Goldman, "Brief Report: Narratives of Personal Events in Children with Autism and Developmental Language Disorders: Unshared Memories," *Journal of Autism and Developmental Disorders* 38 (2008): 1982–1988.

28. See, for an enlightening examination of a number of these issues, N. Eilan, C. Hoerl, T. McCormack, and J. Roessler, *Joint Attention: Communication and Other Minds* (Oxford: Oxford University Press, 2005).

29. For an enlightening and deeply practice-based examination of a number of particular cases, especially in connection with the too-often-overlooked or insufficiently investigated contribution of the rhythm section to ensemble improvisation, see Ingrid Monson, *Saying Something: Jazz Improvisation and Interaction* (Chicago: University of Chicago Press, 1996).

30. For a helpful discussion of attention in its philosophical and experimental contexts, see Christopher Mole, "Attention," *Stanford Encyclopedia of Philosophy* (Palo Alto, Stanford University, 2009, http://plato.stanford.edu/entries/attention/, accessed January 27, 2014); he discusses the Helmholtz case and shows its larger significance for James, which I have followed here.

31. Consider in this light the instructive passage by Berliner in *Thinking in Jazz* 413: "The disruptive experiences [in unsuccessful performances] cited above illustrate why musicians diligently cultivate sensibilities to group interplay on the bandstand. By necessity, the process is a gradual one. Excited by their discovery of jazz, students initially seek opportunities to improvise at every accessible performance venue and in any group that will have them. They are, in the beginning, less particular about the partners with whom they form musical relationships, because they have yet to appreciate the subtle dimensions of interpersonal communication and the intricate meshing entailed in successful improvisation. Many are not immediately attuned to the exceptional moments of performances, nor acclimated to the extramusical experiences that accompany them."

32. There is a deep connection between improvisation in speech and in music that, I believe, music would cast a good deal of light on (rather than, as has become customary, assuming that it is language that will cast light on music). See particularly in this connection the extraordinarily helpful discussion in Monson, *Saying Something*, 73–96. Glenn Gould is also one to note (if in passing) in this direction (i.e., going from music to language and not vice-versa): "[S]o it is with the written word; we all improvise with it continually." *The Glenn Gould Reader*, ed. Tim Page (New York: Alfred A. Knopf, 1984), 257. Regarding the

prerequisite of understanding a person, or more specifically a sensibility, in order to seriously communicate in language, just as is the case in improvised ensemble music (and where the insight that we need such understanding in language extends from the musical experience to language and not vice versa), see the closing remark by Cecil Taylor in the instructively difficult interview with Len Lyons, in his *The Great Jazz Pianists*, reprinted in *Reading Jazz: A Gathering of Autobiography, Reportage, and Criticism from 1919 to Now*, ed. Robert Gottlieb (New York: Pantheon, 1996), 320: "I don't know what language you speak or what you're prepared to hear. If we're going to talk, I need some idea of who you are."

BIBLIOGRAPHY

Berliner, Paul F. *Thinking in Jazz: The Infinite Art of Improvisation*. Chicago: University of Chicago Press, 1994.

Bratman, Michael. "I Intend that We J." In *Contemporary Action Theory*. Vol. 1, *Social Action*, edited by R. Tuomela and G. Holmström-Hintikka, 49–63. Dordrecht: Kluwer, 1997.

Bratman, Michael. "Shared Agency." In *Philosophy of the Social Sciences: Philosophical Theory and Scientific Practice*, edited by Chris Mantzavinos, 42–59. Cambridge: Cambridge University Press, 2009.

Bratman, Michael. "Acting Over Time, Acting Together." http://philosophy.stanford.edu/community/documents-papers/view/Acting_Over_Time_Acting_Together/, accessed January 27, 2014.

Coleman, Ornette. *The Shape of Jazz to Come*. Compact disc. Atlantic Records WPCR13429, 2009. Originally released in 1959.

Coleman, Ornette. *Free Jazz: A Collective Improvisation by the Ornette Coleman Double Quartet*. Compact disc. Warner Jazz 8122736092, 2002. Originally released in 1961.

Coltrane, John. *Ascension, Editions I and II*. Compact disc. Impulse! 1792024, 2009. Originally released in 1965.

Coltrane, John. *John Coltrane and Johnny Hartman*. Compact disc. Impulse! 1764897, 2008. Originally released in 1963.

Coltrane, John. "Chasin' the Trane." *A John Coltrane Retrospective: The Impulse Years*, with notes by David Wild. Compact disc. Impulse! 119, 1992. Originally released in 1962.

Coltrane, John. "You Don't Know What Love Is." *John Coltrane Quartet: Ballads*. Compact disc. Impulse! 1703697, 2007. Originally released in 1962.

Eilan, N., C. Hoerl, T. McCormack, and J. Roessler. *Joint Attention: Communication and Other Minds*. Oxford: Oxford University Press, 2005.

Ellison, Ralph. "The Golden Age, Time Past." In *The Jazz Cadence of American Culture*, edited by Robert G. O'Meally, 448–456. New York: Columbia University Press, 1998.

Giddins, Gary. "Ornette Coleman (This Is Our Music)." In *Visions of Jazz: The First Century*, 467–476. New York: Oxford University Press, 1998.

Goldman, James. *The Lion in Winter*. New York: Penguin Books, 1983; first published in 1966.

Goldman, Sylvie. "Brief Report: Narratives of Personal Events in Children with Autism and Developmental Language Disorders: Unshared Memories." *Journal of Autism and Developmental Disorders* 38 (2008): 1982–1988.

Gottlieb, Robert, ed. *Reading Jazz: A Gathering of Autobiography, Reportage, and Criticism from 1919 to Now*. New York: Pantheon, 1996.

Gould, Glenn. *The Glenn Gould Reader*. Edited by Tim Page. New York: Alfred A. Knopf, 1984.

Hagberg, Garry L. *Describing Ourselves: Wittgenstein and Autobiographical Consciousness*. Oxford: Clarendon Press, 2008.

Hagberg, Garry L. "Imagined Identities: Autobiography at One Remove." *New Literary History* 38, no. 1 (Winter 2007): 163–181.

Hagberg, Garry L. "Jazz Improvisation: A Mimetic Art?" *Revue Internationale de Philosophie* 238 (2006): 469–485.

Hagberg, Garry L. "Jazz Improvisation and Ethical Interaction: A Sketch of the Connections." In *Art and Ethical Criticism*, edited by Garry L. Hagberg, 259–85. Oxford: Blackwell, 2008.

James, William. *The Principles of Psychology*. New York: Dover, 1950. Originally published in 1890.

Levine, Lawrence W. "Jazz and American Culture." In *The Jazz Cadence of American Culture*, edited by Robert G. O'Meally, 431–447. New York: Columbia University Press, 1998.

Mole, Christopher. "Attention." *Stanford Encyclopedia of Philosophy*. Palo Alto: Stanford University Press, 2009. http://plato.stanford.edu/entries/attention/, accessed January 27, 2014.

Monson, Ingrid. *Saying Something: Jazz Improvisation and Interaction*. Chicago: University of Chicago Press, 1996.

Putnam, Hilary. *Philosophical Papers*. Vol. 2, *Mind, Language and Reality*. Cambridge: Cambridge University Press, 1985.

Rosenthal, David H. *Hard Bop: Jazz and Black Music 1955-1965*. New York: Oxford University Press, 1992.

Searle, John. "Collective Intentions and Actions." In *Intentions and Communication*, edited by P. Cohen, J. Morgan, and M. E. Pollack, 401–416. Cambridge, MA: Bradford Books, MIT Press, 1990.

Tollefson, Deborah. "Collective Intentionality." *Internet Encyclopedia of Philosophy* (2004): http://www.iep.utm.edu/coll-int/, accessed January 27, 2004.

Tollefson, Deborah. "Collective Epistemic Agency." *Southwest Philosophy Review* 20, no. 1 (2004): 55–66.

Troupe, Quincy, and Ben Riley. "Remembering Thelonious Monk: When the Music Was Happening Then He'd Get Up and Do His Little Dance." In *The Jazz Cadence of American Culture*, edited by Robert G. O'Meally, 102–110. New York: Columbia University Press, 1998.

Velleman, J. David. "How to Share an Intention." *Philosophy and Phenomenological Research* 57 (March 1997): 29–50.

CHAPTER 28

INTERSPECIES IMPROVISATION

DAVID ROTHENBERG

To explain to you why improvisation between species makes sense, I'll need to say a little bit about why there is so much more music out there in the natural world than that made by humans alone. If we are to make sense of that music as improvisors, we'll need to find some way to join in.

Certain species of birds have very complex songs that they seem to sing for hours at a time. Young male birds usually learn these songs from adult males, not always their fathers. Nightingales, mockingbirds, warblers, great reed warblers, shamas, butcher-birds, and song thrushes are a few of the world's best bird singers. They all listen to what their fellows are up to and thus find their own way to sing, in most species quite stylized, so that we humans can easily identify a species from the precise notes of his song. But in some species, individuality and distinctness are what let us identify what we hear. Left to their own devices, these species are able to improvise the music they need.

What happens if you raise a baby male singing bird alone, with no example for him to hear and to imitate? Donald Kroodsma tried just such an experiment on an American catbird.[1] The gray catbird, *Dumetella carolinensis*, is a common medium-size North American bird known for its flashy, aggressive presence. He sits on an exposed perch (where the phrase "catbird seat" comes from), imitating whoever he likes, adding snatches of pretty melody, and then interjecting short harsh notes in between the chortling phrases. Sometimes these squawks sound a lot like a meowing cat, hence our common name for what the Chippewa called *Ma-ma-dive-bi-ne-shi*, the bird that cries with grief.

Samuel Parker, author of the intriguing nineteenth-century volume *Twelve Months with the Birds and Poets*, includes the following verses on the curious dual quality of the catbird's song:

> You, who would with wanton art
> Counterfeit another's part
> And with noisy utterance claim

Right to an ignoble name,—
Inharmonious!—why must you,
To a better self untrue,
Gifted with the charm of song,
Do the generous gift such wrong?

Oh! you much mistake your duty,
Mating discord thus with beauty,—
'Mid these heavenly sunset gleams,
Vexing the smooth air with screams,—
Burdening the dainty breeze
With insane discordancies.[2]

Catbirds are easy to hear singing during springtime, and not everyone thinks they are musical. To many humans they sound like avant-gardists with no sense of repetition, prettiness, or humane melody. It takes a different kind of human listener to be drawn to the catbird. This cat sounds like an avant-garde jazzman destined to shock the world into something more than pretty melodies. The contemporary poet Richard Wilbur heard the catbird's quirky mix as somewhere in between truth and fiction: ". . . it is tributary / To the great lies told with the eyes half-shut / That have the truth in view. . . ."[3]

We aim for the truth of what we hear, but, when we listen to sounds not meant for us, we eavesdrop with our ears half-closed. What of the catbird behind bars? Kroodsma raised young catbirds in the laboratory in a situation where their song learning could be controlled. Two groups heard only a repeated, 10-second clip of normal catbird song. Two other groups heard a much longer, 16-minute clip of song, repeated over and over. The fifth group heard no taped song at all. Kroodsma expected to discover some correlation between the amount of practice material each bird heard and what it came to sing, which is what had been found in similar studies on other species. However, something rather surprising occurred. Each bird developed its own unique song, using a process Kroodsma decided to call "improvisation," making up a song on its own, with no teacher to help. All the birds in the study developed distinct repertoires of hundreds of separate song syllables. Even the birds that heard no catbird song during the crucial learning period were able to create their own distinct songs that later got a favorable response when the birds were released into the wild. The distinctiveness of the song seemed to ensure success, not any particular sounds being copied or assimilated.

What exactly were the catbirds singing, out there on their seats? Kroodsma says nothing about the particular qualities of the hundreds of sounds his team identified, only that they were diverse, catbirdesque, and appreciated by other catbirds, regardless of how much training each bird had. They were all creative individualists, driven into their own tunes.

Were they in fact improvising? As a musician I might say the catbird is more of a self-taught composer. He worked his song out on his own, not needing to hear others in order to create what he is supposed to create, the song he needs to attract his mate and defend his territory. Each bird species has its own style, its own aesthetic, maybe even its own genre of music that outsiders always strain to hear. Who *cares* if we humans like the catbird song or not? It was never meant for us.

And yet, and yet.... so many bird songs are beautiful to human ears. They preceded our music for millions of years, so they are a kind of bedrock beneath all we have created. This is the real classical music, the truly ancient stuff. We know not exactly what it means for the bird, and we have a hard time figuring out what makes for better or worse nightingale or mockingbird songs. There is rarely any clear correlation between any particular kind of song and more mating success, more strength, or that elusive "male quality" that biologists are always trying to find in the alpha, number one, top birds.

No, more often there is just rampant exuberant individuality, among whole species that have evolved madly complex songs, or, in particular, individuals who just sing and sing, endlessly, expressively, beautifully, without anyone being able to figure out why.

I know this is not a very scientific answer to the question of why birds sing. I wrote a book with that title and I answered on the last page that birds sing because they have to, they must, it is of their very essence as they have evolved.[4] They may do it while they are looking for mates or defending territories, but those tasks do not define the structure and beauty of what is sung. We need to think musically to try to understand that, and as an improviser, I have found that it can be best to jam right along with the birds. And the whales. And even the bugs. The experiential knowledge that one gains from joining in with a foreign music you can barely understand enables a special kind of interspecies communication that can be difficult to understand but easy to appreciate. It can even have some scientific value, confounding what we think we know about what birds do sing and why.

Most birds with complex, extended repertoires surprise us a bit every time. Improvisation, based on certain styles and forms unique to that species, is the name of the game. And most of these male singers are solo performers, more interested in getting their own song out there than listening to anyone else.

Dietmar Todt and Henrike Hultsch have studied nightingales in Germany for decades, both in the wild and in captivity. Because of their work and the work of their students, more is known about the singing behavior of these famous birds than of any other species with so complex a song. Their first studies focused on how the birds sing in the wild, while later experiments examined how the birds learn to sing in controlled circumstances.

One of the first aspects of the nightingale's singing behavior that they uncovered is that there are three distinct ways nightingales sing and countersing to each other, beginning late at night and ending by dawn in the first weeks of spring. Adjacent male nightingales tend to sing back and forth with each other, timing the beginning of each song phrase in a precise way. Most males are "inserters," meaning that they wait about one second after a neighbor's song finishes before starting their own. Songs alternate between one bird and another. Mutual listening occurs, and timing is everything. Then there are "overlappers," who start their song about one second after their neighbor begins, as if to cover up or jam the neighbor's signal. It's some kind of threat or a mask of the first song, cutting into his air time. Then there are "autonomous singers," who sing and sing according to their own schedule, paying no heed to what any nearby nightingales are doing. The top bird listens to no one else. He doesn't care who comes in when, and he is more interested in his own song than anything else. We all know human musicians like that.[5]

The standard evolutionary model of bird song says the males are competing with each other, that they listen to others only to define their own status. Not very cooperative, more like war with music as the weapon. That's the mainstream story, but anyone who goes out in the woods to listen hears much more than this. There are trees full of yellow goldfinches, all in a giant tweeting chorus. A thicket full of European marsh warblers, all cavalcading their collections of African bird song imitations that they have collected on their winter migration to the tropics, a giant jam session where everyone seems to be singing together, not against each other or alone.[6] Erich Jarvis has found that bird brains release dopamine while they are singing, so it's realistic for us to say they like singing, they may even love it. At least they are addicted to it.[7]

An improvising human musician doesn't need to know all of this. Wander through an aviary with your instrument, and listen to what happens. One of the best places is the National Aviary in Pittsburgh, which has a whole rainforest room full of exotic singers. Although most species do have these simple few-note identifying songs that seem mostly the same each time they blurt them out, there are a few with long, extended songs that seem different every time. Are they improvising? Or singing back exact phrases they have learned by rote imitation?

I step through the artificial leaves of the aviary with my clarinet, testing out phrases, throwing up licks. If you want to improvise with birds, you must leave them space. Don't just get up there and play your favorite tune, or show off your arpeggios to the max. And for god's sake don't imitate the songs you hear—that's too close to what scientists call a playback experiment, or what bird watchers call "pishing," making sounds just to get the birds to come out. Take them seriously as musicians, play something you think they might like to join in with. Get them to want to listen to you.

Most of the Aviary birds just kept singing their own songs, showing little interest in my strange and foreign phrases. But one bird, a male white-crested laughing thrush, *Garrulax leucolophus*, suddenly hopped over and began to sing along with me, phrases that seemed to interweave in a truly jazzy way with what I was handing him. More than a few people have seen a clip of this on YouTube,[8] documenting the very first moment I got a real musical response from a bird and the genesis of my interest in interspecies music-making. It was in the year 2000, despite that 1980s-vintage sweater I'm wearing. This bird really seemed to want to join in. He didn't seem to be competing with me, or trying to attract me. We were making music together.

As I played through the net mesh cage, astonished with each new phrase the bird would sing me, I imagined this was a male singing for the usual dual male reasons to sing. Later I learned that it was no accident that the laughing thrush was the one bird that found a way to join in with me. Frederic Vencl and Branko Soucek found in 1975 that male and female laughing thrushes each have a different musical "program," that is, each decides which of 25 different syllables it will sing next after hearing its mate sing a preceding syllable. Their decision trees and transition matrices show a definite pattern that could be reasonably modeled on the vintage computers they had in those ancient days. When I read that this is a species in which the males and females sing precisely structured duets, then the whole thing took on another light. This is a species where the males and females make music together, performing a complex duet that somehow sounds a bit like jazz. Suddenly I could imagine myself part of a pair-bonding ritual, where my phrases were interpreted by the bird within an exact two-part regimen. Science illuminates the experience.

In fact, it is remarkable that, in the 30 years of computer advances since these studies, hardly anyone has conducted an analysis of bird songs into programs as elaborate as this, even though any notebook computer has more than enough processing power to do this kind of work. Vencl and Soucek found a definite order and structure to the duets that they were able to reasonably model with simple computer programs. They described the male and female birds as each having a distinct "song program" that determines what they sing. Bird as machine. What do they think all this exactness means?

> At this time, it is speculation to suggest what the birds are saying to one another. We have noted that certain syllables are given more often under some conditions. For example F_2-M_{23} seem to be called up after a disturbance such as a loud noise. This reply loop might mean something like, "I am OK, how about you?" $M_{6/22}$-F_1 may represent a synchonization which "entrains" both birds for further singing. It may signify, "I'm ready to sing, are you?"[9]

The practical value of this structured duetting, they surmise, must lie in the fact that there is a plan to it all. The birds need to stay in touch with each other in very specific ways.

What does this have to do with my jamming with a thrush in an aviary in Pittsburgh? Now I listen back to the recording of what I did, and then print out my bird/human duet as a sonogram (Figure 28.1). Smack in the middle of our song, the bird begins by delivering a characteristic *dee to deeto dee to dee to deeep* and I respond with a rising arpeggio

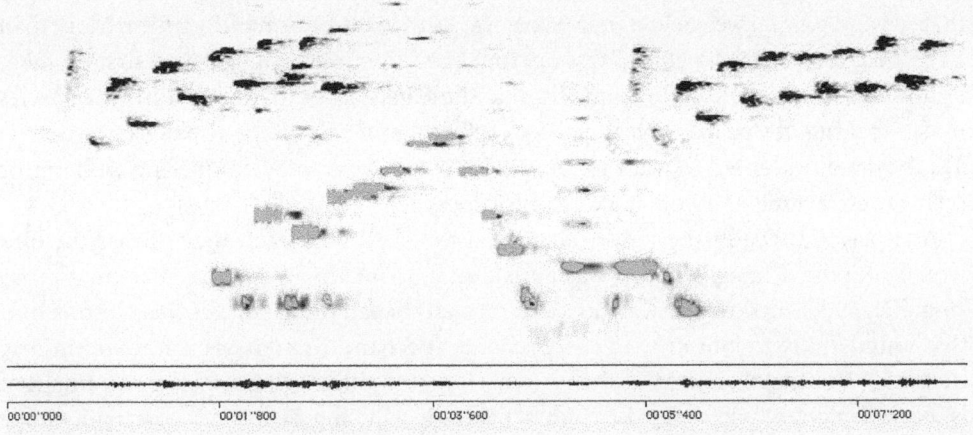

00'00''000   00'01''800   00'03''600   00'05''400   00'07''200

FIGURE 28.1 A fragment of a live duet between clarinet and laughing thrush; bird in black, clarinet in gray.

and fall. Then he repeats his same riff, as if daring me to get it. (The clarinet is the lower, gray phrase that goes up and comes down. The bird's phrases are similar alternating patterns to the left and to the right):

Notice that both the clarinet and laughing thrush tones make simple, clear marks. Maybe that's why so much easy music evolves between us. Later I try a descending slightly syncopated bluesy scale. The bird seems to be trying to match it with high back-and-forth whistles, those parallel marks above mine (Figure 28.2). Does he know I'm not a bird? Most likely he does. Does he hear my clarinet tone as being related to his own? I suspect something about my instrument's overtone series gets to him. Whether I am rising, falling, or slinking down a scale, the bird finds a way to insert his characteristic phrases along with mine. I don't feel he is trying to jam my signal or intimidate me into silence. Will I ever know if this is more than an anthropomorphic hope that someone else in the natural world likes what I play?

Music is made with a mix of control and daring, answering in sound at the moment more questions are raised. That's the nature of art inside nature: we will always hear more music than we can find reason for. Even a tiny bird brain can be attuned to the magic of organized sound, where the form might be greater than the function, beauty ever resonant and present, long before we were able to learn from its ways and hear the opposite of time.

Some who have heard my interactions wonder why I don't just try to copy the bird, to show I admire what he sings. I remind them that music is not at its best as a battle or copycat imitation. We learned from song sparrows that it is most aggressive to parrot back to a bird with exactly his same song. Bending what you hear, weaving it with your own songs—now that is suggestive of much more respect.

Some people laugh at such an approach and consider it wishful thinking or musical self-congratulation. What right have you, they say, to imagine that a bird would care

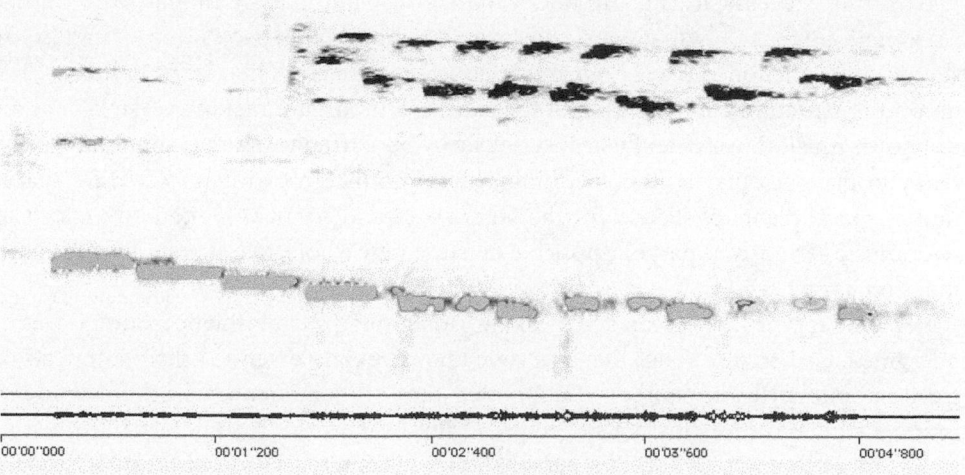

| 00'00''000 | 00'01''200 | 00'02''400 | 00'03''600 | 00'04''800 |

FIGURE 28.2 Laughing thrush begins to respond musically to the clarinet.

about clarinet and saxophone wailing when he has evolved to care only about his own rightful songs? This is why scientists' playback experiments must be done with such rigor and care. You don't want your bird to become assimilated to irreverent human sounds. Look at parrots for goshsakes! They'll imitate anything, if it gets them attention. But only in cages. In the wild, they hardly use their mimicking abilities at all.

Birds are smarter than some scientists give them credit for. In my experience they can be interested in all kinds of sounds, not just their own. As much as we have tried to track birds' behavior while they sing, or when we play sounds back at them, we know very little of how they listen, what sounds in their surrounding world matter to them. We know they have extremely sensitive ears that can detect rhythms five times faster than any human can catch. Tiny nuances in texture can mean a lot to them. It also might not be a coincidence that so many of the sounds they make are right in the range of human hearing. Our musicality is accessible to them, as theirs is to us.

Two musicians from different parts of the planet who might not speak the same language can easily get up on stage and start performing together. This is why we're always told not to shake the hands of anyone in the band we've not met before because the audience doesn't believe it's possible for musicians to make sense together if they haven't rehearsed, or haven't spoken. This is part of the magic of music's ability to communicate—that its rhythms, melodies, and forms can cross cultural lines. Clarinetist Barbaros Erköse tours the world with oud player Anouar Brahem, even though Brahem speaks no Turkish and that's the only language Erköse knows.[10] They make perfect musical sense together, and I have been fortunate to interview Erköse as well, using only my clarinet to ask my questions.

It takes a leap of faith to extend this sense of music's communicative power to use it to cross species lines, not only boundaries of culture. If birds make music, as nearly all human cultures think they do, by virtue of our use of the word *song* to describe their learned, species-specific sounds, then we take their sounds most seriously when we address them musically, and dare to play along.

Now this isn't easy, learning to find a sudden way into the unfamiliar. Still, I think it's something that all human musicians should try, and Interspecies Improvisation 101 should be a sanctioned part of our music education system. First, learn to listen. Pick up on the structure and inflection of the sounds animals are making. Take it in as an unknown musical world, and take it seriously by preparing yourself to join in. If you're ready to play, just play a little, try things out, announce your intention. Leave space, mostly space, plenty of silence, for the other species to admit you—to join in, to take your music seriously as part of a possible music, a new whole, that no one species could make on its own.

Remember why jazz spread across the world and had such influence. Sure, it was at one time based on pop songs that everyone knew, but jazz extended them into feats of freedom and rhythmic coolness. But another part of its influence comes from how it found a way into so many kinds of music around the world. It could learn from anything, adapt to anything, bring a personal, player-centered vision of creativity to any existing genre, introducing originality and exploration into forms that previously might have seem hemmed in. Play fast and loose with Indian music, break the raga rules that tell you to go up the scale one way and down another, and you can quickly make mistakes that the terms of Indian classical music will quickly tell you are wrong. Jazz is more forgiving.

Sure, there can be right and wrong notes for a particular chord progression, but somewhere, sometime, a cat has put forward just those wrong notes and tried as hard as he could to convince you they are right. The successive acceptance of more and more bending of the rules has pushed jazz onward to unexpected directions and innovations. That's why jazz musicians may be the best prepared to take on the music of other species; they have been stepping over boundaries for more than a hundred years.

Some birds even seem like natural jazzers. Consider the song of the veery, *Catharus fuscescens*, a brown, spotted-belly thrush that lives in temperate American forests, known for its querulous, queasy descending line heard every spring in the green wooded forests of Eastern North America. I believe the bird's song is the source of its name, a swirling, *peeooweeeoooweeeooo* descending invisible behind dense green leaves. You will almost never see this bird, but you will often hear him, sometimes from very far away. An early Native American forest guide said, "this sound really makes me sick," but I find it captivating, mysterious.[11]

How are we to represent the sound, to bring it within the realm of human understanding? A pioneering work in this field, F. S. Mathews's *Field Book of Wild Birds and Their Music* (1904), describes it in Figure 28.3, and Aretas Saunders, author of a famous mid-20th century (1951) *Guide to Bird Songs*, represented the sound like so in Figure 28.4. Here the graphic notation of the veery song looks like a sweeping round sigh descending through the trees, or graphic notation by Tibetan monks or Cornelius Cardew. Not as musical to our classical aesthetes, but more like a wash of synthesized atmosphere present in the electronic music of today.

FIGURE 28.3 F. S. Mathews's graphic and musical notations of a veery's song (1904).

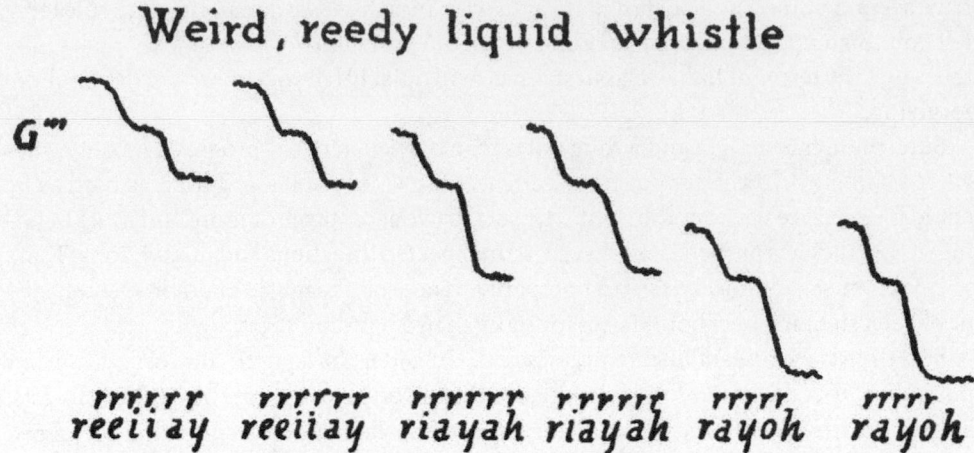

SONG OF THE VEERY

FIGURE 28.4 Aretas Saunders's graphic and mnemonic notation of a veery's song (1951).

FIGURE 28.5 My transcription of a slowed-down veery's song (2005).

How does the veery become a suspected jazz bird? Using the popular computer music software Ableton Live, I slowed the veery's song down and discovered a syncopated line like a phrase out of Miles Davis's electric fusion period, which conventional musical notation can only partially report, in Figure 28.5. I really didn't expect something like that to come out, a melody that changes from C minor to G7 midcourse. And who knew a veery was swinging like that, with the sound so high and too fast for us to hear it.

Modern science prefers computer-generated sonograms, like the one created by the shareware program Amadeus, with frequency on the vertical axis plotted against time in Figure 28.6. That reveals the structure, but not really the sense of syncopation. So we have the wishful-thinking early transcription of the transposed melody into the

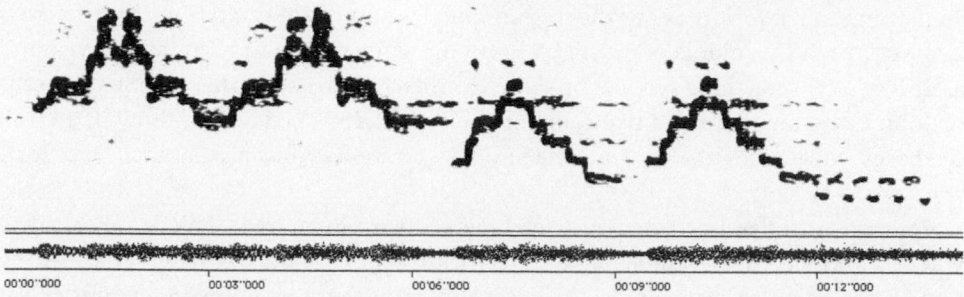

FIGURE 28.6 Sonogram of a slowed-down veery's song, printed out by the program Amadeus (2005).

astonishing realm of a Miles Davis-like cool jazz trumpet phrase, and then a more precise transcription, which in the end demonstrates a very refined sense of musicality in the single utterance of this musical bird. He's veerying with feeling, he means something because he's got that swing. In the end we have the sonogram, produced by a machine seeking no nuance. Is that then our most accurate representation of what this veery sings?

What does the veery song mean? Some call music the language of emotions, pulling our heartstrings the way nothing else can. Others say its meaning is purely musical, to be understood only between precise rules of form and order that most listeners hardly know. There is truth in both these claims, and this is true for both humans and animals.[12]

I haven't played live with veeries and I'm not sure they'd really care for my licks. The coolness of their phrase can only be heard when their distinctive tune is slowed down into our range of rhythm and pitch. Then I can learn with it, and I've certainly played live on stage with recordings of the veery, sliced, diced, moved around, turned into musical material for electronic improvisation. But that is closer to interspecies emulation than interspecies communication. The best dialogue I've had with actual creatures has come, ironically, with an animal thousands of times heavier than me, a humpback whale.

In the case of humpback whales, we have a song that very few humans knew about until the end of the 1960s, so we have only a half-century of attempts to make sense of what it might mean. Once again, only the males do the singing. Their half-hour-long songs are sung mostly during mating season, so sex probably has something to do with it. But unlike in songbirds, we have zero evidence that female whales care—we have never seen them show a whit of interest in the males' amazing singing. So either the sexual selection of whale song is far more subtle than we have been able to see, or something else may be at work.[13]

Humpback whales and nightingales are far apart on the tree of evolution, and yet there is something quite similar about their songs. How can this be? Both of these creatures are outliers, because the sounds they make are particularly intricate, extended, and beautiful. Nightingales sing from twilight long into the dark hours—if you haven't yet heard one you may be surprised that their songs are not immediately melodious, but rhythmic, strange, like a secret pulsed code emitting from an alien star. There is indeed something otherworldly about their clear whistles and ratchety rhythms heard across a forest lake in the middle of the night. From our current listening vantage they sound a bit like a DJ scratching records or some Euro techno artist; perhaps to Shakespeare or John Clare they sounded like something else entirely. Their songs, though, are full of energy, sung all night long while the birds sit motionless on a high branch, easy for a predator to pick off.

Rhythms at different frequencies, interspersed with long, clear whistle tones, a few whoops and bleeps. Definitely organized, with a structure not yet much analyzed by human scientists, or human musicians. But a music is there, an always alien music. Is it beautiful? To the female nightingales, it is supposed to be. To other males? A challenge.

Ask a person what a slowed-down nightingale song sounds like and they might say, "Huh? It sounds a lot like a humpback whale!" Those whoops, blats, chirps, and grumbling rhythms happen at a whole different metabolic scale, in a different medium, the tough-to-see-through tropic underwater world, slow enough that humans again have a hard time paying attention to the whole way it moves. But again, there are clear patterns, rhythms, tones, a definite structure. Speed it up, raise the pitch, and it strangely resembles the nightingale's song in terms of the kinds of different elements, the spacing of the silences between sounds, and the relative complexity of structure. Figure 28.7 presents a small sampling of each, with scale of time and pitch adjusted to see the similarity, ten seconds of bird compared to one minute of whale.

Why should these very different animals have songs with similar attributes? If they are supposed to be the result of sexual selection, a process of evolution that favors extended preference of random qualities, or at least arbitrary qualities, why should the songs of these very animals be so alike instead of wildly divergent? There may be certain sonic patterns that appear in all the music of the animal world, and these musical axioms may be the reason that it is possible to jam with a humpback whale, and why the whale, in the best moments, might actually listen to a clarinet and want to chime in.

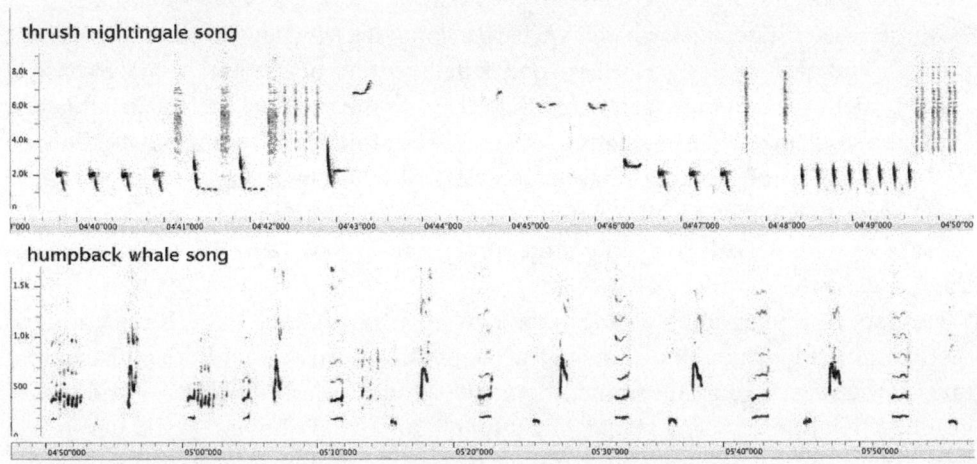

FIGURE 28.7 Thrush nightingale and humpback whale sonograms compared.

The song of the humpback whale is the most extended patterned vocalization produced by any animal. These songs were first described by Roger Payne and Scott McVay, who took a bold step for scientific rhetoric when they praised the "surprising beauty" of these sounds in the prestigious journal *Science* in 1971.[14] The structure of 11 minutes of humpback whale song looks something like McVay's hand-traced sonogram (Figure 28.8) from this famous paper.

During the following decades the astonishing moans of this whale made its way into human culture, becoming the inspiration for famous classical compositions by Alan Hovhaness, George Crumb, and later John Cage and Toru Takemitsu. In the pop world the humpback whale song and the plight of the whale found its way into works by Pete Seeger; Judy Collins; Captain Beefheart; Crosby; Stills and Nash; Jethro Tull; Yes; Paul Winter; Charlie Haden; the Partridge Family; Country Joe and the Fish; Laurie Anderson; Alice in Chains; Tom Waits; and Lou Reed, to name but a few. The original recording assembled by Payne, *Songs of the Humpback Whale,* became a platinum record, selling more than a million copies, and in 1979 an excerpt from it was included as a "sound page," in *National Geographic.* With more than 10 million copies printed at

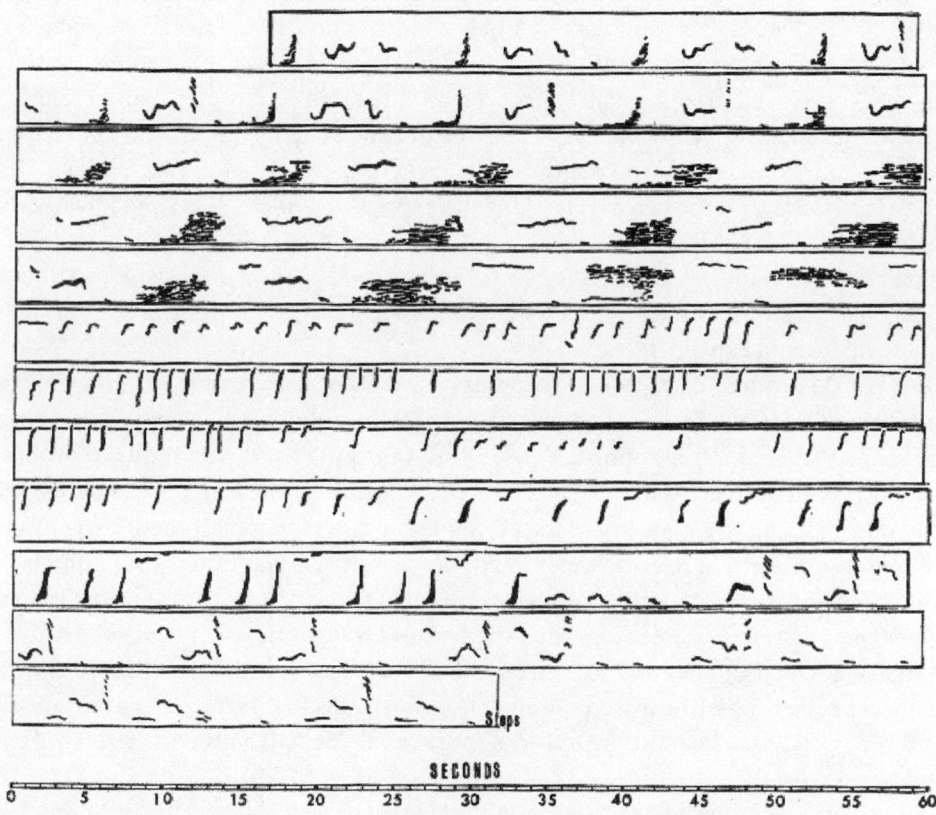

FIGURE 28.8 Scott McVay's hand-traced sonogram from Payne and McVay (1971).

once in many languages, this remains the largest single pressing of any audio recording in history.[15]

Humpback songs are far more musical in structure than the sound of any other dolphin or whale. They consist of repeating patterns, hierarchically organized at the level of unit (or motif), phrase, theme, and song. Each complete song consists of five to seven themes. Some of the phrases end with the same contrasting sound, so they can be said to rhyme, in a way analogous to human poems. A series of these songs can be repeated extensively, up to 23 hours in a single session. Since singing mostly happens only during the winter breeding season, when the whales congregate in specific breeding grounds, such as the Hawaiian Islands, the Silver Bank off the Dominican Republic, and Archipelago Revillagigedo off of Mexico, it is generally assumed to be a male sexual display with the purpose of attracting females, who do not sing. However, no one has ever seen a female humpback whale show any interest in the song whatsoever, but other males do respond to a singing male, in a usually nonaggressive manner. A rival theory, less popular, but the only one with any evidence, says the humpback whale song serves to organize the male whales together in a manner different from any other animal we have yet observed.[16]

The most remarkable aspect of this amazing song is that, unlike nearly all bird songs, it constantly changes during the breeding season. When an innovation appears in the song, all other males strive to copy the new element and in a matter of weeks all are singing the same new song. They all want to sound the same, yet the sameness continually evolves. No one has postulated a good reason for this, and no one can yet explain why whales in any given ocean, say, the North Pacific, change their songs in tandem even though they are likely too many thousands of miles away to hear each other.[17] The whales in Hawaii and Mexico are changing their songs in tandem, in a similar way, even though they can't hear what the other population is doing. In birds, widely separated populations tend to have different dialects in their songs, but widely dispersed humpback whales have the same song, and they are changing it very rapidly in several ways. Again, no one can explain it.

With its extended, clear structure, humpback whale song is more clearly musical than the songs of most birds. And with the uncertainty about who the males are singing for, the song of the humpback whale is full of mysteries impenetrable to humanity. But for our species, a mystery means a challenge. As a musician, I wanted to hear for myself. Having spent several years playing my clarinet to birds, sometimes getting a response, sometimes not, I was eager to try this interspecies jamming with humpback whales. To my surprise, I got a very different result than the researchers did. So different, that when I played my recording of a humpback whale/clarinet duet to several leading humpback scientists, they did not believe the encounter was real. But I assured them it really happened. What surprised my audiences most was that nearly everyone considered the sound they heard to be music: a music made between human clarinetist and humpback whale.

In January–February 2007 I spent several weeks off of Maui, Hawaii, trying to interact musically with humpback whales. The making of these duet recordings does not involve getting the clarinet wet. I'm safely onboard a boat and the whale is, ideally, about 10 meters underwater, directly under us or within 100 meters at most. He can be much further away and still sound loud and clear. In fact, singing humpback males usually situate themselves about one kilometer apart from each other. Figure 28.9 shows how it's done. The chain of technology enables the clarinetist to talk to the whale or, more accurately, use music to cross species lines. Why do I think this is even worth trying? Because music can communicate across cultures in a way language cannot.

Can I do the same with a nameless whale? Humpback males usually suspend themselves motionless underwater in a curved posture, singing continuously in a solo trance. I am essentially interrupting a reverie whose purpose we do not know. In the musical moment I do not care about the purpose, but instead wish to understand the result. Can I prove the whale is responding to me? I will show you the best of such duets I have recorded, and you can judge for yourself.

Many things can go wrong in such an experiment: the whale might stop singing and move away, a loud motorboat might come near and mess up the sound quality. Scientists might call my duet statistically insignificant, because it represents the one best case scenario rather than the probable result of broadcasting a clarinet underwater next to a singing humpback whale male. But even a single interesting improvised performance is worthy of musical analysis. I want to figure out why I like it, why even the skeptics I have played this to have responded to this sudden music.

In the whale/clarinet duet sonograms you are about to look at (Figures 28.10–28.14), I have adjusted the appearance so that the two parts are clearly visible. Here is a summary of the whole mood: The whale sounds have a huge range, from 100 Hz (G2) (in the form of clear *broomphs* [not a technical term]), visible as round, sine-like tones with few overtones. But then the whale may suddenly jump to high, wavering whistles that resemble the timbre of the clarinet, with a series of parallel overtones. The pitch of the whale's high whistles, though, is rarely steady, but warbles about twice a second around 300–600 Hz (E4–D5), in the third octave of the clarinet. Then occasionally there will be an extremely high note, around 4800 Hz, coming almost immediately after the *broomph*, from the

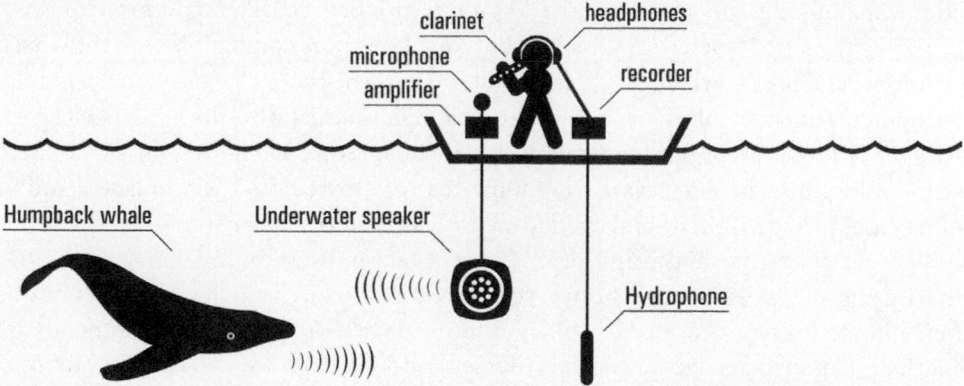

FIGURE 28.9 How to play music live with a humpback whale, from Rothenberg (2008).

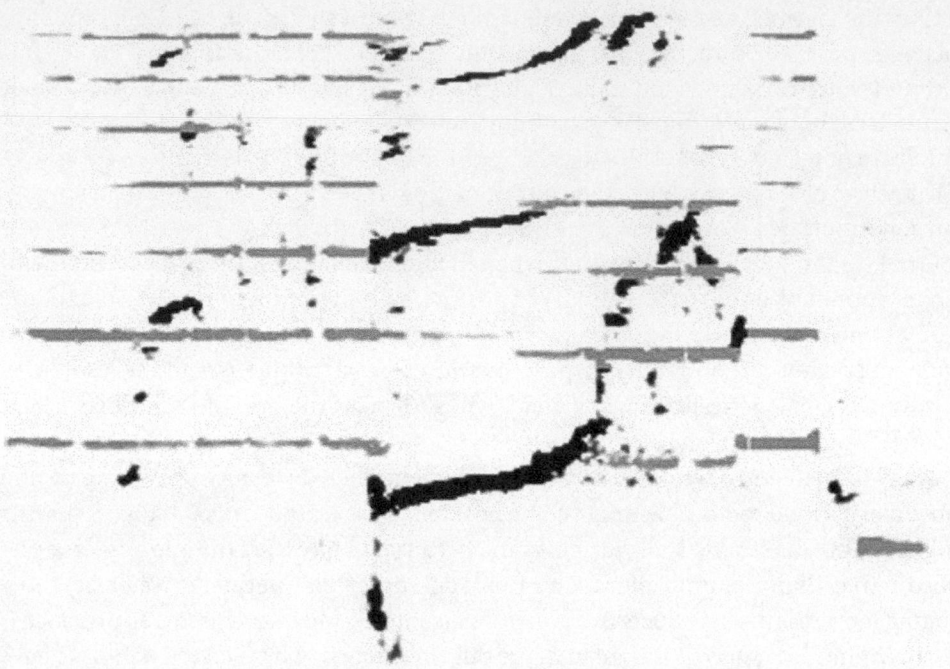

FIGURE 28.10 Whale tried to match the clarinet's steady pitch.

same whale. How can he jump so high so fast? I'm afraid we really have little idea how the humpback whale makes these sounds at all.

The clarinet sounds are often high, held-out notes, more constant in pitch and thus closer to straight horizontal lines on the sonogram printout. There are usually at least a few parallel lines of overtones, more than usual for the instrument because the clarinet is being broadcast underwater, and the properties of underwater sound propagation seems to add overtones to the timbre, making the clarinet more bell-like, closer to a soprano saxophone (which, because of its conical bore, produces more overtones). Yet after some minutes, my clarinet starts to produce higher, shriekier, and more uneven, warbling notes, not exactly like the whale but somehow more compatible with the whale.

And what does the whale do? Does his sound become more clarinet-like during the encounter? I am not really sure, but some of our high squeaks are quite hard to tell apart. And the clearest sign of communication comes when I stop, and he begins with a direct sense of response, in some cases continuing the very same note I just finished, and in other cases trying to join in, and overlap me with a complementary sound.

To truly assess the musicality of this encounter, and decide for yourself whether this interspecies duet is music or not, you should first of all listen to it; an mp3 of this four minute excerpt is available online at http://terrain.org/columns/21/Rothenberg_Clarinet_Humpback.mp3. Listen for yourself, and perhaps we can set up our own Martinellian survey: is this duet music: yes or no? There is a play-by-play account of the

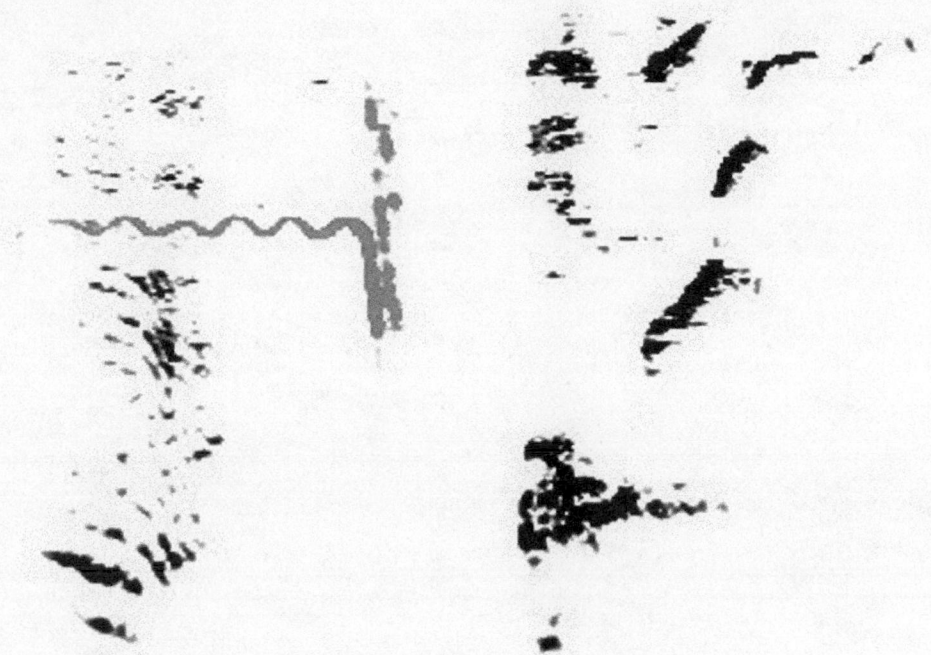

FIGURE 28.11 Whale sings a previously unheard sound.

FIGURE 28.12 Whale matches my sound as I play.

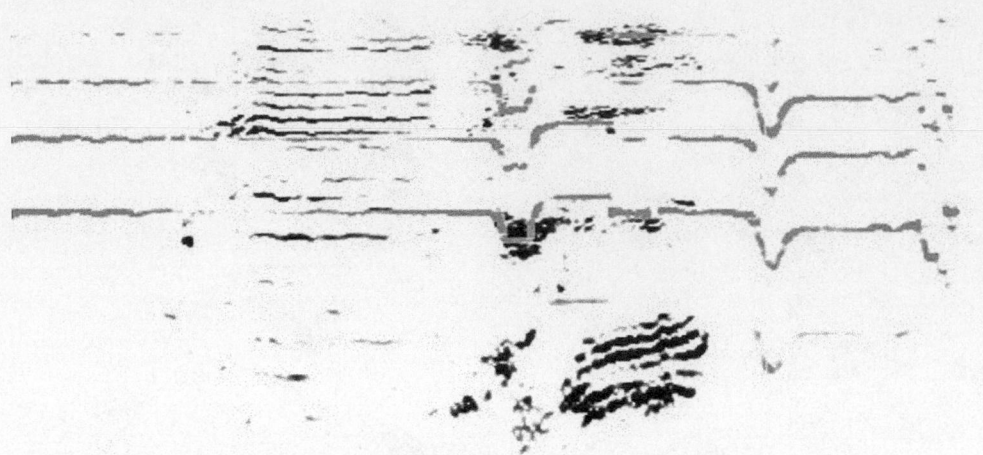

FIGURE 28.13 Whale responds to the steady clarinet tone with a gritty growl.

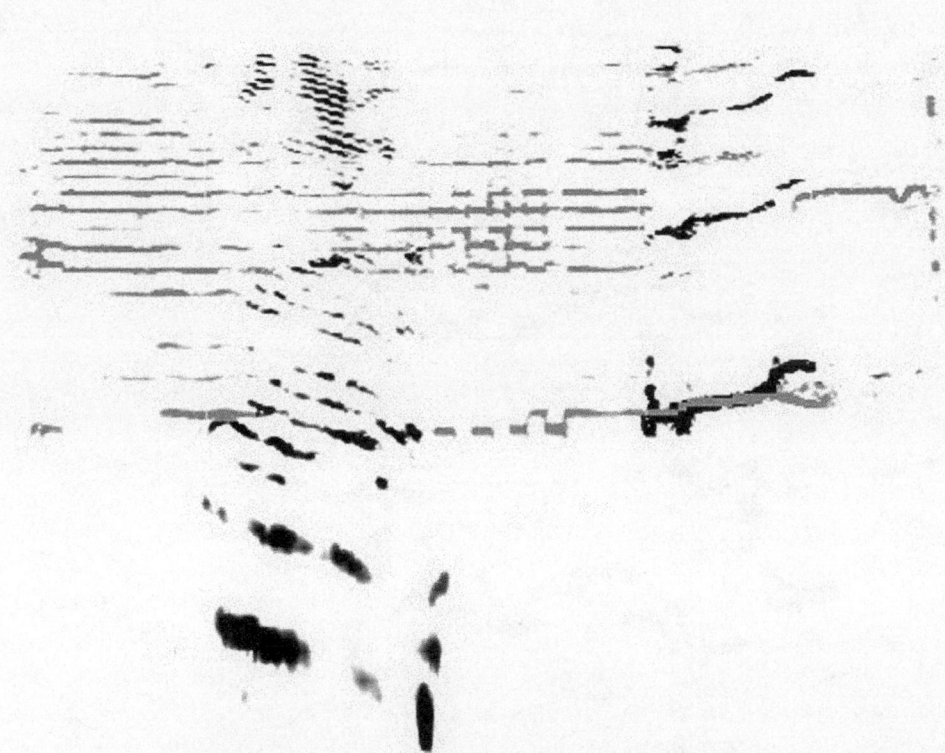

FIGURE 28.14 My own song is changed after hearing the whale.

best part of the duet, including a *complete* sonogram, also online.[18] I have posted this because I am frustrated that in so many scientific papers on animal music, complete sonograms do not appear, only summary statistical analysis. Here you can assess the whole thing, and next is my play-by-play account of the duet as I understand it.

Right at the outset we hear a form of tone and rhythm matching, where the whale seems to match the middle C, 260 Hz (C4) he hears on the clarinet twice (2.1" and 5.5"). Then his successive descending whoops echo the roughly one-second beats suggested by the clarinet. If we compare the pacing of this response with the usual speed of this particular theme, it is faster than usual, suggesting that the clarinet's presence is having an effect on the whale's overall tempo. Now the clarinet moves up to a 370 Hz (G-flat4) for its repeating beats. Note that at 10" and 14" the whale inserts a *whoop* followed by rhythmic descending notes. My approach in the duet is to play tentative, testing notes, leaving space to listen for what the whale does. A skeptical listener could say this makes any interaction sound like a duet, but let's see what happens. At 21" and 23" the whale adds a descending *gulp* after his *whoop*, and then after I play a glissando up to 831 Hz (Ab5) at 26" the whale *clearly* responds with a high cry immediately afterwards at 26.5", the closest acknowledgment from the whale thus far. At 41" the whale sings an insanely high squeak around 4700 Hz (D8), and then at 45.5" I try to imitate it by playing my teeth on the reed. Fellow humans on the boat did not enjoy this sound, and most of them were not listening to the underwater whales through the headphones, so they weren't hearing the whole thing.

As the encounter progressed, I found myself playing fewer phrases that I enjoyed and more that seemed to engage the leaps and plunges of the whales' aesthetic world. Listening to both species, it's unclear just who such music would be for, if neither people nor whales really want it. I guess each of our kinds can expand our awareness through such an alien musical process. At 55" the whale makes two super-high squeaks again, and then after my short bluesy phrase he seems to match with the *booweah* sound, and then we are all together, me and whale, playing almost a single chord at 1'02". In this passage one clearly sees and hears the tendency of the whale to respond with a full spectrum whoop up to the stratosphere as soon as the clarinet stops playing. From 1'12" to 1'14.5" is the grand phrase from whoop to squeak, then with a deep grunt (almost like the boom of a giant bullfrog) showing in a few seconds the full range of humpback music. At 1'15" the clarinet moves from 1175 Hz (D6) to 784 Hz (G5) (only higher overtones appear on the sonogram, so the notes look similar, the movement from three to four parallel lines is the key), and at 1'18" the whale appears to gliss up to join my steady G5 with an up-sliding moan that anticipates my pitch.

In response to two instances of a held-out G5 on the clarinet, the whale offers two responses: first, the great warbling whistle at 1'22.5", and then the upsliding pitch-matching moan at 1'27". At 1'32" we hear the whale attempting to match the changed pitch of the clarinet held note from G5 to 932 Hz (Bb5), a frequency of warble we have not previously heard, a third or so higher, 698 Hz (F5), than a similar warble at 1'12", 587 Hz (D5). At 1'43.5" the whale remarkably matches the earlier pitch, D5, with a warbling that gradually approaches the steady note. At 1'55" a different contoured whale whistle attempts to match the clarinet pitch. Or is this all wishful thinking of an interspecies dreamer? Even the long upsweep from 2'00" to 2'02" seems to strive for that clarinet pitch. From 2'07" to 2'08" we hear the grand culminating seagull scream. And at 2'19" it appears again. And again with greater flourish at 2'30". At 2'38" he responds with a downgrunt and then I seem to match his upsweep at 2'41". At 2'46" comes the newly heard chopping sound, clarinet high on top of it, then more steady notes broken by a whale upsweep, as the rhythmic presence of the low grunts increases.

The choppiness comes again at 2'57", before a blustering clarinet gliss at 3'01" brings another upsweep of whale into a high held note. This is becoming a familiar pattern. A new kind of very high whale sound appears, like rapid bow strokes on the bridge of a violin. This builds the mood for the moment when the situation really draws me in to create a sound quite unlike any I had ever played before. When I look at these dramatic, warbly clarinet things at 3'24" and 3'28", I clearly see that something has happened to me here. I don't know if I am musically becoming a whale, but I have definitely been driven by the encounter to wail in a whole new way. It does look a bit like the klezmer madness of my ancestors, but an octave too high, way up at 2800 Hz (F7).

At this point the rest of the crew was ready to throw me off the ship. At 3'33" the whale is matching with a new kind of high squeak we have not previously heard. I wasn't sure before but now I am convinced that this animal is modifying his song in response to mine, a musical result that is a true surprise. This new and nearly painful shriek is, for me, the climax of this alien musical encounter. When something similar recurs between 3'43" to 3'44", I can no longer quite tell, either by ear or on the page, which is clarinet and which is whale. And at 3'55", for the first time, the held out notes of clarinet and whale occur in tandem, like some kind of high altitude harmonic choir. After a bit of further matching the whale makes a high growl at 4'01" that looks like a fingerprint on the sonogram, and the overlapping continues. Following this, the whale slows down his low phrases to his more usual tempo. Perhaps he is no longer so excited by this strange new clarinet sound. From a low trill the whale upsweeps in and I join in with a final new shriek. The whale stretches out his final moan and is back to his usual self.

The remaining eight minutes of the duet are less dramatic, but there are still moments where the whale seems to change the pacing and nature of his phrasing in relation to clarinet sounds. Since this is a musical, not a scientific experiment, I am sorry I do not have enough data to be conclusive. But I do think it is relevant that a high percentage of scientists I played this recording for, all of whom were familiar with the official line that humpback whales do not reliably respond to human sounds, were shocked by what they heard.

The shock might wear off once they begin to try to explain what they heard, but I believe the music is still there. Back on the boat, the rest of the humans on board got tired of these strange clarinet squeaks, and eventually some jumped in the water to hear the underwater mix for themselves, and the whale didn't seem too pleased with that and slowly moved away.

The engineer listening in on the hydrophones shouted out, "David, stop playing! I need to adjust this equipment," but I told him, "Kent, I stopped a few minutes ago."

Noonan turned to me and was taken aback. By now, at least to Kent, the whale was sounding as much like a clarinet as the clarinet was trying to sound like a whale. My music had become whale-like, and the people could stand it no longer!

Throughout this duet are several clear examples where the whale seems to match the clarinet. Several of my favorites are enlarged in Figures 28.10 to 28.14: at 2'50", where the whale is striving to match the steady clarinet pitch (Figure 28.10); at 3'31", where my whale-like wail garners a never previously heard squeaky response (Figure 28.11); at 3'51", where the whale dares to match my sound as I am playing it. He can't quite hold the pitch but he is wavering up and down around it (Figure 28.12); at 3'58" I am now playing wavering tones as he has taught them to me, he responds with a gritty growl (Figure 28.13); finally, at 4'06" he joins in with my steady note by uttering a deep, complex boom, then after my riff of discrete pitches he comes in with a whistle that finally matches me truly in tune, then I end with that new whale wail I have learned during this performance (Figure 28.14).

As I reflect on the visualization of this experience, which seems to clearly reinforce my hunches that the whale was listening and trying to match me, I remember what I have learned from many years of jamming with birds. Most birds have their own set and specific songs, and when they hear a clarinet, if they respond at all, it will be with their own well-known tunes. Even a bird with a vast repertoire like a nightingale or a mockingbird is going to use its own licks when and if he plays along with you.

No one disagrees with the basic fact that, unlike any other species we know of, male humpback whales constantly change their song, and yet every whale seems to be singing the same song at the same time. How is the song changing, then? The best evidence we have of hearing a change suddenly appear comes from a one-page article in *Nature* by Michael Noad, who reports that at least one, maybe a few Indian Ocean humpback whales from the West Coast of Australia got lost one season and turned up in his research area off Australia's East Coast, in the South Pacific Ocean. They arrived with a completely different song, and in a matter of weeks all those Pacific whales had switched to the Indian Ocean song.[19] In 2010 an even more rapid example of humpback song change was documented, also in the South Pacific.[20]

Is the drive for innovation so strong in this species that any new tune is going to displace the one in action before? This observation suggests it. But the new song probably has to have some particular qualities unknown to us to really become popular. Just as the music industry cannot manufacture a hit, we do not know what makes a catchy whale tune. But there must be some riffs they like and others they do not, explaining why some units stay in the humpback repertoire for decades and others come and go in a matter of months or years.

So if a whale has a penchant to learn from another whale, and be able to take on a new sound very quickly, then *of course* if he hears a clarinet out of the deep blue he's going to try the new sound on for size! Not only should I not be surprised that the whale is imitating me, I should expect it. If he didn't do it, then I would want to question the theory that whales learn songs from other whales. The sounds I was playing were well within the range of possible notes a humpback whale could make. So he tried them on for size.

Would this whale retain some of my phrases, work them into his repertoire? If he did, and all the whales have this real need for a new song that rapidly takes over the airwaves, then in a few months I might hear some of my motifs incorporated as new units in the song of the humpback whale. That would indeed be the highest compliment an interspecies musician could receive. Not praise from one's peers, but a piece of my music in the group mind of the whales.

I imagine it would take a lot more time playing the same phrases for the whales. Jim Darling told me he would like to get a permit to do that kind of research, but he doubts the Office of Marine Mammals would grant it—too much meddling in things we know little about![21] But already there is no doubt that the whale's live music has influenced what *I* play. Performing along with a whale, I try to inhabit the rhythm and shape of the song, which a written or printed description cannot contain.

How to train oneself to be an interspecies improviser? Like any form of improvisation, first of all, just listen. Then only when you feel like there is space to make a musical announcement of your presence, go ahead, do it. Be a bird among birds, a whale among whales. Then leave more space, listen again. Know that most musical creatures will only sing their own, stylized song. The best species to communicate with are those who share with humanity a curious interest in a range of sounds, and who have evolved to want to improvise, to try something new, to enjoy real play with sound. Take a stab at their style and twist the essence of what you do. You may be surprised and just might effect a change in a musical world of which you cannot quite speak. Learn to appreciate more than what your own species has attuned itself to hear. Make a more-than-human music just past the edge of what you expect and could believe. A music greater than the sensibility of one species alone might slightly show us a way to live better with nature and not destroy our planet with rampant human aesthetics, saving the Earth while there still is time.

NOTES

1. Donald Kroodsma et al., "Song Development by Grey Catbirds," *Animal Behavior* 54 (1997): 457–464.
2. Samuel Harper, *Twelve Months with the Birds and Poets* (Chicago: Ralph Fletcher Seymour, 1917), 83–84.
3. Richard Wilbur, "Some Notes on 'Lying,'" in *The Catbird's Song: Prose Pieces 1963–1995* (New York: Harcourt, 1997), 137.
4. David Rothenberg, *Why Birds Sing* (New York: Basic Books, 2005).
5. Silke Kipper, Roger Mundry, Henrike Hultsche, and Dietmar Todt, "Long-Term Persistence of Song Performance Rules in Nightingales," *Behaviour* 141 (2004): 371–390. See also Marc Naguib, "Effects of Song Overlapping and Alternating on Nocturnally Singing Nightingales," *Animal Behaviour* 58, no. 5 (1999): 1061–1067.
6. Françoise Dowsett-Lemaire, "The Imitative Range of the Song of the Marsh Warbler *Acrocephalus palustris*, with Special Reference to Imitations of African Birds," *Ibis* 121 (1979): 453–468. See also Françoise Dowsett-Lemaire, "Vocal Behaviour of the Marsh Warbler," *Le Gerfaut* 69 (1979): 475–502.

7. Erina Hara, Lubica Kubikova, Neal A. Hessler, and Erich D. Jarvis, "Role of Midbrain Dopaminergic System in the Modulation of Vocal Brain Activation by Social Context," *European Journal of Neuroscience* 25 (2007): 3406–3416.
8. http://www.youtube.com/watch?v=zVO4XoGl4EI
9. Fredric Vencl and Branko Soucek, "Structure and Control of Duet Singing in the White-Crested Laughing Thrush," *Behaviour* 57, no. 3–4 (1976): 221.
10. Anouar Brahem, *Conte de l'incroyable amour* (Munich: ECM Records, 1457, 1991), compact disc.
11. Arthur Cleveland Bent, *Life Histories of Familiar North American Birds* (New York: Harper, 1960), 271.
12. Rothenberg, *Why Birds Sing*, 221.
13. David Rothenberg, *Thousand Mile Song* (New York: Basic Books, 2008).
14. Roger Payne and Scott McVay, "Songs of Humpback Whales," *Science* 173, no. 3997 (August 13, 1971): 585-597.
15. Rothenberg, *Thousand Mile Song*, 9.
16. James D. Darling, Meagan E. Jones, and Charles P. Nicklin, "Humpback Whale Songs: Do They Organize Males during the Breeding Season?" *Behaviour* 143 (2006): 1051–1101.
17. Salvatore Cerchio, Jeff Jacobson, and Thomas Norris, "Temporal and Geographical Variation in Songs of Humpback Whales: Synchronous Change in Hawaiian and Mexican Breeding Assemblages," *Animal Behaviour* 62 (2001): 313–329.
18. See David Rothenberg, "To Wail With a Whale: Anatomy of an Interspecies Duet" (2007), http://www.thousandmilesong.com/wp-content/themes/twentyten/images/wail_with_whale.pdf. Accessed October 5, 2014.
19. Michael Noad et al., "Cultural Revolution in Whale Songs," *Nature* 408, no. 6812 (2000): 537.
20. Ellen Garland et al., "Dynamic Horizontal Cultural Transmission of Humpback Whale Song at the Ocean Basin Scale," *Current Biology* 21 (2011): 1–5. doi:10.1016/j.cub.2011.03.019.
21. Rothenberg, *Thousand Mile Song*.

BIBLIOGRAPHY

Bent, Arthur Cleveland. *Life Histories of Familiar North American Birds.* New York: Harper, 1960.
Brahem, Anouar. *Conte de l'incroyable amour.* Munich: ECM Records 1457, 1991. Compact disc.
Cerchio, Salvatore, Jeff Jacobson, and Thomas Norris. "Temporal and Geographical Variation in Songs of Humpback Whales: Synchronous Change in Hawaiian and Mexican Breeding Assemblages." *Animal Behaviour* 62 (2001): 313–329.
Darling, James D., Meagan E. Jones, and Charles P. Nicklin. "Humpback Whale Songs: Do They Organize Males During the Breeding Season?" *Behaviour* 143 (2006): 1051–1101.
Dowsett-Lemaire, Françoise. "The Imitative Range of the Song of the Marsh Warbler *Acrocephalus palustris*, with Special Reference to Imitations of African Birds." *Ibis* 121 (1979): 453–468.
Dowsett-Lemaire, Françoise. "Vocal Behaviour of the Marsh Warbler." *Le Gerfaut* 69 (1979): 475–502.
Garland, Ellen, et al. "Dynamic Horizontal Cultural Transmission of Humpback Whale Song at the Ocean Basin Scale." *Current Biology* 21 (2011): 1–5. doi:10.1016/j.cub.2011.03.019.

Hara, Erina, Lubica Kubikova, Neal A. Hessler, and Erich D. Jarvis. "Role of Midbrain Dopaminergic System in the Modulation of Vocal Brain Activation by Social Context." *European Journal of Neuroscience* 25 (2007): 3406–3416.

Harper, Samuel. *Twelve Months with the Birds and Poets*. Chicago: Ralph Fletcher Seymour, 1917.

Kipper, Silke, Roger Mundry, Henrike Hultsche, and Dietmar Todt. "Long-Term Persistence of Song Performance Rules in Nightingales." *Behaviour* 141 (2004): 371–390.

Kroodsma, Donald, et al. "Song Development by Grey Catbirds." *Animal Behavior* 54 (1997): 457–464.

Naguib, Marc. "Effects of Song Overlapping and Alternating on Nocturnally Singing Nightingales." *Animal Behaviour* 58, no. 5 (1999): 1061–1067.

Noad, Michael, et al. "Cultural Revolution in Whale Songs." *Nature* 408, no. 6812 (2000): 536–548.

Payne, Roger, and Scott McVay. "Songs of Humpback Whales." *Science* 173, no. 3997 (August 13, 1971): 585–597.

Rothenberg, David. *Thousand Mile Song*. New York: Basic Books, 2008.

Rothenberg, David. "To Wail With a Whale: Anatomy of an Interspecies Duet" (2007), http://www.thousandmilesong.com/wp-content/themes/twentyten/images/wail_with_whale.pdf. Accessed October 5, 2014.

Rothenberg, David. *Why Birds Sing*. New York: Basic Books, 2005.

Vencl, Frederic, and Branko Soucek. "Structure and Control of Duet Singing in the White-Crested Laughing Thrush." *Behaviour* 57, nos. 3–4 (1976): 221–229.

Wilbur, Richard. "Some Notes on 'Lying.'" In *The Catbird's Song: Prose Pieces 1963–1995*. New York: Harcourt, 1997.

CHAPTER 29

SPIRITUAL EXERCISES, IMPROVISATION, AND MORAL PERFECTIONISM

With Special Reference to Sonny Rollins

ARNOLD I. DAVIDSON
(Translated from the French by Anton Vishio. Revised by the author.)

The great Irishman Edmund Burke once said: "The only thing necessary for the triumph of evil is for good men to do nothing." We must accept our destiny, the destiny to struggle for the unattainable, because there is nothing absolute, nothing definite, and it is only in struggling for the unattainable that we can conquer evil. I have often wished that the fathers of the American Constitution had affirmed "Life, liberty, and the pursuit of the unattainable."[1]

I simply want to play and speak the truth. Every time I sit down at the drums, I have enough ego to say that what I played last night was good. But not good enough for tonight. I don't play as well as I would like. . . . I have never attained the level of total satisfaction. It is truly impossible. . . . You demand more and still more from yourself. Self-satisfaction is your enemy. It's over for you as an artist if you think "Well, I am so good that I don't need to try anything more difficult." Art Tatum didn't play as well as he wished.[2]

IN this essay I would like to study a model of improvisation that links the practice of spiritual exercises to moral perfectionism and precisely to that perfectionism that aims at the perpetual surpassing of oneself—at an overcoming always renewed, never definitive.[3] This perfectionism is at the heart of recent work by Stanley Cavell: in speaking of it, he often uses the expression "Emersonian perfectionism," since Emerson is the starting point for his elaboration of moral perfectionism.[4] We will see that in ancient philosophy, the idea of wisdom, or better the figure of the sage, could be interpreted as the historico-philosophical origin of this ideal. But we must begin with the practice of spiritual exercises. Regarding the notion of a "spiritual exercise," at the beginning of his book *What Is Ancient Philosophy?*, Pierre Hadot writes:

> By this term, I mean practices which could be physical, as in dietary regimes, or discursive, as in dialogue and meditation, or intuitive, as in contemplation, but which were all intended to effect a modification and a transformation in the subject who practiced them. The philosophy teachers' discourse could also assume the form of a spiritual exercise, if the discourse were presented in such a way that the disciple, as auditor, reader, or interlocutor, could make spiritual progress and transform himself within.[5]

In short, as Hadot said in our book of conversations, a spiritual exercise is "a voluntary, personal practice intended to bring about a transformation of the individual, a transformation of the self," and among the significant examples of such a practice he cites a certain practice of Beethoven, precisely because Beethoven "referred to the exercises of musical composition that he required of his students, and that were meant to allow them to attain a form of wisdom—one that might be called aesthetic—as spiritual exercises."[6]

According to Hadot, in antiquity, philosophy is "that activity by means of which philosophers train themselves for wisdom"; here one must underline the expression "train for wisdom," because wisdom itself is a "transcendent norm."[7] Thus, "philosophy, for mankind, consists of efforts toward wisdom which always remain unfinished."[8] Describing in detail the figure of the sage in ancient philosophy, and especially in the Stoic school, Hadot writes:

> Foremost, for the Stoics, the sage is an exceptional being; there are very few, perhaps one, even none at all. The figure of the sage is thus for them an almost unattainable idea, more a transcendent norm than a concrete figure. . . . The Stoic philosopher knows that he can never realize this ideal figure of the sage, but it exercises on him its attraction, provokes in him enthusiasm and love, allows him to hear a call to live better, to become aware of the perfection which he strives to attain. . . . The philosopher who trains for wisdom will try to form a nucleus of inexpugnable inner freedom via spiritual exercises.[9]

Thus, it could be concluded, I believe, that philosophy as a spiritual exercise toward wisdom is a form of moral perfectionism and therefore a particular way of life.

Now, I can easily imagine your perplexity: spiritual exercises, moral perfectionism, wisdom, what does all of this have to do with the improvisations of the saxophonist Sonny Rollins? From my point of view, philosophy is not primarily a doctrine or a theory, but rather an activity and an attitude. This is why nothing prohibits the attitude that is expressed in certain acts of improvisation from being named, without hesitation or equivocation, "philosophical."[10] The activity of improvisation becomes a philosophical activity when one deploys a practice of spiritual exercises that aims at perfecting oneself. From this perspective, Rollins is a perfect example of a model of moral perfectionism sustained by spiritual exercises.

In a 2006 interview, Rollins said, "I'm dissatisfied and I'm always striving. . . . A lot of guys have learned their craft and they get to a place, and they are satisfied, and the stuff they do is great. . . . In my case, my thing is constantly looking for something else. I'm not satisfied yet. I know there is more there."[11]

Rollins's dissatisfaction is certainly an aesthetic disposition, but it is also and above all an ethical attitude: Rollins is always searching for his "next self"—something beyond himself, a spiritual place never completely reached. In discussing his concerts, famous for their extreme ardor and energy, Rollins affirms:

> There are certain concerts that I play, performances when I do feel that I have reached the higher level. When that happens as a normality rather than rarely, then I will feel that I am there. Then there will probably be something else I need to do, but I do feel that I am getting closer to more of a complete expression. It's a reachable goal, it is not something which is never going to happen, but that doesn't mean that will be the end. There will always be something else to do. I think I can get to a better place.[12]

Here we can glimpse the possibility of a progress that is, so to speak, spiritual ("the higher level," "I am getting closer to a more complete expression"), but, at the same time, the feeling that a definitive end is impossible ("then there will probably be something else I need to do"). Moreover, Rollins makes use of an explicitly ethical vocabulary to characterize his attitude ("I think I can get to a better place").

In another interview, from 2008, Rollins clearly articulates the paradox represented by the duty to attain an end that is indeed impossible to attain—a paradox typical of moral perfectionism: "What I'm looking for perhaps is unattainable. I know that. But I certainly have a right to try to achieve it. It's my duty to achieve it."[13]

This duty of reaching an inaccessible place is no metaphysical abstraction: it is rather a duty that is made concrete in the necessity of exercising oneself. In effect, this existential obligation, with its highly particular structure, is elaborated in various traditions of thought and of practice. Cavell has often insisted on the fact that moral perfectionism is not another moral theory, but rather an attitude, a perspective, a vision of the world that traverses the history of thought and of life. To cite a single unexpected example of this perfectionist dimension: in a system of practices as remote as possible from those of Rollins, namely Orthodox Judaism, one finds, according to Yeshayahou Leibowitz, the idea of a "reality always beyond that which is, that one can never attain, but which, nevertheless, one must ceaselessly strive to attain." What is such a reality called? According to Jewish tradition, its name is precisely "redemption," a redemption therefore that is always still to come.[14] In my opinion, as we will see, in his own tradition Rollins himself is a figure of this redemption, that is to say of this infinite exercise of ourselves.

Rollins is renowned for the periods during which he did nothing other than practice, up to 15 hours per day. That which Rollins dubbed his "relentless practicing" is a way of manifesting his ethical attitude:

> I've taken several sabbaticals from performing and recording. I have a certain ideal
> when I play, and this ideal has changed over the years. I've taken breaks because I've
> been frustrated with a performance or I just wanted to go to the woodshed and exper-
> iment. I always become frustrated when I'm not reaching what I hear for myself. . . . I
> never viewed practicing as a chore. I always saw it as a necessity to improve.[15]

The interminable exercises of Rollins also highlight the priority of a certain relationship with oneself and, in the case of Rollins, the necessity of forming oneself in such a
way that improvisation can become unlimited. This improvisation, infinite in a certain
sense, presupposes, according to Rollins, a very particular relationship with oneself—
strong but at the same time mobile. It is just such a relationship with oneself that occupies the center of Rollins's existential attitude: "This is the struggle of life, to be better
people. That's how I figured out what life is all about. This is what I am trying to do. Life
is an opportunity, but the hardest battle is with ourselves. That is what I realize, and that's
what I am doing. . . . What matters is you winning the battle with yourself."[16]

This attitude is the foundation, the core of Rollins's judgment: "As far as I am concerned, a good band starts with yourself. It starts with me getting my stuff together."[17]
And "getting your stuff together" is a task that one is never finished with.

Let us take the example of the relationship with oneself expressed by Rollins in the
music he created in the 1950s. In this music, one finds what I will call a "horizontal
inexhaustibility" within a form of the self. Let me explain: Rollins created a form of
himself that allowed him never to exhaust an improvisation, to always invent new possibilities, as if the improvisation was, literally, an infinite creation without determinate limits. The form of Rollins's self at the end of the 1950s is a form never filled in,
one that precedes all substance, a form without weight, always in movement, vital, a
form, one might say, whose dimensions are limitless. It is a form that responds precisely
to Rollins's incessant exercises. Consider "I'm an Old Cowhand" from the recording
Way Out West (1957; see Figure 29.1).[18] Rollins's solo is magnificent; one perceives in
it, at the same time, both imagination and organization, yet it is a solo that is in a clear
sense unfinished. However, its felt incompleteness is of a very particular kind; it concerns the inexhaustibility of the improvisation, an inexhaustibility achieved thanks to
a certain practice, a certain form of the self. In listening to the alternate take of "I'm
an Old Cowhand," nearly twice as long as the first version, one understands immediately that Rollins is capable of continuing *ad infinitum*, until the end of the world, without repeating himself. The fadeout of this alternative take is a sign of the interminable
activity of his improvisation, a symbol of his capacity to never fill in his own form of
the self; rather, he is always ready to dilate himself and to prolong himself, to go forward. Without any doubt, in these years, there was a sound, a clear style, that is to say a
distinctive form called *Rollins*, precisely that form which, within a piece, authorized a
beyond, always elsewhere, further on, which knew no permanent pause, no definitive
conclusion, no resting in peace.

Often it is Rollins's cadences that demonstrate in the most unforgettable manner this
horizontal inexhaustibility; these are very evident moments of his infinite creativity. The

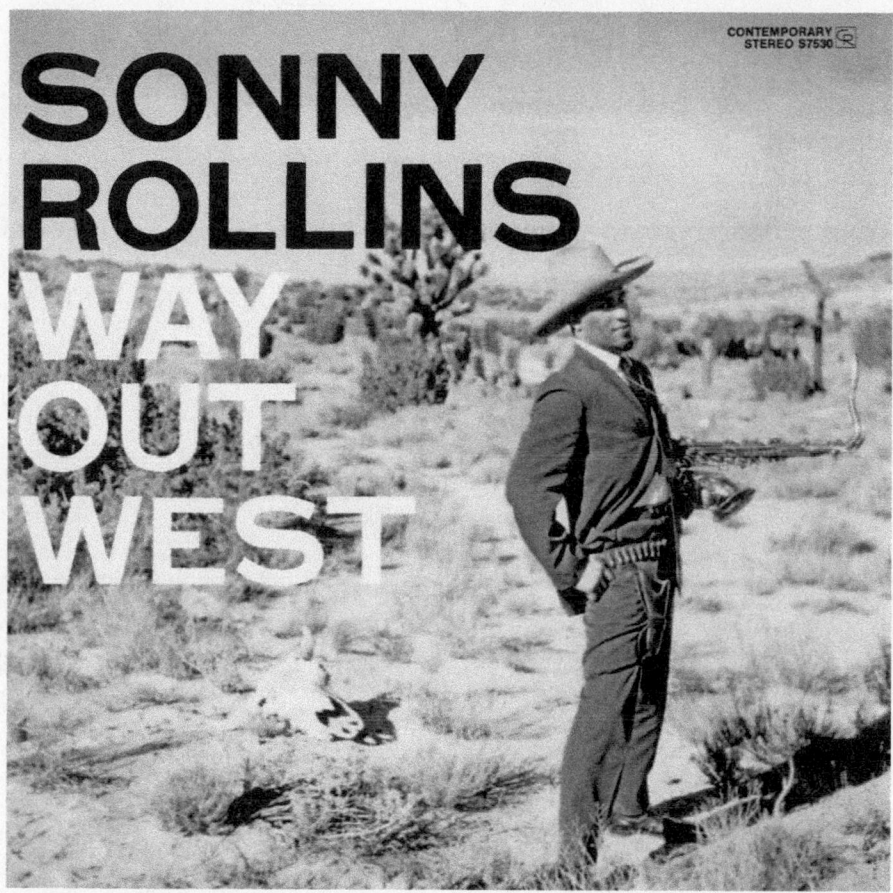

FIGURE 29.1 Sonny Rollins ([1957] 2010).

form that Rollins gives to these cadences expresses, moreover, a musical version of the cosmic consciousness described by Hadot. Among the aspects of this cosmic consciousness that Hadot emphasized, there is the exercise of dilation, of the expansion of the self into the cosmos, that is, the exercise "of becoming aware of his being within the All, as a minuscule point of brief duration, but capable of dilating into the immense field of infinite space and of seizing the whole of reality in a single intuition."[19] At the same time that he describes the ideal of stoic wisdom, Hadot speaks of cosmic consciousness, evoking a connection between each instant and the entire universe:

> By becoming conscious of one single instant of our lives, one single beat of our hearts, we can feel ourselves linked to the entire immensity of the cosmos, and to the wondrous fact of the world's existence. The whole universe is present in each part of reality. For the Stoics, this experience of the instant corresponds to their theory of the mutual interpenetration of the parts of the universe. Such an experience, however, is not necessarily linked to any theory. For example, we find it

expressed in the following verses by Blake: To see a World in a Grain of Sand / And a Heaven in a Wild Flower, / Hold Infinity in the palm of your hand / And Eternity in an hour.[20]

The intuitions, the pulsations of Sonny Rollins unveil the entire musical universe, infinity heard in the mouthpiece of a saxophone. Rollins's breathing is metamorphosized into a short melody of several notes that leads us on to a second melody, and then to yet another, etc.—melodies between which we discover a reciprocal compenetration never imagined. Or else a melody transforms itself into an extended improvisation that links, in a spontaneous and natural manner, "high" music with "popular" music, jazz and classical music, all the different moments of the history of jazz, and so on. All things considered, it seems that a single note of Rollins encompasses, from the outset, all musical worlds, as if his improvisation unravels the cosmos itself. And one can understand that the consciousness of Rollins "is plunged, like Seneca, into the totality of the cosmos: *toti se inserens mundo*."[21]

The greatness of Rollins, however, does not stop here, since there remains another modality of "transcendence," perhaps rarer than that which I have just described, and which I will call the "vertical displacement" of the form of the self: the hard, unexpected and shattering process of *surpassing* oneself. One surpasses not simply a particular content of the self, but even its established structure. This is the invention of a new form of oneself, a transfiguration of one's own identity, of the "ontological" form, so to speak, of the self: it is a self-transcendence in which one goes beyond the sound, the expression, the style, that is to say the form of the self already realized—it is the occasion in which one becomes another. At stake is no longer a horizon that extends without end; instead, the fundamental configuration of the self is transformed. The experience is that of the birth of a new self, lived as an elevation to a new plane of possibility—hence a vertical surpassing, rather than a horizontal dilation (see Figure 29.2).[22]

This arduous, disturbing change is often provoked by an encounter with another, not with just any other but with an exemplary figure, in which is revealed the possibility and necessity of a vertical surpassing of the self. In the case of Rollins, one could interpret in this way his encounter with Coleman Hawkins, on the 1963 album *Sonny Meets Hawk* (see Figure 29.3).[23] In general, Rollins makes a distinction between "copying from" and "learning from": "I didn't try to copy others. I just tried to learn from them." And he continues: "If you have enough talent and you're committed, working with people who are superior to you always will improve your playing."[24] In the specific relationship that interests us here, we must take account of a remarkable letter, written to Hawkins in 1962 after having heard one of his recent concerts, where Rollins expresses his esteem for him utilizing the vocabulary of moral perfectionism: "Such tested and tried musical achievement denotes and is subsidiary to personal character and integrity of being."[25] And then, just after this, Rollins writes a remarkable sentence on the exemplarity of Hawkins, a sentence worthy of Nietzsche in *Schopenhauer as Educator*: "For you have 'lit the flame' of aspiration within so many of us and you have epitomized the superiority of

FIGURE 29.2 Sonny Rollins ([1965, 1968] 2008); hear, in particular, "Darn that Dream" to "Three Little Words" (47:15–49:10).

'excellence of endeavor' and you stand today as a clear living picture and example for us to learn from."[26]

In my view, Hawkins's response to Rollins is found on *Sonny Meets Hawk*. This very same Hawkins indubitably shows here his own capacity to learn, and, more precisely, he makes us hear the lessons that he has learned from Rollins. At this moment,

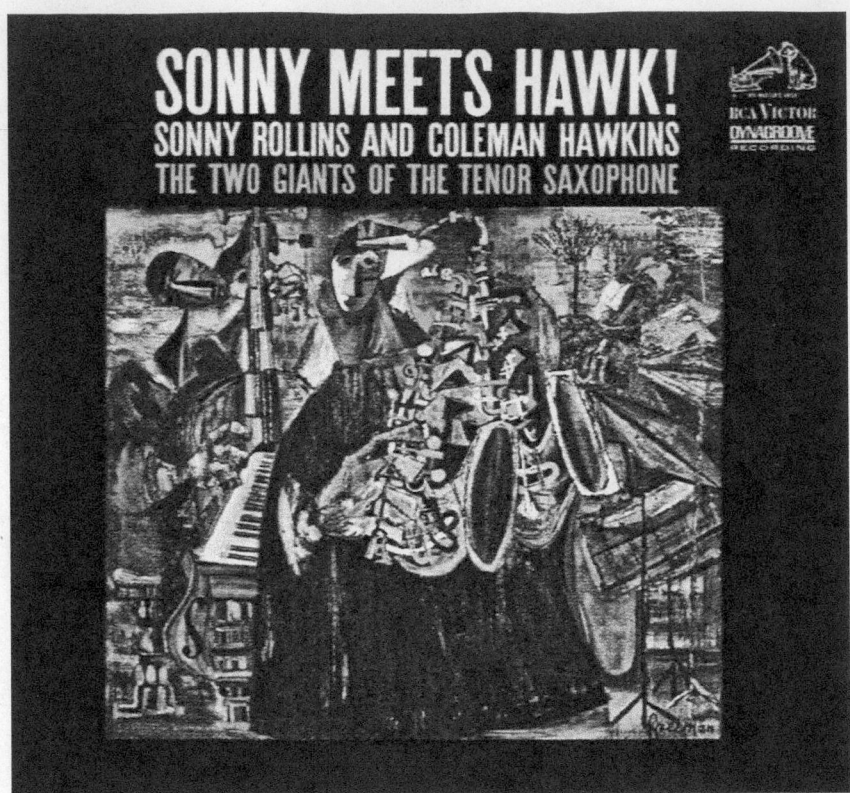

FIGURE 29.3 Coleman Hawkins and Sonny Rollins, ([1963] 2003).

Hawkins transcends the magnificent Hawkins of "Body and Soul" of 1939; this transcendence is also a praise of Rollins's sound (see Figure 29.4). Instead of remaining within his own style, Hawkins demonstrates his force, at one and the same time aesthetic and ethical, through the creation of a new form of himself.[27] This is a Hawkins who, in a dazzling manner, comes *after* Rollins, a Hawkins reformed, renewed, thanks to the practice of Rollins. Hawkins's phrasing, his rhythm, his attitude, are fully modern. In this context, the term *modern* has the sense that Foucault brought to the fore:

> I wonder whether we may not envisage modernity rather as an attitude than as a period of history. And by "attitude," I mean a mode of relating to contemporary reality; a voluntary choice made by certain people; in the end, a way of thinking and feeling; a way, too, of acting and behaving that at one and the same time marks a relation of belonging and presents itself as a task.[28]

In *Sonny Meets Hawk*, Hawkins shows his capacity to put himself into relation with the contemporary, that is with Rollins, given that in 1963 the contemporary tenor saxophone was represented precisely by Sonny Rollins, or, more exactly, Rollins was one of the two

2CDSET

Jazz Ballads 6

C. Hawkins

Body And Soul
I'm In The Mood For Love
If I Could Be With You One Hour Tonight
April In Paris
And many others

24 BIT \ 96 KHZ
HIGH-END MASTERING

FIGURE 29.4 Coleman Hawkins (2004).

reference points of the contemporary tenor saxophone, the other of course being John Coltrane. Hawkins thus manifests a voluntary choice in the new mode of playing that he adopts; in short, he exhibits a manner of thinking and of feeling, of acting and of conducting himself that marks his belonging to what is happening now, and at the same time presents a task to accomplish. If we take the piece "Lover Man," for example, we can see, and the effect is unforgettable, this modern attitude of Hawkins.[29] It is as if Hawkins had said to Rollins, "Thanks to your example, I too have learned to surpass myself, to play beyond my usual style, that style which is the basis for my immense reputation." It is an understatement to say that this ethics of vertical displacement is a risky task. And with his customary light-handedness of expression, Rollins recognizes the success of Hawkins: "Hawkins is timeless and what he plays is beyond style and category. In fact, it's a shame that people tend to categorize music. A fine musician can play with anyone, just as a fine person can get along with anyone."[30]

In reality, very few musicians are "beyond category," in such a way that they can play with "anyone." This is another way of measuring the exemplarity manifested by Hawkins.

This musical response of Hawkins to Rollins finds a disconcerting reaction in the new mode of playing of Rollins himself. In "Lover Man," the enigma is that Rollins no longer plays like the young, and already celebrated, Rollins. He does not compete with Hawkins; on the contrary, he turns away from the new style of Hawkins, that is to say that very Hawkins reformed by the imprint of Rollins himself. Rollins creates here a new form of himself, not only by a phrasing and a rhythm far from that of the 1950s, but by an innovative, unprecedented sonority and tonality. We hear Rollins in the very process that consists of "detaching himself from himself." This radical change could provoke a misunderstanding, as if Rollins had not respected the victory (over himself) of Hawkins. In effect, this is the judgment of Lee Konitz:

> It bothered me what he [Sonny Rollins] did on the recording with Coleman Hawkins and Paul Bley. I thought that he was being disrespectful. Maybe it was necessary for him, to separate himself from Hawk as a father figure. But if he'd played inspired, the way he can, it would have been a great tribute to Hawk, and it wouldn't have sounded like Hawk at all. . . . He just played very out. But I think Paul Bley [the pianist on the date] can do that for you, by playing a cluster or two—I've had that experience with him of just wanting to go out. But why do it when Pappa [Hawkins] is there playing beautifully? Sonny could play beautifully too.[31]

I don't hear Rollins's playing as answering to a psychological necessity, that is, as anxious to "separate himself from Hawk"; on the contrary, I see this recording as a true homage to Hawkins, inspired by the new sound of Hawk—no doubt, it is a very singular homage, an homage rendered to an exemplary creativity, the homage of moral perfectionism. Typically, when the term *beautiful* is pronounced in a judgment directed against someone, it is a question of trying to narrow the possibilities of being creative. We already know the sound of the beautiful; and it is certain that in 1963 it was not the sound of Rollins on *Sonny Meets Hawk*. Rollins wanted to go beyond the "beautiful," beyond his beauty, and create an alternative acoustic space, inventing a form that puts to the test the beauty expected by those who have heard *his recordings*; that is to say he wanted to render less stable and less evident that modern beauty represented on this recording not by Rollins, but by the "post-Rollins" sound of Hawkins. Let us hope that jazz will always remain a privileged site of such creativity, such newness. As Rollins said, "The essence of jazz you know, it's improvisational; you know you do like the creator, there is always something creative, every raindrop is different, so there is always something to do that has not been done in a way that's creative so there is no end to creativity."[32] The practice of jazz as creative improvisation without fixed limits is not in the least banal, but here we must distinguish several levels of improvisation. It may well be that the level of creativity that is the most unusual and the most disquieting is that which gives rise to a new form of oneself, and in this recording it is precisely this level that is attained twice, in two different ways, by Hawkins and then by Rollins.

In my view, the manner in which Rollins responded to the exemplarity of Hawkins manifested the most profound respect. It is as if Rollins had said to Hawkins: "In light of the way in which you have surpassed yourself, I see myself obliged to create new relations with myself, I acknowledge my own incompleteness," and then Rollins creates an unanticipated form. It is precisely in playing with Hawkins that Rollins gives a new and intensified ethical-political attention to *his modernity*, a modernity that, in the terms of Foucault, is at once a limit attitude and an experimental attitude. Rollins's playing poses the central question of the limit-attitude: "In what is given to us as universal, necessary, obligatory, what place is occupied by what is singular, contingent, and due to arbitrary constraints?"[33] The "performance" of Rollins is in effect a philosophical critique, not a Kantian critique exercised "in the form of necessary limitation," but a practical critique brought about "in the form of a possible overcoming."[34] Every form of ourselves that is sedimented in history, that has become rigidified, seems to us to be a natural, inevitable form, and consequently overcoming, considered as "unnatural," never gives rise to the reassuring feelings of beauty and of harmony. The attempt at overcoming is necessarily linked to an experimental attitude: "But if we are not to settle for the affirmation or the empty dream of freedom, it seems to me that this historico-critical attitude must also be an experimental one," that is to say an attitude that must "put itself to the test of reality, of contemporary reality, both to grasp the points where change is possible and desirable and to determine the precise form this change should take."[35] And it is up to Rollins, through his vertical displacement, to give a precise form to the musical transformation. In order to specify Rollins's ethos, it does not seem to me exaggerated to use the description given by Foucault: "I shall thus characterize the philosophical ethos appropriate to the critical ontology of ourselves as a historico-practical test of the limits that we may go beyond, and thus as work carried out by ourselves upon ourselves as free beings."[36]

This putting to the test of oneself as a free being is found again during the performance with Ornette Coleman that took place at the concert for Rollins's 80th birthday. The piece "Sonnymoon For Two," played by Rollins who knows how many times, begins in a very typical manner: after the entry of Coleman and the "freer" sound for which he is known, Rollins begins to detach himself from the melodic and rhythmic contours of the piece, and in the end Rollins attains a level of freedom which magnificently demonstrates the value of his practice of spiritual exercises and his commitment, even at 80 years old, not to rigidify himself, not to let himself become petrified, to be always animated and courageous (see Figure 29.5).[37] Here again one can link Sonny Rollins and Foucault in the precise sense that Rollins is "never completely at ease with his own self-evidences"; he is always looking for the "indispensible mobility."[38] Sonny Rollins is the living image of moral perfectionism.

Let us now return to the work on oneself and to Rollins's spiritual exercises. In a 2005 conversation, Rollins claims, "I'm always trying to prove myself and improve myself. . . . I'm never satisfied with my playing and that's led me into experimenting with lots of different kinds of things."[39]

The availability, the receptivity, the agility of Rollins allow us to see an attitude of experimental freedom, prepared by a constant practice of exercises, exercises that involve the entire spirit. Thanks to these spiritual exercises it is possible to prepare oneself, to make one's spirit open and lively; yet these spiritual exercises in themselves are

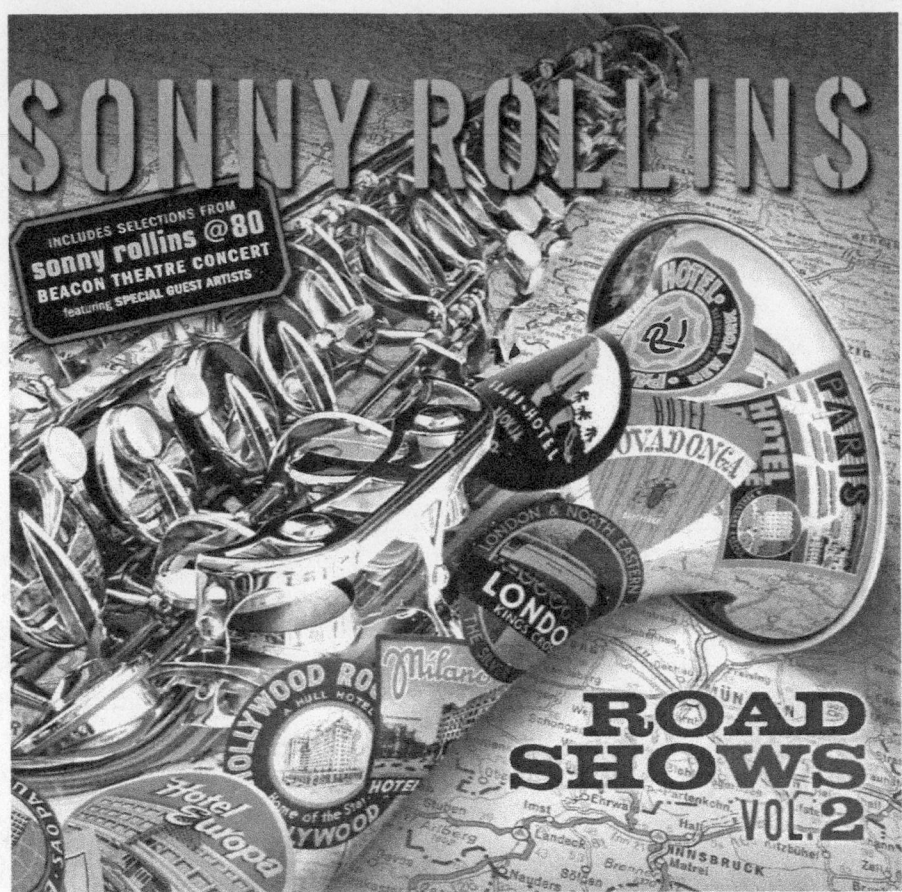

FIGURE 29.5 Sonny Rollins (2011).

not the guarantee of a striking, brilliant, truly creative result. They are, one might say, a condition, a crucial discipline, even if not sufficient, for reaching the summit of improvisation in jazz. Moreover, it is exactly at the moment when one glimpses the possibility of the vertical surpassing of oneself that the fields of uncertainty and risk widen; thus, it is also the moment in which the support and orientation furnished by an exemplary personality provide courage and the strength to put oneself to the test. Nevertheless, we never find ourselves faced with an ineluctable necessity to recognize and accept the exemplarity of someone; at most we perceive the attraction of the exemplary figure, we feel a provocation that provides us more energy: a new *élan*. Without the challenge of exemplarity, our exercises remain static; without the work of spiritual exercises, exemplarity is a nebulous ideal. In the end, it is up to each of us, as individuals, to go forward or to remain in place, that is to say to construct a certain relationship to ourselves. In moral perfectionism, there is no ethical inevitability.

In an interview given in 2007, Sonny Rollins weaves together creativity, the perspective of transcendence, and exercise. I conclude, therefore, with his philosophical intuition, as an emblem of moral perfectionism: "Music itself has no end, there's always more to learn. I know I want to be able to reach a way of playing that transcends everything. I've not done that yet, that's why I keep practicing."[40]

POSTSCRIPT

In this essay I have emphasized the relation between Sonny Rollins's improvisations and certain Stoic spiritual exercises.[41] Other modes of improvisation can be linked to the spiritual exercises of other schools of ancient thought. Elsewhere I have argued that Steve Lacy's last recorded solo concert, *Reflections*, manifests a form of Plotinian spiritual exercise,[42] and I have claimed that the posthumously released duo between Charlie Haden and Jim Hall exhibits a form of epicurean improvisation.[43] I would also not hesitate to say that John Coltrane's *Ascension* exemplifies the existential attitude and spiritual exercises of ancient cynicism.[44] The diversity of kinds of improvisation can be related to the multiplicity of spiritual exercises. All of them, however, aim at self-transformation, which always also has a social dimension. The problem for all of us, as Haden so clearly and compellingly put it in 2014, is that "when I put down my instrument, that's when the challenge starts, because to learn how to be that kind of human being at that level that you are when you're playing—that's the key, that's the hard part."[45] In other words, as I might put it, the spiritual exercises of improvisation must become a way of life.

NOTES

1. Yehudi Menuhin, *Musica e vita interiore* (Palermo: Edizioni rueBallu, 2010), 78.
2. Buddy Rich, quoted in Georges Paczynski, *Une histoire de la batterie de jazz,* (Paris: Outre Mesure, 1997), 1: 276.
3. I would like to insist on the fact that to *understand* the meaning of my text, one absolutely must *listen* to the indicated tracks of music and video.
4. See, for example, Stanley Cavell, *Conditions Handsome and Unhandsome: The Constitution of Emersonian Perfectionism* (Chicago: University of Chicago Press, 1990).
5. Pierre Hadot, translated by Michael Chase, *What Is Ancient Philosophy?* (Cambridge, MA: Harvard University Press, 2002), 6.
6. Pierre Hadot, translated by Marc Djaballah and Michael Chase, *The Present Alone Is Our Happiness: Conversations with Jeannie Carlier and Arnold I. Davidson* (Stanford: Stanford University Press, [2001] 2011), 87, 92. In this connection, Hadot cites a book by Elizabeth Brisson, *Le sacre de musicien: La référence à l'Antiquité chez Beethoven* (Paris: CNRS Éditions, 2000).
7. Hadot, *What Is Ancient Philosophy?*, 220.
8. Hadot, *What Is Ancient Philosophy?*, 265–266.
9. Pierre Hadot, "La figure du sage dans l'Antiquité gréco-latine," in *Études de philosophie ancienne* (Paris: Les Belles Lettres, 1998), 242, 245, 248.

10. Cf. Ludwig Wittgenstein, *Tractatus Logico-Philosophicus*, trans. C.K. Ogden (Mineola, NY: Dover, [1922] 1999), 4, 112, "Philosophy is not a theory but an activity"; and Michel Foucault, "What Is Enlightenment?," in *The Foucault Reader*, trans. Catherine Porter, ed. Paul Rabinow (New York: Pantheon Books, 1984).

11. Sonny Rollins, "Interview," *Academy of Achievement: A Museum of Living History*, http://www.achievement.org/autodoc/page/roloint-4 (2006), accessed March 15, 2015.

12. Rollins, "Interview."

13. Sonny Rollins, with Marc Myers, "Interview: Sonny Rollins, Part 3," *Jazz Wax*, http://www.jazzwax.com/2008/02/sonny-rollins-2.html (February 21, 2008), accessed March 15, 2015.

14. Yeshayahou Leibowitz, *Les fêtes juives. Réflexions sur les solennités du judaïsme* (Paris: Cert, 2008), 112.

15. Rollins, "Interview: Sonny Rollins, Part 3." Also see "Interview: Sonny Rollins, Part 1," *Jazz Wax*, http://www.jazzwax.com/2008/02/sonny-rollins-p.html (February 21, 2008), accessed March 15, 2015.

16. Rollins, "Interview."

17. Franck Médioni, "Sonny Rollins and David S. Ware: Sonny Meets David," *All About Jazz*, http://www.allaboutjazz.com/sonny-rollins-and-david-s-ware-sonny-meets-david-by-franck-medioni.php?&pg=5, (October 21, 2005), accessed March 15, 2015.

18. The alternate take of "I'm an Old Cowhand" is on Sonny Rollins, *Way Out West (with bonus tracks)*, Original Jazz Classics 7231993, [1957] 2010, compact disc.

19. Hadot, *What Is Ancient Philosophy?*, 205.

20. Pierre Hadot, *Philosophy as a Way of Life: Spiritual Exercises from Socrates to Foucault*, trans. Michael Chase (Malden, MA: Blackwell Publishing, 2005), 260.

21. Hadot, *Philosophy as a Way of Life*, 252.

22. Watch Rollins's performance from "Darn that Dream" to "Three Little Words" (47:15–49:10) on Sonny Rollins, *Sonny Rollins Live in '65 & '68*, Jazz Icons 2119011, [1965, 1968] 2008, DVD-video disc.

23. Coleman Hawkins and Sonny Rollins, *Sonny Meets Hawk*, BMG 37349, [1963] 2003, compact disc.

24. Rollins, "Interview: Sonny Rollins, Part 1." Also see "Interview: Sonny Rollins, Part 2," *Jazz Wax*, http://www.jazzwax.com/2008/02/sonny-rollins-1.html (February 21, 2008), accessed March 15, 2015.

25. Rollins, "You Have Lit the Flame of Aspiration Within So Many of Us (letter to Coleman Hawkins)," *Letters of Note*, http://www.lettersofnote.com/2010/10/you-have-lit-flame-of-aspiration-within.html (October 13, 1962), accessed March 15, 2015.

26. Sonny Rollins, "You Have Lit the Flame of Aspiration."

27. The classic performance of "Body and Soul" is on Coleman Hawkins, *Jazz Ballads 6*, Membran 222536, 2004, compact disc.

28. Foucault, "What Is Enlightenment?," 39.

29. The performance of "Lover Man" is on Hawkins, *Sonny Meets Hawk*.

30. Hawkins, *Sonny Meets Hawk*, liner notes.

31. Andy Hamilton, *Lee Konitz: Conversations on the Improviser's Art* (Ann Arbor: University of Michigan Press, 2007), 83.

32. Médioni, "Sonny Rollins and David S. Ware: Sonny Meets David."

33. Foucault, "What Is Enlightenment?," 45.

34. Foucault, "What Is Enlightenment?," 45.

35. Foucault, "What Is Enlightenment?," 46.
36. Foucault, "What Is Enlightenment?," 47.
37. Sonny Rollins, *Road Shows, Vol. 2,* Doxy Records/Emarcy 0015949-02, 2011, compact disc.
38. Michel Foucault, "For an Ethic of Discomfort," in *Essential Works of Foucault, 1954–1984,* vol. 3, *Power,* trans. Robert Hurley and others, ed. James D. Faubion (New York: The New Press, 2000), 448.
39. Hamilton, *Lee Konitz,* 58.
40. Sonny Rollins, "In My Mind, I Haven't Reached My Vision," Inter Press Service, http://www.ipsnews.net/2007/11/qa-39in-my-mind-i-haven39t-reached-my-vision39/ (November 1, 2007), accessed March 15, 2015.
41. In revising this translation, I have sometimes modified published translations of other French texts. My primary concern has been to preserve philosophical precision, even if occasionally at the cost of literary elegance. The author and the editors would like to thank Diane Brentari and Souleymane Bachir Diagne for additional close reading of the text.
42. Arnold I. Davidson, "L'improvvisazione matura," *Il Sole24 Ore Domenica,* http://www.banchedati.ilsole24ore.com/doc.get?uid=domenica-DO20141228032AAA (December 28, 2014), accessed March 15, 2015.
43. Davidson, "Epicuro si curerebbe con il jazz," *Il Sole24 Ore Domenica,* http://www.banchedati.ilsole24ore.com/doc.get?uid=domenica-DO20141228032AAA (March 15, 2015), accessed March 15, 2015.
44. John Coltrane, "Ascension (Editions I and II)," Impulse! #1792024. Compact disc, [1965] 2009.
45. Charlie Haden, "'Live in the Present': Charlie Haden Remembered," National Public Radio (United States), http://www.npr.org/2014/07/18/332544960/live-in-the-present-charlie-haden-remembered (July 18, 2014), accessed March 15, 2015.

Works Cited

Brisson, Elizabeth. *Le sacre de musicien: La référence à l'Antiquité chez Beethoven.* Paris: CNRS Éditions, 2000.

Cavell, Stanley. *Conditions Handsome and Unhandsome: The Constitution of Emersonian Perfectionism.* Chicago: University of Chicago Press, 1990.

Coltrane, John. "Ascension (Editions I and II)." Impulse! #1792024. Compact disc, [1965] 2009.

Davidson, Arnold I. "Epicuro si curerebbe con il jazz." *Il Sole24 Ore Domenica,* http://www.banchedati.ilsole24ore.com/doc.get?uid=domenica-DO20141228032AAA (March 15, 2015), accessed March 15, 2015.

Davidson, Arnold I. "L'improvvisazione matura." *Il Sole24 Ore Domenica,* http://www.banchedati.ilsole24ore.com/doc.get?uid=domenica-DO20141228032AAA (December 28, 2014), accessed March 15, 2015.

Foucault, Michel. "What Is Enlightenment?" In *The Foucault Reader.* Translated by Catherine Porter. Edited by Paul Rabinow, 32–50. New York: Pantheon Books, 1984.

Foucault, Michel. "For an Ethic of Discomfort." In *Essential Works of Foucault, 1954–1984.* Vol. 3, *Power.* Translated by Robert Hurley and others. Edited by James D. Faubion, 443–448. New York: The New Press, 2000.

Haden, Charlie. "'Live in the Present': Charlie Haden Remembered." National Public Radio (United States), http://www.npr.org/2014/07/18/332544960/live-in-the-present-charlie-haden-remembered (July 18, 2014), accessed March 15, 2015.

Hadot, Pierre. "La figure du sage dans l'Antiquité gréco-latine." In *Études de philosophie ancienne*, 233–57. Paris: Les Belles Lettres, 1998.

Hadot, Pierre, translated by Marc Djaballah and Michael Chase. *The Present Alone Is Our Happiness: Conversations with Jeannie Carlier and Arnold I. Davidson*. Stanford: Stanford University Press, 2011.

Hadot, Pierre. *Philosophy as a Way of Life: Spiritual Exercises from Socrates to Foucault*. Translated by Michael Chase. Malden, MA: Blackwell Publishing, 2005.

Hadot, Pierre. *What Is Ancient Philosophy?* Cambridge, MA: Harvard University Press, 2002.

Hamilton, Andy. *Lee Konitz: Conversations on the Improviser's Art*. Ann Arbor: University of Michigan Press, 2007.

Hawkins, Coleman. *Jazz Ballads 6*. Membran #222536. Compact disc, 2004.

Hawkins, Coleman, and Sonny Rollins. *Sonny Meets Hawk*. BMG #37349. Compact disc, 2003.

Leibowitz, Yeshayahou. *Les fêtes juives. Réflexions sur les solennités du judaïsme*. Paris: Cert, 2008.

Médioni, Franck. "Sonny Rollins and David S. Ware: Sonny Meets David." *All About Jazz*, http://www.allaboutjazz.com/sonny-rollins-and-david-s-ware-sonny-meets-david-by-franck-medioni.php?&pg=5 (October 21, 2005), accessed March 15, 2015.

Menuhin, Yehudi. *Musica e vita interiore*. Palermo: Edizioni rue Ballu, 2010.

Paczynski, Georges. *Une histoire de la batterie de jazz*. Vol. 1. Paris: Outre Mesure, 1997.

Rollins, Sonny. "In My Mind, I Haven't Reached My Vision." Inter Press Service, http://www.ipsnews.net/2007/11/qa-39in-my-mind-i-haven39t-reached-my-vision39/ (November 1, 2007), accessed March 15, 2015.

Rollins, Sonny. "Interview." *Academy of Achievement: A Museum of Living History*, http://www.achievement.org/autodoc/page/roloint-4 (2006), accessed March 15, 2015.

Rollins, Sonny. *Road Shows*. Vol. 2. Doxy Records/Emarcy #0015949-02. Compact disc, 2011.

Rollins, Sonny. *Sonny Rollins Live in '65 & '68*. Jazz Icons #2119011. DVD-video disc, [1965, 1968] 2008.

Rollins, Sonny. *Way Out West (with bonus tracks)*. Original Jazz Classics #7231993. Compact disc, [1957] 2010.

Rollins, Sonny. "You Have Lit the Flame of Aspiration Within So Many of Us (letter to Coleman Hawkins)." *Letters of Note*, http://www.lettersofnote.com/2010/10/you-have-lit-flame-of-aspiration-within.html (October 13, 1962), accessed March 15, 2015.

Rollins, Sonny, with Marc Myers. "Interview: Sonny Rollins, Part 1." *Jazz Wax*, http://www.jazzwax.com/2008/02/sonny-rollins-p.html (February 21, 2008), accessed March 15, 2015.

Rollins, Sonny, with Marc Myers. "Interview: Sonny Rollins, Part 2." *Jazz Wax*, http://www.jazzwax.com/2008/02/sonny-rollins-1.html (February 21, 2008), accessed March 15, 2015.

Rollins, Sonny, with Marc Myers. "Interview: Sonny Rollins, Part 3." *Jazz Wax*, http://www.jazzwax.com/2008/02/sonny-rollins-2.html (February 21, 2008), accessed March 15, 2015.

Wittgenstein, Ludwig. *Tractatus Logico-Philosophicus*. Translated by C. K. Ogden. Mineola, NY: Dover Publications, [1922] 1999.

CHAPTER 30

IMPROVISATION AND ECCLESIAL ETHICS

SAMUEL WELLS

IMPROVISATION in the theater is a practice through which actors seek to develop trust in themselves and one another in order that they may conduct unscripted dramas without fear. In my own work I have sought to describe how the Christian church may become a community of trust in order that it may faithfully encounter the unknown of the future without fear. This involves a treatment of how the story and practices of the church shape and empower Christians with the uninhibited freedom sometimes experienced by theatrical improvisers. What is involved is a renarration of Christian ethics, not as the art of performing the Scriptures, but as faithfully improvising on the Christian tradition. To understand that renarration requires a journey through the contemporary field of Christian ethics, an identification of the most fertile territory for Christians seeking to be faithful in challenging times. It then involves a brief outline of what is at stake in improvisatory ethics, and some examples of its promise and challenges in a contemporary context.

CONTEMPORARY CHRISTIAN ETHICS

Universal Ethics. Ethics is conventionally taught as a face-off between two rival conceptions of how to pursue the good. One approach, known as deontological ethics, is based around an absolute sense of right and wrong. Precisely where those qualities of right and wrong are located is understood differently by various proponents. Most obviously, those who follow divine command ethics locate them within God's revealed word—explicitly, the Ten Commandments and other scriptural passages that leave little apparent room for ambiguity. Meanwhile, those who advocate natural law ethics locate right and wrong in the discernment of the precepts, limits, and purposes written into human existence. Then there are those who follow Immanuel Kant, for whom right is equivalent to duty, and duty can be rationally discerned by each individual person's conscience, provided they follow a rule which he calls the categorical imperative.[1]

Another approach, known as consequential ethics, makes relative judgments about right and wrong by evaluating the likely outcomes of different possible actions. In other words, this approach shifts attention from action (or motivation) to outcome. The most common form of consequentialism is utilitarianism, which seeks to calculate the good by assessing what will bring about the greatest happiness for the greatest number.[2] Consequentialism has attracted a great deal of anxiety because in most of its forms it seems to abandon an absolute sense of right and wrong, and thus to open the door to moral relativism. Nonetheless, because it doesn't appear to require commitment to a prior system of belief or reasoning, and because it upholds the subtler quality of common sense over the simpler commitment to consistency, consequentialism has proved to be the dominant style of reasoning in public discourse and policy-making. When Barack Obama said in his 2009 inauguration address that he was committed to "what works," he was propounding the essence of consequentialism.[3]

While these two understandings of ethics long seemed the only players in the game, in the last 50 years they have come under criticism on broadly two grounds, both of which highlight what they have in common; thus, I see them as two versions of the same approach, which I call "universal ethics," rather than two rival approaches.

Subversive Ethics. The first criticism of deontological and consequential ethics is that both are unaware of, or unconcerned by, their common assumption that the white, Western male is the unquestioned universal moral subject. Because they are both fundamentally concerned to offer a perspective that is binding on everybody, these perspectives exclude or ignore information that is particular to agents or circumstances or activities. But such information is, the criticism maintains, the heart of ethics. Moreover, the Jesus of the gospels seems less inclined to overarching theories that work in all circumstances, and more drawn to the plight of the least, the last, and the lost. Jesus, this criticism maintains, exhibits a bias to the poor. Thus, Christian ethics should imitate Jesus in privileging the perspective of those on the underside of class, race and/or gender prejudice, disadvantage, discrimination, or exclusion. I call this criticism, and the field of ethics it inaugurates, "subversive ethics," because it believes ethics is not so much for everybody, but principally for the excluded.

Ecclesial Ethics. The second criticism is that both perspectives assume that the focus of ethics is the agent's moment of decision. But life is not lived lurching from crisis to crisis. What agents even perceive as a dilemma, and the way they would describe that quandary, is dependent on the world in which they imagine themselves to be living, and how they already see that world. When agents do face a crisis, they will act from habit rather than from rule or calculation. On January 15, 2009, US Airways flight 1549 from New York to Charlotte, North Carolina, with 155 passengers and crew on board, was disabled by a flock of Canada geese that flew into its engines three minutes after takeoff. The pilot, Chesley Sullenberger, drawing on countless years of rehearsal for multiple emergencies, calmly surveyed the possible options before ditching safely in the Hudson River, with no loss of life. Sullenberger was not aware at any stage that he had made a decision; he had simply conformed to the best practice in which he had been trained.[4] Hence the significance of the Duke of Wellington's words after the final defeat of Napoleon in 1815: "The battle of Waterloo was won on the playing fields of Eton."[5] By the time the English troops were on the battlefield, the key factors relating to their success or failure were already in place. They had been settled in the formation of character of the commanding officers at English public schools a decade or more previously.

The question then becomes, how does character become formed so that, when a flock of geese hit an aircraft, or soldiers face a battle, the important parts of the story have already happened, and what would otherwise be a crisis no longer appears like the crucial moment? It is this question that is at the root of the third strand of contemporary ethics, which I call "ecclesial ethics." I call it "ecclesial" because the answer many contemporary theologians give to this central question is that this is precisely what the Christian church does: it forms the characters of its members so that they learn to take the right things for granted, and no longer experience life as a sequence of insoluble dilemmas. Sullenberger and the Duke of Wellington are not substitutes for the church, but rather they witness to the fact that the only way in which character is formed is through sustained communities of practice that foster traditions in which the character of members is shaped over time.

How the church actually does this has been the subject of a good deal of my own writing.[6] What binds the diverse field of ecclesial ethics together is that, like subversive ethicists but for slightly different reasons, its proponents are suspicious of the whole project of universal ethics, which they see as an attempt to save the world without the need for the church in general and Jesus in particular. Ecclesial ethicists often share the criticisms subversive ethics makes of universal ethics, but in turn find fault with much of subversive ethics because it seems to be content with criticism and to lack a sufficiently constructive agenda.

Many people in higher education and public life find it easier to incorporate subversive ethics than ecclesial ethics. It has become commonplace to advocate for diversity and promote programs that enhance the accessibility of education to underrepresented social groups. But the fear about ecclesial ethics lingers in two minor and two major keys.

The two minor reservations are, first, that the church the ecclesial proponents talk about does not exist—that it is a fantasy made possible only by ignoring the hopelessly divided contemporary reality and its convoluted and often ignominious history. To this I can only say that I have served as a priest for over 20 years and throughout that time I have always been able to say that the church the ecclesial ethicists describe exists in the congregation I have been with at the time. Critics who say the church of ecclesial ethics doesn't exist seem to assume that Jesus founded the church on the Beloved Disciple, full of grace and truth, whereas all the gospel writers tell us in fact he founded the church on Peter, full of clumsiness and fragility. The second minor reservation is that Christians have no special claim on the good, in theory or in practice. There are plenty of people who are good but not Christian. I have no problem in celebrating vignettes of grace wherever they may dwell, but it seems to me the logic of this version of universal ethics is to assume that Jesus Christ's incarnation, life, death, and resurrection made no material difference to human possibility, and that, while being a respectable philosophical position, is not an orthodox theological one.

The two major reservations are, first, that if it gives up the shared project of universal ethics, Christianity has no public way of advocating that its claims are true. Kantian and consequential ethics are all about seeking grounds for public evaluation that do not depend on revelation. To give up on this quest feels to many like fideism—the holding to truth claims that have no visible means of support. The second, and most widely aired, major reservation is that if Christians are principally concerned with fostering their own virtues, they might be expected to withdraw from the public square into a sequestered space of pious righteousness.

I would respond to both these concerns by asking again, in a postmodern vein, whether there really is such a thing as universal ethics, or such a thing as a unitary public square, that are not the construction of those with the power and interest to claim it is so.[7] If there is no neutral territory for ethics to occupy, no neutral public square for the church to inhabit, surely the church must ensure that, when it is interacting with those of other faiths or none, it is doing so as the church, and when its members are in plural conversations across traditions it is their baptism, rather than their race or nationality or species, that they are regarding as the definitive mark of their own identity. [8]

Simply put, the first characteristic of ecclesial ethics is its fusion of Aristotle and the New Testament. In more contemporary terms, it is the sometimes uneasy meeting-point of two major turns on philosophy and theology: the recovery of virtue, represented by figures such as Alasdair MacIntyre; and the Christocentric turn in ethics inspired by Karl Barth but embodied more specifically by the Mennonite theologian John Howard Yoder. To map the contours of ecclesial ethics I shall, initially, outline these two dimensions in turn, beginning with virtue.

Imagine a European country were to be invaded and overrun by a foreign power. Imagine there remained pockets of resistance. What would the foreign power do? Most likely it would round up such insurgents as it could find, and torture them until it garnered sufficient information to discover the whereabouts of the rest. And what kind of people would it find most threatening? Probably those who had sufficient convictions, and came from sufficiently deep-rooted communities, that they had a profound sense of their own identity and a confidence that their people would still be around long after the invaders had been sent back or been assimilated. In other words, those whose communities had a character that could not be dismantled by simply picking off individuals.

A painful question for those who are members of churches is this: Would they, or would any members of their churches, be considered worth torturing? Have they concentrated so much on aligning themselves with public imagination or developing inner states of the heart that they have lost sight of the communal practices that might constitute a genuine threat to an invader by offering a deeply rooted alternative tradition? Or would they simply be pushovers, ready to accommodate, eager to find influence, personal wellbeing, or a safe place in a dangerous time?

This is what virtue ethics are about.[9] Virtue ethics portray the development of a particular kind of power, known as virtue, which might precisely enable a person or a people to withstand fear and temptation and deprivation and persecution in the face of an invading army. Virtue ethicists examine the "playing fields of Eton" and similar places where character is formed through communal practices shaped over generations in tradition. Such practices are time-honored activities, integral to a whole way of life, which are not only good in themselves, but also manifest training in excellence more broadly. In the 1985 film *Witness*, set in Lancaster County, Pennsylvania, the whole Amish community at the center of the film gathers in one place to raise a barn for a young couple who recently married. Raising the barn combines technical skill, communal interdependence, corporate celebration, and a kind of liturgical focus for the village.[10] These kinds of practices create a tradition—not as a static inheritance from the past, but as a lively ongoing debate about the good, shaped by practices honed over time.[11]

One further dimension of virtue ethics is their teleological character—that is, their orientation to a particular goal. For example, in 1 Corinthians 14, in his discussion of speaking in tongues, Paul insists that his readers follow the telos that says, "Let all things be done for building up," that is, for the building up of the congregation. This then provides an index by which the relative merits of a wide variety of activities and expressions may be evaluated. For virtue ethicists, it is hard to see how a vulnerable person may be enjoined to fulfill an onerous commitment without an explicit articulation of a telos. A frequent criticism of liberal democracies by virtue ethicists is that they strive to forge a society without identifying a telos.

The second major dimension of ecclesial ethics is its Christological turn. The term *narrative* is used in a number of ways in ethics and theology. It can identify the way the agent is inextricably embedded in a network of relationships and commitments, and can also articulate the way in which the self comes to have a coherent identity over time. In these senses, narrative is part of the critique of decisionist ethics. Inspired by figures such as MacIntyre and John Milbank, it has become fashionable for those involved in ecclesial ethics to trace a historical account, known as a declension narrative, of some kind of a fall from a time when ethics and theology were less problematic to their present impoverished state.[12] But the sense of narrative that is most prominent in ecclesial ethics is that which follows Karl Barth in saying that the narrative of Jesus portrayed in the gospels, and more broadly the narrative of Israel and the church that surround it, preceding and flowing from it, constitutes the definitive narrative in relation to which all of Christian ethics takes shape.[13]

This view is most fully articulated in the work of John Howard Yoder, who demonstrates how the particular details of Jesus's life disclose the elements of Christian social ethics. Yoder identifies the key moment as Jesus's nonviolent confrontation with the powers in Jerusalem. It is what Jesus represented—in contrast to what the violent Barabbas, or the accommodating Caiaphas, or the withdrawing Essenes stood for—that, for Yoder, constitutes the heart of Christian ethics.[14] Thus it is a quick leap from Christocentrism to a commitment to nonviolence. Jesus said, "Love your enemies": when he listed the details of what this involved, telling his followers to turn the other cheek and bless those who cursed them, he was outlining an ethic that he himself embodied on his journey to the cross. For those like Stanley Hauerwas who seek to combine Yoder's Christocentrism with MacIntyre's virtue ethic, nonviolence becomes the testing ground, because to be a nonviolent community requires profound practices that train disciples in witness that falls short of violent fight or terrified flight.[15]

Such an emphasis on Jesus's ministry and on the ethical significance of his cross and resurrection challenges conventional notions of politics. Now the church, living in the power of resurrection and Pentecost, has the key to a very different understanding of public life. It offers a transformed notion of the past, based around the forgiveness of sins, and a transformed notion of the future, based on the promise of eternal life. Thus Christians can balance the ways they seek to infuse the social order, as salt, or offer an example, as light, knowing that the possibilities of human interaction have been renewed and charted in Jesus.

Improvisation

I now consider how improvisation fits into the sphere of ecclesial ethics.[16] The first move is to suggest that drama is a better notion than narrative for describing the way the Christian story is embodied.[17] The Bible becomes the neck of an hourglass, situated between the enacted events of which it tells the story, and the embodied action with which the church seeks to respond. While the neck of the hourglass is narrative, the events and the response are both performed; thus drama is a more suitable genre than narrative for understanding the role of the Bible in Christian ethics.

Think of the Biblical drama as a five-act play. Act One is creation; Act Two, Israel; Act Three, Jesus; Act Four, the church; and Act Five, the eschaton. Secular ethics are inclined to assume that they operate in a one-act play, where it is their responsibility to bring about the right outcome. But living in Act Four, the church has an eschatological perspective. The most important things have already happened in the first three acts (notably the third), and all that is unresolved will be completed by God in Act Five. Many of the wrong turns the church makes can be described as living in the wrong act. For example, to live as if the Messiah has not yet come and God's character has not been fully revealed is to live in Act Two; to assume our day is the crucial one and what we do today will determine the future of creation is to live in Act Three; to believe it is our responsibility to make the world come out right is to live in Act Five.

For all the strengths of the metaphor of scripted drama, it is not sufficient. Life continues to present novel and unpredictable challenges that the text does not explicitly allow for. There have been 2,000 years of performances of the script, and these must be included in the discernment of faithful embodiment. The idea of a script implies that ethics is about recreating a golden era when disciples once got the story right. All these shortcomings in the notion of ethics as performance can tend toward the church withdrawing from engagement with the challenges of the world—like the slave with the one talent burying it, rather than trading with it, for fear of getting things wrong.

Thus emerge the themes of theatrical improvisation as a way of understanding the practice of Christian ethics. Scripture offers countless models of improvisation. In particular the Old Testament account of the Exile and the New Testament account of the Acts of the Apostles provide sustained studies in how the people of God may draw on long-practiced habits to act in new circumstances. Jeremiah portrays God as a potter who finds the clay is spoiled in his hands and refashions it into another vessel. This is a simple picture of God as improviser, committed neither to discard, nor destroy, his creation or his people, but to keep the story going through creative adaptation.

As I have written earlier, "Improvisation in the theatre is a practice through which actors seek to develop trust in themselves and one another in order that they may conduct unscripted dramas without fear."[18] Improvisation is not about being clever, witty, spontaneous, or original. Theatrical improvisers find they have to overcome such urges, which in fact kill the drama. Instead they must learn to be obvious, trust in their learned habits, and trust and enjoy one another. Improvisation may be funny, but it is not thereby trivial or self-indulgent. It is an ordered, skilled, and courageous series of practices that offers enormous potential for helping the church become a community of trust in order that it may faithfully encounter the threatening and the unknown.[19]

There are four broad areas where the training of improvisers has sustained analogies with the character of Christian ethics. The first is the formation of habits. In just the same way as advocated by virtue ethics, improvisation requires extensive immersion in learning to take the right things for granted. Unlike decisionist ethics, it does not assume the actor will spontaneously discern the right thing to do; on the contrary, only the actor who has long been shaped to be obvious will be able to keep the story going. Improvisers seek to cultivate a relaxed awareness that in many respects resembles what it means to be a person of character.

The second area is that of status. Status draws attention to the element of power and role in every single interaction between two or more people. Much of the dynamism of improvisation arises from its attention to status interactions, and its recognition that every interaction has a status dimension. "Status informs *every single interaction between people*—no casual movement or gesture is without significance. There are no innocent remarks or meaningless pauses. Status interactions are the ways people try to manoeuvre conversations and interplays into forms that reaffirm their preferred mode of relationship. Behind every status interaction is an implicit incipient story, and in many ways status names the negotiation over what kind of story this might become."[20] Improvisers love to begin with conventional scenes, such as a man asking a woman to marry him, or a person undergoing a police interrogation, or a shop assistant advising a customer on a purchase, and then to transform those scenes by altering the status each character adopts. The crucial point to grasp is that status is something one *chooses*, not something that is imposed. This is a difficult point to grasp for those whose theological commitments have been oriented toward the liberation of the oppressed. The key to understanding status is to grasp the difference between the status a person *has* and the status that person *plays*. The building in which I currently work has a housekeeper who acts in almost every way as if he were the most senior person in the organization. The status he *has* is low, but the status he *plays* is high. The fascination lies in the difference between the two.

Even the oppressed can play high status, because status is something one *plays*, not something one *is*. In the 1983 film *Merry Christmas Mr. Lawrence*, set in the Far East during the Second World War, prisoner of war Major Jack Celliers is being interrogated by the Japanese camp commander.[21] At one point the commander, relishing his power, and determined to play the highest status possible, says to Celliers, "Do you know what I am thinking?" But Celliers responds, "No. Do you?"—an equally high status retort that provokes a predictably brutal reaction. Celliers shows it is perfectly possible to play high status even in the direst circumstances. The expert status player is able to alter status at will to produce the desired effects. When one is aware of a person changing status adeptly and enjoying it, one tends to call it charm; when one is not enjoying it, one tends to call it manipulation.

The third area is known as overaccepting. Whenever a dialogue partner says or does anything, whether friendly, hostile, or indifferent, they are making what is known as an "offer." You have three options in return. You may "accept." This means to accept the premise of the offer and let it shape your subsequent interaction. Or, you may "block" the offer, by rejecting its premise. The third is to "overaccept" the offer. This means to accept the premise of the offer but place the offer on a much larger canvas than had been supposed by the person making the offer. A friend was approached by a sex worker who said, "Would you like a good time?" To have accepted would have been to have said, "Yes, how much?" To have blocked would have been to have said, "No, thank you." Instead my friend overaccepted and said, "I'd like to talk to you. I don't think what you're offering me right now is what I'd call a good time. If I can buy you a drink I'd like to talk to you about what I would call a *really* good time." Improvisers seek to train themselves to accept all offers. This seems a terrifying, even foolish commitment. But sometimes blocking is not an option. Sometimes blocking assumes one has access to superior violent force. In many cases violent blocking is futile, even if it seems justified. Overaccepting is especially significant for those who lack sufficient power simply to block threatening offers.

The fourth area is called reincorporation. One influential writer describes improvisation as like walking backwards.[22] Instead of walking *forwards* to face the daunting emptiness of an unknown future, the improviser walks *backwards*, seeing discarded material, near or far, as a host of gifts enabling the continuance and resolution of troubling narratives. Reincorporation comes about when discarded elements from earlier in the narrative begin to reappear, especially at moments when redeeming these discarded elements offers the resolution to what seemed insurmountable problems. Children are often highly attuned to reincorporation, and refuse to believe they have reached the end of the story until elements and characters earlier set aside finally reappear. Charles Dickens's novels are notable for immense and rapid reincorporation in their closing chapters, where it sometimes seems almost every character in a sprawling narrative comes back into the story in a new way.[23] Act 5 of the Christian drama is entirely made up of discarded elements from earlier parts of the story—the victims of history, the least, the last, and the lost, the hungry, thirsty, naked, stranger, sick, and imprisoned of Jesus's parable of the last judgment in Matthew 25:31–46. This becomes the key motif in Christian eschatology: the study of how God brings back into the story as gifts those elements that have previously been suppressed or oppressed as obstacles or superfluous elements.

Putting Improvisation to Work

I want to illustrate how improvisation works by looking briefly at the sociological place of Christianity in contemporary Western Europe. I want briefly to describe that context and show how ecclesial ethics, specifically the four aspects of improvisation I've just outlined, may be helpful. Charles Taylor describes three dimensions of this context. The modern Western state and all levels of social interaction—in short, the public square—has been, as Taylor points out, largely emptied of a day-to-day connection to faith in God; religion becomes a largely private matter. Meanwhile, Europe has experienced the falling-off of religious belief and practice, with people turning away from faith and no longer going to church. In a more subtle and third sense, there has been a move from a society where belief in God is unchallenged and unproblematic to one in which it is one option among others, and not the easiest one at that.[24] To Taylor's analysis I would add one further dimension. The related cultural, social, and religious challenge of Islam in Europe has countered the universality of these secular assumptions in ways that cause confusion and sometimes evoke clumsy and counterproductive responses.

Let's look at what the practices of improvisation may bring to this context. Taylor's first observation, about the disappearance of religion from the public square, is really about status. In the story of David and Goliath in 1 Samuel 17, David at first tries on Saul's armor. But in the end David goes out to fight Goliath armed with a slingshot and five smooth stones. Everyone reads this story and loves David, identifies with David, applauds David. But if the churches in Europe love David so much, why are they trying so hard to play Goliath? The story of the church in Europe is that once the church was David. But it became Goliath. It became the overblown, inflexible powerbroker it started its life by evading. That's the first irony of the contemporary church in Europe: it's turning back into David, but it doesn't like it. It would much rather remain Goliath. In fact it feels Goliath is its natural God-given status.

The church is being presented with an opportunity to be faithful in a way it hasn't been for a very long time, and all it can do is lament. It would be funny if it weren't so sad. If the church could realize it is called to be David, it could reincorporate all those moments in its past that look like faithful, honest failures, and see them for what they truly are: icons of true holiness. Likewise, it could reincorporate the faithful, honest failures of Christians in parts of the world where the church is distressed and persecuted, and realize that these pangs of suffering are the seed of the church today. God has given the church in Europe everything it needs to look like David—just not everything it needs to look like Goliath.

Here we have the second, even greater irony of the church in contemporary Europe: How did it happen that Christians in Europe lost so much of the respect and trust of people of other faiths and of no expressed faith? It happened by Christians turning Jesus into Goliath. And that's a tragedy. Jesus is not a cosmic or political or cultural bully. Jesus is not Goliath. Goliath is not God. Christians made a terrible theological wrong turn when they started to assume that their role in society was to be in charge, when they decided they imitated Jesus best when they looked like Goliath rather than like David. Right now they are being forced to look more like David, but they keep itching to put on Saul's armor.

And this is where overaccepting comes in. Status analysis points out the difference between trying to be Goliath and trying to be David. The choices are to block and try to be Goliath; to accept and lie down as a dead Goliath; or to overaccept and recognize this isn't about Goliath at all. The churches have a chance to become David like they haven't had for a long time and like maybe they should have been all along.

Let's look for a moment at the challenge of Islam. In the conventional configuration, Islam is a challenge to the secular state and Christians are so invested in the secular state that they perceive Islam as a challenge to them, too. But this is a sign of just how much the church has lost its identity. Rather than attempting to block Islam, the church should be overaccepting Islam. That's to say the church should look at the habits in which it has been forming its people. Why are Christians not as distinctive as Muslims, if not more distinctive? Christians stand for democracy and the rule of law and free speech, it seems. But are there not values more fundamental to Christians than that, values in significant tension with those of the secular state? If the heart of the Christian faith is the forgiveness of sins and the resurrection of the body, should not Christians be most famous for practices that reflect those commitments, practices like restorative justice and partnering with ex-offenders, practices like end-of-life hospice care and cherishing those with learning and mobility difficulties, practices like debt relief and reconciliation of warring parties?

For generations Christians have been formed to be good disciples of the secular state, but the state was never the church; being its disciple is at best a distraction, and at worst, idolatry. Christians seek its welfare, but as an additional activity, not as their main purpose. Islam is challenging Christians to rediscover their Christian identity, not as Goliaths dominating the state but as Davids being renewed in the practices and habits of the disciples of Jesus. When Christians say religion is not a private matter, it should not be because they are claiming some right to state power or influence, but because everywhere Christians are combining around issues at the core of their identity and getting a reputation for being found with the least, the last, and the lost, in all the places the gospels suggest Christ most frequently shows up.

Once, when I was the pastor of a church with a rather small congregation, a woman said to me, "You know, there are so many things we do here that we couldn't do if we were a larger church." It was a breakthrough moment for me because I'd been pastor there about three years and it was the first time anyone had said that. Previously there had solely been lament that we were not larger like other, proper churches. Like Israel, we too much wanted to be like our neighbors. But the fact that it took three years showed how hard it is for old patterns of thought to die. The church in Europe is locked into denial and lament. If only it could wake up and realize it has an opportunity to be what the church hasn't been for a very long time: a distinctive community whose traditions point to the death and resurrection of Christ and which invites strangers to become companions through the beauty of its life, the love of its members, and the hope of its witness.

NOTES

1. Kant's categorical imperative is described in his *Grounding for the Metaphysics of Morals: On a Supposed Right to Lie Because of Philanthropic Concerns*, 3rd ed., trans. James W. Ellington (Indianapolis: Hackett, 1993), 19–48.

2. The classic utilitarianism text is John Stuart Mill, *Utilitarianism*, ed. Roger Crisp (Oxford: Oxford University Press, 1998). See also Jeremy Bentham, *An Introduction to the Principles of Morals and Legislation* (Mineola, NY: Dover, 2009).

3. "Barack Obama's Inaugural Address," *New York Times*, January 20, 2009, http://www.nytimes.com/2009/01/20/us/politics/20text-obama.html?pagewanted=all.

4. Alex Altman, "Chesley B. Sullenberger III," *Time*, January 16, 2009, accessed July 18, 2012, http://www.time.com/time/nation/article/0,8599,1872247,00.html.

5. *The Oxford Dictionary of Quotations*, 3rd ed. (Oxford: Oxford University Press, 1979), 567.

6. See, for example, Samuel Wells, *God's Companions: Reimagining Christian Ethics* (Malden, MA: Blackwell, 2006).

7. In doing so I challenge contemporary thinkers such as Jürgen Habermas, whose notion of "discourse ethics" assumes such a public square. See his *The Theory of Communicative Action* (Boston: Beacon Press, 1984).

8. John Howard Yoder, "The Constantinian Sources of Christian Social Ethics," in *The Priestly Kingdom: Social Ethics as Gospel* (Notre Dame: University of Notre Dame Press, 1984), 135–47. Some ecclesial thinkers have been criticized for a somewhat loose employment of the term *Constantinian* to refer to the church's overextended desire to have a significant influence in public life. But Constantinianism fundamentally means the tendency of Christians to regard themselves as having a mark of identity more fundamental or more consequential than their baptism.

9. The terms *virtue ethics* and *ecclesial ethics* are related but not interchangeable. Virtue ethics is a well-established strand of ethics with a long philosophical and theological history; ecclesial ethics is my own connotation for a distinctly theological form of virtue ethics. The simple distinction between the two is this: virtue ethics are oriented toward a telos and shape actions accordingly; ecclesial ethics are oriented toward the eschaton, which is in many respects like a telos but is fundamentally a new heaven and earth. The eschaton is something that God reveals, rather than one that human effort can bring about, and has already been revealed in the life, death, and resurrection of Jesus Christ.

10. *Witness*, directed by Peter Weir, screenplay by Earl Wallace and William Kelley (Paramount Pictures, 1985).

11. The definitions of practices and tradition draw from Alasdair MacIntyre, *After Virtue: A Study in Moral Theory*, 2nd ed. (London: Gerald Duckworth, 1990), 207, 222.

12. John Milbank, *Theology and Social Theory* (Oxford: Blackwell, 1990).

13. Karl Barth, *Dogmatics in Outline*, trans. G. T. Thomson (London: SCM Press, 1949).

14. John Howard Yoder, *The Politics of Jesus*, 2nd ed. (Grand Rapids, MI: Eerdmans, 1994).

15. Stanley Hauerwas, *The Peaceable Kingdom: A Primer in Christian Ethics* (London: SCM Press, 1983).

16. For a contrasting proposal for how improvisation may chart a vision for Kantian deontological ethics, see J. David Velleman, *How We Get Along* (Cambridge: Cambridge University Press, 2009). For a review of improvisatory tropes in modernist writers Henry James, T. S. Eliot, and Gertrude Stein, see Omri Moses, "Fitful Character: The Ethics of Improvisation in Modernist Writing" (PhD diss., University of California, Berkeley, 2005).

17. This theme is explored in Samuel Wells, *Improvisation: The Drama of Christian Ethics* (Grand Rapids, MI: Brazos Press, 2004).

18. Ibid., 11.

19. The most common way in which improvisation is treated in theological circles is in interpretation generally or, more specifically, preaching. See for example Kirk Byron Jones, *The Jazz of Preaching: How to Preach with Great Freedom and Joy* (Nashville: Abingdon Press, 2004); Bruce Ellis Benson, "The Improvisation of Hermeneutics: Jazz Lessons for Interpreters," in *Hermeneutics at the Crossroads,* ed. Kevin J. Vanhoozer, James K. A. Smith, and Bruce Ellis Benson (Bloomington: Indiana University Press, 2006), 193–210. Thoughtful studies in other spheres also exist, for example, Deborah J. Kapp, "Improvisation and the Practice of Ministry," *Journal of Religious Leadership* 9, no. 1 (2010): 35–57; Steven Spidell, "Improvisation and the Pastoral Conversation," *Chaplaincy Today* 22, no. 2 (2006): 15–19; in relation to liturgy, Cyprian Love, "Musical Improvisation and Eschatology: A Study of Liturgical Organist Charles Tournemire (1870–1939)," *Worship* 81, no. 3 (2007): 227–49; and in relation to community development, Jodi Kanter, *Performing Loss: Rebuilding Community through Theater and Writing* (Carbondale: Southern Illinois University Press, 2007). There is also a helpful checklist of themes in Frank J. Barrett, "Creativity and Improvisation in Jazz and Organizations: Implications for Organizational Learning," *Organization Science* 9 (September/October 1998): 605–22. For a more doctrinal approach, which refers to improvisation but is not closely dependent upon it, see Jeremy Begbie, *Theology, Music and Time* (Cambridge: Cambridge University Press, 2000). In a more popular vein, with an interest in issues of creation/science and creativity, see Ann Pederson, *God, Creation, and All That Jazz: A Process of Composition and Improvisation* (St. Louis, MO: Chalice Press, 2001).

20. Wells, *Improvisation,* 88.

21. *Merry Christmas Mr. Lawrence,* directed by Nagisa Oshima, screenplay by Nagisa Oshima and Paul Mayersburg (Universal Pictures, 1983).

22. Keith Johnstone, *Impro: Improvisation and the Theatre* (London: Methuen, 1981), 116.

23. For example, in *David Copperfield* Dan Peggotty, Little Em'ly, Mrs. Gummidge, and the Micawbers all reappear in the conclusion en route to a new and happier life in Australia.

24. Charles Taylor, *A Secular Age* (Cambridge, MA: Belknap Press of Harvard University Press, 2007), 1–4.

Bibliography

Barrett, Frank J. "Creativity and Improvisation in Jazz and Organizations: Implications for Organizational Learning." *Organization Science* 9 (September/October 1998): 605–22.

Barth, Karl. *Dogmatics in Outline.* Translated by G. T. Thomson. London: SCM Press, 1949.

Begbie, Jeremy. *Theology, Music and Time.* Cambridge: Cambridge University Press, 2000.

Benson, Bruce Ellis. "The Improvisation of Hermeneutics: Jazz Lessons for Interpreters." In *Hermeneutics at the Crossroads*, edited by Kevin J. Vanhoozer, James K. A. Smith, and Bruce Ellis Benson, 193–210. Bloomington: Indiana University Press, 2006.

Bentham, Jeremy. *An Introduction to the Principles of Morals and Legislation*. Mineola, NY: Dover, 2009.

Habermas, Jürgen. *The Theory of Communicative Action*. Boston: Beacon Press, 1984.

Hauerwas, Stanley. *The Peaceable Kingdom: A Primer in Christian Ethics*. London: SCM Press, 1983.

Johnstone, Keith. *Impro: Improvisation and the Theatre*. London: Methuen, 1981.

Jones, Kirk Byron. *The Jazz of Preaching: How to Preach with Great Freedom and Joy*. Nashville: Abingdon Press, 2004.

Kant, Immanuel. *Grounding for the Metaphysics of Morals: On a Supposed Right to Lie Because of Philanthropic Concerns*. 3rd ed. Translated by James W. Ellington. Indianapolis: Hackett, 1993.

Kanter, Jodi. *Performing Loss: Rebuilding Community through Theater and Writing*. Carbondale: Southern Illinois University Press, 2007.

Kapp, Deborah J. "Improvisation and the Practice of Ministry." *Journal of Religious Leadership* 9, no. 1 (2010): 35–57.

Love, Cyprian. "Musical Improvisation and Eschatology: A Study of Liturgical Organist Charles Tournemire (1870–1939)." *Worship* 81, no. 3 (2007): 227–49.

MacIntyre, Alasdair. *After Virtue: A Study in Moral Theory*. 2nd ed. London: Gerald Duckworth, 1990.

Merry Christmas Mr. Lawrence. Directed by Nagisa Oshima, screenplay by Nagisa Oshima and Paul Mayersburg. Universal Pictures, 1983.

Milbank, John. *Theology and Social Theory*. Oxford: Blackwell, 1990.

Mill, John Stuart. *Utilitarianism*. Edited by Roger Crisp. Oxford: Oxford University Press, 1998.

Moses, Omri. "Fitful Character: The Ethics of Improvisation in Modernist Writing." PhD diss., University of California, Berkeley, 2005.

The Oxford Dictionary of Quotations. 3rd ed. Oxford: Oxford University Press, 1979.

Pederson, Ann. *God, Creation, and All That Jazz: A Process of Composition and Improvisation*. St. Louis, MO: Chalice Press, 2001.

Spidell, Steven. "Improvisation and the Pastoral Conversation." *Chaplaincy Today* 22, no. 2 (2006): 15–19.

Taylor, Charles. *A Secular Age*. Cambridge, MA: Belknap Press of Harvard University Press, 2007.

Velleman, J. David. *How We Get Along*. Cambridge: Cambridge University Press, 2009.

Wells, Samuel. *Improvisation: The Drama of Christian Ethics*. Grand Rapids, MI: Brazos Press, 2004.

Wells, Samuel. *God's Companions: Reimagining Christian Ethics*. Malden, MA: Blackwell, 2006.

Witness. Directed by Peter Weir, screenplay by Earl Wallace and William Kelley. Paramount Pictures, 1985.

Yoder, John Howard. *The Priestly Kingdom: Social Ethics as Gospel*. Notre Dame: University of Notre Dame Press, 1984.

Yoder, John Howard. *The Politics of Jesus*. 2nd ed. Grand Rapids, MI: Eerdmans, 1994.

INDEX